3 180375 507

457.

9780904107081

D1742981

A BIBLIOGRAPHY OF
PRINTED WORKS RELATING TO
OXFORDSHIRE
(EXCLUDING THE UNIVERSITY AND CITY OF OXFORD)

Oxford Historical Society
NEW SERIES, VOL. XI

A BIBLIOGRAPHY OF
PRINTED WORKS RELATING TO
OXFORDSHIRE
(EXCLUDING THE UNIVERSITY AND CITY OF OXFORD)

By
E. H. CORDEAUX, M.A.
and
D. H. MERRY, M.A.

OXFORD
At the CLARENDON PRESS *for the*
OXFORD HISTORICAL SOCIETY
MCMLV (*for* MCMXLIX–MCML)

163278
QH 942.57016 COR

OXFORDSHIRE
COUNTY
LIBRARIES

FOREWORD

THE publication of this Bibliography will, it is hoped, supply satisfactorily a need that has long been felt by all students of local affairs in Oxfordshire whatever their special field of interest may be. Although more or less abortive or incomplete attempts have been made in the past to cover some parts of the subject, the material contained in this volume has never been assembled as a whole before, and the authors, both members of the staff of the Bodleian Library, deserve every credit for the successful accomplishment of a very laborious and most useful undertaking. If every county in England could be equipped with such a comprehensive bibliographical tool, the task of many researchers in all the varied branches of local history would be very greatly eased, and it is hoped that the present work may help to indicate both in its scope and its arrangement the general lines on which scholars in other areas may be led to compile their own county bibliography.

Although this is not an official publication of the Bodleian Library and the authors are alone responsible for such merits or defects as it may possess, its production has been made possible by financial co-operation between the Society and the Curators of the Library, who in return for a substantial contribution to the cost of production have obtained a stock of copies for sale to the public. It can therefore be purchased direct from the Library.

All bibliographies of this kind are necessarily out of date even before they are issued but it is intended in the present case to minimize this inevitable defect by publishing supplements at regular intervals in the *Bodleian Library Record*. By purchasing the numbers containing these supplements as they are issued from time to time anyone who cares to do so will be able to keep this Oxfordshire Bibliography as nearly up to date as is humanly possible.

J. N. L. MYRES
Bodley's Librarian

September 1952

PREFACE

As stated on the title-page, this bibliography of the County of Oxford excludes the City and the University, a deficiency which, it is hoped, will be remedied in due course. An attempt to compile a county bibliography was made between 1889 and 1898 by J. and C. J. Parker, but all that survives is a set of proof sheets now in the Bodleian, to which acknowledgements are gratefully recorded. The limiting date is 1951: a few works, however, published early in 1952, have been included. It is only possible to indicate in general the type of material collected. In addition to complete publications, any works containing a topographical division have been listed, but national gazetteers and similar works, arranged alphabetically, have been ignored. The *Transactions* and *Journals* of archaeological and historical societies, both national and regional, have been analysed. In addition, most of the better known periodicals, relating to the various aspects of the classification scheme, and such publications as *Country Life* and the *Gentleman's Magazine*, have been dealt with in detail. Many isolated entries from other periodicals, not otherwise examined, have been included. No attempt, however, has been made to analyse newspapers; and maps, prints, plans, and drawings have normally been excluded. Auction catalogues of real estate have received a formal entry under each place involved. A number of Bodleian 'scrap' collections (picture postcards, societies' circulars, advertisements, and the like) have also been incorporated: although trivial in themselves, as collections they have a definite value. In some cases it has not been possible to compile a complete entry. This applies particularly to school and parish magazines, and the papers of local societies. It was felt, however, that the practical value of identifying an item, even by an incomplete entry, outweighed any other consideration. Information enabling more complete entries to be made would be welcomed.

The rationalization of the County boundaries from time to time has caused some difficulty. In the main the present bounds have been taken as limiting, but material about places no longer in Oxfordshire (such as Stokenchurch, Caversham, &c.) has been recorded to the time of their transfer. Villages which are now within the City of Oxford, but which at some time were autonomous, have been treated separately until they were incorporated in the city.

Throughout the work, within the limits of each section, a chronological arrangement by date of publication has been followed: occasionally, however, convenience has been preferred to consistency, and the rule has been relaxed. At the end of many of the general sections, references are given to works on the same subject which are classified under an individual place. In the section 'Individual Places', the smallest unit has been chosen as the heading—the hamlet rather than the parish which contains it. Detailed classification in this section has been attempted only when it seemed profitable.

Shelfmarks are attached to Bodleian entries, and an attempt has been made to indicate the location of works not in the Bodleian (where possible in a library in Oxford). When more than one edition of a work is recorded, the shelfmarks of the earliest and the latest are given. It should not be assumed, therefore, that the intervening editions are not in the Bodleian.

Similar treatment has been accorded to Acts of Parliament. Most main acts are followed by a series of amending acts, but for these a shelfmark has only been given when the original act is not in the Bodleian. Most of them are to be found in the Bodleian general collection of acts, with the shelfmarks L. Eng. A 69 c. 1 for Public acts; L. Eng. A 69 c. 6 for Local and Personal acts; L. Eng. C 13 c. 1 for Private acts. There seems to be a doubt whether some of the early acts were ever printed, but as they are given in the official indexes, they have been included.

A word of explanation is also needed for the treatment of Parliamentary Accounts and Papers, and the Reports of Commissioners. The Bodleian shelfmark Pp. Eng. (Parliamentary papers, England) has been considered sufficient identification: the year and volume refer to the official bound collection, in agreement with the official index, entitled 'General (alphabetical) index to the bills, reports, accounts and other papers, printed by order of the House of Commons, 1801-' and published by H.M. Stationery Office from 1829 onwards. It has been necessary to select those papers in which the subject has been dealt with on a topographical basis, and from these to make a selection according to size and apparent importance.

In conclusion it is a pleasant duty to thank all those who have given advice and help in the compilation of this work. Our warmest thanks are offered to Strickland Gibson, M.A., for suggesting its inception, and for his constant kindness and encouragement, and to W. O. Hassall, M.A., D.Phil., who provided us with many valuable references, and much helpful advice. Grateful acknowledgements are made to Bodley's Librarian; W. A. Pantin, M.A., Keeper of the University Archives; I. G. Philip, M.A.; W. G. F. Hoskins, M.A.; L. W. Hanson, B.Litt., M.A.; and P. S. Spokes, B.Sc., M.A. Also to Miss P. Pedlar, M.A., for her work on Parliamentary papers and to Miss D. M. Barratt, B.A.,

D.Phil., for her classification of the section Religion. Particular thanks are due to the following for contributing and revising practically the whole of the sections of Natural History with which they are associated: W. B. Alexander, M.A.; W. J. Arkell, M.A., D.Phil., D.Sc.; J. H. Burnett, M.A.; J. M. Edmonds, B.Sc., M.A.; C. S. Elton, M.A.; B. M. Hobby, M.A., D.Phil.; Mrs. A. Smith; and Mr. E. Taylor. For access to collections, thanks are due to Major F. G. Scott, clerk to the Oxford County Council; Mr. S. G. Baker; Miss M. Stanley-Smith; G. H. Spinney, B.A.; R. F. Ovenell, M.A.; Mr. E. Hemmings; Miss M. Nichols; and Miss E. C. Davies. Acknowledgement is also made to R. H. Hill, M.A.; F. J. King, M.A.; E. J. S. Parsons, B.Litt., M.A.; Raymond Smith, F.L.A., F.S.A.; J. D. Stewart, M.B.E., F.L.A.; R. Beesley, M.A.; W. H. Beyer, B.A.; S. G. Burden, M.A.; Mr. R. F. Tandy; W. E. Tate, B.Litt.; and Mrs. J. Howell, for their kind and generous help.

E. H. C.
D. H. M.

September 1952

CLASSIFICATION SCHEME

NATURAL HISTORY

GENERAL   1–8
Floods and drainage   9–16
Water Supply   17–19

GEOLOGY   20–44

BOTANY   45–78

ZOOLOGY
Insecta   79–95
Mollusca   96–104
Fishes   105–06
Reptiles and amphibians   107–08
Birds   109–29
Mammals   130–33

TOPOGRAPHY

GENERAL   134–222

PLACE NAMES   223–26

GUIDE BOOKS

    227–41

HISTORY

SOURCES   242–59

GENERAL   260–307

EARLY MAN   308–32

ROMANO-BRITISH   333–40

ANGLO-SAXON   341–46

MIDDLE AGES   347–62

TUDOR AND EARLY STUART   363–64

CIVIL WAR AND COMMONWEALTH   365–445

RESTORATION TO DATE   446–51

ECONOMIC HISTORY

GENERAL   452–53

COMMUNICATIONS
Canals and Rivers   454–81
Railways   482–93
Roads   494–556
Bridges   557–60

HUSBANDRY AND FARMING
General and Arable 561–79
Enclosures 580–84
Open Fields 585–86
Agricultural Societies 587–96
Smallholdings, allotments, and gardens 597–99
Pasture 600–03
Forestry 604–05

INDUSTRIES AND TRADES
General 606–09
Bee-keeping 610
Gloves
Paper-Mills
Printing 611
Quarries and Stone-working 612–16
Textiles 617
Tradesmen's Tokens 618–21

MARKETS 622–23

POLITICAL AND MILITARY HISTORY
GENERAL 624–32

ADMINISTRATION
General 632A
Boundaries 633–37
County Council 638–39
Finance 640–52
Parliamentary Representation
General 653–58
Poll Books and Registers 659–73
Particular Elections
1690–1710 674–76
1754 677–758
1798 and after 759–76
Public Officers 777–78
Statistics 779–97

MILITARY 798–829

SOCIAL HISTORY
GENERAL 830–54

DIALECT 855

FOLKLORE 856–70

SOCIAL SERVICES
General 871
Charities 872–87
Poor Law 888–913
Education 914–70
Law Courts 971–84

Police   985–88
Prisons   989–1000
Public Health   1001–19
Public Utilities   1020–24

SOCIETIES, CLUBS, ETC.
Cultural Societies and Libraries
Freemasons   1025–28
Friendly Societies   1029–33
Political Societies   1034–35
Savings Associations (incl. Post Office)   1036–37
Temperance Societies   1038–41
Women's Institutes   1042

SPORT AND PASTIME   1043–56

TOWN AND COUNTRY PLANNING   1057–61

RELIGION

GENERAL   1062–71

RELIGIOUS HOUSES   1072–80

MEDIEVAL ARCHDEACONRY

DIOCESE AND ARCHDEACONRY
General History   1081–1115
Diocesan Boards and Societies   1116–45
Ecclesiastical Visitations and Courts   1146–57
Benefices and Incumbents   1158–92
Parishes and Churches   1193–1206

DISSENT
General   1207–08
Protestant   1209–17

ROMAN CATHOLICISM (post-Reformation)   1218–23

BIOGRAPHY, GENEALOGY, AND HERALDRY

BIOGRAPHY AND GENEALOGY   1224–36

FAMILY HISTORIES   1237–67

HERALDRY (including Visitations)   1268–81

MONUMENTS AND RECORDS   1282–98

ARCHITECTURE AND ALLIED ARTS

GENERAL   1299–1310

FONTS   1311

MURAL DECORATION   1312–17

SCREENS   1318

STAINED GLASS   1319–23

TILES   1324–25

NEWSPAPERS 1326–80

DIRECTORIES AND ALMANACS 1381–1408

INDIVIDUAL LOCALITIES 1409–4310

KEY TO LIBRARIES

WHEN a work is not in the Bodleian, the Library or Institution which does possess a copy is indicated by initials (or an abbreviation) in the space usually occupied by the Bodleian shelfmark. The key to these initials, &c., is given here:

A.R.W.   = A. R. Wagner, Richmond Herald, College of Arms, London

Ashm.   = Ashmolean Museum Library

B.M.   = British Museum Library

J.C.   = J. Cheney & Co., Banbury

O.A.H.S. = Oxford Architectural and Historical Society

O.C.L.   = Oxfordshire County Library

O.C.R.L. = Oxfordshire County Record Office Library

O.P.L.   = Oxford City Public Library

Radcl.   = Radcliffe Science Library

R.H.   = Rhodes House

Taylor   = Taylor Institution

NATURAL HISTORY

GENERAL

1. CHILDREY, J., Britannia Baconica: or, The natural rarities of England, Scotland & Wales. (Oxfordshire, p. 83, 84.) Lond., 1661, 8°.
   Gough Nat. hist. 5

2. CHILDREY, J., Histoire des singularitez naturelles d'Angleterre, d'Escosse, tr. par m. P. B. [P. Briot]. (Oxfordshire, p. 121, 22.) Par., 1667, 12°.
   Gough Nat. hist. 11

3. PLOT, R., Quær's to be propounded to the most ingenious of each county in my travels through England, by R. P. [Madan 3022.] [Oxf. ? 1674], 4°. 4 pp.
   Ashm. 1820a (222)

4. PLOT, R., The natural history of Oxford-shire, by R. P. [Madan 3130.] Oxf., 1677, fol. 358+26 pp.
   Gough Oxf. 77
   — [Another ed.]. [1677?].
   Gough Oxf. 76
   — [Another ed.]. 1705.
   Gough Oxf. 78

5. MARTIN, B., The natural history of England. (Oxfordshire, vol. 1, p. 364–400.) Lond., 1759, 8°.
   Gough Nat. hist. 48

6. JORDAN, J., Memoir of the hail storm, that occurred in the county of Oxford, on Wednesday, August 9, 1843. Lond., &c., 1843, 8°. 28 pp.
   G.A. Oxon 8° 636 (3)

7. Oxfordshire natural history society and field club [afterw.] Ashmolean natural history society of Oxfordshire. (Proceedings and) Report. 1900–. Oxf., 1901–, 8°.
   Radcl.

8. WALKER, J. J., ed., The natural history of the Oxford district. Oxf., 1926, 8°. 336 pp.
   G.A. Oxon 8° 1049

Floods and Drainage

9. Report of the Committee on the inundations of the Thames, with an appendix. Oxf., (1853), 8°. 32 pp.
   G.A. Oxon 8° 179 (4)

10. SAUNDERS, J., Oxford valley outfall. Mr. Saunders' letter to mr. Treacher, April 1853. (Oxf., 1853), 8°. 11 pp.
    G.A. Oxon 8° 124 (14)

11. Copy of a letter . . . by the Conservators of the river Thames . . . in reference to the withdrawal of certain clauses of the Thames navigation bill [concerning the removal of flood waters at and above Oxford]. n. pl., 1870, s. sh.
    G.A. Oxon c. 317 (1)

12. An act for the draining of lands adjoining and near to the river Thames and its tributaries, in the counties of Berks, Oxford, Wilts and Gloucester. (34 & 35 V., c. 158, L. & P.) Lond., 1871, fol. [63 pp.]
                                                             L. Eng. A 69 c. 6

    — 37 & 38 V., c. 22, L. & P.
    — 53 & 54 V., c. 30, L. & P.
    — 54 & 55 V., c. 61, L. & P. [Concerns Northmoor.]

13. PALMER, F. I., Floods in the Thames Valley, and the relief of London Bridge and its approaches. Lond., 1877, 8°. 92 pp.   186 h. 89

14. HARCOURT, L. F. VERNON-, The floods around Oxford, a lecture, Feb. 13. Oxf., 1883, 8°. 21 pp.   G.A. Oxon 8° 325

15. Oxford valley drainage committee. [Proceedings of a meeting] Dec. 5, 1885. n. pl., 1885, 4°. 4 pp.   G.A. Oxon c. 317 (1)

16. Thames flood prevention association. Objects (Constitution). n. pl., [1908], fol. 4 pp.   G.A. Oxon c. 317 (1)

Water Supply

17. PRESTWICH, J., On the geological conditions affecting the water supply to houses and towns, with special reference to the modes of supplying Oxford, a lecture. Oxf., &c., 1876, 8°. 48 pp.
                                       G.A. Oxon 8° 199 (11)

18. TIDDEMAN, R. H., The water supply of Oxfordshire, with records of sinkings and borings, with contributions on rainfall by H. R. Mill. (Mem., Geol. survey.) Lond., 1910, 4°. 108 pp.   Radcl.

19. SANDFORD, K. S., Situations of settlements in the country around Oxford with relation to water supply. (South Eastern naturalist and antiquary, 1936, vol. 41, p. 77, 78.)   Soc. 18853 e. 6
See 1637 [Water of Holywell, Tadmarton Heath as drinking-water for Banbury. 1853].
See 1639, 1641, 42 [Banbury water company acts. 1865, 1937, 1942].

GEOLOGY

A SHORT selective bibliography of the geology of Oxfordshire was compiled by W. J. Arkell, M.A., D.Phil., D.Sc., and published in the Victoria county history, volume 1, in 1939. The following list contains some publications prior to that date, with which it is thought the Victoria county history titles should be supplemented, but is mainly concerned to include works issued subsequent to 1939. We express our thanks to J. M. Edmonds, B.Sc., M.A., for providing the following list.

20. HULL, E., The geology of the country around Woodstock. (Mem., Geol. survey of Gt. Brit., sheet no. 45 S.W.). Lond., 1859, 8°. 32 pp.
                                         18850 d. 2

21. HULL, E., and WHITAKER, W., The geology of parts of Oxfordshire and Berkshire. (Mem., Geol. survey of Gt. Brit.) Lond., 1861, 8°. 58 pp. 1885o d. 3

22. GREEN, A. H., The geology of the country round Banbury, Woodstock, Bicester and Buckingham. (Mem., Geol. survey of Gt. Brit., sheet 45.) Lond., 1864, 8°. 62 pp. Radcl.

23. WHITAKER, W., List of works on the geology and palæontology of Oxfordshire [&c.]. (Rept., Brit. assoc., 1882, p. 327–47.) Radcl.
— Repr. G.A. Oxon 4° 375 (4)

24. SPICER, E. C., Solution valleys in the Glyme area. (Quart. journ., Geol. soc., 1908, vol. 64, p. 335–44.) Radcl.

25. SANDFORD, K. S., The river-gravels of the Oxford district. (Quart. journ., Geol. soc., 1924, vol. 80, p. 113–79.) Radcl.

26. TOMLINSON, M. E., The drifts of the Stour–Evenlode watershed and their extension into the valleys of the Warwickshire Stour and Upper Evenlode. (Proc., Birm. nat. hist. and phil. soc., 1929, vol. 15, p. 157–95.) Per. 1996 e. 545

27. SANDFORD, K. S., Some recent contributions to the Pleistocene succession in England [the Upper Thames succession]. (Geol. mag., 1932, vol. 69, p. 1–18.) Radcl.

28. WOOLDRIDGE, S. W., The glaciation of the London basin and the evolution of the lower Thames drainage system (p. 633–39, the drifts between Goring gap and the Colne valley). (Quart. journ., Geol. soc., 1938, vol. 94, p. 627–67.) Radcl.

29. Geology. (Victoria county history, 1939, vol. 1, p. 1–26.)
R. 9. 41s

30. HARDEN, D. B., The geological origin of four stone axes found in the Oxford district. (Oxoniensia, 1940, p. 165.) R. Top. 340

31. ARKELL, W. J., Stratigraphy and structures east of Oxford [Forest Hill and Wheatley]. (Quart. journ., Geol. soc., 1942, vol. 98, p. 187–204.) Radcl.
— Pt. 2. The Miltons and Haseleys. (1944, vol. 100, p. 45–60.) Radcl.
— Pt. 3. Islip. (1944, vol. 100, p. 61–73.) Radcl.

32. ARKELL, W. J., Geology and prehistory from the train, Oxford–Paddington. (Oxoniensia, 1945, p. 1–15.) R. Top. 340

33. WHITEHEAD, T. H., and ARKELL, W. J., Field meeting at Hook Norton and Sibford [Ferris]. (Proc., Geol. assoc., 1946, vol. 57, p. 16–18.) Radcl.

34. RICHARDSON, L., ARKELL, W. J., and DINES, H. G., The geology of the country around Witney. (Mem., Geol. survey.) Lond., 1946, 4°. 150 pp. Radcl.

35. SHERLOCK, R. L., British regional geology: London and the Thames valley. 2nd ed. (Mem., Geol. survey.) Lond., 1947, 8°. 69 pp. Radcl.

36. ARKELL, W. J., The geology of Oxford. Oxf., 1947, 4°. 267 pp. Radcl.

37. ARKELL, W. J., Oxford stone. Lond., 1947, 8°. 185 pp.
G.A. Oxon 8° 1210
— [Review of Oxford stone, by E. M. Jope.] (Oxoniensia, 1949, p. 90–98.) R. Top. 340
[For other works on building stones see 614, 15, 16].

38. ARKELL, W. J., The geology of the Evenlode gorge, Oxfordshire. (Proc., Geol. assoc., 1947, vol. 58, p. 87–113.) Radcl.

39. COX, L. R., and ARKELL, W. J., A survey of the mollusca of the British great oolite series. 2 pt. (Palaeontol. soc., 1948–50.) Radcl.

40. ARKELL, W. J., Monograph of the English Bathonian ammonites. Pt. 1, 2, . (Palaeontol. soc., 1950, 51, , p. 1–76, .) Radcl.

41. ARKELL, W. J., Thames terraces and alpine glaciations, some recent correlations. (Archaeol. news letter, 1951, p. 17–19.) Per. 17572 d. 68

42. DOUGLAS, J. A., A new structure in the forest marble of Oxford [at Bladon]. (Geol. mag., 1951, vol. 88, p. 169–74.) Radcl.

43. FALCON, N. L., and TARRANT, L. H., The gravitational and magnetic exploration of parts of the mesozoic-covered areas of South-Central England. (Quart. journ., Geol. soc., 1951, vol. 106, p. 141–70.) Radcl.

44. PHIZACKERLEY, P. H., A revision of the Teleosauridae [from Enslow bridge] in the Oxford University museum and the British Museum (Natural history). (Annals and mag. of nat. hist., 1951, ser. 12, vol. 4, p. 1169–92.) Radcl.

44A. ARKELL, W. J., and DONOVAN, D. T., The fuller's earth of the Cotswolds, and its relation to the great oolite. (Quart. journ., Geol. soc., 1952, vol. 107, p. 227–53.) Radcl.
See 329 [Three Oxfordshire palaeoliths. 1945].
See 330 [Treacher collection of middle Thames palaeoliths. 1946/7].
See 332 [Ancient channel between Caversham and Henley. 1948].
See 2742 [Palaeolith, Handborough terrace. 1948].
See 4208 [Geol. map of Blenheim, appendix 1 in Green's Blenheim palace. 1952].

BOTANY

Records of additions to, and the distribution of, the flora of Oxfordshire can be found in the Reports of the Botanical society and Exchange club of the British Isles, vol. 1–13, and in Watsonia, vol. 1– under (a) Plant notes, (b) Distributors' Reports.

An annotated index of records for Oxfordshire is maintained in the Druce Herbarium of the University Department of Botany, Oxford.

We wish to thank J. H. Burnett, M.A., for providing the following list.

45. SIBTHORP, J., Flora Oxoniensis, exhibens plantas in agro Oxoniensi sponte crescentes, secundum systema sexuale distributas. Oxon., 1794, 8°. 422 pp.   Gough Oxf. 40

46. BAXTER, W., Stirpes cryptogamae Oxonienses; or, Dried specimens of cryptogamous plants, collected in the vicinity of Oxford. 2 fasc. Oxf., 1825–28, 4°.   Botan.

47. WALKER, R., The flora of Oxfordshire, and its contiguous counties. Oxf., 1833, 8°. cxxxv+338 pp.   19136 e. 16

48. WATSON, H. C., The new botanist's guide to the localities of the rarer plants of Britain. (Oxfordshire, vol. 1, p. 166–73.) Lond., 1835, 8°.   8° G 254 BS.

49. AYRES, P. B., List of cryptogamic plants of Oxfordshire. (The Phytologist, 1844, vol. 1, p. 661–64, 702–04.)   Per. 19131 e. 11

50. MASTERS, M. T., On the flowering plants and ferns of Oxfordshire and the contiguous counties. (Ashmol. soc.) Oxf., 1857, 8°. 16 pp.
G.A. Oxon 8° 503 b

51. BOSWELL, H., Bryology in the neighbourhood of Oxford. (The Phytologist, 1860, new ser., vol. 4, p. 343–47.)   Per. 19131 e. 11

52. DYER, W. T. T., Notes of plants of the neighbourhood of Oxford. (Journ. of botany, 1871, vol. 9, p. 145–48.)   Radcl.

53. TRIMEN, H., Botanical bibliography of the British counties. (Oxfordshire.) (Journ. of botany, 1874, vol. 12, p. 109.)   Radcl.

54. DRUCE, G. C., The flora of Oxfordshire. Oxf., 1886, 8°. 451 pp.
19136 e. 20
— 2nd ed. 1927. 538 pp.   Radcl.

55. DRUCE, G. C., Notes on Oxford plants. (Journ. of botany, 1890, vol. 28, p. 227–34.)   Radcl.
— Repr.   19136 e. 9

56. NAPIER, H., Report on the local moss flora. (Proc. and Rept., Ashmol. nat. hist. soc., 1910, p. 50–59.)   Radcl.

57. DRUCE, G. C., The mosses and liverworts of Oxfordshire. (Proc. and Rept., Ashmol. nat. hist. soc., 1921, p. 25–63.)   Radcl.
— Repr. 1922.   Radcl.

58. CHURCH, A. H., Introduction to the plant-life of the Oxford district. 3 pt. (Oxf. botan. mem., 13–15.) Lond., 1922–25, 8°.   Radcl.

59. CLAPHAM, A. R., Plant communities of the Oxford district. (South-Eastern naturalist and antiquary, 1936, vol. 41, p. 52–55.)
                                                            Soc. 18853 e. 6

60. BAKER, H., Alluvial meadows, a comparative study of grazed and mown meadows. (Journ. of ecology, 1937, vol. 25, p. 408–20.)
                                                                       Radcl.

61. CHAPPLE, J. F. G., Bromus hordeaceus L. × lepidus Holmberg [and] Lolium multiflorum Lam. × perenne L. (Rept., Botan. soc. and exchange club, 1938, vol. 12, p. 31.)   Per. 19131 e. 2

62. Botany. (Victoria county history, 1939, vol. 1, p. 27–55.)
                                                               R. 9. 41 s

63. BAKER, H., and CLAPHAM, A. R., Seasonal variation in the acidity of some woodland soils. (Journ. of ecology, 1939, vol. 27, p. 114–25.)
                                                                       Radcl.

64. MELVILLE, R., The Plot elm, Ulmus Plottii Druce. (Journ. of botany, 1940, vol. 78, p. 181–92.)   Radcl.

65. CLAPHAM, A. R., The role of bryophytes in the calcareous fens of the Oxford district. (Journ. of ecology, 1940, vol. 28, p. 71–80.)
                                                                       Radcl.

66. TIMM, E. W., and CLAPHAM, A. R., The jointed rushes of the Oxford district. (New Phytologist, 1940, vol. 39, p. 1–16.)   Radcl.

67. DANDY, J. E., and TAYLOR, G., Studies of British Potamogetous xii (xiii). (Journ. of botany, 1940, vol. 78, p. 1–11, 49–66.)   Radcl.

68. BRITTON, C. E., Bucks and Oxon notes. (Journ. of botany, 1941, vol. 79, p. 198–200.)   Radcl.

69. ROSE, F., A note on the rediscovery of Orchis simia (Lamarck) in Oxfordshire. (Journ. of botany, 1942, vol. 80, p. 102–04.)   Radcl.

70. HANCOCK, B. L., Cytological and ecological notes on some species of Galium L. em. Scop. (New Phytologist, 1942, vol. 41, p. 70–78.)
                                                                       Radcl

71. TURRILL, W. B., Pulicaria dysenterica (L.) Bernh. vor Hubbardii Turrill. (Naturalist, 1945, p. 51, 52.)   Radcl.

72. HODGMAN, M. G., Galinsaga, a weed of the future. (Gardener's chron., 1945, vol. 117, p. 7.) Radcl.

73. LAMBERT, J. M., Glyceria maxima. Effect of drought on flowering. (Rept., Botan. soc. and exchange club, 1945, vol. 13, p. 41.) Per. 19131 e. 2

74. FITZPATRICK, J. M., A cytological and ecological study of some British species of Glyceria. (New Phytologist, 1946, vol. 45, p. 137-44.) Radcl.

75. BRENAN, J. P. M., Notes on the flora of Oxfordshire and Berkshire. (Rept., Botan. soc. and exchange club, 1946, vol. 12, p. 781-802.) Per. 19131 e. 2

76. BRENAN, J. P. M., [Excursion in the neighbourhood of Oxford. List of plants found.] (Rept., Botan. soc. and exchange club, 1946/7, vol. 13, p. 223-32.) Per. 19131 e. 2

77. CHAPPLE, J. F. G., Allium paradoxum. (Rept., Botan. soc. and exchange club, 1946/7, vol. 13, p. 277.) Per. 19131 e. 2

78. CLAPHAM, A. R., Taxonomic problems in Galium and Juncus. (Brit. flowering plants and mod. systematic methods, ed. by A. J. Wilmott, 1949, p. 72-74.) Botan.
See 1616 [Plants, Banbury area. 1841].
See 2488 [Plants, Ewelme. 1917].
See 3061 [Plants, Kirtlington area. 1839].
See 3394 [Botany of Otmoor. 1900].

ZOOLOGY

Insecta

THE following section is a list of the more important articles issued subsequent to the publication in 1939 of the Insecta section of the Victoria county history (1939, vol. i, p. 62-178 [R. 9. 41 s]). We have to thank Mrs. A. Smith of the Department of Entomology, for providing the following list.

Collembola

79. MILES, P. M., Collembola new to the Oxford district. (Proc., Ashmol. nat. hist. soc., 1940, p. 15, 16.) Radcl.

80. MILES, P. M., Collembola new to the Oxford district. [Supplementary to 79]. (Entomologist's monthly mag., 1942, vol. 78, p. 247.) Radcl.

Orthoptera

81. BROWN, E. S., Some new county records for Orthoptera. Omocestus viridulus, L. (Entomologist's record, 1939, vol. 51, p. 143.) Radcl.

82. GROVE, L. R. A., Notes on the Orthoptera of the Middle Thames basin. (Entomologist's record, 1938, vol. 50, p. 141–44.) Radcl.

Plecoptera

83. GRENSTED, L. W., Trichoptera, Ephemeroptera and Plecoptera in the Oxford district, 1938. (Proc., Ashmol. nat. hist. soc., 1938, p. 16–18.) Radcl.

84. GRENSTED, L. W., Trichoptera and Plecoptera in the Oxford district, 1939. (Proc., Ashmol. nat. hist. soc., 1939, p. 15.) Radcl.

85. GRENSTED, L. W., Trichoptera, Ephemeroptera and Plecoptera new to Oxfordshire, 1940. (Proc., Ashmol. nat. hist. soc., 1940, p. 17.) Radcl.

Ephemeroptera

See 83, 85

Hemiptera

86. BROWN, E. S., The aquatic and semi-aquatic Hemiptera-Heteroptera of Oxfordshire. (Proc., Ashmol. nat. hist. soc., 1941/47, p. 37–43.) Radcl.

87. MACFADYEN, A., Some records of water-bugs (Hemiptera-Heteroptera) in the Oxford district. (Proc., Ashmol. nat. hist. soc., 1941/47, p. 44–46.) Radcl.

Trichoptera

See 83, 84, 85.

Lepidoptera

88. BRETHERTON, R. F., A list of the Macro-lepidoptera of the Oxford district. (Proc., Ashmol. nat. hist. soc., 1939, p. 25–70.) Radcl.

89. BRETHERTON, R. F., Additions to the list of Macro-lepidoptera of the Oxford district. (Proc., Ashmol. nat. hist. soc., 1940, p. 22, 23.) Radcl.

90. BRETHERTON, R. F., Some 'clearwings' in the Oxford district. (Entomologist's monthly mag., 1946, vol. 82, p. 213–17.) Radcl.

91. EMMET, A. M., Second supplement to the list of Macro-lepidoptera of the Oxford district. (Proc., Ashmol. nat. hist. soc., 1941/47, p. 47–55.) Radcl.

Coleoptera

92. DICKER, G. H. L., Additions to the Oxfordshire list of Coleoptera. (Entomologist's monthly mag., 1944, vol. 80, p. 13.) Radcl.

Diptera

93. GRENSTED, L. W., Calamoncosis laminiformis Beck. (Dipt., Chloropidae) new to Oxfordshire. (Entomologist's monthly mag., 1949, vol. 85, p. 192.) Radcl.

94. GRENSTED, L. W., Chymomyza distincta Egg. (Dipt., Drosophilidae) new to Oxfordshire. (Entomologist's monthly mag., 1949, vol. 85, p. 230.) Radcl.

Siphonaptera

95. FREEMAN, R. B., Siphonaptera of the Oxford district. (Proc., Ashmol. nat. hist. soc., 1939, p. 19–24.) Radcl.

Mollusca

96. NORMAN, A. M., Land and fresh-water mollusca of Oxford and its neighbourhood [*afterw.*] Notes on the Oxfordshire shells. (Zoologist, 1853, vol. 11, p. 3761–64, 4126–29; 1857, vol. 15, p. 5609–13.)
Per. 18933 e. 395

97. DALTON, J., Land and fresh water shells in the vicinity of Oxford [signed J. D.]. (Naturalist, 1855, vol. 5, p. 200–03.)
Per. 1996 d. 24

98. WHITEAVES, J. F., On the land and fresh water mollusca inhabiting the neighbourhood of Oxford. (Ashmol. soc.) Oxf., 1857, 8°. 20 pp.
G.A. Oxon 8° 503 *b*

99. PEARCE, S. S., The land and freshwater mollusca in the vicinity of Oxford. (Zoologist, 1883, ser. 3, vol. 7, p. 327–31, 362–70.)
Per. 18933 e. 395

100. COLLINGE, W. E., The land and freshwater mollusca of Oxfordshire. (The Conchologist, 1891, vol. 1, p. 11–14, 19–23, 39–44, 51–53.) Per. 18945 d. 8

101. CARPENTER, G. D. H., Where to find shells round Oxford. (Rept., Ashmol. nat. hist. soc., 1904, p. 42–45.) Radcl.

102. ELLIS, A. E., Notes on some British helicidae [found in Oxfordshire]. (Journ. of conchology, 1924, vol. 17, p. 162–67.)
Per. 18945 d. 18

103. ELLIS, A. E., Additional notes on the mollusca of the Oxford district. (Journ. of conchology, 1927, vol. 18, p. 137–38.)
Per. 18945 d. 18

104. Mollusca. (Victoria county history, 1939, vol. 1, p. 187–91.)
R. 9. 41 *s*

See 1617 [Molluscs, Banbury. 1855].
See 1618 [Shells, Banbury. 1874].
See 2856 [Shells, Henley. 1834].

Fishes

105. CHRISTY, M., Bibliographical note on Oxfordshire fishes. (Zoologist, 1893, ser. 3, vol. 17, p. 257.) Per. 18933 e. 395

106. Fishes. (Victoria county history, 1939, vol. 1, p. 192–98.)
R. 9. 41 s

Reptiles and Amphibians

107. CHRISTY, M., Bibliographical note on Oxfordshire reptiles. (Zoologist, 1893, ser. 3, vol. 17, p. 246.) Per. 18933 e. 395

108. Reptiles and amphibians. (Victoria county history, 1939, vol. 1, p. 199, 200.) R. 9. 41 s
See 3062 [Cetiosaurus at Kirtlington. 1895].

Birds

THE following list was compiled with the help of W. B. Alexander, M.A., to whom we offer our thanks.

109. MATTHEWS, A. and H., The birds of Oxfordshire and its neighbourhood. (Zoologist, 1849, vol. 7, p. 2423–33, 2531–41, 2592–2603, 2623–26; 1850, vol. 8, p. 2736–39.) Per. 18933 e. 395

110. FOWLER, W. W., A year with the birds, by an Oxford tutor [W. W. Fowler]. [Chapters 1 and 2 deal with the Oxford area.] Oxf., 1885, 8°. 18961 e. 24
— 2nd ed. 1886. 18961 e. 25
— 3rd ed. 1889. 18961 e. 40

111. APLIN, O. V., The birds of Oxfordshire. Oxf., 1889, 8°. 217 pp.
Radcl.

112. CHRISTY, M., Bibliographical note on Oxfordshire birds. (Zoologist, 1890, ser. 3, vol. 14, p. 258.) Per. 18933 e. 395

113. APLIN, O. V., [Annual] Notes on the ornithology of Oxfordshire. (Zoologist, 1892, ser. 3, vol. 16– 1915, ser. 4, vol. 20.)
Per. 18933 e. 395

114. STUBBS, C. E., Notes on Oxfordshire ornithology, ed. by O. V. Aplin. (Zoologist, 1903, ser. 4, vol. 7, p. 444–53.)
Per. 18933 e. 395

115. FOWLER, W. W., Acrocephalus palustris [marsh warbler at Kingham] a breeding record of fourteen years. (Zoologist, 1906, ser. 4, vol. 10, p. 401–09.) Per. 18933 e. 395
— [Repr.]. G.A. Oxon 8° 976

116. ATTLEE, H. G., Bird-notes for Oxford district in 1913 and 1914. (Zoologist, 1915, ser. 4, vol. 19, p. 109–12.)   Per. 18933 e. 395

117. Report of the Ornithological section of the Ashmolean society and the Oxford Ornithological society for 1923 and 1924 (1925–). (Oxfordshire, *passim*.)   Radcl.

118. Oxford ornithological society. Report . . . on the birds of Oxfordshire, Berkshire and Buckinghamshire, 1915/22–. Oxf., 1924–, 8°.   Per. 18961 e. 340

119. NICHOLSON, E. M., and B. D., The rookeries of the Oxford district. (Journ. of ecology, 1930, vol. 18, p. 51–66.)   Radcl.
— Repr. 1930.   18961 d. 253

120. SOUTHERN, H. N., Close-ups of birds [herons, &c., on Otmoor, p. 75–88]. Lond., 1932, 8°.   18961 d. 255

121. ALEXANDER, W. B., The bird population on an Oxfordshire farm [Temple farm, Sandford-on-Thames]. (Journ. of animal ecology, 1932, vol. 1, p. 58–64.)   Radcl.

122. ALEXANDER, W. B., The rook population of the Upper Thames region. (Journ. of animal ecology, 1933, vol. 2, p. 24–35.)   Radcl.

123. TUCKER, B. W., The great crested grebe investigation in Oxon, Berks and Bucks. Repr. from Rept., Oxf. ornith. soc., 1932, 33. Oxf., 1934, 8°. 26 pp.   1896125 e. 8

124. TICEHURST, N. F., The swan-marks of Oxfordshire and Buckinghamshire. (Rept., Oxf. archaeol. soc., 1936, p. 97–130.)   R. Top. 330

125. Birds. (Victoria county history, 1939, vol. 1, p. 201–16.)   R. 9. 41s

126. CHAPMAN, W. M. M., The bird population of an Oxfordshire farm Temple farm, Sandford-on-Thames]. (Journ. of animal ecology, 1939, vol. 8, p. 286–99.)   Radcl.

127. ALEXANDER, W. B., The birds of Oxfordshire. (Bird notes, 1947/8, vol. 23, p. 61–63.)   Soc. 18961 d. 278

128. ALEXANDER, W. B., A revised list of the birds of Oxfordshire. Oxf., 1947, 8°. 36 pp.   1896125 e. 8

129. FITTER, R. S. R., I live in a desert [Burford]. (Bird notes, 1950, vol. 24, p. 120–22.)   Soc. 18961 d. 278
See 1619 [Banbury birds. 1882].

Mammals

THE material for Mammalia is based on the Victoria county history, 1939, vol. I, p. 217–22 [R. 9. 41s.]. An ecological survey of animal communities in the Oxford region (with special reference to Wytham woods, Berkshire) is being carried on by the Bureau of Animal Population, Department of Zoological Field Studies, where there is a growing body of information on punch-cards, maps, &c. We are indebted to C. S. Elton, M.A., for the material provided here.

130. MIDDLETON, A. D., The ecology of the American grey squirrel in the British Isles. (Proc., Zool. soc. of Lond., 1930, p. 809–43.)   Radcl.

131. ELTON, C. S., The study of epidemic diseases among wild animals. (Journ. of hygiene, 1931, vol. 31, p. 454–56.)   Radcl.

132. VENABLES, L. S. V., and LESLIE, P. H., The rat and mouse populations of corn ricks. (Journ. of animal ecology, 1942, vol. 11, p. 44–68.)   Radcl.

133. VENABLES, L. S. V., Observations at a pipistrelle bat roost [in Binsey church]. (Journ. of animal ecology, 1943, vol. 12, p. 19–26.)   Radcl.

133A. SHORTEN, M., A survey of the distribution of the American grey squirrel (sciurus carolinensis) and the British red squirrel (s. vulgaris leucourus) in England and Wales in 1944–5. (Journ. of animal ecology, 1946, vol. 15, p. 82–92.)   Radcl.

133B. SOUTHERN, H. N., and LAURIE, E. M. O., The house-mouse (mus musculus) in corn ricks. (Journ. of animal ecology, 1946, vol. 15, p. 134–49.)   Radcl.

133C. CHITTY, D., and SHORTEN, M., Techniques for the study of the Norway rat (rattus Norvegicus). (Journ. of mammology, 1946, vol. 27, p. 63–78.)   Radcl.

133D. SHORTEN, M., Some aspects of the biology of the grey squirrel (sciurus carolinensis) in Great Britain. (Proc., Zool. soc. of Lond., 1951, vol. 121, p. 427–59.)   Radcl.

TOPOGRAPHY

GENERAL

134. A book of the names of all parishes, market towns, villages, hamlets, and smallest places, in England and Wales. (Oxfordshire, p. 129–32.) Lond., 1657, 4°.   Gough Gen. top. 76
— [Another ed. 1662.]   Tanner 273 (3)

135. LEIGH, E., England described. (Oxfordshire, p. 154–58.) Lond., 1659, 8°.   Douce L 99

136. BLOME, R., Britannia; or, A geographical description of . . . England [&c.]. (Oxfordshire, p. 186–89.) Lond., 1673, fol.   fol. Δ 777

137. England's remarques, an exact account of the several shires [&c.]. (Oxfordshire, p. 153–58.) Lond., 1678, 12°.   8° V 81 Art.
— [Another issue in 1682.]

138. CROUCH, N., Admirable curiosities, rarities & wonders in England, Scotland and Ireland, by R. B. (Oxfordshire, p. 173–83.) Lond., 1682, 12°.   8° W 17 Jur.
[Other eds. in 1684, 85. 1811: Sutherland 63.]

139. MIEGE, G., The new state of England. (Oxfordshire, p. 80–91.) Lond., 1691, 12°.   Hope adds. 206
[Other eds. in 1693, 1699, 1702, 03. 1707: Lister F 80.]

140. MORDEN, R., The new description and state of England. 2nd ed. (Oxfordshire, p. 61, 62.) Lond., 1704, obl. 4°.
    G.A. Gen. top. 4° 358

141. MIEGE, G., The present state of Great Britain. (Oxfordshire, p. 176–81.) Lond., 1707, 8°.   Hope adds. 211
[Other eds. in 1711, 1715, 1718, 1723, 1731, 1738, 1745. 1748: G.A. Gen. top. 8° 739.]

142. BEEVERELL, J., Les délices de la Grand' Bretagne, et de l'Irlande. Tom. 3. (Oxfordshire, p. 1–594.) Leide, 1707, 8°.   Douce B 614–17
— Nouv. éd. 1727.   Gough Gen. top. 247–54

143. British curiosities in nature and art. (Oxfordshire, p. 57–64, 150.) Lond., 1713, 12°.   8° L 9 (2) Linc.
[Other eds. in 1721: Gough Gen. top. 297; and 1728: Gough Gen. top. 298.]

144. JONES, D., A new description of England and Wales [by D. Jones]. To which is added a set of maps, by H. Moll. (Oxfordshire, p. 93–100.) Lond., 1724, fol.   Gough Gen. top. 220

145. STUKELY, W., Itinerarium curiosum; or, An account of the antiquitys . . . observed in travels thro' Great Britain. (Oxfordshire, p. 40–45.) Lond., 1724, fol. Douce S 847
— [Another ed.] 1776. Gough Gen. top. 57

146. A description of all the counties in England and Wales, collected by P. W. (Oxfordshire, p. 137–43.) Lond., 1728, 12°.
Gough Gen. top. 302
— 5th ed. [by R. R.], p. 153–59. 1741. B.M.
— 6th ed. 1752. Gough Gen. top. 305

147. SALMON, N., A new survey of England. (Oxfordshire, vol. 2, p. 449–81.) Lond., 1728, 29, 8°. Gough Gen. top. 331, 332
— [Another ed. 1731.] Gough Gen. top. 328

148. A complete system of geography. (Oxfordshire, p. 135–39.) Lond., 1744, fol. Gough Gen. top. 113

149. The geography of England. (Oxfordshire, p. 133–43.) Lond., 1744, 8°. Gough Gen. top. 321

150. SALMON, T., The present state of the universities, and of the five adjacent counties of . . . Oxford [&c.]. (Vol. 1, p. 1–24.) Lond., 1744, 8°. G.A. Oxon 8° 65

151. SIMPSON, S., The agreeable historian, or The complete English traveller. (Oxfordshire, vol. 3, p. 747–804.) Lond., 1746, 8°.
G.A. Gen. top. 8° 571

152. A description of Oxfordshire. (London mag., 1749, p. 21–27.)
Hope adds. 404

153. READ, T., A new description of Lancashire [&c.] . . . Oxfordshire. (The English traveller, vol. 3, p. 416–84.) Lond., 1749, 8°.
G.A. Gen. top. 8° 366

154. An account of Oxfordshire. (Universal mag., 1755, vol. 17, p. 37–40, 49–54, 97–102, 193–201, 258–64, 324–28; vol. 18, p. 14–17, 49–55.) Per. 2705 e. 552

155. TOLDERVY, W., England and Wales described, letters. (Letter xxiii, from Bleachington, p. 203–32.) Vol. 1. Lond., 1762, 8°.
Gough Gen. top. 155 (10)

156. The beauties of England. 2nd ed. (Oxfordshire, p. 129–39.) Lond., 1764, 12°. G.A. Gen. top. 16° 174
— [Another ed. 1767: B.M.]

157. England illustrated, or, A compendium of the natural history, geography, topography and antiquities . . . of England and Wales. (Oxfordshire, vol. 2, p. 157–86.) Lond., 1764, 4°.
G.A. Oxon 4° 348

158. BEAUMONT, G., and DISNEY, H., A new tour thro' England . . .
1765, 1766 and 1767. (Oxfordshire, p. 88–92.) Lond., [1768], 8°.
Gough Gen. top. 180 (1)

159. RUSSELL, P., ed., England displayed, by a society of gentlemen.
2 vols. (Oxfordshire, vol. 1, p. 234–72.) Lond., 1769, fol.
G.A. Gen. top. c. 5, 6

160. A description of England and Wales. (Oxfordshire, vol. 7, p. 173–
263.) Lond., 1770, 12°. Gough Gen. top. 279

161. SANDERS, R., The complete English traveller, by Nathaniel
Spencer [i.e. R. Sanders]. (Oxfordshire, p. 336–55.) Lond., 1771, fol.
B.M.

162. GROSE, F., The antiquities of England and Wales. 4 vols. (Oxford-
shire, vol. 3.) Lond., 1773–87, 4°. G.A. Gen. top. c. 32
— New ed. Vol. 4, p. 169–88; vol. 8, p. 19. 1783–97. B.M.
— New ed., by H. Boswell. 1795. G.A. fol. A 359

163. Britannica curiosa, or, A description of the most remarkable
curiosities . . . of Great Britain. 6 vols. (Oxfordshire, vol. 2, p. 187–
277.) Lond., 1777, 8°. B.M.

164. BURLINGTON, C., The modern universal British traveller. (Oxfordshire, p. 228–45.) Lond., [c. 1779], fol. G.A. Gen. top. b. 26

165 GOUGH, R., British topography. (Oxfordshire, vol. 2, p. 79–180*.)
Lond., 1780, 4°. G.A. Gen. top. 4° 137
— 2nd ed. 1780. Gough Gen. top. 365

166. WALPOOLE, G. A., ed., The new British traveller, or, A complete . . .
display of Great Britain and Ireland. (Oxfordshire, p. 197–210.)
Lond., 1784, fol. G.A. Gen. top. b. 34

167. AIKIN, J., England delineated. (Oxfordshire, p. 172–78.) Lond.,
1788, 8°. Gough Gen. top. 333
[Other eds. in 1790, 1795, 1800, 1803, 1809. 1818, entitled England
described: G.A. Gen. top. 8° 73.]

168. SHAW, S., A tour to the West of England in 1788. (Oxfordshire,
p. 81–122.) Lond., 1789, 8°. Gough Gen. top. 312

169. Topographical miscellanies. Vol. 1. [Not paginated. 40 pp. relate
to Oxfordshire.] Lond., 1792, 4°. G.A. Gen. top. 4° 100

170. LIPSCOMB, G., A journey into South Wales, through the counties
of Oxford [&c.]. (Oxfordshire, p. 19–31, 354.) Lond., 1802, 8°.
Gough Wales 58

171. GREEN, W., The picture of England. (Oxfordshire, vol. 2, p. 96–
105.) Lond., 1804, 8°. B.M.

172. COOKE, G. A., Topographical and statistical description of the county of Oxford. (Topogr. of Gt. Brit., or, British traveller's dir.) Lond., [c. 1805], 12°. 144 pp. G.A. Gen. top. 16° 136
— [Another ed. c. 1830.] 180 pp. G.A. Oxon 8° 184 (1)

173. CRUTTWELL, C., Tours through ; . . Great Britain. (Oxfordshire, vol. 1, p. cliii–clvii; vol. 3, p. 74–105, 163–65, 283, 384, 85.) Lond., 1806, 8°. G.A. Gen. top. 8° 383–88

174. SPENCE, E. I., Summer excursions through parts of Oxfordshire [&c.]. 2 vols. Lond., 1809, 12°. G.A. Gen. top. 8° 57
— 2nd ed. 1809. B.M.

175. NIGHTINGALE, J., English topography, or, A series of historical and statistical descriptions of the several counties of England and Wales. (Oxfordshire, 2 pp. Not paginated.) Lond., 1816, fol.
G.A. Gen. top. c. 1

176. WALFORD, T., The scientific tourist through England, Wales & Scotland. (Oxfordshire, vol. 1, 9 pp. Not paginated.) Lond., 1818, 12°. G.A. Gen. top. 8° 63

177. DUGDALE, J., The new British traveller. (Oxfordshire, vol. 4, p. 54–130.) Lond., 1819, 4°. G.A. Gen. top. 4° 270

178. SPIKER, S. H., Travels through England, Wales, and Scotland. Transl. 2 vols. (Oxfordshire, vol. 1, p. 11–42.) Lond., 1820, 8°.
8° O 28 BS.
[Orig. ed. Reise durch England [&c.]. 1816, and 1818.]

179. BREWER, J. N., The picture of England, or, Historical and descriptive delineations of the most curious works of nature and art in each county. (Oxfordshire, vol. 2, p. 142–80.) Lond., 1820, 8°.
G.A. Gen. top. 8° 9

180. TURNER, SIR G. O. P., Topographical memorandums for the county of Oxford. Lond., 1820, 8°. 44 pp. G.A. Oxon 8° 259
[2 other eds. in 1823: G.A. Oxon 8° 211, 698.]

181. MOULE, T., The English counties delineated. Pt. 1. (Oxfordshire, p. 67–82.) Lond., 1830, 4°. G.A. Gen. top. 4° 60

182. DUGDALE, T., and BURNETT, W., Curiosities in Great Britain. England & Wales delineated, alphabetically arranged. Lond., [c. 1830], 8°. G.A. Gen. top. 8° 447–50
[Other eds. in 1845? 1854: G.A. Gen. top. 4° 99.]

183. TYMMS, S., The family topographer. 7 vols. (Oxford circuit, vol 4, p. 131–92.) Lond., 1834, 12°. G.A. Oxon 8° 810 (18)

184. PIGOT AND CO., Pigot's gazetteer. (Oxfordshire, p. 367–82.) n. pl., [1840], 8°. G.A. Oxon 8° 611 (12)

185. HALL, S. C., and A. M., The book of the Thames. (Oxfordshire, *passim.*) Lond., 1859, 4°. 516 pp.   G.A. Gen. top. 4° 19
— [Another ed.] 1867.   Manning 8° 61
— 2nd ed. 1877.   G.A. Gen. top. 4° 70
— New ed. [*c.* 1880].   G.A. Gen. top. 4° 475

186. Through Oxon [signed C.]. (Temple Bar, Aug. 1865, p. 95–108.)
G.A. Oxon 4° 579 (15)

187. HOUSE, J., Geography of Oxfordshire. (Collins' county geogr.)
Lond., [*c.* 1870], 16°. 32 pp.   G.A. Oxon 16° 153

188. FAUNTHORPE, J. P., The geography of Oxfordshire and Buckinghamshire for use in schools. (Philip's county geogr.) Lond., 1873, 8°. 32 pp.   G.A. Oxon 8° 147 (11)

189. Ordnance survey. Book of reference to the plan of the [parishes] . . . in the county of Oxford. Lond., 1876–82, 4°.
G.A. Gen. top. 4° 400

190. SMITH, W., The particular description of England, 1588, ed. by H. B. Wheatley and E. W. Ashbee. (Oxfordshire, p. 33.) Lond., 1879, 4°.   G.A. Gen. top. 4° 265

191. MASON, C. M., The forty shires. (Oxfordshire, p. 271–76.) Lond., 1881, 8°.   G.A. Gen. top. 8° 353

192. MOWAT, J. L. G., *ed.*, Sixteen old maps of properties in Oxfordshire (with one in Berkshire) . . . illustrating the open field system. Oxf., 1888, fol.   G.A. Oxon a. 11

193. Deacon's Berkshire, Buckinghamshire and Oxfordshire court guide & county blue book. Lond., 1889, 8°.
— 2nd ed. 1890.   Dir. Gen. top. e. 1

194. Oxford: the upper river. (Longman's mag., July 1890, p. 325–32.)
G.A. Oxon 4° 577 (50)

195. The Gentleman's magazine library, a classified collection of the chief contents of the Gentleman's magazine from 1771–1868, ed. by G. L. Gomme. English topography, pt. ix, ed. by F. A. Milne. (Oxfordshire, p. 51–236.) Lond., 1897, 8°.   3974 d. 690 (9)

196. Photographic survey of England and Wales. County of Oxford. [Report of work which the committee proposes to make.] n. pl., (1898), 8°. 4 pp.   G.A. Oxon c. 317 (2)

197. HERBERTSON, A. J., On the one-inch ordnance survey map, with special reference to the Oxford sheet. (Geogr. teacher, 1902, vol. 1, no. 4, p. 150–66.)   G.A. Oxon 4° 383

198. FEA, A., Picturesque old houses, with illustrations. (Oxfordshire, p. 127–49.) Lond., [1902], 8°.   G.A. Gen. top. 8° 647

199. MANNING, P., Manuscript materials for the topography of Oxfordshire, in the library of the Society of antiquaries, London. n. pl., [1902], 8°. 8 pp. G.A. Oxon 4° 186 (1)

200. HUTTON, W. H., By Thames and Cotswold. Westm., 1903, 4°. 288 pp. G.A. Gen. top. 4° 210
— Revised. Lond., 1908, 8°. 310 pp. G.A. Gen. top. 8° 712

201. EVANS, H. A., Highways and byways in Oxford and the Cotswolds. Lond., &c., 1905, 8°. 407 pp. G.A. Gen. top. 8° 676
— 2nd ed. 1938. 396 pp. G.A. Gen. top. 8° 1280

202. HARPER, C. G., Thames valley villages. 2 vols. Lond., 1910, 8°. G.A. Gen. top. 8° 761, 62

203. DITCHFIELD, P. H., Oxfordshire. (Cambr. county geogr.) Cambr., 1912, 8°. 218 pp. G.A. Oxon 8° 836

204. FEA, A., Quiet roads and sleepy villages. (Oxfordshire, p. 88–110, 206–88.) Lond., 1913, 4°. G.A. Gen. top. 8° 814

205. GODLEY, A. D., Of a map, and walks [round Oxford]. (Cornhill mag., 1918, Aug., p. 142–52.) Per. 2705 d. 213

206. MONK, W. J., By road from Cheltenham to Oxford, with some account of the places near the route. Evesham, 1922, 8°. 96 pp. G.A. Eng. roads 8° 76

207. MONK, W. J., A ramble in Oxfordshire. [Oxf., 1925], 8°. 121 pp. G.A. Oxon 8° 1041

208. HEADLAM, C., Oxford & neighbouring churches. (Cathedrals, abbeys & famous churches.) Lond., &c., 1925, 16°. 192 pp. G.A. Eccl. top. 16° 55

209. Hutchinson's Britain beautiful, ed. by W. Hutchinson. (Oxfordshire, vol. 3, p. 1625–60.) Lond., 1926, 4°. G.A. Gen. top. 4° 300

210. FREEBORN, M. E., 'Twixt Cherwell and Glyme. Lond., [1927], 8°. 396 pp. G.A. Oxon 8° 1057

211. MARSHALL, R. M., Oxfordshire by-ways. Oxf., (1935), 8°. 136 pp. G.A. Oxon 8° 1155
— 2nd ed. 1949. 208 pp. G.A. Oxon 8° 1258

212. WILLIAMS, E. C., Companion into Oxfordshire. Lond., 1935, 8°. 268 pp. G.A. Oxon 8° 1147
— Repr. 1951. O.C.L.

213. ROBERTS, C., Gone rambling [in S.E. Oxfordshire]. Lond., 1935, 8°. 336 pp.
— Repr. 1935. G.A. Oxon 8° 1146

214. ROBERTS, C., Gone afield [in S.E. Oxfordshire]. Lond., 1936, 8°.
377 pp.   G.A. Gen. top. 8° 1220

215. MACARTHUR, W., The river Windrush. Lond., &c., 1946, 8°.
184 pp.   G.A. Eng. rivers 8° 129

216. BRIGGS, M. S., Round the shires. (Oxfordshire, p. 138–45.) Lond.,
[1946], 8°.   G.A. Gen. top. 8° 1384

217. PALMER, A., ed., Recording Britain. (Oxfordshire, vol. 3, p. 175–
99.) Oxf., 1948, 4°.   G.A. Gen. top. 4° 419 (3)

218. TURNOR, C., Oxfordshire. (Vision of Engl.) Lond., 1949, 4°.
120 pp.   G.A. Oxon 4° 650

219. WYMER, N., Green hills and grey spires. (Oxfordshire, p. 40–66.)
Lond., 1950, 8°.   G.A. Gen. top. 8° 1455

219A. PEEL, J. H. B., The Chilterns. (Vision of Engl.) (Oxfordshire,
passim.) Lond., &c., 1950, 4°. 112 pp.   G.A. Gen. top. 4° 454

220. WHYTE, D., The Cotswolds. Oxfordshire and Gloucestershire.
Lond., &c., [1951], 8°. p. 1–74.   G.A. Gen. top. 8° 1422 (13)

220A. MAIS, S. P. B., Brittania, 1651–1951. (Oxfordshire, p. 60, 61.)
Lond., &c., 1951, 4°.   G.A. Gen. top. c. 78

221. CANNAN, J., Oxfordshire. (County books.) Lond., [1952], 8°.
276 pp.   G.A. Oxon 8° 1247

222. [Collection of picture postcards of Oxfordshire.]
                                                     G.A. Oxon 4° 548, 49
See also 454, &c. [Communications].

PLACE NAMES

223. EARLE, J., On the names of places in the neighbourhood of Oxford.
(Proc., Oxf. architect. and hist. soc., 1879, N.S. vol. 3, p. 337–39.)
                                                     R. 13. 709

224. ALEXANDER, H., The place-names of Oxfordshire. Lond., &c.,
1912, 8°. 251 pp.   E. 1. 91

225. RITTER, O., Zu einigen Ortsnamen aus Oxfordshire. (Englische
Studien, 1922, vol. 56, p. 292–300.)   E. 7. 6 (56)

226. ARKELL, W. J., Place-names and topography in the Upper
Thames country. (Oxoniensia, 1942, p. 1–23.)   R. Top. 340
See 2480 [Etymology of 'Ewelme'. 1875].

GUIDE BOOKS

227. FLETCHER, W., and NIEMANN, E. J., A tour round Reading, a guide to its environs [p. 5–38 comprising villages in Oxfordshire west of the town]. Reading, [1840], 8°.　　　　G.A. Berks 8° 21

228. The environs of Oxford. (A handbook for Oxfordshire, p. 149–76.) Oxf., 1841, 16°.　　　　G.A. Oxon 16° 103

229. Murray's Handbook for travellers in Berks, Bucks and Oxfordshire. Lond., 1860, 12°.　　　　G.A. Gen. top. 8° 41
— 2nd ed. 1872. 3rd ed. 1882.　　　　G.A. Gen. top. 8° 404, 05

230. Oxfordshire. The official county map and guide. Lond., [c. 1877], 8°. 34 pp.　　　　G.A. Oxon 8° 204 (11)

231. RIMMER, A., Pleasant spots around Oxford. Lond., &c., [1878], 4°. 292 pp.　　　　G.A. Oxon 4° 63

232. Rambles and rides around Oxford. (Shrimpton's popular handbooks.) Oxf., (1885), 8°. 199 pp.
— 2nd ed., enlarged. [c. 1900].　　　　G.A. Oxon 8° 702

233. MURRAY, J., Handbook for travellers in Oxfordshire. Lond., 1894, 8°. 242 pp.　　　　G.A. Oxon 16° 42

234. GRAVES, H., The way about Oxfordshire. (Way-about ser. of gazetteer guides, no. 10.) Lond., [1897], 8°. 221 pp.
　　　　G.A. Oxon 8° 623

235. INMAN, H. T., Near Oxford, handbook to over a hundred places of interest within a radius of about fifteen miles. Oxf., &c., 1904, 16°. 215 pp.　　　　G.A. Oxon 16° 78
[Other eds. in 1913, 1920, 1946: G.A. Oxon 16° 126, 167, 209.]

236. BRABANT, F. G., Oxfordshire. (Little guides.) Lond., 1906, 8°. 282 pp.　　　　G.A. Oxon 16° 85
[Other eds. in 1914, 1919, 1924, 1933: G.A. Oxon 16° 196.]

237. SHUFFREY, J. A., Rural Oxford, sketches of . . . places on the motor bus routes . . . around Oxford. [Letterpress by H. Paintin, sketches by J. A. Shuffrey.] Oxf., [1927], obl. 8°. 41 pp.
　　　　G.A. Oxon 4° 479

238. TYLER, A. A., Guide to the Oxford motorbus country services. 2nd ed. Oxf., [1927], 16°. 137 pp.　　　　G.A. Oxon 16° 175

239. Oxfordshire, an illustrated review of the holiday & sporting attractions and commercial and industrial amenities of the county, by F. T. Dunn and other contributors, ed. by H. E. O'Connor. Cheltenham, [1936], 4°. 50 pp.　　　　G.A. Oxon 4° 563 (1)
— 2nd ed. [1939]. 32 pp.　　　　G.A. Oxon 4° 563 (2)

240. PIPER, J., Oxon. (Shell guides.) (Lond.), [1938], 4°. 45 pp.
G.A. Gen. top. 4° 363

241. MEE, A., Oxfordshire. (King's England.) Lond., 1942, 8°. 415 pp.
G.A. Gen. top. 8° 1228 [35]

241A. City of Oxford motor services. Oxford . . . followed by detailed itineraries. Glouc., [1950], 8°. 56 pp.   G.A. Gen. top. 8° 1524

HISTORY

SOURCES

242. TURNER, W. H., A calendar of charters, and rolls preserved in the Bodleian Library. (Oxfordshire, p. 277–84, 660–62.) Oxf., 1878, 8°.
R. 4. 205

243. Appendices to the Report of the Committee appointed to enquire as to the existing arrangements for the collection and custody of local records. (Oxfordshire, appendix 3, p. 26, 27.)
Pp. Eng. 1902, vol. 49

244. WALTON, H. M., The Oxfordshire County Record Office and its records. (Oxoniensia, 1938, p. 111–22.)   R. Top. 340
— Repr. with additions. (Oxf. county records joint comm., record publ., no. 1.) 1948. 15 pp.   G.A. Oxon 4° 643

245. Oxfordshire county council, county records joint committee. Report. 1947–.   G.A. Oxon 4° 678

ATTENTION is directed to the following general sources, which are too complex to admit of more detailed treatment.

246. State papers [afterw.] Calendar of state papers, domestic series, preserved in the Public record office. 1518–. Vol. 1–. (Lond.), 1830–, 4°. Ψ 2. 12

247. Proceedings and ordinances [afterw.] Acts of the Privy council of England. 1386–. Vol. 1–. Lond., 1834–, 4°.   R. 5. 172

248. Letters and papers, foreign and domestic, of the reign of Henry VIII, preserved in the Public record office. Vol. 1–. Lond., 1862–, 4°. Ψ 2. 19

249. First (–   ) report of the Royal commission on historical manuscripts. Lond., 1874–, fol. & 8°.   R. 6. 1–

250. Publications of the Pipe Roll society. Lond., 1883–, 8°.
R. 5. 145, 46

251. PULLING, A., The law reports. Index to the orders in council, proclamations, royal commissions of inquiry, matter, orders and notices of government departments, and all other published in the London Gazette, 1830–1880. Lond., 1885, 4°.   22858 d. 63

252. Calendar of the proceedings of the Committee for compounding &c. 1643–1660, preserved in the Public record office. 5 pt. Lond., 1889–92, 4°. Ψ 2. 32 f

253. A descriptive catalogue of ancient deeds in the Public record office. 6 vols. Lond., 1890–1915, 4°. R. 5. 166

254. Calendar of entries in the Papal registers relating to Great Britain and Ireland. Papal letters. 1198–. Vol. 1–. Lond., 1893–, 4°. R. 8. 25

255. Calendar of the Patent rolls preserved in the Public record office. 1216–. Lond., 1901–, 4°. R. 5. 164

256. Calendar of the Close rolls preserved in the Public record office. 1227–. Lond., 1902–, 4°. R. 5. 162

257. Calendar of the Charter rolls preserved in the Public record office. 1226–1516. 6 vols. Lond., 1903–27, 4°. R. 5. 163

258. Calendar of Liberate rolls preserved in the Public record office. 1226–. Lond., 1916–, 4°. R. 5. 162a

259. Curia Regis rolls, preserved in the Public record office. Richard I–. Lond., 1922–, 4°. R. 5. 150

GENERAL

260. CAMDEN, W., Britannia, tr. and enlarged by R. Gough. 3 vols. (Oxfordshire, vol. 1, p. 285–312.) Lond., 1789, fol.
Gough Gen. top. 61
— 2nd ed. 1806. vol. 2. G.A. Gen. top. b. 4
[The first Latin ed. was publ. in 1586, and there have been many subsequent eds. in Lat. & Engl. The eds. listed above are the most convenient.]

261. TAYLOR, J., The honorable and memorable foundations, erections, raisings and ruines, of divers cities . . . within ten shires and counties . . . Also, a relation of the wine tavernes . . . in . . . the said severall shires. (Oxfordshire, sig. D 6–8.) Lond., 1636, 8°.
Mal. 506

262. LELAND, J., The itinerary of John Leland the antiquary, publ. by T. Hearne. 9 vols. Oxf., 1710–12, 8°. Mus. Bibl. II 15–23
[Other eds. were publ. in 1745, 1768.]
— [Another ed.] ed. by L. T. Smith. Lond., 1907–10, 4°.
R. 9. 21t
[The Itinerary was made c. 1535–43.]

263. DEFOE, D., A tour through the whole island of Great Britain. (Oxfordshire, vol. 2, letter 3, p. 21–48.) Lond., 1724–27, 8°.
Gough Gen. top. 317
[Other eds. in 1742, 1748, 1753, 1761, 1769, 1778, &c. 1927, vol. 2: G.A. Gen. top. 4° 324.]

264. COX, T., and HALL, A., Magna Britannia et Hibernia [by T. Cox and A. Hall]. (Oxfordshire, vol. 4, p. 209–509.) Lond., 1724, 4°.
Douce C subt. 102
[The Bodleian has a graingerized edition by J. Dunkin of the Oxfordshire portion, in 3 folio vols.; G.A. Oxon a. 115–17.]

265. MOORE, J., A list of the principal castles and monasteries in Great Britain. (Oxfordshire, p. 34.) Lond., 1798, 8°.
Gough Gen. top. 173

266. BREWER, J. N., A topographical and historical description of the county of Oxford. (The beauties of England and Wales, vol. 12.) Lond., (1819), 8°. 545 pp.   G.A. Oxon 8° 598

267. The history and topography of Oxfordshire. (Pinnock's County histories.) Lond., 1819, 16°. 72 pp.   G.A. Oxon 16° 132

268. Oxfordshire, ancient state and remains, present state and appearance. (Gent's. mag., 1820, pt. 2, p. 202–06, 297–301, 394–96.)
Ψ 2. 44

269. Oxfordshire, miscellaneous remarks. (Gent's. mag., 1820, pt. 2, p. 584–87.) Ψ 2. 44

270. Oxfordshire, history, eminent natives (Gent's. mag., 1820, pt. 2, p. 497–502.) Ψ 2. 44

271. Skelton's engraved illustrations of the principal antiquities of Oxfordshire, from original drawings by F. Mackenzie. With descriptive notices, &c. Oxf., 1823, 4°. 142 pp.   R. 9. 98 s

272. Oxfordshire monumental inscriptions, from the MSS. of Anthony à Wood, dr. Hutton and mr. Hinton. [Pedigrees, parochial collections, &c., ed. by sir T. Phillipps. Unfinished.] Evesham, 1825, fol. 98 pp.   Manning fol. 6

273. History, gazetteer and directory of the county of Oxford. (R. Gardner.) Peterborough, 1852, 8°. 862 pp.   G.A. Oxon 8° 64

274. Memoirs chiefly illustrative of the history and antiquities of the county and city of Oxford, communicated to the Archæological institute, 1850. Lond., 1854, 8°. 266 pp.
G.A. Gen. top. 8° 528 (6)

275. Edward Cassey and co.'s History, gazetteer and directory of Berkshire and Oxfordshire. Lond., 1868, 8°. [Oxf. 278 pp.]
G.A. Berks 8° 58

276. DAVENPORT, J. M., Oxfordshire annals. (Oxf.), 1869, 8°. 121 pp.
G.A. Oxon 8° 136

277. TIMBS, J., Abbeys, castles and ancient halls of England and Wales. (Oxfordshire, vol. 1, p. 78-113.) Lond., [1870], 8°.
G.A. Gen. top. 8° 216
— [Another ed.] 1872, vol. 2.   G.A. Gen. top. 8° 256
— [Another ed.] 1892, vol. 2.   G.A. Gen. top. 8° 553

278. EARWAKER, J. P., On recent discoveries in the neighbourhood of Oxford. (Proc., Oxf. architect. and hist. soc., N.S., vol. 3, 1872, p. 1-5; 1874, p. 170.)   R. 13. 709

279. The Gentleman's magazine library, a classified collection of the chief contents of the Gentleman's magazine from 1771-1868, ed. by G. L. Gomme. English topography, pt. ix, ed. by F. A. Milne. (Oxfordshire, p. 51-236.) Lond., 1897, 8°.   3974 d. 690 (9)

280. MARSHALL, E., Wayside, churchyard and market crosses. (Rept., Oxf. archaeol. soc., 1897/8, p. 28-39.)   R. Top. 330

281. FALKNER, J. M., History of Oxfordshire. (Berks, Bucks, & Oxon archaeol. journ., 1899, vol. 5, p. 83-86.)   R. Top. 100

282. FALKNER, J. M., A history of Oxfordshire. (Popular county hist.) Lond., 1899, 8°. 327 pp.   G.A. Oxon 8° 661
— Cheap ed. 1906.   G.A. Oxon 8° 1235

283. GRETTON, M. S., Three centuries in North Oxfordshire, by M. S. Henderson [mrs. Gretton]. Oxf., &c., 1902, 8°. 270 pp.
G.A. Oxon 8° 694

284. DITCHFIELD, P. H., Memorials of old Oxfordshire. Lond., &c., 1903, 8°. 252 pp.   G.A. Oxon 8° 700

284A. South Oxfordshire constitutional review. No. 1, 2. Oxf., 1903, 8°.
G.A. Oxon 8° 874 (16)

285. The Victoria history of the county of Oxford, ed. by L. F. Salzman [&c.]. Vol. 1, 2, . Lond., 1939, 07,   fol.   R. 9. 41 s

286. IRVING, J., Stories from the history of Oxfordshire. Oxf., 1908, 8°. 96 pp.   G.A. Oxon 8° 756

287. LIDDELL, H. A., School history of Oxfordshire. Oxf., 1908, 8°. 256 pp.   G.A. Oxon 8° 758

288. Royal archaeological institute. The Summer meeting at Oxford, July 1910. [Proceedings, containing descriptions, plans, &c., of churches, &c., within the county. Extr. from the Archaeol. journ., vol. 67, no. 268.] Lond., 1910, 4°. 76 pp.   G.A. Oxon 4° 388
— Detailed programme. 41 pp.   G.A. Oxon 4° 389

289. GUNTHER, R. W., ed., The Oxford country, its attractions and associations described by several authors. Lond., 1912, 8°. 319 pp.
G.A. Oxon 8° 844

290. GRANT, J., *ed.*, Berkshire and Oxfordshire, historical, biographical and pictorial. Lond., 1912, fol.   O.A.H.S.

291. DITCHFIELD, P. H., The counties of England, their story and antiquities. (Oxfordshire, vol. 1, p. 346–67.) Lond., 1912, 8°.
G.A. Gen. top. 8° 784

292. Parochial collections, made by Anthony à Wood and Richard Rawlinson, transcr. by F. N. Davis. 2 pt. (Oxf. record soc., vol. 2, 11.) Oxf., 1920, 29, 8°.   R. 13. 702

292A. HODGE, R. T. HERMON-, BARON WYFOLD, The Upper Thames valley, some antiquarian notes. Lond., 1923, 8°. 64 pp.
G.A. Gen. top. 8° 962

293. MONK, W. J., By Thames and Windrush, giving some historical account of Witney, Eynsham, Stanton Harcourt, Bablockhythe, Newbridge, Northmoor, Standlake, Gaunt house, Yelford, Coke-thorpe and Ducklington. Oxf., 1926, 8°. 58 pp.
G.A. Oxon 8° 1047

294. PAINTIN, H., Occasional papers. 1. Wychwood forest. 2. The Wychwood country. 3. The eastern Cotswolds. 4. Wittenham, &c. [Typewritten]. [Oxf., 1929], 4°. 26 pp.   G.A. Oxon 4° 495

295. Tours through literary England: the Matthew Arnold country. (Sat. rev., 1930, July 5, p. 9, 10.)   N. 2288 c. 8

296. BAKER, J. H., The story of the Chiltern Heathlands. Reading, (1931), 8°. 74 pp.   G.A. Oxon 8° 1079 (14)
— 2nd ed. (1932). 104 pp.   G.A. Oxon 8° 1101 (2)

297. MASSINGHAM, H. J., Adventures among [Cotswold] villages. (Contemp. review, 1932, May, p. 603–09.)   Per. 3977 d. 58

298. CAM, H. M., The Hundred outside the North gate of Oxford [&c.]. (Oxoniensia, 1936, p. 113–28.)   R. Top. 340
— [Repr. as chapter 7 of H. M. Cam's Liberties and communities in medieval England. 1944. 2272 d. 9.]

299. HYDE, W., Leaves from an Oxfordshire notebook [by W. Hyde]. Oxf., 1937, 4°. 43 pp.   O.C.L.

300. DAVIES, A. MORLEY, The hundreds of Buckinghamshire and Oxfordshire. (Records of Bucks, Journ. of the architect. and archaeol. soc. of Bucks, 1950, vol. 15, p. 231–49.)   R. Top. 110

301. Historic Oxfordshire. (Oxfordshire rural community council.) Oxf., 1951, 8°. 77 pp.   G.A. Oxon 8° 1252

Societies

302. Archaeological (and natural history) society of North Oxfordshire [*afterw.*] North Oxfordshire [*afterw.*] Oxfordshire archaeological society.
— Rules. Banbury, 1853, 8°. 9 pp.   R. Top. 330 (1)
— Transactions. 1853-. Banbury, 1853-, 8°.   R. Top. 330
— First (-) report. Banbury, 1851-, 8°.   R. Top. 330

303. Oxford society for promoting the study of Gothic architecture [*afterw.*] Oxford architectural (and historical) society.
— (The rules and) Proceedings. 1839–1896/1900. Oxf., 1839–[1901], 8°.   R. 13. 705–11
— Oxoniensia. Vol. 1-. Oxf., 1936-, 4°.   R. Top. 340
— [Miscellaneous papers. 1839-.]   G.A. Oxon 4° 300–302**

304. PANTIN, W. A., The Oxford architectural and historical society, 1839–1939. (Oxoniensia, 1939, p. 174–94.)   R. Top. 340

305. OLLARD, S. L., The Oxford architectural and historical society and the Oxford Movement. (Oxoniensia, 1940, p. 146–60.)
     R. Top. 340

306. Oxford historical society. [Publications. Vol. 1-, 1884-.] Oxf., 1885-, 8°.   R. 13. 700
— [Miscellaneous papers. 1883-.]   G.A. Oxon 4° 104, 104*

307. Oxfordshire record society. Oxfordshire record series. Vol. 1-. Oxf., 1919-, 8°.   R. 13. 702
— [Annual report. 1931-.]   G.A. Oxon 8° 985*

EARLY MAN

308. Observations on certain ancient pillars of memorial called hoarstones. (Archaeologia, 1834, vol. 25. Oxfordshire, p. 54, 55.)
     R. Top. 7

309. GAGE, J., A letter . . . with an account of a British buckler found in the bed of the river Isis between Little Wittenham and Dorchester. (Archaeologia, 1838, vol. 27, p. 298–300.)   R. Top. 7

310. DAWKINS, W. B., On the traces of the Early Britons in the neighbourhood of Oxford [Standlake and Yarnton]. (Proc., Oxf. architect. and hist. soc., 1862, N.S., vol. 1, p. 108–16.)   R. 13. 707
— [Another ed.]. (Gent's. mag., 1862, pt. 2, p. 142–49.)   Ψ 2. 44

311. STEVENS, J., Stone implements found in the Thames river. (Journ., Brit. archaeol. assoc., 1883, vol. 39, p. 344–47.)
     R. Top. 4

312. MANNING, P., Notes on the archaeology of Oxford and its neighbourhood. (Berks, Bucks, & Oxon archaeol. journ., 1898, vol. 4, p. 9-28, 39-47.) R. Top. 100

313. WINDLE, SIR B. C. A., A tentative list of objects of prehistoric and early historic interest in . . . Berks, Bucks and Oxon. (Berks, Bucks, & Oxon archaeol. journ., 1901, vol. 7, p. 45-47.) R. Top. 100

314. Ancient earthworks. (Victoria county history, 1907, vol. 2, p. 303-49.) R. 9. 41 s

315. MANNING, P., and LEEDS, E. T., An archaeological survey of Oxfordshire. (Archaeologia, 1921, vol. 71, p. 227-65.) R. Top. 7

316. CRAWFORD, O. G. S., The long barrows of the Cotswolds. (Oxfordshire, p. 158-66.) Glouc., 1925, 4°. G.A. Gen. top. 4° 305

317. LEEDS, E. T., Early settlement [Neolithic, Bronze age, Iron age, Roman and Saxon] in the Upper Thames basin. (Geography, 1928, vol. 14, p. 527-35.) Per. 263334 d. 11

318. LEEDS, E. T., A bronze cauldron from the river Cherwell. (Archaeologia, 1930, vol. 80, p. 1-36.) R. Top. 7

319. LEEDS, E. T., Recent Bronze age discoveries in Berkshire and Oxfordshire. (Antiquaries journ., 1934, vol. 14, p. 264-76.) R. Top. 2

320. LEEDS, E. T., Rectangular enclosures of the Bronze age in the Upper Thames valley [Benson, Dorchester]. (Antiquaries journ., 1934, vol. 14, p. 414-16.) R. Top. 2

321. LEEDS, E. T., Recent Iron age discoveries in Oxfordshire and North Berkshire. (Antiquaries journ., 1935, vol. 15, p. 30-41.) R. Top. 2

322. LEEDS, E. T., Round barrows and ring-ditches in Berks and Oxon. (Oxoniensia, 1936, p. 7-23.) R. Top. 340

323. LEEDS, E. T., Beakers of the Upper Thames district. (Oxoniensia, 1938, p. 7-30.) R. Top. 340

324. SUTHERLAND, C. H. V., Three ancient British coins found in Oxfordshire. (Oxoniensia, 1938, p. 171, 72.) R. Top. 340

325. LEEDS, E. T., Four polished stone axes [found at Alvescot, Kencot, Bampton and Sutton Courtenay, Berks.]. (Oxoniensia, 1938, p. 168, 69.) R. Top. 340

326. Early man. (Victoria county history, 1939, vol. 1, p. 223-26 a.) R. 9. 41 s

327. LEEDS, E. T., New discoveries of Neolithic pottery in Oxfordshire. (Oxoniensia, 1940, p. 1-12.) R. Top. 340

327A. Council for British archaeology. Archaeological bulletin for the British Isles. 1940–1946. (Oxfordshire, p. 28, 29.)
— 1947. (p. 36, 37.)   G.A. Gen. top. 8° 1476

328. RILEY, D. N., Archaeology from the air in the Upper Thames valley. (Oxoniensia, 1943, 44, p. 64–101.)   R. Top. 340

329. ARKELL, W. J., Three Oxfordshire palaeoliths and their significance for pleistocene correlation. (Proc., Prehist. soc., 1945, N.S., vol. 11, p. 20–31.)   Soc. 247115 d. 124

330. ARKELL, W. J., The Treacher collection of middle Thames palaeoliths. (Oxoniensia, 1946–7, p. 171–73.)   R. Top. 340

331. O'NEIL, B. H. ST. J., War and archaeology in Britain. (Antiquaries journ., 1948, vol. 28, p. 20–45. Oxfordshire, passim.)   R. Top. 2

332. On the ancient channel between Caversham and Henley, and its contained flint implements. Pt. 1, by M. S. Treacher. Pt. 2, by W. J. Arkell and K. P. Oakley. (Proc., Prehist. soc., 1948, vol. 14, p. 126–54.)   Per. 247115 d. 124

See 1714 [Late-Celtic dagger, fibula and jet cameo-bronze fibula, Beckley. 1915].
See 1974 [Middle Bronze age barrow, Cassington. 1946].
See 2041, 42 [Chastleton camp, early Iron age. 1881, 1931].
See 2345 [Flint implements, Ditchley. 1874].
See also entries under Dorchester, 2377, &c.
See 2471 [Hoar stone, Enstone. 1949].
See 2525 [Beaker, Eynsham. 1931].
See 2661 [Prehistoric remains, Grafton. 1905].
See 2711–13 [Grim's Dyke].
See 2742 [Palaeolith, Hanborough. 1946].
See 2751 [Urn (beaker), Hardwick. 1876].
See 2824 [Bronze sword and Iron spearhead, Henley. 1882].
See 2827 [Jersey megalithic monument, Henley. 1919].
See 2829 [Food vessel, Henley. 1938].
See 2982 [Imitation Stone-age monument, Ipsden. 1919].
See 3075 [Excavations. Langford downs. 1946/7].
See also entries under Little Rollright, 3139, &c.
See 3161 [Ring-ditch, Long Hanborough. 1946].
See 3261 [Cave site at Nettlebed. 1915].
See 3401 [Flint-factory, Peppard Common. 1913].
See 3654 [British and Saxon remains. Circular trenches, &c. Standlake.1857].
See 3659 [Early Iron-age settlement, Standlake. 1942].
See 3660 [Late Bronze-age and Iron-age site, Standlake. 1946, 47].
See 3685, 86 [Excavations at Stanton Harcourt. 1943/4, 45].
See 3835 [Thor's stone, Taston. 1949].
See 3979 [Henge monument, Westwell. 1949].
See 4131 [Bronzes, Woodeaton. 1949].

ROMANO-BRITISH

333. POINTER, J., Britannia Romana, or, Roman antiquities in Britain. [Accounts of Roman coins, &c. found in Oxfordshire (p. 12–34) and isolated references to roads, camps, &c. in the county.] Oxf., 1724, 8°. 54 pp.   Gough Oxf. 122 (2)

334. FOX, A. L., On some flint implements found associated with Roman remains in Oxfordshire and the Isle of Thanet. (Journ., Ethnol. soc., 1868, vol. I, p. I–12.) Soc. 247115 e. 61

335. HAVERFIELD, F. J., [Account of some Romano-British remains in the Upper Thames valley]. (Proc., Soc. of antiq., 1899, ser. 2, vol. 18, p. 9–16.) R. Top. 1

336. LYELL, A. H., Bibliographical list of Romano-British remains. (Oxfordshire, p. 102–05.) Cambr., 1912, 8°. 258732 e. 2

337. MANNING, P., and LEEDS, E. T., An archaeological survey of Oxfordshire. (Archaeologia, 1921, vol. 71, p. 227–65.) R. Top. 7

338. STEVENS, C. G., and MYRES, J. N. L., Excavations on the Akeman Street, near Asthally, Oxon, Feb.–June, 1925. (Antiquaries journ., 1926, vol. 6, p. 43–53.) R. Top. 2

339. O'NEIL, B. H. ST. J., Akeman street and the river Cherwell. (Antiquaries journ., 1929, vol. 9, p. 30–82.) R. Top. 2

340. Romano-British remains. (Victoria county history, 1939, vol. 1, p. 267–345.) R. 9. 41 s

See 312 [Notes on archaeology. 1898].
See 313 [List of objects of historic interest. 1901].
See 317 [Early settlement, Upper Thames. 1928].
See 328 [Archaeology from the air. 1943].
See also entries under Alchester, 1431, &c.
See 1491 [Roman altar, Bablock Hythe. 1946].
See 1510 [Romano-British village, Bampton. 1891].
See 1539 [Roman remains, Banbury. 1853].
See 1713 [Roman villa, Beckley. 1868].
See 1766 [Arretine ware, Bicester. 1907].
See 1830, 1833 [Romano-British site, Bloxham. 1929, 1938].
See 2223 [Romano-British potters' field, Cowley. 1941].
See 2224 [Romano-British skeletons, Cowley. 1941].
See 2318 [Romano-British site, Cutteslowe. 1935].
See 2347–50 [Roman villa, Ditchley. 1935, 36].
See also entries under Dorchester, 2377, &c.
See 2526 [Roman coins, Eynsham. 1936].
See 2761 [Roman remains, Headington. 1850].
See 2826 [Roman villa, Henley. 1911].
See 2906 [Romano-Celt brooch, Hook Norton. 1910].
See 3021, 22 [Roman coin-hoard, Kiddington. 1936].
See 3067 [Romano-British finds, Aves ditch, Kirtlington. 1937, 1946].
See 3129A [Roman pottery works, Littlemore. 1884].
See 3138 [Roman finds, Little Rollright. 1940].
See 3169, 70 [Roman coins, &c., Madmarston camp. 1853].
See also entries under North Leigh, 3306, &c.
See 3473 [Pottery, Sandford-on-Thames. 1922].
See 3515 [Roman remains, Shiplake. 1918].
See also entries under Stonesfield, 3747, &c.
See 3989, 90 [Roman villa, Wheatley. 1846].
See 4127 [Coins at Woodeaton. 1931].
See 4129, 30 [Blue pigment, Woodeaton. 1940].
See 4135, 36 [Roman antiquities, Woodperry. 1846, 47].
See 4199 [Roman road, Blenheim park. 1899].

ANGLO-SAXON

341. DAWKINS, W. B., On the traces of the Early Britons in the neighbourhood of Oxford [Standlake and Yarnton]. (Proc., Oxf. architect. and hist. soc., 1862, N.S., vol. 1, p. 108–16.) R. 13. 707
— [Another ed.]. (Gent's. mag., 1862, pt. 2, p. 142–49.) Ψ 2. 44

342. BARING, F., Oxfordshire traces of the Northern insurgents of 1065. (Engl. hist. review, 1898, vol. 13, p. 295–97.) Ψ 2. 38

343. CRAWFORD, O. G. S., A Saxon fish-pond near Oxford. (Antiquity, 1930, vol. 4, p. 480–83.) R. Top. 6

344. LEEDS, E. T., The Early Saxon penetration of the Upper Thames area. (Antiquaries journ., 1933, vol. 13, p. 229–51.) R. Top. 2

345. GRUNDY, G. B., ed., Saxon Oxfordshire, charters and ancient highways. (Oxf. record soc., 15.) Oxf., 1933, 8°. 120 pp. R. 13. 702

346. Anglo-Saxon remains. (Victoria county history, 1939, vol. 1, p. 346–72.) R. 9. 41 s

See 312 [Notes on archaeology. 1898].
See 313 [List of objects of historic interest. 1901].
See 317 [Early settlement, Upper Thames. 1928].
See 1460 [Anglo-Saxon burial ground, Asthall. 1924].
See 1862–65 [Anglo-Saxon cemetery, Brighthampton. 1857, 58, 1860].
See 1901, 02 [Anglo-Saxon remains, Broughton Poggs. 1857].
See 1922 [8th-century stone coffin, Burford. 1814].
See 1973 [Early Saxon cemeteries, Cassington. 1942].
See 2006 [Saxon cemeteries, Chadlington. 1940].
See 2430 [Anglo-Saxon remains, Ducklington. 1859].
See 2483 [Bronze bowl, Ewelme. 1907].
See 3168 [Lyneham barrow. 1895].
See 3234 [Minster Lovell jewel. 1948].
See 3654–56 [British and Saxon remains. Circular trenches, &c., Standlake, &c. 1857, 58].
See 3922 [Weapons from battle between Offa of Mercia and Cenwulph of Wessex, Warborough. 1900].
See 3993 [Photographs of Anglo-Saxon graves, Wheatley. 1883].
See 3994, 95 [Anglo-Saxon cemetery, Wheatley. 1884, 1916].

MIDDLE AGES

347. Domesday-book [ed. by A. Farley]. (Oxfordshire, vol. 1, p. 154–61.) [Lond.], 1783, fol. R. 9. 089
[Publ. in 1783 without title-pages, the title-pages as above were issued in 1816 by the Record Commission, with the 2 vols. containing the Indices and Additamenta.]

347A. KELHAM, R., Domesday book illustrated. (Oxfordshire, p. 81–84.) Lond., 1788, 8°. Gough Gen. top. 159

348. Dom Boc. A translation . . . as far as relates to the counties of Middlesex [&c.] Oxford, by W. Bawden. Doncaster, 1812, 4°.
G.A. Gen. top. 4° 191

349. Domesday book. Facs. of the part relating to Oxfordshire. Southampton, 1862, fol. 15 pp. R. 9. 090 *a*

350. MOWAT, J. L. G., Notes on the Oxfordshire Domesday [by J. L. G. Mowat]. Oxf., 1892, 8°. 32 pp. G.A. Oxon 4° 149

351. Domesday survey. (Victoria county history, 1939, vol. 1, p. 373–428, 491–97.) R. 9. 41 *s*

352. HODGEN, M. T., Domesday water-mills [incl. a detailed map of those in Oxf. area]. (Antiquity, 1939, vol. 13, p. 261–.) R. Top. 6

353. LAMBORN, E. A. GREENING, A problem of the Oxfordshire Domesday [mainly about Chislehampton]. (N. & Q., 1944, vol. 187, p. 203–05.) Ψ 2. 97

See 1172 [Taxatio ecclesiastica, 1290. 1802].
See 1173 [Nonarum inquisitiones in curia scaccarii, temp. Edwardi iii. 1807].

354. Testa de Nevill sive Liber feodorum in curia scaccarii, temp. Hen. iii. & Edw. i. (Oxfordshire, *passim.*) [Lond.], 1807, fol. R. 5. fol. 128
— [Another ed. entitled] Liber feodorum, The book of fees. 1198–1293. 3 pt. Lond., 1920–31, 4°. R. 5. 164 *n*

See 1174 [Valor ecclesiasticus temp. Henr. viii. 1814].

355. Rotuli Hundredorum temp. Hen. iii. & Edw. i. in Turr' Lond' et in curia receptae scaccarii Westm. asservati. (Oxfordshire, vol. 2, p. 30–48, 688–877.) [Lond.], 1818, fol. R. 5. 129 *b*

356. BIRCH, W. DE G., On three lists of monasteries compiled in the thirteenth century. (Journ., Brit. archaeol. assoc., 1872, vol. 28. Oxeneforde, p. 57.) R. Top. 4

357. HALL, H., *ed.*, The Red book of the Exchequer. 3 pt. (Oxfordshire, *passim.*) Lond., 1896, 8°. Rolls ser. 99

358. An Oxfordshire will of 1230–1231 [ed. by H. E. Salter]. (Engl. hist. review, 1905, vol. 20, p. 291, 92.) Ψ 2. 38

359. FARRER, W., Honors and knights' fees. Vol. 2. Chester (p. 240–54 concern Gt. Tew; Tackley; South Weston; Ardley; Churchill and Pirton). Lond., 1924, 4°. G.A. Gen. top. 4° 291

360. SALTER, H. E., *ed.*, The feet of fines for Oxfordshire, 1195–1291. (Oxf. record soc., 12.) Oxf., 1930, 8°. 275 pp. R. 13. 702

361. Inquisitions and assessments relating to feudal aids, 1284–1431. Vol. 4. [Oxfordshire, p. 154–203.] Lond., 1906, 4°. R. 5. 160

362. SALTER, H., Some Oxfordshire surveys of 1387. [Inquisitions of the properties of alien priories, eschaets, &c. of the king, concerning

Kirtlington, Shipton-under-Wychwood, Chadlington Hundred, Broughton Poggs, Benson, Watlington, Nettlebed, Whitchurch and Coggs.] (Rept., Oxf. archaeol. soc., 1910, p. 28–34.) R. Top. 330

362A. The Registrum antiquissimum of the cathedral church of Lincoln, ed. by C. W. Foster. Vol. 1–6. (Lincoln record soc., vol. 27, 28, 29, 32, 34, 41 .) Lincoln, 1931–50, , 4°. R. Top. 260

See 1451 [Excavation at the 12th-century castle, Ascot d'Oilly. 1946].
See 2996A [Late Dark age finds at Islip. 1950]
See 3426 [Campaign of Radcot bridge in 1387. 1927].
See 3861 [15th-century hoard, Thame. 1940].
See 3862 [Gold rings and silver groats, Thame. 1941].

TUDOR AND EARLY STUART

363. The names of the nobility . . . and others who contributed to the defence of this country at the time of the Spanish invasion in 1588. Lond., 1798, 4°. 72 pp. 22853 d. 19

364. LEADAM, I. S., ed., The Domesday of inclosures, 1517–1518, the extant returns to Chancery for Berks . . . Oxon [&c.] by the Commissioners of inclosures in 1517. 2 vols. (Publ., Roy. hist. soc.) Lond., &c., 1897, 8°. 24754 e. 109

CIVIL WAR AND COMMONWEALTH

IN the following section reference has been made to Falconer Madan's Oxford books. When a work has been found which is not listed in Madan, and is not in the Bodleian, we have referred to the printed catalogue of the Thomason collection in the British Museum.

365. Feb. 10. Two petitions of the knights . . . of the best ranke and quality in the county of Oxford. The one to the . . . House of peers. The other to the . . . House of Commons. [Anti-popery petitions.] Lond., 1641, 4°. 8 pp. C 15. 15 Linc.

366. [April 10?] To the . . . House of peers . . . The humble petition of the knights . . . and others, inhabitants of the county of Oxford. [For disarming papists; against abuses of the Church, &c.] Lond., 1641, s. sh. Wood 516 (5)

367. [May?] To the . . . House of commons . . . The humble petition of the baronets . . . and others of good ranke and quality in the county of Oxford. [An anti-popery petition.] [Madan 978.] [Oxf., 1641], s. sh. Wood 373 (26)

368. The Brownist hæresies confuted . . . in a true history of one Mistris Sarah Miller of Banbury. . . . n. pl., 1641, 8°. 6 pp. C 13. 14 (28) Linc.

369. Feb. 8, 9. The two petitions of the knights, gentlemen and free-holders of the county of Oxon: together with Two petitions of the knights . . . of Kent. [Against popery.] Lond., 1642, 4°. 8 pp.
G. Pamph. 2288(7)

370. Feb. 15. To his excellencie, the earl of Forth . . . the humble petition of divers poor prisoners in Oxford-castle . . . to take their distressed condition into your pious consideration . . . that your petitioners may receive some relief from their friends. . . . Lond., 1642, s. sh. Antiq. c. E. 9 (121)

371. [Feb. 16.] The humble petition of the inhabitants of the county of Oxford to his majesty, with his majesties answer thereunto. [Madan 1249.] Oxf., 1642, 4°. 8 pp. Antiq. e. E. 1642. 86

372. [Feb.] To the House of peers, The petition of the county of Oxford [praying that the University be not allowed to be 'over-whelmed with Popery']. [Thomason i. 82.] Lond., 1642, s. sh.
B.M.

373. July 29. The proceedings at Banbury since the Ordnance went down for the Lord Brooks to fortify Warwick Castle. Lond., 1642, 4°. 8 pp. Wood 374 (34)

374. Aug. 3. His majesties two letters, one to the Vice-chancellour and Convocation of the University of Oxford: the other to the High Sheriff of the county and to the major of the city of Oxford. . . . [Madan 1016.] Lond., 1642, 4°. 8 pp. B.M.

375. Aug. 11. The earle of Portlands charge delivered to the Lords house by M. Pym. Also a new plot discovered, being a relation of the earle of Northamptons surprizing the magazine at Banbury by the forging of a false letter [&c.]. [Lond.], 1642, 4°. 6 pp. G. Pamph. 2315 (6)

376. Aug. 17. Exceeding ioyfull news from Oxford-shire, being a true relation of a victorious battell fought by the apprentizes of London against the cavaliers. [Madan 1026.] Lond., 1642, 4°. 8 pp. B.M.

377. Aug. 24. Exceeding good news from Oxfordshire: being a true relation of the manner of the apprehending of the earle of Berkshire . . . and other cavaliers. . . . [Lond.], 1642, 4°. 6 pp.
Antiq. e. E. 1642. 119 (1)

378. [Sept. 1. Account of Sir John Byron's skirmish at Brackley and welcome given to the Cavaliers at Oxford.] (Severall occurrences that have lately happened at Warwicke, Northamptonshire, and Oxfordshire, p. 7.) [Madan 1030.] Lond., 1642, 4°.
Antiq. e. E. 102 (2)

379. Sept. 20. R. (S.), Good news from Banbury in Oxfordshire, relating how two troops of Horse, under . . . my Lord Jay's two sons, pursued divers cavalleers as they fled from Oxford [signed S.R.]. [Thomason i. 170.] Lond., 1642, 4°. B.M.

380. [Oct. 26.] The King's resolution concerning his coming from Banbury to London. [Thomason i. 186.] Lond., 1642, 4°.   B.M.

381. Nov. 2. His maiesties declaration . . . to all his souldiers . . . [*With*] His maiesties speech to the . . . inhabitants of the county of Oxon. [Madan 1060.] [Oxf.], 1642, 4°. 8 pp.   Ashm. 1065 (8)
— [Another ed.] 1642.   4° L 72 (3) Art.

382. Nov. 3. New plots discovered against the Parliament and the peace of the kingdom, in two letters, the one from the marquis of Hartford to sir Ralph Hopton, the other from sir Ralph Hopton to the said Marquis. Also an exact relation [by J. Johnson] of the treachery of master Muntague, who delivered Banbury to the cavaliers. [Thomason i. 190.] Lond., 1642, 4°.   B.M.

383. Nov. 3. By the king. A proclamation of . . . pardon to the inhabitants of . . . Oxon. [Madan 1053.] [Oxf., 1642], s. sh.
                                         Gough Oxf. 138 (2)

384. Nov. 7. Truthes from severall parts of the kingdome, since Munday the one and thirtieth of October to this present. From Warwicke, Banbury, Oxford. [Madan 1064.] Lond., 1642, 4°. 8 pp.
                                         G.A. Berks 4° 3 (2)

385. [Nov. 27. Requisition for horses in order to protect the county of Oxford from dragooners.] [Madan 1090.] [Oxf., 1642], s. sh.
                                              Don. b. 5 (75)
— [Repr.] [Lond., 1642], s. sh.   Arch. G. b. 1 (8)

386. Dec. 9. Exceeding joyfull newes from the earl of Essex, a true and reall relation of his incompassing the king's army neare the citty of Oxford, Decemb. 7, and the great skirmish which they had at that time. [Madan 1113.] [Lond.], 1642, 4°. 8 pp.   8° Z 45 Art.

387. Dec. 9. His majesties proclamation to all the inhabitants of his counties of Oxford [&c.] commanding them to give notice . . . of the approach of any rebells forces neere unto them. [Madan 1116.] [Oxf.], (1642), s. sh.   Don. b. 4 (23)

388. Dec. 19. The requests of the gentlemen of the grandjury of this county of Oxford . . . were read, and considered of: and thereupon the kings commissioners have . . . ordered as followeth. [The Requests are not included.] [Madan 1132.] Oxf., 1642, 4°. 8 pp.
                                              Wood 516 (6*)
— Repr. [Madan 1146] Lond., 1642.   G.P. 2288 (6)

389. Dec. 21. An agreement betwixt his majesty and the inhabitants of the county of Oxford for provisions for his majestie's horses billited in this county. [Madan 1134.] Oxf., 1642, 4°. 6 pp.
                                         G.A. Oxon 4° 15 (1)
— Repr. [Madan 1146.] Lond., 1642.   B.M.

390. [Dec. 26?] A declaration of his maiesties royall pleasure . . . concerning the security of divers parts of this kingdome, especially the city and county of Oxford. Repr. [Madan 1139.] Lond., [1642], 4°. 8 pp.   B.M.

391. [Dec. 29?] An explanation of the agreement of the 21. of December last, betwixt his majesty and the inhabitants of the county of Oxon, for provisions for his majesties horses billited in this county. [Madan 1187.] [Oxf.], 1642, 4°. 8 pp.   Wood 375 (28)

392. The petitions of Northampton-shire and Oxford-shire presented unto . . . parliament. [Anti-popery.] Lond., 1642, 4°. 6 pp.
                                                                          Wood 373 (24)

393. Jan. 5. A proclamation prohibiting all persons within this county of Oxford from buying or receiving horse or armes . . . from any souldiers of his majesties army. [Madan 1167.] Oxf., [1643], s. sh.
                                                                          Don. b. 4 (1)

394. Jan. 11. A proclamation requiring all his majesties tenants within the counties of Oxford and Berks to pay their severall rents . . . at the citty of Oxford. [Madan 1182.] Oxf., [1643], s. sh.
                                                                          Arch. G. b. 1 (24)

395. [Jan. 11?] His majesties speech spoken to . . . the citie of Oxford, and . . . counties of Oxford and Berks . . . requesting . . . money [&c.]. [Madan 1181.] [Lond.], 1643, 4°. 8 pp.   Antiq. e. E. 1643. 6

396. Jan. 11. A declaration of the Agreement of the 11. of January betwixt his majesty and the Inhabitants of the county of Oxon. For provision for his majesties horses billited in this County. [Madan 1188.] Oxf., [really Lond.], 1642[3], 4°. 8 pp.   C 15. 15 (17) Linc.

397. Jan. 12. To our trusty . . . colonells . . . and all other our officers of our army [against waste of crops in Oxon and Berks]. [Madan 1186.] [Oxf.], 1642[3], s. sh.   Don. b. 4 (3)

398. [Jan. 13.] The answer of the city of Oxford to his majesties propositions concerning money and plate: as also, The answer to the counties of Oxford and Berk-shire. [Madan 1185.] Oxf. [really Lond.], 1643, 4°. 8 pp.   Gough Oxf. 138 (9)

399. Jan. 17. A proclamation for the ease of the citty of Oxford, and suburbs, and of the county of Oxford, of unnecessary persons lodging or abiding there. [Madan 1192.] Oxf., [1643], s. sh.
                                                                          Arch. G. b. 1 (26)
— [Repr.] Jan. 20. [Lond. 1643.]   Ashm. H 23 (93)

400. Jan. 26. TURNER, S., A true relation of a late skirmish at Henley upon Thames, wherein a great defeat was given to the Redding cavaliers lately assaulting the aforesaid towne, a letter. Lond., 1643, 4°. 6 pp.   C 14. 3 (35) Linc.

401. [Mar. 14.] A perfect relation of the cause and manner of apprehending, by the king's souldiers, William Needle and mistris Phillips, both dwelling in . . . Banbury . . . together with their inhumaine usage. n. pl., 1643, 4°. 6 pp.   4° X 49 (35) Jur.

402. June 3. A proclamation for the redresse of certaine grievances complained of by the inhabitants of the county of Oxford. [Madan 1370.] Oxf., 1643, s. sh.   Don. b. 5 (45)

403. [June 18.] A true relation of a great fight between the king's forces and the parliament's at Chinner. Lond., [1643], 4°. 8 pp.
      Ashm. 1028 (9)

404. [July 1.] His highnesse prince Ruperts late beating up the rebels quarters at Post-comb & Chinner in Oxford shire, and his victory in Chalgrove feild, Iune 18. 1643. [Madan 1400.] [Oxf.], 1643, 4°. 20 pp.   Wood 376 (14)

405. Sept. 27. The agreements made between his majesty and the knights . . . and inhabitants of the county of Oxford, for the better provision and ordering of his majesties army. [Madan 1458.] Oxf., 1643, 4°. 8 pp.   4° N 11 (21) Art. BS.

406. Dec. 1. A proclamation prohibiting free-quarter, or taking any provisions in the counties of Oxford, Berks and Wilts without paying. [Madan 1498.] [Oxf.], (1643) s. sh.   B.M.

407. [Dec. 29.] R. (s.), An exact and full relation of all the proceedings between the Cavaliers and the Northamptonshire forces at Banbury. . . . Lond., 1643, 4°. 8 pp.   Antiq. e. E. 102 (4)

408. Feb. 9. The desires of the commissioners for the weekly loane to his majesties horse in the county of Oxford. [Madan 1533.] [Oxf.], 1643 [4], 4°. 8 pp.   4° M 15 (23) Art. BS.

409. Feb. 14. A proclamation commanding the due observation of the desires of the commissioners for the contribution of the county of Oxford. [Madan 1537.] Oxf., 1643 [4], s. sh.   Arch. G. c. 5 (1)

410. [Apr. 16? 1644.] A proclamation for the better preservation of the countrey and the garrison at Oxford, and securing of their corne and other provisions. (Repr., Husband's Collection of all the publicke . . . ordinances and declarations . . . of Parliament, 1646, p. 484.) [Madan 1609.]   Douce P subt. 112

411. [April 22.] A declaration of the Lords and Commons . . . concerning his majesties late proclamation threatening fire and sword to all inhabitants in the county of Oxford and Berks . . . that will not bring . . . provisions . . . to . . . Oxford. [cf. Madan 1609.] Lond., 1644, 4°. 6 pp.   C 15. 15 Linc.

412. May 24. Letters by which it is certified that sir Samuell Luke tooke at Islip fiftie horse, and fiftie pound in money [&c.]. Testified by col. Chadwick, [Thomason i. 326.] Lond., 1644, 4°.   B.M.

413. June 3. THOMAS, V., Account of the night-march of king Charles the first from Oxford, by Wolvercot, Yarnton, Hanborough bridge, to Burford and Worcester, June 3, 1644. (Oxf.), [1852], 8°. 29 pp.
G.A. Oxon 8° 73 (7)

414. June 8. An ordinance of the Lords and Commons . . . appointing . . . Richard Brown sergeant major generall of all the forces . . . imployed by . . . parliament for the reducing of the city of Oxford . . . the town and castle of Banbury [&c.] [Madan 1651.] Lond., 1644, 4°. 8 pp.   Ashm. 1069 (17)

415. June 27. An ordinance of . . . Parliament to appoint and enable committees in the severall counties of Buckingham, Oxon and Berks to put in execution this . . . and severall other ordinances [for raising money and troops]. Lond., 1644, 4°. 8 pp.
G.A. Berks 4° 3 (9)

416. June 29. ELLIS, T. An exact and full relation of the last fight between the kings forces and sir William Waller on 29 June [at Cropredy bridge] a letter [signed T. Ellis]. Lond., 1644, 4°. 8 pp.
Wood 377 (15)

417. Sept. 4. A letter: being a full relation of the siege of Banbury-Castle by . . . Colonell Whetham governour of Northampton. Lond., 1644, 4°. 8 pp.   4° D 6 (28) Art. B.S.

418. May 24. The copy of a letter from an eminent commander in sir Thomas Fairfax army dated at Marston . . . wherein is related the return of lieutenant gen. Crumwell and major gen. Brown, and their joyning with sir Thomas Fairfax at Marston. [Thomason i. 377.] Lond., 1645, 4°. 6 pp.   B.M.

419. July 18. An ordinance of Parliament for the releife of . . . Oxon, Bucks [&c.]. Lond., 1645, 4°. 5 pp.   Antiq. e. E. 1645. 9

420. Apr. 5. The manner of the discovering the king at Southwell . . . 5 of April, 1646 . . . Banbury taken in . . . Also The copie of Sir Thomas Fairfax's Proclamation. Lond., 1646, 4°. 6 pp.
Wood 501 (8)

421. Apr. 30. The treaty with the earle of Southampton, the earle of Linsey and other commissioners from Oxford. The taking of Woodstock and of Bridg-North castle. . . . Lond., 1646, 4°. 8 pp.
Wood 501 (6)

422. [May 6?] LLOYD, M., The king found at Southwell, and the Oxford gigg play'd and sung at Witney Wakes. [Madan 1863.] Lond., 1646, 4°. 8 pp   B.M.

423. May 5. VENABLES. The flight of Charles i from Oxford and his surrender . . . at Southwell on the 5th of May, 1646. (Associated archit. socs'. repts. and papers, 1877, vol. 14, p. 9–26.)   R. Top. 3

424. May 6. Articles agreed upon by capt. Gannock and capt. Baylie, deputed on the behalf of sir W. Compton, governour of the castle of Banbury, and col. Whetham, commissioners appointed by col. Whaley, touching the surrender thereof. [Thomason i. 437.] Lond., 1646, s. sh.   B.M.

425. Sept. 14. The copie of three petitions as they were presented to the . . . Commons, Sept. 14th and 15th, 1647. 1. From the county of Bucks . . . 2. From the county of Oxford. 3. From Oxford, Bucks and Hertford, for purging the great fountain of justice. [Thomason i. 557.] Lond., 1647, 4°. 6 pp.   B.M.

426. [Jan. 1.] The Woodstock scuffle; or, Most dreadful aparitions that were lately seen in the Mannor-house of Woodstock. [A ballad.] n. pl., 1649, 4 leaves.   B.M.
   See 4169 A, B [Just devil of Woodstock. 1660, 1802].

427. Jan. 25. The humble advice and earnest desires of certain well-affected ministers, lecturers of Banbury . . . and Brackly . . . to . . . Thomas lord Fairfax. Lond., 1649, 4°. 8 pp.   G. Pamph. 643 (7)
   — [Another ed.]. 1649.   G.A. Oxon 8° 74

428. [Feb. 27.] The Parliament justified in their late proceedings against Charles Stuart. As also, an answer to . . . 'The humble advice of the lecturers of Banbury . . . and Brackley'. By J. Fidoe, T. Jeanes and W. Shaw. [Thomason i. 727.] n. pl., 1648, 4°.   B.M.

429. Apr. 16. The humble representation and petition of divers wel-affected gentlemen . . . and others of the county of Oxon, presented to . . . the Commons. Lond., (1649), 4°. 6 pp.   Wood 515 (13)

430. May 6. THOMPSON, W., England's standard advanced. Or, A declaration from m. Will. Thompson and the oppressed people of this nation now under his conduct in Oxfordshire. [A Leveller's pamphlet.] n. pl., (1649), 8°. 4 pp.   Wood 503 (2)

431. May 18. The declaration of cornet Thompson and the rest of the Levellers executed in Burford churchyard. [Thomason i. 744.] Lond., 1649, 4°.   B.M.
   — [Another ed. in] May 22. The declaration of the prince of Wales to the commissioners . . . of Scotland in reference to their proclaiming him king. . . . Also the declaration of cornet Thompson [&c.]. [Thomason i. 745.] Lond., 1649, 4°.   B.M.

432. May 22. A declaration of the proceedings of . . . general Fairfax in the reducing of the revolted troops, together with the humble petition of the . . . prisoners remaining in the church of Burford . . . Repr. Lond., 1649, 4°. 16 pp.   G.A. Oxon 4° 15 (3)

433. Aug. 20. The Levellers (falsly so called) vindicated, or the case of the twelve troops (which by treachery in a treaty) was lately surprised and defeated at Burford. n. pl., 1649, 4°. 12 pp.
Wood 503 (4)

434. Sept. 17. WHITE, F., A true relation of the proceedings in the businesse of Burford [the Levellers incident]. Lond., 1649, 4°. 16 pp.
Wood 503 (5)

435. [Mar. 3.] AUDLAND, A., A true declaration of the suffering of the innocent, wherein is discovered the zeale of the magistrates and people of Banbury, declared in a letter sent to William Allen . . . by Anne Audland, whom the world scornfully calls Quaker. Lond., 1655, 4°. 6 pp.
110 k. 485 (2)

436. Feb. 13. A declaration of the county of Oxon to his excellency the lord general Monck [concerning a free parliament]. Lond., 1660, s. sh.
Wood 276 a (236)

437. RUSHER, P., Crouch-hill, a descriptive poem, with some account of the sieges of Banbury castle, in the reign of Charles the first [by P. Rusher]. Banbury, 1789, 8°. 34 pp.
Gough Oxf. 45 (7)

438. COMPTON, LORD ALWYNE, Notes on the Civil war and the siege of Banbury. (Trans., North Oxf. archaeol. soc., 1853–55, p. 25–36.)
R. Top. 330

439. RIGAUD, G., The lines formed round Oxford by King Charles I. Oxf., 1880, 8°. 16 pp.
G.A. Oxon 8° 469 (5)

440. FIRTH, C. H., A chronological summary of the Civil war in Oxfordshire, Buckinghamshire and Berkshire, 1642–1646. (Proc., Oxf. architect. and hist. soc., 1890, N.S., vol. 5, p. 280–91.)
R. 13. 711

441. WHETHAM, C. D., and W. C. D., A history of the life of colonel Nathaniel Whetham, a forgotten soldier of the Civil wars. (The siege of Banbury, p. 74–89.) Lond., &c., 1907, 4°.
22856 d. 27

442. VARLEY, F. J., Oxford army list for 1642–1646. (Oxoniensia, 1937, p. 141–51.)
R. Top. 340

443. FRENCH, J. M., Milton in chancery. (Mod. lang. assoc. of Amer., monogr. ser.) New York, 1939, 4°. 428 pp.
3963 d. 106 (10)

444. O'NEIL, B. H. ST. J., A civil war battery at Cornbury. (Oxoniensia, 1945, p. 73–78.)
R. Top. 340

445. LUKE, SIR S., Journal of sir Samuel Luke, ed. by I. G. Philip. Vol. 1–3. (Oxf. record soc., vol. 29, 31, 33.) (Oxf.), 1950–53, 8°.
R. 13. 702

See 4115 [Coin hoard of the Civil war, Wolvercote. 1937].
See 4164 [Parish church, Woodstock, and an episode of the Civil war. 1927].

RESTORATION TO DATE

446. Strange news from Oxfordshire . . . a true . . . account of a wonderful . . . earthquake . . . the 17th of . . . September, 1683 . . . in a letter from Wallingford. Lond., (1683), fol. 2 pp.

Ashm. 1677 (97)

447. GRETTON, M. S., A corner of the Cotswolds, through the 19th century. Lond., 1914, 8°. 289 pp.   G.A. Oxon 8° 881

448. Hearth tax returns, Oxfordshire, 1665, ed. by M. M. B. Weinstock. (Oxf. record soc., vol. 21.) Oxf., 1940, 8°. 264 pp.   R. 13. 702

449. RICKARD, R. L., ed., The progress notes of warden Woodward round the Oxfordshire estates of New college, 1659–1675. (Oxf. record soc., 27.) Oxf., 1949, 8°. 100 pp.   R. 13. 702 (27)

450. WYNDHAM, H., A backward glance. [A reconstruction of the countryside of the Ploughley Hundred in 1793.] Lond., 1950, 8°. 79 pp.   G.A. Oxon 8° 1217

451. [A volume of newspaper cuttings on Oxford and Oxfordshire, c. 1750–1820.]   G.A. Oxon 4° 49

ECONOMIC HISTORY

GENERAL

452. Social and economic history. (Victoria county history, 1907, vol. 2, p. 165–224.) R. 9. 41 *s*

453. Oxford univ., agric. econ. research inst. Country planning, a study of rural problems [in N. Oxfordshire]. Lond., 1944, 8°. 288 pp.
2479115 e. 22

COMMUNICATIONS
Canals and Rivers

Canal

454. A bill for making and maintaining a navigable canal, from the Coventry canal navigation to . . . Oxford. Lond., 1768/9, fol. 61 pp.
L. Eng. B 53 d. Canals 1 (1)
— [Act.]. 9 G. III, c. 70, Pub. L. Eng. B 53 d. Canals 1 (2)
— 15 G. III, c. 9, Pub.
— 26 G. III, c. 20, Pub.
— 34 G. III, c. 103, Pub.
— 39 G. III, c. 5, L. & P.
— 47 G. III, c. 9, Sess. 2, L. & P.
— 48 G. III, c. 3, L. & P.
— 10 G. IV, c. 48, L. & P.

455. Statement of facts in favour of the intended London and Western canal, lately called the Hampton Gay canal. n. pl., (1792), 8°. 24 pp. Gough Oxf. 7 (11)

456. Throp, alias Hampton-Gay, alias, The London and Western canal, a new song. n. pl., [1792?], s. sh.
MS. Top. Oxon c. 200 (f. 160)

457. Oxford canal bill. Case of the Oxford canal company. n. pl., [1829?], fol. 4 pp. G.A. fol. A 139* (6)

458. An act to confirm a provisional order made by the Board of Trade . . . containing the . . . schedule of maximum tolls and charges . . . for the Aberdare canal navigation, and [the Oxford canal]. (57 & 58 V., c. 198, L. & P.) Lond., 1894, fol. 81 pp.   L. Eng. A 69 c. 6

459. An act to convert into stock the share capital of the company of proprietors of the Oxford canal navigation, to change the name of the company, and for other purposes. (25 G. V, c. 15, L. & P.) Lond., 1935, 4°. 28 pp. L. Eng. A 69 c. 6
— [Undertaking acquired by British Transport commission. 10 & 11 G. VI, c. 49, Sch. 3, pt. 2, Pub.]

Thames

460. An acte for clearing the passage by water from London, to and beyond the citie of Oxford. (3 James I, c. 20, Pub.) Lond., 1606, fol. 4 pp.   L. Eng. A. 69 c. 1

461. An act for the making of the river of Thames nauigable for barges, boats and lighters, from . . . Bercot . . . vnto the vniuersitie and citie of Oxon. (21 James I, c. 32, Pub.) Lond., 1624, fol. 6 pp.
                                                    L. Eng. A 69 c. 1

462. An act to prevent exactions of the occupiers of locks and wears upon the river of Thames westward, and for ascertaining the rates of water-carriage upon the said river. (6 & 7 W. & M., c. 16, Pub.) Lond., 1695, fol. 9 pp.   L. Eng. A 69 c. 1
— 3 G. II, c. 11, Pub.

463. Orders and constitutions made by his majesties justices of the peace for the county of Oxon . . . May 1695 . . . in pursuance of . . . An act to prevent exactions of the occupyers of locks and weers upon the river Thames. . . . n. pl., (1695), fol. 4 pp.
                                              G.A. Oxon 4° 6 (12)

464. An essay on the right of angling in the river Thames. . . . Reading, [c. 1787], 8°. 61 pp.   Gough Lond. 13 (12)

465. VANDERSTEGEN, W., The present state of the Thames considered; and a comparative view of canal and river navigation. Lond., 1794, 8°. 76 pp.   Gough Lond. 13 (1)

466. BOYDELL, JOHN, and JOSIAH, An history of the river Thames. (Oxfordshire, vol. 1, *passim*.) Lond., 1794, fol.   O.C.R.L.

467. An act for the purification of the river Thames by the diversion therefrom of the sewage of Oxford, Abingdon [&c.]. (29 & 30 V., c. 319, L. & P.) Lond., 1866, fol. 20 pp.   L. Eng. A 69 c. 6

468. In Parliament, session, 1870. Thames navigation. Petition against [A Bill for extending and amending the acts relating to the navigation of the Thames]. Westm., 1870, fol. 12 pp.
                                              G.A. fol. A 226 (2)

469. TAUNT, H. W., A new map of the river Thames from Oxford to London. (Oxfordshire, *passim*.) Oxf., [1872], 4°.
                                              G.A. Gen. top. 4° 53
— 2nd ed. [1873].   G.A. Gen. top. 4° 62
— Pocket ed. [1873].   G.A. Gen. top. 8° 266

470. TAUNT, H. W., A new map of the river Thames from Thames head to London. 3rd ed. [illustr.]. (Oxfordshire, *passim*.) Oxf., [1879], 8°.
                                              G.A. Gen. top. 8° 328
— 5th ed. 1887.   G.A. Gen. top. 8° 495

471. TAUNT, H. W., Map of the river Thames from Lechlade to London. 4th (pocket) ed. (Oxfordshire, *passim.*) Oxf., 1881, 8°.
G.A. Gen. top. 8° 361

472. TAUNT, H. W., Taunt's shilling map and guide to the river Thames from Oxford to London. Oxf., &c., [1882], 8°. 50 pp.
G.A. Gen. top. 8° 400

473. CHURCH, A. J., Isis and Thamesis. Lond., 1886, 4°. 65 pp.
G.A. Oxon 4° 88

474. Thames preservation league. Draft rules. [Reprod. from typewriting.] [Lond., 1899], fol. 2 pp. G.A. Oxon c. 317 (1)

475. STANFORD, W., A sectional map of the river Thames from Oxford to Richmond. (Homeland pocket books.) Lond., [1907], 16°.
G.A. Eng. rivers 16° 23
— [Another ed. 1920.] Maps. Eng. f. 20

476. THACKER, F. S., The stripling Thames, a book of the river above Oxford. Lond., 1909, 8°. 495 pp. G.A. Eng. rivers 8° 45

477. THACKER, F. S., The Thames highway, a history of the inland navigation. Lond., 1914, 8°. 295 pp. G.A. Eng. rivers 8° 66

478. THACKER, F. S., The Thames highway, a history of the locks and weirs. Lond., 1920, 8°. 525 pp. G.A. Eng. rivers 8° 74

479. The Thames valley from Cricklade to Staines, a survey, prepared by the earl of Mayo [and others]. (Lond.), 1929, fol. 106 pp.
G.A. Eng. rivers c. 20

480. WILLAN, T. S., The navigation of the Thames and Kennet, 1600–1750. (Berks archaeol. journ., 1936, vol. 40, p. 146–56.)
R. Top. 100

481. PHILIP, I. G., River navigation at Oxford during the Civil war and Commonwealth. (Oxoniensia, 1937, p. 152–65.) R. Top. 340

481A. DE MARÉ, E. S., Time on the Thames. [Description of the country and places on the river banks.] Lond., 1952, 8°. 238 pp.
G.A. Eng. rivers 8° 150

See also 9–16 [Floods and drainage].
See also 2974, &c. [Iffley lock].

Railways

482. An act for making a railway from the Great Western Railway [Didcot] to . . . Oxford. (6 & 7 V., c. 10, L. & P.) Lond., &c., 1843, fol. 124 pp. G.A. Oxon c. 107 (74)

483. An act for making a railway from Oxford to Worcester and Wolverhampton. (8 & 9 V., c. 184, L. & P.) n. pl., 1845, fol. 54 pp.
G.A. Oxon c. 179
— 9 & 10 V., c. 278, L. & P.
— 11 & 12 V., c. 133, L. & P.

484. An act for making a railway from the city of Oxford to the town of Rugby. (8 & 9 V., c. 188, L. & P.) Lond., 1845, fol.

485. Oxford and Rugby railway. Report of . . . meeting, held in the Town Hall, Banbury. Repr. from the Banbury Guardian. Banbury, 1846, 4°. 8 pp.
G.A. Oxon 4° 119

486. An act for making a railway from Oxford [through Cutslow, Kidlington, Islip, Oddington, Charlton, Wendlebury, Chesterton, Bicester] to the London and Birmingham railway at Bletchley. (9 & 10 V., c. 82, L. & P.) Lond., 1846, fol. 15 pp.
L. Eng. A 69 c. 6
— 10 & 11 V., c. 236, L. & P.
— 16 & 17 V., c. 205, L. & P.

487. An act to authorize an alteration in the line of the Buckinghamshire railways at Oxford. [Kidlington, Islip, Saint Giles.] (13 & 14 V., c. 6, L. & P.) Lond., 1850, fol. 11 pp.
L. Eng. A 69 c. 6

488. Return of all parishes . . . into which or through any portion of which any public railway passes; shewing the mileage of railway, the total acreage of each parish, the acreage occupied by the railway; the gross amount of Poor's rate collected in each parish in 1851, 1852, and the amount contributed by railway property to the Poor's rate of each parish. (Oxfordshire, p. 80, 81.)
Pp. Eng. 1852/3, vol. 97

489. An act for making a railway from the Oxford, Worcester and Wolverhampton railway [from a junction in the parish of Churchill at the Chipping Norton Junction Station through Kingham] to Bourton-on-the-Water. . . . (23 V., c. 82, L. & P.) Lond., 1860, fol. 14 pp.
L. Eng. A 69 c. 6

490. An act to authorise the construction of a railway from Oxford to Aylesbury. (46 & 47 V., c. 210, L. & P.) Lond., 1883, fol. 23 pp.
L. Eng. A 69 c. 6
— 51 & 52 V., c. 185, L. & P.
— 55 & 56 V., c. 137, L. & P.
— 57 & 58 V., c. 179, L. & P.

491. An act for conferring further powers upon the Great Western railway company for vesting in that company the undertakings of the Whitland and Cardigan and East Gloucestershire and the Witney railway companies for confirming an agreement with the Woodstock railway company. (53 & 54 V., c. 159, L. & P.) Lond., 1890, fol. 65 pp.
L. Eng. A 69 c. 6

492. An act for conferring further powers upon the Great Western railway company . . . and the London and North Western railway company . . . in respect of their undertaking for amalgamating the Buckfastleigh, Totnes and South Devon, Kington and Eardisley, Woodstock, Banbury and Cheltenham Direct [&c.] railway companies with the Great Western railway company. . . . (60 & 61 V., c. 248, L. & P.) Lond., 1897, fol. 145 pp.   L. Eng. A 69 c. 6

493. MOWAT, C. L., The Oxford, Witney and Fairford railway. (Railway mag., March 1931, vol. 68, p. 190–94.)   Per. 247917 d. 39

See 1643 [Act concerning railway. Banbury district. 1873].
See 2125 [Act concerning railway. Chipping Norton. 1854].
See 4080 [Act concerning railway. Witney. 1859].
See 4186 [Act concerning railway. Woodstock. 1886].

Roads

494. TAYLOR, J., The carriers cosmographie, or A briefe relation of the innes, ordinaries, hosteries and other lodgings in and neere London, where the carriers [&c.] doe usually come, from any parts . . . [Bampton?, Banbury, Burford, Dorchester?, Keinton, Oxford, Thame, Witney, Woodstock.] Lond., 1637, 4°.   Tanner 192 (7)
— [Repr.] 1877. (An Engl. garner, by E. Arber. Vol. 1.)
270 f. 781 *a*

495. An act for repairing the road from Becconsfield . . . to Stokenchurch. (5 G. I, c. 2, Private.) [Lond., 1718], fol. 7 pp.
L. Eng. B 53 c. Highways 6
— 9 G. II, c. 11, Pub.
— 33 G. II, c. 37, Pub.
— 15 G. III, c. 70, Pub.
— 34 G. III, c. 142, Pub.
— 4 G. IV, c. 108, L. & P.
— 28 & 29 V., c. 107, Pub.
— 30 & 31 V., c. 121, Pub.

496. An act for repairing the roads from the top of Stoken-church hill to Enslow bridge, and the road leading from Wheatly bridge through . . . Oxon by Begbrooke, to New Woodstock . . . (5 G. I, c. 1, Private.) Lond., 1718, fol.
— 13 G. II, c. 15, Private.   G.A. Oxon c. 188
— 2 G. III, c. 41, Pub.
— 18 G. III, c. 91, Pub.
— 29 G. III, c. 90, Pub.
— 5 G. IV, c. 99, L. & P.
— 8 & 9 V., c. 30, L. & P.
— 40 & 41 V., c. 64, Pub.

497. A list of the subscribers for mending the road from Reading to Caversham. Reading, 1724, 4°. 12 pp. 4° Rawl. 526

498. An act for repairing . . . several roads leading from Woodstock through Kiddington and Enston to Rollright lane, and from Enslow bridge to Kiddington. (3 G. II, c. 21, Pub.) Lond., 1730, fol. 15 pp.
G.A. Oxon c. 199 (1)
— 24 G. II, c. 21, Pub.
— 31 G. II, c. 48, Pub.
— 24 G. III, sess. 2, c. 61, Pub.
— 44 G. III, c. 79, L. & P.
— 3 G. IV, c. 126, Pub.
— 4 G. IV, c. 95, Pub.
— 5 G. IV, c. 69, Pub.
— 6 G. IV, c. 94, L. & P.
— 9 & 10 V., c. 7, L. & P.
— 41 & 42 V., c. 62, Pub.

499. An act for repairing the road leading from Chappel on the Heath . . . to the quarry above Bourton on the Hill . . . (4 G. II, c. 23, Pub.) Lond., 1731, fol. 20 pp. L. Eng. A 69 c. 1
— 17 G. II, c. 10, Pub.
— 5 G. III, c. 80, Pub.
— 31 G. III, c. 111, Pub.
— 56 G. III, c. 1, L. & P.

500. An act for repairing the roads leading from Henley bridge . . . to Dorchester bridge and from thence to Culham bridge, and to . . . Mile-stone in the road leading to Magdalene bridge. (9 G. II, c. 14, Pub.) Lond., 1736, 4°. 29 pp. G.A. Oxon 4° 345
— 28 G. II, c. 42, Pub.
— 21 G. III, c. 77, Pub.
— 41 G. III, c. 79, L. & P.
— 42 G. III, c. 60, L. & P.
— 1 & 2 G. IV, c. 26, L. & P.
— 3 G. IV, c. 36, L. & P.
— 4 & 5 V., c. 100, L. & P.
— 36 & 37 V., c. 90, Pub.

501. An act for repairing the road from . . . Buckingham . . . to Warmington . . . [through Hanwell and Banbury]. (17 G. II, c. 43, Pub.) Lond., 1744, fol. 20 pp. B.M.
— 9 G. III, c. 52, Pub.
— 32 G. III, c. 134, Pub.
— 51 G. III, c. 2, L. & P. L. Eng. A 69 c. 6
— 2 & 3 W. IV, c. 34, L. & P.

502. An act for repairing the road from . . . Crickley Hill . . . to Frogg Mill, through . . . Northleach, Burford and Witney and Handborough and Bladen to Campsfield in . . . Kidlington . . . and also

the road from Witney through Ensham, Cumner and Botley to . . .
Oxford. (24 G. II, c. 28, Pub.) Lond., 1751, fol.
— 8 G. III, c. 41, Pub.
— 38 G. III, c. 13, L. & P.
— 1 & 2 G. IV, c. 109, L. & P.   L. Eng. A 69 c. 6
— 3 & 4 W. IV, c. 73, L. & P.
— 4 & 5 W. IV, c. 94, L. & P.
— 32 & 33 V., c. 90, Pub.

503. An act for repairing . . . the road from . . . Upton Field in the parish
of Burford [through Westwell, &c.] . . . to . . . Dancy's Fancy. . . .
(26 G. II, c. 70, Pub.) Lond., 1753, fol. 31 pp.   B.M.
— 20 G. III, c. 76, Pub.
— 41 G. III, c. 16, L. & P.   L. Eng. A 69 c. 6
— 3 G. IV, c. 47, L. & P.
— 25 & 26 V., c. 72, Pub.
— 30 & 31 V., c. 121, Pub.

504. An act to widen . . . the road from . . . Drayton Lane, near Banbury
. . . to . . . Edge Hill. . . . (26 G. II, c. 78, Pub.) Lond., 1753, fol.
26 pp.   B.M.
— 20 G. III, c. 67, Pub.
— 41 G. III, c. 84, L. & P.   L. Eng. A 69 c. 6
— 3 G. IV, c. 90, L. & P.
— 16 & 17 V., c. 135, Pub.
— 17 & 18 V., c. 58, Pub.
— 34 & 35 V., c. 115, Pub.

505. An act for repairing . . . roads leading from . . . Finford bridge . . .
to . . . Banbury . . . and from the guide post in . . . Adderbury . . .
through Kidlington to the mile-way leading towards . . . Oxford . . .
and also . . . from . . . Two mile tree . . . to . . . Weston on the Green.
(28 G. II, c. 46, Pub.) Lond., 1755, fol. 36 pp.   B.M.
— 17 G. III, c. 87, Pub.

506. An act for repairing . . . the road from The Hand and Post at the
top of Burford Lane in the county of Gloucester, to Stow on the
Wold [&c.] and also the road from The Cross Hands on Salford
Hill [Oxon] to the Hand and Post, Dowdeswell. . . . (28 G. II, c. 47,
Pub.) Lond., 1755, fol. 32 pp.   B.M.
— 27 G. III, c. 77, Pub.
— 44 G. III, c. 13, L. & P.   L. Eng. A 69 c. 6
— 5 G. IV, c. 9, L. & P.

507. An act for repairing the road . . . from Towcester . . . to . . .
Weston on the Green. (30 G. II, c. 48, Pub.) Lond., 1757, fol.
— 18 G. III, c. 87, Pub.
— 41 G. III, 5th sess., c. 1, L. & P.   L. Eng. A 69 c. 6
— 1 G. IV, c. 73, L. & P.
— 14 & 15 V., c. 61, L. & P.

508. An act for repairing and widening the road from Shillingford . . .
through Wallingford and Pangborne to Reading . . . and for building
a bridge over the river Thames at or near Shillingford Ferry.
(4 G. III, c. 42, Pub.) Lond., 1764, fol. 35 pp. B.M.
— 24 G. III, c. 22, Pub.
— 45 G. III, c. 25, L. & P. L. Eng. A 69 c. 6
— 7 & 8 G. IV, c. 19, L. & P.
— 15 & 16 V., c. 79, L. & P.
— 37 & 38 V., c. 95, Pub.

509. An act to continue the term . . . of an act . . . for repairing the road
from Wallingford . . . to Wantage . . . and for repairing the road
leading from . . . Nuffield Common . . . to . . . Wallingford. (5 G.
III, c. 55, Pub.) Lond., 1765, fol. 13 pp. B.M.
— 39 G. III, c. 37, L. & P. L. Eng. A 69 c. 6
— 59 G. III, c. 100, L. & P.
— 4 & 5 V., c. 107, L. & P.
— 36 & 37 V., c. 90, Pub.

510. An act for repairing . . . the road from . . . Banbury . . . through
Daventree and Cottesbach . . . to Lutterworth. . . . (5 G. III, c. 105,
Pub.) Lond., 1765, fol. 28 pp. B.M.
— 25 G. III, c. 128, Pub.
— 47 G. III, sess. 2, c. 91, L. & P. L. Eng. A 69 c. 6
— 9 G. IV, c. 86, L. & P.
— 3 & 4 V., c. 38, L. & P.
— 33 & 34 V., c. 73, Pub.

511. An act for repairing . . . the road leading from Reading . . . through
Henley . . . to Hatfield. (8 G. III, c. 50, Pub.) Lond., 1768, fol.
— Repr. 1818. 27 pp. B.M.
— 27 G. III, c. 81, Pub.
— 49 G. III, c. 97, L. & P. L. Eng. A 69 c. 6
— 10 G. IV, c. 133, L. & P.
— 22 & 23 V., c. 11, L. & P.
— 43 & 44 V., c. 12, Pub.

512. An act to enlarge . . . an act for repairing and widening the road
from . . . Oxford over Botley Causeway to the turnpike road near
Fifield in the county of Berks; and to provide more effectually for
repairing . . . the ancient horse road from . . . Botley Causeway to
Witney. (8 G. III, c. 34, Pub.) Lond., 1768, fol. 12 pp. B.M.
— 18 G. III, c. 81, Pub.
— 54 G. III, c. 186, L. & P. L. Eng. A 69 c. 6
— 5 & 6 W. IV, c. 103, L. & P.
— 40 & 41 V., c. 64, Pub.

513. An act for repairing the road from Stoney Stratford in the county
of Bucks, through . . . Buckingham and Bicester, to . . . Woodstock,
in the county of Oxford. (9 G. III, c. 88, Pub.) Lond., 1769, fol.
27 pp. G.A. Oxon 4° 350

514. An act for repairing . . . the road from Burford to Banbury . . . and from Burford . . . to the turnpike road leading to Stow . . . and from Swerford Gate . . . to . . . Aynho. . . . (10 G. III, c. 101, Pub.) [Lond.], 1770, fol. 25 pp.　　　　L. Eng. B 53 c. Highways 5 (3)
— 31 G. III, c. 128, Pub.
— 50 G. III, c. 210, L. & P.
— 2 & 3 W. IV, c. 16, L. & P.
— 35 & 36 V., c. 85, Pub.

515. An act for amending the road from Aylesbury . . . through Thame and Little Milton to the turnpike road between Bensington and Shillingford. . . . (10 G. III, c. 58, Pub.) Lond., 1770, fol. 30 pp.
　　　　　　　　　　　　　　　　　　　　　　　　　　B.M.
— 25 G. III, c. 127, Pub.
— 31 G. III, c. 136, Pub.
— 3 & 4 W. IV, c. 86, L. & P.
— 1 & 2 V., c. 46, L. & P.
— 38 & 39 V., c. 194, L. & P.

516. An act for repairing . . . the road from Bicester . . . to Aylesbury . . . (10 G. III, c. 72, Pub.) Lond., 1770, fol. 26 pp.　　　　B.M.
— 31 G. III, c. 101, Pub.
— 53 G. III, c. 199, L. & P.　　　　G.A. Oxon a. 117 (f. 6. iii)
— 3 & 4 W. IV, c. 24, L. & P.
— 27 & 28 V., c. 75, Pub.
— 28 & 29 V., c. 107, Pub.
— 38 & 39 V., c. 194, L. & P.

517. An act for amending . . . the road from the bottom of Galley Hill, near Witney, to Clanfield. (11 G. III, c. 73, Pub.) n. pl., 1771, fol. 21 pp.　　　　L. Eng. B 53 c. Highways 5 (2)
— 33 G. III, c. 137, Pub.
— 55 G. III, c. 38, L. & P.
— 17 & 18 V., c. 58, Pub.
— 18 & 19 V., c. 98, Pub.
— 19 & 20 V., c. 49, Pub.
— 20 & 21 V., c. 24, Pub.
— 21 & 22 V., c. 63, Pub.
— 37 & 38 V., c. 95, Pub.

518. An act for repairing . . . the road from the market house in Great Farringdon, Berks, to Burford. (11 G. III, c. 84, Pub.) n. pl., 1771, fol. 28 pp.　　　　L. Eng. B 53 c. Highways 5 (1)
— 32 G. III, c. 150, Pub.
— 52 G. III, c. 155, L. & P.
— 3 & 4 W. IV, c. 73, L. & P.
— 4 & 5 W. IV, c. 94, L. & P.
— 38 & 39 V., c. 194, L. & P.

519. An act for amending . . . the road leading from the turnpike road in the parish of Asthall . . . to Buckland. (17 G. III, c. 105, Pub.) [Lond.], 1777, fol. 26 pp.   Vet. A 5 c. 9
— 39 G. III, c. 76, L. & P.
— 1 G. IV, c. 81, L. & P.
— 15 & 16 V., c. 139, L. & P.
— 37 & 38 V., c. 95, Pub.

520. An act for continuing . . . an act [28 G. II, c. 46] . . . so far as the same relates to the road leading from the Cross of Hand near Finford Bridge . . . through . . . Southam . . . to Banbury. (20 G. III, c. 69, Pub.) Lond., 1780, fol.
— 42 G. III, c. 14, L. & P.   L. Eng. A 69 c. 6
— 3 G. IV, c. 95, L. & P.
— 21 & 22 V., c. 63, Pub.
— 22 & 23 V., c. 92, L. & P.
— 41 & 42 V., c. 62, Pub.

521. An act for repairing . . . the road from . . . Weston on the Green . . . to . . . Kidlington Green. (21 G. III, c. 87, Pub.) Lond., 1781, fol. 33 pp.   B.M.
— 41 G. III, c. 137, L. & P.   L. Eng. A 69 c. 6
— 1 & 2 G. IV, c. 86, L. & P.

522. An act for repairing . . . the road from . . . Bicester . . . to the Buckingham Turnpike road in Aynho. . . . (31 G. III, c. 103, Pub.) Lond., 1791, fol. 29 pp.   B.M.
— 53 G. III, c. 200, L. & P.   G.A. Oxon a. 117 (f. 6. i)
— 26 & 27 V., c. 94, Pub.
— 27 & 28 V., c. 79, Pub.

523. An act for amending . . . several pieces of road . . . and making . . . new road . . . from Buckingham through Brackley to join the Daventry Turnpike road near Banbury. . . . (31 G. III, c. 105, Pub.) Lond., 1791, fol. 12 pp.   B.M.
— 50 G. III, c. 133, L. & P.   L. Eng. A 69 c. 6
— 1 G. IV, c. 73, L. & P.
— 14 & 15 V., c. 61, L. & P.
— 36 & 37 V., c. 90, Pub.

524. An act for amending . . . the roads from Great Marlow . . . to Stokenchurch. . . . (31 G. III, c. 135, Pub.) Lond., 1791, fol. 37 pp.   B.M.
— 53 G. III, c. 44, L. & P.   L. Eng. A 69 c. 6

525. An act for repairing . . . the road leading from . . . Burford . . . to Leachlade . . . and . . . thence to the river Isis. . . . (32 G. III, c. 153, Pub.) Lond., 1792, fol. 52 pp.   B.M.
— 53 G. III, c. 42, L. & P.   L. Eng. A 69 c. 6
— 16 & 17 V., c. 104, L. & P.
— 38 & 39 V., c. 194, L. & P.

526. An act for amending . . . the road from Clay Hill in the turnpike-road between Neat Enstone and Chipping Norton . . . over Heyford Bridge . . . to Bicester . . . and from Bicester . . . to . . . Weston on the Green. (33 G. III, c. 180, Pub.) Lond., 1793, fol. 34 pp.   B.M.
— 53 G. III, c. 133, L. & P.   G.A. Oxon a. 117 (f. 6. ii)
— 14 & 15 V., c. 38, Pub.
— 18 & 19 V., c. 98, Pub.
— 19 & 20 V., c. 49, Pub.
— 20 & 21 V., c. 9, Pub.
— 21 & 22 V., c. 63, Pub.
— 39 & 40 V., c. 39, Pub.

527. An act for more effectually repairing, improving and keeping in repair the road leading from the guide post in . . . Adderbury . . . through Kidlington to the end of the mileway in the city of Oxford. (37 G. III, c. 170, L. & P.) Lond., 1797, fol. 28 pp.   B.M.
— 59 G. III, c. 122, L. & P.   L. Eng. A 69 c. 6
— 28 & 29 V., c. 107, Pub.
— 38 & 39 V., c. 194, L. & P.

528. Crickley Hill and Campsfield road, Oxfordshire district. [Petition to parliament for permission to take over 320 yards of a road held by Faringdon trust, and to make it a Turnpike road. With plans.] (Witney), [18–], fol. 4 pp.   G.A. Oxon c. 317 (10)

529. An act for amending . . . the road leading from . . . Witney to . . . Swerford Heath, and also . . . from the turnpike road from Wood-stock to Birmingham through Charlbury to the turnpike road from Chipping Norton to Burford. (39 & 40 G. III, c. 16, L. & P.) Lond., 1800, fol. 28 pp.   L. Eng. A 69 c. 6
— 1 G. IV, c. 82, L. & P.
— 17 & 18 V., c. 58, Pub.
— 18 & 19 V., c. 85, L. & P.
— 40 & 41 V., c. 64, Pub.

530. An act for amending . . . the road leading from . . . Banbury . . . through Swalcliffe . . . to . . . Barcheston. . . . (42 G. III, c. 38, L. & P.) Lond., 1802, fol. 28 pp.   L. Eng. A 69 c. 6
— 4 G. IV, c. 105, L. & P.
— 35 & 36 V., c. 85, Pub.

531. Case of the intended turnpike road from Culham . . . to Streatley. [Lond.], 1802, fol. 4 pp.   G.A. Oxon b. 113 (27)

532. Report from the select committee appointed to consider the acts now in force regarding turnpike roads and highways. (Oxfordshire, p. 178–82.)   Pp. Eng. 1821, vol. 4

533. Turnpike trusts. Copies of the several accounts transmitted to the clerks of the peace of the . . . counties . . . from the clerks of . . . the several turnpike trusts. . . . (Oxfordshire, p. 495–509.)
                                          Pp. Eng. 1824, vol. 20

534. A bill for repairing the road from Aylesbury ... to Thame ... and the roads ... from ... Thame to Shillingford, Postcomb and Bicester. n. pl., 1833, fol. 19 pp.

L. Eng. B 53 c. Highways 1 (1)

— Act. (3 & 4 W. IV, c. 86, L. & P.)
— Act. (1 & 2 V., c. 46, L. & P.)

L. Eng. B 53 c. Highways 1 (2)

535. An abstract of the general statements of the income and expenditure of the several turnpike trusts. 1834. (Oxfordshire, p. 66–69.)

	Pp. Eng. 1836, vol. 47
— 1835, p. 66–69.	Pp. Eng. 1837, vol. 51
— 1836, p. 78–80.	Pp. Eng. 1837/8, vol. 46
— 1837, p. 79–81.	Pp. Eng. 1839, vol. 49
— 1838, p. 78–81.	Pp. Eng. 1840, vol. 45
— 1839, p. 78–81.	Pp. Eng. 1841, vol. 27
— 1840, p. 78–81.	Pp. Eng. 1842, vol. 37
— 1841, p. 78–81.	Pp. Eng. 1843, vol. 48
— 1842, p. 78–81.	Pp. Eng. 1844, vol. 42
— 1843, p. 78–81.	Pp. Eng. 1845, vol. 41
— 1844, p. 78–81.	Pp. Eng. 1846, vol. 40
— 1845, p. 78–81.	Pp. Eng. 1847, vol. 44
— 1846, p. 78–81.	Pp. Eng. 1849, vol. 46
— 1847, p. 78–81.	Pp. Eng. 1850, vol. 49
— 1848, p. 78–81.	Pp. Eng. 1851, vol. 48
— 1849, p. 78–81.	Pp. Eng. 1852, vol. 44
— 1850, p. 78–81.	Pp. Eng. 1852/3, vol. 97
— 1851, p. 52–55.	Pp. Eng. 1854, vol. 64
— 1852, p. 52–56.	Pp. Eng. 1854, vol. 64
— 1853, p. 50–57.	Pp. Eng. 1854/5, vol. 49
— 1854, p. 50–53.	Pp. Eng. 1856, vol. 58
— 1856, p. 50–53.	Pp. Eng. 1859, vol. 23
— 1857, p. 50–57.	Pp. Eng. 1860, vol. 61
— 1858, p. 52–57.	Pp. Eng. 1861, vol. 57
— 1859, p. 52–57.	Pp. Eng. 1862, vol. 53
— 1860, p. 50–57.	Pp. Eng. 1863, vol. 50
— 1861, p. 50–57.	Pp. Eng. 1864, vol. 50
— 1862, p. 50–57.	Pp. Eng. 1865, vol. 47
— 1863, p. 52–57.	Pp. Eng. 1866, vol. 60
— 1864, p. 52–57.	Pp. Eng. 1866, vol. 60
— 1865, p. 52–57.	Pp. Eng. 1867, vol. 62
— 1866, p. 50–57.	Pp. Eng. 1867/8, vol. 2
— 1867, p. 50–57.	Pp. Eng. 1868/9, vol. 54
— 1868, p. 50–57.	Pp. Eng. 1870, vol. 59
— 1869, p. 46–49.	Pp. Eng. 1871, vol. 60
— 1870, p. 46–49.	Pp. Eng. 1872, vol. 52
— 1871, p. 46–49.	Pp. Eng. 1873, vol. 58
— 1872, p. 46–49.	Pp. Eng. 1874, vol. 59

— 1873, p. 42–45.   Pp. Eng. 1875, vol. 67
— 1874, p. 42–45.   Pp. Eng. 1876, vol. 65
— 1875, p. 42–45.   Pp. Eng. 1877, vol. 73
— 1876, p. 34–37.   Pp. Eng. 1878/9, vol. 63
— 1877, p. 34–37.   Pp. Eng. 1880, vol. 64
— 1878–9, p. 26–29.   Pp. Eng. 1880, vol. 64
— 1879–80, p. 26–29.   Pp. Eng. 1881, vol. 81
— 1880–1, p. 26, 27.   Pp. Eng. 1882, vol. 61
— 1881–2, p. 26, 27.   Pp. Eng. 1883, vol. 61

536. Auction catal. One third part of £100 secured on the Postcombe turnpike road. 1 May 1838.   G.A. fol. B 71

537. Report of the Commissioners for inquiring into the state of the roads in England and Wales. (Oxfordshire, p. 326–37.)
Pp. Eng. 1840, vol. 27

538. HUSSEY, R., An account of the Roman road from Allchester to Dorchester, and other Roman remains in the neighbourhood. (Ashmolean soc.) Oxf., 1841, 8°. 47 pp.   G.A. Oxon 8° 503

539. General statement of the income and expenditure of the Gosford turnpike road trust. 1850.   G.A. Oxon c. 73 (377)
1851.   G.A. Oxon c. 75 (401)
1856.   G.A. Oxon c. 76 (417)
1858.   G.A. Oxon c. 65 (180)
1859.   G.A. Oxon c. 67 (177)
[Oxf.], 1850–59, fol.

540. Turnpike trusts. Buckingham, Brackley and Banbury road. n. pl., 1851, fol. 3 pp.   Pp. Eng. 1851, vol. 48

541. An abstract of the general statements of the receipts and expenditure on account of the highways of the several parishes, townships, &c. in England and Wales for the year ending 25th March, 1850. (Oxfordshire, p. 372–85.)   Pp. Eng. 1852, vol. 43
— 1852, p. 26, 27.   Pp. Eng. 1852/3, vol. 97
— 1853, p. 26, 27.   Pp. Eng. 1854/5, vol. 49
— 1854, p. 26, 27.   Pp. Eng. 1856, vol. 58
— 1855, p. 26, 27.   Pp. Eng. 1857, sess. 2, vol. 37
— 1856, p. 26, 27.   Pp. Eng. 1857/8, vol. 52
— 1857, p. 26, 27.   Pp. 1859, sess. 2, vol. 26
— 1858, p. 22, 23.   Pp. Eng. 1860, vol. 61
— 1859, p. 22, 23.   Pp. Eng. 1861, vol. 57
— 1860, p. 22, 23.   Pp. Eng. 1862, vol. 53
— 1861, p. 22, 23.   Pp. Eng. 1863, vol. 50
— 1862, p. 22, 23.   Pp. Eng. 1864, vol. 50
— 1863, p. 22, 23.   Pp. Eng. 1865, vol. 47
— Year ending 25 Mar. 1864, p. 16. 17.   Pp. Eng. 1867, vol. 62
— From 25 Mar. to 31 Dec. 1864, p. 14, 15.
Pp. Eng. 1866, vol. 60

— 1865, p. 16, 17.	Pp. Eng. 1867, vol. 62
— 1866, p. 18, 19, 46, 47.	Pp. Eng. 1867/8, vol. 62
— 1867, p. 18, 19, 46, 47.	Pp. Eng. 1868/9, vol. 54
— 1868, p. 18, 19, 46, 47.	Pp. Eng. 1870, vol. 59
— 1869, p. 18, 19, 46, 47.	Pp. Eng. 1871, vol. 60
— 1870, p. 18, 19, 46, 47.	Pp. Eng. 1872, vol. 52
— 1871, p. 18, 19, 46, 47.	Pp. Eng. 1873, vol. 58
— 1872, p. 18, 19, 60–63.	Pp. Eng. 1874, vol. 59
— 1873, p. 18, 19, 60–63.	Pp. Eng. 1875, vol. 67
— 1874, p. 18, 19, 58–61.	Pp. Eng. 1876, vol. 65
— 1875, p. 18, 19, 58–61.	Pp. Eng. 1877, vol. 73
— 1876, p. 18, 19, 58–61.	Pp. Eng. 1878, vol. 66
— 1877, p. 18, 19.	Pp. Eng. 1878/9, vol. 63
— 1878, p. 18, 19, 58–61.	Pp. Eng. 1878/9, vol. 63
— 1879, p. 18, 19, 58–61.	Pp. Eng. 1880, vol. 64
— 1880, p. 18, 19, 42, 43.	Pp. Eng. 1881, vol. 81
— 1881, p. 22, 23, 50, 51.	Pp. Eng. 1882, vol. 61
— 1882, p. 22, 23, 50, 51.	Pp. Eng. 1883, vol. 61
— 1883, p. 22, 23, 52, 53.	Pp. Eng. 1884, vol. 70

542. Turnpike trusts. Reports of the secretary of state. No. 3. Shilling-ford, Wallingford, and Reading road.　　Pp. Eng. 1852, vol. 44

543. Turnpike trusts. Reports of the secretary of state. No. 9. Burford, Leachlade, and Swindon roads.　　Pp. Eng. 1852/3, vol. 97

544. Turnpike trusts. Report . . . relating to the circumstances of the under-mentioned Turnpike trusts applying for local acts in the present session of parliament, made by the Home department. 1. Finford Bridge and Banbury road.　　Pp. Eng. 1859, vol. 13

545. The Highway acts 25 & 26 Vict. c. 61 and 27 & 28 Vict. c. 101. 'Bullingdon' highway district. Provisional order. [Oxf., 1864], fol. 4 pp.　　G.A. fol. A 139* (25)
— Final order. [Oxf.], 1865, fol. 2 pp.　　G.A. fol. A 139* (26)

546. Bullingdon highway district. Specification and contract. (Oxf., 1866), fol. 4 pp.　　G.A. fol. A 139* (22)

547. Return of Turnpike trusts, continued by annual continuance acts in 1864, 1865, 1866 and 1867, giving name of trust and county, date of expiry of last local act, amount of interest per cent. payable [&c.]. (Oxfordshire, p. 45–48.)　　Pp. Eng. 1867/8, vol. 62

548. Return showing the several highway districts in each county . . . constituted under the highway acts 1862 and 1864 and the names of the parishes comprised in each district. (Oxfordshire, p. 40–41.)
　　Pp. Eng. 1873, vol. 58

549. Disturnpiked roads . . . Return of the names of the several turn-pike roads which have become disturnpiked between 31 Dec. 1870 and 30 June 1878 in each county [&c.]. (Oxfordshire, p. 7, 14.)
　　Pp. Eng. 1878, vol. 66

550. County of Oxford. List of the main roads. 1879. [Oxf., 1879], fol.
10 pp. O.C.R.L.

551. TURRELL, W. J., and GRAVES, H., The roads round Oxford. Oxf.,
1892, 12°. 47 pp. G.A. Eng. roads 16° 5
— 2nd ed., by H. Graves and A. B. Evans. (Oxf. univ. bicycle club.)
1896. 82 pp. G.A. Eng. roads 16° 10

552. Berks, South Oxon and North Hants society for the preservation
of public rights of way and open spaces. Occasional paper. No. 1–12.
n. pl., 1898–1900, 4°. G.A. Berks 4° 65

553. Oxford and district footpaths, bridlepaths and commons preserva-
tion society. Rules. [1926, 1930]. G.A. Oxon b. 128
— Balance sheet. 1926, 1929, 30. G.A. Oxon b. 128
— Annual report. 1928, 1930–38. O.P.L.

554. Oxford and district footpaths, bridlepaths and commons preservation society. Short walks round Oxford. (Oxf.), [1927], 8°. 12 pp.
O.P.L.
— 3rd ed. [1935]. 47 pp. O.P.L.

555. Oxfordshire county council, county surveyor's office. An investigation and report on four years fatal accidents in Oxfordshire. Oxf.,
1937, fol. 65 pp. 247913 c. 27

556.

See 3017 [Lines on Kiddington turnpike house. 1879].

Bridges

557. An act for building a bridge over the river Thames from . . .
Sutton Courtney . . . to . . . Culham. . . . (47 G. III, sess. 2, c. 43,
L. & P.) Lond., 1807, fol. 29 pp. L. Eng. A 69 c. 6

558. Oxford county council. List of county and other bridges. [Oxf.],
1845, fol. 4 pp. G.A. fol. A 137 (1)

559. Oxfordshire bridges (repaired at the expense of the county). n. pl.,
1869, fol. 17 pp. G.A. Oxon c. 107 (19)
— 1885. 32 pp. O.C.R.L.
— Bridges repairable by the County council. 1889. O.C.R.L.
— Bridges repairable by the County council. 1905. O.C.R.L.

560. TOLLIT, H. J., 1878. Report . . . upon all the bridges in the county
of Oxford recognised as 'county bridges' . . . [Oxf.], 1878, fol. 92 pp.
G.A. Oxon c. 141

See also Caversham, Clifton Hampden, Cropredy, Culham, Eynsham,
Goring, Henley, Kidlington, Lower Heyford, Newbridge, Northmoor,
Osney, Radcot, Shillingford, Shilton, Whitchurch, Witney, Wolvercote.

HUSBANDRY AND FARMING

General and Arable

561. DAVIS, R., General view of the agriculture of the county of Oxford. Lond., 1794, 4°. 39 pp.   Gough Oxf. 103 (3)

562. YOUNG, A., View of the agriculture of Oxfordshire, drawn up for the . . . Board of agriculture, by the secretary of the board [A. Young]. Lond., 1809, 8°. 362 pp.   G.A. Oxon 8° 901
— [Another ed. *entitled*] General view [&c.]. Lond., 1813, 8°. 362 pp.   G.A. Oxon 8° 288

563. LOUDON, J. C., Observations on laying out farms in the Scotch style, adapted to England . . . The introduction of the Berwickshire husbandry into Middlesex and Oxfordshire. Lond., 1812, fol. 105 pp.   19197 b. 1

564. MARSHALL, W., A review . . . of the reports to the Board of Agriculture from the Midland department of England. (Oxfordshire, p. 444–94.) York, 1815, 8°.   G.A. Gen. top. 8° 424

565. COBB, T., Agricultural distress, the causes assigned and a remedy suggested to the owners in the county of Oxford. Lond., &c., 1835, 8°. 15 pp.   G.A. Oxon 8° 938

566. READ, C. S., On the farming of Oxfordshire. (Journ., Roy. agric. soc., 1854, vol. 15, p. 189–276.)   Soc. 19195 e. 298

567. Association for the preservation of agriculture and our other industries for . . . Berks, Bucks and Oxon. [Aims & rules.] Oxf., (1887), 4°. 4 pp.   G.A. Oxon c. 317 (3)

568. Agriculture. (Victoria county history, 1907, vol. 2, p. 279–92.)
                    R. 9. 41 s

569. GRAY, H. L., Yeoman farming in Oxfordshire from the sixteenth century to the nineteenth. (Quart. journ. of econ., 1910, vol. 24, no. 2, p. 293–326.)   G.A. Oxon 4° 387

570. GRAY, H. L., The later history of the Midland system in Oxfordshire. (English field systems, 1915, p. 109–56.)   24754 e. 182

571. ORR, J., Agriculture in Oxfordshire, a survey, by J. Orr, with a chapter on soils by C. G. T. Morison. Oxf., 1916, 8°. 239 pp.
                    Radcl.

572. GUNTHER, R. T., Report on agricultural damage by vermin and birds in the counties of Norfolk and Oxfordshire in 1916. (Oxfordshire, p. 56–92.) Lond., &c., 1917, 8°.   1639 d. 18

573. FUSSELL, G. E., Crop husbandry in the 18th century: Oxford, Bucks and Berks. (Journ., Min. of agric., 1938, vol. 45, p. 563–69.)
Soc. 19192 d. 12

574. MARSHALL, M., Land of Britain. Pt. 56. Oxfordshire. (Land utilization survey of Britain, p. 195–240.) Lond., 1943, 4°.
23213 d. 2 (56)

575. Reading univ., dept. of agric. econ. Miscellaneous cost studies. No. 1–. [Reprod. from typewriting.] 1944–. [Many of the surveys concern Oxfordshire farms.]
23213 d. 111

576. Oxford univ., agric. econ. research *inst.* Country planning, a study of local problems [in N. Oxfordshire]. Lond., 1944, 8°. 288 pp.
2479115 e. 22

577. BURR, H., Farming club movement in Oxfordshire. (Journ., Min. of agric., 1946/7, vol. 53, p. 275, 76.)
Per. 19192 d. 12

578. HUTHNANCE, S. L., Farming in Berkshire and Oxfordshire. (Journ., Roy. agric. soc., 1949, vol. 110, p. 1–15.)
Soc. 19195 d. 201

579. GARDNER, T. W., The farms and estates of Oxfordshire. (Reading univ., dept. of agric. econ., misc. studies, 5.) Reading, [1951], 8°. 80 pp.
23213 d. 146 (5)

See 1250 [Plan for employment of farm labourers, Cropredy. *c.* 1820].
See 788A [Return of owners of land. 1874].

Enclosures

580. County of Oxford. Inclosure awards enrolled in the office of the Clerk of the peace of the county, or at Westminster. [Oxf.], 1869, fol. 16 pp.
G.A. fol. A 137 (5)

581. Inclosures. Return of the acreage of — 1. Waste lands subject to rights of common. 2 Common field lands in which the tithes have been commuted [&c.]. (Oxfordshire, p. 161–65.)
Pp. Eng. 1874, vol. 52

582. LEADAM, I. S., *ed.*, The Domesday of inclosures, 1517–1518, the extant returns to Chancery for Berks . . . Oxon [&c.] by the Commissioners of inclosures in 1517. 2 vols. (Publ., Roy. hist. soc.) Lond., &c., 1897, 8°.
24754 e. 109

583. TATE, W. E., Members of parliament and their personal relations to enclosures, a study with special reference to Oxfordshire enclosures, 1757–1843. (Agric. hist., July 1949, vol. 23, p. 213–20, publ. by the Agric. hist. soc. of Chicago.)
G.A. Oxon 4° 679 (1)

584. TATE, W. E., Oxfordshire enclosure commissioners, 1737–1856.
(Journ. of mod. hist., 1951, vol. 23, no. 2, p. 137–45.)
S. Hist. per. 11
— Repr. G.A. Oxon 4° 504 (13)

See 3187 [Enclosure by agreement, Marston. 1927].
For enclosure acts, &c., see under separate places.

Open Fields

585. BALLARD, A., Notes on the open fields of Oxfordshire. (Rept.,
Oxf. archaeol. soc., 1908, p. 22–31.) R. Top. 330

586. BALLARD, A., The management of open fields [relates to Chipping
Norton and Steeple Aston]. (Rept., Oxf. archaeol. soc., 1913,
p. 131–44.) R. Top. 330

See 192 [Maps illustrating open field system. 1888].
See 2036 [Charlton-on-Otmoor open fields. 1907].
See 2590 [Open fields at Fritwell. 1907].
See 2707 [Gt. Tew. Open field system and bye-laws. 1907].
See 3185 [Open field and inclosure, Marston. 1924].

Agricultural Societies

587. Oxfordshire agricultural society. [Proceedings &c.] At a meeting
of the committee . . . 20th Oct. 1824. G.A. Oxon b. 112 (82)
— 12th Oct. 1839. G.A. Oxon c. 56 (7)
— 13th Oct. 1849. G. A. Oxon b. 96 (24)
— [Proceedings &c.] At a general meeting, 14th Jan., 1857.
G.A. Oxon b. 96 (31)

588. Oxfordshire agricultural society. Prize list, regulations, &c. of the
show of stock and implements [*afterw.*] Annual report and prize
list, 1882–1912. n. pl., (1882–1912), 8°. Per. 19192 e. 151

589. Oxfordshire agricultural society. [Catalogue of] the show of stock
and implements. 1882–. n. pl., (1882–), 8°. Per. 19192 e. 151

590. Oxfordshire agricultural society. Specification tender and agreement for works at Show yard. [Oxf., *c.* 1910], fol. 10 pp.
G.A. Oxon c. 262

591. Oxfordshire agricultural society. Revenue account and balance
sheet for the year ended 31 Aug. 1912 (–25). (Oxf., 1912–25), 8°.
Per. 19192 e. 151

592. Oxfordshire agricultural society. Catalogue of the annual show.
1920–. Oxf., 1920–, 8°. Per. 19192 e. 151

593. Oxford, Oxfordshire and neighbouring counties' horticultural society [*afterw.*] Royal Oxfordshire horticultural society. Rules (and regulations). 1830.   G.A. Oxon 8° 900 (24)
— 1838.   G.A. Oxon 8° 1132 (13)
— 1846.   G.A. Oxon c. 54 (141)
— 1851.   G.A. Oxon c. 62 (114)
— 1859.   G.A. Oxon c. 66 (184)

594. Oxford, Oxfordshire, and neighbouring counties' horticultural society. The first report. Oxf., 1832, 8°. 24 pp.
          G.A. Oxon 8° 1046 (4)

595. Royal Oxfordshire horticultural society. [Shows.] 1832.
          G.A. Oxon c 48 (119)
— 1833.   G.A. Oxon c. 49 (122)
— 1835.   G.A. Oxon c. 51 (133)
— 1836.   G.A. Oxon c. 52 (130)
— 1837.   G.A. Oxon c. 53 (143)
— 1838.   G.A. Oxon c. 54 (147)
— 1840.   G.A. Oxon c. 56 (10)
— 1842.   G.A. Oxon c. 58 (126)
— 1843.   G.A. Oxon c. 59 (137)
— 1844.   G.A. Oxon c. 60 (147)
— 1845.   G.A. Oxon c. 61 (145)
— 1846.   G.A. Oxon c. 62 (113)
— 1847.   G.A. Oxon c. 63 (1)
— 1849.   G.A. Oxon c. 65 (195)
— 1850.   G.A. Oxon c. 66 (170)
— 1851.   G.A. Oxon c. 66 (183)
— 1852.   G.A. Oxon c. 68 (184)
— 1853.   G.A. Oxon c. 69 (211)

596. Royal Oxfordshire horticultural society. (Schedule of prizes, rules, instructions, and list of members.) 1860.
          G.A. Oxon 4° 405* (3)
— 1876–1939.   G.A. Oxon 8° 1051

See also Banbury agricultural society.
     Begbroke, Cassington, and Yarnton horticultural society.
     Benson horticultural society.
     Bicester agricultural and horticultural association.
     Dorchester and Burcot horticultural society.
     Hanborough and Freeland horticultural society.
     Headington horticultural, cottage garden, and poultry society.
     Henley horticultural society.
     Standlake and Stanton Harcourt horticultural and cottage garden society.
     Thame horticultural society.
     Thame Show.
     Witney and West Oxfordshire horticultural society.
     Woodstock agricultural and horticultural society.

Smallholdings, Allotments, and Gardens

597. A return of the numbers of allotments under 1 acre in extent detached from cottages, and of small holdings of $\frac{1}{4}$ acre to 50 acres inclusive, in each parish or township. (Oxfordshire, p. 330–42.)
Pp. Eng. 1890, vol. 57

598. ASHBY, A. W., Allotments and small-holdings in Oxfordshire, a survey. Oxf., 1917, 8°. 198 pp. 24754 e. 179

599. Oxfordshire garden produce committee. Food production bulletin. New ser. No. 1–. [Previous issues not printed.] Oxf., 1945–, 8°.
Radcl.

See 961 [School gardens. 1910].
See 2764 [Terms for letting allotments, Headington. 1876].

Pasture

600. Oxfordshire fat cattle show, 1846. [Conditions and list of awards.] (Oxf., 1846), fol. 3 pp. G.A. Oxon b. 96 (22)

601. Oxford down sheep breeders' assoc. The Oxford down flock book [*afterw.*] Flock book of the Oxford down sheep. Vol. 1–. Lond., 1889–, 8°. 18973I e. 8

602. HOBBS, J. T., Oxford downs, history of the breed. (Journ., Roy. agric. soc., 1908, vol. 69, p. 44–48.) Soc. 19195 e. 298

603. Oxford county, educ. comm. Report of the staff instructor in agriculture on the epizootic abortion experiments . . . 1911 to 1913. — 2nd report. 1911 to 1916. n. pl., (1913, 1916), 8°. 1632 d. 1

See 1827 [Division of common land. Bloxham. 1912].
See 3004 [Dairy. Kelmscott. 1917].
See 4296–98 [Lot meadows. Yarnton. 1910, 1912].

Forestry

604. Forestry. (Victoria county history, 1907, vol. 2, p. 293–301.)
R. 9. 41 s

605. WATT, A. S., The vegetation of the Chiltern hills, with special reference to the beechwoods and their seral relationships. (Journ. of ecology, 1934, vol. 22, p. 230–70, 445–507.) Radcl.

See 3424 [Pyrton papers and Saxon woodlands on the Chilterns. 1949].
See 4269, &c. [Wychwood forest].

INDUSTRIES AND TRADES

General

606. Industries of Oxfordshire, Berks, Bucks, etc. (British industries business review. A guide to leading commercial enterprises, p. 1–34.) Lond., &c., [1895], 4°. G.A. Gen. top. 4° 181

607. Industries. (Victoria county history, 1907, vol. 2, p. 225–77.)
R. 9. 41 s

608. PROSSER, R. B., A list of patents granted under the old law, 1617 to 1852, to persons resident in Oxfordshire, compiled from the official indexes. [Title-leaf & preface printed, the rest in MS.]
MS. Top. Oxon d. 175

609. WOODS, K. S., The rural industries round Oxford, a survey. Oxf., 1921, 8°. 180 pp.   232311 e. 62

See 1472, 73 [Aston training school for young girls for domestic service. 1913, 14].
See 4051 [Witney church registry for placing and assisting unemployed servants. 1890].
See 2111, 12 [Strike at Chipping Norton. 1914].

Bee-keeping

610. Oxfordshire bee-keepers' assoc. Report, list of members and balance sheet. 1883–88. Chipping Norton, 1883–88, 8°.
G.A. Oxon 8° 497

Gloves

See 4167, 68 [Woodstock. 1898, 1938].

Paper Mills

See 2523 [Eynsham. 1888].
See 2726 [Hampton Gay. 1849].
See 3330 [North Newington. 1833].
See 4116 [Wolvercote. 1849].

Printing

611. CHENEY, J., Printers and printing in Oxford and district [F. H. Castle & co., ltd., Thame and Cheney & sons, Banbury]. (Our bulletin, South Western alliance of Master printers' assoc., Jan. 1931, p. 19.)   G.A. Oxon b. 175

See 1511 [Bampton. Private printing press. 1900].
See 1608A [J. Cheney and sons, Banbury. 1936].
See 3756, 57 [Stonor. Private printing press. 1854, 1896].

Quarries and Stone-working

612. DAVIS, R. H. C., Masons' marks in Oxfordshire and the Cotswolds. (Rept., Oxf. archaeol. soc., 1938, p. 69–84.)   R. Top. 330

613. ARKELL, W. J., Oxford stone. Lond., 1947, 8°. 185 pp.
G.A. Oxon 8° 1210
— [Review of Oxford stone, by E. M. Jope.] (Oxoniensia, 1949, vol. 14, p. 90–98.)   R. Top. 340

614. JOPE, E. M., Abingdon abbey craftsmen and building stone supplies [mainly from Taynton and Wheatley]. (Berks archaeol. journ., 1948/9, vol. 51, p. 53–64.) R. Top. 100

615. ARKELL, W. J., The future of English building-stones. (Endeavour, 1950, vol. 9, p. 40–44.) Radcl.

616. ARKELL, W. J., The building-stones of Blenheim palace, Cornbury park, Glympton park and Heythrop house. (Oxoniensia, 1950, vol. 15, p. 49–54.) R. Top. 340

See 3742, 45 [Stonesfield slate. 1894, 1936].

Textiles

617. BECKINSALE, R. P., Factors in the development of the Cotswold woollen industry. (Oxfordshire. Plush industry at Banbury. Blanket trade at Witney.) (Geogr. journ., 1937, vol. 90, p. 357–61.)
Soc. 2017 d. 60

See 4068, &c. [Witney Blanket industry].

Tradesmen's Tokens

618. BOYNE, W., Tokens issued in the seventeenth century in England, Wales and Ireland, by corporations, merchants, tradesmen, &c. (Oxfordshire, p. 371–82.) Lond., 1858, 8°.
Arch. Num. inf. III a. 19, 19*
— New ed. [entitled] Trade tokens [ed.] by G. C. Williamson. 2 vols. (Oxfordshire, vol. 2, p. 919–38.) Lond., 1889–91, 8°.
Num. Gen. top. d. 1, 2

619. MILNE, J. G., ed., Catalogue of Oxfordshire seventeenth century tokens. Oxf., &c., 1935, 8°. 49 pp. +16 pl. Num. Oxon e. 2

620. ATKINS, J., The tradesmen's tokens of the eighteenth century. (Oxfordshire, p. 163.) Lond., 1892, 8°. Num. Gen. top. d. 11

621. MILNE, J. G., Oxfordshire traders' tokens. (Oxoniensia, 1945, p. 104, 05.) R. Top. 340

MARKETS

622. Royal commission on market rights and tolls. First report. Appendix. (List of fairs, Oxfordshire, p. 192, 93.)
Pp. Eng. 1888, vol. 53

623. Royal commission on market rights and tolls. Vol. 13, pt. 1. Statistics relating to . . . markets owned by local authorities. (Oxfordshire, p. 212–19.) Pp. Eng. 1890/1, vol. 39

POLITICAL AND MILITARY HISTORY

GENERAL

624. Votes of the House of Commons. 1689–1776/77. 22772 d. 1–56
— [MS. index in the Bodleian. 3 vols.] 22772 d. 57–59
Numerous references to Oxfordshire.

625. A declaration of the nobility . . . of the county of Oxon which have adhered to the late king. Lond., 1660, s. sh. Wood 276 *a* (221)
— [Repr.] (Somers tracts, 1751, ser. 3, vol. 2, p. 209.)
GG 141 Art.
— [Repr.] (Somers tracts, 1812, vol. 7, p. 392.) Σ III 17

626. The declaration of the county of Oxon to his excellency the lord general Monck. We, the gentlemen [&c.] . . . of the county of Oxon . . . do now hereby declare the resentments we have of our grievances . . . [Feb. 13, 1660]. Lond., 1660, s. sh. O.C.R.L.

627. To the . . . House of Commons . . . the humble petition of the baronets [&c.] . . . in the county of Oxford [praising the Church and asking for laws against papists &c.]. n. pl., [1679?], s. sh.
Wood 276 *a* (188)

628. An address to the Oxfordshire addressors, and all others of the same strain [against Jacobites and papists]. Lond., 1710, 8°. 15 pp.
G.A. Oxon 8° 218 (1)

629. An authentick copy of the association entered into by part of the nobility [&c.] . . . of the county of Oxford at the . . . rebellion in . . . 1745, together with the names of all the persons who subscribed (and who would not subscribe) thereto. n. pl., (1745), s. sh.
Gough Oxf. 101 (26)

630. DUCKETT, SIR G. F., *ed.*, Penal laws and Test act, questions touching their repeal propounded in 1687–8 by James ii. (Oxfordshire, p. 327–44.) Lond., 1882, 4°. G.A. Gen. top. 4° 459

631. Oxfordshire preparations for the prince of Orange. (Rept., Oxf. archaeol. soc., 1902, p. 27–29.) R. Top. 330

632. Political history. (Victoria county history, 1939, vol. 1, p. 429–56.)
R. 9. 41 *s*

ADMINISTRATION

General

632A. The Oxford blue book and elector's companion, ed. by W. Rowbottom. 1888–90. Oxf., 1888–90, 8°. Dir. Oxon e. 8

Boundaries

See 189 [Book of reference to the Ordnance Survey plan of the parishes in the County. 1876–82].

633. Local government boundaries commission. Report. 1888. 2 vols. (Oxfordshire, *passim*.) Pp. Eng. 1888, vol. 51

634. An act to confirm certain provisional orders of the Local government board relating to the city of Oxford and to the counties of Oxford and Berks. (52 & 53 V., c. 15, L. & P.) Lond., 1889, fol. 19 pp. L. Eng. A 69 c. 6

635. An act to confirm certain provisional orders of the Local government board relating to the counties of Buckingham ... Oxford [&c.]. (59 V., c. 8, L. & P.) [Concerns the boundaries of Stokenchurch, Kingsey and Mollington.] Lond., 1895, fol. 25 pp.
L. Eng. A 69 c. 6

636. Local government board. A statement of the county boroughs, other boroughs, urban districts other than boroughs and rural districts. (Oxfordshire, p. 108–11.) Lond., 1896, fol. O.C.R.L.

637. Oxfordshire county council. Local government act, 1933, section 141. The County of Oxford (alteration of rural parishes) (No. 1) Order, 1951. Parishes in the Henley rural district. [Oxf.], (1951), 8°. 22 pp. L. Eng. B 33 d. Par. 1

County Council

638. Oxfordshire county council. [Reports. 8 May 1889–.] O.C.R.L.

639. Oxfordshire county council. Quarterly meeting. Feb. 1947–. [Oxf.], 1947–, 8°. G.A. Oxon 4° 640

Finance

640. An act for making an equal county rate for the county of Oxford. (53 G. III, c. 78, L. & P.) Lond., 1813, fol. 6 pp.
L. Eng. A 69 c. 6

641. Report from the select committee on the expenditure of county rates. 1825. (Oxfordshire, p. 381–88, 738.) Pp. Eng. 1825, vol. 6

642. County rates. An account of the latest valuation of every parish, township or place. (Oxfordshire, p. 154–56.)
Pp. Eng. 1831/2, vol. 44

643. County rates. Accounts from the respective treasurers of the counties in England and Wales, of the several sums received by them for county rates, during 1821(–32) with statements of the application thereof. (Oxfordshire, p. 96.) Pp. Eng. 1833, vol. 32

644. A comparative statement of the expenditure of the county rates in the several counties of England . . . 1792, 1802, 1812, 1822 and 1832. (Rept., Select comm. of the House of lords appointed to inquire into the charges of the county rates. Oxfordshire, p. 178, 79.)
Pp. Eng. 1835, vol. 14

645. A return, showing the annual value of real property in each parish . . . assessed to the Property and Income tax, for the year ending April 1843, [&c.]. (Oxfordshire, p. 54–56.)
Pp. Eng. 1844, vol. 32
— showing the quota of Land tax assessed in 1798. (Oxfordshire, p. 164–66.) Pp. Eng. 1844, vol. 32

646. Abstract of i) Returns of all rates, other than poor rates, levied, and of all sums, other than those for the relief of the poor, expended out of the poor rates . . . in 1843. ii) . . . of all sums expended out of the rates . . . in 1843 on each of the following accounts:—Expense of gaol and maintenance of prisoners, administration of justice, county expenses, coroner and county rates. (Oxfordshire, p. 137–41.)
Pp. Eng. 1847, vol. 40

647. Statement shewing the population, area, number of inhabited houses, and rateable value to the county rate, of the parishes and places in the county of Oxford. [Oxf.], 1863, fol. 11 pp.
G.A. fol. A 139 (13)

648. Returns of the amount levied for the purposes of the county rate . . . in each of the last seven years, showing the amount per cent levied on property assessed to the county rate . . . and of the number of head of cattle . . . and of any income derived by any county . . . from any other source than the county rate. 1867 (Oxfordshire, p. 21.) Pp. Eng. 1867, vol. 58

649. Rating act, 1874. Return (with respect to the several hereditaments rendered rateable by the above act, &c.). (Oxfordshire, p. 132–37.)
Pp. Eng. 1877, vol. 71

650. An act to confirm certain provisional orders of the Local government board relating to the counties of Oxford and Worcester [relating to additional borrowing powers]. (3 Edw. VII, c. 60, L. & P.) Lond., 1903, fol. 4 pp. L. Eng. A 69 c. 6
— Amended by 4 & 5 G. V, c. 46, L. & P.

651. Oxfordshire county council. Estimates of income and expenditure. May 1910–. O.C.R.L.
[Bodleian 1945/50–. Per. 232971 d. 79]

652. Ministry of health. Proposals for reform in Local government and in the financial relations between the Exchequer and local authorities. (Oxfordshire, p. 15, 16.) Pp. Eng. 1928/9, vol. 15

See also 888, &c. [Poor rates].

Parliamentary Representation
General

653. [Letter to Viscount Quarendon and sir J. Dashwood from the High Sheriff and Grand jury, concerning representation and instructions.] (London mag., 1742, p. 133, 34.) Hope adds. 397

654. WILLIS, B., Notitia Parliamentaria, an account of the first returns and incorporations of the cities, towns and boroughs . . . that send members to Parliament, their returning officers, number of electors and coats of arms [&c. Vol. 3. Oxfordshire, *passim*]. Lond., 1750, 8°. 8° E 102 BS.

655. CUNNINGHAM, T., An historical account of the rights of election of the several counties, cities and boroughs of Great Britain. (Oxfordshire, p. 408-10, &c.) Lond., 1783, 8°. 8° A 14. 9 Jur.

655A. Parliamentary representation. Reports from commissioners on proposed division of counties and boundaries of boroughs. (Oxfordshire, vol. 2, pt. 2, p. 189-97.) Pp. Eng. 1831/2, vol. 39

655B. A letter to the freeholders of Oxfordshire [concerning the Reform Bill. Signed A small farmer]. [Oxf., 1831], 8°. 8 pp.
G. Pamph. 789 (11)

656. SMITH, H. S., The parliaments of England from 1st George i. to the present time. (Oxfordshire, vol. 2, pp. 1-12.) [List of members for Oxon, Banbury and Woodstock.] Lond., 1845, 8°.
G.A. Gen. top. 8° 207

656A. County of Oxford. Polling districts. n. pl., 1868, 8°. 15 pp.
G.A. Oxon 8° 100 (6)

657. WING, W., Oxfordshire elections in the present century. Repr. from the Oxf. chronicle. (Oxf.), 1878, 12°. 30 pp.
G.A. Oxon 8° 220 (1)

657A. Report (suppl. report) of the Boundary commissioners. 1885. (Oxfordshire, pt. 1, p. 139.) Pp. Eng. 1884/5, vol. 19

657B. Elections. Redistribution of seats act, 1885 (contents of county divisions). County of Oxford. Pp. Eng. 1884/5, vol. 63

658. WILLIAMS, W. R. J., The Parliamentary history of the county of Oxford, including the city and university . . . and the boroughs of Banbury, Burford, Chipping Norton, Dadington, Witney and Woodstock, 1213-1899. Brecknock, 1899, 8°. 235 pp.
G.A. Oxon 8° 662

658A. Report of the Boundary commission. (Oxfordshire, vol. 2, p. 149-52.) Pp. Eng. 1917/18, vol. 13

Poll Books and Registers

659. A copy of the poll for knights of the shire for the county of Oxford, taken at Oxford on the 17th of April 1754. Oxf., 1754, 4°. 35 pp.
G.A. Oxon 4° 6 (4)

660. A copy of the poll for knights of the shire . . . of Oxford . . . 17th, 18th, 19th, 20th, 22d and 23d of April 1754. Oxf., 1754, 4°. [65 pp.]
Gough Oxf. 101 (16)

661. The poll of the freeholders of Oxfordshire, taken at the County court, 17th April, 1754. Oxf., (1754), 8°. 115 pp.
Gough Oxf. 101 (17)

— [Another ed.] Oxf., 1754, 4°. 116 pp. Gough Oxf. 101 (15)

662. The poll of the freeholders of Oxfordshire, taken at Oxford on 17th, 18th, 19th, 20th, 22nd and 23rd of April 1754. Oxf., 1754, 4°. 155 pp.
G.A. Oxon 4° 346

663. A list of the several persons who voted for . . . viscount Wenman . . . and sir James Dashwood, or for one of them, at the last election of knights to serve in Parliament for the county of Oxford, intended to be objected to by . . . viscount Parker, and sir Edward Turner. n. pl., [1754], fol. 23 pp. G.A. Oxon 4° 6 (1)

664. The copy of the poll for knights of the shire for the county of Oxford, taken 16th, 17th, and 19th June, 1826. Oxf., &c., 1826, 4°. 75 pp.
G.A. Oxon 4° 110

665. The copy of the poll of the freeholders for knights of the shire . . . 5th–7th August 1830. Oxf., 1830, 4°. 82 pp. G.A. Oxon 4° 68

666. The copy of the poll of the freeholders for knights of the shire for the county of Oxford, taken . . . 9th, 10th, and 11th May, 1831. Oxf., &c., 1831, 4°. 82 pp. G.A. Oxon 4° 36 (1)

667. The register of electors to vote in the choice of a member . . . to serve in Parliament. Oxf., (1836), obl. fol. 140 pp.
G.A. Oxon c. 132

668. The poll of the electors who voted at the election of three knights of the shire to serve in the first parliament of queen Victoria, for the county of Oxford, on the 1st and 2nd August, 1837. Oxf., 1837, 4°. 122 pp.
G.A. Oxon 4° 36 (2)

669. The register of persons entitled to vote at any election of a member . . . to serve in Parliament for the county of Oxford (Northern-, Southern-, Mid-division) 1843/44–1915. Oxf., (1844–1915), 4°.
1843/44, O.C.R.L.; 1844/45–1915, G.A. Oxon 4° 136

670. The register of persons entitled to vote at any election of a member or members to serve in parliament for the county of Oxford between . . . November 1859 and . . . December 1860. Witney polling district. [Oxf.], (1859), 4°. 19 pp. MS. Top. Oxon d. 213 (f. 106–25)

671. The poll of the electors . . . of a knight of the county of Oxford, 31st January 1862. Oxf., 1862, 4°. 99 pp.   G.A. Oxon 4° 45 (5)

672. Banbury division of . . . Oxford. Register of parliamentary electors . . . and of local government electors. [*With*] Absent voters list. 1918–. [Oxf.], 1918–, 4°.
         1918–, O.C.R.L.; 1920–, G.A. Oxon 4° 136*

673. Henley division of . . . Oxford. Register of parliamentary electors . . . and of local government electors. [*With*] Absent voters list. 1918–. [Oxf.], 1918–, 4°.
         1918–, O.C.R.L.; 1920–, G.A. Oxon 4° 136**

Particular Elections

1690–1710

674. A letter from a person of honour at London in answer to his friend in Oxfordshire, concerning the ensuing election of knights of the shire for that county. n. pl., [1690], s. sh.   G.A. Oxon c. 107 (29)

675. [Begin.] To the copyholders or customary tenants of the county of Oxford. [Warning of punishment of perjurers at elections.] n. pl., [17—], s. sh.   G.A. fol. A 248 (3)

676. The Oxfordshire election [a satire in verse]. Lond., 1710, s. sh.
     Antiq. b. E. 15 (29)

1754

IN the following section, where possible, the political bias of the work has been indicated by [T.] for Tory and [W.] for Whig. The contemporary election literature is arranged alphabetically by title.

677. WING, W., The great Oxfordshire election of 1754. Repr. from the Oxford Chronicle. n. pl., 1881, 8°. 11 pp.
     G.A. Oxon 8° 220 (3 *a*)

678. WING, W., Oxfordshire in the eighteenth century, and the county election of 1754. Repr. from the Bicester Herald. An appendix to Brief annals of the Bicester poor law union. Bicester, (1881), 8°. 20 pp.   G.A. Oxon 8° 220 (36)

679. ROBSON, R. J., The Oxfordshire election of 1754. (Oxf. hist. ser., Brit. ser.) Lond., 1949, 8°. 192 pp.   22774 d. 16

680. An address to . . . dr. Huddesford . . . occasioned by what is called his proper reply to the Defence of the rector and fellows of Exeter-college. [W.] Lond., 1755, 8°. 37 pp.   Gough Oxf. 106 (9)

681. An address to the freeholders of the county of Oxford on the subject of the present election. [W.] Lond., 1753, 8°. 19 pp.
     Gough Oxf. 129 (3)

682. An address to the gentlemen of the grand-jury for the county of Oxford, on their late presentment of a libel against his majesty's person and government. [W.] Lond., [1754], 8°. 54 pp.
G.A. Oxon 4° 347

683. Advice from Horace to lady S-s-n. [T.] n. pl., [1753], s. sh.
G.A. fol. A 248 (41)

684. Advice to a certain dowager high-sheriff, a rhapsody. [T.] n. pl., [1754], s. sh.
G.A. Oxon 4° 31

685. The blackest of all black jokes, or, No joke like a true joke, a ballad. [T.] n. pl., [1755?], s. sh.
Gough Oxf. 39 (10)

686. Boots and shoes: or, Advice to a lady. [T.] n. pl., [1753], s. sh.
G.A. fol. A 248 (6)

687. The bump reviv'd. [T.] n. pl., [1753], s. sh.
G.A. fol. A 248 (31)

688. The case stated on both sides [concerning the Oxfordshire election]. (London mag., 1755, p. 204, 05.)
Hope adds. 410
— [Repr.]
G.A. Oxon 4° 31

689. The Christian's new warning piece: or, A full and true account of the circumcision of sir E. T. bart. as it was perform'd at the Bear-inn in the city of Oxford. [T.] Lond., 1753, 8°. 14 pp.
G.A. Oxon 8° 53 (10)

690. Circumcision not murder, but, Jews no Christians. [T.] n. pl., [1753], s. sh.
G.A. fol. A 248 (43)

691. The conduct of - - - - coll. consider'd; with some reflections upon ... A defence of the rector and fellows of Exeter college, in a letter from a Cambridge soph [signed Cantabrigiensis.] [T.] Lond., (1754), 4°. 16 pp.
Gough Oxf. 106 (10)

692. The cow of Haslemere; or, The conjuror's scrutiny at Oxford. [In verse.] [T.] Lond., 1754, fol. 12 pp.
Gough Oxf. 101 (20)

693. The curate and cobler, a third dialogue [signed T. P. i.e. Thomas Bray?] [T.] Lond., 1754, 8°. 32 pp.
G.A. Oxon 8° 53 (5)

694. [Debate concerning the Oxfordshire election.] (Journal of the proceedings and debates of the Political club. London mag., 1755, p. 265–76, 313–20, 361–67, 409–19, 465–72.)
Hope adds. 410

695. WEBBER, F., A defence of the rector and fellows of Exeter college from the accusations brought against them by ... dr. Huddesford. [By F. Webber.] [W.] Lond., 1754, 8°. 63 pp.
Gough Oxf. 106 (8)

696. KING, W., Doctor King's apology: or, Vindication of himself from the several matters charged on him by the Society of informers. [T.] Oxf., 1755, 4°. 46 pp.   Gough Oxf. 81 (10)
— 2nd ed. 47 pp.   Gough Oxf. 81 (11)

697. KING, W., The dreamer [by W. King. The 5th dream, p. 111–52, relates to Oxford under the name of Pallantis. The MS. notes in the Bodleian copy are those of Horace Walpole who identifies Cornix as sir E. Turner, Porcus as visct. Parker, the Onocentaurs as the Whigs, and their governor-general as the Duke of Marlborough]. Lond., 1754, 8°.   270 f. 62

698. The election magazine; or, The Oxfordshire register . . . a . . . collection of all the pieces in prose and verse lately published, in favour of the old and new interest; and not inserted in any other collection. Oxf., 1753, 8°. 78 pp.   G.A. Oxon 8° 53 (8)

699. An expedition to Oxford, a new song. [W.] n. pl., [1753], s. sh.
                                                                   G.A. fol. A 248 (30)

700. Fifty queries concerning the present Oxfordshire contest. [W.] Oxf., 1754, 8°. 31 pp.   G.A. Oxon 8° 53 (9)

701. The fishermen, a fable. [T.] n. pl., [1753?], s. sh.
                                                                   G.A. fol. A 248 (35)

702. The fryar's petition, a new song. [T.] n. pl., [1753], s. sh.
                                                                   G.A. fol. A 248 (24)

703. Hue and cry after the Greens. [T.] n. pl., [1753], s. sh.
                                                                   G.A. fol. A 248 (44)

704. Informations and other papers relating to the treasonable verses found at Oxford, July 17, 1754. Oxf., 1755, 8°. 45 pp.
                                                                   Gough Oxf. 39 (16)
— 2nd ed. 1755. 44 pp.   G.A. Oxon 8° 126

705. Informations &c. [concerning treasonable verses found at Oxford, July 17, 1754. p. 9–35 of a larger work].   Gough Oxf. 39 (16*)

706. The jolly brewer. [W.] n. pl., [1753], s. sh.
                                                                   G.A. fol. A 248 (23)

707. The jolly brewer's reply to the lean friar. [T.] n. pl., [1753], s. sh.
                                                                   G.A. fol. A 248 (25)

708. The Kiddlington canvas: or, The candidates in the mud. [T.] n. pl., [1753], s. sh.   G.A. fol. A 248 (42)

709. The knight arrant: or, The candidate, a tragedy . . . taken from Shakespeare. [T.] n. pl., [1753], s. sh.   G.A. fol. A 248 (34)

710. The last blow: or, An unanswerable vindication of the society of Exeter college in reply to the vice-chancellor, dr. King, and the . . . London Evening Post. [T.] Lond., 1755, 4°. 32 pp.
Gough Oxf. 89 (13)
— 2nd ed.   Gough Oxf. 106 (11)

711. [Letter, signed An English Christian supporting lord Parker and sir E. Turner.] [W.] n. pl., [1754?], 4°. 4 pp.   Gough Oxf. 55 (3)

712. M., A., A letter from a member of the University of Oxford to a gentleman in the country; containing a particular account of a watch-plot lately discovered there [signed A. M.]. [T.] Lond., 1755, 8°. 16 pp.   Gough Oxf. 131 (9)

713. A letter to doctor King, occasion'd by his late Apology; and, in particular, by such parts of it as are meant to defame mr. Kennicott, by a friend to mr. Kennicott and lately a member of the university of Oxford. [W.] Lond., 1755, 8°. 148 pp.   G.A. Oxon 8° 60 (8)

714. A letter to the author of the Defence of Exeter college, by way of notes upon his pamphlet, interspersed with serious advice. [T.] Lond., 1755, 8°. 74 pp.   G.A. Oxon 8° 60 (7)

715. A letter to the printer; with a letter to the freeholders of Oxford-shire, containing . . . remarks on . . . An address to the freeholders of the county of Oxford. [Signed D. G.] [T.] Oxf., 1753, 8°. 19 pp.
Gough Oxf. 39 (7)

716. [List of persons supporting the nomination of lord Parker and sir Edw. Turner as candidates at the meeting on 15 Feb., 1753.] [W.] n. pl., (1753), s. sh.   G.A. Oxon b. 112 (3)

717. A list of the several objections respectively made by lord Wenman and sir James Dashwood . . . to the voters who voted for lord Parker and sir Edward Turner. n. pl., [1755?], fol. 14 pp.
G.A. Oxon c. 318

718. Μάχιμος καὶ καλὸς ἀλέκτωρ, or, Billingsgates's ghost. [W.] n. pl., [1755], s. sh.   G.A. Oxon b. 112 (5)

719. The masters of extraordinary merit, or, all the recommendations and qualifications of the candidates of the old interest, as they are made public and asserted, by their secretary D. G. of Burford, in his letter to the freeholders of Oxfordshire, now first proved and clearly explained. Together with the political creed of the modern true-blues in O - - - shire. [W.] Lond., 1754, 8°. 25 pp.
G.A. Oxon 8° 53 (7)

720. BRAY, T., Mr. Boots's [T. Bray] apology for the conduct of the late h - - - h sh - - - ff [T. Blackhall, sheriff of Oxfordshire] in answer to a late infamous libel, intituled The blackest of all black jokes. [T.] Lond., [1755], 8°. 24 pp.   Gough Oxf. 39 (10)

721. The new interest display'd; a dialogue between a curate and a cobler, address'd to the freeholders of Oxfordshire. [T.] Lond., 1753, 8°. 22 pp. G.A. Oxon 8° 53 (2)

722. The new interest display'd: or, A second dialogue between a curate and a cobler, address'd to the freeholders of Oxfordshire. [T.] Lond., 1753, 8°. 22 pp. G.A. Oxon 8° 53 (4)

723. New interest moderation, or, A short account of some extra-ordinary proceedings at Banbury . . . and at Chipping-Norton. Lond., 1754, 4°. 8 pp. G.A. Oxon 8° 927

724. A new song [praising the duke of Marlborough & others, and pro-testing loyalty to king George]. [W.] n. pl., [1753], s. sh. G.A. fol. A 248 (8)

725. A new song to the tune of The three drunken maidens. [W.] n. pl., [1753?], s. sh. G.A. fol. A 248 (37)

726. The new way of overturning the old interest, with proper direc-tions. [T.] n. pl., [1753], s. sh. G.A. fol. A 248 (36)

727. The old and new interest: or, A sequel to the Oxfordshire contest, a collection of all the pieces that have appear'd since the nomination of the new candidates. Lond., 1753, 8°. 72 pp. Gough Oxf. 39 (3)

728. GREENWOOD, G., Old interest: a farce of three and forty acts as it is perform'd with great disaffection at the th—e in O–f–d [by G. Greenwood]. [W.] Lond., 1753, 8°. 27 pp. Gough Oxf. 39 (4)

729. The old interest display'd; a dialogue between an alderman and a cobler, address'd to the freeholders of Oxfordshire [by W. Black-stone?]. [W.] Lond., [1753], 8°. 19 pp. G.A. Oxon 8° 53 (3)

730. Old interest fury; or, A full and true account of some extraordinary proceedings . . . at Banbury . . . and Chipping Norton. [W.] n. pl., 1754, 8°. 15 pp. B.M.

731. The Oxford rag-plot: or, A rag-a-muffin song of Tag, rag, and bob-tail. [T.] n. pl., [1753], s. sh. G.A. fol. A 248 (29)

732. The Oxfordshire contest: or, The whole controversy between the old and new interest, containing, great variety of wit, humour, and argument . . . &c. Lond., 1753, 8°. 64 pp. G.A. Oxon 8° 53 (1)

733. The Oxfordshire garland, being a new dialogue between a turner and a twister. [T.] n. pl., [1753], s. sh. G.A. fol. A 248 (9)

734. Oxfordshire in an uproar; or, The election magazine. Oxf., [1754], 8°. 74 pp. G.A. Oxon 8° 62 (12)

735. The Oxfordshire voters for the old country interest, made by an honest freeholder. [T.] n. pl., [1753], s. sh. G.A. fol. A 248 (10)

736. The Oxf-rd- election. [T.] n. pl., [1753], s. sh.
G.A. fol. A 248 (47)

737. Political arithmetic, or, The old and new interest numbers. [T.]
n. pl., (1755), s. sh.   Gough Oxf. 101 (25)

738. The poor cobler's advice to the Oxfordshire freeholders. [W.]
n. pl., [1753], s. sh.   G.A. fol. A 248 (33)

739. The poor old interest supporters payment of the rich new interest
in their own coin. [T.] n. pl., [1753], s. sh.   G.A. fol. A 248 (28)

740. The poor supporters of the poor old interest, a song, by an Oxfordshire freeholder. [W.] n. pl., [1753], s. sh.
G.A. fol. A 248 (7)

741. BUCKLER, B., A proper explanation of the Oxford almanack for
. . . 1755. [By B. Buckler.] [T.] Lond., (1755), 8°. 30 pp.
G.A. Oxon 8° 60 (9)

742. HUDDESFORD, G., A proper reply to . . . A defence of the rector
and fellows of Exeter college, &c. [T.] Oxf., 1755, 4°. 17 pp.
Gough Oxf. 106 (7)

743. The ragged uproar: or, The Oxford roratory: a new dramatic
satire. [T.] Lond., [1755], 4°. 32 pp.   G.A. Oxon 4° 31 (3)

744. The rich supporters of the poor new interest, or, Tag, rag, and
bob-tail, a new ballad. [T.] n. pl., [1753], s. sh.
G.A. fol. A 248 (27)

745. The rump-worthies: or, The new-interest supporters in their true
colours, by an honest freeholder. [T] n. pl., [1753], s. sh.
G.A. fol. A 248 (32)

746. A second address to the freeholders of the county of Oxford, in
vindication of a former address against the writer of A letter to the
printer, &c. [W.] Lond., 1753, 8°. 32 pp.   G.A. Oxon 8° 218 (2)

747. SMITH, GYLES, pseud., Serious reflections on the dangerous tendency of the common practice of card-playing; especially of the
game of all-fours, as it hath been publickly play'd at Oxford, in 1754.
By Gyles Smith [i.e. W. Hawkins or W. King?]. [T.] Lond., (1754),
8°. 24 pp.   Gough Oxf. 39 (13)

748. Some queries from a public spirited cobler of Hampton-Wick . . .
in which are considered some queries from a cobler of Woodstock,
and one recommended to the serious perusal of . . . the honest freeholders in the county of Oxford. [T.] n. pl., [1753], s. sh.
G.A. Oxon b. 112 (4)

749. A song in season. [T.] n. pl., [1753], s. sh.   G.A. fol. A 248 (13)

750. A song not out of season, by one of the new interest. [T.] n. pl., [1753], s. sh. G.A. fol. A 248 (20)

751. The spy: or, Pasquin at Oxford. Lond., 1755, 8°. 48 pp.
Vet. A 5 e. 177 (1)

752. A summary of the . . . affairs in . . . Parliament [incl. the Oxford-shire election]. (London mag., 1755, p. 336–39.) Hope adds. 410

753. The terrors of conscience: or, The she - - - ff in Newgate. [T.] Lond., 1754, 4°. 16 pp. Gough Oxf. 39 (13)

754. FREINSHEMIUS, J., Threnodia: or, An elegy on the . . . death of the m— of B—. [T.] Oxf., 1753, 4°. 16 pp. 2799 d. 157

755. To the gentlemen, clergy and freeholders of the county of Oxford. [Election manifesto by lord Parker and sir Edward Turner.] [W.] n. pl., 1753, s. sh. Gough Oxf. 39 (2)

756. True-blue: or, A letter to the gentlemen of the old interest in . . . Oxford, by an A—n. [W.] Lond., 1754, 12°. 38 pp.
G.A. Oxon 8° 62 (10)

757. A true blue song upon true blue paper. [T.] n. pl., [1753], s. sh.
G.A. fol. A 248 (11)

758. Votes of the House of Commons . . . 1754 (1755). [Oxfordshire election, passim.] Lond., 1754 (55), fol. 22772 d. 35
[The Bodleian has a MS. index, with the shelfmark 22772 d. 57.]

1798 and after

759. COKER, J., A letter addressed to the freeholders and inhabitants of the county of Oxford, occasioned by A letter addressed to them by sir C. C. Dormer. Oxf., 1798, 8°. 20 pp.
G.A. Oxon 8° 611 (33)

760. TIT FOR TAT, *pseud.*, An account of a subscription entered into in order to defray the election expenses of l-rd S-nd-rl-nd [G. S. Churchill, afterw. 6th duke of Marlborough]. [A satire, signed Tit for Tat.] Oxf., [1815], s. sh. fol. Θ 673 (3)

761. TAUNTON, R. C., To John Coker, esq. [A letter in reply to his observations in Jackson's Oxford Journal upon sir W. Taunton's 'Refutation of the charges brought against him', in connection with the Oxfordshire parliamentary election of 1815. Signed Tenax, i.e. R. C. Taunton?] Oxf., [1815], s. sh. fol. Θ 673 (1)

762. [Oxfordshire election bills, &c., 1815–70.] G.A. Oxon b. 15, 95

763. To Timothy Homespun [a letter signed Ezakiel Homespun, concerning the candidature of lord Norreys in the county election]. Oxf., (1830), s. sh. G.A. Oxon c. 317 (26)

764. [Election bills, &c. 1830.]   G.A. Oxon b. 114

765. [Election papers, &c. 1830–32.]   G.A. Oxon b. 38 (2)

766. [Election bills, &c. chiefly relating to the county election of 1831.]
                                                                        G.A. Oxon a. 118

767. Electoral returns. Summary of electoral returns relating to counties . . . 1865–66. (Oxfordshire, p. 46.)
                                                                Pp. Eng. 1866, vol. 57

768–773.

774. County of Oxford, Mid division, Registration of voters. The corrupt and illegal practices list . . . List of persons . . . named as having been guilty of any bribery . . . at an election in 1880. n. pl., (1881), s. sh.   G.A. Oxon c. 107 (12)

775. [Oxfordshire political scrapbook, 1892–1910.]
                                                                G.A. Oxon b. 38 (3)

776.

> See also Banbury elections, 1620, &c.
> See also Woodstock elections, 4181, &c.

Public Officers

777. DAVENPORT, J. M., Lords lieutenant and high sheriffs of Oxfordshire 1086–1868. [By J. M. Davenport]. n. pl., [1868], 8°. 80 pp.
                                                                G.A. Oxon 8° 112

778. DAVENPORT, J. M., Oxfordshire. Lords lieutenant, high sheriffs, and members of Parliament, revised by T. M. Davenport. Oxf., 1888, 8°. 156 pp.   G.A. Oxon 8° 440

Statistics

779. Abstract of the answers and returns made pursuant to . . . An act for taking an account of the population of Great Britain. 1801.
Enumeration.   Pp. Eng. 1801, vol. 02
— Parish registers abstract.   Pp. Eng. 1801, vol. 03

780. Abstract of the answers and returns made pursuant to . . . An Act for taking an account of the population of Great Britain. 1811.
Enumeration.   Pp. Eng. 1812, vol. 11
— Parish registers abstract.   Pp. Eng. 1812, vol. 11

781. Abstract of the answers and returns made pursuant to . . . An act for taking an account of the population of Great Britain. 1821. Parish registers abstract.   Pp. Eng. 1822, vol. 11
— Enumeration.   Pp. Eng. 1822, vol. 15

782. Abstract of the answers and returns made pursuant to . . . An act for taking an account of the population of Gt. Britain. 1831.
— Comparative account of the population . . . in . . . 1801, 1811, 1821 and 1831. Pp. Eng. 1831, vol. 18
— Enumeration. Pp. Eng. 1833, vol. 36
— Parish registers abstract. Pp. Eng. 1833, vol. 38

783. First (–) annual report of the Registrar General of births, deaths and marriages (publ. in Repts. from Commissioners). 1839–.
Pp. Eng. 1839, vol. 16 (&c.)
— Quarterly return of the marriages, births and deaths (infectious diseases, weather, survey of sickness, population estimates) registered. 1849–. B.M.
[The Bodleian set commences No. 9, 1851–. Per. 24761 d. 83.]
— Weekly return of births and deaths (marriages) registered in county boroughs . . . and of . . . infectious diseases (weather). 1922–. [Previously confined to large towns.] Per. 24761 d. 84

784. Abstract of the answers and returns made pursuant to . . . An act for taking an account of the population of Great Britain. 1841.
Enumeration. Pp. Eng. 1843, vol. 22
— Age abstract. Pp. Eng. 1843, vol. 23
— Occupational abstract. Pp. Eng. 1844, vol. 27

785. Census, 1851. Population tables. Ages, civil condition, occupations and birth-place of the people. Vol. 1.
Pp. Eng. 1852/3, vol. 58, pt. 1.
— Population tables. i. Number of the inhabitants, in the years 1801, 1811, 1821, 1831, 1841, 1851. Vol. 1. South Midland division.
Pp. Eng. 1852/3, vol. 85
— Religious worship. Report and tables. Table C and detailed tables. Pp. Eng. 1852/3, vol. 89
— Education. Report and tables. Pp. Eng. 1852/3, vol. 90

786. A return of the following information in respect of each parish . . . not within the limits of any city or parliamentary borough, for the year ended at Lady-day 1856, viz.:— 1. Name; 2. Population; 3. Gross estimated rental of the property assessed to the Poor rate; 4. Rateable value [&c.]. (Oxfordshire, p. 129–33.)
Pp. Eng. 1857/8, vol. 50

787. Census of England and Wales. 1861. Population tables. Numbers and distribution of the people. Vol. 1. Pp. Eng. 1862, vol. 50
— Tables of the ages, civil conditions, occupations and birth-places of the people. Division 3. Pp. Eng. 1863, vol. 53, pt. 1

See 647 [Statement shewing population, &c. 1863].

788. Census of England and Wales. 1871. Population tables. Area, houses and inhabitants. Vol. 1. Pp. Eng. 1872, vol. 66, pt. 1

— Population tables. Area, houses and inhabitants. Vol. 2. Registration or union counties. Pp. Eng. 1872, vol. 66, pt. 2
— Population abstracts. Ages, civil conditions, occupations and birth-places of the people. Pp. Eng. 1873, vol. 71, pt. 1

788A. Return . . . of every owner of one acre and upwards, with the estimated acreage and annual gross estimated rental of land, &c. of individual owners, and of the number of owners of less than one acre, &c. . . . with the estimated extent of commons and waste lands. (Oxfordshire, vol. 2, 23 pp.) Pp. Eng. 1874, vol. 72

789. Census of England and Wales. 1881. Vol. 1. Area, houses and population. Counties. Pp. Eng. 1883, vol. 78
— Vol. 2. Area, houses and population. Registration counties.
Pp. Eng. 1883, vol. 79
— Vol. 3. Ages, conditions as to marriage, occupations and birth-places of the people. Pp. Eng. 1883, vol. 80

790. Census of England and Wales. 1891. Vol. 1. Area, houses and population. Administrative and ancient counties.
Pp. Eng. 1893/4, vol. 104
— Vol. 2. Registration areas and sanitary districts.
Pp. Eng. 1893/4, vol. 105
— Vol. 3. Ages, condition as to marriage, occupations, birth-places and infirmities. Pp. Eng. 1893/4, vol. 106

791. Census of England and Wales. 1901. County of Oxford. Area, houses and population, also population classified by ages, condition as to marriage, occupations, birthplaces and infirmities. Lond., 1903, fol. 58 pp. Pp. Eng. 1902, vol. 120

792. Census of England and Wales. 1911.
— Vol. 1. Area, families or separate occupiers, and population. Administrative areas. Counties, urban and rural districts, &c.
Pp. Eng. 1912/13, vol. 111
— Vol. 2. Area, families [&c.] Registration areas.
Pp. Eng. 1912/13, vol. 111
— Vol. 3. Area, families [&c.] Parliamentary areas.
Pp. Eng. 1912/13, vol. 112
— Vol. 4. Families or separate occupiers, and population. Ecclesiastical areas. Pp. Eng. 1912/13, vol. 112
— Vol. 5. Index to the population tables.
Pp. Eng. 1912/13, vol. 112
— Vol. 6. Buildings of various kinds. Pp. Eng. 1912/13, vol. 113
— Vol. 7. Ages and condition as to marriage in administrative counties, urban and rural district and registration counties and districts. Pp. Eng. 1912/13, vol. 113
— Vol. 8. Tenements in administrative counties and urban and rural districts. Pp. Eng. 1913, vol. 77

— Vol. 9. Birthplaces of persons enumerated in administrative counties, county boroughs &c. Pp. Eng. 1913, vol. 78
— Vol. 10. Occupations and industries. Pt. 1, 2.
Pp. Eng. 1913, vol. 78, 79
— Vol. 11. Infirmities. Pp. Eng. 1913, vol. 79

793. The Registrar-General's statistical review of England and Wales. (Oxfordshire, *passim.*) Lond., 1921–, 8°. Per. 24761 d. 119

794. Census of England & Wales, 1921. County of Oxford. Lond., 1924, fol. 46 pp. 24761 c. 63

795. Census of England and Wales. 1931. County of Oxford. 2 pt. Lond., 1933, fol. 31+17 pp. 24761 c. 84

796. National registration of England and Wales 1939. Population statistics. (Oxfordshire, p. 79, 80.) [Reprod. from typewriting.] (Lond.), [1949], fol. 24761 c. 95

797. Local government boundary commission. Administrative county of Oxford. Review of county districts, June 1948. General statistics (Supplementary statistics) and other information relating to the county and county districts. Oxf., (1948), fol.
G.A. Oxon c. 305, 306
See also 888, &c. [Poor rate returns].

MILITARY

798. Useful instructions for the First Regiment of Oxfordshire Yeomanry cavalry. Witney, 1831, 24°. 21 pp. 23187 g. 110

799. The standing orders of the 52nd Light Infantry. Cork, 1853, 8°. 48 pp. 23181 f. 46

800. Army (Drying rooms) . . . Copy of report made by colonel Gordon upon mr. Huthname's drying room at Chipping Norton, inspected . . . 25 October 1856. Pp. Eng. 1861, vol. 36

801. Oxford loyal volunteer rifle club. [Report of a meeting, 10 Nov. 1859, initiating the corps.] G.A. Oxon b. 131 (3)

802. Oxfordshire (volunteer) rifle corps. Minutes of meeting of 19th Nov., 1859. G.A. Oxon b. 131 (4)
— Memoranda, Dec., 1859. G.A. Oxon b. 131 (5)

803. Oxfordshire volunteer rifle corps. [Draft] rules. (Oxf., 1859), fol. 3 pp. G.A. Oxon b. 131 (6)

804. Second battalion of the Oxfordshire rifle volunteers. Rules. 5 Feb., 1860. (Oxf., 1860), fol. 4 pp. G.A. Oxon b. 131 (7)
— June, 1860. G.A. Oxon b. 131 (12)
— 1 Oct., 1860. G.A. Oxon b. 131 (18)
— 20 Mar., 1868. 8°. 8 pp. G.A. Oxon b. 131 (36)

805. Second battalion, Oxfordshire rifle volunteer corps. [List of donations and subscriptions. 1860.]   G.A. Oxon b. 131 (22)

806. Second Oxon rifle volunteer corps. Accounts for 1860.
     G.A. Oxon b. 131 (20)
— 1862.   G.A. Oxon b. 131 (31)
— 1868.   G.A. Oxon b. 131 (40)
— 1870.   G.A. Oxon b. 131 (41)

807. Fourth Oxfordshire rifle volunteer corps. Rules. (Henley-on-Thames, 1860), fol. 2 pp.   G.A. Oxon b. 131 (10)

808. Deddington, or Sixth corps of the Oxfordshire rifle volunteers. Rules and regulations. (Deddington, 1860), fol. 4 pp.
     G.A. Oxon b. 131 (21)

809. MOORSOM, W. S., ed., Historical record of the Fifty second regiment (Oxfordshire Light Infantry) from 1755–1858. Lond., 1860, 4°. 437 pp.   231 d. 7

810. Oxfordshire militia, sketch of the history of the regiment. n. pl., 1869, 8°. 36 pp.   G.A. Oxon 8° 139

811. Oxfordshire and Buckinghamshire Light Infantry. The 43rd & 52nd Light Infantry chronicle. 1892–. Lond., 1892–, 8°.
     23168 e. 23

812. FERRYMAN, A. F. MOCKLER-, The Oxfordshire Light Infantry calendar. 1894. Lond., 1894, 8°. 32 pp.   Cal. 23168 e. 31

813. The Oxfordshire Light Infantry. [A short history.] Lond., [c. 1895], 8°. 8 pp.   G.A. Oxon c. 317 (2)

814. WILLAN, F., History of the Oxfordshire regiment of militia, 1778–1900, including the diary of Thomas Mosley Crowder, 1852–1885. Oxf., 1900, 4°. 185 pp.   23172 d. 15

815. FERRYMAN, A. F. MOCKLER-, ed., The Oxfordshire Light Infantry in South Africa. Lond., 1901, 8°. 314 pp.   24691 e. 121

816. Oxfordshire Light Infantry, 2nd volunteer battalion. Regimental orders. 15 July 1893; 12 July 1900; 11 July 1901.
     G.A. Oxon b. 131

817. NEWBOLT, SIR H. J., The story of the Oxfordshire and Buckinghamshire Light Infantry. Lond., &c., [1915], 8°. 224 pp.
     23168 d. 41

818. FERRYMAN, A. F. MOCKLER-, Regimental war tales, 1741–1914, told for the soldiers of the Oxfordshire and Buckinghamshire Light Infantry. Oxf., 1915, 8°. 253 pp.   23168 f. 4
— [Another ed.] With a chapter on the Great War by R. B. Crosse. Oxf., 1942, 8°. 240 pp.   O.P.L.

819. TON, *pseud.*, Oxfordshire Light Infantry. (Field, Mar.–May 1916, p. 490, 91, 547, 48, 556, 57, 592, 660, 664, 65, 714, 744, 45.)
N. 3993 b. 5

820. Oxfordshire volunteer regiment . . . 2nd Volunteer battalion, the Oxfordshire & Buckinghamshire Light Infantry. [Muster roll.] n. pl., [*c.* 1919], s. sh. MS. Top. Oxon d. 257 (f. 169)

821. PICKFORD, P., War record of the 1/4th Battalion Oxfordshire & Buckinghamshire Light Infantry. (Banbury), 1919, 8°. 127 pp.
22281 f. 79

822. ROSE, G. K., The story of the 2/4th Oxfordshire and Buckinghamshire Light Infantry. Oxford, 1920, 8°. 226 pp. 22281 e. 1122

823. Oxfordshire and Buckinghamshire Light Infantry regimental assoc. Rules. Oxf., [*c.* 1920], 8°. 6 pp. 23168 e. 40 (4)

824. WHEELER, C., *ed.*, Memorial record of the Seventh (service) battalion the Oxfordshire and Buckinghamshire Light Infantry. Oxf., 1921, 8°. 223 pp. O.P.L.

825. Oxfordshire and Buckinghamshire Light Infantry. Journal. Vol. 1, no. 1–. (Bristol), 1925–, 8°. Per. 23168 d. 75

826. CROSSE, R. B., A short history of the Oxfordshire and Buckinghamshire Light Infantry, 1741–1922, for the young soldiers of the regiment. Aldershot, 1925, 8°. 47 pp. 23168 e. 86

827. KEITH-FALCONER, A., The Oxfordshire Hussars in the Great War, 1914–1918. 1st ed. Lond., 1927, 8°. 391 pp. 22281 e. 1572

828. GRAHAM, C., Record of 4th Oxfordshire (Bullingdon) battalion Home Guard, 1940–1944. (Oxf.), [1945?], 8°. 101 pp.
231714 d. 33

829. The Oxfordshire & Buckinghamshire Light Infantry chronicle, the records of the 43rd, 52nd, 4th, 5th & 1st Buckinghamshire battalions in the Second German war, ed. by J. E. H. Neville. Vol. 1–. Aldershot, 1949–, 8°. 22283 e. 457

See 1530 [Appeal for clothing for military, Banbury. 1794].
See 1533 [Cavalry regulations, Banbury and Bloxham. 1803].
See 2231, &c. [Oxford military college, Cowley].

SOCIAL HISTORY

GENERAL

830. An act to enable William Batson esq; to sell lands in . . . Oxon and to purchase . . . an estate in . . . Suffolk. (1 Will. & Mary, c. 8, Private.) 1689.

831. An act to confirm articles of partition made between the earl and countess of Wemyss, of the one part, and Anne Robinson . . . of the other part, of their estates in the counties of Oxon, Northampton, and Kent, and for vesting their respective moieties in trustees, to be sold. (8 Anne, c. 16, Private.) [Estates are specified in an agreement of 17 June 1709 but are not listed here. Nuneham Courtenay is mentioned.] Lond., 1710, fol. 7 pp.   B.M.

832. An act to enable Arthur lord viscount Irwyn, to raise money by mortgage or sale of certain estates in the cowties [sic] of York, Lincoln, Oxon. . . . (11 G. I, c. 17, Private.) n. pl., [1725], fol. 7 pp.
L. Eng. C 13 c. 1 (1714/27. 66)

833. An act for vesting in trustees divers lands in the several counties of Berks [&c.] Oxford . . . the estate of David, earl of Buchan. . . . (1 G. II, c. 15, Private.) n. pl., 1727, fol. 8 pp.   B.M

834. An act for vesting the undivided fourth part of Edward Webb and Elizabeth Frances Webb . . . in estates in the counties of Buckingham, Middlesex and Oxford, in trust to be sold. . . . (53 G. III, c. 19, Private.) Lond., 1813, fol.

835. Oxfordshire anecdotes, with historical and topographical notes. [No. 1, 2.] n. pl., [c. 1826], 8°. 16 pp.   G.A. Oxon 8° 934

836. Report of the collection and administration of the Hail storm relief fund for the county of Oxford, 1844. (Chipping-Norton, 1844), 8°. 39 pp.   G.A. Oxon 8° 636 (4)

837. FERGUSON, W., The impending dangers of our country; or, Hidden things brought to light. Lond., 1848, 8°. 124 pp.   48. 902

838. Oxford and county society for the prevention of cruelty to children. Report. April 1–Dec. 31, 1898. Oxf., [1899], 8°. 12 pp.   O.P.L.

839. BUCKELL, R. AND SON, The Oxford and district register of properties to be let and sold. Oct. 1902–Apr. 1912.   Per. 247553 d. 5

840. HAMLET AND DULAKE, The Oxford house, property and estate register. Dec. 1902–Feb. 1903. [Includes the county.]
Per. 247553 d. 4

841. BALLARD, A., The assize of bread in Oxfordshire in the nineteenth century. (Rept., Oxf. archaeol. soc., 1906, p. 22–25.) R. Top. 330

842. Social and economic history. (Victoria county history, 1907, vol. 2, p. 165–224.) R. 9. 41 s

843. E. J. Brooks & sons register of furnished and unfurnished residences, and of . . . estates [&c.] to let or for sale. [Including city and county.] 1909, 1912. G.A. Oxon c. 256 (4, 5)

844. A rural community council in being. An account of some work in Oxfordshire villages. Banbury, 1929, 8°. 36 pp. O.P.L.

845. THOMPSON, F., An Oxfordshire hamlet in the 'eighties. (National review, 1937, Aug., p. 222–28.) Per. 22775 d. 14

846. Oxfordshire federation of women's institutes. Old times exhibition, 27–30 April, 1937. (Oxf.), 1937, 8°. 16 pp. 177 d. 92 (8)

847. Oxfordshire rural community council. Village life in Oxfordshire, a report. Oxf., (1937), 8°. 12 pp. O.C.R.L.

848. BUXTON, L. H. D., TREVOR, J. C., and BLACKWOOD, B., Measurements of Oxfordshire villagers. (Journ., Roy. anthrop. inst., vol. 69, 1939, p. 1–10.) Soc. 247115 d. 98

849. HIGGINS, C., Social life in Georgian days in Berkshire and Oxfordshire. (Country Life, 1940, vol. 87, p. 92–97.) Per. 384 b. 6

850. Oxford univ., agric. econ. research inst. Country planning, a study of local problems [in N. Oxfordshire]. Lond., 1944, 8°. 288 pp. 2479115 e. 22

851. THOMPSON, F., Lark Rise to Candleford, a trilogy. [Orig. publ. as Lark Rise; Candleford Green; Over to Candleford. Reminiscences of North Oxfordshire village life in the late 19th century.] Lond., &c., 1945, 8°. 556 pp. 247126 e. 229

852. GREEN, DAVID, Country neighbours. 1st ed. [Reminiscences, mainly about the Evenlode country.] Lond., 1948, 8°. 203 pp. G.A. Oxon 8° 1215

853. THOMPSON, F., Still glides the stream. [A description of life in a North Oxfordshire village at the end of the 19th century.] Lond., &c., 1948, 8°. 233 pp. 247126 e. 238

854. ALLEN, A. B., Rural education. 2 vols. [Vol. 1 consisting mainly of general material about village customs &c.] Lond., (1950), 8°. 2621 e. 397

See 2830 [Hearth-blowers, Henley. 1947].

DIALECT

855. PARKER, A., A glossary of words used in Oxfordshire. (Engl. dialect soc., 1876, ser. C. 5, p. 110–21.)
— Suppl. (1881, ser. C. 24, p. 65–102.) Soc. 30205 e. 2
— [The Bodleian has an interleaved copy with MS. additions.]
G.A. Oxon 8° 960
See 2038 [Charlton-on-Otmoor, words and sayings. 1911].

FOLK-LORE

856. Oxfordshire mummers. (Folk-lore, 1894, vol. 5, p. 88, 89.)
Per. 93 d. 36

857. MANNING, P., Some Oxfordshire seasonal festivals: with notes on morris-dancing in Oxfordshire. (Folk-lore, 1897, vol. 8, p. 307–24.)
G.A. Oxon 4° 399 b (14)

858. BUSBY, G., Oxfordshire village rhymes. Lond., 1899, 12°. 12 pp.
G.A. Oxon 8° 963 (3)

859. MANNING, P., Stray notes on Oxfordshire folklore. (Folk-lore, 1902, vol. 13, p. 288–95; 1903, vol. 14, p. 65–74, 167–77, 410–14.)
Per. 93 d. 36

860. HEWITT, W. H., Oxfordshire folklore. (Folk-lore, 1903, vol. 14, p. 183–85.)
Per. 93 d. 36

861. PRIOR, C. E., Dedications of churches, with some notes as to village feasts and old customs. (Rept., Oxf. archaeol. soc., 1903, p. 20–42; 1904, p. 23–53; 1905, p. 11–25; 1906, p. 14–22.)
R. Top. 330

862. SHARP, C. J., and MACILWAINE, H. C., The morris book, with a description of dances. 5 pt. [Many references are made to dances and dancers in Oxfordshire.] Lond., 1907–13, 8°. 38434 e. 12
— 2nd ed. 3 pt. 1912–24. 38434 e. 20

863. SHARP, C. J., Folk-dance airs collected and arranged for the pianoforte. [The dance-airs in this collection were noted down in Oxfordshire, and 4 other counties.] Lond., 1909, fol.
[Mus.] 119 c. S. 24

864. FIELD, J. E., The myth of the pent cuckoo. (Oxfordshire, passim.) Lond., 1913, 8°. 215 pp. 930 d. 165

865. PARKER, A., Oxfordshire village folklore, 1840–1900. (Folk-lore, 1913, vol. 24, p. 74–91.)
Per. 93 d. 36

866. EMSLIE, J. P., Scraps of folklore collected by J. P. Emslie. (Folk-lore, 1915, vol. 26, p. 158–60.)
Per. 93 d. 36

867. PARKER, A., Oxfordshire village folklore, II. (Folk-lore, 1923, vol. 34, p. 322–33.) Per. 93 d. 36

868. HEUMAN, G., CORBETT, E., and ANTROBUS, A. A., Scraps of English folklore, xvii. (Folk-lore, 1929, vol. 40, p. 77–83.) Per. 93 d. 36

869. BUXTON, L. H. D., and BLACKWOOD, B., An introduction to Oxfordshire folklore. (Folk-lore, 1934, vol. 45, p. 29–46.) Per. 93 d. 36

870. Oxfordshire and district folklore society. Annual record. No. 1–. Oxf., 1949–, 8°. Per. 930 e. 807

See 1811 [Bladon feast. 1883].
See 2474 [Maypole at Ewelme. 1702].
See 2968 [Mayday at Iffley. 1934].
See 3155, 56 [Little Tew ghost. 1854, 1933].
See 3299 [North Leigh, folklore. 1929].

SOCIAL SERVICES

General

871. Oxford city, Barnett house. A survey of the social services in the Oxford district [ed. by A. F. C. Bourdillon]. [Vol.] 1, 2, . Lond., 1938, 1940, , 8°. 24725 e. 845

See 1131 [Oxford diocesan social service committee. 1908].

Charities

872. Commissioners for charitable uses. [Notice from the Charity commissioners, that the Oxfordshire members will meet at the Bear inn, Oct. 3, to redress the misemployment of charities.] [Madan 2774.] [Oxf., 1667], s. sh. Wood 423 (43)

873. Rules and orders for the management and disposal of a charitable contribution, proposed to be raised for the relief of the widows and orphans of clergymen within the diocese, or county of Oxford, agreed on at a meeting . . . Jun. 27, 1770. n. pl., (1770), fol. 4 pp. G.A. Oxon b. 126 (1)

874. The state of the charity for the relief of the widows and orphans of clergymen, within the diocese and county of Oxford. 1803, 1817, 1831, 32, 1838, 39, 1841, 1870, 71, 1878, 79, 1881–88, 1891–97, 1899–1911, 1919. (Oxf., 1803–1919), fol. G.A. Oxon b. 126

875. Abstract of the returns of charitable donations for the benefit of poor persons, made by the ministers . . . of the several parishes and townships in England . . . 1786–1788. (Repts. from comm. of the House of commons, Suppl. vol. 2. Oxfordshire, p. 965–1000.) Lond., 1816, fol. Pp. Eng. 1786, &c., vol. 2

876. Report of the Commissioners appointed . . . to inquire concerning charities . . . for the education of the poor. 1819. (Oxfordshire, p. 198–206, 326–41.)   Pp. Eng. 1819, vol. 10 *a*
— 4th rept. 1820, p. 199–225.   Pp. Eng 1820, vol. 5
— 6th rept. 1821, p. 379–462.   Pp. Eng. 1822, vol. 9
— 8th rept. 1823, p. 437–560.   Pp. Eng. 1823, vol. 8
— 10th rept. 1824, p. 337–416.   Pp. Eng. 1824, vol. 13
— 12th rept. 1825, p. 159–358.   Pp. Eng. 1825, vol. 10
— 27th rept. 1834, p. 711, 712.   Pp. Eng. 1834, vol. 21
— 29th rept. 1835, p. 892.   Pp. Eng. 1835, vol. 21
— 32nd rept. 1837, p. 654–701.   Pp. Eng. 1837/8, vol. 26

877. Reports of the Commissioners appointed . . . to inquire concerning charities and education of the poor. 1815 to 1839. [A made-up volume for Oxfordshire.]   R. 6. fol. 8 *a*

878. Reports from Commissioners, &c. Charitable donations [&c.]. (Oxfordshire, p. 100–02.)   Pp. Eng. 1820, vol. 6

879. Reports of the Commissioners for inquiring concerning charities in the hundreds of Banbury & Bloxham, also some places in the hundreds of Wootton, Ploughley, Chadlington & Bullington . . . from the twelfth and thirteenth reports. 2 vols. Banbury, 1826, 1844, 4°. 188+229 pp.   G.A. Oxon 8° 170, 171

880. Charities. A list of the counties reported upon and not reported upon by the Commissioners of inquiry into charities, with the income of each charity. (Oxfordshire, p. 137–51.)
     Pp. Eng. 1828, vol. 21

881.

882. Digest of the reports made by Commissioners of inquiry into charities, so far as relates to the county of Oxford. Lond., 1841, fol. 59 pp.   Manning fol. 14

883. EDWARDS, H., A collection of old English customs, and curious bequests and charities. [Burford, Cropredy, Horley, Swerford, Woodstock.] Lond., 1842, 8°.   42. 355

884. Public charities. i. Analytical digest of the reports made by the Commissioners of inquiry into charities. (Oxfordshire, p. 146–85.)
     Pp. Eng. 1843, vol. 16

885. Public charities . . . iii. Return of charities to be distributed to the poor. (Oxfordshire, p. 199–204.)   Pp. Eng. 1843, vol. 18

886. Endowed charities . . . Copies 'of the general digest of endowed charities for the counties and cities mentioned in the Fourteenth report of the charity commissioners' . . . County of Oxford. n. pl., 1871, fol. 77 pp.   Pp. Eng. 1871, vol. 55

887. Oxfordshire mendicity society. An account of its formation and objects [&c.]. n. pl., 1879, 8°. 23 pp.　　　　G.A. Oxon 8° 1046 (1)

See 1157 [Answers to ecclesiastical visitation questionnaires, 1738 &c.].
See 1414 [Town lands charity, Adderbury. 1872].
See 1496 [St. Michael's orphanage, Balscote. 1884].
See 1498 [Bampton and Weald charities. 1801].
See 1685A [Banbury Charitable society for visiting and relieving the sick and distressed poor. 1841].
See 1687 [Banbury Old charitable society. 1890].
See 1688 [Banbury Refuge for the afflicted. 1845].
See 1713A [Sir G. Croke's charity, Beckley. 1880].
See 1770 [Gray house, Bicester. 1934].
See 1953, 54 [Burford charities. 1861].
See 2003 [Chadlington. Alice Hemming charity. 1905].
See 2466 [Enstone. Church estate and Thomas Davis' charity. 1887].
See 2502, &c. [Ewelme almshouse. 1732 &c.].
See 2640 [Goring. Allnutt's charity. 1877].
See 2646 [Goring. Whistler and Simmons charities. 1937].
See 2772 [Headington charity organisation society. 1908].
See 2820 [Henley corporation charities. 1858].
See 3480, 3480A [Sandford St. Martin charities. 1885].
See 3702 [Steeple Aston charities. 1873].
See 3997 [Eliza Carey Biscoe Home of rest, Wheatley. 1902].
See 4285 [Yarnton. Alderman Fletcher's charities. 1843].

Poor Law

888. Report from the committee appointed to inspect and consider the returns made by the overseers of the poor . . . together with abstracts of the said returns. 1777. (Oxfordshire, p. 436–39.)
　　　　　　　　　　　　　　　　　　Pp. Eng. 1715, &c., vol. 9
— 1787, p. 654–57.　　　　　　　　Pp. Eng. 1715, &c., vol. 9

889. Abstract of the returns made by the overseers of the poor. (Oxfordshire, p. 140–43.) n. pl. 1777, fol.　　　　Gough Gen. top. 222

890. Abstract of the answers and returns made pursuant to . . . An act for procuring returns relative to the expense and maintenance of the poor in England, 1803. (Repts. from comm. of the House of commons, suppl. vol. 3. Oxfordshire, p. 397–408.)
　　　　　　　　　　　　　　　　　　Pp. Eng. 1804, vol. 1

891. Abridgement of the abstract of the answers and returns made pursuant to . . . An act for procuring returns relative to the expense and maintenance of the poor. (Oxfordshire, p. 351–62.)
　　　　　　　　　　　　　　　　　　Pp. Eng. 1818, vol. 19

892. Poor rate returns for 1830, 1831, 1832, 1833 and 1834. (Oxfordshire, p. 153–57.)　　　　　　　　Pp. Eng. 1835, vol. 47

816. Report from his majesty's Commissioners for inquiring into the administration and practical operation of the poor laws. Appendix A. Pt. 1 (Oxfordshire, p. 1–4.)　　　　Pp. Eng. 1834, vol. 28

894. Report from his majesty's Commissioners for inquiring into the administration and practical operation of the poor laws. Appendix B. 1. Answers to rural queries. 5 pt. (Oxfordshire, *passim.*)
Pp. Eng. 1834, vol. 30–34.
— Appendix B. 2. Answers to town queries. 5 pt. (Oxfordshire, *passim.*)
Pp. Eng. 1834, vol. 35, 36

895. Report from his majesty's Commissioners for inquiring into the administration and practical operation of the poor laws. Appendix D. Labour rate. (Oxfordshire, p. 84–92.)
Pp. Eng. 1834, vol. 38

896. Labour rate. Copy of any documents which may be in the possession of the Poor law commissioners with regard to the Labour rate bill. (Oxfordshire, p. 44–48.)
Pp. Eng. 1833, vol. 32

897. Poor law commissioners. 1st annual report. Appendix D. List of unions formed and parishes included therein [&c.]. (Oxfordshire, p. 237–39).
Pp. Eng. 1835, vol. 25
— 2nd annual report. (Oxfordshire, p. 544.)
Pp. Eng. 1836, vol. 29

898. Account of the money levied and expended for the maintenance and relief of the poor . . . 1835 and 1836. (2nd annual report of the Poor law commissioners, Appendix E. Oxfordshire, p. 290–99.)
Pp. Eng. 1836, vol. 29, pt. 2
— 1837. (3rd annual report. Appendix D, p. 147–52.)
Pp. Eng. 1837, vol. 31
— 1838. (4th annual report. Appendix D, *passim.*)
Pp. Eng. 1840, vol. 18

899. A return of all debts, liabilities and engagements claimed against the Poor rates of any parish [&c.]. (Oxfordshire, p. 66–69.)
Pp. Eng. 1842, vol. 35

900. A return showing the amount of property assessed to the relief of the poor . . . for the year ending 25th March, 1850. (Oxfordshire, p. 74–76.)
Pp. Eng. 1852, vol. 45

901. Return of all parishes . . . into which . . . any public railway passes; showing . . . the gross amount of Poor's rate collected in each parish in 1851, 1852, and the amount contributed by the railway property to the Poor's rate of each parish. (Oxfordshire, p. 80, 81.)
Pp. Eng. 1852/3, vol. 97

902. Poor rate assessments, &c. Returns from the several parishes [&c.] of the number of separate assessments in the rate for the relief of the poor, specifying the amount of such rate, number of assessments . . . with the number of persons [and] premises assessed: and of the number of municipal electors on the burgess list. (Oxfordshire, p. 206–12.)
Pp. Eng. 1852, vol. 45

903. Return of the names of the different unions . . . into which, for the purposes of the Poor law, the counties are divided; specifying the parishes included in each union, together with the population and extent, the sums of money raised for the relief of the poor in each parish, for the year ending 25th March, 1852. (Oxfordshire, *passim.*)
Pp. Eng. 1854, vol. 55

904. Returns of the number, in the last week of September 1852 and in the last week of January 1853, in each workhouse in England and Wales, of the paupers of each religious denomination; specifying . . . the religious accommodation . . . and the provision made for the religious instruction of the children within the workhouse; and, of the number of children placed or farmed out in any establishment. (Oxfordshire, p. 62–64.)
Pp. Eng. 1854/5, vol. 55

905. Poor law medical relief . . . A return of the medical officers under the Poor law acts . . . for 1853, 1854 and 1855. (Oxfordshire, p. 45, 46.)
Pp. Eng. 1856, vol. 49

906. A return of the following information in respect of each parish . . . not within the limits of any city or parliamentary borough for the year ended at Lady-day 1856, viz.:—1. Name; 2. Population; 3. Gross estimated rental of the property assessed to the Poor rate; 4. Rateable value [&c.]. (Oxfordshire, p. 129–33.)
Pp. Eng. 1857/8, vol. 50

907. Poor relief. A return of the several particulars (medical poor relief etc.) as respects the unions, parishes under boards of guardians, incorporations and parishes under local acts and Gilbert's act [&c.]. (Oxfordshire, p. 40–42.)
Pp. Eng. 1857/8, vol. 49A

908. Poor rate, &c. . . . A return as respects the year ended at Lady-day 1856 of . . . The gross estimated rental of property rated to the Poor rate in each parish [and other statistics]. (Oxfordshire, p. 153–58.)
Pp. Eng. 1861, vol. 54

909. Poor rate exemption . . . A return 'of all houses and buildings and lands which are exempted . . . from the payment of Poor rate . . .'. (Oxfordshire, p. 109–11.)
Pp. Eng. 1861, vol. 54

910. Poor law unions . . . Return 'of the number of parishes in each poor law union and incorporation in England and Wales'. 'And with reference to single parishes not in union, as well as to unions . . . statement of the area, population and gross estimated rental of each . . . '. (Oxfordshire, p. 20.)
Pp. Eng. 1868/9, vol. 53

911. Poor law unions. Contested election of guardians. Returns showing the number of parishes in every union, the number of guardians for each parish . . . number of contests at the annual elections during the last three years [&c.]. (Oxfordshire, p. 70–72.)
Pp. Eng. 1876, vol. 73

912. OLDHAM, C. R., Oxfordshire poor laws. (Econ. hist. review, 1932–34, vol. 4, p. 470–74; 1934–35, vol. 5, p. 87–97.)   Per 232 d. 155

913. Oxfordshire county council. Public assistance year book. 1932–39/40, 1946. Oxf., 1932–46, 8°.   O.C.R.L.

> See 999 [Return of number of persons from each union workhouse committed to prison. 1875].
> See 1786, 87 [Bicester poor law union. 1854, 1877].
> See 1850 [Election of a guardian, Bodicote. 1840].
> See 4102 [Witney poor law union. 1891].
> See 4255 [Woodstock poor law union. 1841].

Education

> For the Reports of the Commissioners appointed to inquire concerning charities for the education of the poor, see *Charities, 872* &c.

914. A digest of parochial returns made to the select committee appointed to inquire into the education of the poor; session 18. (Oxfordshire, vol. 2, p. 717–34. Suppl., vol. 3, p. 1474.)
     Pp. Eng. 1819, vol. 9 B, C

915. Education enquiry. Abstract of the answers and returns. (Oxfordshire, vol. 2, p. 738–59.)   Pp. Eng. 1835, vol. 42

916. Oxford diocesan board of education. First(–Fortieth) annual report. Oxf., 1840–79, 8°. [Contd. in 1133.]   G.A. Oxon 8° 489

917. Public charities . . . ii. Digest of schools and charities for education. Grammar schools. (Oxfordshire, p. 89–91.) Schools not classical. (Oxfordshire, p. 216–23.) Charities . . . not attached to endowed schools. (Oxfordshire, p. 82–85.)   Pp. Eng. 1843, vol. 18

918. Minutes of the Committee of council on education, reports of her majesty's inspectors of schools. 1850–1, vol. 2. (Oxfordshire, p. 66, &c.)   Pp. Eng. 1851, vol. 44
— 1852–3, p. 93, &c.   Pp. Eng. 1852, vol. 39
— 1852–3, p. 93, &c.   Pp. Eng. 1852/3, vol. 80
— 1853–4, p. 71, &c.   Pp. Eng. 1854, vol. 52
— 1854, p. 398, &c.   Pp. Eng. 1854/5, vol. 42
— 1855, p. 240, &c.   Pp. Eng. 1856, vol. 47
— 1856–7, p. 149, &c.   Pp. Eng. 1856/7, vol. 33
— 1857–8, p. 157, &c.   Pp. Eng. 1857/8, vol. 45
— 1858–9, p. 35, &c.   Pp. Eng. 1859, sess. 1, vol. 21
— 1859–60, p. 26, &c.   Pp. Eng. 1860, vol. 54
— 1860–1, p. 26, &c.   Pp. Eng. 1861, vol. 49
— 1861–2, p. 25, &c.   Pp. Eng. 1862, vol. 2
— 1862–3, p. 12, &c.   Pp. Eng. 1863, vol. 47
— 1863–4, p. 186, &c.   Pp. Eng. 1864, vol. 45
— 1864–5, p. 14, &c.   Pp. Eng. 1865, vol. 42
— 1865–6, p. 570, &c.   Pp. Eng. 1866, vol. 27
— 1866–7, p. 16, &c.   Pp. Eng. 1867, vol. 22

— 1867–8, p. 693, &c.   Pp. Eng. 1867/8, vol. 25
— 1868–9, p. 20, &c.   Pp. Eng. 1868/9, vol. 20
— 1869–70, p. 140, &c.   Pp. Eng. 1870, vol. 22
— 1870–1, p. 22, &c.   Pp. Eng. 1871, vol. 22
— 1871–2, p. 31, &c.   Pp. Eng. 1872, vol. 22
— 1872–3, p. 474, &c.   Pp. Eng. 1873, vol. 24
— 1873–4, p. 394, &c.   Pp. Eng. 1874, vol. 18
— 1874–5, p. 110, &c.   Pp. Eng. 1875, vol. 24
— 1875–6, p. 611, &c.   Pp. Eng. 1876, vol. 23
— 1876–7, p. 849, &c.   Pp. Eng. 1877, vol. 29
— 1877–8, p. 471, &c.   Pp. Eng. 1878, vol. 28
— 1878–9, p. 660, &c.   Pp. Eng. 1878/9, vol. 23
— 1879–80, p. 674, &c.   Pp. Eng. 1880, vol. 22
— 1880–1, p. 661, &c.   Pp. Eng. 1880/1, vol. 32
— 1881–2, p. 720, &c.   Pp. Eng. 1882, vol. 23
— 1882–3, p. 402, &c.   Pp. Eng. 1883, vol. 25
— 1883–4, p. 52, &c.   Pp. Eng. 1884, vol. 24
— 1884–5, p. 52, &c.   Pp. Eng. 1884/5, vol. 23
— 1885–6, p. 52, &c.   Pp. Eng. 1886, vol. 24
— 1886–7, p. 58, &c.   Pp. Eng. 1887, vol. 28
— 1887–8, p. 58, &c.   Pp. Eng. 1888, vol. 38
— 1888–9, p. 58, &c.   Pp. Eng. 1889, vol. 29
— 1889–90, p. 58, &c.   Pp. Eng. 1890, vol. 28
— 1890–1, p. 58, &c.   Pp. Eng. 1890/1, vol. 27
— 1891–2, p. 690, &c.   Pp. Eng. 1892, vol. 28
— 1892–3, p. 779, &c.   Pp. Eng. 1893/4, vol. 26
— 1893–4, p. 654, &c.   Pp. Eng. 1894, vol. 29
— 1894–5, p. 968, &c.   Pp. Eng. 1895, vol. 27
— 1895–6, p. 59, &c.   Pp. Eng. 1896, vol. 26
— 1897–8, p. 201, &c.   Pp. Eng. 1898, vol. 22
— 1899–1900, vol. 3, p. 243, &c.   Pp. Eng. 1900, vol. 19
— 1901, p. 85, &c.   Pp. Eng. 1902, vol. 25

919. Diocesan association of schoolmasters. The report of the annual meeting. 1857, 58, 61, 62. Oxf., 1857–62, 8°.   G.A. Oxon 8° 496

920. Oxford diocesan board of education. Diocesan inspection of schools [afterw.] Oxford diocesan inspection. Report. 1859/60–1910. Oxf., 1860–1911, 8°.   G.A. Oxon 8° 490

921. Endowed grammar schools. Return. (Oxfordshire, p. 164–69.)   Pp. Eng. 1865, vol. 43

922. School enquiry commission. Report. 21 vols. (Oxfordshire, vol. 12).   Pp. Eng. 1867/8, vol. 28

923. Return . . . of the number of children in inspected schools in the year ending the 31st Aug. 1867, distinguishing how many of such children belong to families which are considered as poor. (Oxfordshire, p. 336–48.)   Pp. Eng. 1867/8, vol. 53

924. Education (Building grants) . . . Returns of the total number of the building grants applied for during . . . 1870 by managers of elementary schools [&c.]. (Oxfordshire, p. 318–28.)

Pp. Eng. 1871, vol. 55

925. School fees (England and Wales) . . . Return . . . of all public elementary schools under inspection . . . distinguishing . . . 1. Board schools . . . 2. Other schools . . . and showing . . . the ordinary rates of fee per week [&c.]. (Oxfordshire, p. 266–68.)

Pp. Eng. 1875, vol. 59

926. Oxford diocesan board of education. Report on expenses of village schools. Wallingford, 1878, 8°. 12 pp.   G.A. Oxon 8° 611 (5)

927. Oxford diocesan board of education. Report of committee on finance. n. pl., [1881?], 8°. 3 pp.   G.A. Oxon 4° 268

928. Return (List) of school districts in England and Wales with the standards fixed by the bye-laws of each district. (Oxfordshire, *passim*.)   Pp. Eng. 1881, vol. 72
— Revised to Feb. 1890.   Pp. Eng. 1890, vol. 56
— Revised to 1st Mar. 1895.   Pp. Eng. 1895, vol. 76

929. Education department. List of school boards and school attendance committees. 1st April 1882. (Oxfordshire, p. 56, 57.)

Pp. Eng. 1882, vol. 50

— 1883, p. 62, 63.   Pp. Eng. 1883, vol. 53
— 1884, p. 62, 63.   Pp. Eng. 1884, vol. 61
— 1885, p. 62, 63.   Pp. Eng. 1884/5, vol. 61
— 1886, p. 62, 63.   Pp. Eng. 1886, vol. 51
— 1887, p. 62, 63.   Pp. Eng. 1887, vol. 65
— 1888, p. 63, 64.   Pp. Eng. 1888, vol. 78
— 1889, p. 63, 64.   Pp. Eng. 1889, vol. 59
— 1890, p. 64, &c.   Pp. Eng. 1890, vol. 55
— 1891, p. 64, &c.   Pp. Eng. 1890/1, vol. 61
— 1893, p. 60, &c.   Pp. Eng. 1893/4, vol. 68
— 1894, p. 66, &c.   Pp. Eng. 1894, vol. 66
— 1895, p. 66, &c.   Pp. Eng. 1895, vol. 76
— 1896, p. 68, &c.   Pp. Eng. 1896, vol. 64
— 1897, p. 68, &c.   Pp. Eng. 1897, vol. 68
— 1898, p. 69, &c.   Pp. Eng. 1898, vol. 70
— 1899, p. 69, &c.   Pp. Eng. 1899, vol. 75
— 1900, p. 69, &c.   Pp. Eng. 1900, vol. 65, pt. 1
— 1901, p. 69, &c.   Pp. Eng. 1901, vol. 56
— 1902, p. 73, &c.   Pp. Eng. 1902, vol. 79

930. Oxford diocesan board of education. Higher education in religious knowledge. 4th, 5th, 7th, 13th, 14th report. Oxf., 1886, 8°.

G.A. Oxon 8° 1124

931. Oxford diocesan training college for mistresses. Report. 1887, 88.
n. pl., [1888, 89], 8°. G.A. Oxon 4° 268

932. Return of all public elementary schools examined during the year
ending 31 August 1889, giving denomination, number of scholars
[&c.]. (Oxfordshire, p. 212–17.) Pp. Eng. 1890, vol. 56

933. Endowed schools acts foundations (England) . . . Return of foundations . . . the endowments . . . of which are . . . recorded in the books
of the Charity Commissioners . . . as subject to the . . . Endowed
schools acts, showing . . . name, place, county, gross income [&c.]
for . . . 1890. (Oxfordshire, p. 57, 58.) Pp. Eng. 1892, vol. 60

934. Diocesan conference committee on church school councils. Report.
n. pl., [1891], 4°. 4 pp. G.A. Oxon 4° 268

935. Elementary education. Return showing by counties for each public
elementary school examined . . . the name and denomination . . . the
number of scholars . . . the annual grant paid; and particulars of
school income . . . for . . . 1893. (Oxfordshire, p. 490–501.)
Pp. Eng. 1894, vol. 65
— 1899, p. 92–95, 666–79. Pp. Eng. 1900, vol. 65

936. Education department. 1. Schools in receipt of parliamentary
grants. 2. Grants paid to school boards . . . 3. School board accounts
and list of loans. 1895–6. (Oxfordshire, p. 188–92.)
Pp. Eng. 1896, vol. 65
— 1896–7, p. 196–201, &c. Pp. Eng. 1897, vol. 69
— 1897–8, p. 196–201. Pp. Eng. 1898, vol. 69
— 1898–9, p. 197–202. Pp. Eng. 1899, vol. 74
— 1899–1900, p. 197–202. Pp. Eng. 1900, vol. 64
— 1900–01, p. 197–202. Pp. Eng. 1901, vol. 55
— 1901–2, p. 168–71. Pp. Eng. 1902, vol. 78
— 1902–3, p. 168–71. Pp. Eng. 1903, vol. 51
— 1903–4, p. 174–77. Pp. Eng. 1905, vol. 59

937. Oxford diocesan assoc. of voluntary schools. Report. 1897.
26235 e. 41 (17)
— 1901/2. G.A. Oxon 8° 721
Oxf., &c., 1898, 1902, 8°.

938. Oxford county council, techn. instr. comm. Annual report. 1899–
1902/3. [Oxf.], 1899–1903, 4°. G.A. Oxon 4° 308

939. Return showing the occupation of the parents of the winners of
county council scholarships during the past three years [1896–
1899] the amount of each scholarship . . . the name of the school in
which the scholarship was won [&c.]. (Oxfordshire, p. 103, 04.)
Pp. Eng. 1900, vol. 73

940. Board of education. Lists of schools under the administration of
the Board. 1901–1902. (Oxfordshire, p. 197–202.)
Pp. Eng. 1902, vol. 79

941. Oxford county council, techn. instr. comm. Technical instruction
directory. Oxf., 1902, 8°. 36 pp.   G.A. Oxon 8° 835

942. Report of the standing committee of the Oxford diocesan association of voluntary schools. 1901–02. Berks., 1902, 8°. 33 pp.
G.A. Oxon 8° 721

943. Board of Education. Statement under administrative counties . . .
of public elementary schools which have received building grants,
shewing . . . the amount of such . . . grants and the amount subscribed by the promoters at the time [&c.]. (Oxfordshire, p. 104–06.)
Pp. Eng. 1902, vol. 78

944. [A collection in the Bodleian of reports, papers &c. of the county
education authority. c. 1903–15, G.A. Oxon c. 134–38**; 1916–22,
G.A. Oxon c. 219.]

945. Board of education. Lists of public elementary schools and training
colleges under the administration of the Board. 1902–1903. (Oxfordshire, p. 197–202.)   Pp. Eng. 1903, vol. 51
— 1903–4, p. 196–200.   Pp. Eng. 1904, vol. 75

946. Board of Education. List of evening schools under the administration of the Board. 1903–1904. (Oxfordshire, p. 73, 74.)
Pp. Eng. 1906, vol. 85
— 1904–5, p. 73, 74.   Pp. Eng. 1907, vol. 62
— 1905–6, p. 72, 73.   Pp. Eng. 1908, vol. 82

947. Board of Education. General report on the instruction and training
of pupil-teachers 1903–1907. (Oxfordshire, p. 117, 18, &c.)
Pp. Eng. 1907, vol. 64

948. The Education authorities directory (and annual). 1st– ed. Lond.,
&c., 1903–, 8°.   Dir. 26011 e. 75

949. Oxfordshire county council. [Education reports. 1904–.]
O.C.R.L.

950. Oxford county council, educ. comm. Directory 1905–1906, 1909
to 1910. Oxf., 1905, 1909, 16°.   G.A. Oxon 16° 118
— 1913 to 1914. Oxf., 1913, 12°. 124 pp.   O.P.L.

951. The public elementary schools in the diocese [signed J.P.].(Oxf.
diocesan mag., 1906/8, vol. 3, p. 267–71.)   Per. 11126 d. 78

952. Education. (England and Wales). . . . Return of the schools . . .
recognised on the 1st . . . January 1906 as non-provided public
elementary schools, showing . . . the tenure of the premises . . . and
the character of the trusts . . . to which the premises are subject . . .
Oxfordshire. Lond., 1906, fol. 36 pp.   Pp. Eng. 1906, vol. 88

953. Board of education. List of public elementary schools in England and Wales on 1st Jan., 1906. (Oxfordshire, p. 524–32.)
Pp. Eng. 1906, vol. 86

954. Board of education. List of public elementary schools and certified efficient schools in England. 1906. (Oxfordshire, p. 524–32.)
Pp. Eng. 1907, vol. 63
— 1907, p. 524–32. Pp. Eng. 1908, vol. 84

955. Education act, 1902 . . . Return 'by the county council of each administrative county . . . of particulars as to the amounts received during the year ended . . . 1906 . . . from rates raised under section 18 (1) (c) and (d) of the Education act, 1902 . . .'. (Oxfordshire, p. 45–46.) Pp. Eng. 1907, vol. 62

956. Board of Education. List of secondary schools in England recognised as efficient with a list of recognised pupil-teacher centres. 1907–1908. (Oxfordshire, p. 52–53, 130–31.)
Pp. Eng. 1908, vol. 83

957. Board of Education. Public elementary schools in 'single-school parishes'. . . . (Oxfordshire, p. 76–78.) Pp. Eng. 1908, vol. 82

958. Oxford county council, educ. comm. Quarterly reports (of subcommittees). 1908–21. [Oxf.], 1908–21, 4°. G.A. Oxon 4° 305

959. Oxford county council, educ. comm. Medical adviser's [afterw.] School medical officer's report. 1908–. [From 1934 included in no. 1007.] [Oxf.], (1909–), 4°. O.C.R.L.
[Bodley has 1908–14; G.A. Oxon 4° 307]

960. Oxford county council, educ. comm. Chairman's review of some of the work of the Oxfordshire education committee from March 1907, to 31st December, 1909. [Oxf.], 1910, 4°. 13 pp.
G.A. Oxon 4° 306

961. Oxford county council, educ. comm. Report on the school gardens. 1909, 1912–19. [Oxf.], 1910–19, 4°. G.A. Oxon 4° 304

962. Oxford county council. Oxfordshire local education authority. Education act, 1918. Scheme. (Draft). n. pl. (1918), fol. 58 pp.
G.A. Oxon c. 220

963. HADOW, G., A county experiment [formation of the Oxfordshire rural community committee]. (Oxf. diocesan mag., 1922, vol. 17, p. 284–87.) Per. 11126 d. 78

964. Schools . . . directory of schools, arranged in order of counties. 1924–. Lond., 1924–, 8°. Dir. 26011 e. 130

965. Oxford county council, educ. comm. Syllabus of religious instruction for council schools. Lond., 1927, 8°. 28 pp. 13215 d. 23

966. Oxfordshire education committee. Programme for . . . 1930–33 called for by the Board of Education in circular 1397. n. pl. [1930], 8°. 26 pp.   O.P.L.

967. Oxford, univ., delegacy for extra-mural studies, comm. for furthering adult educ. in Oxfordshire, Berkshire and Buckinghamshire. Thirteenth annual report, 1937–38. Oxf. (1938), 8°. 42 pp.
                                                            O.C.R.L.

968. Schools. (Victoria county history, 1939, vol. I, p. 457–90.)
                                                            R. 9. 41 s

969. Oxfordshire county council education committee. Scheme of further education and plan for county colleges, for submission . . . under . . . the Education act, 1944. Oxf., 1948, 4°. 74 pp.
                                                            2624 d. 121

970. ALLEN, A. B., Rural education. 2 vols. [Vol. 2 entitled The country school, an account of the Endowed school, Great Haseley.] Lond., (1950), 8°.   2621 e. 397

See 1157 [Answers to ecclesiastical visitation questionnaires. 1738, &c.].
See also schools under the following places: Bampton, Banbury, Benson,
   Bicester, Caversham, Charlbury, Chipping Norton, Cowley, Dorchester,
   Hailey, Headington, Henley, Horspath, Kingham, Littlemore, Sandford
   St. Martin, South Leigh, Thame, Witney.

Law Courts

971. [*Begin.*] At the General Quarter sessions of the Peace . . . in the third year [1691] . . . of . . . William and Mary [&c. An order enforcing the law against drunkenness, &c.]. Repr. Oxf., 1711, s. sh.
                                                   fol. Θ 662 (14)

972. Game law commitments. Return of the number of commitments . . . from 1 Nov. 1829 to 1 Feb. 1830; from 1 Nov. 1830 to 1 Feb. 1831; and from 1 Nov. 1831 to 1 Feb. 1832. (Oxfordshire, p. 16.)
                                                   Pp. Eng. 1831/2, vol. 33
— 1 Nov. 1831 to 1 Nov. 1832, p. 26.   Pp. Eng. 1833, vol. 29
— 1 Nov. 1832 to 1 Nov. 1833, p. 7.   Pp. Eng. 1834, vol. 47
— since 1st Nov. 1833, p. 65–70.   Pp. Eng. 1836, vol. 41
— 5 May 1846–1 Aug. 1848, p. 69, 70.   Pp. Eng. 1849, vol. 44
— 1857–62, p. 257–63.   Pp. Eng. 1864, vol. 49

973. Criminal offenders. Return . . . showing the number of criminal offenders committed for trial or bailed for appearance at the assizes and sessions in each county. 1834. (Oxfordshire, p. 58, 59.)
                                                   Pp. Eng. 1835, vol. 45
— 1835, p. 60, 61.   Pp. Eng. 1836, vol. 41
— 1836, p. 60, 61.   Pp. Eng. 1837, vol. 46
— 1837, p. 58, 59.   Pp. Eng. 1837/8, vol. 43

— 1838, p. 58, 59.   Pp. Eng. 1839, vol. 38
— 1839, p. 58, 59.   Pp. Eng. 1840, vol. 38
— 1840, p. 26, 27.   Pp. Eng. 1841, vol. 18
— 1841, p. 26, 27.   Pp. Eng. 1842, vol. 32
— 1842, p. 27.   Pp. Eng. 1843, vol. 42
— 1843, p. 27.   Pp. Eng. 1844, vol. 39
— 1844, p. 27.   Pp. Eng. 1845, vol. 37
— 1845, p. 27.   Pp. Eng. 1846, vol. 34
— 1846, p. 27.   Pp. Eng. 1847, vol. 47
— 1847, p. 27.   Pp. Eng. 1847/8, vol. 52
— 1848, p. 27.   Pp. Eng. 1849, vol. 44
— 1849, p. 27.   Pp. Eng. 1850, vol. 45
— 1850, p. 27.   Pp. Eng. 1851, vol. 46
— 1851, p. 27.   Pp. Eng. 1852, vol. 41
— 1852, p. 27.   Pp. Eng. 1852/3, vol. 81
— 1853, p. 27.   Pp. Eng. 1854, vol. 54
— 1854, p. 27.   Pp. Eng. 1854/5, vol. 43
— 1855, p. 28.   Pp. Eng. 1856, vol. 49
— 1856, p. 41. Judicial statistics, pt. 1.
                                   Pp. Eng. 1857, sess. 2, vol. 35
— 1857, p. 51. Judicial returns.   Pp. Eng. 1857/8, vol. 57
[Thereafter reports do not admit of detailed treatment.]

974. Abstract return of the Courts of request, Courts of conscience, and all other courts . . . having jurisdiction in personal actions . . . and the extent of their jurisdiction. (Oxfordshire, p. 128–31.)
                                        Pp. Eng. 1840, vol. 41

975. Justices of the peace. Return . . . of the number of justices in the commission of the peace for each county . . . in 1852, 1853 and 1854. (Oxfordshire, p. 210–16.)   Pp. Eng. 1856, vol. 50

976. COOPER, W. D., ed., The expenses of the judges of Assize, riding the Western and Oxford circuits, temp. Elizabeth 1596–1601. (Camden misc., vol. 4, pt. 2, p. 44–57.) (Lond.), 1858, 4°.
                                            Ψ 2. 112 (73)

977. County of Oxford. A calendar of prisoners for trial at the assizes . . . 2nd March 1863. [Oxf.], (1863), fol. 8 pp.
                                        G.A. Oxon b. 113 (168)

978. List of the (acting) magistrates of Oxfordshire [afterw.] List of justices of the peace [afterw.] List of magistrates, 1863–. [Oxf.], 1863–, fol. & 4°.   G.A. Oxon c. 24*; G.A. Oxon 4° 425

979.

980. County of Oxford. List of persons exempted from service on juries. [Oxf.], 1866, fol. 4 pp.   MS. Top. Oxon c. 290 (38)

981. Judicature commission. Oxfordshire quarter sessions. [Oxf.], 1870,
     fol. 6 pp.   MS. Top. Oxon c. 290 (51)

982. DAVENPORT, J. M., County of Oxford. Notes upon the jurisdiction
     of the county justices within the city of Oxford; and cognate matters
     [signed J. M. D.]. [Oxf.], 1872, 8°. 14 pp.   G.A. Oxon 8° 164 (5)
     — [Another ed. enlarged.] 16 pp.   G.A. Oxon 8° 164 (6)

983.

984. GRETTON, M. S., Oxfordshire justices of the peace in the seven-
     teenth century. [*With*] Appendix of the earliest extant Oxfordshire
     quarter sessions record, 1687–1689. (Oxf. record soc., 16.) Oxf.,
     1934, 8°. 101+34 pp.   R. 13. 702

     See 2494A [Honour court leets, Ewelme. 1950].
     See 3452 [Rousham. Leet juries. 1870].
     See 3679 [Stanton Harcourt. Manor courts. 1913].
     See 3703 [Steeple Aston. Law deed curiosities. 1874].

                              Police

985. A proposal offered to the gentlemen, tradesmen . . . within the
     county of Oxford, for the discovery, punishment and prevention for
     the future of all murder, robbery, theft and all unlawful invasion of
     any one's property. n. pl., [1756], s. sh.   fol. Θ 673 (13)

986. County of Oxford constabulary. Orders and regulations. n. pl.,
     1857, 16°. 49 pp.   G.A. Oxon 16° 152

987. Oxfordshire Michaelmas quarter sessions, 1875. Order appointing
     committee to treat with a Berkshire committee as to the reciprocal
     police supervision of riparian places. [Oxf.], 1875, fol. 2 pp.
                                                 G.A. fol. A 139 (7*)

988. Police (counties and boroughs). Reports of the inspectors of con-
     stabulary for the year ending 29th Sept. 1857. (Oxfordshire, p. 18.)
                                                 Pp. Eng. 1857/8, vol. 47
     — 1858, p. 31, 32.   Pp. Eng. 1859, session 1, vol. 22
     — 1859, p. 29, 30.   Pp. Eng. 1860, vol. 57
     — 1860, p. 28, 29.   Pp. Eng. 1861, vol. 52
     — 1861, p. 31, 32.   Pp. Eng. 1862, vol. 45
     — 1862, p. 36, 37.   Pp. Eng. 1863, vol. 50
     — 1863, p. 41–43.   Pp. Eng. 1864, vol. 48
     — 1864, p. 46, 47.   Pp. Eng. 1865, vol. 45
     — 1865, p. 47–49.   Pp. Eng. 1866, vol. 34
     — 1866, p. 35, 36.   Pp. Eng. 1867, vol. 36
     — 1867, p. 37, 38.   Pp. Eng. 1867/8, vol. 36
     — 1868, p. 36, 37.   Pp. Eng. 1868/9, vol. 31
     — 1869, p. 24, 25.   Pp. Eng. 1870, vol. 36
     — 1870, p. 32–34.   Pp. Eng. 1871, vol. 28
     — 1871, p. 42–44.   Pp. Eng. 1872, vol. 30

— 1872, p. 47–50.	Pp. Eng. 1873, vol. 31
— 1873, p. 50–52.	Pp. Eng. 1874, vol. 28
— 1874, p. 54–57.	Pp. Eng. 1875, vol. 36
— 1875, p. 54–57.	Pp. Eng. 1876, vol. 34
— 1876, p. 53–55.	Pp. Eng. 1877, vol. 42
— 1877, p. 55–58.	Pp. Eng. 1878, vol. 40
— 1878, p. 57–58.	Pp. Eng. 1878/9, vol. 33
— 1879, p. 59–63.	Pp. Eng. 1880, vol. 34
— 1880, p. 60–63.	Pp. Eng. 1881, vol. 51
— 1881, p. 61–64.	Pp. Eng. 1882, vol. 33
— 1882, p. 63–65.	Pp. Eng. 1883, vol. 31
— 1883, p. 63–65.	Pp. Eng. 1884, vol. 42
— 1884, p. 62–64.	Pp. Eng. 1884/5, vol. 37
— 1885, p. 59–61.	Pp. Eng. 1886, vol. 34
— 1886, p. 61–63.	Pp. Eng. 1887, vol. 40
— 1887, p. 62–64.	Pp. Eng. 1888, vol. 57
— 1888, p. 59–61.	Pp. Eng. 1889, vol. 40
— 1889, p. 59–62.	Pp. Eng. 1890, vol. 36
— 1890, p. 51–54.	Pp. Eng. 1890/1, vol. 42
— 1891, p. 54–56.	Pp. Eng. 1892, vol. 41
— 1892, p. 45–47.	Pp. Eng. 1893/4, vol. 45
— 1893, p. 39–41.	Pp. Eng. 1894, vol. 42
— 1894, p. 36–38.	Pp. Eng. 1895, vol. 55
— 1895, p. 36–38.	Pp. Eng. 1896, vol. 42
— 1896, p. 37–39.	Pp. Eng. 1897, vol. 39
— 1897, p. 38–40.	Pp. Eng. 1898, vol. 46
— 1898, p. 37–39.	Pp. Eng. 1899, vol. 42
— 1899, p. 38–40.	Pp. Eng. 1900, vol. 40
— 1900, p. 38–40.	Pp. Eng. 1901, vol. 32
— 1901, p. 33–35.	Pp. Eng. 1902, vol. 41
— 1902, p. 42–45.	Pp. Eng. 1903, vol. 28
— 1903, p. 40–42.	Pp. Eng. 1904, vol. 34
— 1904, p. 41–43.	Pp. Eng. 1905, vol. 36
— 1905, p. 40–42.	Pp. Eng. 1906, vol. 49
— 1906, p. 40–42.	Pp. Eng. 1907, vol. 31
— 1907, p. 37–39.	Pp. Eng. 1908, vol. 89
— 1908, p. 69, 70.	Pp. Eng. 1909, vol. 72
— 1909, p. 33, 34.	Pp. Eng. 1910, vol. 75
— 1910, p. 34, 35.	Pp. Eng. 1911, vol. 65
— 1911, p. 84, 85.	Pp. Eng. 1912/13, vol. 69
— 1912, p. 91, 92.	Pp. Eng. 1913, vol. 52
— 1913, p. 92, 93.	Pp. Eng. 1914, vol. 67
— 1914, p. 103, 104.	Pp. Eng. 1914/16, vol. 32

[Thereafter the reports become too general to warrant detailed treatment.]

See 1630 [Banbury police instructions. 1836].
See 2515 [Eynsham. Mutual assistance against felony. 1816].
See 2568 [Forest Hill. Mutual assistance against felony. 1836].

Prisons

989. Oxfordshire, to wit. A calendar of the prisoners . . . in the castle
goal, March 6th 1776. n. pl. (1776), s. sh.
                                        G.A. Oxon b. 113 (19)

990. Oxfordshire, to wit. Sentences of the prisoners . . . in the Castle
goal for the said county, Summer assizes, July 17th, 1776.
                                        G.A. Oxon b. 113 (18)
— 1826, 1840, 1844, 1848.   G.A. Oxon b. 96 (8, 19, 23)
— 1862, 1863.   G.A. Oxon b. 113 (147, 169)
n. pl., (1776–1863), s. sh.

991. HOWARD, J., The state of prisons in England and Wales.
(Oxfordshire, p. 315–20.) Warrington, 1777, 4°.
                                        .Gough Gen. top. 102
— 2nd ed. 1780 (p. 302–05).   Gough Gen. top. 112

992. Rules and regulations for the government of the common gaol
and Bridewell of the County of Oxford. Oxf., 1820, 8°. 32 pp.
                                        G.A. Oxon 8° 124 (22)

993. Gaols. Copies of . . . reports. 1823. (Oxfordshire, p. 187–90.)
                                        Pp. Eng. 1824, vol. 19
— 1824, p. 212–15.   Pp. Eng. 1825, vol. 23
— 1825, p. 210, 211.   Pp. Eng. 1826, vol. 24
— 1826, p. 187–89.   Pp. Eng. 1826/7, vol. 19
— 1827, p. 220–22.   Pp. Eng. 1828, vol. 20
— 1828, p. 195–98.   Pp. Eng. 1829, vol. 19
— 1829, p. 194–96.   Pp. Eng. 1830, vol. 24
— 1830, p. 187–89.   Pp. Eng. 1830/1, vol. 12
— 1831, p. 187–89.   Pp. Eng. 1831/2, vol. 33
— 1832, p. 201–03.   Pp. Eng. 1833, vol. 28
— 1833, p. 187–90.   Pp. Eng. 1834, vol. 46
— 1834, p. 183, 184.   Pp. Eng. 1835, vol. 44
— 1835, p. 121, 122.   Pp. Eng. 1836, vol. 42
— 1836, p. 121, 122.   Pp. Eng. 1837, vol. 45
— 1837, p. 126, 127.   Pp. Eng. 1837/8, vol. 43
— 1838, p. 121–23.   Pp. Eng. 1839, vol. 38
— 1839, p. 129–31.   Pp. Eng. 1840, vol. 38
— 1840, p. 134–36.   Pp. Eng. 1841, vol. 18
— 1841, p. 136–38.   Pp. Eng. 1842, vol. 32
— 1842, p. 137, 138.   Pp. Eng. 1843, vol. 43
— 1843, p. 139, 140.   Pp. Eng. 1844, vol. 39
— 1844, p. 167, 168.   Pp. Eng. 1845, vol. 37
— 1845, p. 162, 163.   Pp. Eng. 1846, vol. 34
— 1846, p. 176, 177.   Pp. Eng. 1847, vol. 47
— 1847, p. 177–79.   Pp. Eng. 1847/8, vol. 52
[Later reports do not concern Oxfordshire.]

994. Fourth report of the inspectors appointed . . . to visit the different prisons of Great Britain. Southern and Western district. (Oxford county gaol, p. 193–200.)   Pp. Eng. 1839, vol. 22
— 7th rept., p. 153–64.   Pp. Eng. 1842, vol. 21
— 9th rept., p. 331–51.   Pp. Eng. 1844, vol. 29
— 11th rept., p. 308–26.   Pp. Eng. 1846, vol. 21
— 12th rept., p. 309–24.   Pp. Eng. 1848, vol. 35
— 15th rept., p. 43–54.   Pp. Eng. 1851, vol. 27
— 22nd rept., p. 93–95.   Pp. Eng. 1857/8, vol. 29
— 25th rept., p. 50.   Pp. Eng. 1860, vol. 35
— 27th rept., p. 61–63.   Pp. Eng. 1862, vol. 25
— 29th rept., p. 60.   Pp. Eng. 1864, vol. 26
— 30th rept., p. 179–81.   Pp. Eng. 1865, vol. 23
— 31st rept., p. 160–62.   Pp. Eng. 1866, vol. 37
— 33rd rept., p. 151–53.   Pp. Eng. 1868/9, vol. 29
— 34th rept., p. 163–66.   Pp. Eng. 1870, vol. 37
— 35th rept., p. 204–12.   Pp. Eng. 1871, vol. 29
— 36th rept., p. 118–20.   Pp. Eng. 1872, vol. 31
— 37th rept., p. 237–41.   Pp. Eng. 1873, vol. 32
— 38th rept., p. 272–78.   Pp. Eng. 1874, vol. 29
— 39th rept., p. 293–99.   Pp. Eng. 1875, vol. 37
— 40th rept., p. 289–95.   Pp. Eng. 1876, vol. 35
— 41st rept., p. 292–98.   Pp. Eng. 1877, vol. 43
— 42nd rept., p. 292–98.   Pp. Eng. 1878, vol. 41
[Thereafter limited information may be found in the reports of the Commissioners of prisons.]

995. Rules of the government of the prison of the County of Oxford, called the Oxford Castle. [Oxf.], 1855, 8°. 55 pp.
G.A. Oxon 8° 352

996. Returns relating to dietaries in the county gaols. (Oxfordshire, p. 90, 91.)   Pp. Eng. 1857, vol. 14

997. Regulations and rules for the government of the prison of the County of Oxford, called the Oxford Castle. [Oxf.], 1867, 46 pp.
G.A. Oxon 4° 13 (7)
— Additional rules and dietary table . . . 1867. 25 pp.   O.C.R.L.

998. Oxford county prison. Benefactions. n. pl., 1872, fol. 16 pp.
G.A. fol. A 139 (8)
— [Another ed. *With* Order of visiting justices, 30th Nov., 1872.]
G.A. fol. A 139 (9)

999. Workhouses (Commitments to prison) . . . Return of the number of persons . . . committed to prison from each union workhouse . . . for the half-year ending on the 25th . . . March 1874 . . . (Oxfordshire, p. 34, 35.)   Pp. Eng. 1875, vol. 62

1000. Prisons, Great Britain. Return from all county and borough prisons for 1874, showing 1. Daily average number of prisoners in custody. 2. Average annual cost per prisoner [&c.]. (Oxford-shire, p. 77.) Pp. Eng. 1876, vol. 61

See 1631 [Banbury prison. 1837–].

Public Health

1001. Rules and orders [against the spread of the plague] made by the vice-chancellor of the University of Oxford, and Iustices of peace, for the good and safety of the Vniversity, city and county of Oxford. [Madan 2713.] [Oxf., 1665], s. sh. Wood 276 *a* (313)

1002. ROWELL, G. A., On the effects of elevation and floods on health; and the general health of Oxford compared with that of other districts. Lond., &c., 1866, 8°. 46 pp. G.A. Oxon 8° 100 (2)

1003. CHILD, G. W., Report upon the sanitary condition of the dis-tricts of the combined sanitary authorities of Oxfordshire, from Lady-day 1873 to Lady-day 1874. Lond., 1874, 8°. 63 pp.
15012 e. 13
— Second report. 1874 to 1875. 88 pp. G.A. Oxon 8° 200
— Third report. 1875 to 1876. 48 pp. Radcl.

1004. SIMMS, G., Oxonia [account of the treatment of people of Oxford & the surrounding area with Oxonia, a patent medicine, used in cases of cancer and lupus]. Lond., (1893), 8°. 8 pp. 1693 d. 108

See 959 [School medical officer's report. 1908].

1004A. Oxfordshire county council. Annual report of the County medical officer of health, 1911–. [From 1934 included in no. 1007.] Oxf., 1912–, 8°. O.C.R.L.

1005. Oxfordshire rural community council, health group. A report on the existing health services in Oxfordshire. Oxf., [1928?], 8°. 26 pp.
O.P.L.

1006. JENNINGS, H. C., An inquiry into some factors affecting the incidence of tuberculosis in Oxfordshire. Repr. from the Annual report in county health services, Oxfordshire. n. pl., 1933, 4°. 23 pp.
15697 d. 104 (7)

1007. Oxfordshire county council. Annual report on the county health services. 1934–. Pt. 1. Report of the School medical officer.
— Pt. 2. Report of the County medical officer. [Formerly publ. separately. See 959, 1004A.] Oxf., 1935–, 8°. Radcl.

1008. PINSENT, E. F., The mental health services in Oxford city, Oxfordshire and Berkshire. Oxf., 1937, 8°. 87 pp. 1535 e. 243

1009. Nuffield provincial hospitals trust. The Berks, Bucks and Oxon regional hospital council. First annual report, 1941/42. O.P.L.
— Report for the 3 years ended 31 Mar. 1944. O.P.L.

1010. Nuffield provincial hospitals trust. The Berks, Bucks and Oxon regional hospital council. Report of the sub-committee on the ophthalmic services in the region. n. pl., 1943, 8°. 8 pp.   O.P.L.

1011. Nuffield provincial hospitals trust. The Berks, Bucks and Oxon regional hospitals council, medical advisory committee. A cancer service for Berks, Bucks, Northants & Oxon. Nov. 1945. (Oxf., 1945), 4°. 25 pp.   O.P.L.

1012. Ministry of Health. Hospital survey. The hospital services of Berkshire, Buckinghamshire and Oxfordshire. Lond., 1945, fol. 92 pp.   2279 c. 10

1013. Nuffield provincial hospitals trust. The Berks, Bucks and Oxon regional hospitals council. Report for Jan. 1943 to Mar. 1946. (Oxf., 1946), 4°. 39 pp.   O.P.L.

1014. Nuffield provincial hospitals trust. The Berks, Bucks and Oxon regional hospitals council, medical advisory committee. A comprehensive maternity service for Berks, Bucks & Oxon. Apr. 1946. (Oxf., 1946), 4°. 32 pp.   O.P.L.

1015. Oxford and district joint hospitals board. Report of the *ad hoc* planning committee on the planning of hospital services in the board's area. Sept. 1946. (Oxf., 1946), 4°. 31 pp.   O.P.L.

1016. Nuffield provincial hospitals trust. Report on the planning of hospital services in Berks, Bucks & Oxon region. Jan. 1947. (Oxf., 1947), 4°. 39 pp.   O.P.L.

1017. Nuffield provincial hospitals trust. The Berks, Bucks and Oxon regional hospitals council. Child health services. May 1948. (Oxf., 1948), 4°. 85 pp.   O.P.L.

1018. Oxfordshire county council, publ. health dept. Health services. (Oxf.), 1949, 8°. 80 pp.   15012 e. 85

1019. South Oxfordshire combined districts. Annual report of the medical officer of health. 1949–. Oxf., (1950–), 4°.   Radcl.

See 905, 907 [Poor law medical relief. 1856, 57].
See 1632, &c. [Public health, Banbury].
See 1762 [Bicester. Report on enteric fever. 1896].
See 1928 [Burford district. Report on sanitary conditions. 1872].
See 2259A [Crowmarsh, Culham, and Goring rural sanitary district. Report. 1911].
See 4288 [Yarnton. Anti-cholera precautions. 1853].

Asylums

1019A. Bucks, Oxon and Reading Joint board for the mentally defective. Annual report. 1935–47. [Previously issued as an Appendix to the reports of the Mental deficiency committee of the County council, included in no. 638.] Oxf., [1936–48], 8°.   O.C.R.L.
See Headington, Hook Norton, Littlemore.

Hospitals

See 2212 [Cowley. National hospital. 1869].
See 2773 [Headington infectious hospital. 1908].
See 2825 [Henley. Smith hospital. 1900].
See 2852, 54 [Henley and Wallingford (Crowmarsh; Whitchurch) joint hospital districts. 1904, 15].
See 1636 [Horton infirmary for Banbury. 1877].
See 2811, 12 [Wingfield convalescent home. 1873].
See 2813 [Wingfield orthopaedic hospital. 1923].

Nursing associations

See 1635 [Banbury nursing assoc.].
See 1745 [Benson, Ewelme, and Berwick nursing assoc.].
See 2484 [Ewelme nursing, and maternity benefit soc.].
See 2739 [Hanborough nursing assoc.].
See 2893 [Heythrop, N. Oxon benefit nursing soc.].
See 4050 [Witney, medical club].

Public Utilities

1020. An act for better enabling the mayor, aldermen and citizens of Oxford to supply Oxford and other places [Cowley, Headington, Iffley, Wolvercot, and Littlemore] with water. (38 & 39 V., c. 41, L. & P.) Lond., 1875, fol. 12 pp.   L. Eng. A 69 c. 6

1021. An act for incorporating and conferring powers on the South Oxfordshire water and gas company. (5 E. VII, c. 32, L. & P.) Lond., 1905, fol. 41 pp.   L. Eng. A 69 c. 6

1022. An act for incorporating and conferring powers on the United District Gas company [with works at Bicester, Adderbury, Charlbury and Shipton-under-Wychwood &c. The limits of the company are set out, and the Banbury Gas Light & Coke company is prohibited from supplying W. and E. Adderbury, Milton and Bloxham]. (3 & 4 G. V, c. 40, L. & P.) Lond., 1913, fol. 40 pp.   L. Eng. A 69 c. 6

1023. An act to consolidate and reduce the capital of the South Oxfordshire Water and Gas company. . . . (13 G. V, c. 2, L. & P.) Lond., 1923, 8°. 22 pp.   L. Eng. A 69 c. 6

1024. An act to confirm a provisional order of the Minister of Health relating to the South Oxfordshire water and gas company. (25 & 26 G. V, c. 74, L. & P.) Lond., 1935, 8°. 11 pp.   L. Eng. A 69 c. 6

For publications concerning the natural history aspect of the water-supply see 17–19.
See 1637, &c., 1679, &c. [Public utilities, Banbury].
See 2109 [Electric lighting, Chipping Norton. 1913].
See 2641 [Goring gas and water works. 1888].
See 2861, &c. [Public utilities, Henley].
See 2959, 3132, 3472 [Sewage works, Iffley, Littlemore, Sandford-on-Thames. 1874].
See 4076, &c. [Public utilities, Witney].

SOCIETIES, CLUBS, ETC.

Cultural Societies and Libraries

See 1678 [Banbury church choral society. 1843].
See 1571, 72 [Banbury fine art exhibition. 1881].
See 4046, 47 [Witney choral society. 1875, 1896].
See 4071, &c. [Witney natural history and literary society. 1870 &c.].
See 4150 [Woodstock debating society. 1894].
See 1501 [Bampton reading society. 1815].
See 1763 [Chained library. Bicester. 1896/1900].
See 1995, 96 [Caversham public library. 1907].
See 2181, 82 [Coombe reading room. 1892].
See 2819 [Henley old library. 1852].
See 2961 [Iffley reading room. 1895].
See 3211 [Middleton Stoney state library. 1893].
See 3854 [Thame institute library. 1882].

Freemasons

1025. The Freemasons calendar & directory for the province of Oxford-shire. 1867-. (Oxf.) 1867-, 12°.   Dir. 24791 f. 28

1026. HAWKINS, E. L., A history of freemasonry in Oxfordshire. Oxf., 1882, 8°. 57 pp.   G.A. Oxon 8° 314

1027. By-laws of the Provincial Grand Lodge of Oxfordshire. [Free-masons.] Oxf., 1884, 12°. 28 pp.   24791 g. 30

1028. [2 volumes preserved in the Bodleian, of circulars and notices connected with Oxfordshire freemasonry.]   G.A. Oxon c. 124

Friendly Societies

1029. Return of the number of Friendly societies filed by the Clerks of the Peace of each county since 1st January 1793 to [1831]. (Oxford-shire, p. 21.)   Pp. Eng. 1831/2, vol. 26

1030. A return relating to Friendly societies enrolled in the several counties. (Oxfordshire, p. 21.)   Pp. Eng. 1837, vol. 51
— 1842, p. 30.   Pp. Eng. 1842, vol. 26
— 1851, p. 13.   Pp. Eng. 1852, vol. 28

1031. Report of the Registrar of Friendly societies in England. 1856–1939. [Later reports include information concerning number of members, pecuniary position, addresses, &c. Also included are Valuations and Quinquennial returns. They are published in Accounts and Papers of the House of Commons.]
      Pp. Eng. 1856, vol. 58 (&c.)

1032. Central Oxfordshire friendly society. Rules and tables. Oxf., 1860, 8°. 15 pp.   G.A. Oxon 8° 208 (1)
— [Another ed.] [Oxf., 1860?]. 15 pp.   G.A. Oxon 8° 208 (2)

1033. Friendly and benefit building societies' commission. Reports of the assistant commissioners: Southern and Eastern counties. (Oxfordshire, p. 92–119.)   Pp. Eng. 1874, vol. 23, pt. 2.

See 1445 [Ambrosden. Amicable society of tradesmen].
See 1692 [Banbury. Beneficial society].
See 1693 [Banbury. British queen benefit society].
See 1694 [Banbury. Female friendly society].
See 1695 [Banbury. Friendly society].
See 1686, 96, 97 [Banbury. Oddfellows].
See 1690 [Banbury. Sick fund society].
See 1698 [Banbury. Tradesmens' benefit society].
See 1691 [Banbury. United Christian benefit society].
See 1705, 06 [Barton. Friendly society].
See 1823 [Bloxham. Friendly society].
See 1923 [Burford. Friendly institution].
See 2142 [Clanfield. Prince of Wales Friendly society].
See 2557 [Filkins. Benefit society].
See 2930 [Horspath. Rent and shoe club].
See 3026 [Kidlington. Friendly society].
See 3113 [Little Milton. Lamb inn slate club].
See 3249 [Neithrop. Working men's club].
See 3590 [Somerton. Friendly and benefit society].
See 3674 [Stanton Harcourt. Victoria club].
See 2939 [Studley. Hand in glove benefit society].
See 4040 [Witney. Benevolent society].

Political Societies

1034. Mid-Oxfordshire Conservative assoc. (Rules and regulations.) Kiddington, 1909, 8°. 24 pp.   G.A. Oxon 8° 1101 (9)

1035. The South Oxfordshire pioneer. The official organ of the South Oxfordshire Divisional Labour party. No. 1–6. (Shiplake), 1929, 30, 4°.   Per. 22775 d. 56

See 1736 [Benson. Conservative club].

Savings Associations, &c.

1036. Peoples savings association. Oxfordshire branch. [Draft scheme.] n. pl., 1873, 8°. 24 pp.   G.A. Oxon 8° 803

1037. Return . . . showing the number of accounts of depositors in Post office savings banks . . . remaining open . . . 31st Dec. 1873 to 1878. (Oxfordshire, p. 66, 67.)   Pp. Eng. 1878/9, vol. 42
— 1879, p. 21, 22.   Pp. Eng. 1881, vol. 57
— 1880, 81, p. 56.   Pp. Eng. 1882, vol. 37
— 1882, 83, p. 62, 63.   Pp. Eng. 1884, vol. 47
— 1884, p. 28, 29.   Pp. Eng. 1886, vol. 38
— 1885, p. 30.   Pp. Eng. 1886, vol. 38
— 1886, p. 31, 32.   Pp. Eng. 1887, vol. 49
— 1887, p. 32, 33.   Pp. Eng. 1888, vol. 65
— 1888, p. 34, 35.   Pp. Eng. 1889, vol. 47

— 1889, p. 36.   Pp. Eng. 1890, vol. 41
— 1894, p. 45.   Pp. Eng. 1895, vol. 61

See 1683, 84 [Banbury bank for savings].
See 1689 [Banbury saving's bank annuity society].

Temperance Societies

1038. Oxfordshire Band of hope and temperance union. 1st–32nd annual report. Oxf., 1876–1908, 8°. [Bodleian set is imperf.]
G.A. Oxon 4° 213

1039. Oxfordshire Band of hope and temperance union. Speakers' plan [*afterw.*] Quarterly manual and speakers' plan [*afterw.*] Speakers' appointments. 1892–1916. (Oxf., 1892–1916), s. sh., &c.
G.A. Oxon 4° 213

1040. Oxfordshire Band of hope review. Vol. 1, 2. Oxf., 1903, 04, 4°.
Per. 16871 d. 13

1041. International order of Good Templars. Quarterly guide to lodges in Oxfordshire. Sept. to Nov., 1913. Oxf. (1913), 16°. 32 pp.
G.A. Oxon c. 317 (2)

See 2774 [British Workman, Headington. 1924].

Women's Institutes

1042. [Oxfordshire Women's institutes. Home & country, *passim.* 1919–.]
Per. 2474 d. 78

SPORT AND PASTIME

General

1043. Sport. (Victoria county history, 1907, vol. 2, p. 351–72.)
R. 9. 41 *s*

1044. MANNING, P., Sport and pastime in Stuart Oxford. (Oxf. hist. soc., vol. 75, p. 85–135.) Oxf., 1923, 8°.
R. 13. 700

1045. BONNETT, F., Sport in the counties. No. 16. Oxfordshire. (Badminton mag., 1915, vol. 42, p. 104–21.)
Per. 3843 d. 5

See 4045 [Witney Athenaeum. 1874].

Boy Scouts

1045A. Oxford & district boy scouts' chronicle. Vol. 1, no. 1, 2. Oxf., 1909, 8°.
Per. 38483 e. 11

1046. Oxfordshire Boy scouts association. Oxfordshire Boy scouts [*afterw.*] The Oxfordshire Boy scout (ed. A. R. Masters). Vol. 1, no. 1–4. [No more publ.] Canterbury, 1936, 37, 8°.

Per. 38483 d. 46

1047. Oxfordshire Boy scouts association. Year book. 1948–. Oxf., 1948–, 8°. Per. 38483 f. 35

Chess

1048. Oxfordshire chess association. Constitution and rules. First year's report. Oxf., 1909, 8°. 8 pp. 38472 e. 69 (9)

Cricket

1049. Oxfordshire county cricket club. Rules and report. 1891. n. pl., (1891), 8°. 8 pp. 38454 e. 17 (10)

See 2213 [Cowley cricket club. 1870].

Dancing

See 4009 [Whitchurch dancing assemblies. 1860].

Horse-racing

See 1917 [Burford downs. 1753].

Hunting

See 2890 [Places of meeting of Heythrop hunt. *c.* 1840].

1050. VENABLES, A. M., Hunts in the neighbourhood of Oxford, with the places of meeting. Oxf., [*c.* 1845], obl. 16°. 22 pp.

G.A. Oxon 16° 136 (17)

1051. List of masters and Hunt servants, and pedigrees of the Heythrop fox hounds, 1835 to 1886. Chipping Norton, 1886, 8°. 71 pp.

G.A. Oxon 8° 965

1052. BARROW, A. S., The Heythrop. The Bicester and Warden Hill. (More shires & provinces by 'Sabretache', 1928, p. 27–38, 55–66.)

38445 c. 7

Morris dancing

See Folk-lore, 862, 63.

Rowing

See Henley, 2866, &c.
See Iffley, 2957A.

Rugby Football

1053. Oxfordshire Nomads Rugby union F.C. [Rules and misc. papers, in the Bodleian. 1909–11.] G.A. Oxon c. 265

Shooting

1054. Oxfordshire rifle association. Report. 1863, 1864/5, 1878, 1899, 1908, 09. Oxf. (1863–1909), 8°. G.A. Oxon 8° 896

1055. Oxfordshire rifle association. Prizes to be shot for . . . 1898, 1901, 02, 1905, 1908, 09. Oxf., 1898–1909, s. sh. G.A. Oxon c. 119

1056. Oxfordshire miniature rifle association. A winter prize meeting, Dec. 1909. [Oxf.], 1909, s. sh. G.A. Oxon c. 119

TOWN AND COUNTRY PLANNING

1057. MAYO, EARL OF, ADSHEAD, S. D., and ABERCROMBIE, P., Regional planning report on Oxfordshire. Oxf., &c., 1931, 4°. 80 pp.+plates. 2479115 d. 44

1058. Council for the preservation of rural England. An appeal from the Oxfordshire branch. (Oxf., 1936), 8°. 23 pp. O.P.L.

1059. Council for the preservation of rural England. Oxfordshire branch. Report. 1937–. Oxf. [1938–], 8°. O.C.R.L.

1060. MARSHALL, M., Land of Britain. Pt. 56. Oxfordshire. (Land utilization survey of Britain, p. 195–240.) Lond., 1943, 4°. 23213 d. 2 (56)

1061. Oxford univ., agric. econ. research inst. Country planning, a study of rural problems [in N. Oxfordshire]. Lond., 1944, 8°. 288 pp. 2479115 e. 22

See 1645 [Banbury. 1933].
See 3360 [Nuneham Courtenay and Marsh Baldon. Town planning survey. 1937].

RELIGION

GENERAL

1062. LE NEVE, J., Fasti Ecclesiæ Anglicanæ: or, An essay towards deducing a regular succession of all the principal dignitaries in each cathedral . . . in England and Wales. (Oxfordshire, *passim*.) (Lond.), 1716, fol. Gough Eccl. top. 69
— [Another ed.] corrected and continued by T. D. Hardy. 3 vols. (Oxfordshire, vol. 2, *passim*.) Oxf., 1854, 8°. R. 3. 50

1063. WILLIS, B., A survey of the cathedrals of Lincoln, Ely, Oxford [&c.] containing an history of their foundations, . . . endowments . . . patronages [&c.]. Lond., 1730, 4°. Vet. A 4 d. 135

1064. Account of benefices and population; churches, chapels, and their capacity; number and condition of glebe houses; and income of all benefices not exceeding £150 per ann. (Oxfordshire, p. 163–68.) Pp. Eng. 1818, vol. 18

1065. To the . . . Commons . . . the humble petition of the . . . archdeacon and clergy of the archdeaconry of Oxford [against the Births and deaths registration act, 1836]. n. pl. [*c.* 1837], 8°. 4 pp.
G.A. Oxon 8° 77 (8)

1066. Churches, chapels, &c. . . . Return of the churches, chapels . . . in the registration districts of Great Britain showing the religious denomination to which such . . . buildings belong. (Oxfordshire, *passim*.) Pp. Eng. 1882, vol. 50

1067. DEARMER, P., The cathedral church of Oxford . . . and A brief history of the episcopal see. (p. 126–36.) Lond., 1897, 8°.
G.A. Eccl. top. 8° 39 (5)

1068. Ecclesiastical history. (Victoria county history, 1907, vol. 2, p. 1–63.) R. 9. 41 *s*

1069. Registrar General. List . . . of places of meeting for religious worship certified . . . under provisions of the acts 15 & 16 Vict. c. 36 [&c.]. (Official list of the Registrar general, pt. 3.) [Oxfordshire, *passim*.] 1910–. Lond., 1910–, fol. 24761 c. 43; B.M. 1899–

1070. The resolutions of the Oxford and Oxfordshire auxiliary Bible society, which were passed at its formation on June 25, 1813: together with a statement of the proceedings on that occasion. Oxf., (1813), 8°. 73 pp. G. Pamph. 627

1071. Oxford and Oxfordshire auxiliary society for promoting Christianity among the Jews. [1st]–77th Annual report. Oxf., 1827–1904, 8°. G.A. Oxon c. 43 (100); c. 74 (324); 8° 486

See 2196 [Coate and Leafield colportage assoc. 1877].
See 3288 [Letter proposing disestablishment of the Church. North Aston. c. 1900].
See 3762 [Catholic sanctuary at Stonor. 1951].

RELIGIOUS HOUSES

1072. DODSWORTH, R., and DUGDALE, SIR W., Monasticon Anglicanum. 3 vols. [An account of the abbeys and priories of England, which, although not arranged by counties, contains much information about Oxfordshire.] Lond., 1655–73, fol.
Gough. Eccl. top. 90–92
— [Other eds. in 1682, 1693, 1718. 1817, R. 9. 090 *m*; 1846, G.A. Eccl. top. b. 12–19.]

1073. TANNER, T., Notitia monastica, or, A short history of the religious houses in England and Wales. (Oxfordshire, p. 177–86.) Oxf., 1695, 8°. Gough Eccl. top. 1
[Other eds. 1744, Gough Eccl. top. 85; 1787, R. 9. 090 *o*.]

1074. STEVENS, J., The history of the antient abbeys, monasteries [&c.]. Being two additional volumes to sir W. Dugdale's Monasticon Anglicanum. Lond., 1722, fol. Gough Eccl. top. 88, 89

1075. WARBURTON, J., Some account of the alien priories, and of such lands as they are known to have possessed in England and Wales [by J. Warburton, ed. by J. Nichols &c.]. 2 vols. (Oxfordshire, *passim*.) Lond., 1779, 8°. Douce W 138, 139

1076. MOORE, J., List of the abbies, priories, and other religious houses, castles, &c. in England and Wales. (Oxfordshire at sig. G.) Lond., 1786, 8°. Gough Eccl. top. 16

See also 265, 277 [Monasteries].

1077. The cartulary of the Monastery of st. Frideswide at Oxford, ed. by S. R. Wigram. Vol. 2. The chantry and country parish charters. (O.H.S., 31.) Oxf., 1896, 4°. R. 13. 700 (31)

1078. BOUCHIER, E. S., Monastic remains near Oxford. Oxf., &c., 1905, 16°. 44 pp. G.A. Eccl. top. 16° 34

1079. Religious houses. (Victoria county history, 1907, vol. 2, p. 64–163.) R. 9. 41 *s*

1080. BASKERVILLE, G., The dispossessed religious of Oxfordshire [at the time of the Suppression]. (Rept., Oxf. archaeol. soc., 1930, p. 327–47.) R. Top. 330

See 1150, 1154 [Religious houses, Lincoln diocese].
See 356 [Three lists of monasteries in 13th century. 1872].
See also Religious houses under the following places:

1777, 78 Bicester	2941, 42 Horton cum Studley
1955, &c. Burford	3129 A, B, 3130, 31 Littlemore
2162 Cogges	3231 Minster Lovell
2174–76 Cold Norton	3370, &c. Osney
2391, &c. Dorchester	3491 Sandford St. Martin
2542, &c. Eynsham	3865, &c. Thame
2615, &c. Godstow	4267 Wroxton.
2650, &c. Goring	

MEDIEVAL ARCHDEACONRY

Oxfordshire was an archdeaconry in the diocese of Lincoln until 1546, when the diocese of Oxford was founded. For works on this medieval archdeaconry see:

362A The Registrum antiquissimum of the Cathedral church of Lincoln.
1107 History of the diocese of Lincoln, by Venables and Perry.
1113 Lincoln diocese documents, 1450–1544.
1150 Visitations of religious houses in the diocese of Lincoln, 1420–49.
1154 Visitations in the diocese of Lincoln, 1517–31.
1182 Liber antiquus de ordinationibus vicariarum, 1209–35.
1183, 84 Rotuli Hugonis de Welles, 1209–35.
1185 Subsidy collected in the diocese of Lincoln, 1526.
1186 Rotuli Roberti Grosseteste, 1235–53.
1191 Rotuli Ricardi Gravesend, 1258–79.
1192A The rolls and register of bishop Oliver Sutton, 1280–99.

DIOCESE AND ARCHDEACONRY

General History

1081. SECKER, T., bp. of Oxford, Notice . . . that the bishop will confirm at the places, and on the days following. . . . n. pl., 1738, s. sh. Gough Eccl. top. 82 (14)

1082. [Volumes of miscellaneous circulars, notices, &c., 1804–.] G.A. Oxon b. 127, c. 114

1083. Oxford diocesan calendar and clergy list. 1858–. Oxf., 1858–, 8°. Cal. 11126 e. 150

1084. The diocese of Oxford and its management . . . by an Oxfordshire idler. Lond., 1858, 4°. 32 pp. G.A. Oxon 4° 372 (3)

1085. 'An Oxfordshire idler', in a matter of fact point of view, by an Oxfordshire rustic. [An answer to The diocese of Oxford and its management.] London., 1858, 8°. 15 pp. G.A. Oxon 8° 70 (10)

1086. PAYNE, E., A letter to the Church laity of the rural deanery of Deddington [in reply to the Oxfordshire idler]. Oxf., 1858, 8°. 23 pp. G.A. Oxon 4° 372 (6)

1087. WILSON, J. H., Thoughts on church matters in the diocese of Oxford, by a layman and magistrate for that county [J. H. Wilson]. Lond., 1858, 4°. 34 pp. G.A. Oxon 4° 372 (2)
— 2nd ed. 1858. 100 f. 76 (9)

1088. Further thoughts upon the diocese of Oxford, with especial reference to Cuddesdon college, in reply to mr. Twopeny, by an Oxfordshire idler. Lond., 1858, 8°. 25 pp. 100 f. 76 (10)

1089. Counter-thoughts on Church matters in the diocese of Oxford, a letter by a clergyman of that diocese. With observations on Some remarks on the visitation of Cuddesdon college by R. Twopeny. Lond. [1858], 8°. 59 pp. 100 f. 76 (12)

1090. GOLIGHTLY, C. P., Facts and documents, shewing the alarming state of the diocese of Oxford, by a senior clergyman of the diocese [C. P. Golightly]. Lond., 1859, 4°. 40 pp. G.A. Oxon 4° 372 (7)

1091. An examination of 'Facts and documents, shewing the alarming state of the diocese of Oxford', by one who has a regard for truth. Oxf., 1859, 8° 10 pp. G.A. Oxon 8° 1130* (15)

1092. CUST, A. P. PUREY-, A letter addressed to the author of 'Facts and documents shewing the alarming state of the diocese of Oxford'. Oxf., &c., 1859, 8°. 8 pp. G.A. Oxon 8° 179 (14)

1093. ISHAM, A., A letter to archdeacon Clerke by . . . A. Isham . . . stating his reasons for refusing to sign the address of Feb. 25th, in reference to . . . 'Facts and documents, &c.' [With the Address]. (Oxf., 1859), 4°. 13 pp. G.A. Oxon 4° 372 (8)

1094. LITTON, E. A., Address to the bishop of Oxford of . . . E. A. Litton and other clergymen of the diocese, together with his lordship's reply. n. pl., (1859), 8°. 16 pp. G.A. Oxon 8° 403

1095. To the . . . bishop of Oxford [a petition by certain clergy of the diocese protesting against a 'Romanizing' tendency in the diocese]. n. pl. [1859], s. sh. 11126 e. 408 (10)

1096. To the . . . bishop of Oxford [a letter refuting the accusations of 'Romanizing' made in Facts and documents. Signed by the archdeacons of Oxford, Bucks, and Berks, and by 24 rural deans. Mar. 1. *With* The Bishop's answer]. n. pl., (1859), fol. 4 pp.
G. Pamph. 2839 (9).

1097. TUCKER, J., A letter to the lord bishop of Oxford; a rejoinder to his reply to the address of E. A. Litton, and other clergymen of the diocese. Lond., 1859, 4°. 17 pp. G.A. Oxon 4° 372 (12)

1098. An impartial account of the recent agitation in the diocese of Oxford, with the addresses to the bishop, and his lordship's replies. Lond., 1859, 4°. 34 pp.   G.A. Oxon 4° 372 (9)

1099. BULL, H., Some remarks upon the remonstrance . . . to the arch-deacons . . . of the diocese of Oxford, a letter to W. R. Fremantle. Oxf., &c., 1859, 4°. 14 pp.   G.A. Oxon 4° 372 (10)

1100. FREMANTLE, W. R., Reasons for signing the remonstrance . . . to the archdeacons . . . of the diocese of Oxford, a reply to H. Bull. Oxf., &c., 1859, 4°. 16 pp.   G.A. Oxon 4° 372 (11)

1101. A watchman's remarks upon . . . 'Thoughts on church matters in the diocese of Oxford, by a layman and magistrate of that county'. Lond., 1859, 8°. 16 pp.   100 f. 81
See also 2275, &c. [Cuddesdon college].

1102. Oxford diocesan conference. [Reports of committees, &c. 1873–1909.]   G.A. Oxon 4° 557

1103. Oxford diocesan conference. Minutes. 1874–1931. (Oxf., 1874–1931), 8°.   GA. Oxon 8° 618

1104. Oxford diocesan conference, 1878. Ceremonial regulation. Paper read by . . . J. G. Hubbard. Lond., 1878, 8°. 16 pp.
G.A. Oxon 8° 199 (25)

1105. MARSHALL, E., Oxford. (Diocesan histories.) Lond., 1882, 12°. 302 pp.   111 f. 58

1106. The Oxford diocesan gazette. 1890, 91. Oxf., 1891, 92, 4°.
Per. G.A. Oxon 4° 143

1107. VENABLES, E., and PERRY, G. G., Lincoln. (Diocesan histories.) Lond., &c., 1897, 8°. 371 pp.   111 f. 55

1108. Oxford diocesan missionary loan exhibition and sale of work, in connection with the C.M.S. centenary. Oxf., 1899, 8°. 132 pp.
G.A. Oxon 8° 848

1109. Oxford diocesan magazine. 1902–. Oxf., 1902–, 8°.
Per. 11126 d. 78

1110. CLAYTON, H. E., The division of the diocese. (Oxf. diocesan mag., 1906/8, vol. 3, 89–91, 104–07, 250–53.)   Per. 11126 d. 78

1111. Division of the diocese of Oxford, a letter from the bishop of Oxford to members of the Diocesan conference. Oxf., 1912, 8°. 8 pp.
G.A. Oxon 8° 850 (21)

1112. Church finance, report of the advisory committee appointed by the Diocesan conference. [Oxf., 1912], 4°. 16 pp.
G.A. Oxon 4° 403 (2)

1113. CLARK, A., *ed.*, Lincoln diocese documents, 1450–1544, with notes and indexes. (E.E.T.S., no. 149.) Lond., 1914, 8°. 382 pp.
E. 2. 96 (149)

1114. Our diocese. No. 1–. Oxf., 1936–, 8°. Per. 11126 d. 180

1115. PHILIP, I. G., Diocesan records in the Bodleian library. (Geneal. mag., 1939, vol. 8, p. 7–9.) Soc. 2183 e. 10
See 2302 [Culham diocesan training college].
See 2410, &c. [Dorchester missionary college].

Diocesan Boards and Societies

1116. Oxford diocesan assoc. in aid of the Church missionary soc. 1st–82nd report. Oxf., 1826–1907, 8°. [The Bodleian set is imperf.]
G.A. Oxon 8° 483

Oxford diocesan assoc. of schoolmasters.
See under Education, 919.

Oxford diocesan assoc. of voluntary schools.
See under Education, 937, 942.

1117. Oxford diocesan board. Sixth report. Oxf., 1918, 8°. 29 pp.
G.A. Oxon 4° 399A (11)

Oxford diocesan board of education.
See under Education, 916, 920, 926, 27, 930.

1118. Oxford diocesan board (of finance). Reports and statement of accounts of the diocesan fund, the four diocesan societies, and other diocesan organisations, which receive grants from the diocesan fund. 1917–. Oxf., 1918–, 8°. [The Bodleian has 1917, 1923, and 1947–.] G.A. Oxon 8° 986

1119.

1120. Oxford diocesan board of missions. Report. 1904–24. Windsor, &c., 1904–24, 8°. Per. 133 e. 318

1121. Diocesan society for the increase of church accommodation and of the number of parsonage houses within the diocese of Oxford. The rules, proceedings and list of subscribers. [1848–78.] Oxf., 1849–79, 8°. [Contd. in 1133.] G.A. Oxon 8° 492, 494

1122. Oxford diocesan church building society. [Summary of operations, 1847 to 1889.] G.A. Oxon 4° 268

1123. Oxford diocesan church mission to the deaf and dumb. First (–third) annual report. Oxf., 1899–1901, 8°. G.A. Oxon 8° 680

1124. Oxford diocesan church societies. [Account.] Oxf., 1896, 8°. 7 pp.
G.A. Oxon 4° 268

1125. Oxford diocesan clergy sustentation fund. Objects, funds . . .
statement of accounts. 1897. n. pl., 1897, 4°. 2 pp.   1229 d. 4

1126. Oxford diocesan guild of church bell-ringers. 1st(–23rd) annual
report. Reading, 1881–1904, 8°. [The Bodleian set is imperf.]
Per. 1743 e. 27

1127. Oxford diocesan missionary candidates' association. [Aims and
Rules.] (Oxf.), 1867, 8°. 4 pp.   G.A. Oxon 4° 268

1128. Oxford diocesan missionary candidates' association. Second
(–sixtieth) report. Oxf., (1870–1927), 8°.   G.A. Oxon 8° 518

1129. Oxford diocesan missionary union. Report. 1903. Windsor, 1903,
8°.   Per. 133 e. 296

1130. Oxford diocesan prize assoc. 1st(–17th) annual report. Oxf.,
1859–75, 8°. [The Bodleian set is imperf.]   G.A. Oxon 8° 616

1131. Oxford diocesan social service committee. Report. 1908, 09, 12.
Lond. &c., (1908–12), 8°.   G.A. Oxon 8° 1152

1132. Oxford diocesan society.
— 2nd, 12th report.   G.A. Oxon c. 59 (130, 145)
— 3rd, 6th report.   G.A. Oxon c. 107 (100, 101)
    Oxf., 1834–43, fol.

1133. Reports of the Diocesan church building, Education and Spiritual
help societies [afterw.] Three diocesan (church) societies [afterw.]
Four diocesan societies, and General fund (and the church ele-
mentary schools assoc.) [afterw.] Bishop of Oxford's fund and
Four diocesan societies. 1879–1911. Oxf., 1880–1912, 8°.
Soc. G.A. Oxon 8° 494

1134. Oxford diocesan societies. Agenda paper for the quarterly meeting. 1876–91. Oxf., 1876–91, 8°.   G.A. Oxon 8° 478

1135. The Oxford diocesan general fund in support of the diocesan
societies and for the maintenance and building of mission and parish
rooms. Report for 1888. Oxf., 1889, 8°. 9 pp.
G.A. Oxon 8° 761 (24)

1136. GARRY, N. T., The (four) diocesan societies. (Oxf. diocesan mag.,
1904/5, vol. 2, p. 265–67.)   Per. 11126 d. 78

1137. JOHNSTON, J. O., The funds of the diocesan societies. (Oxf.
diocesan mag., 1908/9, vol. 4, p. 2–5.)   Per. 11126 d. 78

1138. Oxford diocesan spiritual help society. [Foundation rules &c.]
Oxf., 1857, 4°. 2 pp.   G.A. Oxon c. 73 (163)

1139. Oxford diocesan spiritual help society. Report. 1858–78. Oxf.,
1859–79, 8°. [Contd. in 1133.]   G.A. Oxon 8° 493

1140. Oxford diocesan Sunday school association. Occasional paper. No. 1. Oxf., 1911, 8°. 24 pp.   G.A. Oxon 8° 850 (35)

1141. Oxford diocesan Sunday school assoc. Sunday school festival, 1927. Official handbook, with daily programme. Oxf. (1927), 8°. 80 pp.   G.A. Oxon 8° 1055 (2)

Oxford diocesan training college for mistresses.
See under Education, 931.

1142. Oxfordshire society for promoting the education of the children of the poor in the principles of the established Church. [Proceedings of a meeting held March 7, 1833.] n. pl. (1833), 4°. 4 pp.
                    G.A. Oxon c. 49 (119)

1143. Oxfordshire society for promoting the education of the children of the poor in the principles of the established Church. First report. n. pl. [1834], s. sh.   G.A. Oxon c. 50 (118 b)
— 8th report. 1840.   G.A. Oxon c. 114 (3)

1144. Society for augmenting small benefices in the diocese of Oxford. First(–35th) report. Eton, &c., 1862–96, 8°. [Contd. in 1133. The Bodleian set is imperf.]   G.A. Oxon 8° 491

1145. The Young men's Union for the diocese of Oxford. Report of the committee appointed by the Diocesan conference of 1878, with additions. Oxf., 1879, 8°. 35 pp.   G.A. Oxon 8° 850 (34)

Ecclesiastical Visitations and Courts

1146. Oxford diocese. Visitation articles.

1604.	Vet. A 2 e. 74
1619.	4° E 2 (8) Art. BS.
1622.	Wood 516 (18)
1628.	Vet. A 2 e. 82
1629.	Vet. A 2 e. 84
1632.	Vet. A 2 e. 89
1635.	Vet. A 2 e. 94
1638.	Vet. A 2 e. 100
1662.	Wood 516 (10)
1666.	C 8. 22 (2) Linc.
1672.	C 8. 22 (26) Linc.
1679.	C 8. 22 (19) Linc.
1682.	B.M.
1781.	G.A. Oxon 4° 42 (4)
1838.	G.A. fol. A 133 (10)
1842.	G.A. fol. A 133 (9)

1147. TURNER, W. H., On the Ecclesiastical court-books of the diocese of Oxford. (Proc., Oxf. architect. and hist soc., N.S., vol. 3, 1873, p. 130–38.)   R. 13. 709

1148. Articles of inquiry . . . at the visitation of the . . . archdeacon of Oxford in . . . 1877. Bicester, (1877), fol. 5 pp.

G.A. Oxon c. 11

1149. Peculiars in Oxfordshire. (Oxf. diocesan mag., 1906/8, vol. 3, p. 491–93.)   Per. 11126 d. 78

1150. Visitations of religious houses in the diocese of Lincoln, 1420–(49), ed. by A. H. Thompson. Vol. 1–3. (Lincoln record soc., vol. 7, 14, 21.) Lincoln, 1914–29, 4°.   R. Top. 260
— [Another issue.] (Cant. and York soc., vol. 17, 24, 33.) Lond., 1915–27, 4°.   R. 8. 26

1151. Churchwarden's presentments, 1520 [ed. H. E. Salter]. (Rept., Oxf. archaeol. soc., 1925, p. 75–117.)   R. Top. 330

1152. PEYTON, S. A., The Churchwardens' presentments in the Oxfordshire peculiars of Dorchester, Thame and Banbury. (Oxf. record soc., 10.) [Oxf.], 1928, 8°. 340 pp.   R. 13. 702

1153. SALTER, H. E., ed., A visitation of Oxfordshire in 1540. (Rept., Oxf. archaeol. soc., 1930, p. 289–307.)   R. Top. 330

1154. Visitations in the diocese of Lincoln, 1517–1531, ed. by A. H. Thompson. Vol. 1–3. (Lincoln record soc., vol. 33, 35, 37.) Lincoln, 1940–47, 4°.   R. Top. 260

1155. BRINKWORTH, E. R., ed., The archdeacon's court, liber actorum, 1584. 2 vols. (Oxf. record soc., 23, 24.) Oxf., 1942, 46, 8°.

R. 13. 702

1156. BRINKWORTH, E. R., The study and use of archdeacons' court records: illustrated from the Oxford records, 1566–1759. (Trans., Roy. hist. soc., 1943, 4th ser., vol. 25, p. 93–119.)

Soc. 2262 e. 45

1157. [Answers of the clergy to printed questionnaires circulated by the bishops of Oxford before holding visitations, giving information about residence of incumbents, church services, dissenters, schools, charities and population, from 1738 onwards are to be found in the Bodleian collection of MSS. Oxf. Dioc. papers.]

See 2398 [Austin canons, Dorchester].
See 3865 [Thame monastery. 1526].

Benefices and Incumbents

1158. Valor beneficiorum, or, A valuation of all ecclesiastical preferments in England and Wales. (Oxford diocese, p. 241–47.) Lond., 1695, 12°.   Gough Eccl. top. 8

1159. CALAMY, E., An abridgment of mr. Baxter's History of his life and times. With an account of many others of those worthy ministers who were ejected after the Restauration of king Charles the

second . . . and a continuation of their history till . . . 1691. (Oxfordshire, p. 335, 36, &c.). Lond., 1702, 8°. 8° D 249 BS.
— 2nd ed. . . . the continuation to 1711. (Oxfordshire, vol. 2, p. 540–
44, &c.) Lond., 1713, 8°. Tanner 780

1160. CALAMY, E., A continuation of the account of the ministers,
lecturers . . . who were ejected and silenced after the Restoration in
1660, by or before the Act for uniformity. (Oxfordshire, vol. 2,
p. 704–20.) Lond., 1727, 8°. 11123 e. 28

1161. CALAMY, E., The Nonconformist's memorial: being an account
of the ministers who were ejected or silenced after the Restoration
. . . now abridged and corrected by S. Palmer. [A recast of Calamy's
Abridgment.] (Oxfordshire, vol. 2, passim.) Lond., 1775, 8°. B.M.
— 2nd ed. 1777. B.M.
— [Another issue.] 1778. 210 n. 238
— [Another ed.] 1802, 03. 11123 e. 23

1162. CALAMY, E., Calamy revised, by A. G. Matthews. (Oxfordshire,
passim.) Oxf., 1934, 8°. R. 3. 54

1163. ECTON, J., Liber valorum et decimarum, an account of the
valuations and yearly tenths of such ecclesiastical benefices in England and Wales, as now stand charged with, or lately were discharged from the payment of tenths. (Oxfordshire, p. 284–90.)
Lond., 1711, 8°. 8° Rawl. 449
— 2nd ed. 1723. 8° Z 54 Jur.
— 3rd ed. 1728. 8° H 103 Linc.

1164. LLOYD, J., Thesaurus ecclesiasticus, an improved edition of the
Liber valorum et decimarum [of J. Ecton]. (Oxford diocese, p. 285–
90.) n. pl., 1791, 8°. 1229 e. 57

1165. ECTON, J., A state of the . . . bounty of queen Anne, for the
augmentation of the maintenance of the poor clergy, 1704 to 1718.
Lond., 1719, 8°. B.M.
— 2nd ed. to 1720. (Oxfordshire, p. 227, 28.) Lond., 1721, 8°.
8° Z 55 Jur.

1166. ECTON, J., Thesaurus rerum ecclesiasticarum, an account of the
valuations of . . . benefices in the dioceses . . . of England and Wales.
(Oxford diocese, p. 467–81.) Lond., 1742, 4°.
G.A. Eccl. top. 4° 54
— 2nd ed. 1754. Gough Eccl. top. 61

1167. WALKER, J., An attempt towards recovering an account of the
numbers and sufferings of the clergy of the Church of England . . .
in the late grand rebellion. (Oxfordshire, passim.) Lond., 1744, fol.
G. 2. 15 Jur.
— Epitomised. 1862. 110 k. 615
— Abridged by R. Whittaker. 1863. 110 k. 620

1168. WALKER, J., Walker revised, by A. G. Matthews. (Oxfordshire, p. 295–301.) Oxf., 1948, 8°.   R. 3. 53 *m*

1169. BATEMAN, T., The royal ecclesiastical gazetteer, an alphabetical list of all the livings . . . in the gift of the king [&c.]. (Oxford diocese, p. 91, 92.) Lond., [1774], 12°.   Gough Eccl. top. 37 (1)

1170. BATEMAN, T., The ecclesiastical patronage of the Church of England. (Oxfordshire, p. 209, 10.) Lond., 1783, 12°.
Gough Eccl. top. 37 (2)

1171. BACON, J., Liber regis vel thesaurus rerum ecclesiasticarum. (Oxford diocese, p. 785–809.) Lond., 1786, 4°.
Gough Eccl. top. 60

1172. Taxatio ecclesiastica Angliæ et Walliæ auctoritate p. Nicholai iv circa 1290. (Oxfordshire, *passim.*) [Lond.], 1802, fol.
R. 5. fol. 133

1173. Nonarum inquisitiones in curia scaccarii, temp. Edwardi iii. (Oxfordshire, p. 132–42.) [Lond.], 1807, fol.   R. 5. fol. 138

1174. Valor ecclesiasticus temp. Henr. viii. Vol. 2. (Oxfordshire, p. 159–66.) [Lond.], 1814, fol.   R. 5. fol. 139

1175. Papers relating to queen Anne's bounty, and to parliamentary grants for the augmentation of the maintenance of the poor clergy, 1703–1815. (Oxford diocese, p. 97, 98.)   Pp. Eng. 1814/15, vol. 12

1176. Report of the commissioners appointed . . . to inquire into the ecclesiastical revenues of England and Wales. (Oxford diocese, p. 774–91.)   Pp. Eng. 1835, vol. 22

1177. A return of the net annual revenue of each of the several . . . ecclesiastical benefices in England and Wales, on an average three years ending 31st Dec., 1831, of a clear annual income of £250 and upwards [&c.]. (Oxford diocese, p. 78–80.)   Pp. Eng. 1837, vol. 41

1178. Returns of all tithes commuted and apportioned under the act 6 & 7 Will. 4 c. 71 distinguishing between those assigned to clerical appropriators, lay appropriators, parochial incumbents, schools and colleges. And, of all tithes commuted but not yet apportioned. (Oxford diocese, p. 144–46, 286, 87.)   Pp. Eng. 1847/8, vol. 49
— 1856, p. 34, 35.   Pp. Eng. 1856, vol. 46

1179. Vicarages and curacies . . . Return from the registrars of each diocese in England and Wales of all augmentations granted to poor vicarages and curacies . . . (Oxford diocese, p. 8–11.)
Pp. Eng. 1866, vol. 55

1180. Return of all glebe lands . . . showing parishes in which they are respectively situate, and the estimated annual value of the respective glebes. (Oxford diocese, p. 116–23.)   Pp. Eng. 1887, vol. 64

1181. Tithes commutation. Return of all tithes commuted and apportioned under the acts for the commutation of tithes distinguishing
between those assigned to clerical appropriators and their lessees,
lay impropriators, parochial incumbents, and schools, colleges, &c.
... to 1887. (Oxfordshire, p. 160–63.)   Pp. Eng. 1887, vol. 64

1182. GIBBONS, A., ed., Liber antiquus de ordinationibus vicariarum
tempore Hugonis Wells, Lincolniensis episcopi, 1209–1235. (Oxfordshire, p. 1–11.) (Linc. record ser., 2.) Lincoln, 1888, 8°.
Soc. G.A. Lincs 8° 88 (2)

1183. Rotuli Hugonis de Welles, 1209–1235. Vol. 2. Institutions in the
archdeaconry of Oxford. (Cant. and York soc., 1907, vol. 3, p. 1–47.)
R. 8. 26
— [Another issue.] (Lincoln record soc., 1913, vol. 6, p. 1–47.)
R. Top. 260

1184. Rotuli Hugonis de Welles, 1209–1235. Vol. 1. Vicarages ordained
in the archdeaconry of Oxford. (Cant. and York soc., 1909, vol. 1,
p. 177–84.)   R. 8. 26
— [Another issue.] (Lincoln record soc., 1912, vol. 3, p. 177–84.)
R. Top. 260

1185. SALTER, H., ed., A subsidy collected in the diocese of Lincoln in
1526. (Oxford diocese, p. xi–xvi, 249–86.) Oxf., &c., 1909, 4°.
G.A. Lincs 8° 123
— [Another issue.] (O.H.S., vol. 63.)   R. 13. 700
— [Repr. of pt. 4.] Bucks and Oxon.   G.A. Oxon 4° 284

1186. Rotuli Roberti Grosseteste, 1235–1253. Institutions, Archdeaconry of Oxford. (Cant. and York soc., 1913, vol. 10, p. 443–
507.)   R. 8. 26
— [Another issue.] (Lincoln record soc., 1914, vol. 11, p. 443–507.)
R. Top. 260

1187. A certificate of the Oxford clergy, 1593 [ed. by S. S. Pearce].
(Rept., Oxf. archaeol. soc., 1913, p. 145–70.)   R. Top. 330

1188. PEEL, A., ed., A seconde parte of a register, being a calendar of
manuscripts under that title intended for publication by the Puri-
tans about 1593. (A survaie of the state of the ministerie in Oxfordshire, 1586, p. 130–42.) Cambr., 1915, 4°.   258876 d. 13, 14

1189. PEARCE, S. S., The clergy of the rural deanery of Oxford and of
the peculiar of Newington with Britewell, at the time of the settlement of 1559 and afterwards. (Rept., Oxf. archaeol. soc., 1919,
p. 198–234.)   R. Top. 330
See 4101 [Clergy. Deaneries of Witney and Bicester. 1914].
See 2881 [Clergy. Deaneries of Henley and Aston. 1918].

1190. GRAHAM, R., *ed.*, The chantry certificates (Oxfordshire, 1548). (Oxf. record soc., vol. 1, p. 1–56.) Oxf., 1919, 8°. R. 13. 702
— [Another ed.] (Alcuin club collections, 23.) Lond., &c., 1920, 8°. Soc. 137 d. 38 (23)

1191. Rotuli Ricardi Gravesend, 1258–1279. Institutions, archdeaconry of Oxford. (Lincoln record soc., 1925, vol. 20, p. 213–35.) R. Top. 260
— [Another issue.] (Cant. and York soc., 1925, vol. 31, p. 213–35.) R. 8. 26

1192. COPE, E. E., Chantries of Oxfordshire. [Quest of the donors.] (N. & Q., 1928, Dec. 29, p. 458, 59.) Ψ 2. 97

1192A. The rolls and register of bishop Oliver Sutton, 1280–1299, ed. by R. M. T. Hill. Vol. 1, 2 . (Lincoln record soc., vol. 39, 43 .) Lincoln, 1948, 1950 , 4°. R. Top. 260

See 873, 74 [Charities, widows and orphans of clergy. 1770, 1803].
See 2116 [Chipping Norton vicarage in 1683. 1945].
See 3362 [Diary of a parish rector, Nuneham Courtenay. 1945].
For works on tithes see also:
  2022 [Charlbury. 1842].
  4021 [Wickham. Auction catal. 1806].

Parishes and Churches

1193. Church rates. Abstract of . . . return of every church rate . . . within the last two years, in every parish. (Oxford diocese, p. 186–92.) Pp. Eng. 1845, vol. 41

1194. Church rates. A return from each parish . . . setting forth the gross amount expended during the last seven years for church purposes. (Oxford diocese, p. 186–91.) Pp. Eng. 1859, vol. 20

1195. Local taxation returns. Return of all sums received in respect of church or chapel rates for 12 months terminating at Easter, 1862. (Oxford diocese, p. 190–97.) Pp. Eng. 1863, vol. 30
— 1864, p. 172–87. Pp. Eng. 1865, vol. 46
— 1866, p. 152–60. Pp. Eng. 1867, vol. 58

For works on Church accounts see also:
  3186 [Marston, Spelsbury, Pyrton. Churchwarden's accounts. 1925].
  3642 [Spelsbury. Churchwarden's account. 1910].
  3801 [Swyncombe. Churchwarden's accounts. 1910].
  3867 [Thame. Proctors and stewards accounts. 1852].
  3874 [Thame. Churchwarden's accounts. 1902–14].

1196. A return of all parishes . . . in which any new portion of ground has been consecrated to serve as a churchyard during the last thirty years. (Oxford diocese, p. 43.) Pp. Eng. 1863, vol. 46
— during the last ten years. (Oxford diocese, p. 21–23.) Pp. Eng. 1873, vol. 52

— since the return in 1863. (Oxford diocese, p. 27–29.)
Pp. Eng. 1877, vol. 66

1197. New parishes and church building acts, &c. . . . Returns of parishes divided and districts assigned to churches under the . . . Church building acts . . . by the Ecclesiastical commissioners for England since the 31st . . . October 1866 [&c.] (Oxford diocese, p. 92.) Pp. Eng. 1870, vol. 54

1198. Church building and restoration. Returns showing the number of churches (including cathedrals) in every diocese . . . built or restored at a cost exceeding £500 since . . . 1840. (Oxford diocese, p. 49–55.) Pp. Eng. 1876, vol. 58

1199. BAVERSTOCK, E. P., Church bells. (Oxfordshire, *passim*.) (Oxf. diocesan mag., 1926, vol. 20, p. 173–77, 189–93.)
Per. 11126 d. 78

1200. SHARPE, F., The Church bells of Oxfordshire. Vol. 1, 2, 3, 4. (Oxf. record soc., 28, 30, 32, 34). Oxf., 1949–53, 8°. 112 pp.
R. 13. 702

For works on Church bells see also:
1652 [Banbury. 1901].
1785 [Bicester deanery. 1932].
2216 [Rules, Cowley parish church ringers. 1874].
2837 [Henley bell ringers, rules. 1857].
3652 [Standlake bell ringers club. 1890].
3829 [Tadmarton. 1898].
3869, 70 [Thame. 1876].

1201. PRIOR, C. E., Dedications of churches, with some notes as to village feasts and old customs. Deaneries of Islip and Bicester. (Rept., Oxf. archaeol. soc., 1903, p. 20–42.)
— Woodstock, Deddington & Witney. (1904, p. 23–53.)
— Chipping Norton, Cuddesdon, Oxford. (1905, p. 11–25.)
— Aston and Henley. (1906, p. 14–22.) R. Top. 330

1202. KIRK, K. E., Church dedications of the Oxford diocese. Oxf., 1946, 8°. 92 pp. G.A. Oxon 8° 1206

1203. STAPLETON, B. J., An inventory of the church plate in the deanery of Oxford, with notes. (Trans., Oxf. archaeol. soc., 34.) Banbury, 1896, 8°. 44 pp. R. Top. 330

1204. HONE, N. Oxfordshire church goods. (Berks, Bucks, & Oxon archaeol. journ., 1897, vol. 3, p. 29, 30, 52, 53; 1898, vol. 4, p. 75–77; 1899, vol. 5, p. 27, 28, 48, 49; 1900, vol. 6, p. 52, 53, 73; 1902, vol. 8, p. 86, 87; 1903, vol. 9, p. 71–73; 1904, vol. 10, p. 58, 59.)
R. Top. 100

1205. GRAHAM, R., *ed.*, The Edwardian inventories of church goods (for Oxfordshire). (Oxf. record soc., vol. 1, p. 57–147.) Oxf., 1919, 8°. R. 13. 702

1206. EVANS, J. T., The church plate of Oxfordshire. Oxf., 1928, 4°. 223 pp. 1371 d. 27

For works on Church goods and plate see also:
3109 [Little Faringdon chalice. 1882].
4099 [Witney. 1890].
4251 [Woodstock. 1894].
See also 1299, &c. Architecture and allied arts.

DISSENT

General

1207. FERGUSON, W., Spiritual ruin and practical Romanism in the diocese of Oxford. Lond., &c. 1849, 8°. 31 pp. 49. 1978

1208. HASSALL, W. O., Dissent at Aston Rowant, Kingston Blount, Crowell and Chinnor. (Thame Gazette, Jan. 30, 1951.)
N.G.A. Oxon a. 120

Protestant

For editions of Calamy's Abridgment, &c., see 1159, &c.

1209. TURNER, G. L., ed., Original records of early nonconformity under persecution and indulgence. [Contains the classified summary of meeting houses of the 17th century in vol. 2, p. 826–30, vol. 3, p. 829–36; and the Episcopal return of conventicles, 1669 in vol. 3, p. 823–28, &c.] Lond., 1911, 14, 8°. 11123 d. 6, 7, 7 a

See 1659 [Defence of non-belief in divine authority of Bible. 18—].

1210. Oxford and district free church magazine. Vol. 1, no. 1–vol. 22, no. 267. Oxf., 1897–1919, 4°. G.A. Oxon 4° 195

See 1660 [Free Church Leader. Banbury. 1899].

1211. SUMMERS, W. H., History of the Congregational churches in the Berks, South Oxon and South Bucks association, with notes on the earlier Non-conformist history of the district. Newbury, 1905, 8°. 331 pp. 11136 e. 17

See 4087 [Witney congregational church. 1935].
See 1828 [Presbyterians of Bloxham and Milton. 1920].
See 3976 [Weston on the Green, Methodist church centenary. 1938].

1212. Oxfordshire association of Baptist churches. The Christian law of love, the circular letter from the ministers and messengers of the Baptist churches in the Oxfordshire Association, assembled . . . June 20th and 21st, 1848. Chipping-Norton, 1848, 8°. 16 pp.
11135 e. 27 (6)

1213. Oxfordshire association of Baptist churches. Family religion in relation to Church life, the circular letter from the ministers and messengers of the Baptist churches of the Oxfordshire association. To which are added: Breviates of the 85th meeting . . . [and] extracts from letters. Oxf., 1887, 8°. 23 pp. G.A. Oxon 8° 761 (25)

1214. Oxfordshire association of Baptist churches. 'The priestly ministry of the Church', the presidential address, May 31st and June 1st, 1904, with the breviates of the 102nd meeting . . . and brief extracts from the letters of the churches, and statistics for the year 1903–1904. Stow-on-the-Wold, 1904, 8°. 25 pp.   11135 e. 94 (3)

1215. Oxfordshire (and East Gloucestershire) Baptist assoc. 110th-annual report. Stow-on-the-Wold, 1912–, 8°.   Per. 11135 e. 88
See 2198 [Baptist church, Coate. 1936].

1215A. BESSE, J., A brief account of many of the prosecutions of the people call'd Quakers. (Oxfordshire, p. 98–101, 184.) [By J. Besse.] Lond., 1736, 8°.   G. Pamph. 73

1215B. An examination of . . . A brief account [by J. Besse] of many of the prosecutions of the . . . Quakers, so far as the clergy of the dioceses of Oxford, Glocester and Chester are concerned in it. Lond., 1740, 8°.   B.M.

1215C. A vindication of . . . A brief account of many of the prosecutions of the . . . Quakers, in answer to a late Examination thereof. (Oxford diocese, p. 6–24.) Lond., 1740, 8°.   G. Pamph. 894 (4)

1216. BRAITHWAITE, W. C., The first planting of Quakerism in Oxfordshire, a lecture. Banbury, 1908, 8°. 18 pp.
      G.A. Oxon 8° 900 (32)

1217. FOX, S., and PICKARD, E., The hat crusade. Vol. 1. [An account of the refusal by certain Quakers to remove their hats in church. Charlbury (where Fox lived for a time) and Witney churches are particularly mentioned.] Flushing, Cornw., 1896, 8°.   11141 e. 8

See 1656–1658 [Quakers at Banbury. 1655, 1702, 03].
See 2030 [Quaker community, Charlbury. 1942].

ROMAN CATHOLIC (POST REFORMATION)

1218. Recusants in Oxfordshire, 1603–1633 [ed. by H. E. Salter]. (Rept., Oxf. archaeol. soc.. 1924, p. 7–71.)   R. Top. 330

1219. The English Catholic non-jurors of 1715, a summary of the register of their estates, ed. by E. E. Estcourt and J. O. Payne. (Oxfordshire, p. 211–18.) Lond., &c., (1885), 8°.   11131 d. 1

1220. Records of the English Catholics of 1715, ed. by J. O. Payne. (Oxfordshire, p. 50, 51.) Lond., &c., 1889, 8°.   11131 d. 2

1221. STAPLETON, MRS. B., A history of the post-reformation Catholic missions in Oxfordshire. Lond., 1906, 8°. 371 pp.   11127 d. 8

1222. The martyrs of Oxfordshire, by students of Heythrop college. (Cath. truth soc.) Lond., (1933), 8°. 32 pp.

G.A. Oxon 8° 1184 (15)

1223. HASSALL, W. O., Papists in early eighteenth-century Oxfordshire. (Oxoniensia, 1948, vol. 13, p. 76–82.) R. Top. 340

See 1662, &c. [Dispute between G. Harris and W. Tandy. 1838].
See 1674 [Letter to inhabitants of Banbury in defence of Roman Catholicism. 1856].
See 1675 [Catholicity in Banbury. 1898].
See 3128 [Newman and Littlemore. 1945].
See 3762 [Stonor. Catholic sanctuary. 1951].

BIOGRAPHY, GENEALOGY, AND HERALDRY

BIOGRAPHY AND GENEALOGY

1224. FULLER, T., The history of the worthies of England. [Arranged by counties in alphabetical order. Oxfordshire, 21 pp.] Lond., 1662, fol.   Gough Gen. top. 138
— [Another ed.] 2 vols. 1811.   R. 9. 20
— New ed., with notices of worthies since the time of Fuller, by dr. Nuttall. 3 vols. 1840.   40. 893–95

1225. A true copy of the last will and testament of James Leverett, late of Witney. [Concerns Witney, Hailey, Standlake, Bampton, Curbridge, Minster Lovell, Crawley and Ducklington.] n. pl., (1783), 8°. 12 pp.   G.A. Oxon 8° 364

1226. Oxfordshire, history, eminent natives. (Gent's. mag., 1820, pt. 2, p. 497–502.) Ψ 2. 44

1227. PHILLIPPS, SIR T., Additional particulars for the biography of three Oxfordshire writers. Geffrey of Monmouth, Walter Map and Alexander de Swerford. (Mem. chiefly illustr. of the county and city of Oxford, Archaeol. inst., p. 91–100.) Lond., 1854, 8°.   G.A. Gen. top. 8° 528 (6)

1228. [Begin.] Who was the rev. John Horseman? [Signed W.] n. pl., [1872], s. sh.   G.A. Oxon 16° 33 (18)

1229. Deacon's . . . Oxfordshire court guide and county blue book. Lond., 1889, 8°.
— 2nd ed. 1890.   Dir. Gen. top. e. 1

1230. GATFIELD, G., Guide to printed books and manuscripts relating to . . . genealogy. (Oxfordshire, p. 171–74.) Lond., 1892, 8°.   R. 14. 309

1231. GASKELL, E., Oxfordshire leaders, social and political. Lond., [c. 1900], 4°.   G.A. Oxon 4° 249

1232. JEUNE, M. D., Pages from the diary of an Oxford lady [M. D. Jeune] 1843–1862, ed. by M. J. Gifford. Oxf., 1932, 4°. 141 pp.   G.A. Oxon 4° 511

1233. MANSFIELD, E., Famous women of Oxfordshire. [Ser. 1], 2. Oxf., [1932], 8°. 32 & 34 pp.   211 e. 697

1234. Who's who in Oxfordshire. Limited ed. (Who's who in the counties ser.) Lond., 1936, 4°. 396 pp.   G.A. Oxon 4° 567

1235. WINSTEDT, E. O., Sineta Lambourne and Sineta Smith [Oxfordshire gipsies]. (Journ., Gypsy lore soc., 1944, 3rd ser., vol. 23, p. 106–14.)   Per. 2471865 d. 11

1236. GRETTON, M. S., Re-cognitions [an autobiography]. Oxf., 1951, 8°. 155 pp.   211 e. 1244

See 272 [Oxfordshire pedigrees].
See also 1268, &c. [Pedigrees from visitations].

FAMILY HISTORIES

1237. GUPPY, H. B., Homes of family names. (Oxfordshire, p. 327–35.) Lond., 1890, 8°.   E. 1. 108

1237A. MARSHALL, G. W., The genealogist's guide. [Index of family pedigrees.] Guildford, 1903, 8°. 880 pp.   R. 14. 311

1238. WHITMORE, J. B., A genealogical guide. 3 pt. (Harleian soc., vol. 99, 101, 102.) [Suppl. to Marshall.] Lond., 1947–50, 4°.
                                                                                            Ψ 2. 11
Arsic family.
See 2163.

Babington family.
See 3016.

Barentine family.
See 2017, 18.

1239. BARTELOT, R. G., Our family surname (The Oxfordshire Bartelots, p. 38–40.) n. pl., 1944, 8°.   2182 B. d. 98

1240. SMITH, L. G. H. H., The Bayley family of . . . Oxon [&c.]. Repr. from Notes & queries for Somerset & Dorset. Sherborne, 1947, 8°. 10 pp.   2182 B. d. 99

Beazley family.
See 3271.

Blount family.
See 3058.

Brookes family.
See 3710.

Browne-Mostyn family.
See 3016.

Burford, Barony of.
See 1925.

Burrows family.
See 3809, 10.

Chaucer family.
See 2489.

Cornwall, family of.
See 1925 [Burford barony. 1868].

Cottrell-Dormer.
See Dormer.

1241. CROKE, SIR A., The genealogical history of the Croke family.
2 vols. Oxf., 1823, 4°.   4° BS. 815, 16
— [Another ed.] 1823.   2182 C. d. 50, 51

Curzon family.
See 3939.

Danvers family.
See 2169.

1242. TOWNSEND, J., The Oxfordshire Dashwoods. Oxf., 1922, 8°.
52 pp.   2182 D. d. 32

1243. DAVEY, E. C., Memoirs of an Oxfordshire old Catholic family [the
Daveys] and its connections from 1566 to 1897. Lond., (1897), 8°.
78 pp.   2182 D. e. 7

1244. ROUND, J. H., Note on the De la Pole pedigree. (Genealogist,
1886, new ser., vol. 3, p. 112.) Ψ 2. 10 i

De la Pole family.
See 2487, 2491.

1245. Visitation of Oxfordshire, 1668–9. Dormer. (Misc. geneal. et
heraldica, 1916/17, 5th ser., vol. 2, p. 201.) Ψ 2. 10 f

1246. MACLAGAN, M., The family of Dormer in Oxfordshire and
Buckinghamshire. (Oxoniensia, 1946–7, p. 90–101.)   R. Top. 340

Dormer [Cottrell-] family.
See 3451, 3456.

Druce family.
See 2636.

Dunkin family.
See 3198, 99.

Elers family.
See 1798.

Fermor family.
See 3585, 3587, 88.

1247. Visitation of Oxfordshire, 1668–9. Fettiplace. (Misc. geneal. et heraldica, 1916/17, 5th ser., vol. 2, p. 241.) Ψ 2. 10 f

Fettiplace family.
See 3733, 3794, 3795, 3802.

Fynmore family.
See 3031.

Giffard family.
See 3631.

Goodwin family.
See 2915.

1248. Visitation of Oxfordshire, 1668–9. Halloway pedigree. (Misc. geneal. et heraldica, 1916/17, 5th ser., vol. 2, p. 121.) Ψ 2. 10 f

Harcourt family.
See 3357.

1249. E., W. S., Pedigree of the family of Hord, of Salop, Oxon and Surrey. (Topogr. and geneal., 1846, vol. 1, p. 33–42.) Ψ 2. 10 b

Horde family.
See 1505.

1250. Pedigree of Hungerford of Wiltshire, Oxfordshire [&c.]. [Middlehill], 1855, s. sh.   Caps. 6. 47 (46)

Hungerford family.
See 1798.

Keck family.
See 2705.

Knollys family.
See 3434, 37, 38.

1251. [Knollys family.] The case of Charles [called 4th] earl of Banbury. n. pl., [1692?], s. sh.   Wood 276 b (74)

1252. KNOLLYS, W., called 8th earl of Banbury. Some remarks on the claim to the earldom of Banbury, by the present claimant. Lond., 1835, 8°. 57 pp.   21851 e. 9 (8)

1253. [Knollys family.] The true countess of Banbury's case relating to her marriage. Lond., 1696, fol. 34 pp.   Gough Oxf. 103 (16)

1254. [Knollys family.] PEARMAN, M. T., The Banbury peerage. (Genealogist, 1884, new ser., vol. 1, p. 42–45; 1885, new ser., vol. 2, p. 239.) Ψ 2. 10 i

1255. [Knollys family.] The petition of William, earl of Banbury . . . claiming the earldom of Banbury, with his majesty's reference thereof to the House of peers, and the report of his majesty's attorney general annexed. n. pl., 1808, fol. 56 pp.

G. Pamph. 1677 (18)

1256. LEE, F. G., Pedigree of the family of Lee, cos. Chester, Bucks, and Oxon. [With] Notes. n. pl., [1884], fol. 4+3 pp.

MS. Top. Bucks c. 1 (f. 162)

Lee family.

See 1415, 3855.

Lenthall family.

See 1955.

1257. Visitation of Oxfordshire, 1668–9. Lybbe and Napier. (Misc. geneal. et heraldica, 1918/19, 5th ser., vol. 3, p. 2, 3.) Ψ 2. 10f

1258. COOKE, A. H., The family of Meols. (Berks, Bucks, & Oxon archaeol. journ., 1929, vol. 33, notes, p. 49, 50.)   R. Top. 100

Napier family.

See Lybbe family, 1257.

1259. O'CONOR, N. J., Godes peace and the queenes, vicissitudes of a house [Norreys family of Weston on the Green], 1539–1615. Lond., 1934, 8°. 154 pp.   G.A. Oxon 4° 553

Peniston family.

See 2192.

1260. BARNWELL, E. L., Perrot notes; or Some account of the various branches of the Perrot family. Lond., 1867, 8°. 216 pp.   218 d. 24

Perrot family.

See 3301.

Phillips family.

See 2114.

Plowden family.

See 3517.

1261. MORIARTY, G. A., The Poure family of Oxfordshire. (Misc. geneal. et heraldica, 1926/28, 5th ser., vol. 6, p. 363–75.)

Ψ 2. 10f

Pudsey family.

See 2460.

1262. CARTER, W. F., The Quartremains of Oxfordshire. Oxf. 1936, 8°. 146 pp.   2182 Q. d. 1

1263. READE, C., A record of the Redes of Barton court, Berks [and Oxfordshire]. Hereford, 1899, 4°. 148 pp.   2182 R. d. 6

1264. Visitation of Oxfordshire, 1668–9. Sheldon. (Misc. geneal. et heraldica, 1916/17, 5th ser., vol. 2, p. 281.) Ψ 2. 10 f

Stonor family.
See 3754, 55, 3760.

1265. MORIARTY, G. A., Stretley family of Bucks and Oxon. (Bucks records, 1939, vol. 13, p. 379–97.)   R. Top. 110

Tipping family.
See 3734.

Trinder family.
See 2900.

1266. WACE, E. G., The history of the Wace family. Gloucester [c. 1934], 4°. 112 pp.   O.C.L.

1267. Visitation of Oxfordshire, 1668–9. Washington. (Misc. geneal. et heraldica, 1918/19, 5th ser., vol. 3, p. 83.) Ψ 2. 10 f

Weston family.
See 4300.

Wickham family.
See 3772A, 3774.

Wilcote family.
See 2708.

Wilder family.
See 3516.

Williams family.
See 2195.

Wilmot family.
See 1415.

Wykeham family.
See 3772A, 3774.

Wynslowe family.
See 1801.

HERALDRY (INCLUDING VISITATIONS)

1268. Oxfordshire [heraldic] visitation, by Lee, in 1574. (The Topographer, 1790, vol. 5, p. 14–53.) Salisbury, 1821, 8°.
Gough Gen. top. 179*

1269. NICOLAS, SIR N. H., Catalogue of the Heralds' Visitations with references to many other valuable genealogical and topographical manuscripts in the British Museum. [By sir N. H. Nicolas.] 2nd ed. (Oxfordshire, p. 58, 59.) Lond., 1825, 8°. 2590 e. Lond. 1a.1

1270. Visitations of Oxfordshire, 1574 and 1634. [ed. by sir T. Phillipps.] Typis Medio-Montanis, [184–], fol. 33 pp.
Caps. 6. 38

1271. Indexes to county visitations in the library at Middle Hill, 1840, and to a few others in the British Museum, the Bodleian library, and Queen's college, Oxford. (Oxfordshire, 1583, p. 2, 3.) Typis Medio-Montanis, 1841, fol. Caps. 6. 22*

1272. SIMS, R., An index to the pedigrees and arms contained in the heralds' visitations, and other genealogical manuscripts in the British Museum. (Oxfordshire, p. 224–30.) Lond., 1849, 8°.
R. 13. 291

1273. TURNER, W. H., ed., The visitations of Oxford, taken in the years 1566, 1574 and 1634 &c. (Publ., Harleian soc., vol. 5.) [204 pedigrees of Oxfordshire families.] Lond., 1871, 4°. Ψ 2. 11

1274. GATFIELD, G., Guide to printed books and manuscripts relating to . . . heraldry. (Oxfordshire, p. 171–74.) Lond., 1892, 8°.
R. 14. 309

1275. Pedigrees from the visitation of Oxfordshire, 1634. (Misc. geneal. et heraldica, 1912, ser. 4, vol. 5, p. 97–104, 141–49, 193–200, 254–60.) Ψ 2. 10 e
— Repr. 1913. 35 pp. Ψ 2. 11 (ii. 5*)

1276. The commission issued to Richard Lee for the visitation of Oxfordshire and Buckinghamshire in 1574. (B.Q.R., 1920, 3rd quarter, p. 71–73.) R. 13. 178 f

1277. Heraldry in Oxfordshire [arms in churches and old houses]. (N. & Q., 1928, vol. 154, p. 137, 195, 233.) Ψ 2. 97

1278. COPE, E. E., Heraldry: two Oxfordshire discoveries [at North Aston and Westwell]. (N. & Q., 1929, July 27, p. 59, 60.) Ψ 2. 97

1279. COPE, MRS. H., Selections from notes on heraldry in Oxfordshire churches. (Rept., Oxf. archaeol. soc., 1929, p. 233–52.)
R. Top. 330

1280. LAMBORN, E. A. GREENING, 'The Complete peerage' and 'The History of parliament' [comments on heraldic inaccuracies affecting Oxfordshire families]. (N. & Q., 1945, vol. 188, p. 11, 12.)
Ψ 2. 97

1281. LAMBORN, E. A. GREENING, Heraldry and the 'History of parliament' [comments on heraldic inaccuracies affecting Oxfordshire families]. (N. & Q., 1945, vol. 189, p. 125–27.) Ψ 2. 97

See 1319, &c. [Armorial glass].
See 2492 [Arms on Chaucer tomb, Ewelme. 1941].
See 3593, 94 [Juxon coat of arms, Somerton. 1902].
See 3819 [Arms in the nave roof, Tackley church. 1938].
See 4287 [Heraldic notices, Yarnton church. 1844].

MONUMENTS AND RECORDS

1282. A list of the monumental brasses remaining in England. (Oxfordshire, p. 65–69.) Lond., 1846, 8°.   G.A. Eccl. top. 8° 31

1283. HAINES, H., A manual of monumental brasses [vol. 2, p. 163–76 cover Oxfordshire]. Oxf. &c., 1861, 8°.   G.A. Eccl. top. 8° 20

1284. Monumental Brass Society. Transactions of the Cambridge university association of brass collectors [afterw.] Monumental brass society. [Vol. 1] no. 1–. Cambr. &c., 1887–, 8°.   Soc. 2184 d. 85

1285. MACKLIN, H. W., Monumental brasses. (Oxfordshire, p. 138, 39.) Lond., 1890, 8°.   2183 e. 1
[Other eds. in 1905, 1913.]

1286. Oxford univ., brass-rubbing soc. The Oxford portfolio of monumental brasses. Pt. 1–5. Oxf., 1898–1901, fol.   2184 b. 1

1287. STEPHENSON, M., A list of palimpsest brasses. Oxfordshire. (Trans., Monumental brass soc., 1903, vol. 4, pt. 7, p. 251–62.)
Soc. 2184 d. 85

1288. MACKLIN, H. W., The brasses of England. (Oxfordshire, passim.) Lond., 1907, 8°. 336 pp.   G.A. Eccl. top. 8° 139

1289. STEVENSON, M., A list of monumental brasses in the British Isles. (Oxfordshire, p. 397–426, Appendix, p. 789, 90.) Lond., 1926, 4°.
R. 14. 311*

1290. GAWTHORPE, W. E., Restorations of brasses (Oxfordshire, p. 45.) (Trans., Monumental brass soc., 1934, vol. 7, pt. 1.)
Soc. 2184 d. 85

See 1418 [Brasses. Adderbury. 1897].
See 1737 [Brasses. Benson. 1898].
See 1871 [Brasses. Brightwell Baldwin. 1908].
See 1970 [Brasses. Cassington. 1898].
See 3646 [Brasses. Chalgrove. 1897].
See 2059 [Brasses. Checkendon. 1897].
See 2080 [Brasses. Chinnor. 1935].
See 2105 [Brasses. Chipping Norton. 1897].
See 2332 [Brasses. Deddington. 1938].
See 2352 [Brasses. Ditchley. 1898].
See 2482 [Brasses. Ewelme. 1897].
See 2675 [Brasses. Great Haseley. 1898].

See 2879 [Brasses. Henley deanery. 1898].
See 2910 [Brasses. Hook Norton. 1949].
See 2980 [Brasses. Ipsden. 1909].
See 1970 [Brasses. Kidlington. 1898].
See 3336 [Brasses. North Stoke. 1939].
See 3340 [Brasses. North Weston. 1900].
See 3367 [Brasses. Oddington. 1938].
See 3646 [Brasses. Stadhampton. 1897].
See 3695 [Brasses. Stanton St. John. 1912].
See 3794 [Brasses. Swinbrook. 1911].
See 3873 [Brasses. Thame. 1898].
See 3938, 3646, 3941, 42 [Brasses. Waterperry. 1846, 1897, 1914, 1949].
See 1970 [Brasses. Woodstock. 1898].
See 1970 [Brasses. Yarnton. 1898].

1291. Report of the commissioners appointed to inquire into the state, custody, and authenticity of registers of records of births or baptisms, deaths or burials, and marriages, in England and Wales, other than the parochial registers. (Oxfordshire, p. 49.)
Pp. Eng. 1837/8, vol. 28

1292. FAULKNER, C., A brief history of parish registers, with remarks on a few of the registers of the North of Oxfordshire. (Trans., N. Oxf. archaeol. soc., 1853–55, p. 101–11.)   R. Top. 330

1293. SIMS, R., A manual for the genealogist, topographer, antiquary, and legal professor, consisting of descriptions of public records; parochial and other registers [&c.]. (Oxfordshire, passim.) Lond., 1856, 8°.   258795 e. 4
— New ed. 1888.   R. 14. 310

1294. GIBBONS, A., Early Lincoln wills. An abstract of all the wills & administrations recorded in the episcopal registers of the old diocese of Lincoln. (Oxford diocese, passim.) (Linc. record ser., 1.) Lincoln, 1888, 8°.   Soc. G.A. Lincs 8° 88 (1)

1295. SHERWOOD, G. F. T., Bucks and Oxon marriage bonds [abstracts of records embracing the years 1617–1735, preserved in Somerset House]. (Berks, Bucks, and Oxon archaeol. journ., 1896, vol. 2, p. 52–58, 77–82, 117–19.)   R. Top. 100

1296. MARSHALL, G. W., Parish registers: a list of those printed, or of which MS. copies exist in public collections. (Index—Oxfordshire, p. 117, 18.) [With] Appendix. Lond., 1900, 1908, 8°.
G.A. Eccl. top. 8° 56, 56*

1297. Oxfordshire parish registers. Marriages, ed. by W. P. W. Phillimore (and W. J. Oldfield). Vol. 1, 2. [Covers Chipping Norton, Wootton, Pyrton, Crowell, Eynsham, Stanton Harcourt, Standlake, Handborough, Northmoor, Yarnton, Cassington, over various periods to the year 1837.] Lond., 1909, 10, 8°.
G.A. Oxon 4° 279

1298. Extracts from the parish registers of Oxfordshire, transcr. by W. J. Oldfield. (Berks, Bucks, and Oxon archaeol. journ., 1910, vol. 16, p. 57, 58, 71–74, 117, 118; 1911, vol. 17, p. 44–48.)

R. Top. 100

See 1446 [Parish register, Ambrosden. 1612–1757. 1888].
See 2016 [Parish register, Chalgrove. 1911].
See 2093 [Parish register, Chipping Norton. 1560–1686. 1830].
See 2307 [Parish register, Culham. 1933].
See 2333C [Parish register, Deddington. Notes from. 1951].
See 2435 [Parish register, Ducklington, Index. 1881].
See 3200 [Parish register, Merton. Account. 1902].
See 3440 [Parish register, Rotherfield Greys. Account. 1908].
See 3694 [Parish register, Stanton St. John. Notes from. 1904/5].
See 3940 [Catholic register, Waterperry. 1701?–1834. 1909].
See 4108 [Parish register, Wolvercote, 16th, 17th cent. 1888].

ARCHITECTURE AND ALLIED ARTS

GENERAL

1299. A guide to the architectural antiquities in the neighbourhood of Oxford [ed. by J. H. Parker and W. Grey]. 4 pt. [Pt. 1, deanery of Bicester: pt. 2, deanery of Woodstock: pt. 3, 4, deanery of Cuddesdon.] Oxf., 1842–46, 8°. 398 pp.   Manning 8° 41
— [Another issue. 1846. G.A. Oxon 8° 57.]
— [2nd ed. of pt. 1, 1860. G.A. Oxon 8° 703.]

1300. Ecclesiastical and architectural topography. Oxfordshire. Oxf., 1850, 8°. 84 pp.   G.A. Gen. top. 8° 83

1301. TURNER, T. H., Some account of domestic architecture in England from the Conquest to the end of the 13th century. (Oxfordshire, *passim*.) Oxf., 1851, 8°. 287 pp.   173 e. 51

1302. PARKER, J. H., Some account of domestic architecture in England from Edward i to Richard ii [by J. H. Parker]. (Oxfordshire, p. 260–70.) Oxf., 1853, 4°.   173 e. 52

1303. PARKER, J. H., Some account of domestic architecture in England from Richard ii to Henry viii [by J. H. Parker]. (Oxfordshire, p. 270–77.) Oxf., 1859, 8°.   173 e. 54

1304. Church notes [taken between 1835 and 1840]. (Oxfordshire, *passim*; Archaeological journ., 1887, vol. 44, p. 43–50, 185–93, 294–303, 397–402.)   R. Top. 5

1305. Around Oxford. (The Builder, 1890, vol. 59, no. 2480, p. 119–24.)   G.A. Oxon 4° 577 (45)

1306. GARNER, T., and STRATTON, A., The domestic architecture of England during the Tudor period, illustrated in a series of photographs & measured drawings, with text. 2 vols. (Oxfordshire, *passim*.) Lond., 1911, fol.   17363 b. 4
— 2nd ed. 1929.   17363 b. 19, 20

1307. BARLOW AND ALDEN LTD., Country houses around Oxford. [Booklet advertising installation of lighting and heating, with illustr. of country houses owned by satisfied customers.] Oxf., [1921], 8°. 18 pp.   G.A. Oxon 8° 1000 (4)

1308. Working drawings of an Oxfordshire house designed by W. Cave. (Building news, 1922. Nov. 29.)   N. 1863 c. 4

1309. BIRD, W. H., Old Oxfordshire churches. Lond., (1932), 8°. 182 pp.   G.A. Oxon 8° 1091

1310. LONG, E. T., Mediæval domestic architecture in Oxfordshire. (Rept., Oxf. archaeol. soc., 1938, p. 45–56; 1939, p. 97–105; 1940, p. 3–17.)   R. Top. 330
— [Repr. 3 pt. 1939–41.]   G.A. Oxon 8° 1236 (1)

See 198 [Oxfordshire old houses. 1902].
See 1553 [Banbury district. Sculptured cornices. 1924].
See 2186 [Coombe. Church clock. 1938].
See 2481 [Ewelme. Carved corbel. 1896].
See 2678 [Gt. Haseley. Mass clock. 1926].
See 3071 [Langford. Unusual doorways in church. 1890].
See 3152 [Little Tew. Paper roofs. 1811].
See 3153 [Little Tew. Farm buildings design. 1824].
See 3843 [Tetsworth. Sculpture, tympanum. 1853].

FONTS

1311. LAMBORN, E. A. GREENING, The armorial fonts of the Oxford diocese. (Berks archaeol. journ., 1941, vol. 45; Oxfordshire, p. 114–19.)   R. Top. 100

See 2183 [Coombe. 1895].
See 3344 [Nuffield. 1916].

MURAL DECORATION

1312. SODEN-SMITH, R. H., A first list of buildings in England (Oxfordshire, *passim*) having mural or other painted decorations of dates previous to the middle of the 16th century [compiled by R. H. Soden-Smith]. (Comm. of council on educ., South Kensington mus., Sci. and art dept.) Lond., 1871, 8°. 24 pp.
                                                                      17006 e. 51 (5)
— [2nd ed.] 1872. 57 pp.   17006 e. 51 (6)
— 3rd ed., by C. E. Keyser, 1883. 402 pp.   17032 e. 2

1313. KEYSER, C. E., On recently discovered mural paintings . . . in the south of England. (Oxfordshire, *passim*. Archaeological journ., 1896, vol. 53, p. 178–81; 1901, vol. 58, p. 53, 54.)   R. Top. 5

1314. HURST, H., Remains of pargetting in Oxford. (Berks, Bucks, & Oxon archaeol. journ., 1898, vol. 4, p. 105–11.)   R. Top. 100

1315. LONG, E. T., Some wall-paintings in Oxfordshire. (Burlington mag., 1934, vol. 65, p. 80–83.)   Per. 170 e. 25

1316. TRISTRAM, E. W., English medieval wall painting. The twelfth century, with a catalogue. (Oxfordshire, *passim*.) Lond., &c., 1944, fol.   1373 c. 33

1317. TRISTRAM, E. W., English medieval wall painting. The thirteenth century. Text [and] Plates. (Oxfordshire, *passim.*) Lond., 1950, fol.
1373 c. 35, 36
See 2010 [Chalgrove. Church murals. 1860].
See 2055 [Checkendon. Church murals. 1868].
See 2184 [Coombe. Church murals. 1906, 07].
See 2295 [Cuddesdon. Church murals. 1879].
See 2527 [Eynsham. Church murals. 1937].
See 2762 [Headington. Church murals. 1863].
See 2990 [Islip. Church murals. 1842].
See 3007 [Kelmscott. Church murals. 1936].
See 3366 [Oddington. Church murals. 1926].
See 3550 [Shorthampton. Church murals. 1937].
See 3613, 15, 16 [South Leigh. Church murals. 1872, 73, 1900].
See 3629, 3632 [South Newington. Church murals. 1907, 1933].
See 3669 [Stanton Harcourt. Church murals. 1846].

SCREENS

1318. HOWARD, F. E., Screens and rood-lofts in the parish churches of Oxfordshire. (Archaeological journ., 1910, vol. 67, p. 151–201.)
R. Top. 5
— Repr. 1910.
1736 d. 44
See 1946 [Burford. Reredos and screen. 1922].
See 2035 [Charlton-on-Otmoor. Rood screens. 1900].

STAINED GLASS

1319. BOUCHIER, E. S., Notes on the stained glass of the Oxford district. Oxf., 1918, 8°. 106 pp.
1373 e. 28

1320. BOUCHIER, E. S., Old stained glass in Oxfordshire. (Journ., Brit. soc. of Master glass-painters, 1932, Apr. 4, p. 122–33.)
Soc. 17031 d. 6

1321. LAMBORN, E. A. GREENING, The armorial glass of the Oxford diocese. (Berks archaeol. journ., 1942, vol. 46, Oxfordshire, p. 46–53, 88–96; 1943, vol. 47, p. 24–45).
R. Top. 100

1322. WOODFORDE, C., Some medieval English glazing quarries painted with birds. [8 quarries in Yarnton church]. (Journ., Brit. archaeol. assoc., 1944, 3rd ser., vol. 9, p. 7, 8.)
R. Top. 4

1323. LAMBORN, E. A. GREENING, The armorial glass of the Oxford diocese, 1250–1850. Lond., 1949, 8°. 178 pp.+64 plates.
17031 e. 15

See 2068 [Protest about images in Chesterton Church windows. 1867].
See 3127 [Littlemore. 1898].
See 3272 [Newington. 1938].
See 3441 [Rotherfield Greys. Armorial glass. 1938].
See 3593, 94 [Somerton. Armorial glass. 1902].
See 3633 [South Newington. Stained glass. 1938].

TILES

1324. CHURCH, W. A., Patterns of inlaid tiles from churches in the diocese of Oxford. [South Stoke, Crowmarsh Gifford, Dorchester and Newnham Murren.] Wallingford, 1845, 4°. 24 pl.   2 ⊿ 478

1325. HABERLY, L., Mediaeval English pavingtiles. [An illustr. survey of decorated tiles surviving within 15 miles of Oxford.] Oxf., 1937, 4°. 326 pp.   17513 d. 37

See 2623 [Encaustic tiles at Godstow. 1873].

NEWSPAPERS

1326. Banbury Advertiser. July 5, 1855–.   B.M.

1327. Banbury Beacon. 1860–1905.   [June 5, 1868– B.M.]

1328. Banbury Evening news. Jan. 1–Dec. 31st, 1877. [Discontinued.]
     B.M.

1329. Banbury Guardian and general advertiser. July 6, 1843–. [Formerly The Guardian.]   B.M.
[Bodleian: 1843–56, 1916–. imperf.   N.G.A. Oxon a. 6.]

1330. Banbury Herald. Jan. 10, 1861–Feb. 27, 1869. [Incorporated with Oxfordshire Weekly news.]   B.M.

1331. Banbury Telegraph. March 2, 1893–May 9, 1895. [Discontinued.]
     B.M.

1332. Berks and Oxon Advertiser. 1855–1941.   B.M.

1333. Bicester Advertiser. No. 20, July 7, 1855–Jan. 26, 1866. [Discontinued.]   B.M.

1334. Bicester Advertiser (and Mid-Oxon Chronicle). [Incorporating the Bicester Herald and the Brackley Observer.] Jan. 10, 1879–.
     N.G.A. Oxon a. 127; B.M.

1335. Bicester Herald. June 1855–1917. [Incorporated with the Bicester Advertiser.]   N.G.A. Oxon a. 128; B.M.

Chipping Norton Advertiser.
See 1336 Chipping Norton News.

1336. Chipping Norton News. 1930–32. [*Contd. as*] Chipping Norton Advertiser. 1933–.

1337. Farmer's gazette. Nov. 7, 1843–July 2, 1844. [Discontinued.]
     B.M.

1338. The Guardian; or, Monthly poor law register, for the district comprised in the unions of Banbury, Bicester, Brackley, Chipping-Norton, . . . Witney, and Woodstock. No. 1–63. [*Afterw.* The Banbury Guardian.] Banbury, 1838–43, 4°.   Per. G.A. Oxon 4° 129

1339. Hall's Oxonian Advertiser. Jan. 1853–Mar. 26, 1856.   B.M.
The Oxonian Advertiser [publ. by Hall & Son]. Vol. 17, no. 230, 231. June & July, 1871.   N.G.A. Oxon a. 112

1340. Henley Advertiser. 1868–1908. [No. 142, May 7, 1870–.   B.M.]

1341. Henley and South Oxfordshire Standard [incorporating Henley Free press from 1892]. 1879–.   B.M.

1342. Henley Chronicle. 1904–13. [*Contd. as*] Oxford Chronicle (Henley and South Oxon edition). 1914–29.

1343. Henley (Reading) Express. 1879–Dec. 1884.

1344. Henley Free press. 1885–92. [Incorp. in Henley and South Oxfordshire Standard.]   B.M.

Illustrated Oxford Messenger.
See 1363 Oxford Messenger.

1345. Illustrated Oxfordshire Telegraph. Dec. 29, 1858–June 18, 1859. [*Contd. as*] Oxfordshire (Buckinghamshire and Northamptonshire) Telegraph. June 25, 1859–June 20, 1894.   B.M.

1346. Jackson's Oxford Journal. 1753–1909. [*Contd. as*] Oxford Journal illustrated. 1909–1928. [Incorp. in Oxford Times.]
N.G.A. Oxon a. 4, 4*

1347. GOVE, P. B., Jackson's Oxford Journal. (Notes, Oxoniensia, 1940, p. 171.)   R. Top. 340

1348. Midland Mail. June 9, 1899–Oct. 27, 1899. [*Contd. as*] South Midland Mail. Nov. 3, 1899–Oct. 5, 1900. [Discontinued.]   B.M.

1349. North Oxfordshire Monthly times and agricultural advertiser. No. 1–31. Deddington, 1849–52, fol.   G.A. Oxon b. 102

1350.

1351. Oxford and district Morning echo. No. 25, Oct. 22, 1898–no. 112, Feb. 3, 1899. [*Contd. as*] Oxford Morning echo. Feb. 4, 1899– Jan. 30, 1900. [Discontinued.]   N.G.A. Oxon b. 42

Oxford Chronicle (Henley and South Oxon edition).
See 1342 Henley Chronicle.

Oxford Chronicle and Berks and Bucks Gazette.
See 1352 Oxford City and County Chronicle.

Oxford Chronicle and Reading Gazette.
See 1352 Oxford City and County Chronicle.

1352. Oxford City and County Chronicle. Feb. 4, 1837–July 16, 1842. [*Contd. as*] Oxford Chronicle and Reading Gazette. July 23, 1842– Dec. 1845. [*Contd. as*] Oxford Chronicle and Berks and Bucks Gazette. Jan. 1846–1929.   N.G.A. Oxon a. 2

1353. Oxford Conservative. July 5, 1834–June 27, 1835.   B.M.
— [Bodleian. No. 4–37. July 26, 1834–Mar. 14, 1835. Imperf.
N.G.A. Oxon a. 27.]

1354. Oxford Evening times. Dec. 1, 1928–Mar. 16, 1929. [Discontinued.]   N.G.A. Oxon a. 107

1355. Oxford Flying post. Jan. 7–Aug. 26, 1859. [*Contd. as*] Oxford Post, Sept. 3–Nov. 19. 1859. [Discontinued.]   B.M.

1356. The Oxford Flying weekly journal and Cirencester Gazette. Vol. 2, no. 79. March, 1747–8. Oxf., 1748, fol. 4 pp.   fol. Δ 755 (19)

1357. Oxford Free press. Jan. 2–Aug. 21, 1858. [Discontinued.] B.M.

Oxford Gazette and Reading Mercury.
See 1373 Reading Mercury.

1358. Oxford Guardian. 1872–Jan. 27, 1892. [Discontinued.] [B.M. has 1884–. Bodleian 1888–.   N.G.A. Oxon a. 13.]

Oxford Journal illustrated.
See 1346 Jackson's Oxford Journal.

1359. Oxford Leader. Labour and Socialist news. No. 2, 3, 1909.
                                           N.G.A. Oxon a. 113 (1, 2)

1360. Oxford Mail. 1928–. Oxf., 1928–, fol.   N.G.A. Oxon a. 108

1361. Prospectus of the Oxford Mercury, and Midland County Chronicle. Oxf., 1795, s. sh.   N.G.A. Oxon a. 7★

1362. Oxford Mercury, and Midland County Chronicle. Aug. 5, 1795.
                                           N.G.A. Oxon a. 7★

1363. Oxford Messenger. No. 14, June 4, 1873–Apr. 21, 1877. [*Contd. as*] Illustrated Oxford Messenger. Apr. 27–Oct. 26, 1877. [Discontinued.]   B.M.

Oxford Morning echo.
See 1351 Oxford and district Morning echo.

Oxford Post.
See 1355 Oxford Flying post.

1364. Oxford (Oxfordshire) Telegraph and news of the district. Feb. 17, 1900–03.   N.G.A. Oxon a. 26

1365. Oxford Times. Sept. 1862–. B.M. [Bodleian: Mar. 21, 1863; 1887–.   N.G.A. Oxon a. 5.]

1366. Oxford University and City Herald. May 31, 1806–Dec. 1830. [*Contd. as*] Oxford University, City and County Herald. Jan. 1831–Feb. 1852. [*Contd. as*] Oxford University Herald. Mar. 1852–Jan. 30, 1892. [Discontinued.]   N.G.A. Oxon a. 3

Oxford University, City and County Herald.
See 1366 Oxford University and City Herald.

Oxford University Herald.
See 1366 Oxford University and City Herald.

1367. Oxford Weekly record. Dec. 1, 1882–June 8, 1883. [Discontinued.]   B.M.

1368. Oxfordshire Advertiser. No. 1, Feb. 1908.
N.G.A. Oxon. a. 112

Oxfordshire, Buckinghamshire and Northamptonshire Telegraph.
See 1345 Illustrated Oxfordshire Telegraph.

1369. Oxfordshire County news. Feb. 25–May 27, 1898. [Incorp. with Jackson's Oxford Journal.]   B.M.
[Bodleian. No. 2.   N.G.A. Oxon a. 112.]

1370. Oxfordshire Free press. 1906–19.

Oxfordshire Telegraph.
See 1345 Illustrated Oxfordshire Telegraph.

Oxfordshire Telegraph and news of the district.
See 1364 Oxford Telegraph and news of the district.

1371. Oxfordshire Up-to-date farmer. No. 1, 1909–No. 26, 1910.
N.G.A. Oxon a. 112

1372. Oxfordshire Weekly news [incorporating Witney Telegraph: and Banbury Herald, 1870] 1865–1929.   B.M.

Oxonian Advertiser.
See 1339 Hall's Oxonian Advertiser.

1373. Reading Mercury [*contd. as*] Oxford Gazette and Reading Mercury [*contd. as*] Reading Mercury, Berks county paper, Oxford Gazette, Newbury Herald. 1723–.
[*For collation & Bodleian shelfmarks of issues see* Milford and Sutherland, A catalogue of English newspapers.]

South Midland Mail.
See 1348 Midland Mail.

1374.

1375. South Oxfordshire News. Jan. 1, 1887–May 19, 1894. [Discontinued.]   B.M.

1376. Thame Gazette (and Oxfordshire and Bucks Advertiser). No. 1–. March 11, 1856–.   B.M.
[Bodleian has no. 4963, Dec. 5, 1950–.   N.G.A. Oxon a. 120.]

1377. Witney Express. 1861–Nov. 15, 1888. [Incorporated with Witney Gazette.] [No. 416, July 15, 1869–88. B.M.]

1378. Witney Gazette (Burford, Bampton and West Oxon Advertiser) Dec. 30, 1882–. B.M.

1379. Witney Telegraph. Oct. 13, 1866–Feb. 20, 1869. [Incorporated in Oxfordshire Weekly news.] B.M.

1380. Woodstock Herald and Charlbury Messenger. No. 1–6. Sept. 1875–Feb. 1876. (Lond.), 1875, 76, fol. N. 1126 b. 15

DIRECTORIES AND ALMANACS

DIRECTORIES

1381. Bailey's Western & midland directory for . . . 1783 containing [towns in Oxfordshire &c.]. Birm., 1783, 8°. [2 issues.]
Guildhall Libr.

1382. Bailey's British directory . . . for . . . 1784. 1st ed. Vol. 2. The Western directory, containing [towns in Oxfordshire &c.] (Lond.), 1784, 8°.
B.M. and Guildhall Libr.

1383. The Universal British directory of trade, commerce & manufacture. Vol. 2–5. [Arranged alphabetically by towns.] Lond., 1790–[98], 8°.
G.A. Gen. top. 8° 239–42

1384. Pigot and co.'s London & provincial new commercial directory for 1823–24. (Oxfordshire, p. 435–53.)
Dir. Middl. d. 8

1385. Pigot and co.'s London and provincial directory, 1830. (Oxfordshire, p. 633–64.)
G.A. Oxon 4° 262 (12)

1386. County of Oxford. (The Oxf. univ., city and county dir. for 1835, publ. by J. Vincent, p. 57–70.)
G.A. Oxon 16° 147

1387. Robson's Commercial directory of the six counties forming the Norfolk circuit, with Oxfordshire [82 pp.] (Lond.), 1839, 8°.
Norwich and A.R.W.

1388. Pigot and co.'s National and commercial directory and topography of . . . Derbyshire, Dorsetshire, Gloucestershire. [Oxfordshire, 40 pp.] Lond., 1842, 8°.
A.R.W.
— [Another issue.]
B.M.
— [Another issue.]
Reading

1389. SLATER, I., Pigot and co.'s Royal national and commercial directory and topography of . . . Berkshire [&c.] Oxfordshire. Lond., &c., 1844, 4°. 40 pp.
Dir. Gen. top. d. 25

1390. Hunt and co.'s City of Oxford directory, including the . . . residents . . . in Abingdon, Banbury, Bicester, Deddington, Thame, Witney, Woodstock, &c. (Lond.), 1846, 8°.
Dir. Oxon e. 3

1391. Post office directory of Berkshire . . . Oxfordshire [&c.]. [1847], 1854.
— 1864, 69. (Post office directory of Northamptonshire, &c.).
— 1877. (Post office directory of Bedford, &c.)
Lond., [1847]–77, 4°.
Dir. Gen. top. d. 2

1392. Slater's directory. Oxfordshire. n. pl., [1850], 4°. 46 pp.
G.A. Oxon 4° 507

1393. History, gazetteer and directory of the county of Oxford. (R. Gardner.). Peterborough, 1852, 4°. 862 pp. G.A. Oxon 8° 64

1394. Lascelles and co.'s Directory and gazetteer of the county of Oxford. Birm., 1853, 8°. 405 pp.

1395. M. Billing's Directory & gazetteer of the counties of Berks and Oxon. Birm., 1854, 8°. 406 pp. Dir. Berks d. 1

1396. Dutton and Allen's History, directory, and gazetteer of Oxford, Berks and Bucks. Manch., 1863, 8°. G.A. Gen. top. 8° 23

1397. Edward Cassey and co.'s History, gazetteer and directory of Berkshire and Oxfordshire. Lond., 1868, 8°. 278 pp.
G.A. Berks 8° 58

1398. Webster's Oxford directory, including Banbury, Eynsham, Wallingford, Witney and Woodstock: also the principal villages in the vicinity. Oxf., 1872, 8°. 329 pp. Dir. Oxon e. 7

1399. Mercer & Crocker's General topographical and historical directory for Oxfordshire [&c.]. Leicester, 1873, 4°. 127 pp.

1400. Berks, Bucks and Oxon, Bennett's business directory. 1881–1918. [Oxfordshire. Bodleian, 1898, 1904/5. Dir. Gen. top. d. 29.]

1401. Kelly's Directory of Berkshire, Bucks and Oxon. 1883, 1887, 1891, 1895, 1899, 1903, 1907, 1911, 1915, 1920, 1924. Lond., 1883–1924, 4°. Dir. Gen. top. d. 3

1402. Kelly's Directory of Oxfordshire. [12th ed.–.] Lond., &c., 1928–, 4°. [Earlier eds. in 1401.] Dir. Oxon d. 2

1403. Deacon's Berkshire, Buckinghamshire, and Oxfordshire court guide and county blue book. Lond., 1889, 8°.
— 2nd ed. 1890. Dir. Gen. top. e. 1

1404. VALTERS, J. C., Valters' Oxford and district post office directory. 1889–99. Oxf., 1889–99, 8°.
[1889–96/7, Dir. Oxon e. 5; 1891/2–99, O.C.R.L.]

1405. Kelly's Oxford directory, with Abingdon, Woodstock and neighbourhood. 1889/90–. Lond., 1889–, 8°. Dir. Oxon e. 1

See 1579, &c. [Banbury directories].
See 1776 [Bicester directory. 1857].
See 1923A [Packer's Burford directory. 1860, &c.].
See 2840 [Henley-on-Thames directory. 1932–42].

ALMANACS

1406. The Oxfordshire, Berkshire and Buckinghamshire almanack for
. . . 1784, 1788. Lond., 1784, 1788, s. sh.   Alm. 1777–97 a. 1

1407. Wiltshire, Hampshire, Oxfordshire, Berkshire and Buckinghamshire almanack for 1791, 1794–97. Lond., 1791–97, s. sh.
                                        Alm. 1777–97 a. 1
— 1822–27, 1831–48.   B.M.

1408. The Oxford city and county almanack for . . . 1858, containing
a list of the . . . county officers [&c.], list of conveyances from
Oxford [&c.]. Oxf., (1858), 8°. 47 pp.   (Alm.) Oxon 8° 1038

See 1923A [Packer's Burford almanack. 1860, &c.].
See 2104 [Chipping Norton illustrated almanack. 1897].

INDIVIDUAL LOCALITIES

ADDERBURY

1409. God's strange and terrible judgement in Oxfordshire: being a true relation how a woman at Atherbury . . . was suddenly burn'd to ashes. Lond., 1677, 4°. 8 pp.   Vet. A 3 e. 237 (3)
See 505, 527 [Turnpike acts. 1755, &c.].

1410. An act for dividing and inclosing certain . . . fields and commonable lands in the parish of Adderbury. (6 G. III, c. 90, Private.) n. pl., 1766, fol. 35 pp.   G.A. Oxon c. 113 (7)

1411. An act for vesting the legal estate . . . in . . . Adderbury . . . now vested in Charles Townsend . . . in . . . Henry, Duke of Buccleugh. . . . (12 G. III, c. 79. Private.) n. pl., 1772, fol. 7 pp.
L. Eng. C 13 c. 1 (1772. 23)

1412. An act for rendering effectual a proposal or agreement made between the duke of Buccleugh and the lord bishop of Winchester for exchanging and enfranchising certain leasehold and copyhold lands . . . in . . . Adderbury . . . (15 G. III, c. 88, Private.) n. pl., 1775, fol. 21 pp.   L. Eng. C 13 c. 1 (1775. 11)

1413. Adderbury. (Gent's. mag., 1792, pt. 1, p. 111, 12; 1800, pt. 1, p. 209; 1834, pt. 1, p. 161–65.) Ψ 2. 44

1414. Scheme established . . . 1871 by the authority of the Charity commissioners for the regulation of the feoffees, or town lands charity, in the parish of Adderbury. Banbury, 1872, 8°. 14 pp.   O.P.L.

1415. GREENFIELD, B. W., ed., Wilmot and Lee. Extract from the register of the parish church of Adderbury. (Misc. geneal. et heraldica, 1874, new ser., vol. 1, p. 420, 21.) Ψ 2. 10 f

1416. The restoration of Adderbury church [appeal for funds]. n. pl., 1885, s. sh.   G.A. Oxon c. 22 (3)

1417. Adderbury church. (Trans., Bristol and Glouc. archaeol. soc., 1895–96, vol. 20, p. 359–64.)   R. Top. 210

1418. FEARSON, W. W., A catalogue of the brasses in Adderbury church. (Journ., Oxf. univ. brass-rubbing soc., 1897, vol. 1, p. 79–80.)
Soc. 2184 d. 50

1419. Painted wooden memorial tablet in Adderbury church. (Proc., Soc. of antiq., 1905, 2nd ser., vol. 20, p. 221, 22.)   R. Top. 1
See 1022 [Act concerning supply of gas. 1913].

1420. GEPP, H. J., Adderbury. Banbury, 1924, 8°. 93 pp.
G.A. Oxon 8° 1030

1421. HOBSON, T. F., ed., Adderbury 'rectoria'. (Oxf. record soc., 8.)
[Oxf.], 1926, 8°. 127 pp. R. 13. 702

1422. Adderbury. (Archaeol. notes. Oxoniensia, 1936, p. 202.)
R. Top. 340

1423. Adderbury. (Country Life, 1949, vol. 105, p. 30–33.)
Per. 384 b. 6
See 449 [Estates of New college, 1659–75, p. 17–27].

1424. Auction catal. 3 cottages. 15 Mar. 1833.
G.A. Oxon b. 85 a (27)

1425. Auction catal. Nell bridge wharf. 20 July, 1899.
G.A. Oxon b. 90 (1)

1426. Auction catal. Manor. 29 Sept. 1910. G.A. Oxon c. 317 (4)

1427. Auction catal. Sydenham farm. 5 May 1911.
G.A. Oxon b. 90 (2)

1428. Auction catal. Manor house. 7 Sept. 1922.
G.A. Oxon 4° 403 (12)

ALBURY

1429. An act for appointing jointures for the wives and . . . portions for
the younger children of . . . Willoughby, earl of Abingdon, and
Peregrine Bertie his brother. [Albury &c.]. (9 G. III, sess. 2, c. 10,
Private.) n. pl., 1769, fol. 43 pp. G.A. Oxon c. 192

1430. Auction catal. Rycote estate. 31 May 1911.
G.A. Oxon b. 91 (44)

ALCHESTER

1431. KENNETT, W., bp. of Peterborough, The history of Allchester.
(Parochial antiquities . . . of Ambrosden, Appendix, p. 683–703.)
Oxf., 1695, 4°. Douce K 114
— [Copy in the Bodleian with MS. notes by the author].
Don. d. 56
— New ed. 1818. (Appendix No. 1, p. 417–42.)
G.A. Oxon 4° 118

1432. DUNKIN, J., The history and antiquities of Bicester . . . to which
is added, an inquiry into the history of Alchester, a city of the
Dobuni, the site of which now forms part of the common field of
Wendlebury. Lond., 1816, 8°. 270 pp. G.A. Oxon 8° 257 (1)
See 538 [Roman road from Alchester to Dorchester, by R. Hussey. 1841].

1433. Antiquities found at Alchester. (Journ., Brit. archaeol. assoc., 1856, vol. 12, p. 176–78, 240.)   R. Top. 4

1434. MARSHALL, J., and BROWN, W. L., Alchester. (Trans., N. Oxf. archaeol. soc., 1857–58, p. 123–41.)   R. Top. 330

1435. MYRES, J. L., On excavations at Alchester. (Proc., Oxf. architect. and hist. soc., N.S., vol. 5, 1891, p. 355.)   R. 13. 711

1436. HAWKES, C., Excavations at Alchester, 1926. (Antiquaries journ., 1927, vol. 7, p. 154–84.)   R. Top. 2

1437. Excavations at Alchester. (Antiquity, 1928, vol. 2, p. 467, 68.)
                    R. Top. 6

1438. ILIFFE, J. H., Excavations at Alchester, 1927. (Antiquaries journ., 1929, vol. 9, p. 105–36.)
— 1928. (Antiquaries journ., 1932, vol. 12, p. 35–67.)   R. Top. 2

1439. HARDEN, D. B., Excavations at Chesterton Lane, Alchester, 1937. (Rept., Oxf. archaeol. soc., 1937, p. 23–39.)   R. Top. 330

1440. Alchester. (Archaeol. notes. Oxoniensia, 1941, p. 84.)
                    R. Top. 340

ALVESCOT

1441. An act for dividing, allotting and inclosing the . . . fields . . . of Alvescot . . . (36 G. III, c. 8, Private.) n. pl., 1796, fol. 30 pp.
                    L. Eng. C 13 c. 1 (1796. i. 1)
See 325 [Account of stone axe found at Alvescot, by E. T. Leeds. 1938].

1442. Sale catal. Estate. May 1812.   G.A. fol. B 71

1443. Auction catal. Home and Shill farms, Plough inn, and Vine cottage. 8 June 1909.   G.A. Oxon b. 90 (3)

AMBROSDEN

1444. KENNETT, W., bp. of Peterborough, Parochial antiquities attempted in the history of Ambrosden, Burcester, and other adjacent parts in the counties of Oxford and Bucks. Oxf., 1695, 4°. 703 pp.   Douce K 114
— [Copy in the Bodleian with MS. notes by the author.]
                    Don. d. 56
— New ed., enlarged. 2 vols. Oxf., 1818, 4°. 583 & 526 pp.
                    G.A. Oxon 4° 117, 18
See 3403 [Account of endowments, by the bp. of Oxford. 1807].

1445. Amicable society of tradesmen. Rules and orders. Oxf., 1818, 8°. 16 pp.   G.A. Oxon 8° 900 (34)

1446. BLAYDES, F. A., *ed.*, Extracts from the parish registers of Ambrosden [1612–1757]. (Misc. geneal. et heraldica, 1888, 2nd. ser., vol. 2, p. 303, 04.) Ψ 2. 10 f

ARDLEY

1447. BLOMFIELD, J. C., History of Ardley, [&c.] (Hist. of . . . deanery of Bicester. Pt. 8. Ardley. 37 pp.) Lond., 1894, 4°.
G.A. Oxon 4° 71
See 359 [Honors and knight's fees. 1924].

1448. ARKELL, W. J., RICHARDSON, L., and PRINGLE, J., The lower oolites exposed in the Ardley and Fritwell railway-cuttings, between Bicester and Banbury. (Proc., Geol. assoc., 1933, vol. 44, p. 340–54.)   Radcl.

1449. Auction catal. Outlying portions of the Blenheim estates. 3 July 1894.   G.A. Oxon b. 90 (12)

ARNCOT

1450. An act for inclosing lands in Arncott. (54 G. III, c. 207, L. & P.) Lond., 1814, fol. 27 pp.   G.A. Oxon a. 117 (f. 42)
See 3735 [Windmill, Arncot. 1925].

ASCOT D'OYLEY

1451. Excavations at the 12th century castle at Ascot-D'Oilly, 1946. (Oxoniensia, 1946–47, p. 165–67.)   R. Top. 340

ASCOT UNDER WYCHWOOD

1452. An act to authorize the inclosure of certain lands . . . [Ascot]. (21 V., c. 8, Pub.) Lond., 1858, fol. 2 pp.   L. Eng. A 69 c. 1

1453. Auction catal. Manor. 29 Jan. 1858.   G.A. Oxon b. 85 *b* (42)

ASTHALL

See 519 [Turnpike act. 1777, &c.].

1454. An act for inclosing lands . . . of Asthal. . . . (52 G. III, c. 131, Private.) (Lond.), 1812, fol. 33 pp.
L. Eng. C 13 c. 1 (1812, vol. 1)

1455. An act to authorize the inclosure of certain lands . . . [Asthall]. (21 & 22 V., c. 61, Pub.) Lond., 1858, fol. 2 pp.
L. Eng. A 69 c. 1

1456. An act to authorize the inclosure of certain lands . . . [Asthall]. (22 V., c. 3, Pub.) Lond., 1859, fol. 2 pp.   L. Eng. A 69 c. 1

1457. Notes of an excursion to . . . Asthall. . . . (North Oxf. archaeol. soc., 1870.) Banbury, [1870], 8°. 37 pp.   R. Top. 330

1458. Asthall church. (Trans., Bristol and Glouc. archaeol. soc., 1895–96, vol. 20, p. 368–69.)   R. Top. 210

1459. Asthall. (Rept., Oxf. archaeol. soc., 1904, p. 9.)   R. Top. 330

1460. LEEDS, E. T., An Anglo-Saxon cremation-burial of the seventh century in Asthall Barrow, Oxfordshire. (Antiquaries journ., 1924, vol. 4, p. 113–26.)   R. Top. 2

1461. PRICE, E. R., Two effigies in the churches of Asthall and Cogges. (Oxoniensia, 1938, p. 103–10.)   R. Top. 340

1462. HUSSEY, C., Asthall manor. (Country Life, 1945, vol. 97, p. 1124–27.)   Per. 384 b. 6

1463. Asthall. (Archaeol. notes. Oxoniensia, 1946–7, p. 163.)   R. Top. 340

1464. Auction catal. Kitesbridge farm, 27 Nov. 1810.   G.A. fol. A 273*

1465. Auction catal. Kilkenny farm. 17 June 1908.   G.A. Oxon b. 90 (14)

1466. Auction catal. Arable land. 18 Sept. 1913.   G.A. Oxon b. 91 (1)

1467. Auction catal. Asthall and Swinbrook estates. 23 Sept. 1925.   G.A. Oxon c. 238

ASTHALL LEIGH

See 338 [Excavations on Akeman Street near Asthally. 1926].

1468. Auction catal. Kitesbridge farm. 27 Nov. 1810.   G.A. fol. A 273*

ASTON

1469. An act for the vesting . . . several manors and lands [in Aston &c.] late the inheritance of W. Jennens . . . in trustees to be sold. (8 Anne, c. 10, Private.) n. pl., [c. 1709], 8°. 52 pp.   Radcl. e. 127

1470. The Home visitor for Aston, Coggs, and Ducklington. June, 1879. Lond., (1879), 8°.   G.A. Oxon 8° 578

1471. Deddington, Heyford & Aston permanent building society. Rules. Lower Heyford, 1889, 8°. 32 pp.   G.A. Oxon 8° 567

1472. Aston school for training girls for domestic servants. [Report on opening of new buildings &c.] Repr. from Oxf. Times and from Witney Gazette of July 12th, 1913. n. pl., (1913), s. sh.
G.A. Oxon c. 317 (4)

1473. The Aston training school [for young girls for domestic service]. 27th annual report. n. pl., (1914), obl. 8°. 19 pp.
G.A. Oxon c. 317 (4)

1474. Auction catal. J. H. Usill estate. 26 July 1894.
G.A. Oxon b. 6 (31)

1475. Auction catal. Manor farm. 12 July 1898.
G.A. Oxon b. 90 (4)

1476. Auction catal. Manor farm. 24 May 1900.
G.A. Oxon c. 317 (4)

1477. Auction catal. Cote house. 21 July 1920.
G.A. Oxon b. 92* (2)

ASTON ROWANT

1478. An act for inclosing lands . . . of Aston Rowant. . . . (2 Will. IV, c. 1, Private.) Lond., 1832, fol. 38 pp.   L. Eng. C 13 c. 1

1479. Aston Rowant. (Rept., Oxf. archaeol. soc., 1886, p. 9–14.)
R. Top. 330

1480. HASSALL, W. O., Dissent at Aston Rowant [&c.]. (Thame Gazette, Jan. 30, 1951.)   N.G.A. Oxon a. 120

1481. HASSALL, W. O., History and Aston Rowant. (Thame Gazette, Mar. 27, 1951.)   N.G.A. Oxon a. 120

1482. Auction catal. Aston house. 19 Oct. 1859.
G.A. Oxon b. 85 a (1)

1483. Auction catal. Aston Rowant estate. 30 Oct. 1889.
G.A. Oxon b. 85 a (2)
— 22 July 1890.   G.A. Oxon b. 85 a (3)
— 1 July 1891.   G.A. Oxon b. 85 a (4)

1484. Auction catal. Outlying portions of Thame park estate. 24, 25 Sept. 1917.   G.A. Oxon b. 92 (23)

1485. Auction catal. Glebe farm, &c. 28 Sept. 1920.
G.A. Oxon b. 92* (18)

ASTON DEANERY

1486. The Aston Deanery magazine (with Benson). Nov. 1900–Nov. 1909. Watlington, 1900–09, 4°.   G.A. Oxon 4° 211

1487. PRIOR, C. E., Dedications of churches, with some notes as to village feasts and old customs. Deaneries of Aston and Henley. (Rept., Oxf. archaeol. soc., 1906, p. 14–22.)   R. Top. 330

1488. PEARCE, S. S., The clergy of the deaneries of Henley and Aston and of the peculiar of Dorchester, during the settlement of 1559 and afterwards. (Rept., Oxf. archaeol. soc., 1918, p. 127–89.)
R. Top. 330

ATTINGTON

1489. Auction catal. Attington house &c. 21 June 1907.
G.A. Oxon b. 90 (7)

1490. Auction catal. Outlying portions of Thame park estate. 24, 25 Sept. 1917.   G.A. Oxon b. 92 (23)

BABLOCK HYTHE

See 3318, 19 [Provision of bridge at Northmoor. 1910].
See 293 [History, by W. J. Monk. 1926].

1491. A Roman altar from Bablock Hythe. (Oxoniensia, 1946–47, p. 181.)
R. Top. 340

BAINTON

1492. Auction catal. Agricultural and sporting estate of J. S. Mansfield. 20 Mar. 1903.   G.A. Oxon b. 92 (7)

BALDON ESTATE

1493. Auction catal. 1,800 trees on Baldon estate. 16 Dec. 1869.
G.A. Oxon 8° 956 (1)

1494. Auction catal. 800 trees on Baldon estate. 5 Jan. 1871.
G.A. Oxon 8° 956 (2)

BALSCOTT

1495. An act for inclosing lands . . . of . . . Balscot. (43 G. III, c. 146, L. & P.) n. pl., [1803], fol. 24 pp.
L. Eng. C. 13 c. 1 (1803. ii. 42)

1496. St. Michael's orphanage, Balscote. (Our waifs & strays, 1884, new ser., no. 7.)   G.A. Oxon c. 317 (4)

BAMPTON

See 494 [London inns frequented by Bampton [? Oxon] carriers. 1637].

1497. An act for the vesting . . . several manors and lands [in Bampton &c.] . . . late the inheritance of W. Jennens . . . in trustees to be sold. (8 Anne, c. 10, Private.) n. pl., [c. 1709], 8°. 52 pp.
Radcl. e. 127

See 1225 [J. Leverett's will. 1783].

1498. HUDSON, R., A brief statement of the several charitable gifts and donations for the benefit of the poor of Bampton and Weald . . . . To which is added, An account of the lands appropriated for the use of repairing the church, &c. [By R. Hudson.] Bampton, 1801, 8°. 16 pp.
— Repr. 1814. [Reprod. in No. 1503, appendix 21.]

1499. An act for vesting part of the settled estates of . . . Charles, earl of Shrewsbury in the counties of Salop [&c.] . . . and Oxford [parish of Bampton] in trustees to be sold . . . (43 G. III, c. 40, L. & P.) Lond., 1803, fol. 22 pp.   L. Eng. A 69 c. 6

1500. An act for inclosing lands in the parish of Bampton. (52 G. III, c. 46, L. & P.) Lond., 1812, fol. 30 pp.   L. Eng. B 53 c. Land 2

1501. Bampton reading society. A catalogue of the books of the . . . society. n. pl., 1815, 8°. 24 pp.   G. Pamph. 540 (2)

1502. Oxfordshire anecdotes, with historical and topographical notes. [No. 1, 2 Bampton, &c.] n. pl., [c. 1826], 8°. 16 pp.
                                              G.A. Oxon 8° 934*

1503. GILES, J. A., History of the parish and town of Bampton. [With] Appendix. Oxf., 1847, 8°. 124+66 pp.   Manning 8° 317
— 2nd ed. enlarged. [With] Suppl. Bampton, 1848, 8°. 178+16 pp.
                                              G.A. Oxon 8° 14

1504. An act to authorize the inclosure of certain lands . . . [Bampton]. (16 & 17 V., c. 3, Pub.). Lond., 1853, fol. 2 pp.
                                              L. Eng. A 69 c. 1

1505. The manor of Bampton, and family of Horde. [Deeds, ed. by H. G.] (Topogr. and geneal., 1853, vol. 2, p. 515–20.) Ψ 2. 10 b

1506. DREWE, G. H., S. Mary's college, Bampton. [Appeal, signed G. H. Drewe, for funds for repair work.] (Oxf., 1860), s. sh.
                                              G.A. Oxon c. 22 (2)

1507. Bampton, St. Mary's coll. [Account of annual commemoration, 1861. Extr. from Oxford journ. Dec. 21st.]

Bampton, 1861, s. sh.   G.A. Oxon 8° 1130* (8)

1508. DREWE, G. H., The public school brought within the reach of the upper middle classes at one-fourth the expense, with an account of the work now being carried on at St. Mary's college, Bampton. Oxf., [1862], 8°. 16 pp.   G.A. Oxon 8° 1130* (9)

1509. Notes of an excursion to Ducklington, Cokethorpe, Stanlake, Yelford and Bampton. (North Oxf. archaeol. soc., 1871.) Banbury, [1871], 8°. 73 pp.   R. Top. 330

1510. ELLIS, F., Some account of a Romano-British village at Bampton. (Antiquary, vol. 23, 1891, p. 155–58.) Per. 17572 d. 32

1511. PLOMER, H. R., The private press of dr. J. A. Giles at Bampton vicarage. (The Library, new ser., vol. 1, 1900, p. 421, 22.) Per. 2589 d. 21

1512. KEYSER, C. E. An architectural description of Bampton church. (Journ., Brit. archaeol. assoc., 1916, new ser., vol. 22, p. 1–12, 113–22+43 plates.) R. Top. 4

1513. RODWELL, G. E. C., The flight of st. Frideswide [attempting to justify the claim of Bampton as the place which offered her sanctuary]. (Journ., Brit. archaeol. assoc., 1916, new ser., vol. 22, p. 85–89.) R. Top. 4

See 325. [Stone axe found 1938].

1514. Bampton. (Country Life, 1946, vol. 100, p. 118–21, 166–69, 266.) Per. 384 b. 6

1515. Auction catal. Lew farm. 13 May 1824. G.A. fol. B 71

1516. Auction catal. Baker's otherwise Macey's ground. 2 Aug. 1866. G.A. fol. B 71

1517. Auction catal. Estate. 31 May 1893. G.A. Oxon b. 6 (23)

1518. Auction catal. Outlying portions of the Blenheim estates. 3 July 1894. G.A. Oxon b. 90 (12)

1519. Auction catal. Upper Haddon farm. 2 May 1907. G.A. Oxon c. 317 (5)

1520. Auction catal. Calais farm. 14 June 1907. G.A. Oxon c. 317 (4)

1521. Auction catal. Pasture land. 18 Sept. 1913. G.A. Oxon b. 91 (1)

1522. Auction catal. Valetta lodge. 28 June 1917. G.A. Oxon c. 317 (4)

1523. Auction catal. Weald farm. 12 Sept. 1917. G.A. Oxon c. 317 (4)

BANBURY

General

1524. WHATELY, W., Sinne no more, or, A sermon preached in the parish church of Banbury . . . vpon occasion of a terrible fire. Lond., for G. Edwards, 1628, 4°. 56 pp. 4° M 45 (2) Th. [Other eds. in 1628, 2nd time publ. Antiq. e. X. 12 (6); 1630, Antiq. e. E. 8 (4); repr. 1824, G.A. Oxon 8° 169.]

1525. [Facsimile of the appeal for funds, dated 1628, after the great fire in Banbury in that year. The Appeal begins 'To our wel-beloued friends . . .' and is signed Epiphan Hill, maior, William Whately, minister (and 25 others).] G.A. Oxon c. 317 (16)

For works relating to incidents at Banbury during the Civil War see 368, 373, 375, 379, 80, 382, 384, 401, 407, 414, 417, 420, 424, 427, 28, 437, 38, 441.

1526. The Banb - - - y apes: or, The monkeys chattering to the mag-pye, a letter [satirising the arrival in Banbury of dr. Sacheverell]. Lond., [1710], 8°. 8 pp. G.A. Oxon 8° 4
— 3rd ed. 1710. G.A. Oxon 8° 637 (1)
— 4th ed. 1710. Douce PP 182

1527. An act for indemnifying Thomas Twisleton and Francis Twisle-ton . . . the purchasers of certain lands . . . [Banbury, &c.] belonging to James Ness . . . (9 G. III, c. 88, Private.) n. pl., 1769, fol. 7 pp. L. Eng. C. 13 c. 1 (1769, 76)

1528. RUSHER, P., Crouch-hill, a descriptive poem, with some account of the sieges of Banbury castle, in the reign of Charles the first [by P. Rusher]. Banbury, 1789, 8°. 34 pp. Gough Oxf. 45 (7)

1529. The Banbury miscellany, containing many interesting particulars . . . of persons . . . &c. that do, or that have existed, or happened in Banbury and the adjacent country, with prose pieces, and a variety of poetical compositions, by several hands. Banbury, 1789, 21°. 60 pp. G.A. Oxon 8° 162

1530. [Begin.] Banbury, 4th November, 1794. At a crisis like the present . . . [An appeal for clothing for the troops, signed] R. Bignell, J. Rushworth [and others]. [Banbury], (1794), s. sh. J.C.
— [Facsimile in no. 1608A, plate 39.]

1531. An act for vesting part of the estates of the late sir James Dash-wood in trustees, in trust to sell the same. [Banbury.] (37 G. III, c. 101, Private.) n. pl., 1797, fol. 30 pp. L. Eng. C 13 c. 1 (1797)

1532. The loyal signs of Banbury. [A ballad, naming many of the signs.] [Banbury, c. 1800], s. sh. J.C.
— [Facsimile in no. 1608A, plate 41.]

1533. Extracts from the cavalry regulations, with reference thereto; and directions for the sword exercise, for the use of the Bloxham and Banbury squadron of Oxfordshire Light-Horse Volunteers. Ban-bury, 1803, 8°. 58 pp. J.C.

1534. BELL, G., Rejoice and do good . . . a charity sermon, preached at Banbury, Mar. 17th, 1805. With an appendix of notes and refer-ences, explanatory of some local parish concerns. Banbury, (1805), 8°. 64 pp. G.A. Oxon 8° 637 (17)

1535. [A collection of newspaper cuttings &c., 1833–1848.]
G.A. Oxon 8° 989–94

1536. Banbury. (Gent's. mag., 1834, pt. 2, p. 300.) Ψ 2. 44

1537. BEESLEY, A., The history of Banbury. Lond., (1841), 8°. 667 pp.
G.A. Oxon 8° 5

1538. Reviews of . . . English topography. The history of Banbury . . .
by A. Beesley. (Archaeologist, no. 7, p. 1–9.) [Lond.], (1842), 4°.
G.A. Oxon 4° 360 (4)

1539. BEESLEY, T., On Roman remains in the neighbourhood of Banbury. (Trans., North Oxf. archaeol. soc., 1853–55, p. 15–22.)
R. Top. 330

1540. CADBURY, J., A new history of Banbury before and after a Maine
liquor law. Lond., 1855, 8°. 8 pp. B.M.

1541. RAWLINSON, R., Notes relating to the town and church of
Banbury, printed from the MSS. collections of dr. Rawlinson.
(North Oxf. archaeol. soc., 1860/61.) Banbury, (1861), 8°. 15 pp.
R. Top. 330

1542. JOHNSON, W. P., The history of Banbury and its neighbourhood.
Banbury, [c. 1865], 8°. 256 pp. G.A. Oxon 8° 604

1543. The Glow-worms amateur dramatic entertainment at the Corn
exchange, Banbury, April 20th, 1871 in aid of the funds of the New
Hospital. [Programme.] [Banbury, 1871], 8°. 4 pp.
G.A. Oxon 8° 360 (20)

1544. The Midland garner, a quarterly journal containing a selection
of local notes and queries from the 'Banbury Guardian', ed. by
J. R. Wodhams. 1st ser., vol. 1, 2. Banbury, 1884, 4°.
Per. G. A. Gen. top. 4° 155

1545. WALFORD, E. A., Edge Hill: the battle & battlefield; together with
some notes on Banbury and thereabouts. Banbury, 1886, 8°. 36 pp.
G.A. Warw. 8° 130
— 2nd ed. Banbury, &c., 1904. 102+ix pp. G.A. Warw. 16° 32
— (3rd ed.) With the Battle of Cropredy bridge and notes on the
countryside. Banbury, (1923), 8°. 57 pp. 22856 f. 25

1546. PEARSON, E., Banbury chap books and nursery toy book literature of the 18th and early 19th centuries. Lond., 1890, 4°. 116 pp.
2703 d. 2

1546A. CHENEY, C. R., Early Banbury chap-books and broadsides. (The
Library, 1937, ser. 4, vol. 17, p. 98–108.) E. Per. 26

1547. BOWEN, C. J., The hospitaller knights of St. John of Jerusalem,
with some account of St. John's ancient gate and priory, Banbury,
Oxon. (p. 18–32.) Lond., &c., 1894, 4°. G.A. Oxon 4° 399 b (12)

1548. Programme of the public celebration of the diamond jubilee of . . . Queen Victoria. Banbury, (1897), fol. 8 pp.   G.A. Oxon c. 100
See 658 [Parliamentary history by W. R. Williams. 1899].

1549. W., E., The pathways of Banburyshire. Banbury, &c., 1900, 8°. 57 pp.   G.A. Oxon 16° 64

1550. POTTS, W., Notes on the Globe room at the Reindeer inn, Banbury. (Rept., Oxf. archaeol. soc., 1905, p. 26–31.)   R. Top. 330

1551. The Reindeer inn, Banbury. (Berks, Bucks, & Oxon archaeol. journ., 1912, vol. 18, notes, p. 56, 57.)   R. Top. 100

1552. BRAITHWAITE, W. C., Banbury, the town & village community of the Middle Ages, a lecture. Banbury, 1913, 8°. 20 pp.
G.A. Oxon 8° 900 (33)

1553. KEYSER, C. E., Sculptured cornices in churches near Banbury, and their connexion with William of Wykeham. (Antiquaries journ., 1924, vol. 4, p. 1–10.)   R. Top. 2

1554. POTTS, W., Banbury in the coaching days. Banbury, 1929, 8°. 46 pp.   O.A.H.S.

1555. POTTS, W., Banbury through a hundred years. Banbury, 1942, 8°. 130 pp.   G.A. Oxon 8° 1188

1556. Auction catal. Crouch hill estate. 15 March 1833.
G.A. Oxon b. 85 a (27)

1557. Auction catal. Residences and business premises. 12 July 1880.
G.A. Oxon b. 85 a (7)

1558. Auction catal. Accommodation pasture. 28 July 1892.
G.A. Oxon b. 85 a (35)

1559. Auction catal. Overthorpe. 29 June 1899.
G.A. Oxon c. 317 (16)

1560. Auction catal. Springfields. 29 July 1903.
G.A. Oxon b. 6 (62)

Administration

1561. First report of the Commissioners appointed to inquire into the municipal corporations in England and Wales. (Banbury, Appendix, p. 7–15.)   Pp. Eng. 1835, vol. 23
— Protest of Sir F. Palgrave in the matter of the report. (p. 22, 33, 34).   Pp. Eng. 1835, vol. 40

1562. Report of the Commissioners appointed to report . . . upon the boundaries and wards of certain boroughs and corporate towns. (Banbury, pt. 1, p. 36–38.)   Pp. Eng. 1837, vol. 26

1563. COCKBURN, A. E., Corporations of England and Wales. (Banbury, vol. 1, p. 199–201.) Lond., 1835, 8°.

G.A. Gen. top. 8° 727 (1)

1564. An act to confirm certain provisional orders under the Local government act 1858 relating to . . . Banbury [&c., concerning rates]. (23 & 24 V., c. 44, Pub.) Lond., 1860, fol. 27 pp.

L. Eng. A 69 c. 1

1565. Memorandum as to the proposed bill for extending the municipal boundary. Banbury, 1883, fol. 4 pp.   G.A. Oxon 4° 360 (34)

1566. POTTS, J., The bailiffs and mayors of the borough of Banbury, 1554 to 1904. [Banbury, 1904], 8°. 12 pp.   G.A. Oxon 8° 715 (22)

Banbury Cross

1567. LOVELL, W., Banbury cross. (Archaeological journ. 1889, vol. 46, p. 159–64.)   R. Top. 5

1568. BROOKS, H. R. F., Borough of Banbury. Coronation of . . . George V. memorial committee. Completion of Banbury Cross. [An appeal, signed H. R. F. Brooks & others, for funds to complete the Cross by addition of 3 statues.] n. pl., (1911), 4°. 3 pp.

G.A. Oxon c. 22 (5)

1569. DITCHFIELD, P. H., Banbury cross. (Oxf. diocesan mag., 1923, vol. 18, p. 38–42.)   Per. 11126 d. 78 (18)

1570. POTTS, W., Banbury cross and the rhyme. Banbury, 1930, 8°. 70 pp.   G.A. Oxon 8° 1138

Banbury Fine Art Exhibition, 1881

1571. Banbury fine art exhibition, 1881. [MS. letters, handbills, &c.]
G.A. Oxon 4° 360 (21–32)

1572. Banbury fine art exhibition, 1881. Official catalogue. Banbury, 1881, 4°. 44 pp.   G.A. Oxon 4° 360 (33)

Biography

1573. The histories of four young gentlemen, now living in Banbury, containing also Anecdotes of several persons of Banbury, &c., &c., with a description of a journey to Crouch-Hill. n. pl., [c. 1789].

1574. CADBURY, J., A tribute of affection to the memory of . . . Caleb Clarke, of Banbury. Banbury, (1851), 8°. 8 pp.

G.A. Oxon 8° 637 (22)

1575. REDFORD, E., 'Dieu veult' ... The Banbury female martyr, composed by herself. [Banbury? *c.* 1865], 8°. 83 pp.

G.A. Oxon 8° 98

1576. BEESLEY, S., My life. [Banbury? 1892], 16°. 259 pp. B.M.

1577. Thomas Beesley, J.P., F.C.S., of Banbury. Repr. from the Banbury Guardian, Apr. 8th 1897. Banbury, (1897), 8°. 11 pp.

G.A. Oxon 8° 970

1578. HERBERT, G., Shoemaker's window, recollections of a Midland town [Banbury], before the railway age, ed. by C. S. Cheney. Oxf., 1948, 8°. 139 pp. 211 e. 1162

Banbury peerage.
See 1251–55 [Knolly family].

Directories

1579. RUSHER, J. G., Rusher's Banbury list. 1812–26. [*Afterw.*] Rusher's Banbury list and directory. 1827–31. [*Afterw.*] Rusher's Original Banbury list and directory. 1831–96. Banbury, 1812–96, 8°.

G.A. Oxon 8° 932, 33; Dir. Oxon e. 6

1580. The Banbury directory. 1832. n. pl., (1832), 8°.

Dir. Oxon e. 10

1581. Pott's companion to the almanack and Banbury directory. 1842. Banbury, 1842, 8°. 16 pp. G.A. Oxon 8° 634
See 1390 [Directory. 1846].

1582. The Banbury almanack and local directory for 1851.
— 1852 [*entitled*] Potts's Banbury almanack. Banbury, 1851, 52, 8°.
(Alm.) G.A. Oxon 8° 634

1583. Webster's Oxford, Wallingford, Abingdon and Banbury directory. 1869. Oxf., (1869), 8°. Dir. Oxon e. 7

1584. Banbury and neighbourhood directory. 1932–40. [Publ. biennially].

Education

1585. Banbury British school society. Second (— fourth, seventh) annual report. Banbury, 1842–47, 8°. G.A. Oxon 8° 638

1586. Banbury elementary school of art. [Proposed course of lessons, January, 1867.] Banbury, 1866, s. sh. G.A. Oxon 4° 360 (18)

1587. Banbury High street science school. [Proposed course in inorganic chemistry of Thomas Beesley, October 1866.] [Banbury], 1866, s. sh. G.A. Oxon 4° 360 (17)

1588. International high school, Banbury. [Prospectus.] (Banbury), [1890?], 8°. 8 pp.   G.A. Oxon c. 317 (16)

1589. Banbury mechanics' institution. A catalogue of the library, with the bye-laws for the regulation of the library. Banbury, 1836, 8°. 41 pp.   G.A. Oxon 8° 632 (1)
— [Another ed.] Banbury, 1837, 8°. 39 pp.
     G.A. Oxon 8° 632 (2)

1590. Catalogue of articles contained in the exhibition of the Banbury mechanics' institution, 1840. Banbury, (1840), 4°. 32 pp.
     G.A. Oxon 4° 360 (3)

1591. Banbury municipal school. Abstract of the accounts. 1893–98. Banbury, 1895–99, fol.   G.A. Oxon c. 100

1592. Banbury municipal school. Prospectus. 1898/99, 1899. Banbury, 1898, 99, 4°.   G.A. Oxon c. 100

1593. Banbury municipal school. Science & art division. Head master's opening lecture . . . with the pass list for session 1898–99. Banbury, 1899, 16°. 29 pp.   G.A. Oxon c. 317 (16)

1594. Banbury national schools. Eighty-second annual report. Banbury, 1898, fol. 4 pp.   G.A. Oxon c. 100

1595. Banbury science school. [Proposed course of Thomas Beesley, certificated teacher of chemistry for the winter session of 1862–63.] [Banbury], (1862), 4°. 4 pp.   G.A. Oxon 4° 360 (15)

1596. Banbury science school. Report. 1864. Banbury, 1864, s. sh.
     G.A. Oxon 4° 360 (16)

1597. Proposed school of art, in Banbury. [Circular, signed by various citizens of Banbury and vicinity, notifying a meeting to advocate the foundation of a school of art.] [Banbury, c. 1860], s. sh.
     G.A. Oxon 4° 360 (14)

1598. Banbury school of art and science classes. Prospectus for first session, 1884–5. Banbury, (1884), 4°. 8 pp.   G.A. Oxon 4° 360 (35)

1599. Banbury university students' association library. [Rules. c. 1900]
     G.A. Oxon c. 100 (29)

1600. South Banbury national schools. Report, 1897/98, 1898/99. Banbury (1897–99), 4°.   G.A. Oxon c. 100

1601. [Letter from the town clerk calling a meeting of managers of Elementary schools to discuss a communication from the Educ. Dept. concerning overcrowding of schools]. n. pl., (1899), fol. 4 pp.
     G.A. Oxon c. 100

Guide Books and Photographs

1602. STANLEY, H. B., Photographic view album of Banbury and vicinity. Banbury [18—], 8°. 16 pp.   G.A. Oxon 4° 333

1603. JOHNSON, W. P., The stranger's guide through Banbury and neighbourhood. 2nd ed. Banbury, [1866], 12°. 24 pp.   B.M.

1604. Photographic view album of Banbury and neighbourhood. (Dainty ser.). Banbury, [c. 1890], 4°. 17 photos.
G.A. Oxon 8° 550

1605. The illustrated guide to Banbury and district. Banbury, [c. 1910], 16°. 56 pp.   G.A. Oxon 16° 138

1606. Walford's album of photographic views of Banbury. Banbury, [1917?], 8°. 6 pp.   G.A. Oxon 8° 834

1607. Official guide. 3rd–6th ed. Lond., [1929–36], 8°.
G.A. Oxon 8° 1065

Industries and Trades

1608. LICKORISH, W. H., 'Our balance sheet', an exposition of the report and balance sheet of the Banbury Co-operative industrial society limited. Banbury, 1909, 8°. 22 pp.   23223 e. 16

1608A. John Cheney and his descendants, printers in Banbury since 1767. Banbury, 1936, 4°. 81 pp.+70 plates.   25823 d. 119

See 617 [Plush industry, by R. P. Beckinsale. 1937].

Natural History
Geology

1609. WILSON, W., The geology of the neighbourhood of Banbury. (Rept., Oxf. archaeol. soc., 1857, p. 5–8.)   R. Top. 330

See 22 [Geology, by A. H. Green. 1864].

1610. BEESLEY, T., A sketch of the geology of the neighbourhood of Banbury. (Geol. mag., 1872, vol. 9, p. 279–82.)   Radcl.

1611. WALFORD, E. A., On some upper and middle lias beds in the neighbourhood of Banbury. (Proc., Warwickshire N.F.C., suppl. for 1878, p. 1–23.)   Radcl.
— Repr. 1879.   Radcl.

1612. WALFORD, E. A., The lias ironstone of north Oxfordshire, around Banbury. Lond., &c., 1899, 8°. 36 pp.   Radcl.

1613. DOUGLAS, J. A., The Oxford and Banbury district. (Geology in the Field, 1909, publ. by the Geol. assoc., pt. 1, p. 192–209.)
188505 d. 8

1614. RICHARDSON, L., Excursion to the Banbury and Towcester districts. (Proc., Geol. assoc., 1921, vol. 32, p. 109–22.)   Radcl.

1615. RICHARDSON, L., Certain jurassic, aalenian-vesulian, strata of the Banbury district. (Proc., Cots. N.F.C., 1922, vol. 21, p. 109–32.)   Per. 18855 d. 58

Botany

1616. GULLIVER, G., A catalogue of plants collected in the neighbourhood of Banbury. Lond., &c., 1841, 8°. 37 pp.   19136 f. 1

Zoology

1617. STRETCH, R., List of land and fresh water mollusca found in the neighbourhood of Banbury. (The Zoologist, 1855, vol. 13, p.4540–43.)   Per. 18933 e. 395

1618. PIDGEON, D., A list of the land and freshwater shells found in the neighbourhood of Banbury. (Quarterly journ. of conchology, 1874, vol. 1, p. 54–57.)   Per. 18945 d. 18

1619. APLIN, F. C., B. D., and O. V., A list of birds of the Banbury district. Banbury, 1882, 8°. 29 pp.   18961 e. 6

Newspapers

Banbury Advertiser.
See 1326.

Banbury Beacon.
See 1327.

Banbury Evening news.
See 1328.

Banbury Guardian.
See 1329.

Banbury Herald.
See 1330.

Banbury Telegraph.
See 1331.

Guardian.
See 1338.

Parliamentary Representation

See 723, 730 [Electioneering at Banbury. 1754].

1620. The election and riots at Banbury. (John Bull, May 9th, 1831, vol. 11.)   G.A. Oxon 4° 362 (1)

1621. Parliamentary representation. Reports from Commissioners on proposed division of counties and boundaries of boroughs. (Banbury, p. 189, 90.)   Pp. Eng. 1831/2, vol. 39

1622. Trance of an Oxfordshire corn dealer, related by himself. [Political satire.] n. pl., [1832?], 8°. 8 pp.   G.A. Oxon 8° 637 (2)

1623. PYE, H. J., The speech of H. J. Pye, esq., delivered to the electors of Banbury, Neithrop, and the hamlets, at the Flying Horse inn, on . . . Tuesday, 25th Sept., 1832. Banbury, (1832), 8°. 16 pp.
                                   G.A. Oxon 8° 631 (4)

1624. A copy of the poll of the electors for a burgess in Parliament for . . . Banbury, 5th January, 1835. Banbury, (1835), 8°. 16 pp.
                                   G.A. Oxon 4° 362 (2)

1625. The poll taken for the election of a member to serve in parliament for the borough of Banbury, on Tuesday, 25 July, 1837. Banbury, (1837), 8°. 16 pp.   G.A. Oxon 8° 631 (2)

1626. [Banbury elections, 1841–47. Notices, bills, &c.].
                                   G.A. Oxon b. 101

1627. List of persons whose names are upon the register of electors for . . . Banbury . . . together with the poll, 30th June 1841, for the election of a member . . . in Parliament. Banbury, (1841), 4°. 12 pp.
                                   G.A. Oxon 4° 362 (3)

1628. A copy of the poll of the electors for a burgess in parliament, for the borough of Banbury, taken 31st July, 1847. Banbury, (1847), 12°. 23 pp.   G.A. Oxon 8° 631 (1)
— [Another ed.], 8°. 12 pp.   G.A. Oxon 8° 631 (3)

1629. List of persons whose names are upon the register of electors for . . . Banbury . . . together with the poll, 31st July 1847, for the election of a member to serve in Parliament. Banbury, (1847), 4°. 12 pp.   G.A. Oxon 4° 362 (5)

See 672 [Register of electors, Banbury division. 1918–].

Police

1630. Instructions for the Police force of the borough of Banbury. Banbury, 1836, 8°. 12 pp.   G.A. Oxon 8° 637 (18)

Police (counties and boroughs). Reports of the inspectors of constabulary. 1857–1912. (Banbury).
See 988.

Prisons

1631. Third report of the inspectors appointed . . . to visit the different prisons of Great Britain. Southern and Western district. (Banbury, p. 82–84.) Pp. Eng. 1837/8, vol. 31
— 5th rept., p. 35, 36. Pp. Eng. 1840, vol. 25
— 7th rept., p. 153, &c. Pp. Eng. 1842, vol. 21
— 9th rept., p. 331, &c. Pp. Eng. 1844, vol. 29
— 11th rept., p. 308, &c. Pp. Eng. 1846, vol. 21
— 12th rept., p. 309, &c. Pp. Eng. 1848, vol. 35

Public Health

1632. An act to confirm certain provisional orders of the general board of health, and to amend the Public health act, 1848. [Includes Banbury.] (15 & 16 V., c. 42, Pub.) Lond., 1852, fol. 4 pp.
L. Eng. A 69 c. 1
— 23 & 24 V., c. 44, Pub.

1633. BEESLEY, T., A report to the Local board of health for the district of Banbury. Banbury, (1857), 8°. 16 pp. G.A. Oxon 8° 939 (6)

1634. BUCHANAN, DR., Dr. Buchanan's report on [the sanitary condition of] Banbury: 1870. [Lond.], (1870), fol. 4 pp.
G.A. Oxon 4° 360 (19)

1635. Banbury nursing association. First–(23rd) annual report. Banbury, 1876/7–98/9, 8°. [Bodleian set is imperfect.]
G.A. Oxon 8° 675

1636. Horton infirmary for Banbury and its neighbourhood. Rules. Banbury, 1877, 8°. 21 pp. G.A. Oxon 8° 893

Public Utilities

1637. BEESLEY, T., A chemical analysis of the water of Holywell, Tadmarton Heath, with an inquiry as to its fitness for the water-supply of . . . Banbury. Banbury, 1853, 8°. 9 pp. G.A. Oxon 8° 948

1638. The Banbury local board of health and the Canal company [concerning the purchase of ground for sewage works]. Oxf., 1863, s. sh. G.A. Oxon c. 79 (455)

1639. An act to incorporate the Banbury water company (limited) and to make further provision for the supply of water to . . . Banbury . . . (28 & 29 V., c. 16, L. & P.) Lond., 1865, fol. 14 pp.
L. Eng. A 69 c. 6

1640. An act to incorporate the Banbury Gaslight and coke company (limited) and to make further provision for lighting Banbury and places in the neighbourhood . . . (29 & 30 V., c. 4, L. & P.) Lond., 1866, fol. 18 pp. L. Eng. A 69 c. 6

See 1022 [Act concerning supply of gas. 1913].

1641. An act to authorise the Banbury Water company to construct new works and raise additional capital to alter the limits of supply of the company to confer further powers . . . to empower them to acquire . . . the Bloxham and District Water company limited . . . (1 E. VIII & 1 G. VI, c. 88, L. & P.) Lond., 1937, fol. 65 pp.

L. Eng. A 69 c. 6

1642. Ministry of Health provisional order confirmation (Banbury Water) act. 1942/43. (6 & 7 G. VI, c. 11, Pub.)

L. Eng. A 69 c. 6

Railways

See 485, 492 [Railway. 1846, 1897].

1643. An act to incorporate a company for the construction of the Banbury and Cheltenham Direct railway . . . (36 & 37 V., c. 172, L. & P.) Lond., 1873, fol. 33 pp.   L. Eng. A 69 c. 6
— 40 & 41 V., c. 109, L. & P.
— 41 & 42 V., c. 223, L. & P.
— 42 & 43 V., c. 212, L. & P.

1644. Cheney's Railway guide, list of carriers and postal guide for Banbury and the district. October, 1898. [Banbury], (1898), 8°. 45 pp.   G.A. Oxon c. 317 (16)

Regional Planning

1645. Banbury and district joint regional planning committee. The regional planning of Banbury and district. (Banbury, 1933), 8°. 24 pp.   2479115 d. 34 (5)

Religion

Church of England

1646. An act for taking down the Church chancel and tower . . . of Banbury . . . and for rebuilding the same. (30 G. III, c. 72, Pub.) n. pl., 1790, fol. 17 pp.   Gough Oxf. 103 (20)

1647. The present state of Banbury church building trust, described by a trustee. Lond., 1839, 4°. 14 pp.   G.A. Oxon 4° 360 (2)

1648. Church of England Protestant institution, for Banbury and its vicinity. An address to the operative classes. Banbury, [c. 1845], 8°. 6 pp.   G.A. Oxon 8° 637 (16)

1649. FORBES, C., An address to the parishioners in South Banbury, on the present times, in connection with the anomalous position of pastor and people without a church. Banbury, 1850, 8°. 12 pp.

G.A. Oxon 8° 637 (20)

1650. The churchwardens of the parish of Banbury in account with the subscribers to the fund for defraying the expenses of public worship . . . 1865/66. [Oxf.], (1866), 4°. 4 pp.   G.A. Oxon 4° 119 (7)

1651. DRAPER, E., Notes on the parish church, S. Mary's, Banbury. Banbury, 1892, 8°. 23 pp.   G.A. Oxon 8° 527

1652. DRAPER, E., Gleams of interest across the parish church chimes of S. Mary's, Banbury . . . Together with the words and airs of the chimes. Banbury, 1901, 4°. 41 pp.   Mus. 211 d. 1

1653. DRAPER, E., and POTTS, W., The parish church, S. Mary's, Banbury. Banbury, 1907, 16°. 91 pp.   G.A. Oxon 16° 100

1654. Borough of Banbury, Open spaces act, 1906. Conversion of the disused burial ground of the parish church of St. Mary the virgin, Banbury, into a 'garden of rest'. Statement of tombstones and monuments . . . in the . . . burial ground [giving names, date of death &c. Reprod. from typescript. 1950. 23 fol. sheets]
G.A. Oxon c. 304

1655. Auction catal. Pew of the first class, Banbury church. 15 March 1833.   G.A. Oxon b. 85 a (27)

Nonconformist

1656. The saints' testimony finishing through sufferings: or the proceedings of the Court against the Servants of Jesus . . . at the late Assizes . . . in Banbury . . . 1655; also a relation of Margaret Vivers going to the Steeple house in Banbury after the assize as aforesaid. Lond., 1655, 4°. 44 pp.   4° L 63 Art.

1657. BUGG, F., Distinct advice on two different heads given to the . . . Quakers. First with respect to a conference to be had . . . at Banbury. . . . Lond., 1702, 8°. 16 pp.   110 k. 321 (5)
— 2nd ed. 1703.

1658. BUGG, F., Quakerism drooping and its cause sinking. Also a reply . . . by Ben. Loveling [entitled The spirit of Quakerism rebuked. To which is annex'd the late proceedings with the Quakers at Banbury, by F. Bugg]. Lond., 1703, 8°. 184 pp.   G. Pamph. 840 (4, 5)

1659. BUNTON, W., Passing events! ! To the working and thinking men and women of Banbury. [A letter defending non-believers in the divine authority of the Bible.] n. pl., [18—], 4°. 4 pp.
G.A. Oxon 4° 360 (10)

1660. North Bucks and North Oxon federation of Free church councils. Banbury district free church leader. No. 2, 3. Banbury, (1899), 8°.
G.A. Oxon 8° 656

1661. TYSSEN, A. D., The old meeting house, Banbury and its successor, the Unitarian church. (Trans., Unitarian hist. soc., 1918, Dec., p. 276–302.)   Per. 1116 d. 11

Roman Catholic

1662. HARRIS, G., The spirit of Popery; or, Threats exposed in a copy of a letter from . . . dr. Tandy . . . and a reply to the same. Banbury, 1838, 8°. 8 pp.   G.A. Oxon 8° 637 (4)
— 4th 500. 1838.   G.A. Oxon 8° 637 (5)

1663. TANDY, W., An address to the people of Banbury touching a late production of mr. George Harris, coal dealer. Banbury, 1838, 8°. 15 pp.

1664. HARRIS, G., The abominations of Popery displayed, in remarks upon the Address of the rev. dr. Tandy, 'Catholic pastor of St. John's' to the people of Banbury. Banbury, 1838, 8°. 20 pp.
     G.A. Oxon 8° 637 (6)

1665. CATTON, W., A protest against Popery, in reply to dr. Tandy's address to the people of Banbury [&c.]. Banbury, 1838, 8°. 20 pp.

1666. TANDY, W., The second address to the people of Banbury, exposing the ignorance and falsification of mr. G. Harris in The abominations of Popery displayed. Banbury, 1838, 8°. 26 pp.

1667. HARRIS, G., The second chapter of the abominations of Popery displayed, with some remarks on mr. Tandy's Second address. 2nd 500. Banbury, 1838, 8°. 22 pp.   G.A. Oxon 8° 637 (7)

1668. HARRIS, G., Dr. Tandy and Tristram Shandy. To the inhabitants of Banbury. Banbury, 1838, 8°. 2 pp.   G.A. Oxon 8° 637 (7*)

1669. TANDY, W., To the people of Banbury. [A reply to 'Dr. Tandy and Tristram Shandy'.] Banbury, 1838, 8°. 2 pp.

1670. TANDY, W., A sample of the veracity of mr. Harris. Banbury, 1838, 8°. 2 pp.

1671. TANDY, W., A parting word for mr. Harris [by W. Tandy]. Banbury, [1838], 8°. 8 pp.

1672. HARRIS, G., The defeat of Popery, a reply to the Parting word of dr. Tandy. Banbury, 1838, 8°. 8 pp.

1673. Extract from the 'Aylesbury News', Nov. 10, 1838 [supporting W. Tandy against G. Harris]. n. pl., (1838), s. sh.
     G.A. Oxon 8° 637 (3**)

1674. STONE, J., To the inhabitants of Banbury and its vicinity. [A letter defending Roman Catholicism against A. Gavazzi.] [Banbury], (1856), 4°. 6 pp.   G.A. Oxon 4° 360 (13)

1675. BOWEN, C. J., Catholicity in Banbury since the Reformation. Birm., [1898], 8°. 8 pp. 2182 D. e. 7

1676. St. John's Church, Banbury. A brief history . . . in commemoration of the centenary, June 19th, 1938. (Banbury, 1938), 4°. 48 pp. G.A. Oxon 4° 655

Church Societies

1677. Banbury auxiliary bible society. The twenty first (24th, 25th, 27th) report. Banbury, 1838–44, 4°. G.A. Oxon 8° 637 (8); 133 e. 191 (12–14)

1678. Banbury church choral society. A selection of sacred music, to be performed in the National school room, Feb. 14th, 1843. Banbury, (1843), 8°. 8 pp. G.A. Oxon 8° 637 (19)

Roads

See 494 [London inns frequented by Banbury carriers. 1637].
See 501, 504, 05, 510, 514, 520, 523, 530 [Turnpike acts. 1744, &c.].

1679. An act for paving, cleansing, lighting, watching and otherwise improving the several streets, lanes, public passages and places in the borough of Banbury. . . . (6 G. IV, c. 130, L. & P.) Lond., 1825, fol. 50 pp. O.C.R.L.

1680. The Commissioners appointed by the act of parliament for paving and lighting the borough of Banbury . . . regulations. Banbury, 1825, s. sh. G.A. Oxon c. 317 (16)

1680A. Commissioners for paving the town of Banbury. Report . . . by E. O. Tregelles. Bristol, 1849, 12°. 15 pp. B.M.

Societies

1681. Banbury agricultural assoc. Premiums . . . offered . . . at the annual meeting. 1839–49. Banbury, 1839–49, 4° &c. G.A. Oxon 4° 185

1682. Banbury agricultural assoc. Report of the sub-committee . . . on the method of cultivating flax in Norfolk, with a view to its introduction into this neighbourhood. Banbury, 1844, 8°. 4 pp. G.A. Oxon 4° 185 (1)

1683. Banbury bank for savings. Rules and regulations. Banbury, 1840, 8°. 12 pp. G.A. Oxon 8° 637 (10)
— 1844. G.A. Oxon 4° 360 (6)
— 1847. G.A. Oxon 8° 637 (14)

1684. Banbury bank for savings. [Information for depositors.] [Banbury], 1844, 4°. 4 pp. G.A. Oxon 4° 360 (7)

1685A. General account of the Banbury charitable society for visiting and relieving the sick and distressed poor in the town and parish of Banbury at their own habitations. Banbury, 1841, 8°. 12 pp.
G.A. Oxon 8° 635 (8)

1685B. Banbury clerical society. Fixtures for the centenary year, 1952. Deddington, 1951, 8°. 4 pp.   G.A. Oxon 8° 1259 (1)

1686. Rules and regulations of the Banbury district widow and orphans' fund, of the Independent order of oddfellows, Manchester Unity. Banbury, [1846?], 8°. 8 pp.   G.A. Oxon 8° 635 (3)

1687. Banbury old charitable society. Report. 1890, 1892, 1894, 1896. Banbury, 1890–96, fol.   G.A. Oxon c. 100

1688. Banbury refuge for the afflicted. Rules. Banbury, [1845], 8°. 15 pp.   G.A. Oxon 8° 635 (6)

1689. Banbury savings' bank annuity society. Rules. Banbury, 1834, 4°. 16 pp.   G.A. Oxon 4° 360 (1)
— 1845. 16 pp.   G.A. Oxon 8° 637 (11)

1690. Banbury sick fund society. Laws, rules, and regulations. Banbury, 1846, 8°. 16 pp.   G.A. Oxon 8° 635 (5)

1691. Banbury United Christian benefit society. Rules. Banbury, 1841, 8°. 35 pp.   G.A. Oxon 8° 635 (7)

1692. Beneficial society. Rules, orders, & regulations. Banbury, 1838, 8°. 17 pp.   G.A. Oxon 8° 635 (12)

1693. British queen benefit society. Rules and articles. Banbury, 1849, 8°. 24 pp.   G.A. Oxon 8° 635 (9)

1694. Female friendly society. Rules and orders to be observed and kept by the members. Banbury, 1806, 8°. 12 pp.   J.C.

1695. Rules for the regulation and government of a Friendly society, established at Banbury, Oct. 1837. Banbury, 1837, 8°. 13 pp.
G.A. Oxon 8° 635 (10)

1696. Funded laws for the government of the [blank] lodge of the Independent order of odd fellows . . . Banbury district. Banbury, (1846), 8°. 8 pp.   G.A. Oxon 8° 635 (2)

1697. Bye-laws for the government of the Banbury district of the Independent order of odd fellows. Banbury, (1846), 8°. 7 pp.
G.A. Oxon 8° 635 (4)

1698. Tradesmen's benefit society. Rules . . . established 28th June, 1839. Banbury, 1840, 8°. 19 pp.   G.A. Oxon 8° 635 (11)

BANBURY HUNDRED

1699. Reports of the Commissioners for inquiring concerning charities in the hundreds of Banbury, [&c.]. 2 vols. Banbury, 1826, 44, 4°.
G.A. Oxon 8° 170, 171

BANBURY (Peculiar jurisdiction of)

See 2130 [Peculiar of Banbury, clergy of, during 1559 and afterwards by S. S. Pearce. 1916].

1700. PEYTON, S. A., The Churchwardens' presentments in the Oxford-shire peculiars of Dorchester, Thame and Banbury. (Oxf. record soc., 10.). [Oxf.], 1928, 8°. 340 pp.
R. 13. 702

BARFORD ST. JOHN

1701. An act for dividing and inclosing the . . . fields . . . of Little Barford, otherwise Barford Saint John. . . . (33 G. III, c. 28, Private.) n. pl., 1793, fol. 32 pp.
L. Eng. C 13 c. 1 (1793. i. 13)

1702. Auction catal. Manorial estate. [1st], 2nd ed. 6 June 1891.
G.A. Oxon b. 85 b (60, 61)
— 15 Sept. 1894.
G.A. Oxon b. 92 (43)

BARFORD ST. MICHAEL

1703. An act for inclosing lands . . . of . . . Great Barford, otherwise Barford Saint Michael. . . . (47 G. III, sess. 2, c. 44, Private.) n. pl., [1807], fol. 29 pp.
L. Eng. C 13 c. 1 (1806–7. i. 24)

1704. Auction catal. Land, old Manor house, Buttermilk and Rignell farms, watermill and four cottages. 8 July 1909.
G.A. Oxon c. 317 (5)

BARTON

1705. Barton friendly society. Rules. Oxf., 1868, 8°. 16 pp.
G.A. Oxon 8° 596
— Revised ed. Oxf., 1895, 8°. 24 pp.
G.A. Oxon 8° 596

1706. MARSHALL, E., To the members of the Barton Friendly society. [A letter, signed E. Marshall, urging the cessation of an alcoholic licence for the club.] n. pl., (1878), s. sh.
G.A. Oxon c. 22 (6)

1707. Barton Women's Institute. It happened in the Dorn valley, 1939–45. (Oxf.), [1946], 8°. 71 pp.
G.A Oxon 8° 1250

1708. Auction catal. Pasture land. 13 June 1855.
G.A. Oxon b. 4 (18)

1709. Auction catal. Cottage. 2 Sept. 1868.   G.A. Oxon b. 4 (35)

1710. Auction catal. Barton farm. 24 May 1911.
G.A. Oxon b. 90 (10)

BECKLEY

1711. An act for appointing jointures for the wives and . . . portions for the younger children of . . . Willoughby, earl of Abingdon, and Peregrine Bertie his brother. [Beckley &c.]. (9 G. III, sess. 2, c. 10, Private.) n. pl., 1769, fol. 43 pp.   G.A. Oxon c. 192

1712. An act for inclosing lands . . . of Beckley [&c.] (7 & 8 G. IV, c. 15, Private.) (Lond.), 1827, fol. 31 pp.
L. Eng. C 13 c. 1 (1826/7. i. 9)

1713. WESTWOOD, PROFESSOR, [Roman villa]. (Archaeological journ., 1868, vol. 20, p. 73, 74.)   R. Top. 5

1713A. Charity commission. In the matter of the charity founded and endowed in . . . 1640, by sir George Croke, knight; and In the matter of 'The Charitable trusts act, 1853 to 1869. [The charity affects Beckley and Horton.] Lond., 1880, fol. 10 pp.   Dep. b. 43

1714. EVANS, SIR A., Late-Celtic dagger, fibula and jet cameo. Bronze fibula from Beckley, Oxon. (Archaeologia, 1915, vol. 66, p. 570–72.)
R. Top. 7

1715. HUSSEY, C., Beckley park. (Country Life, 1929, vol. 65, p. 400–08.)   Per. 384 b. 6

1716. Beckley church. (Rept., Oxf. archaeol. soc., 1933, p. 15, 18.)
R. Top. 330

1717. MILLEN, E. L., [Report on Beckley church and request for subscriptions for new churchyard, &c.]. (Oxf.), [1934], 8°. 4 pp.
G.A. Oxon c. 317 (5)

1718. Auction catal. Beckley park, Beckley village. 16 July 1844.
G.A. fol. A 266 (25)

1719. Auction catal. Studley priory estate. [3 eds.] 19 June 1897.
G.A. Oxon b. 85 b (51–53)

1720. Auction catal. Little fields, Water's field. 30 July 1902.
G.A. Oxon b. 90 (20)

1721. Auction catal. New inn farm. 24 May 1911.
G.A. Oxon b. 90 (10)

1722. Auction catal. Entire parish. 25 June 1919.
G.A. Oxon b. 92* (4)

BEGBROKE

1723. An act for confirming a partition made between Robert Dashwood . . . and Cholmley Turner . . . of certain . . . lands . . . in . . . [Begbroke &c.]. (3 G. I, c. 22, Private.) n. pl., 1717, fol. 7 pp.
B.M.
See 496 [Turnpike act. 1718, &c.].

1724. Begbroke. (Gent's. mag., 1808, pt. 1, p. 390, 91.) Ψ 2. 44

1725. Begbroke, Cassington and Yarnton horticultural society. Rules, list of subscribers, and schedule of prizes . . . for 3rd annual show. Oxf., 1887, 8°. 12 pp.   G.A. Oxon c. 317 (5)

1726. STAPLETON, MRS. B., Three Oxfordshire parishes. A history of Kidlington, Yarnton and Begbroke. (Oxf. hist. soc., vol. 24.) Oxf., 1893, 8°. 400 pp.   R. 13. 700

1727. Auction catal. Estate. 6 Sept. 1848.   G.A. Oxon c. 317 (5)

1728. Auction catal. Pixey mead. 10 July 1849.   G.A. Oxon b. 6 (27)

1729. Auction catal. Yarnton estate. 6 June 1891. [1st], 2nd ed.
G.A. Oxon b. 85 b (60, 61)
— 15 Sept. 1894.   G.A. Oxon b. 92 (43)

1730. Auction catal. The Elms, Begbroke hall farm. 5 June 1897.
G.A. Oxon b. 90 (11)

1731. Sale catal. Begbroke place. 1919.   G.A. Oxon c. 317 (5)

BENSON

See 515 [Turnpike act. 1770].

1732. Bensington. (Gent's. mag., 1793, p. 2, pt. 716–19.) Ψ 2. 44

1733. An act to authorize the inclosure of certain lands . . . [Benson.] (16 & 17 V., c. 3, Pub.) Lond., 1853, fol. 2 pp.   L. Eng. A 69 c. 1

1734. PEARMAN, M. T., A history of the manor of Bensington, Benson, Oxon, a manor of ancient demesne. Lond., 1896, 8°. 147 pp.
G.A. Oxon 8° 624

1735. FIELD, J. E., Benson, or Bensington. (Berks, Bucks, & Oxon archaeol. journ., 1896, vol. 2, p. 44–50, 73–76; 1897, vol. 3, p. 6–14.)
R. Top. 100

1736. Benson Conservative club. (Annual report.) 1897, 1899, 1900, 1902. n. pl., 1897–1902, s. sh.   G.A. Oxon c. 317 (17)

1737. FIELD, J. E., Monumental brasses at Benson. (Journ., Oxf. univ. brass-rubbing soc., 1898, vol. 1, p. 208–10.)   Soc. 2184 d. 50

1738. Benson horticultural society. The annual show. [Programme. 1899.]   G.A. Oxon c. 317 (17)
— [1904.]   G.A. Oxon c. 105 (28)
(Wallingford), [1899, 1904], 8°.

1739. Benson national school. [Appeal for funds to enlarge the school, consequent upon the impending closure of the British school in June 1901.] n. pl., (1900), 4°. 4 pp.   G.A. Oxon c. 317 (17)

1740. The Aston Deanery magazine (with Benson). Nov. 1900–Nov. 1909. Watlington, 1900–09, 4°.   G.A. Oxon 4° 211

1741. [Posters, notices, &c. relating to Benson parish. 1902–04.]   G.A. Oxon c. 105

1742. FIELD, J. E., Fifield in Benson. (Berks, Bucks, & Oxon archaeol. journ., 1903, vol. 9, p. 23–28.)   R. Top. 100

     See 362 [Survey of 1387. H. Salter. 1910].

1743. FIELD, J. E., [Note concerning a series of blocks of free stone included in a malthouse at Preston Crowmarsh, and now identified as part of Benson church.] (Berks, Bucks, & Oxon archaeol. journ., 1911, vol. 16, notes, p. 119.)   R. Top. 100

1744. FIELD, J. E., Some notes of Benson or Bensington. (Berks, Bucks, & Oxon archaeol. journ., 1912, vol. 18, p. 10–13.)
     R. Top. 100

1745. Benson, Ewelme & Berrick nursing association. Report. 1920/21. n. pl., (1921), 4°. 4 pp.   G.A. Oxon c. 317 (17)

1746. Auction catal. Estate of John Sedgley. 8 Sept. 1763.
     G.A. Oxon a. 22 (92)

1747. Auction catal. Farm. 7 Feb. 1812.   G.A. fol. B 71

1748. Auction catal. Munday's field. 22 July 1890.
     G.A. Oxon b. 92* (28)

1749. Sale catal. Fifield manor estate [in Benson]. Upper farm. 1900.
     G.A. Oxon b. 90 (45)

1750. Auction catal. Fifield manor estate [in Benson]. 9 June 1902.
     G.A. Oxon b. 90 (46)

1751. Auction catal. The Paddock. 24 Apr. 1925.
     G.A. Oxon c. 224 (18)

BERRICK PRIOR

1752. An act for inclosing lands in the liberty of Berrick Prior. (50 G. III, c. 114, L. & P.) Lond., 1810, fol. 21 pp.
     L. Eng. A 69 c. 6

BERRICK SALOME

1753. An act to authorize the inclosure of certain lands . . . [Berrick Salome.] (16 & 17 V., c. 3, Pub.) Lond., 1853, fol. 2 pp.
L. Eng. A 69 c. 1

1754. Benson, Ewelme & Berrick nursing association. Report. 1920/21. n. pl., (1921), 4°. 4 pp. G.A. Oxon c. 317 (17)

1755. Sale catal. Fifield manor estate. Upper farm. 1900.
G.A. Oxon b. 90 (45)

BICESTER

General

1756. An act for dividing and inclosing the common field . . . of Burchester, otherwise Burcester, otherwise Bissiter Market-end. . . . (30 G. II, c. 7, Private.) n. pl., 1757, fol. 19 pp.
G.A. Oxon a. 117 (f. 4)

1757. Church notes from Burcester. (The Topographer, 1790, vol. 2, p. 305–10.) Douce VV 15

1758. A more full account of the descent of the manor of Burcester. (The Topographer, 1790, vol. 2, p. 311, 12.) Douce VV 15

1759. An act for dividing and inclosing the . . . lands . . . of Burcester King's End, otherwise, Bicester King's End. . . . (33 G. III, c. 45, Private.) n. pl., 1793, fol. 30 pp. L. Eng. C 13 c. 1 (1793. ii. 4)

1760. DUNKIN, J., The history and antiquities of Bicester. Lond., 1816, 8°. 270 pp. G.A. Oxon 8° 257 (1)

1761. Oxfordshire anecdotes, with historical and topographical notes. [Bicester, &c.] n. pl., [c. 1826], 8°. 16 pp. G.A. Oxon 8° 934*

1761A. BLOMFIELD, J. C., The history of Bicester, its town and priory. (Hist. of . . . deanery of Bicester. Pt. 2). Bicester, 1884, 4°. 212 pp.
G.A. Oxon 4° 71 (2)

See 22 [Geology, by A. H. Green. 1864].

1762. Dr. Theodore Thomson's Report to the Local government board on an outbreak of enteric fever in the urban district of Bicester. Aug. 6, 1896. (Rept., Med. inspectors of Local govt. board, 107.) Lond., 1896, fol. 10 pp. Per. 15012 c. 43

1763. MANNING, P., Chained library at Bicester. (Proc., Oxf. architect. and hist. soc., 1896/1900, p. 118–21.) R. 13. 711 (6)
— Repr. G.A. Oxon 8° 705 (5)

1764. CRAWFURD, G. P., The parish church, Bicester, by the vicar [G. P. Crawfurd] (Oxf.), 1898, 8°. 8 pp. G.A. Oxon 8° 972

1765. WARNER, R. T., A seventeenth-century school at Bicester [kept by a mr. Blackwell]. (Home counties mag., 1904, p. 32–37.)
Per. G. A. Gen. top. 4° 176

1766. HAVERFIELD, F., [Note on a fragment of Arretine ware found at Bicester.] (Proc., Soc. of antiq., 1907, ser. 2, vol. 21, p. 461, 62.)
R. Top. 1

1767. The vicar's school at Bicester in the 17th century. (Rept., Oxf. archaeol. soc., 1907, p. 23–33.)
R. Top. 330

See 1022 [Act concerning supply of gas. 1913].

1768. BARROW, A. S., The Bicester and Warden Hill [hunt]. (More shires & provinces by 'Sabretache', 1928, p. 55–66.) 38445 c. 7

1769. CRAWFURD, G. P., Recollections of Bicester, 1894–1907. Reading, [1932], 4°. 92 pp.
G.A. Oxon 4° 512

1770. Gray House association. Gray House, Bicester. Annual report and accounts. 1933/4, 34/5 [and] Final report. n. pl., 1934–36, 8°.
O.P.L.

1771. Bicester (King's end). (Archaeol. notes. Oxoniensia, 1937, p. 202.)
R. Top. 340

1772. Festival of Britain, 1951. Bicester. Historical notes and souvenir programme. Bicester, 1951, 8°. 20 pp. 38493 d. 15 (32)

1773. Auction catal. Bicester hall. 29 July 1885.
G.A. Oxon b. 85 a (10)

1774. Auction catal. Gowell farm. 8 Aug. 1919.
G.A. Oxon c. 317 (18)

1775. Auction catal. La Casita. 22 June 1951. G.A. Oxon b. 92*

Directories

See 1390 [Directory. 1846].

1776. The Bicester directory for 1857. Bicester, 1857, s. sh.
G.A. Oxon b. 96 (32)

Newspapers

See 1333 Bicester Advertiser.
1334 Bicester Advertiser (and Mid-Oxon Chronicle).
1335 Bicester Herald.
1338 Guardian.

Priory

1777. The visitation of the priory of Bicester, 28th May, 1445. (Lincoln record soc., 1918, vol. 14, p. 34–36.)
R. Top. 260
— [Another issue.] (Cant. and York soc., 1919, vol. 24, p. 34–36.)
R. 8. 26

1778. Visitations. Bicester priory. (i) 25 April 1520 (ii) 12 May 1525. (Lincoln record soc., 1944, vol. 35, p. 79–82.)   R. Top. 260

Railways

See 486 [Railway. 1846].

Roads

See 513, 516, 522, 526, 534 [Turnpike acts. 1769, &c.].

Societies

1779. Bicester agricultural and horticultural association. Schedule of premiums for 1871, with list of officers and members. Bicester, 1871, 8°. 16 pp.   G.A. Oxon 8° 355

1780. Bicester agricultural and horticultural association. Smith & Pankhurst's Official list of entries for the horse show. (1886). Bicester, (1886), 8°. 8 pp.   G.A. Oxon c. 317 (18)

1781. Bicester agricultural and horticultural and hunt show. Catalogue of the annual show. 1935. (Bicester, 1935), 8°. 96 pp.
G.A. Oxon c. 317 (18)

BICESTER DEANERY

See 1299 [Guide to architectural antiquities. Deanery of Bicester, by J. H. Parker and others. 1842].

1782. BLOMFIELD, J. C., History of the present deanery of Bicester. 8 pt. Oxf., &c., 1882–94, 4°.   G.A. Oxon 4° 71

1783. PRIOR, C. E., Dedications of churches, with some notes as to village feasts and old customs. Deaneries of Islip & Bicester. (Rept., Oxf. archaeol. soc., 1903, p. 20–42.)   R. Top. 330

1784. PEARCE, S. S., The clergy of the deaneries of Witney and Bicester during the settlement of 1559 and afterwards. (Rept., Oxf. archaeol. soc., 1914, p. 180–237.)   R. Top. 330

1785. SHARPE, F., The church bells of the deanery of Bicester. Brackley, 1932, 8°. 76 pp.   1743 e. 40

BICESTER POOR LAW UNION

1786. Bicester Union. A statement of the Union accounts for the half-year ended Lady-day, 1854, with a list of paupers relieved. Bicester, 1854, 8°. 63 pp.   G.A. Oxon 8° 224

1787. WING, W., Brief annals of the Bicester poor law union and its component parishes, by a local secretary of the North Oxfordshire archaeological society [W. Wing] assisted by friends. Repr. from the Bicester Herald. 4 pt. [With 2 appendices] Bicester 1877–81, 8°. 192 pp.+20+16.   G.A. Oxon 8° 239

BIGMORE COMMON

1788. An act to authorize the inclosure of certain lands . . . [Bigmore Common]. 20 & 21 V., c. 20, Pub.) Lond., 1857, fol. 2 pp.
                                                         L. Eng. A 69 c. 1

BINSEY

1789. [*Begin*] A Hallelujah army has been formed for the parish of Binsey [fly-sheet]. n. pl., [18—], s. sh.   G.A. Oxon c. 317 (5)

1790. TAUNT, H. W., Godstow, with its legend of Fair Rosamund, Medley, Wytham & Binsey. Oxf., [*c.* 1900], 8°. 28 pp.
                                                        G.A. Oxon 8° 709
See 133 [Pipistrelle bat roost in Binsey church. 1943].

1791. RHODES, P. P., New archaeological sites at Binsey and Port Meadow. (Oxoniensia, 1949, vol. 14, p. 81–84.)   R. Top. 340

BIX

1792. MORLEY, H. T., Old ruined church at Bixbrand. (Rept., Oxf. archaeol. soc., 1931, p. 365, 66.)   R. Top. 330

1793. LAMBORN, E. A. GREENING, The churches of Bix. (Oxoniensia, 1936, p. 129–39.)   R. Top. 340

1794. Auction catal. Stonor estate. 26 Sept. 1894.
                                                      G.A. Oxon b. 92 (8)

1795. Auction catal. 'Red Pitts' estate.
— 27 July 1899.   G.A. Oxon b. 92 (11)
— 15 Aug. 1901.   G.A. Oxon b. 92 (12)

BLACKBOURTON

1796. An act for dividing and inclosing certain . . . fields . . . in . . . Blackbourton. (10 G. III, c. 14, Private.) n. pl., 1770, fol. 20 pp.
                                                         G.A. Oxon c. 181

1797. An act for establishing . . . articles of agreement between . . . George duke of Marlborough . . . and . . . Lincoln college [concerning Black Bourton]. (33 G. III, c. 22, Private.) n. pl., 1793, fol. 6 pp.
                                        L. Eng. C 13 c. 1 (1793. ii. 46)

1798. NAPIER, E. H. D. ELERS, Memoir of the Elers family and . . . their connexion with the Hungerfords of Black Bourton place. Lond., 1870, 8°. 23 pp. O.P.L.

1799. LUPTON, M. G., History of the parish of Black Bourton. (Trans., Oxf. archaeol. soc., 43.) Banbury, 1903, 8°. 123 pp. R. Top. 330

1800. KEYSER, C. E., Notes on the churches of Brize Norton and Black Bourton. (Journ., Brit. archaeol. assoc., 1915, new ser., vol. 21, p. 1–12, 89–96+30 plates.) R. Top. 4

1801. Pedigree of Wynslowe of Burton [? Blackbourton], co. Oxon. (Misc. geneal. et heraldica, 1926/28, 5th ser., vol. 6, p. 138, 39.) Ψ 2. 10 f.

1802. Auction catal. Outlying portions of the Blenheim estates. 3 July 1894. G.A. Oxon b. 90 (12)

BLACKTHORN

1803. An act for dividing and inclosing the . . . fields . . . within . . . Blackthorn. (16 G. III, c. 21, Private.) n. pl., 1776, fol. 26 pp. G.A. Oxon c. 187

1804. Blackthorn (Heath Bridge). (Archaeol. notes. Oxoniensia, 1937, p. 202.) R. Top. 340

1805. Auction catal. Howe farm and Farr farm. [18—.] G.A. fol. B 71

BLADON

1806. An act for confirming a partition made between Robert Dashwood . . . and Cholmley Turner . . . of certain . . . lands . . . in . . . [Bladon &c.]. (3 G. I, c. 22, Private.) n. pl., 1717, fol. 7 pp. B.M.

See 502 [Turnpike act. 1751].

1807. An act for dividing and inclosing the common fields . . . of Bladon . . . (6 G. III, c. 4, Private.) n. pl., 1766, fol. 18 pp. L. Eng. C 13 c. 1 (1776, p. 78)

1808. Catalogue of the . . . library . . . of . . . William Mavor, rector of Bladon, with Woodstock, which will be sold by auction, 4th–7th June 1838. Oxf., (1838), 4°. 34 pp.

1809. MARSHALL, E., The early history of Woodstock Manor, and its environs in Bladon [&c.]. Oxf., &c., 1873, 8°. 474 pp. G.A. Oxon 8° 177

1810. MOORE, J. J., Rambles and rides around Oxford, by rail, river and road. Sect 2. Bladon [&c.]: (Shrimpton's hist. county handbooks.) Oxf., 1882, 8°. 103 pp. G.A. Oxon 8° 964

1811. BROWN, G. J., To the parishioners of Bladon [letter on Bladon feast]. n. pl., (1883), 8°. 4 pp.   G.A. Oxon c. 317 (5)

1812. The Bladon with Woodstock parish magazine. May, 1889. Woodstock, 1889, 8°.   G.A. Oxon c. 317 (19)

1813. Restoration of S. Martin's, Bladon. Woodstock, 1891, fol. 4 pp.   G.A. Oxon c. 22 (37)

1814. In memoriam Arthur Majendie, rector of Bladon & Woodstock. Woodstock, (1895), 8°. 24 pp.   11126 e. 171 (9)

1815. BALLARD, A., An Oxfordshire village in the thirteenth century [Bladon]. (The Antiquary, 1907, new ser., vol. 3, no. 4, p. 128–33.)   G.A. Oxon 4° 386

1816. BALLARD, A., Three surveys of Bladon. (Rept., Oxf. archaeol. soc., 1910, p. 20–27.)   R. Top. 330

1817. The Hanborough, Bladon and Freeland news, ed. by F. B. Greenway. No. 1, 3–5, 7, 8. [Reprod. from typewriting.] Hanborough, 1921, 22, 4°.   G.A. Oxon c. 317 (9)

1818. ARKELL, W. J., New evidence on the great oolite succession at Bladon. (Proc., Geol. assoc., 1933, vol. 44, p. 177–83.)   Radcl.

See 42 [New structure in the forest marble of Oxford. 1951].

1819. Auction catal. 20 cottages. 4 May 1920.   G.A. Oxon c. 317 (5)

BLENHEIM PALACE

See WOODSTOCK.

BLETCHINGTON

1820. WING, W., Annals of Bletchingdon. Repr. from the Oxford Chronicle. [Oxf.], 1872, 8°. 63 pp.   G.A. Oxon 8° 147 (14)

1821. Auction catal. Warland's estate and Coxe's estate. 14 Dec. 1810.   G.A. fol. B 71

1822. Auction catal. Estate. 11 May, 1910.   G.A. Oxon b. 90 (13)

BLOXHAM

General

1823. Articles to be observed by a friendly society at Bloxham . . . united the 29th day of January, 1763. Banbury, [c. 1775], s. sh.   J.C.

— [Facsimile in no. 1608A, plate 30.]

1824. An act for vesting part of the estates of the late sir James Dashwood in trustees, in trust to sell the same. [Bloxham.] (37 G. III c. 101, Private.) n. pl., 1797, fol. 30 pp.
L. Eng. C 13 c. 1 (1797. iv)

1825. An act for dividing . . . and inclosing the . . . fields . . . and other commonable lands lying within . . . Bloxham. (39 & 40 G. III, c. 12, Private.) n. pl., 1800, fol. 34 pp.　　　　　G.A. Oxon c. 113 (6)

1826. Bloxham church. (Trans., Bristol and Glouc. archaeol. soc., 1895–96, vol. 20, p. 352–54.)　　　　　R. Top. 210

1827. MACRAY, W. D., Old method of annual division of common land at Bloxham. (Rept., Oxf. archaeol. soc., 1912, p. 111–13.)
R. Top. 330
See 1022 [Act concerning supply of gas. 1913].

1828. TYSSEN, A. D., The Presbyterians of Bloxham and Milton. (Trans., Unitarian hist. soc., 1920, vol. 2, p. 9–32.)
Per. 1116 d. 11

1829. RICHARDSON, L., Ammonites from the upper lias, railway-cutting, Bloxham. (Geol. mag., 1921, vol. 58, p. 426–28.)　　Radcl.

1830. KNIGHT, W. F. J., A Romano-British settlement near Bloxham. (Rept., Oxf. archaeol. soc., 1929, p. 229–32.)　　　R. Top. 330

1831. An act to authorise the Banbury Water company to construct new works and raise additional capital to alter the limits of supply to the company to confer further powers . . . to empower them to acquire . . . the Bloxham and District Water company limited. . . . (1 E. VIII & 1 G. VI, c. 88, L. & P.) Lond., 1937, fol. 65 pp.
L. Eng. A 69 c. 6 (1937)

1832. Bloxham. (Archaeol. notes. Oxoniensia, 1938, p. 165.)
R. Top. 340

1833. KNIGHT, W. F. J., A Romano-British site at Bloxham. (Oxoniensia, 1938, p. 41–56.)　　　　　R. Top. 340

1834. Auction catal. Manor of Bloxham Beauchamp and Bloxham Fiennes. 20 May 1802.　　　　　G.A. fol. A 266 (28)

1835. Auction catal. Old Barn farm &c. 2 Dec. 1879.
G.A. Oxon b. 85 a (9)

1836. Auction catal. Accommodation pasture. 28 July 1892.
G.A. Oxon b. 85 a (35)

1837. Auction catal. Pasture & arable land. 20 July 1922.
G.A. Oxon b. 92* (17)

Grammar School

1838. [Prospectus.] n. pl., 1853, s. sh.　　MS. Top. Oxon f. 40 (f. 83)
　— 1898. 4 pp.　　　　　　　　　　　　　G.A. Oxon c. 317 (5)
　— [c. 1905]. 8°. 24 pp.　　　　　　　　　G.A. Oxon 8° 715 (12)

1839. An office for the admission of scholars. n. pl., 1853, 12°. 12 pp.
　　　　　　　　　　　　　　　　　　　　G.A. Oxon 8° 147 (17)

1840. An office to be used at the laying of the foundation stone, 7th June, 1855. Lond., (1855), 12°. 16 pp.　　MS. Top. Oxon f. 40

1841. A catalogue of books presented to the library, by the rev. J. W. Hewett. [Bloxham? 1855?], 8°. 44 pp.　　G.A. Oxon 8° 72 (6)

1842. An office for the admission of choristers. n. pl., 1856, 16°. 12 pp.
　　　　　　　　　　　　　　　　　　　　MS. Top. Oxon f. 40

1843. Calendar. 1856. Lond., 1856, 8°.　　　Cal. Oxon 8° 480

1844. Benedictio mensae. Grace before and after meat, as said in All saints grammar school, Bloxham. n. pl., 1856, 24°. 8 pp.
　　　　　　　　　　　　　　　　　　　　MS. Top. Oxon f. 40

1845. An office to be used at the dedication of the new buildings. n. pl., 1856, 16°. 20 pp.　　　　　　　　　　MS. Top. Oxon f. 40

1846. The Bloxhamist. 1875–. (Oxf.), 1875–, 4°.
　　　　　　　　　　　　　　[No. 2 only in G.A. Oxon 4° 121]

1847. Dedication festival, 1896. Order of service [&c.] [Partly lithographed, partly newspaper-cuttings.]　　G.A. Oxon c. 22 (40)

1848. WARD, G. H., Gymnasium fund. [An appeal.] n. pl., (1900), 8°. 2 pp.　　　　　　　　　　　　　　G.A. Oxon c. 22 (7)

BLOXHAM HUNDRED

1849. Reports of the Commissioners for inquiring concerning charities in the hundreds of Banbury & Bloxham [&c.] from the twelfth and thirteenth reports. 2 vols. Banbury, 1826, 44, 4°. 188+229 pp.
　　　　　　　　　　　　　　　　　　　　G.A. Oxon 8° 170, 71

BODICOTE

1850. WILSON, J., The new poor law a dead letter in the Banbury Union, an account of the ... proceedings resorted to in the election of a guardian for the township of Boddicot ... 1835, 1836, 1837 and 1838. Banbury, [1840], 8°. 44 pp.　　G.A. Oxon 8° 636

1851. Parish of Bodicote ... Table of fees, &c. Banbury, (1877), s. sh.
　　　　　　　　　　　　　　　　　　　　G.A. Oxon c. 22 (7)

1852. Auction catal. map of estate in Boddicot & Neithrop. 1838.
G.A. Oxon b. 85 *a* (11)

1853. Auction catal. Bodicot Grange estate. 24 July 1860.
G.A. Oxon b. 85 *a* (14-18)
— 8 July 1890. G.A. Oxon b. 85 *a* (22)

1854. Auction catal. Land and farm. 10 Aug. 1888.
G.A. Oxon b. 85 *a* (21)

1855. Auction catal. Manor house estate. 20 May 1898.
G.A. Oxon b. 85 *a* (23)

BOLNEY

1856. Bowney. (Gent's. mag., 1751, p. 602; 1757, p. 603.) Ψ 2. 44

1857. PEARMAN, M. T., Notes on Bolney church and manor, and other lands of Walter Giffard. (Trans., Oxf. archaeol. soc., 39.) Banbury, 1900, 8°. 15 pp. R. Top. 330

1858. Auction catal. Bolney court. 8 July, 1901. G.A. Oxon b. 91 (3)

BOWLD

1859. An act for dividing and inclosing the ... fields ... of Bowld [&c.]. (19 G. III, c. 78, Private.) n. pl., 1779, fol. 16 pp.
L. Eng. C 13 c. 1 (1779. ii. 12)

BOWNEY

See BOLNEY.

BRIGHTHAMPTON

1860. An act for the vesting ... several manors and lands [in Brighthampton &c.] ... late the inheritance of W. Jennens ... in trustees to be sold. (8 Anne, c. 10, Private.) n. pl., [*c.* 1709]. 8°. 52 pp.
Radcl. e. 127

1861. An act to authorize the inclosure of certain lands ... [Brighthampton]. (11 & 12 V., c. 109, Pub.) Lond., 1848, fol. 3 pp.
L. Eng. A 69 c. 1 (1848)

1862. PHILLIPS, PROFESSOR, Discoveries at Brighthampton. (Proc., Soc. of antiq., 1857, ser. 1, vol. 4, p. 70, 71.) R. Top. 1

1863. AKERMAN, J. Y., Report of researches in a cemetery of the Anglo-Saxon period at Brighthampton. (Archaeologia, 1857, vol. 37, p. 391-98.) R. Top. 7

1864. AKERMAN, J. Y., [Account of finds of Anglo-Saxon remains at Brighthampton.] (Proc., Soc. of antiq., 1858, ser. 1, vol. 4, p. 231, 233, 329.) R. Top. 1

1865. AKERMAN, J. Y., Second report of researches in a cemetery of the Anglo-Saxon period at Brighthampton. (Archaeologia, 1860, vol. 38, p. 84–97.) R. Top. 7

1866. Brighthampton. (Archaeol. notes. Oxoniensia, 1949, vol. 14, p. 75.) R. Top. 340

1867. Auction catal. Brighthampton manor estate, comprising Manor farm, Malthouse farm and Florey's farm. 3 Sept. 1924. G.A. Oxon c. 224 (16)

BRIGHTWELL BALDWIN

1868. An act for vesting certain . . . lands [in Baldwin Brightwell] . . . of Toby Hodson . . . in trustees for payment of his debts. . . . (1 Anne, c. 32, Private.) 1701.

1869. An act for the more effectual settlement of the estate of John Stone, of Baldwin Brightwell . . . in his family and name. (13 & 14 W. III & 1 Anne, c. 32, Private.) 1701.

1870. An act for dividing, allotting and inclosing the . . . fields . . . of Baldwin Brightwell. . . . (42 G. III, c. 30, Private.) (Lond.), [1802], fol. 14 pp. L. Eng. C 13 c. 1 (1802. i. 4)

1871. Notes [on a vernaculari nscription]. (Trans., Monumental brass soc., 1908, vol. 5, pt. 20, p. 337–39.) Soc. 2184 d. 85

1872. COXE, H., St. Bartholomew's, Baldwin Brightwell [by H. Coxe]. n. pl., [1934], 8°. 4 pp. G.A. Oxon 8° 1130* (3)

BRITTENTON

1873. An act for vesting the several manors and lands therein mentioned in [Brittenden &c.] late the inheritance of W. Jennens . . . in trustees to be sold. (8 Anne, c. 10, Private.) n. pl., [c. 1709], 8°. 52 pp. Radcl. e. 127

BRITWELL PRIOR

1874. An act for inclosing lands in . . . Britwell Prior. (5 & 6 V., c. 13, Private.) n. pl., 1842, fol. 41 pp. L. Eng. C 13 c. 1 (1842. 13)

1875. Auction catal. Land. 17 June, 1897. G.A. Oxon b. 92 (26)

BRITWELL SALOME

1876. An act for vesting the real estate of Thomas Reade and Elizabeth Reade . . . situate in Brittwell Sallome [&c.] . . . in Thomas, earl of Macclesfield. . . . (28 G. III, c. 6, Private.) n. pl., 1788, fol. 10 pp.
L. Eng. C 13 c. 1 (1788. 49)

1877. An act for inclosing lands in . . . Britwell Salome [&c.] (5 & 6 V., c. 13, Private.) n. pl., 1842, fol. 41 pp. L. Eng. C 13 c. 1 (1842. 13)

1878. Auction catal. Land. 17 June, 1897. G.A. Oxon b. 92 (26)

BRIZE NORTON

1879. An act for dividing, alloting and inclosing . . . fields . . . in . . . Brize Norton . . . (15 G. III, c. 80, Private.) n. pl., 1775, fol. 33 pp.
L. Eng. C 13 c. 1 (1775. 52)

1880. KEYSER, C. E., Notes on the churches of Brize Norton and Black Bourton. (Journ., Brit. archaeol. assoc., 1915, new ser., vol. 21, p. 1–12, 89–96+30 plates.) R. Top. 4

1881. Auction catal. Astrop manor farm. 13 May 1824. G.A. fol. B 71

1882. Auction catal. Upper Haddon farm. 2 May 1907.
G.A. Oxon c. 317 (5)

1883. Auction catal. Kilkenny farm. 17 June 1908.
G.A. Oxon b. 90 (14)

BROADWELL

1884. An act for dividing, allotting and inclosing the . . . fields . . . in . . . Broadwell [&c.] (15 G. III, c. 40, Private.) n. pl., 1775, fol. 24 pp. L. Eng. C 13 c. 1 (1775. 8)

1885. Valuation of timber on estates . . . belonging to the marquis of Thomond. [Broadwell.] [Lond., 18—], s. sh.
G.A. fol. A 266 (28 A)

1886. PAINTIN, H., Three Oxfordshire churches, Kencot, Broadwell and Langford. Oxf., 1911, 4°. 24 pp. G.A. Oxon 4° 276 (16)

1887. Auction catal. Broadwell and Kelmscot manors. 11 Nov. 1802.
G.A. fol. A 273*

BROUGHTON

1888. An act for indemnifying Thomas Twisleton and Francis Twisleton . . . the purchasers of certain lands . . . [Broughton &c.] belonging to James Ness. . . . (9 G. III, c. 88, Private.) n. pl., 1769, fol. 7 pp. L. Eng. C 13 c. 1 (1769. 76)

1889. The case of colonel Thomas Twiselton, of Broughton castle . . . in relation to the barony of Say and Sele. n. pl., [c. 1780], fol. 4 pp.
Gough Oxf. 103 (26)

1890. Miscellaneous epitaphs, in the church of Broughton, by Banbury. (The Topographer, 1790, vol. 2, p. 110, 11.) Douce VV 15

1891. Broughton. (Rept., Oxf. archaeol. soc., 1867, p. 10; 1901, p. 10–12.) R. Top. 330

1892. Broughton. Notes. (Trans., Cambr. univ. assoc. of brass collectors, 1888, no. 6, p. 44.) Soc. 2184 d. 85

1893. METCALFE, G., Some account of Broughton and North Newington. Lond., 1893, 8°. 18 pp. G.A. Oxon 8° 968

1894. WATSON, E. H. L., Broughton castle. (Country Life, 1898, vol. 4, p. 756–62.) Per. 384 b. 6

1895. FIENNES, T. TWISTLETON-WYKEHAM-, 17th baron Saye & Sele, Notes on Broughton Castle. (Berks, Bucks, & Oxon archaeol. journ., 1901, vol. 7, p. 23–25.) R. Top. 100

1896. Broughton castle (Country Life, 1901, vol. 9, p. 112–19.)
Per. 384 b. 6

1897. HARPER, E. J., Broughton church. (Oxf. diocesan mag., 1923, vol. 18, p. 105–11.) Per. 11126 d. 78

1898. TIPPING, H. A., Broughton castle. (Country Life, 1930, vol. 67, p. 50–57, 84–91, 126–34.) Per. 384 b. 6.

See 4208A [Broughton castle in 'English country houses', by C. Hussey. 1951].

1899. Auction catal. Contents of Broughton castle. 4–7 July, 1837.
G.A. Oxon c. 317 (5)

BROUGHTON POGGS

1900. An act for the vesting the several manors and lands therein mentioned in [Powges i.e. Broughton Poggs? &c.] late the inheritance of W. Jennens . . . in trustees to be sold. (8 Anne, c. 10, Private.) n. pl., [c. 1709], 8°. 52 pp. Radcl. e. 127

1901. AKERMAN, J. Y., Note on some further discoveries of Anglo-Saxon remains at Broughton Poggs. (Proc., Soc. of antiq., 1857, ser. 1, vol. 4, p. 73, 74.) R. Top. 1

1902. AKERMAN, J. Y., An account of researches in Anglo-Saxon cemeteries at Filkins, and at Broughton Poggs. (Archaeologia, 1857, vol. 37, p. 140–46.) R. Top. 7

See 362 [Manor. Survey of 1387. 1910].

1903. PAINTIN, H., Three village churches, Broughton-Pogis, Kelmscott and Little Faringdon. Oxf., 1913, 4°. 21 pp.
G.A. Oxon 4° 262 (15)

1904. Auction catal. Broadwell and Kelmscot manors. 11 Nov. 1802.
G.A. fol. A 273*

BUCKNELL

1905. An act for dividing and inclosing the . . . fields . . . of Bucknell. (19 G. III, c. 59, Private.) n. pl., 1779, fol. 28 pp.
L. Eng. C 13 c. 1 (1779. i. 17)

1906. BLOMFIELD, J. C., History of . . . Bucknell [&c.]. (Hist. of . . . deanery of Bicester. Pt. 8. Bucknell. 64 pp.) Lond., 1894, 4°.
G.A. Oxon 4° 71

1907. Auction catal. Bucknell manor estate. 14 May, 1888. 23 July, 1888.
G.A. Oxon b. 85 a (24, 25)

BULLINGDON HUNDRED

1908. DUNKIN, J., The history and antiquities of the hundreds of Bullingdon and Ploughley. 2 vols. Lond., 1823, 4°. 319 & 261 pp.
G.A. Oxon 4° 5
See 879 [Charities. 1826].
See 545 [Bullingdon highway district. Provisional (final) order. 1864, 65].
See 546 [Bullingdon highway district. Specification and contract. 1866].

BULLINGDON RURAL DISTRICT

1909. Official guide to the Bullingdon rural district. Croydon, [1951], 8°. 40 pp.
G.A. Oxon 8° 1248

1910. Bullingdon rural district council. The Bullingdon bulletin. No. 1–. [Oxf.], 1951–, 8°.
Per. G.A. Oxon 8° 1249

BURCOT

1911. An act for dividing and inclosing the . . . fields . . . within . . . the hamlet of Burcot. (15 G. III, c. 4, Private.) n. pl., 1775, fol. 21 pp.
L. Eng. C 13 c. 1 (1775. 9)

1912.

1913. Auction catal. Burcott estate. 16 July, 1844.
G.A. Oxon b. 90 (33)

1914. Auction catal. Burcot farm and freehold property. 16 July 1897.
G.A. Oxon c. 317 (5)

1915. Auction catal. Freehold land. 28 May 1902.   G.A. Oxon b. 6 (64)

BURDROP

1916. An act for dividing and inclosing the open and common field . . .
within . . . Burdrup. . . . (13 G. III, c. 60, Private.) n. pl., 1773, fol.
25 pp.   L. Eng. C 13 c. 1 (1773. 80)

BURFORD

General

For works relating to the Levellers at Burford during the Civil War, May–
Sept. 1649, see 430–34.

1917. Horses entered to run on Seven downs near Burford. n. pl., 1753,
s. sh.   MS. Top. Oxon c. 290

1918. June 17, 1644. Burford church. (The Topographer, 1789, vol. 1,
p. 416, 17.)   Douce VV 14

1919. Some account of Burford . . . with church notes (June 9th 1660)
from a MS. in the Brit. Mus. (The Topographer, 1790, vol. 2,
p. 348–53.)   Douce VV 15

1920. Burford. (Gent's. mag., 1791, pt. 2, p. 896.) Ψ 2. 44

1921. An act for dividing and inclosing the . . . fields . . . of Burford. . . .
(34 G. III, c. 48, Private.) n. pl., 1794, fol. 28 pp.
           L. Eng. C 13 c. 1 (1794. 41)

1922. HUNT, T. H., [Discovery of large stone coffin of the 8th century
during repairs to road.] (Gent's. mag., 1814, pt. 2, p. 597, 98.)
           Ψ 2. 44

1923. Burford friendly institution. Rules and regulations. Burford,
1826, 8°. 29 pp.   G.A. Oxon 8° 438

See 413 [Account of night march of Charles i., June 3, 1644, by V. Thomas.
1852].

1923A. (Packer's) Burford almanack, compendium, directory & diary,
1860–. Burford, 1860–, 8°.
           [Bodleian has 1914, 1918: Dir. Oxon e. 11]

1924. FISHER, J., A history of . . . Burford. Chelt., 1861, 8°. 114 pp.
           G.A. Oxon 8° 12

1925. LEVIEN, E., On the barony of Burford. (Journ., Brit. archaeol.
assoc. 1868, vol. 24, p. 136–50.)   R. Top. 4

1926. PARKER, J. H., On Shipton-under-Wychwood and Burford.
(Proc., Oxf. architect. and hist. soc., N.S., vol. 2, 1869, p. 132–35.)
           R. 13. 708

1927. Notes of an excursion to . . . Burford. . . . (North Oxf. archaeol. soc., 1870.) Banbury, [1870], 8°. 37 pp. R. Top. 330

1928. CHEATLE, T. H., Report on the sanitary condition of the Burford district of the Witney union. (Bampton), 1872, fol. 4 pp.
G.A. Oxon c. 317 (5)

1929. Burford (Rept., Oxf. archaeol. soc., 1891, p. 14–22; 1930, p. 255, 56.) R. Top. 330

1930. MONK, W. J., History of Burford. Burford, &c., 1891, 8°. 197 pp.
G.A. Oxon 8° 475

1931. HOPE, W. H. ST. J., [Description of maces and common seal of the ancient borough of Burford.] (Proc., Soc. of Antiquaries, 1892, 2nd ser., vol. 14, p. 163–65.) R. Top. 1

1932. Visit to Burford. (Trans., Bristol and Glouc. archaeol. soc., 1892–93, vol. 17, p. 326–29.) R. Top. 210

1933. Burford church. (Trans., Bristol and Glouc. archaeol. soc., 1895–96, vol. 20, p. 369–71.) R. Top. 210

1934. MONK, W. J., Walks and drives around Burford. Burford, &c., 1896, 8°. 129 pp. G.A. Oxon 8° 639

1935. Views in & around Burford. Burford, [c. 1897], 8°. 20 pp.
G.A. Oxon 8° 923

1936. MONK, W. J., Burford. Burford, 1897, 8°. 100 pp.
G.A. Oxon 8° 642
See 658 [Parliamentary history, by W. R. Williams. 1899].

1937. HUTTON, W. H., Burford papers, letters of Samuel Crisp to his sister at Burford; and other studies, 1745–1845. Lond., 1905, 8°. 335 pp. 27001 d. 4

1938. RICHARDSON, L., The inferior oolite and contiguous deposits of the district between Rissington and Burford. (Quart. journ., Geol. soc., 1907, vol. 63, p. 437–44.) Radcl.

1939. S., C. R., Burford. (Country Life, 1908, vol. 23, p. 191–97.)
Per. 384 b. 6

1940. MONK, W. J., The story of Burford. Burford, 1909, 8°. 93 pp.
G.A. Oxon 8° 769

1941. Burford church. (Trans., Bristol and Glouc. archaeol. soc., 1911, vol. 34, p. 29–31.) R. Top. 210

1942.

1943. GRETTON, R. H., The Burford records, a study in minor town government. Oxf., 1920, 8°. 736 pp. G.A. Oxon 4° 411

1944. GRETTON, M. S., Burford, past and present. Oxf., 1920, 8°.
135 pp.   G.A. Oxon 8° 988
— [Another ed.] Lond., 1929, 8°. 255 pp.   G.A. Oxon 8° 1069
— New, revised ed. 1945. 158 pp.   G.A. Oxon 8° 1203
— New, revised ed. Repr. 1950.   G.A. Oxon 8° 1220

1945. JOURDAIN, M., Burford. (Architect. rev., 1922, Apr., p. 85–89.)
Per. 17356 c. 8

1946. HOARE and WHEELER, Burford, reredos and screen. (Architect.
rev., 1922, Apr. 28, p. 310.)   Per. 17356 c. 8

1947. MONK, W. J., Guide to Burford. Otley, [1929], 8°. 30 pp.
G.A. Oxon 8° 1056 (6)

1948. MONK, W. J., Burford, the official guide. [1st], 2nd, 3rd, 4th ed.
Chelt., 1934–40, 8°.   G.A. Oxon 8° 1125

1949. Burford. (Country Life, 1945, vol. 98, p. 288–91, 332–35, 376–
79.)   Per. 384 b. 6

1950. HUSSEY, C., The Great house, Burford. (Country Life, 1945,
vol. 98, p. 508–11.)   Per. 384 b. 6

1951. Burford in the war of 1939–45. (Women's inst.) Burford, &c.,
1947, 8°. 63 pp.   G.A. Oxon 8° 1212

1952. Auction catal. Bury barns and Sturt estates. 6 June 1896.
G.A. Oxon b. 90 (15)

Charities

See 883 [Customs and charities. 1842].

1953. The case of the charities in the town and parish of Burford.
(Appendix, 8th rept. of The Charity commissioners, p. 9–12.)
Pp. Eng. 1861, vol. 20

1954. An act for confirming a scheme of the Charity commissioners for
certain charities in . . . Burford. (24 & 25 V., c. 22, Pub.) Lond.,
1861, fol. 4 pp.   L. Eng. A 69 c. 1

Priory

1955. PAINTIN, H., Burford priory and its association with the Lenthall
family. Also a brief account of the church and parish of Besselsleigh.
Repr. from the Oxford Times. Oxf., 1907, 4°. 22 pp.
G.A. Oxon 4° 186 (22)

1956. DE SALES LA TERRIÈRE, B., Burford priory. (Trans., Bristol and
Glouc. archaeol. soc., 1911, vol. 34, p. 90–96.)   R. Top. 210

1957. Burford priory. (Country Life, 1911, vol. 29, p. 306–15.)
Per. 384 b. 6

1958. OSWALD, A., Burford priory. (Country Life, 1939, vol. 85, p. 586–91, 616–21.) Per 384 b. 6

1959. GODFREY, W. H., Burford priory. (Oxoniensia, 1939, p. 71–88.) R. Top. 340

Roads

See 494 [London inns frequented by Burford carriers. 1637].
See 502, 514, 518, 525, 529 [Turnpike acts 1751, &c.].

BURFORD SIGNET

See UPTON AND SIGNET.

CALCUTT

1960. An act for dividing, allotting and inclosing . . . lands . . . of . . . Calcott. . . . (41 G. III, c. 71, Private.) n. pl., 1801, fol. 35 pp.
L. Eng. C 13 c. 1 (1801. iii. 15)

CALTHORPE

1961. An act for vesting part of the estates of the late sir James Dashwood in trustees, in trust to sell the same. [Calthorpe.] (37 G. III, c. 101, Private.) n. pl., 1797, fol. 30 pp.
L. Eng. C 13 c. 1 (1797. iv)

1962. DRAPER, E., Notes on Calthorpe manor house, Banbury, and its inhabitants. Banbury, 1915, 4°. 25 pp. G.A. Oxon 4° 329

1963. Auction catal. Manor of Calthorpe. 15 March 1833.
G.A. Oxon b. 85 a (27)

CAMPSFIELD

See 502 [Turnpike act. 1751, &c.].

1964. WING, W., Annals of Kidlington and its annexes, Campsfield [&c.]. Repr. from the Oxf. chronicle. (Oxf.), 1881, 8°. 31 pp.
G.A. Oxon 8° 220 (5)

CANE END

1965. HUSSEY, C., A converted regency farm-house, Kempwood, Cane End. (Country Life, 1943, vol. 94, p. 994–95.) Per. 384 b. 6

CASSINGTON

1966. An act for confirming a partition made between Robert Dashwood . . . and Cholmley Turner . . . of certain . . . lands . . . in [Cassington &c.]. (3 G. I, c. 22, Private.) n. pl., 1717, fol. 7 pp.
B.M.

B 3239　　　　　　　　　O

1967. An act for dividing, allotting and inclosing certain heath lands and ... fields ... of Cassington ... (40 G. III, c. 60, Private.) n. pl., 1800, fol. 32 pp. L. Eng. C 13 c. 1 (1800. i. 10)

1968. WING, W., A church and parish beyond the neighbourhood of Banbury, Cassington. Repr. from the Banbury Guardian. n. pl., [c. 1880], 8°. 4 pp. G.A. Oxon 8° 1184 (19)

1969. Begbroke, Cassington and Yarnton horticultural society. Rules, list of subscribers, and schedule of prizes ... for 3rd annual show. Oxf., 1887, 8°. 12 pp. G.A. Oxon c. 317 (5)

1970. MANNING, P., Monumental brasses in the churches of St. Mary Magdalene, Oxford, and Cassington [&c.] (Journ., Oxf. univ. brass-rubbing soc., 1898, vol. 1, p. 176–89.) Soc. 2184 d. 50

1971.

See 1297 [Parish registers. Marriages. 1909].

1972. Cassington. (Archaeol. notes. Oxoniensia, 1936, p. 201; 1937, p. 201; 1938, p. 164; 1939, p. 196; 1940, p. 163; 1941, p. 84; 1942, p. 103–07; 1943/4, p. 193–96; 1945, p. 93; 1946/7, p. 164; 1950, vol. 15, p. 104–06.) R. Top. 340

1973. LEEDS, E. T., and RILEY, M., Two early Saxon cemeteries at Cassington. (Oxoniensia, 1942, p. 61–70.) R. Top. 340

1974. ATKINSON, R. J. C., A Middle Bronze age barrow at Cassington. (Oxoniensia, 1946–7, p. 5–26.) R. Top. 340

1974A. ROBERTS, D. F., Skeletal material from Radley and Cassington. (Oxoniensia, 1950, vol. 15, p. 109–10.) R. Top. 340

1975. Auction catal. Begbroke estate. 5 June 1897. G.A. Oxon b. 90 (11)

1976. Auction catal. Wharf farm, Day's farm. 14 July 1920. G.A. Oxon b. 92* (3)

CASTLE HILL

See WHEATLEY.

CAVERSFIELD

1977. An act for dividing and inclosing the ... fields ... of ... Caversfield. (21 G. III, c. 50, Private.) n. pl., 1780, fol. 17 pp. L. Eng. C 13 c. 1 (1780. 40)

1978. DRYDEN, H., Caversfield church. (Rept., Oxf. archaeol. soc., 1893–4, p. 15–23.) R. Top. 330

1979. BLOMFIELD, J. C., History of . . . Caversfield [&c.] (Hist. of . . . deanery of Bicester. Pt. 8. Caversfield. 47 pp.) Lond., 1894, 4°.
G.A. Oxon 4° 71

1980. Auction catal. Caversfield estate. 10 Sept. 1919.
G.A. Oxon b. 92* (2)

CAVERSHAM

1981. CAMPION, T., A relation of the late royall entertainment giuen by . . . lord Knowles, at Cawsome house . . . to queen Anne, in her progresse towards the Bathe. Lond., I. Budge, 1613, 4°.
Mal. 187 (5)
— [Another issue.] 1613.   Wood 537 (8)
— Repr. 1828. (Nichols, J., Progress of king James i, vol. 2, p. 630–39.)   4° BS. 378

1982. Caversham park in Oxfordshire. The seat of major Marsac. [Account of.] n. pl., [17—], s. sh.   G.A. Oxon c. 317 (6)

  See 497 [List of subscribers for mending the road from Reading to Caversham. 1724].

1983. An act for vesting the mannor of Okeley and other lands . . . in trust for Charles lord Cadogan . . . and for settling other lands . . . in the counties of Berks and Oxon [Caversham &c.] to the same uses. (3 G. II, c. 8, Private.) n. pl., [1730], fol. 10 pp.
G.A. Oxon c. 198

1984. A particular of the Manor of Caversham . . . late the estate of the . . . earl of Cadogan. n. pl., [c. 1750]. fol. 4 pp.   4° Rawl. 526

1985. An act for vesting certain tenements and hereditaments in the counties of Oxford, Berks and Wilts, part of the settled estates of the earl of Macclesfield, in trustees, to be sold, or exchanged. [Caversham &c.]. (13 G. III, c. 49, Private.) n. pl., 1773, fol. 26 pp.
L. Eng. C 13 c. 1 (1773)

1986. An act for enabling William Blackall Simonds to sell or mortgage his estate and interest in the impropriate rectory of Caversham . . . free from the claims of the crown. (1 G. IV, c. 114, Pub.) Lond., 1820, fol. 4 pp.   L. Eng. A 69 c. 1
— 2 G. IV, c. 86, Pub.

1987. Caversham park. (Views of the seats of noblemen, by J. P. Neale, 2nd ser., 1824, vol. 1. 2 pp.)   G.A. Gen. top. 4° 43

1988. An act for inclosing lands in . . . Caversham. (2 W. IV, c. 2, Private.) Lond., 1832, fol. 27 pp.   L. Eng. C 13 c. 1
— 18 & 19 V., c. 61, Pub.

1989. RIDGWAY, J., Brief account of Caversham. (Journ., Brit. archaeol. assoc., 1861, vol. 17, p. 198–208.)   R. Top. 4

1990. An act to empower the Corporation of Reading to alter and improve or rebuild Caversham bridge in the counties of Berks and Oxford. (31 & 32 V., c. 60, L. & P.) Lond., 1868, fol. 16 pp.
L. Eng. A 69 c. 6

1991. Oxfordshire Epiphany sessions 1868. Caversham bridge. Resolution of the court. [Oxf.], 1868, fol. 6 pp.   G.A. fol. A 137 (7)

1992. Caversham. (Rept., Oxf. archaeol. soc., 1888/9, p. 19, 20.)
R. Top. 330

1993. PEARMAN, M. T., Historical notices of Caversham. (Trans., Oxf. archaeol. soc., 32.) Lond., 1894, 8°. 54 pp.   R. Top. 330

1994. MARGRETT, E., St. Ann's well and chapel, Caversham. (Berks, Bucks, & Oxon archaeol. journ., 1906, vol. 12, p. 25-27.)
R. Top. 100

1995. Caversham urban district council. *publ. libr. comm.* [Appeal for funds to buy books &c. for the library now being built. 1907.]
G.A. Oxon c. 317 (6)

1996. [Lithographed appeal for funds and announcement of opening of the Public library, Caversham. Dec. 5, 1907.]
G.A. Oxon c. 317 (6)

1997. Queen Anne's school. Chronicle. Vol. 10, no. 2. (Oxf., 1909), 8°.
G.A. Oxon 4° 403* (5)

1998. MASTERS, J. E. SMITH-, The history of Kidmore End, with notes of . . . Caversham [&c.]. (Leighton Buzzard, 1933), 8°. 87 pp.
G.A. Oxon 8° 1131

1999. Diocese of Oxford. Guide to the parish church of St. Peter, Caversham, ed. by E. T. Long. (Berkshire churches, 4.) Oxf., 1938, 8°. 16 pp.   G.A. Berks 8° 243

See 332 [Ancient channel between Caversham and Henley, with flint implements. 1948].

2000. Auction catal. Rose hill estate. 21 Sept. 1906.
G.A. Oxon b. 90 (17)

2001. Auction catal. Balmore. 24 Oct. 1917.   G.A. Oxon c. 317 (6)

CHADLINGTON

2002. An act for inclosing lands . . . of Chadlington West, Chadlington East, and Chilson . . . (51 G. III, c. 25, Private.) n. pl., 1811, fol. 28 pp.   L. Eng. C 13 c. 1 (1811. 1)

2003. Charity commissioners. In the matter of the charity of Alice Hemming . . . applicable as to one moiety in the township of Chadlington [&c.] [Draft scheme.] Lond., 1905, fol. 7 pp.
G.A. Oxon c. 208

2004. KIBBLE, J., Historical and other notes on the ancient manor of Charlbury, and its nine hamlets, Chadlington [&c.]. Oxf., 1927, 8°. 100 pp. G.A. Oxon 8° 1053

2005. PAYNE, J. D., Notes on the history of the parish of Charlbury with Chadlington [&c.] Oxf., 1935, 8°. 52 pp. G.A. Oxon 4° 702

2006. LEEDS, E. T., Two Saxon cemeteries in North Oxfordshire [Chadlington and North Leigh]. (Oxoniensia, 1940, p. 21–30.) R. Top. 340

CHADLINGTON HUNDRED

See 879 [Charities. 1826].
See 362 [Survey of 1387. 1910].

CHALFORD

2007. An act to authorize the inclosure of certain lands . . . [Chalford]. (17 & 18 V., c. 48, Pub.) Lond., 1854, fol. 2 pp. L. Eng. A 69 c. 1

2008. LOBEL, M., The history of Dean and Chalford (Oxf. record soc., 17.) Oxf., 1935, 8°. 171 pp. R. 13. 702

CHALGROVE

See 404 [Prince Rupert's victory. Chalgrove field. 1643].

2009. An act for inclosing lands in . . . Chalgrove . . . (6 & 7 V., c. 7, Private.) n. pl., 1843, fol. 42 pp. L. Eng. C 13 c. 1 (1843. 7)

2010. BURGES, W., On mural paintings in Chalgrove church. (Archaeologia, 1860, vol. 38, p. 431–38). R. Top. 7
— [Repr.] 1861. G.A. Oxon c. 178

2011. GAMMON, L. M. P., Chalgrove, a sketch. (The Pelican, 1883, vol. 5, no. 25, p. 3–8.) G.A. Oxon c. 317 (6)

2012. MONEY, W., A walk to Chalgrove field. (Berks, Bucks, & Oxon archaeol. journ., 1895, vol. 1, p. 14–22.) R. Top. 100

See 3646 [Catalogue of brasses in the church. 1897].

2013. STALLWOOD, J. ST. L., [Letter concerning religious instruction in Chalgrove church, instead of in the school.] n. pl., [c. 1900], s. sh. G.A. Oxon c. 317 (6)

2014. SWINSTEAD, J. H., A village and a battlefield [Chalgrove]. (Oxf. diocesan mag., 1904/5, vol. 2, p. 389–91.) Per. 11126 d. 78

2015. SWINSTEAD, J. H., Chalgrove, Oxon., and John Hampden. n. pl., (1906), 8°. 22 pp. G.A. Oxon 8° 744 (2)

2016. SWINSTEAD, J. H., A quaint register [extracts from Chalgrove parish register]. (Oxf. diocesan mag., 1911, vol. 6, p. 180, 204.)
Per. 11126 d. 78

2017. LAMBORN, E. A. GREENING, History of Parliament. The Barentines [of Chalgrove]. (N. & Q., 1942, vol. 183, p. 190–92.)
Ψ 2. 97

2018. BROOKS, E. ST. J., History of Parliament, the Barentines [of Chalgrove]. (N. & Q., 1942, vol. 183, p. 350.) Ψ 2. 97

2019. Auction catal. Estates of John Sedgley. 8 Sept. 1763.
G.A. Oxon a. 22 (92)

2020. Auction catal. Roffard farm.
— 28 June 1837. G.A. fol. A 273*
— 30 July 1902. G.A. Oxon b. 90 (19)

2021. Auction catal. Houndswell farm. 26 June 1901.
G.A. Oxon b. 90 (18)

CHARLBURY

2022. SILVER, T., A letter to the duke of Marlborough and baron Churchill, lay rectors of . . . Charlbury, on the sacrilege and impolicy of the forced commutation of tithes. Oxf., 1842, 8°. 180 pp.
42. 1075

2023. DAVIES, G. J., A farewell letter to the parishioners of Charlbury. Lond., 1857, 12°.

2024. FOX, S., and PICKARD, E., The hat crusade. Vol. 1. [An account of the refusal by certain Quakers to remove their hats in church. Charlbury (where Fox lived for a time) and Witney churches are particularly mentioned.] Flushing, Cornw., 1896, 8°. 11141 e. 8

2025. TAUNT, H. W., Charlbury Oxon, and round it, including Corbury park, Ditchley &c. Oxf., [1906], obl. 8°. 24 pp.
G.A. Oxon 8° 730

2026. Charlbury grammar school. Scheme for exhibitions. [3rd & 5th proofs.] (Lond., 1908, 09), fol. 4 pp. G.A. Oxon c. 135
See 1022 [Act concerning supply of gas. 1913].

2027. KIBBLE, J., Historical and other notes on the ancient manor of Charlbury, and its nine hamlets. Oxf., 1927, 8°. 100 pp.
G.A. Oxon 8° 1053

2028. KIBBLE, J., Charming Charlbury: a Wychwood gem. Charlbury, 1930, 8°. 110 pp. G.A. Oxon 8° 1077

2029. PAYNE, J. D., Notes on the history of the parish of Charlbury [&c.] Oxf., 1935, 8°. 52 pp. G.A. Oxon 4° 702

2030. ALBRIGHT, M. C., Reminiscences of a Quaker community [at Charlbury]. (Friends Quart. examiner, 1942, p. 271–83.)
Per. 11141 e. 5

2031. Auction catal. Lee place.
— 31 Oct. 1812.   G.A. fol. B 71
— 4 Aug. 1868.   G.A. Oxon b. 85 *a* (29)

2032. Auction catal. Pintle Barn farm and Conygree farm. 14 July 1920.
G.A. Oxon b. 92* (3)

CHARLTON ON OTMOOR

2033. AIRAY, H., The iust and necessary apologie . . . touching his suite in law for the rectorie of Charleton. [*Followed by*] For the farther clearing, and inlarging of some passages in the preceeding apologetique . . . [signed T. W.] Lond., 1621, 8°. 44+13 pp.
Gough Oxf. 7 (1)
See 486 [Railway. 1846].

2034. Rectors of the church of S. Mary-the-virgin, Charlton-super-Otemore from 1240. n. pl., [*c.* 1900], s. sh.   G.A. Oxon c. 317 (6)

2035. PRIOR, C. E., 'Rood screen' in the parish church of St. Mary the virgin, Charlton-on-Otmoor. (Rept., Oxf. archaeol. soc., 1900, p. 18.)   R. Top. 330

2036. PRIOR, C. E., Charlton-on-Otmoor open fields. (Trans., Oxf. archaeol. soc., 51.) Banbury, 1907, 8°. 10 pp.   R. Top. 330

2037. PRIOR, C. E., Notes on an Oxford benefice. (Rept., Oxf. archaeol. soc., 1910, p. 13–19.)   R. Top. 330

2038. PRIOR, C. E., Words and sayings from a mid-Oxon parish [Charlton-on-Otmoor]. (Rept., Oxf. archaeol. soc., 1911, p. 18–23.)
R. Top. 330

2039. Auction catal. Manor farm and Holt farm. 30 July 1902.
G.A. Oxon b. 90 (20)

2040. Auction catal. Manor farm. 24 July 1909.
G.A. Oxon b. 92* (28)

CHASTLETON

2041. PRICE, J. E., Chastleton camp. (Journ., Anthrop. inst., 1881, vol. 10, p. 124–27.)   Soc. 247115 e. 55

2042. LEEDS, E. T., Chastleton camp, Oxfordshire, a hill-fort of the early Iron age. (Antiquaries journ., 1931, vol. 11, p. 382–98.)
R. Top. 2

2043. Excursion to Barton-on-the-heath, the Rollwrights, and Chastleton. (Trans. of the Birm. archaeol. assoc. for 1888, p. 67–70.)
G.A. Warw. c. 2

2044. Chastleton church and manor house. (Trans., Bristol & Glouc. archaeol. soc., 1891–2, vol. 16, p. 36, 37.)
R. Top. 210

2045. DICKINS, M., A history of Chastleton. Banbury, 1938, 4°. 83 pp.
G.A. Oxon 4° 611

2046. JONES, M. WHITMORE, Chastleton house. [Banbury, 19—], 8°. 8 pp.
Ashm.

2047. Chastleton house. (Country Life, 1902, vol. 12, p. 80–89.)
Per. 384 b. 6

2048. JONES, M. WHITMORE, The Gunpowder plot and life of Robert Catesby, also an account of Chastleton house. Lond., 1909, 8°. 120 pp.
22854 e. 35

2049. JOHNSTON, P. M., Chastleton house. (Country Life, 1919, vol. 45, p. 90–96, 116–23.)
Per. 384 b. 6

2050. HUMPHREYS, J., Recently discovered Elizabethan Sheldon tapestries [at Chastleton house]. (Country Life, 1920, vol. 48, p. 463–65.)
Per. 384 b. 6

2051. JOURDAIN, M., Chastleton house [early 17th cent.] (Architect. rev., 1922, Feb., p. 48–50.)
Per. 17356 c. 8

2052. DICKINS, M., Chastleton house. Stratford-upon-Avon, [c. 1935], 8°. 32 pp.
G.A. Oxon 16° 212

See 4208A [Chastleton house in 'English country houses' by C. Hussey. 1951].

2053. Auction catal. Brookend house 17 May 1895.
G.A. Oxon c. 317 (6)

CHECKENDON

2054. An act to authorize the inclosure of certain lands . . . [Checkendon]. (23 & 24 V., c. 55, Pub.) Lond., 1860, fol. 2 pp.
L. Eng. A 69 c. 1

2055. BRUTON, E. G., Recent discovery of wall-paintings in the apse of Checkendon church. (Proc., Oxf. architect. and hist. soc., N.S., vol. 2, 1868, p. 75–78.)
R. 13. 708

2056. Report of proceedings at the re-opening of Checkendon church as restored from the design of Edward G. Bruton, August 2, 1869. (Repr. from the 'Reading Mercury'.) n. pl., (1869), 8°. 10 pp.
G.A. Oxon 8° 147 (5)

2057. PEARMAN, M. T., Notices, manorial and ecclesiastical, of the parish of Checkenden. (Trans., Oxf. archaeol. soc., 29) Lond., 1893, 8°. 47 pp. R. Top. 330

2058. PEARMAN, M. T., Additional notices of Checkenden rectory. (Trans., Oxf. archaeol. soc., 36.) Lond., 1898, 8°. 11 pp. R. Top. 330

2059. STEPHENSON, M., A palimpsest brass at Checkenden. (Trans., Monumental brass soc., 1897, vol. 3, pt. 1, p. 87, 88.) Soc. 2184 d. 85

2060. ABBEY, C. J., On the Chilterns [chiefly history of Checkendon]. (Oxf. diocesan mag., 1902/3, vol. 1, p. 119–21, 138, 39.) Per. 11126 d. 78

2061. COOKE, A. H., Some early Checkendon documents. (Berks, Bucks, & Oxon archaeol. journ., 1928, vol. 32, p. 1–7, 53–62.) R. Top. 100

2062. KEYSER, C. E., Notes on the churches of . . . Checkendon [&c.]. (Journ., Brit. archaeol. assoc., 1918, new ser., vol. 24, p. 1–32+67 plates.) R. Top. 4

2063. Auction catal. One moiety of the Manor of Checkendon. 28 Aug. 1800. G.A. fol. A 266 (3)

2064. Auction catal. Freehold estate, consisting of capital beech and oak wood land.
— 28 Sept. 1801. G.A. fol. A 266 (29)
— 9 Nov. 1801. G.A. fol. A 266 (30)

2065. Auction catal. Little Stoke estate.
— 22 July 1901. G.A. Oxon b. 92 (2)
— 7 Sept. 1917. G.A. Oxon b. 92 (3)

CHEQUERS

See STOKENCHURCH

CHESTERTON

2066. An act for dividing and inclosing . . . fields . . . within . . . Chesterton. . . . (7 G. III, c. 7, Private.) n. pl., [1767], fol. 25 pp. L. Eng. C 13 c. 1 (1767, p. 466)

2067. An act for confirming exchanges of lands in . . . Chesterton . . . made between the trustees of the earl and countess of Jersey and the vicar of Chesterton. . . . (10 G. IV, c. 47, Private.) [Lond.], 1829, fol. 23 pp. L. Eng. C 13 c. 1 (1829)

See 486 [Railway. 1846].

2068. Images in the windows of churches. Protest against them. [Corre-
spondence between G. R. Clark and the bishop of Oxford concerning Chesterton church.] n. pl., (1867), fol. 4 pp.
G.A. Oxon c. 317 (6)

CHILSON

2069. An act for inclosing lands . . . of . . . Chilson. (51 G. III, c. 25,
Private.) n. pl., 1811, fol. 28 pp.   L. Eng. C 13 c. 1 (1811. 1)

2070. An act to authorize the inclosure of certain lands . . . [in Chilson
&c.]. (21 V., c. 8, Pub.) Lond., 1858, fol. 2 pp.   L. Eng. A 69 c. 1

2071. KIBBLE, J., Historical and other notes on the ancient manor of
Charlbury, and its nine hamlets . . . Chilson [&c.]. Oxf., 1927, 8°.
100 pp.   G.A. Oxon 8° 1053

2072. Auction catal. Manor. 29 Jan. 1858.   G.A. Oxon b. 85 b (42)

CHILTERN HUNDREDS

2073. PEARMAN, M. T., Historical account of the Hundreds of Chiltern
in Oxfordshire. (Trans., Oxf. archaeol. soc., 25.) Banbury, 1890, 8°.
20 pp.   R. Top. 330

CHILWORTH

2074. Auction catal. Freehold estate, consisting of two farms. 17 July
1794.   G.A. fol. A 273*

2075. Auction catal. Freehold estate occupied by J. Simon and messrs.
Tyrrell and Brooks. 28 June 1837.   G.A. fol. A 273*

2076. Auction catal. Farm. 4 June 1841.   G.A. fol. B 71

CHINNOR

See 403, 04 [Civil War battle. 1643].

2077. An act to authorize the inclosure of certain lands . . . [Chinnor].
(11 & 12 V., c. 27, Pub.) Lond., 1848, fol. 4 pp.
L. Eng. A 69 c. 1

2078. ROYCE, D., Chinnor [by D. Royce]. (North Oxf. archaeol. soc.,
1874.) Banbury, [1874], 8°. 20 pp.   R. Top. 330

2079. Parish church of St. Andrew, Chinnor. List of rectors. n. pl.,
[c. 1920], s. sh.   G.A. Oxon c. 317 (6)

2080. GAWTHORP, W. E., Chinnor. (Trans., Monumental brass soc.,
1935, vol. 7, pt. 2, p. 65.)   Soc. 2184 d. 85

2081. MANCHESTER, A. J., A short guide to the church of St. Andrew, Chinnor. (Frome), 1936, 8°. 8 pp. O.C.L.

2082. Chinnor. (Archaeol. notes. Oxoniensia, 1942, p. 108; 1946/7, p. 164.) R. Top. 340

2083. HASSALL, W. O., Dissent at . . . Chinnor [&c.] (Thame Gazette, Jan. 30, 1951.) N.G.A. Oxon a. 120

2084. Auction catal. Chinnor estate. 30 Oct. 1889.
G.A. Oxon b. 92* (26)

2085. Auction catal. Outlying portions of the Thame park estate. 24, 25 Sept. 1917. G.A. Oxon b. 92 (23)

CHIPPINGHURST

2086. BAYLEY, W. D'OYLY, *ed.*, Ancient deeds. [D'Oyly's estates; manor of Chislehampton, Chibenhurst manor]. (Topogr. and geneal., 1853, vol. 2, p. 340–44.) Ψ 2. 10 *b*

2087. Auction catal. Chippinghurst manor. 6 June 1903.
G.A. Oxon b. 90 (21)

CHIPPING NORTON

General

2088. FORD, S., An epistle to the Church of Christ in Chippin-Norton. [Madan 2336.] Oxf., 1657, 4°. 46 pp. Pamph. C 104 (18)

2089. Strange and wonderful news from Chipping-Norton . . . of certain dreadful aparations, which were seen in the air on the 28th of July. [Lond., 1680], fol. 4 pp. Ashm. 309 (19)

2090. A full account of a . . . murther committed on . . . William Culliford by George Cruff . . . together with the . . . account of a lamentable fire . . . in a town called Church-Hill within two miles of Chipping-Norton . . . on Wednesday the 30th. of July last. Lond., 1684, s. sh. Ashm. F 5 (113)

See 723, 730 [Electioneering at Chipping Norton. 1754].

2091. An act for dividing and inclosing certain . . . fields . . . in . . . Chipping Norton. (9 G. III, c. 75, Private.) n. pl., [1769], fol. 26 pp.
G.A. Oxon c. 185

2092. Case of the bailiffs and burgesses of Chipping Norton . . . and others, relating to the intended inclosure of the common fields, &c. there. n. pl., 1769, fol. 4 pp. G.A. Oxon 4° 115

2093. Chipping-Norton register, (1560–1686). [Extracts from parish registers.] [Middlehill, 1830], fol. 4 pp. Caps. 6. 24
— [Another ed. 1830.] Caps. 6. 54 (1)

2094. COCKBURN, A. E., Corporations of England and Wales. (Chipping Norton, vol. I, p. 201, 02.) Lond., 1835, 8°.

G.A. Gen. top. 8° 727 (1)

2095. First report of the Commissioners appointed to inquire into the municipal corporations in England and Wales. (Chipping Norton, Appendix p. 31–36.)   Pp. Eng. 1835, vol. 23

2096. Report of the Commissioners appointed to report . . . upon the boundaries and wards of certain boroughs and corporate towns. (Chipping Norton, pt. I, p. 270–72.)   Pp. Eng. 1837, vol. 26

2097. An act for vesting part of the settled estates of . . . John, earl of Shrewsbury [in Chipping Norton &c.] . . . in trustees to be sold. (6 & 7 V., c. 28, Private.) Lond., 1843, fol. 60 pp.

L. Eng. C 13 c. 1 (1843. i. 28)

2098. Army (Drying rooms) . . . Copy of report made by colonel Gordon upon mr. Huthname's drying room at Chipping Norton, inspected . . . 25 October 1856.   Pp. Eng. 1861, vol. 36

2099. KIRTLAND, C., Brief memorials of the early history of Chipping Norton. Chipping Norton, 1871, 8°. 75 pp.   G.A. Oxon 8° 210

2100. Chipping Norton parish church restoration, 1880. [Appeal for funds.] [Chipping Norton?], (1880), s. sh.

MS. Eng. hist. d. 37 (542)

2101. Chipping Norton union & rural district council. Parochial compendium. n. pl., 1887/8–, 16°. [1922/23 only in G.A. Oxon c. 317 (6).]

2102. HOPE, W. H. ST. J., [Description of mace formerly belonging to the old corporation of Chipping Norton.] (Proc., Soc. of Antiquaries, 1892, 2nd ser., vol. 14, p. 66, 67.)   R. Top. 1

2103. BALLARD, A., Notes on the history of Chipping Norton, a lecture. Oxf., 1893, 8°. 40 pp.   G.A. Oxon 8° 542

2104. Chipping Norton illustrated almanack and diary. 1897. Chipping Norton, 1897. 8°.   G.A. Oxon 8° 810 (6)

2105. MANNING, P., Notes on the monumental brasses in Chipping Norton church. (Journ., Oxf. univ. brass-rubbing soc., 1897, vol. I, p. 3–10.)   Soc. 2184 d. 50

See 658 [Parliamentary history, by W. R. Williams. 1899].

2106. LITTLEDALE, G. A., Chipping Norton, S. Mary the Virgin. List of rectors and vicars. n. pl., [1904], s. sh.   G.A. Oxon b. 46

2107. Chipping Norton. (Rept., Oxf. archaeol. soc., 1905, p. 8.)

R. Top. 330

See 1297 [Parish registers, Marriages. 1909].

2108. PEARSON, M. K., Chipping Norton in by-gone days. Chipping Norton, 1909, 8°. 63 pp.   G.A. Oxon 8° 782

2109. An act to confirm certain provisional orders made by the Board of Trade under the Electric Lighting acts 1882 to 1909 relating to . . . Chipping Norton. . . . (3 & 4 G. V, c. 149, L. & P.) Lond., 1913, fol. 40 pp.   L. Eng. A 69 c. 6

2110. BALLARD, A., The management of open fields [orders of the manorial court at Chipping Norton, 22nd Oct. 1764]. (Rept., Oxf. archaeol. soc., 1913, p. 131–44.)   R. Top. 330

2111. CLARK, G. N., and COLE, G. D. H., The strike at Chipping Norton. n. pl., [1914], 8°. 4 pp.   G.A. Oxon c. 317 (6)

2112. Ruskin college, Oxford. Appeal on behalf of the Chipping Norton strikers [signed H. Allen]. n. pl., (1914), s. sh.
G.A. Oxon c. 317 (6)

2113. Official guide. 3rd(–9th) ed. Lond., [1928–41], 8°.
G.A. Oxon 8° 1059

2114. PHILLIPPS, SIR T., bart., Pedigree of Phillips family of Chipping Norton . . . compiled . . . 1852, revised by W. A. Phillips, 1910, revised and publ. by E. Phillips, 1929. (Croydon), 1929, s. sh.
2182 P. d. 34

2115. SALTER, H. E., Rev. John Thorley, of Chipping Norton. (Rept., Oxf. archaeol. soc., 1936, p. 131–32.)   R. Top. 330

2116. BARRATT, D. M., Chipping Norton vicarage in 1683. (Oxoniensia, 1945, p. 105–07.)   R. Top. 340

2117. MEADES, E., The history of Chipping Norton. Oxf., 1949, 8°. 87 pp.   G.A. Oxon 8° 1218

2118. Auction catal. Estate adjoining the common of Primedown. 30 July 1801.   G.A. fol. A 266 (40)

2119. Auction catal. Freehold pleasure farm and shooting box, known as Foxhole's. 8 Aug. 1899.   G.A. Oxon b. 90 (47)

2120. Auction catal. Manor house, West Street. 2 Apr. 1913.
G.A. Oxon c. 317 (6)

2121. Auction catal. Residence in New Street, together with Ivy Croft, New Street. 11 Sept. 1918.   G.A. Oxon b. 92★ (7)

Geology

2122. HUDLESTON, W. H., Excursion to Chipping Norton, April 22nd and following day. (Proc., Geol. assoc., 1878, vol. 5, p. 378–89.)
Radcl.

2123. WOODWARD, H. B., Note on some pits near Chipping Norton. [Geol. note.] (Essex naturalist, 1887, vol. 1, p. 265–66.)
Soc. 18854 d. 18

2124. RICHARDSON, L., The inferior oolite and contiguous deposits of the Chipping Norton district. (Proc., Cots. N.F.C., 1911, vol. 17, p. 195–231.)
Per. 18855 d. 58

Newspapers

See 1336 [Chipping Norton News].
　1338 [Guardian].

Railways

2125. An act for enabling the Oxford, Worcester and Wolverhampton Railway company to construct a branch line of railway to . . . Chipping Norton. . . . (17 & 18 V., c. 209, L. & P.) Lond., 1854, fol. 8 pp.
L. Eng. A 69 c. 6

See 489 [Railway. 1860].

Roads

See 526, 529 [Turnpike acts. 1793, &c.].

2126. Enclosure awards, extracts relating to the roads, bridleways, footways, stone pits, watercourses, etc. . . . within the rural district of Chipping Norton. Chipping Norton, 1903, 8°. 138 pp.　　O.C.R.L.

Schools

2127. Chipping Norton national schools. Appeal for the building fund. n. pl., 1896, 4°. 2 pp.
G.A. Oxon c. 317 (6)

2128. National schools, Chipping Norton. Appeal for funds towards alteration and enlargement. n. pl., [c. 1900], 4°. 4 pp.
G.A. Oxon c. 317 (6)

CHIPPING NORTON DEANERY

2129. PRIOR, C. E., Dedications of churches, with some notes as to village feasts and old customs. Deaneries of Chipping Norton, Cuddesdon. (Rept., Oxf. archaeol. soc., 1905, p. 11–25.)
R. Top. 330

2130. PEARCE, S. S., The clergy of the deaneries of Chipping Norton and Deddington, and the peculiars of Banbury and Cropredy during the settlement of 1559 and afterwards [by S. S. Pearce]. (Rept., Oxf. archaeol. soc., 1916, p. 15–86.)
R. Top. 330

CHISLEHAMPTON

2131. BAYLEY, W. D'OYLY, *ed.*, Ancient deeds [D'Oyly's estates; manor of Chislehampton; Chibenhurst manor]. (Topogr. and geneal. 1853, vol. 2, p. 340–44.) Ψ 2. 10 *b*

2131A. Chiselhampton. (Archaeol. notes. Oxoniensia, 1940, p. 161.)
                    R. Top. 340

2132. LAMBORN, E. A. GREENING, A problem of the Oxfordshire Domesday [mainly about Chislehampton]. (N. & Q., 1944, vol. 187, p. 203–05.) Ψ 2. 97

CHURCH ENSTONE

2133. An act for vesting part of the settled estates of . . . John, earl of Shrewsbury [in Church Enstone &c.] . . . in trustees to be sold. (6 & 7 V., c. 28, Private.) Lond., 1843, fol. 60 pp.
                    L. Eng. C 13 c. 1 (1843. i. 28)

2133A. MARSHALL, E., An account of the township of Church Enstone. Oxf., &c., 1868, 8°. 88 pp.   G.A. Oxon 8° 109

2134. Auction catal. Broad Close. 2 May 1951.
                    G.A. Oxon b. 92*

CHURCH HANDBOROUGH

2135. Church-Handborough. (Gent's. mag., 1793, pt. 2, p. 608, 09.)
                    Ψ 2. 44

2136. OSBORN, G., The duke of Marlborough versus Osborn. Extraordinary disclosures concerning an ejectment case, & excessive game-preserving. Oxf., 1863, 8°. 34 pp.   G.A. Oxon 8° 92 (8)

2137. Auction catal. Coullings, Freeland, Hudson's ground. 10 June 1911.   G.A. Oxon b. 91 (27)

CHURCHILL

2138. A full and true account of two wonderful prodigies [the second seen at Churchill] that were seen at several times in the element. [An account of several 'mock suns' witnessed by T. Davis, R. Davis, R. Brooks, J. Smith, all of Churchill, and T. Smith of Idbury.] (Lond.), 1710, s. sh.   Gough Lond. 42 (4)

2139. PHILIPS, J., Mr. Phillips' letter and representation to . . . lord Harcourt; with an account of the cruel treatment mr. Phillips met with from sir John Walter [respecting the living of Churchill]. n. pl., 1721, 8°.   B.M.

2140. An act for dividing and inclosing the . . . fields . . . in . . . Sarsden and Churchill. . . . (28 G. III, c. 27, Private.) n. pl., [1787], fol. 23 pp.   L. Eng. C 13 c. 1 (1787. 17)

See 489 [Railway. 1860].
See 359 [Honors and knights' fees. 1924].

2141. ROSE, L., The history of Churchill. Brackley, 1934, 8°. 79 pp.
G.A. Oxon 8° 1130* (4)

CLANFIELD

See 517 [Turnpike act. 1771, &c.].

2142. Clanfield. Prince of Wales friendly society. Rules. Bampton, 1875, 8°. 11 pp.   G.A. Oxon 8° 688 (2)

2143. Auction catal. High house farm, Comins farm and Manor farm. 12 July 1898.   G.A. Oxon b. 90 (4)

2144. Auction catal. Windmill farm. 20 July 1901.
G.A. Oxon b. 91 (22)

2145. Auction catal. High house farm, Adams' farm, Windmill farm. 20 Aug. 1908.   G.A. Oxon b. 90 (22)

2146. Auction catal. Pasture land. 8 June 1909.
G.A. Oxon b. 90 (3)

CLATTERCOTE

2147. Clattercote. (Gent's. mag., 1866, pt. 2, p. 286–88.) Ψ 2. 44

CLAYDON

2148. An act for dividing and inclosing the . . . fields . . . of Claydon. . . . (15 G. III, c. 82, Private.) n. pl., [1775], fol. 30 pp.
L. Eng. C 13 c. 1 (1775. 16)

2149. St. James the greater, Cleydon. A memorial of the re-opening of the church, March 7th, 1861. Banbury, (1861), 8°. 10 pp.
G.A. Oxon 8° 636 (11)

CLIFTON

2150. WILSON, W., An address delivered at the laying of the corner-stone of the new church of S. James, at Clifton, in the parish of Deddington, Sept. 8th, 1851. Deddington, 1851, 8°. 8 pp.
G.A. Oxon 8° 636 (12)

CLIFTON HAMPDEN

2151. HEATH, J., Clifton Chapel hill, a poem, with historical annotations. Oxf., 1818, 8°. 43 pp. G.A. Oxon 8° 434

2152. An act for the making and maintaining a bridge over the river Thames . . . near the ferry at Clifton Hampden. . . . (27 & 28 V., c. 44, L. & P.) Lond., 1864, fol. 15 pp. L. Eng. A 69 c. 6

2152A. Clifton Hampden. (Archaeol. notes. Oxoniensia, 1950, vol. 15, p. 106.) R. Top. 340

COGGES

2153. An act for the vesting . . . several manors and lands [in Cogges &c.] . . . late the inheritance of W. Jennens . . . in trustees to be sold. (8 Anne, c. 10, Private.) n. pl., [c. 1709], 8°. 52 pp.
Radcl. e. 127

2154. An act for dividing and inclosing the . . . commonable lands . . . of Coggs. (27 G. III, c. 12, Private.) n. pl., 1787, fol. 25 pp.
L. Eng. C 13 c. 1 (1787. 3)

2155. GILES, J. A., History of Witney, with notices of . . . Cogges [&c.]. Lond., 1852, 8°. 107 pp. G.A. Oxon 8° 13

2156. Cogges. (Excursion. Archaeol. and nat. hist. soc. of N. Oxf., 1868.) Manning 8° 3

2157. BRUTON, E. G., On Cogges church. (Proc., Oxf. architect. and hist. soc., N.S., vol. 2, 1870, p. 141–43.) R. 13. 708

2158. PAYNE, J., Coggs parish. Statement of accounts. 1873. (Witney), 1873, s. sh. G.A. Oxon c. 22 (8*)

2159. The Home visitor for Aston, Coggs, and Ducklington. June, 1879. Lond., (1879), 8°. G.A. Oxon 8° 578

2160. Cogges, Ducklington & Hardwick parish magazine. Jan. 1892–Dec. 1903. (Witney), 1892–1903, 4°. Per. G.A. Oxon 4° 182

See 362 [Survey of 1387. 1910].

2161. PAINTIN, H., The church and village of Coggs. n. pl., [1915], s. sh. G.A. Oxon a. 22 (72)

2162. SALTER, H., Coggs priory. (Rept., Oxf. archaeol. soc., 1930, p. 321–25.) R. Top. 330

2163. MORIARTY, G. A., The barony of Coggs [Arsic family]. (Rept., Oxf. archaeol. soc., 1930, p. 309–20.) R. Top. 330

2164. PRICE, E. R., Two effigies in the churches of Asthall and Cogges. (Oxoniensia, 1938, p. 103–10.) R. Top. 340

2165. Auction catal. Pasture field. 10 June 1911.
G.A. Oxon b. 91 (27)

COKETHORPE PARK

2166. An act for the vesting . . . several manors and lands [in Coke-thorpe &c.] . . . late the inheritance of W. Jennens . . . in trustees to be sold. (8 Anne, c. 10, Private.) n. pl., [c. 1709], 8°. 52 pp.
Radcl. e. 127

2167. MAY, T., An excursion to Cockthorp park, near Witney, in Oxfordshire . . . To which are added, verses written after seeing the gardens of Park-place, near Henley, in Oxfordshire [by T. May. In verse]. [Henley, 1769], 8°. 21 pp. Gough Oxf. 45 (13)

2168. Cokethorpe park. (Views of the seats of noblemen and gentlemen, by J. P. Neale, 1820, vol. 3. 2 pp.) G.A. Gen. top. 4° 42
— 2nd ser., 1824, vol. 1. 2 pp. G.A. Gen. top. 4° 43

2169. Pedigree of Danvers, of Cotherop, co. Oxon . . . &c. (Extr. from Aske's collections. Collectanea topogr. & geneal., 1834, vol. 1, p. 324–30.) Ψ 2. 10

2170. Notes of an excursion to . . . Cokethorpe [&c.], 1871. (North Oxf. archaeol. soc., 1871.) Banbury, [1871], 8°. 73 pp.
R. Top. 330
See 293 [History, by W. J. Monk. 1926].

2171. Cokethorpe park. A catalogue of the Cokethorpe library and collection of pictures . . . which will be sold by auction . . . 12th of Nov., 1908. Lond., 1908, 8°. 10 pp. MS. Top. Oxon b. 78 (325)

2172. Auction catal. Cokethorpe estate. 4 July 1912.
G.A. Oxon b. 92★ (2)

COL D'ARBRES ESTATE
See CROWMARSH GIFFORD

COLD NORTON

2173. Cold Norton. (Gent's. mag., 1845, pt. 2, p. 589, 90.) Ψ 2. 44

2174. WING, W., Cold Norton priory. (Trans., North Oxf. archaeol. soc., 1853–55, pp. 75–78.) R. Top. 330

2175. HOOKINS, P., Notes on [Cold Norton priory]. (Trans., North Oxf. archaeol. soc., 1853–55, pp. 79–88.) R. Top. 330

2176. LEADAM, I. S., The estates of the priory of Cold Norton. (Brasenose coll. quatercent. monogr., vol. 2, p. 54–77. O.H.S. vol. 53.) Oxf., 1909, 8°. R. 13. 700

COMBE

2177. An act for establishing . . . articles of agreement between . . . George, duke of Marlborough . . . and . . . Lincoln college [concerning Combe]. (33 G. III, c. 22, Private.) n. pl., 1793, fol. 6 pp.
L. Eng. C 13 c. 1 (1793. ii. 46)

2178. [Begin] The humble petition of Edward Collett [and others, concerning the attempt by Dr. Tatham to evict the Rev. B. Lee from the curacy of Coombe church]. n. pl., [1823], s. sh.
G.A. Oxon a. 22 (102)

2179. Correspondence, &c. [between the churchwardens of Coombe and the rector of Lincoln coll., concerning the burial of the dead in Coombe churchyard]. 2nd ed., enlarged. (Oxf.), [1850], 8°. 32 pp.
G.A. Oxon 8° 164 (1)

2180. Long Combe parish magazine. January 1892–May 1914. n. pl., 1892–1914, 4°. G.A. Oxon 4° 199

2181. GEE, C. F. A., Catalogue of the Coombe reading room and coffee house library, founded by Adela Brooke. Oxf., 1892, 8°. 48 pp.
2590 d. Coombe 1. 1

2182. MANNERS, J., duchess of Rutland, Miss Adela Brooke's Village institute and reading room at Coombe. Repr. from the 'Queen', Dec. 3rd, 1892. n. pl., (1892), 8°. 8 pp. G.A. Oxon c. 22 (39)

2183. Font at Long Combe. (Berks, Bucks, & Oxon archaeol. journ., 1895, vol. 1, Notes & Queries, p. 93, 94.) R. Top. 100

2184. PEARCE, S. S., A short account of the church of St. Laurence, Long Combe, with a description of its mural paintings uncovered in 1894. Oxf., 1906, 8°. 21 pp. G.A. Gen. top. 8° 865 (18)
— 2nd ed., 1907. G.A. Oxon 8° 884 (17)

2185. PAINTIN, H., Oxford architectural and historical society. Visit to Coombe [&c.]. (Repr. from Oxf. journ. illustr.) n. pl., (1922), s. sh.
G.A. Oxon a. 22

2186. The ancient clock from Combe church. (Oxoniensia, 1938, p. 175; 1946–7, p. 181.) R. Top. 340

2187. EMDEN, C. S., Coombe, church & village. (Oxf.), 1951, 8°. 31 pp.
G.A. Oxon 8° 1204 (14)

2187A. [Nash's cottage, Coombe.] (Ideal home, 1952, vol. 65, no. 5, p. 48–51.) Per. 17525 c. 12

CORNBURY PARK

See 444 [Civil War battery, Cornbury. 1945].
See 2025 [History, by H. W. Taunt. 1906].

2188. WATNEY, V. T., Cornbury and the forest of Wychwood. Lond.,
1910, fol. 296 pp.   G.A. Oxon b. 75

2189. ARKELL, W. J., The building-stones of . . . Cornbury park. . . .
(Oxoniensia, 1948, vol. 13, p. 49–54.)   R. Top. 340

2190. HUSSEY, C., Cornbury park. (Country Life, 1950, vol. 108,
p. 922–26.)   Per. 384 b. 6

2191. Auction catal. Cornbury estate. 7 July 1896.
G.A. Oxon b. 90 (24)

CORNWELL

2192. Genealogy of sir Thomas Peniston of Cornwell. [Middlehill],
1833, s. sh.   Caps. 6. 47 (77)

2193. HUSSEY, C., A Cotswold village reconditioned. Cornwell manor.
(Country Life, 1941, vol. 89, p. 432–36, 454–57, 476–79.)
Per. 384 b. 6

2194. WINSTONE, R., A Cotswold village modernised [Cornwell].
(Homes and gardens, 1952, vol. 33, no. 9, p. 24, 25.)
Per. 17525 c. 11

COTE

2195. WILLIAMS, B., Memorials of the family of Williams of Cote, or
Coate. Norwich, 1849, 4°. 40 pp.   G.A. Oxon 4° 368

2196. Coate and Leafield colportage assoc. Annual report. 1876–7.
n. pl., 1877, 4°. 4 pp.   G.A. Oxon 4° 208 (34)

2197. CYGNUS, pseud., Cote house. (Country Life, 1904, vol. 15, p. 567–
69.)   Per. 384 b. 6

2198. STANLEY, J., The church in the hop garden, a chatty account of
the Longworth-Coate Baptist meeting, ante 1485–1935, and its
ministers. Lond., [1936], 8°. 261 pp.   11133 e. 29

2199. OSWALD, A., Coate house. (Country Life, 1946, vol. 99, p. 1176–
79.)   Per. 384 b. 6

2200. Auction catal. Claywell farm. 22 Feb. 1900.
G. A. Oxon b. 90 (25)

2201. Auction catal. Cote house. 21 July 1920.
G.A. Oxon b. 92* (2)

COTON

2202. An act for dividing and inclosing the . . . fields . . . within . . . Coton, otherwise Cotes. (2 G. III, c. 30, Private.) n. pl., 1761, fol. 24 pp.   G.A. Oxon c. 113 (2)

2203. CHAMBERLIN, W. H., Valuation of Wardington, Wilscote and Coton. Banbury, 1833, 4°. 52 pp.

COTTISFORD

2204. An act to authorize the inclosure of certain lands . . . [Cottisford]. (11 & 12 V., c. 109, Pub.) Lond., 1848, fol. 3 pp.
                                                           L. Eng. A 69 c. 1

2205. BLOMFIELD, J. C., History of Cottisford, Hardwick and Tusmore. (Hist. of . . . deanery of Bicester. Pt. 3.) Bristol, (1887), 4°. 95 pp.   G.A. Oxon 4° 71

2206. CHIBNAL, M., ed., Select documents of the English lands of the abbey of Bec. (Custumal, Cottisford, p. 97–99.) (Camden soc., 3rd ser., vol. 73.) Lond., 1951, 8°. Ψ 2. 112 (iii. 73)

2207. Auction catal. Estate. 15 July 1857.   G.A. Oxon b. 85 b (57)

2208. Auction catal. Manor farm. 29 Oct. 1898.
                                                     G.A. Oxon c. 317 (7)

COWLEY

General

2209. CHAPMAN, MR., The measurement of Cowley farm and rectory and Hines's copyhold, taken from the terrier made by mr. Chapman. Lond., [1837 ?], fol. 3 pp.   MS. Top. Oxon c. 123 (f. 132)

2210. An act to authorize the inclosure of certain lands . . . [Cowley]. (12 & 13 V., c. 7, Pub.) Lond., 1849, fol. 2 pp.
                                                           L. Eng. A 69 c. 1

2211. [Miscellaneous papers, newspaper cuttings &c. 1861–1904.]
                                     G.A. Oxon b. 155; c. 11; 4° 272

2212. Prospectus of a national hospital for incurables. [Appeal for funds.] [Oxf.?, 1869], 8°. 4 pp.   G.A. Oxon c. 85 (446)

2213. Rules of the Cowley cricket club. n. pl., [1870], s. sh.
                                                        G.A. Oxon c. 11

2214. COLEY, J., Parish of Cowley [report of vicar]. 1870, 72–74. Oxf., 1871–75, 8°.   G.A. Oxon c. 9, 11

2215. [The Cowley burial case, involving the rev. J. Coley. A collection of newspaper cuttings &c. 1871–75.]   G.A. Oxon c. 9

2216. Rules for the ringers of Cowley parish church [signed J. Coley]. n. pl., [1874], s. sh.   G.A. Oxon c. 317 (7)

See 1020 [Act concerning supply of water. 1875].

2217. An act to extend the boundaries of the city of Oxford and for other purposes [affecting Cowley &c.]. (18 & 19 G. V., c. 84, L. & P.) Lond., 1928, 8°. 68 pp.   L. Eng. A 69 c. 6

2218. BEAUCHAMP, M. H., St. Francis of Assisi, Cowley. [Details of proposed new church and appeal for funds.] n. pl., [1929], 8°. 16 pp.
          G.A. Oxon b. 155

2219. BEAUCHAMP, M. H., [Appeal for funds to pay staff of the church of St. Francis of Assisi.] n. pl., 1936, 8°. 4 pp.   G.A. Oxon b. 155

2220. St. Luke's church, Cowley. [Plan and views.] n. pl., 1936, 8°. 4 pp.
          G.A. Oxon b. 155

2221. Rose Hill, Cowley. (Archaeol. notes. Oxoniensia, 1937, p. 202.)
          R. Top. 340

2222. Cowley. (Archaeol. notes. Oxoniensia, 1940, p. 163.)
          R. Top. 340

2223. ATKINSON, R. J. C., A Romano-British potters' field at Cowley. (Oxoniensia, 1941, p. 9–21.)   R. Top. 340

2224. Romano-British skeletons from Cowley. (Archaeol. notes. Oxoniensia, 1941, p. 89.)   R. Top. 340

2225. Auction catal. Cowley house. 5 Feb. 1821.   G.A. Oxon b. 4 (6)

2226. Auction catal. Freehold estates. 30 Sept. 1837.   G.A. fol. B 71

2227. Auction catal. Cowley rectory farm. 30 Sept. 1837.
          G.A. Oxon b. 4 (10)

2228. Auction catal. Building land. 8 Mar. 1866.   G.A. Oxon b. 4

2229. Auction catal. Building land. 13 June 1874.
          G.A. Oxon b. 4 (50)

2230. Auction catal. Temple farm. 24 July 1909.
          G.A. Oxon b. 92* (28)

Military College

2231. [Prospectus, 1876, 77.] n. pl., (1876, 77), 4°.   G.A. Oxon 4° 272

2232. [Report. 1880, 1885.] Lond., 1880, [1885], 8°.
          G.A. Oxon 4° 272

2233. The Trumpeter. April. 1888.   G.A. Oxon c. 317 (7)
— April, 1889–July 1891.   O.P.L.

2234. Catalogue of the contents . . . which will be sold by auction, May 4, 5, 6, 7, 1897. [Oxf.], (1897), 8°. 42 pp.   G.A. Oxon 4° 378

2235. Auction catal. Oxford Military college. 17 Nov. 1905.
G. A. Oxon c. 317 (7)

Schools

2236. Oxford diocesan school. Report of the examination held Dec. 1859(–1873) with examination papers. Oxf., 1861–73, 8°.
G.A. Oxon 8° 790

2237. Oxford diocesan central school, Cowley. [Report of a public meeting, 22nd Nov., 1861.] n. pl., 1861, 8°. 3 pp.
G.A. Oxon 4° 272 (1)

2238. The [Oxford diocesan board of education] school committee, to whom was referred the question of the maintenance of the [Oxford diocesan central] school at Cowley . . . submit the following report. n. pl., [1871?], 4°. 4 pp.   G.A. Oxon 4° 272 (2)

2239. Oxford diocesan school. [Brief history]. n. pl., [1871], 8°. 4 pp.
G.A. Oxon c. 317 (7)

2240. Oxford diocesan school, Cowley. [Report by R. Hurman, headmaster.] n. pl., [1872], 8°. 4 pp.   G.A. Oxon 4° 272 (4)

2241. [Report of the sub-committee appointed by the Oxford diocesan board of education school committee to report on the financial aspects of removing the Oxford diocesan central school from Cowley &c.] n. pl., [1872], fol. 8 pp.   G.A. Oxon 4° 272 (3)

2242. Order of the Poor law board for the government of the industrial school at Cowley, 1854. Oxf., (1854), 8°. 23 pp.
G.A. Oxon 8° 791

2243. ACLAND, SIR H. W., Report on the sanitary condition of Cowley industrial school. Oxf., &c., 1863, 8°. 17 pp.   G.A. Oxon 8° 262 (5)

2244. Poor law commissioners. [Orders for the government of Temple Cowley school.] (Lond.), 1854, fol. 14 pp.   G.A. Oxon c. 236

2245. [Appeal, signed G. Moore, for funds to extend the infant school at Temple Cowley.] n. pl., [1893], 8°. 4 pp.   G.A. Oxon c. 317 (7)

CRAWLEY

See 1225 [J. Leverett's will. 1783].

2246. An act to authorize the inclosure of certain lands . . . [Crawley]. (12 & 13 V., c. 57, Pub.) Lond., 1849, fol. 2 pp.
L. Eng. A 69 c. 1

2247. GILES, J. A., History of Witney, with notices of . . . Crawley [&c.]. Lond., 1852, 8°. 107 pp. G.A. Oxon 8° 13

2248. Crawley. (Archaeol. notes. Oxoniensia, 1940, p. 162; 1942, p. 109.) R. Top. 340

CROPREDY

See 416, 1545 [Battle of Cropredy bridge. 1644].

2249. An act for dividing and inclosing certain . . . fields, pastures and waste grounds, called Cropredy field and Ast mead, within the parish of Cropredy. (14 G. III, c. 23, Private.) n. pl., 1774, fol. 43 pp. G.A. Oxon c. 113 (8)

2250. CHAMBERLIN, W. H., A plan for the employment of labourers as adopted in Cropredy [by W. H. Chamberlin]. Banbury, [c. 1820], 8°. 12 pp. G.A. Oxon 8° 935

See 883 [Customs and charities. 1842].

2251. ROYCE, D., Historical notices of the parish of Cropredy. (Trans., North Oxf. archaeol. soc., 1879.) Oxf., 1880, 8°. 56 pp. R. Top. 330

2252. TOYNBEE, M. R., and LEEMING, J. J., Cropredy bridge (Oxoniensia, 1938, p. 123–38.) R. Top. 340

2253. Auction catal. Prescott manor farm, Appletree farm. 6 Apr. 1797. G.A. fol. A 273*

CROPREDY (Peculiar jurisdiction of)

See 2130 [Peculiar of Cropredy, during 1559 and afterwards, by S. S. Pearce. 1916].

CROUCH

2254. RUSHER, P., Crouch-hill, a descriptive poem, with some account of the sieges of Banbury castle, in the reign of Charles the first [by P. Rusher]. Banbury, 1789, 8°. 34 pp. Gough Oxf. 45 (7)

2255. An act for vesting part of the estates [Crouch, &c.] of the late sir James Dashwood in trustees, in trust to sell the same. (37 G. III, c. 101, Private.) n. pl., 1797, fol. 30 pp. L. Eng. C 13 c. 1 (1797. iv)

CROWELL

2256. An act for appointing jointures for the wives and . . . portions for the younger children of . . . Willoughby, earl of Abingdon, and . . . Peregrine Bertie, his brother. [Crowell &c.] (9 G. III, sess. 2, c. 10, Private.) n. pl., 1769, fol. 43 pp. G.A. Oxon c. 192

See 1297 [Parish registers. Marriages. 1909].

2257. HASSALL, W. O., Dissent at . . . Crowell [&c.]. (Thame Gazette, Jan. 30, 1951.) N.G.A. Oxon a. 120

2258. HASSALL, W. O., The history of Crowell. (Thame Gazette, June 26, July 3, 1951.) N.G.A. Oxon a. 120

2259. Auction catal. Crowell estate. 16 July 1844.
G.A. Oxon c. 317 (7)

CROWMARSH GIFFORD

See 1324 [Patterns of inlaid tiles from churches. 1845].
See 2852 [Act affecting Wallingford and Crowmarsh joint hospital district. 1904].

2259A. Crowmarsh, Culham & Goring rural sanitary districts. Report, 1911. By G. T. Cattell. Lond., [1912], 8°. 24 pp. B.M.

2260. CLACK, T. S., A history of Crowmarsh-Gifford. Wallingford, 1922, 8°. 40 pp. G.A. Oxon 8° 1026

2261. Auction catal. Col d'Arbres estate. 28 June 1900.
G.A. Oxon b. 90 (27)

2262. Auction catal. Howbery park and Col d'Arbres. 17 June 1901.
G.A. Oxon b. 90 (28)

2263. Auction catal. Village and manor. 28 May 1902.
G.A. Oxon b. 6 (35)

CROWSLEY PARK

2264. Auction catal. Mansion and grounds of Crowsley park. 15 Oct. 1844. G.A. Oxon b. 92* (1)
— Portion of Crowsley estate. 29 July 1896.
G.A. Oxon b. 91 (48)

CUDDESDON

General

2265. WELLES, P., The humble petition of Paul Welles of Cuddesden . . . [to be allowed to compound with his creditors]. n. pl., [c. 1750], s. sh. Gough Oxf. 103 (4)

2266. An act for enabling William Hall . . . to assign or surrender a term of one thousand years in estates [in Cuddesdon &c.] . . . unto . . . Elisha Biscoe. (53 G. III, c. 203, L. & P.) Lond., 1813, fol. 4 pp.
L. Eng. A 69 c. 6

2267. Cuddesdon. (Gent's. mag., 1821, pt. I, p. 201, 02, 394, 95.)
Ψ 2. 44

2268. Proposals for the restoration of Cuddesdon church. n. pl., (1848), s. sh.   G.A. Oxon c. 317 (7)

2269. All Saints' Cuddesdon. Choir rules [signed C. W. Furse]. n. pl., [*c.* 1880], s. sh.   G.A. Oxon c. 317 (7)

2270. DAVIES, E. A., Cuddesdon: its story. [Reprod. from typewriting.] n. pl., [1950], 4°. 14 pp.   G.A. Oxon 4° 652

2271. HASSALL, W. O., The history of Cuddesdon. (Thame Gazette, Feb. 20, 1951.)   N.G.A. Oxon a. 120

2272. Auction catal. Sale of timber. 2 Mar. 1812.   G.A. fol. B 71

2273. Auction catal. Freehold estates. 26 Oct. 1812, 14 Dec. 1812.   G.A. fol. B 71

2274. Auction catal. Denton house. 25 Oct. 1892.   G.A. Oxon b. 85 *a* (29)

Cuddesdon College

2275. To the clergy and laity of the diocese of Oxford. [Letter, signed A clergyman of the diocese, concerning Romanism in Cuddesdon college.] n. pl., (1858), s. sh.   G.A. Oxon c. 74 (336)

2276. GOLIGHTLY, C. P., Letter to the bishop of Oxford [concerning Cuddesdon college and the commission to the archdeacons]. n. pl., (1858), s. sh.   G.A. Oxon c. 74 (340)

2277. The bishop of Oxford's commission to the archdeacons, with their report, *in re* Cuddesdon college [with remarks by C. P. Golightly]. n. pl., (1858), 4°. 4 pp.   G.A. Oxon c. 74 (338)

2278. GOLIGHTLY, C. P., To the clergy and laity of the diocese of Oxford. [A letter, intended to accompany the Report of the commissioners on Cuddesdon college.] n. pl., (1858), s. sh.   G.A. Oxon c. 74 (341)

2279. The bishop of Oxford, and the principal of Cuddesdon college. [Letters.] n. pl., (1858), s. sh.   G.A. Oxon c. 74 (339)

2280. Correspondence relating to Cuddesdon theological college, in answer to the charges of . . . C. P. Golightly, and the report of the commissioners thereon. Oxf., 1858, 8°. 24 pp.   G.A. Oxon 4° 372 (1)

2281. TWOPENY, R., Some remarks upon the visitation of Cuddesdon college, and the state of the Church in the diocese of Oxford. Lond., 1858, 4°. 23 pp.   G.A. Oxon 4° 372 (4)

2282. Counter-thoughts on Church matters in the diocese of Oxford. With observations on Some remarks on the visitation of Cuddesdon college by R. Twopeny. Lond., [1858], 8°. 59 pp.   100 f. 76 (12)

2283. Further thoughts upon the diocese of Oxford, with especial reference to Cuddesdon college, in reply to mr. Twopeny, by an Oxfordshire idler. Lond., 1858, 8°. 25 pp. 100 f. 76 (10)

2284. SHUTE, H., Cuddesdon college, by one who knows it [H. Shute]. Oxf., &c., 1858, 4°. 20 pp. G.A. Oxon 4° 372 (5)

2285. From the Quarterly review, January 1858. On 'Church extension' [relative to theological colleges and specially to ritualism at Cuddesdon college]. n. pl., (1858), s. sh. G.A. Oxon c. 74 (337)

2286. SWINNY, H. H., Address [on the objects of the college] to the students in the theological college at Cuddesdon, May 8, 1859. n. pl., (1859), 12°. 15 pp. G.A. Oxon 8° 184 (3)

See also 1084–1101 [Diocesan aspect of dispute].

2287. [Regulations.] n. pl., [c. 1860], s. sh. G.A. Oxon 8° 184 (3*)

2288. The Cuddesdon college annual record. 1876–1902. Oxf., 1876–1903, 8°. Cal. 26332 e. 30

2289. GOLIGHTLY, C. P., A solemn warning against Cuddesdon college, addressed to the laity and . . . lay members of the Oxford diocesan conference. Lond., &c., [1878], 4°. 8 pp. G.A. Oxon 4° 372 (14)

2290. [A memorial giving details of the gradual 'Protestantising' of the college since 1859.] n. pl., [1878], s. sh. G.A. Oxon 4° 372 (16)

2291. [An address to the bishop of Oxford from members of the diocese concerning Cuddesdon college.] n. pl., [1878], s. sh.
G.A. Oxon 4° 372 (17)
— [Another ed. with additional signatories.] (Suppl., Oxf. Times, Dec. 21st 1878). G.A. Oxon 4° 372 (19)
— [Another ed.] Oxf., 1878, 4°. 31 pp. G.A. Oxon 4° 372 (20)

2292. Cuddesdon college. 1878. Address of old students to the . . . bishop of Oxford, on the subject of the recent charges brought against the college: together with his lordship's reply. Oxf., &c., 1878, 8°. 16 pp. G.A. Oxon 8° 236 (6)

2293. KNOX, E. A., An address respecting Cuddesdon college intended to have been delivered at the Oxford diocesan conference. Lond., [1878], 4°. 8 pp. G.A. Oxon 4° 372 (15)

2294. GOLIGHTLY, C. P., A letter . . . containing strictures on The life of bishop Wilberforce with special reference to the Cuddesdon college enquiry and the pamphlet 'Facts and documents' [shewing the alarming state of the diocese of Oxford, by C. P. Golightly]. Lond., 1881, 4°. 99 pp. G.A. Oxon 4° 372 (21)

2295. The mural paintings in the Wilberforce memorial chapel, Cuddesdon College. n. pl., [c. 1879], 8°. 16 pp.

2296. The foundation of Cuddesdon college. (Oxf. diocesan mag., 1902/3, vol. I, p. 112–14.)   Per. 11126 d. 78

CUDDESDON DEANERY

See 1299 [Guide to architectural antiquities. Deanery of Cuddesdon, by J. H. Parker, and others. 1842].

2297. PRIOR, C. E., Dedications of churches, with some notes as to village feasts and old customs. Deaneries of Chipping Norton, Cuddesdon. (Rept., Oxf. archaeol. soc., 1905, p. 11–25.)   R. Top. 330

2298. PEARCE, S. S., The clergy of the deanery of Cuddesdon and of the peculiars of Langford, Thame and Great Milton during the settlement of 1559 and afterwards. (Rept., Oxf. archaeol. soc., 1920, p. 242–89.)   R. Top. 330

CULHAM

See 500 [Turnpike act. 1736, &c.].
See 531 [Case of the intended turnpike road from Culham to Streatley. 1802].

2299. Arguments and objections against the Bill for building a bridge across the river . . . at Culham . . . and the making a new turnpike road from thence to Streatley. Reading, [1802], fol. 4 pp.   G.A. Oxon b. 113 (28)

2300. An act for building a bridge over the river Thames from . . . Sutton Courtney . . . to . . . Culham. . . . (47 G. III, sess. 2, c. 43, L. & P.) Lond., 1807, fol. 29 pp.   L. Eng. A 69 c. 6

2301. An act for inclosing lands . . . of Culham . . . (50 G. III, c. 140, L. & P.) n. pl., [1810], fol. 24 pp.   L. Eng. C 13 c. 1 (1810. i. 2)

2302. D., J., A few thoughts upon national education, and upon the Culham diocesan training college. Oxf., 1890, 8°. 30 pp.
       26011 e. 23 (3)
— 2nd ed. 1890.   26011 e. 189 (4)

2303. The Culhamite. March 1890–.   Culham coll.

2304. The Culham club magazine. No. 1–3. Lond., 1894, 4°.
       G.A. Oxon 4° 295
— 1898–.   Culham coll.

2305. PEARMAN, M. T., Culham sanctuary. (Rept., Oxf. archaeol. soc., 1901, p. 25–28.)   R. Top. 330

2306. WHITE, H. J. O., Excursion to Culham and Wallingford. (Proc., Geol. assoc., 1903–4, vol. 18, p. 300–06.)   Radcl.

See 2259A [Rural sanitary district. Report. 1911].

2307. BRADBROOKE, W., Culham. The parish register. (Rept., Oxf. archaeol. soc., 1933, p. 22–28.)   R. Top. 330

2308. NARES, G., Culham manor. (Country Life, 1950, vol. 108, p. 130–34, 210–14.)   Per. 384 b. 6

CURBRIDGE

See 1225 [J. Leverett's will. 1783].

2309. An act for inclosing lands . . . of Curbridge . . . (1 & 2 V., c. 17, Private.) (Lond.), 1838, fol. 38 pp.   L. Eng. C 13 c. 1 (1838. 17)

2310. GILES, J. A., History of Witney, with notices of . . . Curbridge [&c.]. Lond., 1852, 8°. 107 pp.   G.A. Oxon 8° 13

2311. Auction catal. Caswell manor farm and Lower Caswell farm. 13 May 1824.   G.A. fol. B 71

2312. Auction catal. Estate. 26 July 1888.
MS. Top. Oxon b. 78 (f. 236)

2313. Auction catal. Downs farm. 31 May 1900.
G.A. Oxon b. 90 (30)

2314. Auction catal. Grass farm. 5 July 1900.
MS. Top. Oxon b. 78 (f. 258)

2315. Auction catal. Meadow and arable land. 18 Sept. 1913.
G.A. Oxon b. 91 (1)

CUTTESLOWE

See 486 [Railway. 1846].

2316. An act to extend the boundaries of the city of Oxford and for other purposes [affecting Cutteslowe, &c.] (18 & 19 G. V., c. 84, L. & P.) Lond., 1928, 8°. 68 pp.   L. Eng. A 69 c. 6

2317. CAM, H. M., The Hoga of Cutteslowe. (Antiquity, 1935, vol. 9, p. 96–98.)   R. Top. 6

2318. WILLMOT, G. F., A Romano-British site at Cutteslowe, near Oxford. (Journ., Brit. archaeol. assoc., 1935, new ser., vol. 40, p. 203–05.)   R. Top. 4

DEAN

2319. An act for dividing, allotting and inclosing the . . . fields . . . of Dean. (19 G. III, c. 62, Private.) n. pl., 1779, fol. 24 pp.
L. Eng. C 13 c. 1 (1779. i. 37)

2320. Spelsbury Women's institute. A history of Spelsbury, including Dean [&c.] ed. by E. Corbett. Shipston-on-Stour, 1931, 8°. 272 pp.
G.A. Oxon 8° 1081

2321. LOBEL, M., The history of Dean and Chalford. (Oxf. record soc., 17.) Oxf., 1935, 8°. 171 pp.   R. 13. 702

2322. Dean. (Archaeol. notes. Oxoniensia, 1938, p. 168.)
                                                              R. Top. 340

DEDDINGTON

2323. Deddington. (Gent's. mag., 1783, pt. 2, p. 761, 62; 1795, pt. 2, p. 737.) Ψ 2. 44

2324A. An act for inclosing lands . . . of Deddington [&c.] (47 G. III, sess. 2, c. 44, L. & P.) n. pl., [1807], fol. 29 pp.
                                              L. Eng. C 13 c. 1 (1806/7. i. 24)
See 1390 [Directory. 1846].

2324B. BROGDEN, J., A letter relating to the restoration of the national schools of . . . Deddington. Deddington, 1850, 8°. 23 pp.
                                                          G.A. Oxon 8° 1255 (1)

2324C. Deddington national school buildings (Report and financial statement). Deddington, 1854, 8°. 16 pp.   G.A. Oxon 8° 1230 (13)

2325. MARSHALL, E., Historical and descriptive notices of the parish of Deddington. (Trans., North Oxf. archaeol. soc., 1878.) Oxf., 1879, 8°. 46 pp.   R. Top. 330
— [Repr.]   G.A. Oxon 8° 683 (1)

2326. WING, W., Supplement to Marshall's Deddington. Repr. from the 'Oxf. Chronicle'. [Oxf.], 1879, 8°. 8 pp.
                                                          G.A. Oxon 8° 683 (15)

2327. Deddington, Heyford and Aston permanent building society. Rules. Lower Heyford, 1889, 8°. 32 pp.   G.A. Oxon 8° 567

2328. Deddington parish church. Restoration of the tower and bells. n. pl., 1893, s. sh.   G.A. Oxon c. 317 (8)
See 658 [Parliamentary history, by W. R. Williams. 1899].

2329. The Castle house, Deddington. (Country Life, 1908, vol. 23, p. 906–14).   Per. 384 b. 6

2330. HOWARD, F. E., Architectural notes on [Deddington church and castle]. (Rept., Oxf. archaeol. soc., 1931, p. 363, 64.)   R. Top. 330

2331. TURNER, M. V., The story of Deddington. Brackley, 1933, 8°. 95 pp.   G.A. Oxon 8° 1126

2332. TORR, V. J. B., An early citizen at Deddington. (Trans., Monumental brass soc., 1938, vol. 7, pt. 5, p. 235–39.)   Soc. 2184 d. 85

2333A. Excavations at Deddington castle, 1947. (Oxoniensia, 1946–7, p. 167, 68.)   R. Top. 340

2333B. Deddington church schools, 1550–1950. [Appeal for funds.] [Deddington, 1950], 8°. 8 pp. G.A. Oxon 8° 1259 (6)

2333C. FROST, M., ed., Briefs, and other notes from Deddington church registers [extr. by M. Frost]. Deddington, 1951, 8°. 8 pp.
G.A. Oxon 8° 1259 (3)

2333D. FROST, M., A day's worke overtyme for the schole: or, ¶ The old schole-tye to turn the tyde: a plan for past pupills to paye towards ye retaynynge of Deddington church schole. [By M. Frost.] Deddington, 1951, 8°. 4 pp. G.A. Oxon 8° 1259 (4)

2333E. FROST, M., A touchestone for this time present, setting forthe ye demands & expenses wch afflict ye Churche of God in this place in the matter of the education of the young. Together with a statement of the progress made towards ye meeting of ye same. [By M. Frost.] Deddington, 1951, 8°. 8 pp. G.A. Oxon 8° 1259 (5)

2333F. FROST, M., Deddington parish church. Notes on the tower & bells [by M. Frost.] Deddington, 1952, 8°. 8 pp.
G.A. Oxon 8° 1259 (2)

2334. Auction catal. Freehold land in Earls lane. 6 Mar. 1914.
G.A. Oxon c. 317 (8)

2335. Auction catal. Castle house. 18 July 1918.
G.A. Oxon b. 90 (32)

2336. Auction catal. The Hermitage. 22 May 1929.
G.A. Oxon c. 224*

2337. Auction catal. 'The Laurels'. 25 Apr. 1951.
G.A. Oxon b. 92*

DEDDINGTON DEANERY

2338. PAYNE, E., A letter to the church laity of the rural deanery of Deddington. Oxf., &c., 1858, 8°. 23 pp. G.A. Oxon 4° 372 (6)

2339. The Deddington deanery magazine. No. 1–35. (Banbury), 1893–95, 4°. G.A. Oxon 4° 339

2340. PRIOR, C. E., Dedications of churches, with some notes as to village feasts and old customs. Deaneries of Woodstock, Deddington & Witney. (Rept., Oxf. archaeol. soc., 1904, p. 23–53.)
R. Top. 330

2341. PEARCE, S. S., The clergy of the deaneries of Chipping Norton and Deddington, and the peculiars of Banbury and Cropredy during the settlement of 1559 and afterwards [by S. S. Pearce]. (Rept., Oxf. archaeol. soc., 1916, p. 15–86.) R. Top. 330

DENTON

2342. Auction catal. Freehold estate. 4 June 1841.   - G.A. fol. B 71

DITCHLEY
General

2343. A new Oxford guide . . . To which is added A tour to Blenheim, Ditchley and Stow. By a gentleman of Oxford. Oxf., 1759, 12°. p. 77–120.   G.A. Oxon 16° 27
[Other eds. in 1759, 1763, 64, 65, 1768, 1771?, 1776, 77, 1785, 86, 87, 88, 1792, 1794, 1797, 1803, 1805, 1810, 1813, 1817.]

2344. A pocket companion [*afterw.*] A new pocket companion for Oxford . . . To which are added, Correct descriptions of the buildings . . . at Blenheim, Ditchley and Stow. New ed. Oxf., &c., 1759, 12°, p. 109–37.   G.A. Oxon 8° 176
[Other eds. in 1762, 63, 64, 1766, 1768, 69, 1772, 1776, 1782, 83, 1785, 1787, 88, 89, 90, 1793, 94, 95, 96, 97, 1799, 1800, 01, 02, 03, 04, 05, 06, 07, 08, 09, 10, 1812, 1814, 1816.]

2345. DILLON, H., On flint implements, &c. found in the neighbourhood of Ditchley, Oct. 1874–Feb. 1875. (Journ., Anthrop. inst., 1876, vol. 5, p. 30–32.)   Soc. 247115 e. 55

See 2025 [History, by H. W. Taunt. 1906].

2346. Spelsbury women's institute. A history of Spelsbury, including . . . Ditchley, ed. by E. Corbett. Shipston-on-Stour, 1931, 8°. 272 pp.   G.A. Oxon 8° 1081

2347. RADFORD, C. A. R., A Roman villa at Ditchley. (Antiquity, 1935, vol. 9, p. 472–76.)   R. Top. 6

2348. RADFORD, C. A. R., Roman villa site at Ditchley. (South Eastern naturalist and antiquary, 1936, vol. 41, p. 31, 32.)   Soc. 18853 e. 6

2349. RADFORD, C. A. R., The Roman villa at Ditchley [signed C. A. R. R.]. (Oxf. mag., 1936, vol. 54, p. 399–401.)
Per. G. A. Oxon 4° 141

2350. RADFORD, C. A. R., The Roman villa at Ditchley. (Oxoniensia, 1936, p. 24–69.)   R. Top. 340

Ditchley Park

2351. Ditchley park. (Views of the seats of noblemen and gentlemen, by J. P. Neale, 1820, vol. 3. 2 pp.)   G.A. Gen. top. 4° 42

2352. DILLON, VISCOUNT, Brass plates at Ditchley house. (Journ., Oxf. univ. brass-rubbing soc., 1898, vol. 1, p. 234–36.)
Soc. 2184 d. 50

2353. Ditchley. (Country Life, 1904, vol. 16, p. 594–603.)
Per. 384 b. 6

2354. J., M., Furniture from Ditchley. (Country Life, 1933, vol. 73, p. 515–17.)
Per. 384 b. 6

2355. OSWALD, A., Ditchley. (Country Life, 1934, vol. 75, p. 590–95, 622–28.)
Per. 384 b. 6

2356. CHAMBERS, E. K., Sir Henry Lee. [References to Ditchley and Woodstock manor.] Oxf., 1936, 8°. 328 pp.
22853 d. 37

2357. Ditchley [illustr.]. (Antique collector, vol. 16, 1945, p. 2–10.)
N. 1758 c. 5

2357A. WHITEMAN, G. W., Some famous English country homes. (Ditchley, p. 121–30.) Lond., 1951, 4°.
G.A. Gen. top. c. 77

DORCHESTER

General

2358. HEARNE, T., A letter, containing an account of some antiquities between Windsor and Oxford. (Itinerary of John Leland, vol. 5. Dorchester, p. 125–33.) Oxf., 1711, 8°.
Mus. Bibl. II 19
— 1744, 1769.
Mus. Bibl. II 35, 40
— Repr. 1725. 46 pp.
Gough Oxf. 45 (1)

2359. An act for appointing jointures for the wives, and . . . portions for the younger children of . . . Willoughby, earl of Abingdon, and . . . Peregrine Bertie, his brother. [Dorchester &c.] (9 G. III, sess. 2, c. 10, Private.) n. pl., 1769, fol. 43 pp.
G.A. Oxon c. 192

2360. An act for dividing and inclosing the . . . fields . . . within . . . the . . . parish of Dorchester. (15 G. III, c. 4, Private.) n. pl., 1775, fol. 21 pp.
L. Eng. C 13 c. 1 (1775. 9)

2361. Dorchester. (Gent's. mag., 1785, pt. 2, p. 434, 513; 1796, pt. 1, p. 105; 1802, pt. 1, p. 124; 1816, pt. 2, p. 297; 1818, pt. 1, p. 105; 1823, pt. 1, p. 297, 98.)
Ψ 2. 44

2362. MORITZ, K. P., Travels, chiefly on foot, through several parts of England in 1782, tr. from the Germ. by a lady. (Dorchester, p. 159.) Lond., 1795, 8°.
Gough Gen. top. 293
[Orig. entitled Reisen eines Deutschen in England, 1782.]
G.A. Gen. top. 16° 27
— [Repr. in W. Mavor's British tourist's companion, vol. 4. 1798, 1809.]
— [Repr. in J. Pinkerton's Collection of travels, 1808, vol. 2. 4° BS. 897.]
— [Another ed.] 1886. (Cassell's nat. hist.)

Q

2363. An act to authorize the inclosure of certain lands . . . [Dorchester]. (22 & 23 V., c. 47, Pub.) Lond., 1859, fol. 2 pp.   L. Eng. A 69 c. 1

2364. MACFARLANE, W. C., A short account of Dorchester. Oxf. &c., 1881, 8°. 22 pp.   G.A. Oxon 8° 264 [Other eds. 1884; G.A. Oxon 8° 874 (10). 1892; G.A. Oxon 8° 1148 (15).]

2365. The history of Dorchester . . . with intr. by J. H. Parker. Oxf., &c., 1882, 8°. 48+104 pp.   G.A. Oxon 8° 343 (1)

2366. [Appeal for funds for the building of a new boys' school, Dorchester.] n. pl., 1895, 4°. 2 pp.   G.A. Oxon c. 317 (8)

2367. DAVEY, E. C., Memoirs of an Oxfordshire old Catholic family, and its connections from 1566–1897. [The Daveys of Dorchester.] Lond., [1898], 8°. 78 pp.   2182 D. e. 7

2368. [Appeal for funds to enlarge the infants' school-room, Dorchester.] n. pl., 1900, s. sh.   G.A. Oxon c. 317 (8)

2369. Ægilbert and Wini at Dorchester and Winchester, A.D. 650–670 [signed P.]. (Oxf. diocesan mag., 1902/3, vol. 1, p. 158–61.)
    Per. 11126 d. 78

2370. The parish magazine, Dorchester. No. 188–259. Wallingford, 1904–09, 8°.   G.A. Oxon 8° 1187

2371. TAUNT, H. W., Dorchester, Oxon, and its abbey church. (Taunt's new ser. of hist. handbooks.) Oxf., [1906], 8°. 48 pp.
    G.A. Oxon 8° 737

2372. Dorchester and Burcote horticultural society. Rules. n. pl., 1921, 8°. 4 pp.   G.A. Oxon c. 317 (8)

2373. Auction catal. Dorchester and Overy estates. 16 July 1844.
    G.A. Oxon b. 90 (33)

2374. Auction catal. Manor farm. 31 Oct. 1889.
    G.A. Oxon b. 92* (27)

2375. Auction catal. Queensford mill farm. 16 July 1897.
    G.A. Oxon c. 317 (5)

2376. Auction catal. Farm field farm. 29 Oct. 1898.
    G.A. Oxon b. 90 (34)

Early History

See 309 [Account of British buckler. 1838].

2377. PARKER, J. H., On the Roman occupation of Dorchester. (Proc., Oxf. architect. and hist. soc., N.S., vol. 2, 1868, p. 90–99.)
    R. 13. 708

2378. FOX, A. L., On the threatened destruction of the British earthworks near Dorchester. (Journ., Ethnol. soc., vol. 2, 1870, p. 413–15.)
Soc. 247115 e. 61

2379. Do[r]chester dykes (Extr. from an article in the Saturday review of July 2, 1870, and, a letter to the ed. of the Pall Mall gazette, July 11, 1870). (Journ., Ethnol. soc., N.S., 1870, vol. 2, p. 477–82.)
Soc. 247115 e. 61

2380. BARNS, T., Dorchester in British and Roman times. (Proc., Oxf. architect. and hist. soc., N.S., vol. 4, 1881, p. 33, 34.) R. 13. 710

2381. COZENS, W., Notes on pre-historic and Roman Dorchester. (Berks, Bucks, & Oxon archaeol. journ., 1898, vol. 4, p. 78–81.)
R. Top. 100

2382. CRAWFORD, O. G. S., Air-photographs near Dorchester. (Antiquity, 1927, vol. 1, p. 469–74.) R. Top. 6

2383. STEVENS, C. E., and KEENEY, G. S., Ramparts of Dorchester (plan). (Antiquity, 1935, vol. 9, p. 217–19.) R. Top. 6

2384. HARDEN, D. B., Two Romano-British potters' fields near Oxford [Dorchester & Rose-Hill]. (Oxoniensia, 1936, p. 81–102.)
R. Top. 340

2385. MYRES, J. N. L., A prehistoric and Roman site on Mount Farm, Dorchester. (Oxoniensia, 1937, p. 12–40.) R. Top. 340

2386. Dorchester. (Archaeol. notes. Oxoniensia, 1936, p. 201; 1937, p. 201; 1938, p. 165; 1941, p. 84; 1943/4, p. 196; 1946/7, p. 162, 164; 1949, vol. 14, p. 75; 1950, vol. 15, p. 106, 07.) R. Top. 340

2387. HOGG, A. H. A., and STEVENS, C. E., The defences of Roman Dorchester. (Oxoniensia, 1937, p. 41–73.) R. Top. 340

2388. ALLEN, G. W. G., Marks seen from the air in the crops near Dorchester. (Oxoniensia, 1938, p. 169–71.) R. Top. 340

2389. BRADFORD, J. S. P., An early Iron age site at Allen's pit, Dorchester. (Oxoniensia, 1942, p. 36–60.) R. Top. 340

2390. ATKINSON, R. J. C., PIGGOTT, C. M., and SANDARS, N. K., Excavations at Dorchester. 1st report. Oxf., 1951, 4°. 151 pp.+10 pl.
G.A. Oxon 4° 665

Abbey

See 1324 [Patterns of inlaid tiles from churches, by W. A. Church. 1845].

2391. ADDINGTON, H., Some account of the abbey church of St. Peter and St. Paul at Dorchester [by H. Addington]. Oxf., 1845, 8°. 104 pp. G.A. Oxon 8° 3
— Re-issue, with additional notes by W. C. Macfarlane. 1860. 176 pp. G.A. Oxon 8° 2

2392. Oxford architectural society. Proposed restoration of Dorchester abbey church. n. pl., (1845), 8°. 4 pp.   G.A. Oxon 8° 343 (3)

2393. Oxford architectural society. Dorchester church. [Circular asking for subscriptions for the restoration of part of the church.] (Oxf., 1845), 4°. 2 pp.   G.A. Oxon 4° 186 (7)

2394. Restoration of Dorchester abbey church. [Statement of work executed, together with list of subscribers, issued by the Oxford architectural society.] n. pl., [c. 1850], 8°. 11 pp.
    G.A. Oxon 8° 78 (13)

2395. HANNAM, H. J., Reasons for not taking part in the appropriation of sittings in the lately restored church of Dorchester, by one of the churchwardens [H. J. Hannam.] Oxf., 1853, 8°. 16 pp.
    G.A. Oxon 8° 285 (5)

2396. FREEMAN, E. A., On the architecture of the abbey church of Dorchester. (Mem. chiefly illustr. of the county and city of Oxford, communicated to the Archaeol. inst., 1850, p. 229–66.) Lond., 1854, 8°.   G.A. Gen. top. 8° 528 (6)
— Repr.   G.A. Oxon 8° 715 (2)

2397. A song for the bazaar in aid of the funds for the restoration of the abbey church of Dorchester, held at the Star hotel, Oxford, June 18 and 19, 1855. Oxf., (1855), 8°. 8 pp.
    G.A. Oxon 8° 135 (1)

2398. Episcopal visitations of the Austin canons of Leicester and Dorchester, Oxon. (Engl. hist. review, 1889, vol. 4, p. 304–13.)
    Ψ 2. 38

2399. POYNTZ, W. C. S., Notes on the abbey church of Dorchester, Oxon. (Journ., Brit. archaeol. assoc., 1891, vol. 47, p. 222–59.)
    R. Top. 4

2400. A short history, and brief description of Dorchester abbey. Wallingford, [c. 1900], 4°. 4 pp.   G.A. Oxon c. 317 (8)
— [Another ed. c. 1910.]   G.A. Oxon 8° 1175 (11)

2401. PAUL, R. W., Dorchester abbey [lithographed picture and ground plan. 2 sheets]. (Builder, 1900, Jan. 6.)   N. 1863 c. 1

2402. SALTER, H. E., A charter of Dorchester abbey. (Rept., Oxf. archaeol. soc., 1909, p. 11–16.)   R. Top. 330

2403. FIELD, J. E., Abbot Beauforest of Dorchester. (Berks, Bucks, & Oxon archaeol. journ., 1909, vol. 15, notes, p. 61, 62.)
    R. Top. 100

2404. The visitation of the monastery of Dorchester, 27th March, 1441. (Lincoln record soc., 1918, vol. 14, p. 68–78.)   R. Top. 260
— [Another issue.] (Cant. and York soc., 1919, vol. 24, p. 68–78.)
    R. 8. 26

2405. The visitation of the monastery of Dorchester, 22nd May, 1445.
(Lincoln record soc., 1918, vol. 14, p. 78–83.)   R. Top. 260
— [Another issue.] (Cant. and York soc., 1919, vol. 24, p. 78–83.)
R. 8. 26

2406. KIRKPATRICK, H. F., Dorchester-on-Thames and the abbey
church of Saint Peter and Saint Paul. Lond., [1927], 8°. 16 pp.
G.A. Oxon 8° 1002 (14)
— [Another ed. 1930.] (Notes on famous churches and abbeys, 38.)
G.A. Eccl. top. 16° 45 (38)

2407. ROBERTS, H. V. M., Dorchester. (Builder, 1930, Sept. 5, p. 378,
79.)   N. 1863 c. 1

2408.

2409. Visitations. Dorchester abbey. (i) 18 June 1517 (ii) 19 Sept. 1530.
(Lincoln record soc., 1944, vol. 35, p. 115–22.)   R. Top. 260

Missionary College

2410. Annual report. 1878/9–. [The 1st report is printed in no. 3903,
'Obedience and perseverance', by J. C. Ross, 1879, p. 41–61.]
Wallingford, &c., (1879–), 8°. [Bodleian set is imperf.]
G.A. Oxon 8° 379

2411. Dorchester letters. 1st–23rd ser. Oxf., &c., 1883–1906, 8°. [Bod-
leian set is imperf.]   G.A. Oxon 8° 646

2412. Rules and regulations. Oxf., &c., [c. 1890–], 8°.   26332 e. 104

2413. Dorchester missionary college [account]. (Oxf. diocesan mag.,
1902/3, vol. 1, p. 219, 20.)   Per. 11126 d. 78

2414. Dorchester college magazine. No. 31–74. [Dorchester], 1903–15,
8°.   Per. 26332 e. 103

2415. Extension fund [appeal] n. pl., [1908], s. sh.
G.A. Oxon c. 317 (8)

Roads

See 494 [London inns frequented by Dorchester carriers. 1637].
See 500 [Turnpike act. 1736, &c.].
See 538 [Account of Roman road from Alchester to Dorchester, by
R. Hussey. 1841].

DORCHESTER (Peculiar jurisdiction of)

2416. PEARCE, S. S., The clergy of the deaneries of Henley and Aston
and of the peculiar of Dorchester, during the settlement of 1559
and afterwards. (Rept., Oxf. archaeol. soc., 1918, p. 127–89.)
R. Top. 330

2417. PEYTON, S. A., The Churchwarden's presentments in the Oxfordshire peculiars of Dorchester, Thame and Banbury. (Oxf. record soc., 10.) [Oxf.], 1928, 8°. 340 pp. R. 13. 702

DRAYCOTT

2418. A catalogue of all the household furniture . . . horses, calves [&c.] of John Allen, which will be sold by auction at his late farmhouse at Draycott, 5th and 6th April, 1780. n. pl., 1780, 8°. 12 pp.

DRAYTON

2419. An act for dividing, allotting, and inclosing . . . lands . . . of Drayton. . . . (41 G. III, c. 43, L. & P.) n. pl., 1801, fol. 29 pp.
L. Eng. C 13 c. 1 (1801. i. 30)

2420. Drayton. (Gent's. mag., 1831, pt. 2, p. 298–300.) Ψ 2. 44

2421. An act to authorize the inclosure of certain lands . . . [Drayton]. (22 V., c. 3, Pub.) Lond., 1859, fol. 2 pp. L. Eng. A 69 c. 1

2422. Auction catal. Drayton estate. 16 July 1844.
G.A. Oxon b. 90 (33)

2423. Auction catal. Estate. 20 Aug. 1877. G.A. Oxon b. 85 b (38)

2424. Auction catal. Freehold agricultural estate. 17 June 1901.
G.A. Oxon b. 90 (35)
— 2nd ed. 9 June 1902. G.A. Oxon b. 90 (36)

2425. Auction catal. Hanwell castle estate. 22 June 1904.
G.A. Oxon b. 91 (2)

DUCKLINGTON

2426. An act for the vesting . . . several manors and lands [in Ducklington, &c.] . . . late the inheritance of W. Jennens . . . in trustees to be sold. (8 Anne, c. 10, Private.) n. pl., [c. 1709], 8°. 52 pp.
Radcl. e. 127

2427. An act for vesting in Simon lord viscount Harcourt, certain lands in Ducklington . . . discharged from the trusts limited in the marriage settlement of George Hart with Susannah his now wife, and for purchasing other lands to be settled in lieu thereof. (19 G. II, c. 13, Private.) [Lond.], 1746, fol. O.C.R.L.

See 1225 [J. Leverett's will. 1783].

2428. Ducklington. (Gent's. mag., 1815, pt. 2, p. 491, 92.) Ψ 2. 44

2429. GILES, J. A., History of Witney, with notices of . . . Ducklington [&c.] Lond., 1852, 8°. 107 pp. G.A. Oxon 8° 13

2430. STONE, S., Anglo-Saxon remains at Ducklinton near Witney. (Proc., Soc. of Antiq., 1859, 2nd ser., vol. I, p. 100, 01.)
R. Top. 1

2431. [Ducklington and Hardwick church and charity accounts.] n. pl., 1871–1908/9, 4°. G.A. Oxon 4° 183

2432. Parish school accounts, 1871–95. n. pl., (1871–95), 8°. G.A. Oxon 8° 622

2433. Notes of an excursion to Ducklington [&c.] (North Oxf. archaeol. soc., 1871.) Banbury, [1871], 8°. 73 pp. R. Top. 330

2434. The Home visitor for Aston, Coggs, and Ducklington. June, 1879. Lond., (1879), 8°. G.A. Oxon 8° 578

2435. MACRAY, W. D., An index to the registers of baptisms, marriages, and burials in the parish of Ducklington. (Trans., North Oxf. archaeol. soc., 1880.) Oxf., 1881, 8°. 70 pp. R. Top. 330

2436. MACRAY, W. D., Our parish church, a sermon preached in the Church of st. Bartholomew, Ducklington, 26th Aug., 1888. Oxf., (1888), 8°. 8 pp. G.A. Oxon 8° 469 (6)

2437. Ducklington. (Rept., Oxf. archaeol. soc., 1891, p. 9–12.)
R. Top. 330

2438. Cogges, Ducklington and Hardwick parish magazine. Jan. 1892–Dec. 1903. (Witney), 1892–1903, 4°. Per. G.A. Oxon 4° 182

2439. Final account of receipts and payments for enlargement of infants' class room [Ducklington]. [Oxf., 1896], 8°. 2 pp.
G.A. Oxon 8° 622

2440. Balance sheet. Ducklington celebration of queen's diamond jubilee, June 22, 1897. n. pl., (1897), s. sh. G.A. Oxon 4° 183

See 293 [History, by W. J. Monk. 1926].

2441. Auction catal. 2 farm houses and land. 21 Oct. 1808.
G.A. Oxon b. 4 (3)

2442. Auction catal. Houses and land. 8 Aug. 1879.
MS. Top. Oxon b. 78 (227)

2443. Auction catal. Estate. 26 July 1888.
MS. Top. Oxon b. 78 (236)

2444. Auction catal. J. U. Usill estate. 26 July 1894.
G.A. Oxon b. 6 (31)

2445. Auction catal. Property of J. Beaumont. 8 Nov. 1894.
MS. Top. Oxon b. 78 (252)

2446. Auction catal. Claywell farm. 22 Feb. 1900.
G.A. Oxon b. 90 (25)

2447. Auction catal. Grass farm. 5 July 1900.
MS. Top. Oxon b. 78 (258)

2448. Auction catal. Cokethorpe estate, comprising Coursehill farm, Barley park farm, Field Grace's piece, California allotments, meadow land and the Moors. 4 July 1912.
G.A. Oxon b. 90 (23)

2449. Auction catal. The Manor house, 16 cottages, enclosure of meadow land, between the village and Witney. 23 June 1921.
G.A. Oxon c. 224 (10)

DUNS TEW

2450. The case of mr. [Meredith] Vaughan, vicar of Dunchtew, Oxon, truly stated, and his innocence vindicated against the aspersions of Tho. Overton and the misrepresentations of sir Thomas Weale. n. pl., 1705, 4°. [viii]+16 pp.   G.A. Oxon 8° 206

2451. An act for dividing and inclosing the ... fields ... of Dunstew.... (33 G. III, c. 29, Private.) n. pl., 1793, fol. 33 pp.
L. Eng. C 13 c. 1 (1793. i. 12)

2452. Report from his majesty's Commissioners for inquiring into the administration and practical operation of the poor laws. Appendix A. Pt. 1. (Dunstew, p. 3, 4.)   Pp. Eng. 1834, vol. 28

2453. Auction catal. Land sold by Duns Tew friendly society. 6 Mar. 1914.   G.A. Oxon c. 317 (8)

2454. Auction catal. Duns Tew manor estate, embracing the whole of the village. 25 Nov. 1926.   G.A. Oxon c. 224 (20)

2455. Auction catal. Duns Tew estate. 20 Oct. 1948.
G.A. Oxon b. 92*

EASINGTON

2456. An act for vesting part of the estates of the late sir James Dashwood in trustees, in trust to sell the same. [Easinden.] (37 G. III, c. 101, Private.) n. pl., 1797, fol. 30 pp.
L. Eng. C 13 c. 1 (1797. iv)

2457. BUCKLAND, M. W., A history of Easington. n. pl., [c. 1945], 8°. 4 pp.   O.P.L.

ELSFIELD

2458. Elsfield. (Gent's. mag., 1799, pt. 2, p. 837–40.) Ψ 2. 44

2459. GORDON, R., [Appeal for funds to restore Elsfield parish church, June, 1848.] n. pl., (1848), 4°. 2 pp.   MS. Top. Oxon d. 22 (114)

2460. Visitation of Oxfordshire. 1668–9. Pudsey of Elsfield (Misc. geneal. et heraldica, 1916, 5th ser., vol. I, p. 311.) Ψ 2. 10 f

2461. CLARK, G. N., The manor of Elsfield. Oxf., 1927, 8°. 38 pp.
G.A. Oxon 4° 478

EMMINGTON

2462. HASSALL, W. O., The history of Emmington. (Thame Gazette, Apr. 10, 1951.) N.G.A. Oxon a. 120

ENSLOW

2463. DOUGLAS, J. A., and ARKELL, W. J., On a section of fossiliferous upper cornbrash of North Eastern facies at Enslow bridge, near Oxford. (Quart. journ., Geol. soc., 1935, vol. 91, p. 318–22.) Radcl.
See 44 [Teleosauridae from Enslow bridge. 1951].

ENSTONE

See 498 [Turnpike act. 1730, &c.].

2464. JORDAN, J., A parochial history of Enstone. Lond., &c., 1857, 8°. 465 pp. G.A. Oxon 8° 21

2465.

2466. Charity commissioners. In the matter of the charities called the Church estate and Thomas Davis' charity in ... Enstone. (Authority to erect farm buildings.) (Lond., 1887), fol. 4 pp.
L. Eng. B 53 c. Charities 1

2467. DRYDEN, SIR H., The Dolmens at Rollright and Enstone. (Rept., Oxf. archaeol. soc., 1897/8, p. 40–51.) R. Top. 330

2468. COBB, A. K., A parochial history of Enstone. Shipston-on-Stour, [1936], 8°. 11 pp. G.A. Oxon 8° 1148 (9)

2469. COBB, A. K., The parish and church of St. Kenelm, Enstone. Enstone, 1946, 8°. 12 pp. O.A.H.S.

2470. Pottery from Enstone [&c.] (Oxoniensia, 1946–7, p. 169.)
R. Top. 340

2471. LATTEY, R. T., The 'hoar stone' at Enstone. (Oxoniensia, 1949, vol. 14, p. 87.) R. Top. 340

EPWELL

2472. An act for dividing and inclosing the open and common field ... of Epwell. (12 G. III, c. 30, Private.) n. pl., 1772, fol. 27 pp.
L. Eng. C 13 c. 1 (1772. i. 41)

2473. Auction catal. Land, 2 cornmills, 3 cottages. 4 May 1899.
G.A. Oxon b. 91 (51)

EWELME

General

2474. The history of the famous may-pole at Ewelm . . . or, A true . . . relation how it was first begg'd [&c. In verse]. n. pl., 1702, 8°. 34 pp.
G.A. Oxon 8° 11

2475. The case of mr. Thomas Wise, against whom a complaint has been made by William Hucks . . . for a breach of privilege, in having forcibly entred upon a coppice in the parish of Ewelme . . . and lopped several trees. n. pl., 1722, s. sh.   G.A. Oxon c. 317 (8)

2476. [Recommendation of the sufferers by the fire which broke out, May 23, 1755, to the charity of well disposed persons.] n. pl., 1755, s. sh.   MS. Top. Oxon a. 8 (40)

2477. An act to authorize the inclosure of certain lands . . . [Ewelme]. (16 & 17 V., c. 3, Pub.) Lond., 1853, fol. 2 pp.
L. Eng. A 69 c. 1

2478. NAPIER, H. A., Historical notices of the parishes of Swyncombe and Ewelme. Oxf., 1858, fol. 454 pp.   G.A. Oxon c. 168

2479. A bill intituled, An act for re-vesting in her majesty . . . the rectory of Ewelme. n. pl., 1871, fol. 2 pp.
MS. Top. Oxon a. 8 (71)
— [Another ed.]   Pp. Eng. 1871, vol. 2
— Act. (34 V., c. 23, Pub.) Lond., 1871, fol. 2 pp.
L. Eng. A 69 c. 1

2480. HARVEY, W. W., Letter respecting the etymology of 'Ewelme'. (Proc., Oxf. architect. and hist. soc., N.S., vol. 3, 1875, p. 221.)
R. 13. 709

2481. HUGGINS, M. L., Study of a carved corbel in Ewelme church. (Berks, Bucks, and Oxon archaeol journ., 1896, vol. 2, p. 1-8.)
R. Top. 100
— Repr.   G.A. Oxon 8° 683 (4)

2482. BARKER, W. R., A catalogue of the brasses in Ewelme church. (Journ., Oxf. univ. brass-rubbing soc., 1897, vol. 1, p. 11-22.)
Soc. 2184 d. 50

2483. Ewelme. [Account of finding a bronze bowl.] (Proc., Soc. of antiq., 1907, ser. 2, vol. 22, p. 71-73.)   R. Top. 1

2484. Ewelme nursing and maternity benefit society. Rules. n. pl., [c. 1910], s. sh.   G.A. Oxon 4° 487

2485. DODD, J. A., A historical guide to Ewelme church and the adjacent buildings. Oxf., &c., 1912, 8°. 54 pp.   G.A. Oxon 8° 840
— 2nd ed., revised. Bath, 1916, 8°. 58 pp.
       G.A. Oxon 8° 1184 (16)

2486. W., L., Ewelme down. (Country Life, 1912, vol. 31, p. 430–36.)
       Per. 384 b. 6

2487. PAINTIN, H., Ewelme and the De-la-Poles. (Repr. from Oxf. journ. illustr.) n. pl., [1915], s. sh.   G.A. Oxon a. 22 (74)

2488. DRUCE, G. C., Ewelme plants, recorded from 1796 to 1799 by John Randolph, bishop of Oxford. (Proc. and Rept., Ashmolean nat. hist. soc., 1917, p. 23–42.)   G A. Oxon 8° 501

2489. DODD, J. A., Ewelme, school, almshouse and church, with account of the descendants of Thomas Chaucer. (Trans., St. Paul's Ecclesiol. soc., 1920, vol. 8, pt. 5, p. 194–206.)   G.A. Oxon c. 317 (8)

2490. Benson, Ewelme & Berrick nursing association Report. 1920/21. n. pl., (1921), 4°. 4 pp.   G.A. Oxon c. 317 (17)

2491. HUMPHREYS, A. T., A short guide to Ewelme church, together with some brief notes on the almshouse, school, manor and advowson and the De la Pole family. Wallingford, 1926, 8°. 45 pp.
       G.A. Oxon 8° 1046 (11)

2492. LAMBORN, E. A. GREENING, The arms on the Chaucer tomb at Ewelme. (Oxoniensia, 1940, p. 78–93; 1941, p. 90.)   R. Top. 340

2493. PAUL and VIRGINIA, *pseud.*, and HUSSEY, C., Ewelme. (Country Life, 1941, vol. 89, p. 254–58, 275–80.)   Per. 384 b. 6

2494. Ewelme. (Archaeol. notes. Oxoniensia, 1943, 44, p. 196.)
       R. Top. 340

2494A. HASSALL, W. O., Ewelme honour court leets, 1712–20. (Oxoniensia, 1950, vol. 15, p. 114–16.)   R. Top. 340

2495. Auction catal. Eyre's farm. 5th Sept. 1872.

2496. Auction catal. Ewelme park farm. 31 Oct. 1889.
       G.A. Oxon b. 92* (27)

2497 Auction catal. Farms known as Huntingland's, Lower, Eyres, Cottesmore, Down, and Ewelme park, also Munday's field and the Lamb Inn [&c.]. 22 July 1890.   G.A. Oxon b. 92* (28)

2498. Auction catal. Ewelme park farm, The Lamb inn, cottages and shop. 1 July 1891.   G.A. Oxon b. 92* (2)

2499. Auction catal. Ewelme park farm. 26 July 1894.
       G.A. Oxon b. 92 (10)

2500. Sale catal. Fifield manor estate. Upper farm. 1900.
G.A. Oxon b. 90 (45)

2501. Auction catal. Day's farm and Warren farm. 10 June 1904.
G.A. Oxon b. 90 (38)

Almshouse

2502. DE LA POLE, W., The foundation of the almshouse of Ewelme
. . . (Duo rerum Anglicarum script. veteres, e codicibus MSS. eruit
T. Hearnius, 1732, vol. 2, p. 541–73.)   Mus. Bibl. II 96

2503. Scheme for the management and regulation of the almshouse . . .
and the application of the income thereof. Lond., 1860, 8°. 13 pp.
G.A. Oxon 8° 950

2504. Report on the estates vested in the trustees of the almhouse.
Oxf., 1906, 8°. 33 pp.   G.A. Oxon 8° 872

2505. Account of income and expenditure. 1905–09. n. pl., [1906–10],
s. sh.   G.A. Oxon c. 251

2506. Ewelme exhibition endowment. Account of income and expenditure. 1905–19. n. pl., [1906–20], s. sh. [Bodleian set is imperf.]
G.A. Oxon c. 251

2507. Ewelme almshouse charity. Report and accounts. 1910–13. (Oxf.,
1910–13), 4°.   G.A. Oxon 4° 487

2508. Quadrangle, 'God's house' or almshouse, Ewelme. (Building
news, 1916, 27 Dec., p. 594.)   N. 1863 c. 1

See 2489, 2491.

EYE AND DUNSDEN

2509. An act for vesting certain tenements and hereditaments in the
counties of Oxford, Berks and Wilts, part of the settled estates of the
earl of Macclesfield, in trustees, to be sold or exchanged. [Eye and
Dunsden &c.] (13 G. III, c. 49, Private.) n. pl., 1773, fol. 26 pp.
L. Eng. C 13 c. 1 (1773)

2510. MASTERS, J. E. SMITH-, The history of Kidmore End, with notes
of . . . Eye and Dunsden [&c.]. (Leighton Buzzard, 1933), 8°. 87 pp.
G.A. Oxon 8° 1131

EYNSHAM

General

2511. An act for building a bridge cross the river Thames from Swyn-
ford, in the county of Berks, to Eynsham in the county of Oxford.
(7 G. III, c. 63, Pub.) Lond., 1767, fol. 8 pp.   B.M.

See 502 [Turnpike act. 1751, &c.].

2512. An act for inclosing certain lands . . . of Ensham. . . . (21 G. III, c. 38, Private.) n. pl., 1781, fol. 17 pp.
L. Eng. C 13 c. 1 (1780–81. 37)

2513. Some account of Einsham. (The Topographer, 1791, vol. 3, p. 111–14.)   ·   Douce VV 16

2514. An act for dividing . . . open common fields . . . within the parish of Ensham. (40 G. III, c. 63, Private.) n. pl., [1800], fol. 28 pp.
G.A. Oxon c. 247 (8)

2515. Ensham prosecution association. [The members pledge themselves to prosecute anyone detected in any felony, and offer rewards for information concerning specific offences.] (Oxf., 1816), s. sh.
G.A. Oxon c. 317 (20)

2516. Ensham. (Gent's. mag., 1851, pt. 1, p. 191, 92.) Ψ 2. 44

2517. [Paper, signed J. Druce, suggesting that the collection made by the vicar of Eynsham, W. S. Bricknell, on behalf of the Indian relief fund, had not been received by the London Committee.] n. pl., (1858), s. sh.   G.A. Oxon c. 317 (20)

2518. BRICKNELL, W. S., A letter to the lord bishop of Oxford in reference to a complaint made to his lordship against the vicar of Eynsham [by W. S. Bricknell]. [Oxf.], (1858), 4°. 4 pp.
G.A. Oxon 8° 124 (8*)

2519. DAVENPORT, J. M., Reply to the bishop of Oxford's answer to a letter addressed to his lordship in reference to a complaint against the vicar of Eynsham [by J. M. Davenport]. [Oxf.], (1858), 4°. 4 pp.
G.A. Oxon 8° 124 (8)

2520. [Begin.] Parish of Eynsham. [A publication accusing Joseph Druce of negligence in his duty as churchwarden.] n. pl., (1863), s. sh.   MS. Top. Oxon d. 214 (11)

2521. [Begin.] Parish of Eynsham. Facts and figures for an Easter vestry. [Another publication against Joseph Druce.] (Eynsham, 1864), s. sh.   MS. Top. Oxon d. 214 (16)

2522. Eynsham. (Excursion. Archaeol. and nat. hist. soc. of N. Oxf., 1868.)   Manning 8° 3

2523. The Eynsham paper mill company, limited. Prospectus. (Lond., 1888), fol. 4 pp.   G.A. Oxon c. 317 (20)

2524. Eynsham church restoration. n. pl., [1892], 4°. 4 pp.
G.A. Oxon c. 22 (10)
See 1297 [Parish registers. Marriages. 1909].
See 293 [History, by W. J. Monk. 1926].

2525. LEEDS, E. T., A handled beaker from Eynsham. (Antiquaries journ., 1931, vol. 11, p. 280, 81.)   R. Top. 2

2526. SUTHERLAND, C. H. V., A Roman hoard from Eynsham. (Num. chron., 1936, 5th ser., vol. 16, p. 251.)　　　Num. 03 d. 10

2527. Eynsham church mural paintings. (Oxoniensia, 1937, p. 204.)
R. Top. 340

2528. Eynsham. (Archaeol. notes. Oxoniensia, 1937, p. 201; 1938, p. 163, 167; 1940, p. 85, 86.)　　　R. Top. 340

2529. To be let . . . the following part of the estate . . . of James Wastie, situate at Ensham. (Nov. 18th, 1803.) (Oxf., 1803), fol. 4 pp.
MS. Top. Oxon c. 200 (161)

2530. Auction catal. Arable and pasture land. 7 Dec. 1821.
G.A. Oxon b. 4 (5)

2531. Auction catal. Pasture land. 2 June 1828.　　G.A. Oxon b. 4 (8)

2532. Auction catal. Premises. 3 Dec. 1830.　　G.A. Oxon b. 4 (11)

2533. Auction catal. House and land. 23 Sept. 1831.
MS. Top. Oxon c. 200 (87)

2534. Auction catal. Landed property. 19 Apr. 1837.
G.A. fol. B 71

2535. Auction catal. Land and house. 19 May 1855.
G.A. Oxon b. 90 (39)

2536. Auction catal. Eynsham Hall. 9 July 1862.
G.A. Oxon b. 85 a (30)

2537. Auction catal. Acre Hill and Middle farms. 15 Sept. 1900.
G.A. Oxon b. 92* (27)
— 23 Aug. 1911.　　　　　G.A. Oxon b. 90 (41)

2538. Auction catal. Watkins farm. 8 June 1904.
G.A. Oxon b. 6 (37)

2539. Auction catal. Home farm. 29 July 1905.
G.A. Oxon b. 90 (40)

2540. Auction catal. Cuckoo, Means and Millers closes. 10 June 1911.
G.A. Oxon b. 91 (27)

2541. Auction catal. Abbey farm. 14 July 1920.
G.A. Oxon b. 92* (3)

Abbey

2542. [Grant from Godfrey, the abbot, and the convent of Egneshaime to Walter their servant of a virginate of land in Muclintune [Mickleton] at a yearly rent of 5s. Facs.]. n. pl., [c. 1750], s. sh.
Gough maps 41 n (p. 49)

2543. Eynsham cartulary, ed. by H. E. Salter. 2 vols. (Oxf. hist. soc., vol. 49, 51.) Oxf., 1907, 08, 8°.　　　　　　　　　　R. 13. 700

2544. Eynsham abbey. (Lincoln record soc., 1914, vol. 7. Visitations of religious houses, 1420–1436, vol. 1, p. 54–63)　　　R. Top. 260
— [Another issue.] (Cant. and York soc., 1915, vol. 17, p. 54–63.)
　　　　　　　　　　　　　　　　　　　　　　　　　R. 8. 26

2545. The visitation of the monastery of Eynsham, 5th June, 1445. (Lincoln record soc., 1918, vol. 14, p. 90, 91.)　　　R. Top. 260
— [Another issue.] (Cant. and York soc., 1919, vol. 24, p. 90, 91.)
　　　　　　　　　　　　　　　　　　　　　　　　　R. 8. 26

2546. CHAMBERS, SIR E., Eynsham under the monks. (Oxf. record soc., 18.) Oxf., 1936, 8°. 125 pp.　　　　　　　　　R. 13. 702

2547. Visitations. Eynsham abbey. (i) 10 June 1517 (ii) 30 April 1520. (Lincoln record soc., 1944, vol. 35, p. 138–43.)　　　R. Top. 260

FAWLER

2548. BATHER, F. A., Notes on some recent openings in the liassic and oolitic rocks of Fawler. (Quart. journ., Geol. soc., 1886, vol. 42, p. 143–46.)　　　　　　　　　　　　　　　　　　Radcl.

2549. RICHARDSON, L., Excursion to Stonesfield and Fawler. (Proc., Cots. N.F.C., 1910, vol. 17, p. 28–31.)　　　　Per. 18855 d. 58

2550. Excursion to Oxford, Stonesfield and Fawler. (Proc., Geol. assoc., 1910, vol. 21, p. 25–29.)　　　　　　　　　　　　Radcl.

2551. KIBBLE, J., Historical and other notes on the ancient manor of Charlbury, and its nine hamlets . . . Fawler [&c.]. Oxf., 1927, 8°. 100 pp.　　　　　　　　　　　　　　　G.A. Oxon 8° 1053

FEWCOTT

2552. An act for dividing and inclosing the . . . fields . . . of Stoke Lyne and Fewcott. (33 G. III, c. 27, Private.) n. pl., 1793, fol. 29 pp.
　　　　　　　　　　　　　　　　L. Eng. C 13 c. 1 (1793. i. 14)

2553. Auction catal. Fewcott farm. 22 May 1896.
　　　　　　　　　　　　　　　　　　G.A. Oxon b. 90 (43)
— 6 June 1907　　　　　　　　　　　　G.A. Oxon b. 90 (44)

FIFIELD

2554. Auction catal. Fifield manor estate [in Fifield]. 25 June 1872. 2nd ed.　　　　　　　　　　　　　　G.A. Oxon b. 88 (1)
— 25 June 1884. [1st], 2nd ed.　　　　　G.A. Oxon b. 88 (2, 3)

FILKINS

2555. An act for dividing, allotting and inclosing the . . . fields . . . in . . . Broadwell and Filkins. (15 G. III, c. 40, Private.) n. pl., 1775, fol. 24 pp.   L. Eng. C 13 c. 1 (1775. 8)

2556. AKERMAN, J. Y., An account of researches in Anglo-Saxon cemeteries at Filkins [&c.]. (Archaeologia, 1857, vol. 37, p. 140–46.) R. Top. 7

2557. Rules & orders for the government of the benefit society, entitled 'The red, white and blue' held at the Bull inn, Filkins. Oxf., 1907, 8°. 11 pp.   G.A. Oxon 8° 744 (25)

2558. Pottery from . . . Filkins [&c.]. (Oxoniensia, 1946–7, p. 169.) R. Top. 340

2559. Auction catal. Broadwell and Kelmscott manors. 11 Nov. 1802. G.A. fol. A 273*

2560. Auction catal. Filkins Hall estate. 20 July 1842. G.A. fol. B 71

2561. Auction catal. Moat farm and Minchin's Barn farm. 10 Sept. 1898.   G.A. Oxon b. 90 (48)

FINMERE

2562. ROBINSON, C. J., Church notes from Finmere. (Genealogist 1885, new ser., vol. 2, p. 48, 49, 103–06.) Ψ 2. 10 i

2563. BLOMFIELD, J. C., History of Finmere. Buckingham, 1887, 8°. 91 pp.   G.A. Oxon 8° 393

2564. Auction catal. Painter estate. 10 June 1913. G.A. Oxon b. 90 (49)

FINSTOCK

2565. An act to authorize the inclosure of certain lands . . . [Finstock common allotment]. (21 V., c. 8, Pub.) Lond., 1858, fol. 2 pp. L. Eng. A 69 c. 1

2566. KIBBLE, J., Historical and other notes on the ancient manor of Charlbury and its nine hamlets . . . Finstock [&c.]. Oxf., 1927, 8°. 100 pp.   G.A. Oxon 8° 1053

FOREST HILL

2567. An act for enabling William Hall . . . to assign or surrender a term of one thousand years in estates [in Forest-hill &c.] . . . unto . . . Elisha Biscoe. (53 G. III, c. 203, L. & P.) Lond., 1813, fol. 4 pp. L. Eng. A 69 c. 6

2568. Forest hill, &c. association [for defraying the expenses of apprehending and prosecuting felons and thieves]. [Statement of aims, rewards &c.] (Oxf.), 1836, s. sh.   G.A. fol. A 139* (7)

2569. GREAVES, E., John Milton and Foresthill. (Rept., Oxf. archaeol. soc., 1906, p. 9–13.)   R. Top. 330

2570. Forest Hill with Shotover. The village book. Oxf., 1933, 4°. 73 pp.   G.A. Oxon 4° 547

2571. FRENCH, J. M., Milton in chancery. (Mod. lang. assoc. of Amer., monogr. ser.) New York, 1939, 4°. 428 pp.   3963 d. 106 (10)

2572. GRAVES, R., The story of Mary Powell, wife to mr. Milton. Lond., &c., 1943, 8°. 372 pp.   25435 e. 310

See 31 [Stratigraphy at Forest Hill. 1942].

2573. ROWSE, A. L., The Milton country. (The English past, 1951, p. 85–112.)   228 e. 858

2574. BAKER, G. BARRINGTON-, The story of St. Nicholas' church, Forest Hill with Shotover. Oxf., [1951], 8°. 16 pp.
G.A. Oxon 8° 1230 (12)

2575. Auction catal. Forest Hill manor. 25 Sept. 1807.
G.A. Oxon b. 4 (2)

2576. Auction catal. Sandhill farm and Bayswater mill. 31 May 1876.
G.A. Oxon b. 85 *b* (42)

2577. Auction catal. Farm, building sites, cottages. 15 June 1895.
G.A. Oxon b. 90 (50)

FOSCOT

2578. An act for dividing and inclosing the . . . fields . . . of . . . Foscott. (19 G. III, c. 78, Private.) n. pl., 1779, fol. 16 pp.
L. Eng. C 13 c. 1 (1779. 12)

FOXTON LODGE

2579. Auction catal. Foxton lodge. 23 July 1924.
G.A. Oxon c. 224 (15)

FREELAND

2580. BRICKNELL, W. S., Protest against the consecration of a stone altar crucifix and other illegal ornaments in the new church at Freeland. [Oxf.?], (1869), 8°. 18 pp.   G.A. Oxon 8° 884 (10)

2581. Hanborough and Freeland horticultural association. Show, Sept. 12, 1908. Schedule of prizes. n. pl., 1908, s. sh.

G.A. Oxon c. 317 (9)

2582. The Hanborough, Bladon and Freeland news, ed. by F. B. Greenway. No. 1, 3–5, 7, 8. [Reprod. from typewriting.] Hanborough, 1921, 22, 4°.   G.A. Oxon c. 317 (9)

FRINGFORD

2583. An act for dividing and inclosing certain . . . fields in . . . Fringford. (1 G. III, c. 35, Private.) [Lond.], 1760, fol.   O.C.R.L.

2584. An act for exchanging the advowson of the church of Hinton Mertell . . . Dorset . . . for the advowson of the church of Fringford. (15 G. III, c. 27, Private.) [Lond.], 1775, fol. 4 pp.

L. Eng. C 13 c. 1 (1775. 35)

2585. BLOMFIELD, J. C., History of Fringford [&c.]. (Hist. of . . . deanery of Bicester. Pt. 5. Fringford. 54 pp.) Lond., [1890], 4°.

G.A. Oxon 4° 71

FRITWELL

2586. An act for inclosing lands . . . of Fritwell. . . . (47 G. III, sess. 1, c. 27, L. & P.) n. pl., [1807], fol. 24 pp.

L. Eng. C 13 c. 1 (1806–7. i. 29)

2587. HOOKINS, P., Fritwell. 3 pt. (N. Oxf. archaeol. soc., 1884–9.) Banbury, 1884–89, 8°.   Manning 8° 3

2588. BLOMFIELD, J. C., History of Fritwell. (Hist. of . . . deanery of Bicester. Pt. 7.) Lond., 1893, 4°. 62 pp.   G.A. Oxon 4° 71

2589. B., G. E., Fritwell. Restoration of the parish church in 1864. (Rept., Oxf. archaeol. soc., 1903, p. 17–19.)   R. Top. 330

2590. BALLARD, A., The open fields of Fritwell. (Rept., Oxf. archaeol. soc., 1907, p. 16–22.)   R. Top. 330

2591. ARKELL, W. J., RICHARDSON, L., and PRINGLE, J., The lower oolites exposed in the Ardley and Fritwell railway-cuttings, between Bicester and Banbury. (Proc., Geol. assoc., 1933, vol. 44, p. 340–54.)   Radcl.

2592. Auction catal. Manor house. 31 Oct. 1855.

G.A. Oxon b. 85 a (31)

2593. Auction catal. Land. 15 July 1857.   G.A. Oxon b. 85 b (57)

2594. Auction catal. Court farm. 14 June 1901.

G.A. Oxon b. 90 (51)

2595. Auction catal. Fritwell farm. 14 June 1901.
G.A. Oxon b. 90 (52)

2596. Auction catal. Inkerman farm. 24 July 1902.
G.A. Oxon b. 6 (60)

2597. Auction catal. Fritwell manor. 8 Nov. 1911.
G.A. Oxon b. 90 (53)

2598. Auction catal. Horwell farm, 4 cottages and arable land. 14 May
1919. G.A. Oxon c. 224 (5)

FULBROOK

2599. A bill for inclosing lands in . . . Fulbrook. n. pl., 1817, fol. 21 pp.
G.A. Oxon c. 266 (2)
— Act. (57 G. III, c. 26, Private.) L. Eng. C 13 c. 1 (1817)

2600. An act to authorize the inclosure of certain lands . . . [Fulbrook].
(22 V., c. 3, Pub.) Lond., 1859, fol. 2 pp. L. Eng. A 69 c. 1

2601. Auction catal. Foss Grove coppice. 27 Nov. 1810.
G.A. fol. A 273*

2602. Sale catal. Estate. May 1812. G.A. fol. B 71

2603. Auction catal. Westhall hill farm. 29 Apr. 1914.
G.A. Oxon b. 90 (55)

FULWELL

2604. Spelsbury women's institute. A history of Spelsbury, including
. . . Fulwell [&c.] ed. by E. Corbett. Shipston-on-Stour, 1931, 8°.
272 pp. G.A. Oxon 8° 1081

GARSINGTON

2605. An act for effectuating an exchange between . . . Saint John Baptist college . . . and Christopher Hull . . . [Garsington]. (48 G. III,
c. 149, L. & P.) Lond., 1808, fol. 12 pp. L. Eng. A 69 c. 6

2606. An act for inclosing lands . . . of Garsington. . . . (51 G. III, c. 85,
L. & P.) n. pl., 1811, fol. 24 pp. L. Eng. C 13 c. 1 (1811. 1)

2607. Garsington. (Gent's. mag., 1817, pt. 2, p. 9; 1841, pt. 1, p. 21, 22;
1841, pt. 2, p. 38.) Ψ 2. 44

2608. Auction catal. 19 Jan. 1820. G.A. fol. B 71

2609. Auction catal. Estate of T. B. Morrell. 20 June 1903.
G.A. Oxon b. 91 (16)

2610. Auction catal. The Manor. 15 Mar. 1913.
G.A. Oxon b. 90 (56)

GLYMPTON

2611. BARNETT, H., Glympton. (Oxf. record soc., 5.) Oxf., 1923, 8°. 141 pp. R. 13. 702

2612. ARKELL, W. J., The building-stones of . . . Glympton park. . . . (Oxoniensia, 1948, vol. 13, p. 49-54.) R. Top. 340

GODINGTON

2613. An act for making an allotment or allotments of land in lieu of tythes and common rights within the parish of Goddington. (56 G. III, c. 53, L. & P.) [Lond.], (1816), 4°. 13 pp.
L. Eng. C 23 d. Land 1

2614. Auction catal. Moat farm and Goddington Hall farm. 15 July 1857. G.A. Oxon b. 85 b (57)

GODSTOW

2615. RAWLINSON, T., Fragmentum hocce monumenti pervetusti in hortis Prioratus de Godestowe prope Oxoniam anno 1703 . . . erutum . . . in aes incidi curavit Thomas Rawlinson . . . 1711. n. pl., (1711), s. sh. Rawl. prints A 6 (f. 95)

2616. Anonymi chronicon Godstovianum. (Roperi Vitae Tho. Mori, ed. T. Hearnio, p. 180-246.) Oxon., 1716, 8°.
Mus. Bibl. 8° II 55

2617. An act for confirming a partition made between Robert Dashwood . . . and Cholmley Turner . . . of certain . . . lands . . . in . . . [Godstow &c.]. (3 G. I, c. 22, Private.) n. pl., 1717, fol. 7 pp.
B.M.

2618. Some curious observations relating to fair Rosamund, and Godstow nunnery. (Memoirs of the antiq. of Gt. Brit., pp. vii–xii, 25-46.) Lond., 1723, 12°. Bliss A 160

2619. Godstow nunnery. (The beauties of British antiquity, by J. Collinson, p. 237-43.) Lond., 1779, 8°. Gough Gen. top. 184

2620. Godstow. (Gent's. mag., 1783, pt. 1, p. 462, 481; 1791, pt. 2, p. 985, 86; 1792, pt. 1, p. 529; 1797, pt. 1, p. 124.) Ψ 2. 44

2621. Godstow nunnery, and the tomb of Rosamund. (Gent's. mag., Nov. 1791, p. 985, 86.) Ψ 2. 44

2622. PARKER, J. H., On Godstow nunnery. (Proc., Oxf. architect. and hist. soc., 1870, N.S., vol. 2, p. 144-49.) R. 13. 708

2623. TROUSDALE, W. G., On a recent discovery at Godstow [encaustic tiles]. (Proc., Oxf. architect. and hist. soc., 1873, N.S., vol. 3, p. 127, 28.) R. 13. 709

2624. SIMMS, G., On Godstow as a fortress. (Proc., Oxf. architect. and hist. soc., 1886, N.S., vol. 5, p. 9–13.) R. 13. 711

2625. Fair Rosamunds cross. (Berks, Bucks, & Oxon archaeol. journ., 1896, vol. 2, notes, p. 62.) R. Top. 100

2626. TAUNT, H. W., Godstow, with its legend of Fair Rosamund; Medley, Wytham & Binsey. Oxf., [c. 1900], 8°. 28 pp.
G.A. Oxon 8° 709

2627. CLARK, A., ed., The English register of Godstow nunnery . . . written about 1450. 3 pt. (E.E.T.S., orig. ser., 129, 130, 142.) Lond., 1905, 8°. E. 2. 96 (129, 30, 142)

2628. SEGELHORST, W., Die Sprache des 'English register of Godstow nunnery' . . . in ihrem Verhältnis zu Oxford und London. Inaug.-Diss. Marburg, 1908, 8°. 86 pp. 3021 e. 32

2629. Godstow abbey: commission to inquire into irregularities, 1434, with schedule of injunctions, 1432. (Lincoln record soc., 1914, vol. 7, p. 64–68.) R. Top. 260
— [Another issue.] (Cant. and York soc., 1915, vol. 17, p. 64–68.)
R. 8. 26

2630. Picture postcard souvenir and guide to Godstow. Oxf., [1916], 16°. 6 pp. G.A. Oxon 16° 136 (4)

2631. The visitation of the monastery of Godstow, 29th May, 1445. (Lincoln record soc., 1918, vol. 14, p. 113–16.) R. Top. 260
— [Another issue.] (Cant. and York soc., 1919, vol. 24, p. 113–16.)
R. 8. 26

2632. Godstow. (Archaeol. notes. Oxoniensia, 1943, 44, p. 197.)
R. Top. 340

2633. Visitations. Godstow abbey. (i) 12 June 1517 (ii) 4 May 1520. (Lincoln record soc., 1944, vol. 35, p. 152, 53.) R. Top. 260

2634. Auction catal. The Trout inn, site and ruins of the Nunnery and chapel, and land in Pixey meadow. 13 Nov. 1897.
G.A. Oxon c. 224 (1)

GORING
General

2635. Sad and deplorable news from Oxfordsheir & Bark-sheir, being a . . . relation of the drowning of about sixty persons . . . in the lock, near Goring in Oxfordsheir; as they were passing by water from Goring-feast, to Stately [sic] in Barksheir. Lond., 1674, 4°. 6 pp.
Gough Oxf. 45 (2)

2636. DRUCE, G., A genealogical account of the family of Druce of Goreing. n. pl., 1735, 4°.
— Repr. [ed. by C. Bridges]. 1853, 4°. 30 pp. 218 d. 57

2637. An act for dividing and inclosing the . . . fields . . . in Goring. . . . (27 G. III, c. 5, Private.) n. pl., 1787, fol. 21 pp.
L. Eng. C 13 c. 1 (1787. 6)

2638. An act for inclosing Goring Common or Goring Heath and certain waste lands . . . of Goring. . . . (49 G. III, c. 154, L. & P.) n. pl., 1809, fol. 27 pp.
L. Eng. C 13 c. 1 (1809. i. 51)

2639. An act for building a bridge over the river Thames from Streatley . . . to . . . Goring. . . . (7 W. IV & 1 V., c. 31, L. & P.) Lond., 1837, fol. 49 pp.
B.M.

2640. READE, E. A., Allnutt's charity, the schools at Goring Heath. (Walilngford [sic], 1877), 8°. 22 pp.
G.A. Oxon 8° 243

2641. An act to confirm certain provisional orders made . . . under the Gas and water works facilities act, 1870, relating to Goring and Streatley district gas and water. . . . (51 & 52 V., c. 127, L. & P.) Lond., 1888, fol. 35 pp.
L. Eng. A 69 c. 6

2642. TAUNT, H. W., Goring, Streatley and the neighbourhood. Oxf., (1894), 8°. 122 pp.
G.A. Oxon 8° 605

2643. Berks, South Oxon, and North Hants society for the preservation of public rights of way and open spaces. The proposed diversion of a Thames footpath [from Goring to South Stoke]. Repr. from the Reading Standard, Jan. 7th, 1898. n. pl., (1898), 8°. 4 pp.
G.A. Oxon c. 317 (1)

2644. FIELD, J. E., ed., An illustrated guide to Wallingford, Goring and district. Wallingford, [c. 1902], 8°. 60 pp.   G.A. Berks 8° 119

See 2259A [Rural sanitary district. Report. 1911].

2645. An act to empower the Commissioners of the Streatley and Goring bridge and approaches to construct a new bridge across the Thames between Streatley and Goring and for other purposes. (5 & 6 G. V, c. 24, L. & P.) Lond., 1915, fol. 24 pp.
L. Eng. A 69 c. 6

2646. WILLIAMS, E. C., Notes on Whistler and Simmons charities at Goring. (Berks archaeol. journ., 1937, vol. 41, p. 58–67.)
R. Top. 100

2647. BAKER, J. H., Land of The Gap [the Goring district]. Oxf., 1937, 8°. 211 pp.
G.A. Gen. top. 8° 1275

2648. Goring and Streatley official guide. Lond., [1937], 8°. 18 pp.
G.A. Gen. top. 8° 1247
— 2nd ed. [entitled] Official guide to Goring-on-Thames. Lond., [1951], 8°. 17 pp.

2649. Auction catal. Newhouse farm, 2 woods adjoining called Wood-croft and Bustcroft Shaw, 2 proprietors shares of £100 each on the tolls of the New Bridge over the Thames from Whitchurch to Pangbourn. 8 Oct. 1800.   G.A. fol. A 266 (31)

Church and Priory

2650. STONE, P. G., An exact account of the church & priory at Goring. Goring, 1893, 8°. 54 pp.   G.A. Oxon 4° 172
— 2nd ed., 1893.   G.A. Oxon 4° 635

2651. The visitation of the priory of Goring, 21st May, 1445. (Lincoln record soc., 1918, vol. 14, p. 117, 18.)   R. Top. 260
— [Another issue.] (Cant. and York soc., 1919, vol. 24, p. 117, 18.)
          R. 8. 26

2652. COOKE, A. H., ed., A rent roll of the suppressed priory of Goring, 1546. (Berks archaeol. journ., 1931, vol. 35, p. 120–23.)
          R. Top. 100

2653. PARRY, T. R. GAMBIER, ed., A collection of charters relating to Goring, Streatley and the neighbourhood, 1181–1546. (Oxf. record soc., 13, 14.) Oxf., 1931, 8°. 282 pp.   R. 13. 702

2654. WILLIAMS, E. C., The church & priory, Goring-on-Thames. n. pl., 1933, 8°.
— Revised ed. (Henley-on-Thames), 1948, 8°. 24 pp.
          G.A. Oxon 8° 1204 (8)

2655. Visitations. Goring priory. (i) 19 June 1517 (ii) 6 Oct. 1530. (Lincoln record soc., 1944, vol. 35, p. 155–57.)   R. Top. 260

Geology

2656. CHATWIN, C. P., and WITHERS, T. H., The zones of chalk in the Thames valley between Goring and Shiplake. (Proc., Geol. assoc., 1908, vol. 20, p. 390–421.)   Radcl.

2657. Excursion to Goring and Streatley. (Proc., Geol. assoc., 1916, vol. 27, p. 105–07.)   Radcl.

2658. STRAHAN, SIR A., Geology of the Thames valley near Goring, as illustrated by the model in the Museum of practical geology. (Mem., Geol. survey.) Lond., 1924, 4°. 22 pp.   Radcl.
— [Another ed.] (Berks, Bucks, & Oxon archaeol. journ., 1925, vol. 29, p. 129–36.)   R. Top. 100

GOSFORD

See 539 [Gosford turnpike road trust statements, 1850–59].

2659. WING, W., Annals of Kidlington and its annexes . . . Gosford [&c.]. Repr. from the Oxf. Chron. (Oxf.), 1881, 8°. 31 pp.
          G.A. Oxon 8° 220 (5)

GRAFTON

2660. An act for inclosing lands within the manor and hamlet of Grafton. (6 & 7 V., c. 3, Private.) n. pl., 1843, fol. 38 pp.

L. Eng. C 13 c. 1 (1843. 2)

2661. MARGRETT, E., Prehistoric remains in the Thames valley [found at Grafton in 1896, when a cutting was made for the new lock]. (Berks, Bucks, & Oxon archaeol. journ., 1905, vol. 11, p. 27–29.)

R. Top. 100

GREAT BARFORD

See BARFORD ST. MICHAEL

GREAT BOURTON

2662. An act for vesting the two undivided fourth parts, of Priscilla Allett [and others] . . . children of Alice Warner . . . of . . . the manors . . . of Great Bourton and Little Bourton . . . in trustees to sell. . . . (10 G. III, c. 84, Private.) n. pl., 1770, fol. 18 pp.

L. Eng. C 13 c. 1 (1770. 4)

2663. An act for dividing and inclosing the . . . field and commonable lands lying within . . . Great Bourton and Little Bourton in the parish of Cropredy. (17 G. III, c. 74, Private.) n. pl., [1777], fol. 31 pp.   G.A. Oxon c. 113 (5)

GREAT HASELEY

2664. Proposals for surveying land, by William Burgess, of Great Hasely. n. pl., [17—], s. sh.   MS. Top. Oxon c. 290 (28)

2665. A bill for vesting the equity of redemption of the mannor . . . of Great Haseley with . . . lands in Haseley and Latchford . . . the estate of William Lenthall . . . to be sold for the discharging of incumbrances thereupon. n. pl., [1707], fol. 4 pp.

G.A. Oxon c. 247 (6)

— Act. (6 Anne, c. 23, Private.)

2666. An act for annexing the rectory, or parsonage of Hasely . . . to the deanery of Windsor. (7 Anne, c. 38, Private.) n. pl., [1708], fol. 3 pp.   MS. Top. Oxon d. 88 (f. 39)

2667. An act for allotting lands . . . of Great Haseley. . . . (1 G. IV, c. 62, Private.) (Oxf.), 1820, fol. 23 pp.   L. Eng. C 13 c. 1 (1820. ii. 30)

2668. An act to effect an exchange of estates [in Gt. Hasely] in the county of Oxford between John Blackall . . . and the trustees of Cutler Boulter's charity, near the city of Oxford. (7 & 8 G. IV, c. 24, Private.) Lond., 1827, fol. 15 pp.

L. Eng. C 13 c. 1 (1826/7. 2)

2669. A descriptive list of pictures belonging to John Wastie at Great Hasely house, Tetsworth. (Bury St. Edmunds), 1834, 16°. 25 pp.
1706 g. 1

2670. WEARE, T. W., Some remarks upon the church of Great Haseley. Together with copious extracts from Delafield's MS. entitled Notitia Hasleiana. [By T. W. Weare.] (Mem. of Gothic churches, no. 1.) Oxf., 1840, 8°. 56 pp. G.A. Oxon 8° 268
— 2nd ed. [With] Some account of Rycote chapel. Oxf., 1848, 8°. 159 pp. G.A. Oxon 8° 70 (8)

2671. PEARMAN, M. T., The descent of the manors of Pirton and Haseley. (Trans., Oxf. archaeol. soc., 27.) Lond., 1892, 8°. 24 pp.
R. Top. 330

2672. Haseley parochial report, Nov. 1892 to Nov. 1893. n. pl., (1893), 8°. 16 pp.

2673. BILLSON, A., [Description of a tilting-helm of the 16th century, preserved in Haseley Church.] (Proc., Soc. of antiquaries, 1895, 2nd ser., vol. 16, p. 53–58.) R. Top. 1

2674. Haseley. (Rept., Oxf. archaeol. soc., 1895/6, p. 17, 18.)
R. Top. 330

2675. DE WATTEVILLE, H. G., Monumental brasses in the church of Great Haseley. (Journ., Oxf. univ. brass-rubbing soc., 1898, vol. 1, p. 170–75.) Soc. 2184 d. 50 (1)

2676. Haseley church restoration. (Oxf., 1898), 8°. 4 pp.
G.A. Oxon c. 317 (9)

2677. EDWARDS, W. G., Haseley church. (Oxf. diocesan mag., 1909/10, vol. 5, p. 269, 70.) Per. 11126 d. 78 (5)
— [Repr. with additions.] (Oxf. diocesan mag., 1922, vol. 18, p. 206–10.) Per. 11126 d. 78 (18)
— Repr. Oxf., (1922), 8°. 4 pp. G.A. Oxon 4° 504 (11)

See 3735 [Windmill, Great Haseley. 1925].

2678. EDWARDS, W. G., The mass clock of Great Haseley. (Oxf. diocesan mag., 1926, vol. 21, p. 302, 03.) Per. 11126 d. 78 (21)

See 31 [Stratigraphy at Great Haseley. 1944].

2679. ALLEN, A. B., Rural education. 2 vols. [Vol. 2 entitled, The country school, an account of the Endowed school, Great Haseley.] Lond., (1950), 8°. 2621 e. 397

2680. Auction catal. Rycote estate. 31 May 1911.
G.A. Oxon b. 91 (44)

GREAT MILTON

2681. An act to subject and charge the prebend manor of Mych Milton [? Great Milton] . . . and the lands . . . thereunto belonging, with the payment of two several perpetual yearly rent-charges . . . to John Wheeldon and his successors . . . and for divesting the fee-simple and inheritance thereof out of him, and for vesting the same in Charles Sturges. (15 G. III, c. 55, Private.) Lond., 1775, fol. 8 pp.
L. Eng. C 13 c. 1 (1774/5. 48)

2682. Some account of Great Milton. Oxf., 1819, 8°. 48 pp.
G.A. Oxon 8° 72 (4)

2683. Great Milton. (Gent's. mag., 1820, pt. 1, p. 9–11, 106–08; 1828, pt. 2, p. 203, 04.)   Ψ 2. 44

2684. An act for inclosing lands in . . . Great Milton . . . (3 & 4 V., c. 9, Private.) n. pl., 1840, fol. 38 pp.   L. Eng. C 13 c. 1 (1840. 9)

2685. [Restoration of the church. Appeal, with plan.] n. pl., [c. 1890], fol. 2 pp.   G.A. fol. A 139* (70)

2686. DRYDEN, SIR H., Recess in Great Milton church. (Rept., Oxf. archaeol. soc., 1895/6, p. 23–24.)   R. Top. 330

2687. Great Milton. (Rept., Oxf. archaeol. soc., 1895/6, p. 17.)
R. Top. 330

2688. PAINTIN, H., Brief notes on Great Milton. [Typewritten.] [Oxf., 1929], 4°. 11 pp.   G.A. Oxon 4° 496 (2)

See 31 [Stratigraphy at the Miltons. 1944].

2689. Pottery from . . . Great Milton [&c.]. (Oxoniensia, 1946–47, p. 169.)   R. Top. 340

2690. Auction catal. Prebendal manor. 3 Nov. 1810.   G.A. fol. B 71

2691. Auction catal. Arable land. 26 Mar. 1811.   G.A. fol. B 71

2692. Auction catal. Farms. 25 Aug. 1832.   G.A. fol. B 71

2693. Auction catal. Prebendal Manor farm. 7 Oct. 1837.
G.A. fol. B 71

2694. Auction catal. Manor farm. 29 July 1905.
G.A. Oxon b. 91 (31)

GREAT MILTON (Peculiar jurisdiction of)

2695. PEARCE, S. S., The clergy of the deanery of Cuddesdon and of the peculiars of Langford, Thame and Great Milton during the settlement of 1559 and afterwards. (Rept., Oxf. archaeol. soc., 1920, p. 242–89.)   R. Top. 330

GREAT ROLLRIGHT

2696. An act for dividing and inclosing the . . . fields . . . within . . . Great Rolewright. . . . (15 G. III, c. 41, Private.) n. pl., 1775, fol. 29 pp.   L. Eng. C 13 c. 1 (1775. 67)

2697. KEYSER, C. E., Notes on the architecture of the churches of Great Rollright [&c.]. (Journ., Brit. archaeol. assoc., 1919, N.S., vol. 25, p. 1–23+55 plates.)   R. Top. 4

2698. JEFFERY, R. W., The manors and advowson of Great Rollright. (Oxf. record soc., 9.) [Oxf.], 1927, 8°. 207 pp.   R. 13. 702

2699. RENDALL, M. J., The bells of Great Rollright. [An account, in verse and prose, of the village in the 1870's.] Winchester, 1947, 8°. 167 pp.   28001 e. 7047

GREAT TEW

2700. An act for annexing the late duke of Shrewsbury's estate to the earldom of Shrewsbury and confirming Gilbert, earl of Shrewsbury's settlement. [Concerns Great Tew &c.] (6 G. I, c. 29, Private.) n. pl., [1720], fol.
— Repr. 1858. 16 pp.   L. Eng. C 13 c. 1 (1714–27)
— 43 G. III, c. 40, Private.
— 1 G. IV, c. 40, Private.

2701. An act for dividing and inclosing certain . . . fields in . . . Great Tew. (6 G. III, c. 5, Private.) n. pl., 1766, fol. 18 pp.
       G.A. Oxon c. 180

2702. An act concerning certain estates heretofore of Francis Keck . . . in . . . Oxford and Wilts . . . [Great Tew &c.] (18 G. III, c. 109, Private.) n. pl., 1778, fol. 46 pp.   L. Eng. C 13 c. 1 (1778. ii. 8)

2703. An act for discharging the estate of George Frederick Stratton, esquire, in the parish of Great Tew. . . . (50 G. III, c. 178, L. & P.) Lond., 1810, fol. 15 pp.   L. Eng. A 69 c. 6

2704. An act for vesting part of the settled estates of . . . John, earl of Shrewsbury [in Great Tew &c.] . . . in trustees to be sold. (6 & 7 V., c. 28, Private.) Lond., 1843, fol. 60 pp.
       L. Eng. C 13 c. 1 (1843. i. 28)

2705. Pedigree of Keck of Long Marston, Glouc. & Great Tew. [Middlehill], 1857, s. sh.   Caps. 6. 47 (49)

2706. ROYCE, D., History of Great Tew [&c.] [by D. Royce]. (Trans., North Oxf. arch. soc., 1875.) Oxf., 1877, 8°. 22 pp.   R. Top. 330
— Suppl. [by W. Wing]. Repr. from Oxf. Chron. 7 pp.
       G.A. Oxon 8° 1230 (7)

See 3873 [Monumental brasses in the church. 1898].

2707. VINOGRADOFF, SIR P., An illustration of the continuity of the open field system. [*With*] Appendix. (Quarterly journ. of econ., 1907, vol. 22, p. 62–82.)   Per. 23211 d. 32
— [Repr., *entitled*] By-laws of an Oxfordshire manor [Great Tew].
G.A. Oxon 4° 504 (15)

2708. CARTER, W. F., The Wilcotes monument in Great Tew church. Reading, 1907, 8°. 31 pp.   G.A. Oxon 4° 718

2709. MALLESON, J. P., A paper on lord Falkland, read . . . near the site of lord Falkland's house in Great Tew park. Banbury, 1913, 8°. 16 pp.   G.A. Oxon c. 317 (14)

See 359 [Honors and knights' fees. 1924].

2709A. LAMBORN, E. A. GREENING-, Great Tew: a link with Sterne. (N. & Q., 1948, vol. 193, p. 512–15.) Ψ 2. 97

2709B. LAMBORN, E. A. GREENING-, Great Tew and the Chandos portrait. (N. & Q., 1949, vol. 194, p. 71, 72.) Ψ 2. 97

2710. HUSSEY, C., Great Tew. (Country Life, 1949, vol. 106, p. 254–57, 324–27.)   Per. 384 b. 6

2710A. Great Tew. (Archaeol. notes. Oxoniensia, 1950, vol. 15, p. 107.)
R. Top. 340

GRIM'S DYKE

2711. CRAWFORD, O. G. S., Grim's ditch in Wychwood. (Antiquity, 1930, vol. 4, p. 303–15.)   R. Top. 6

2712. CRAWFORD, O. G. S., The Chiltern Grim's ditches. (Antiquity, 1931, vol. 5, p. 161–71.)   R. Top. 6

2713. HARDEN, D. B., Excavations on Grim's Dyke, North Oxfordshire. [Between Woodstock & Charlbury.] (Oxoniensia, 1937, p. 74–92.)
R. Top. 340

HAILEY

See 1225 [J. Leverett's will. 1783].

2714. An act for allotting lands . . . of Hailey. . . . (1 & 2 G. IV, c. 46, L. & P.) n. pl., 1821, fol. 23 pp.   L. Eng. C 13 c. 1 (1821. i. 1)

2715. An act to authorize the inclosure of certain lands . . . [Hailey]. (12 & 13 V., c. 57, Pub.) Lond., 1849, fol. 2 pp.
L. Eng. A 69 c. 1

2716. GILES, J. A., History of Witney, with notices of . . . Hailey [&c.]. Lond., 1852, 8°. 107 pp.   G.A. Oxon 8° 13

2717. Hailey national school. Balance sheet and reports, year ending 30th June 1897. n. pl., (1897), 8°. 4 pp.   G.A. Oxon 4° 183

2718. Auction catal. Mansion and estate. 26 Apr. 1814.
G.A. fol. B 71

2719. Auction catal. New Yatt farm. 13 May 1824.　　G.A. fol. B 71
— 31 July 1902.　　　　　　　　　　　　　　　　G.A. Oxon c. 317 (9)

2720. Auction catal. Freehold and copyhold estate. 16 May 1895.
G.A. Oxon b. 92 (35)

2721. Auction catal. Hailey farm. 18 Sept. 1896.
MS. Top. Oxon c. 232 (234)

2722. Auction catal. Pasture land. 31 May 1900.
G.A. Oxon b. 90 (30)

2723. Auction catal. Estate. 18 Sept. 1913.　　　G.A. Oxon b. 91 (1)

HAMPTON GAY

2724. Miscellanious epitaphs of the 16th and 17th century. Hampton
Gey. May 12, 1660. (The Topographer, 1790, vol. 2, p. 369, 70.)
Douce VV 15
See 455, 56 [Canal. 1792].

2725. WING, W., Two churches and parishes beyond the neighbourhood of Banbury. Hampton Gay and Hampton Poyle. Repr. from
the Banbury Guardian. [First] Second paper. [Signed W. W.] n. pl.,
[1881], 8°. 3+3 pp.　　　　　　　　G.A. Oxon 8° 220 (6, 7)

2726. Auction catal. Estate and Paper mill. 13 July 1849.
G.A. Oxon b. 85 a (33)

2727. Auction catal. Estate. 15 June 1910.　　　G.A. Oxon c. 317 (9)

HAMPTON POYLE

2728. An act for dividing, allotting, and inclosing the . . . commonable
lands . . . of Hampton Poyle. (36 G. III, c. 91, Private.) n. pl.,
[1796], fol. 30 pp.　　　　　　L. Eng. C 13 c. 1 (1796. i. 27)

2729. Hampton Poyle. (Gent's. mag., 1800, pt. 2, p. 809–12; 1806, pt. 1,
p. 524–28.)　　　　　　　　　　　　　　　　Ψ 2. 44

2730. GREENFIELD, B. W., The descent of the manor and advowson of
Hampton-Poyle, from the 15th century. (Herald and genealogist,
1863, vol. 1, p. 209–24, 321–44; 1865, vol. 3, p. 296–307.)
Ψ 2. 10 d
— [Repr.] 1865.　　　　　　　　　　　　G.A. Oxon 8° 952

2731. WING, W., Two churches and parishes beyond the neighbourhood of Banbury. Hampton Gay and Hampton Poyle. Repr. from
the Banbury Guardian. [First] Second paper. [Signed W. W.]
n. pl., [1881], 8°. 3+3 pp.　　　　G.A. Oxon 8° 220 (6, 7)

2732. Auction catal. Estate. 15 June 1910.   G.A. Oxon c. 317 (9)

2733. Auction catal. Freehold properties. 24 May 1911.
G.A. Oxon c. 317 (10)

HANDBOROUGH

See 502 [Turnpike act. 1751, &c.].

2734. An act for dividing and inclosing the common fields . . . of Handborough. . . . (12 G. III, c. 22, Private.) n. pl., 1772, fol. 28 pp.
L. Eng. C 13 c. 1 (1772. i. 51)

See 413 [Account of the night march of Charles i, June 3rd, 1644, by V. Thomas. 1852].

2735. Oxford univ., St. John's coll., Statement respecting [the Living of] Hanborough, &c. [Oxf.], (1867), 4°. 7 pp.
G.A. Oxon 4° 262 (19)

2736. COOKE, S. M., Some Oxfordshire churches. 1. Handborough. Repr. from the Oxford mag. n. pl., (1907), 8°. 8 pp.
G.A. Oxon 8° 611 (9)

2737. Hanborough and Freeland horticultural association. Show, Sept. 12, 1908. Schedule of prizes. n. pl., 1908, s. sh.
G.A. Oxon c. 317 (9)

See 1297 [Parish registers. Marriages. 1909].

2738. Hanborough parish monthly magazine. June, July, 1910. n. pl., 1910, 4°.   G.A. Oxon c. 317 (9)

2739. Hanborough nursing association. Annual report. 1912/13. n. pl., (1913), 12°. 4 pp.   G.A. Oxon c. 317 (9)

2740. The Hanborough, Bladon and Freeland news, ed. by F. B. Greenway. No. 1, 3–5, 7, 8. [Reprod. from typewriting.] Hanborough, 1921, 22, 4°.   G.A. Oxon c. 317 (9)

2741. PAINTIN, H., Oxford architectural and historical society. Visit to . . . Hanborough [&c.]. (Repr. from Oxf. journ. illustr.) n. pl., (1922), s. sh.   G.A. Oxon a. 22

2742. ARKELL, W. J., A palaeolith from the Hanborough terrace. (Oxoniensia, 1946–7, p. 1–4.)   R. Top. 340

2743. Sale catal. 'Park view.' 1919.   G.A. Oxon c. 317 (9)

2744. Auction catal. Blenheim estate, comprising Shepherd's, Manor, Cook's corner, Wastie's and Smith's farm. 14 July 1920.
G.A. Oxon b. 92* (3)

2745. Auction catal. The Cottage. 30 May 1934.
G.A. Oxon c. 224*

HANWELL

See 501 [Turnpike act. 1744, &c.].

2746. KEYSER, C. E., A visit to the churches of . . . Hanwell [&c.]. (Journ., Brit. archaeol. assoc., 1921, new ser., vol. 27, p. 129–58+76 plates.)   R. Top. 4

2747. Auction catal. Hanwell estate. 22 June 1904.
G.A. Oxon b. 91 (2)

HARDWICK

2748. An act for the vesting . . . several manors and lands [in Hardwick &c.] late the inheritance of W. Jennens . . . in trustees to be sold. (8 Anne, c. 10, Private.) n. pl., [c. 1709], 8°. 52 pp.   Radcl. e. 127

2749. An act to authorize the inclosure of certain lands . . . [Hardwick]. (11 & 12 V., c. 109, Pub.) Lond., 1848, fol. 3 pp.   L. Eng. A 69 c. 1

2750. Ducklington (and Hardwick) church accounts. 1873–1908/9. n. pl., 1873–1909, 4°.   G.A. Oxon 4° 183

2751. MACRAY, W. D., [British urn found at Hardwick.] (Proc., Soc. of antiq., 1876, ser. 2, vol. 7, p. 100.)   R. Top. 1

2752. BLOMFIELD, J. C., History of . . . Hardwick [&c.]. (Hist. of . . . deanery of Bicester. Pt. 3.) Bristol, (1887), 4°. 95 pp.
G.A. Oxon 4° 71

2753. Cogges, Ducklington & Hardwick parish magazine. Jan. 1892– Dec. 1903. (Witney), 1892–1903, 4°.   Per. G.A. Oxon 4° 182

2754. Auction catal. Whole parish. 15 July 1857.
G.A. Oxon b. 85 b (57)

2755. Auction catal. Estate. 31 May 1899.   G.A. Oxon b. 91 (37)

HARPSDEN

2756. Auction catal. Estate. 15 Oct. 1844.   G.A. Oxon b. 92* (1)

HASELEY

See GREAT HASELEY

HEADINGTON

General

2757. An act to enable an exchange to be made between Lionel, duke of Dorset and the trustees of Henry Smith . . . of land . . . in . . . Kent . . . for . . . part of a fee farm rent of forty pounds per annum issuing out of the manor of Heddington, with the hundred of Bullingdon. . . . (13 G. I, c. 10, Private.) n. pl., 1726, fol. 4 pp.
L. Eng. C 13 c. 1 (1714/27. 112)

2758. An act for dividing, allotting, and laying in severalty . . . common fields . . . of Headington. (41 G. III, c. 72, Private.) (Oxf.), [1801], fol. 32 pp.   L. Eng. C 13 c. 1 (1801. ii. 20)

2759. An act for enabling William Hall . . . to assign or surrender a term of one thousand years in estates [in Headington &c.] . . . unto . . . Elisha Biscoe. (53 G. III, c. 203, L. & P.) Lond., 1813, fol. 4 pp.
                                                                 L. Eng. A 69 c. 6

2760. Headington. (Gent's. mag., 1816, pt. 1, p. 9, 10.) Ψ 2. 44

2761. JEWITT, LL., On Roman remains recently discovered at Heading-ton. (Journ., Brit. archaeol. assoc., 1850, vol. 5, p. 159; 1851, vol. 6, p. 52–67.)   R. Top. 4

2762. PARKER, J. H., On the wall paintings recently discovered in Headington church. (Proc., Oxf. architect. and hist. soc., N.S., vol. 1, 1863, p. 302.)   R. 13. 707

2763. The Headington parish magazine. (St. Andrew's church). Jan. 1869–Dec. 1889. Oxf., 1869–89, 8°.   G.A. Oxon 8° 539

    See 1020 [Act concerning supply of water. 1875].

2764. Terms and conditions of letting an enclosure of glebe land situate at the cross roads near the Headington mill, in allotments, to sober and industrious labourers. n. pl., [1876], s. sh.
                                                          G.A. Oxon c. 317 (21)

2765. [Report on completion of the additional schoolroom, Headington quarry.] n. pl., (1882), s. sh.   G.A. Oxon c. 317 (21)

2766. Headington quarry school account. 1881/2, 1887/8, 1889/90, 1890–91. (Oxf., 1882–91), s. sh.   G.A. Oxon c. 317 (21)

2767. Headington horticultural, cottage garden, and poultry society. Catalogue of the 10th (23rd, 25th, 27th) annual show. Oxf., 1890–1907, 8°.   G.A. Oxon 8° 816

2768. Headington horticultural. cottage garden, and poultry society. Rules, list of subscribers, and schedule of prizes to be competed for at the 21st (23rd, 24th, 27th) annual show. Oxf., 1901–07, 8°.
                                                              G.A. Oxon 8° 816

2769. BLAKE, J. F., Excursion to Headington [&c.]. (Proc., Geol. assoc., 1902, vol. 17, p. 383–85.)   Radcl.

2770. Headington Baptist chapel. [Appeal for funds.] n. pl., (1904), s. sh.   G.A. Oxon c. 317 (21)

2771. Board of education. Mather foundation, Headington. (Scheme—including appointment of trustees.) Lond., 1907, fol. 4 pp.
                                                              G.A. Oxon c. 135

2772. Headington charity organisation society's report, 1908. n. pl., (1908), 8°. 8 pp. G.A. Oxon c. 317 (21)

2773. Headington rural district council. Infectious hospital and administration block at Headington. Specification and general conditions. Oxf., [1908], fol. 15 pp. G.A. Oxon c. 123

2774. The British workman, Headington [a temperance society. Report and statement of accounts]. n. pl., [1924], 8°. 4 pp.
G.A. Oxon c. 317 (21)

2775. An act to extend the boundaries of the city of Oxford and for other purposes [affecting Headington &c.] (18 & 19 G. V, c. 84, L. & P.) Lond., 1928, 8°. 68 pp. L. Eng. A 69 c. 6

2776. EVANS, E., The manor of Headington. (Rept., Oxf. archaeol. soc., 1928, p. 161–216.) R. Top. 330

2777. COPPOCK, G. A., and HILL, B. M., Headington quarry and Shotover, a history. Oxf., 1933, 8°. 84 pp. G.A. Oxon 8° 1115

2778. Bayswater hill, Headington. (Archaeol. notes. Oxoniensia, 1946–7, p. 163, 165.) R. Top. 340

2779. Auction catal. Estate. 29 June 1813. G.A. fol. B 71

2780. Auction catal. Headington manor. 3 Aug. 1836.
G.A. fol. A 139* (8)

2781. Auction catal. Oxford field and Holley's farms. 28 Oct. 1846.
G.A. Oxon b. 91 (4)

2782. Auction catal. Headington manor. 2 June 1848.
G.A. Oxon b. 85 a (33)

2783. Auction catal. Manor house. 27 May 1895.
G.A. Oxon b. 91 (5)

2784. Auction catal. Manor of Headington and Plowman's farm &c. 20 May 1911. G.A. Oxon b. 91 (7)

2785. Auction catal. Arable land and, in Headington quarry, a house. 13 June 1855. G.A. Oxon b. 4 (18)

2786. Auction catal. Estate at Headington quarry. 18 May 1870.
G.A. Oxon b. 4 (36)

2787. Auction catal. Land. 2 Sept. 1868. G.A. Oxon b. 4 (35)

2788. Auction catal. 70 acre estate. 14 Dec. 1870.
G.A. Oxon b. 4 (39)

2789. Auction catal. Southfield farm &c. 13 June 1874.
G.A. Oxon b. 4 (50)

2790. Auction catal. Bury Knowle house. 6–9 June 1899.
G.A. Oxon 4° 320

2791. Auction catal. Headington house. 6 June 1906.
G.A. Oxon b. 91 (6)

2792. Auction catal. Burton farm. 24 May 1911.
G.A. Oxon b. 90 (10)

Warneford Asylum

2793. Radcliffe infirmary. [Resolutions of the Governors concerning the proposed foundation of a lunatic asylum.] [Oxf.], (1813), 4°. 4 pp.
G.A. Oxon b. 112 (53)

2794. Governors of the Radcliffe Infirmary. Minutes of proceedings relative to a proposal for establishing a lunatick asylum in the vicinity of Oxford by voluntary contributions. Oxf., 1814, 4°. 26 pp.
G.A. Oxon 4° 629

2795. Lunatic asylum . . . January 27th, 1825. [Announcement of partial completion of building, and appeal for funds.] Oxf., 1825, s. sh.
G.A. Oxon b. 112 (86)

2796. Lunatic asylum near Exeter. Abstract of the rules relating to the admission and discharge of patients, proposed to be followed at present for the asylum near Oxford. Oxf., [1825], s. sh.
G.A. Oxon c. 42 (101 k)

2797. Lunatic asylum. [Notice of general meeting and Abstract of accounts to Nov. 28, 1825.] Oxf., 1825, s. sh.
G.A. Oxon c. 41 (101)

2798. Oxford lunatic asylum. [Notice summarising the state of affairs on Jan. 11, 1826.] Oxf., 1826, s. sh.   G.A. Oxon c. 42 (2)

2799. THOMAS, VAUGHAN, An account of the origin, nature and objects of the asylum on Headington Hill, near Oxford. [By V. Thomas.] Oxf., (1827), 4°. 47 pp.   G.A. Oxon 4° 171

2800. Radcliffe lunatic asylum. [Report.]

1828.	G.A. Oxon c. 44 (127)
1836.	G.A. Oxon c. 52 (120)
1837.	G.A. Oxon c. 54 (146 b)
1838.	G.A. Oxon c. 55 (149)
1839.	G.A. Oxon c. 56 (6)
1840.	G.A. Oxon c. 56 (149)
1841.	G.A. Oxon c. 57 (146)
1842.	G.A. Oxon c. 58 (129)
1847.	G.A. Oxon c. 63 (175)
1848.	G.A. Oxon c. 64 (150)
1849.	G.A. Oxon c. 65 (199)

1853, 1855–62.   G.A. fol. B 80
1863–70, 1872.   G.A. Oxon 8° 182
1877, 1909, 1912–14.   G.A. Oxon 8° 205

2801. Useful information concerning the origin, nature, and purpose of the Radcliffe lunatic asylum, on Headington hill, near Oxford. Oxf., 1840, 8°. 10 pp.   G.A. Oxon 8° 204 (10)

2802. Refutation of the assertions made by the writer of the Quarterly review for October 1844, entitled Report of the Metropolitan commissioners in lunacy, pp. 436–441, as far as they relate to the conduct and practice of the Warneford asylum [&c.]. Oxf., (1844), 8°. 52 pp.
                                              G.A. Oxon 8° 1200
See 3122 [Reports of the Commissioners in lunacy. 1852–   ].

2803. CONOLLY, J., Report drawn up for the committee of management of the Warneford lunatic asylum, 1847. Oxf., 1857, 8°.

2804. Rules and orders of the Warneford lunatic asylum. 1848, 1854, 55, 1857. Oxf., 1848–57, 8°.   G.A. Oxon 8° 182

2805. THOMAS, V., Christian philanthropy exemplified in a memoir of ... Samuel Wilson Warneford. Oxf., 1855, 8°. 139 pp.   210 h. 60

2806. THOMAS, V., [Biographical note on] . . . dr. Warneford. Oxf., 1855, 8°. 4 pp.   200 h. 141 (17)

2807. An address to the trustees and governors . . . and to the gentry interested in the distribution of the Warneford gifts. Oxf., [1856], 8°. 14 pp.   G.A. Oxon 8° 659 (15)

2808. The general rules and orders for the government and regulation of the Warneford lunatic asylum, adopted Feb. 12, 1857. (Oxf., 1857), 8°. 26+24 pp.   G.A. Oxon 8° 1130* (10)

2809. The regulations of the Warneford lunatic asylum, 1872. (Oxf., 1872), 8°. 20 pp.   G.A. Oxon 8° 1130* (11)
— Amended 1914. (Oxf., 1914), 8°. 20 pp.
                                              G.A. Oxon 8° 1130* (12)

2810. Brief history of the Warneford lunatic asylum. Compiled by the Committee of management. n. pl., 1875, 8°. 15 pp.
                                              G.A. Oxon 4° 466

Home and Hospital

2811. Wingfield convalescent home. Report. 1872–87, 1894, 95, 1898– 1902, 1907, 1914, 15. Oxf., [1873–1916], 8°.   G.A. Oxon 8° 557
— 1896, 97.   O.P.L.

2812. Wingfield convalescent home, Headington. [First appeal for funds to enlarge the home.] n. pl., (1900), 4°. 4 pp.
                                              G.A. Oxon c. 317 (21)

2813. Wingfield orthopaedic hospital. Report. 1923–. (Oxf.), 1924–, 8°.
                                              Per. 1614 d. 54

HEADINGTON POOR LAW UNION

2814. Financial & statistical statement for the year ended 25th March, 1888, with a list of the guardians and the officers for the current year. Oxf., (1888), 8°. 10 pp.   G.A. Oxon 8° 828 (25)

HENLEY

General

See 400 [Skirmish at Henley. 1643].
See 500, 11 [Turnpike act. 1736, &c.].

2815. An act for building a bridge over the river Thames at . . . Henley upon Thames. (21 G. III, c. 33, Private.) Lond., 1781, fol. 47 pp.
                                                       G.A. Oxon c. 189

— 35 G. III, c. 79, Pub.
— 48 G. III, c. 111, L. & P.
— 6 & 7 W. IV, c. 40, L. & P.
— 28 V., c. 24, Pub.

2816. Henley. (Gent's. mag., 1793, pt. 2, p. 716–19; 1814, pt. 1, p. 121.)
                                                       Ψ 2. 44

2817. MORITZ, K. P., Travels, chiefly on foot, through several parts of England in 1782, tr. from the Germ. by a lady. (Henley, p. 145.) Lond., 1795, 8°.   Gough Gen. top. 293
[*Orig. entitled* 'Reisen eines Deutschen in England, . . . 1782.]
                                                       G.A. Gen. top. 16° 27
— [Repr. in W. Mavor's British tourists companion, vol. 4, 1798, 1809.]
— [Repr. in J. Pinkerton's Collection of travels, 1808, vol. 2. 4°
BS. 897.]
— [Another ed.] 1886. (Cassell's nat. hist.)

2818. Henley, a poem. Henley-on-Thames, 1827, 8°. 77 pp.
                                                       G.A. Oxon 8° 95

2819. Catalogue of the Old Library at Henley-on-Thames, with remarks on lending libraries for rural districts. Lond., 1852, 8°. 20 pp.   2590 e. Henley 1. 1

2820. COOPER, J., An account of the charities under the management of the corporation of . . . Henley-upon-Thames. Lond., 1858, 8°. 41 pp.   G.A. Oxon 8° 915

2821. BURN, J. S., A history of Henley-on-Thames. Lond., &c., 1861, 8°. 352 pp.   G.A. Oxon 8° 7

2822. Henley Horticultural society. Schedules and regulations . . . for the shows, 1864–67. Henley, 1864–67, 8°.
                                                       G.A. Oxon 8° 900 (43–46)

2823. Henley and Remenham Record. 1881, 82.

2824. STEVENS, J., On a bronze sword and an iron spear-head found at Henley-on-Thames. (Journ., Brit. archaeol. assoc., 1882, vol. 38, p. 275–78.)   R. Top. 4

2825. The 'Smith' hospital, Henley-on-Thames. Rules and regulations. Reading, [c. 1900], 8°. 11 pp.   1519 e. 24 (22)

2826. ASHBY, T., A Roman villa near Henley. (Archaeological journ., 1911, vol. 68, p. 43–48.)   R. Top. 5

See 673 [Register of electors, Henley division. 1918–].

2827. SMITH, R. A., A Jersey megalithic monument at Henley-on-Thames. (Proc., Soc. of antiq., 1919, ser. 2, vol. 31, p. 133–45.)
R. Top. 1

2828. Phyllis Court club, Henley. Plans and particulars of the proposed new golf course construction and other improvements & extensions. Lond., [1934], fol. 6 pp.+plan.   G.A. Oxon c. 317 (22)

2829. HAWKES, C. F. C., Food vessel from near Henley-on-Thames. (Antiq. journ., 1938, vol. 18, p. 412.)   R. Top. 2

2830. PATTERSON, R., Two hearth-blowers from Henley-on-Thames and Basingstoke. (Berks archaeol. journ., 1947, vol. 50, p. 98–101.)
R. Top. 100

See 332 [Ancient channel between Henley and Caversham, with flint implements. 1948].

2831. PETERS, G. H., This glorious Henley. Lond., 1950, 8°. 104 pp.
G.A. Oxon 8° 1219

2831A. Henley. (Archaeol. notes. Oxoniensia, 1950, vol. 15, p. 107.)
R. Top. 340

2832. Auction catal. Estate. 15 Oct. 1844.   G.A. Oxon b. 92* (1)

2833. Auction catal. Red Lion. 22 May 1901.   G.A. Oxon b. 6 (35*)
— 30 July 1902.   G.A. Oxon b. 6 (36)

2834. Auction catal. Highmoor hall. 8 June 1909.
G.A. Oxon b. 91 (10)

Church

2835. The parish church of Henley-on-Thames. [Announcement of the approaching completion of repair work, and appeal for help in reducing a deficit in the funds.] (Henley, 1854), s. sh.
G.A. Oxon c. 317 (22)

2836. Henley church. [Announcement of the completion of repair work, and further appeal for funds.] n. pl., [c. 1854], fol. 2 pp.
G.A. Oxon c. 317 (22)

2837. The parish church, Henley-on-Thames. Rules for the ringers. (Henley, 1857), s. sh.   G.A. Oxon c. 317 (22)

2838. [Appeal for funds to purchase ground at Northfield-End to serve as a burial ground, and to erect a church on it.] n. pl., (1865), 8°. 3 pp.   G.A. Oxon c. 317 (22)

2839. [*Begin.*] The Ghost and Goblin burial board give notice . . . [A satire against borrowing £3,000 to purchase a burial ground on the outskirts of Henley.] n. pl., [1867], s. sh.   G.A. Oxon c. 317 (22)

Directories

2840. Henley-on-Thames and neighbourhood directory. 1932–42.

Guides

2841. The Henley guide. Henley-on-Thames &c., 1826, 8°. 80 pp.   G.A. Oxon 8° 192
— [Another ed.] (1838). 112 pp.   G.A. Oxon 16° 148
— 3rd ed. 1850. 132 pp.   G.A. Oxon 8° 351 (1)
— 4th ed. 1850. 132 pp.   G.A. Oxon 8° 953

2842. HEYWOOD, ABEL, Guide to Henley-on-Thames. Henley-on-Thames, [1886], 8°. 16 pp.

2843. CLIMENSON, E. J., A guide to Henley-on-Thames. Henley-on-Thames, 1896, 8°. 120 pp.   G.A. Oxon 8° 629

2844. Friar park, Henley-on-Thames. Guide for the use of visitors. 2nd ed. [Henley], 1908, 4°. 103 pp.   G.A. Oxon 4° 399 *b* (4)

2845. Official guide. [1st–7th ed.] Lond., [1928–52], 8°.   G.A. Oxon 8° 1061

Local Government

2846. An act for better assessing and collecting the poor and parochial rates within . . . Henley-upon-Thames. . . . (6 G. IV, c. 174, L. & P.) Lond., 1825, fol. 12 pp.   O.C.R.L.

2847. First report of the Commissioners appointed to inquire into the municipal corporations in England and Wales. (Henley, Appendix, p. 69–74.)   Pp. Eng. 1835, vol. 23

2848. COCKBURN, A. E., Corporations of England and Wales. (Henley, vol. 1, p. 202, 03.) Lond., 1835, 8°.   G.A. Gen. top. 8° 727 (1)

2849.

2850. An act to confirm certain provisional orders of the Local government board relating to the [boundaries of the] boroughs of Chard and Henley-upon-Thames [p. 9–14]. (55 & 56 V., c. 197, L. & P.) Lond., 1892, fol.   L. Eng. A 69 c. 6

2851. An act to confirm certain provisional orders of the Local government board [in connection with the compulsory purchase clauses of the Land clauses acts] relating to the urban sanitary districts of Bristol, Dover, Henley-upon-Thames [&c.] (57 & 58 V., c. 21, L. & P.) Lond., 1894, fol. 19 pp. L. Eng. A 69 c. 6

2852. An act to confirm certain provisional orders of the Local government board relating to the . . . Henley and Wallingford (Wallingford and Crowmarsh; Whitchurch and district joint hospital) districts. (4 E. VII, c. 44, L. & P.) Lond., 1904, fol. 26 pp.
L. Eng. A 69 c. 6

2853. An act to incorporate a body of conservators for the preservation and management as public open spaces of certain commons in the rural district of Henley. . . . (6 E. VII, c. 184, L. & P.) Lond., 1906, fol. 12 pp. L. Eng. A 69 c. 6

2854. An act to confirm certain provisional orders of the Local government board relating to the . . . Henley and Wallingford joint smallpox hospital. (5 & 6 G. V, c. 94, L. & P.) Lond., 1915, fol. 19 pp.
L. Eng. A 69 c. 6

2855. Oxfordshire county council. Local government act, 1933, section 141. The County of Oxford (alteration of rural parishes) (No. 1) Order, 1951. Parishes in the Henley rural district. [Oxf.], (1951), 8°. 22 pp. L. Eng. B 33 d. Parishes 1

Natural History

2856. STRICKLAND, H. E., A list of some land and freshwater species of shells which have been found in the neighbourhood of Henley on Thames. (Mag. of nat. hist., 1834, vol. 7, p. 494–95.)
Per. 1996 e. 155

2857. WHITE, H. J. O., Notes on the westleton beds near Henley-on-Thames. (Proc., Geol. assoc., 1892, vol. 12, p. 379–84.) Radcl.

2858. WHITE, H. J. O., Excursion to Henley. (Proc., Geol. assoc., 1903–4, vol. 18, p. 414–18.) Radcl.

2859. JUKES-BROWNE, A. J., and WHITE, H. J. O., The geology of the country around Henley-on-Thames and Wallingford. (Mem., Geol. survey.) Lond., 1908, 4°. 113 pp. Radcl.

2860. HAWKINS, H. L., Excursion to Henley and Watlington. (Proc., Geol. assoc., 1912, vol. 23, p. 250–53.) Radcl.

Newspapers

See 1340 Henley Advertiser.
1341 Henley and South Oxfordshire Standard.
1342 Henley Chronicle.
1343 Henley Express.
1344 Henley Free Press.

Public Utilities

2861. An act for incorporating & conferring powers on the Henley-on-Thames Gas company. (51 & 52 V., c. 75, L. & P.) Lond., 1888, fol. 20 pp.   L. Eng. A 69 c. 6

2862. An act to confirm certain provisional orders made by the Board of Trade under the Gas and Water works facilities act 1870 relating to Frimley and Farnborough District water, Henley-on-Thames water [&c.]. . . . (1 E. VII, c. 164, L. & P.) Lond., 1901, fol. 27 pp.   L. Eng. A 69 c. 6

2863. An act to confirm certain provisional orders made by the Board of Trade under the Electric lighting acts 1882 and 1888 relating to Aylesbury . . . Henley-on-Thames [&c.]. . . . (6 E. VII, c. 129, L. & P.) Lond., 1906, fol. 47 pp.   L. Eng. A 69 c. 6

2864. An act to confirm certain provisional orders made by the Board of Trade . . . relating to . . . Henley-on-Thames water [&c.] (2 & 3 G. V, c. 163, L. & P.) Lond., 1912, fol. 57 pp.   L. Eng. A 69 c. 6

2865. An act to confirm a provisional order of the Minister of Health relating to Henley-on-Thames water. (22 & 23 G.V, c. 62, L. & P.) Lond., 1932, fol. 26 pp.   L. Eng. A 69 c. 6

Regatta

2866. Reminiscences of Henley regatta, by an Oxford man. [Extr. from Bentley's miscellany, vol. 34.] n. pl., [1853], 8°. 4 pp.   G.A. Oxon 4° 354 (2)

2867. Henley royal regatta, the official programme. 1886–. Henley, 1886–, 16°.   Per. 38442 g. 1

2868. Racing at Henley from reports printed in The 'Field' from 1903 onwards, (to 1913) ed. by T. A. Cook. Lond., 1911(–13), 8°.   38442 e. 25–31

2869. COOK, SIR T., Henley races. Lond., &c., 1919, 8°. 519 pp.   G.A. Oxon 8° 979

2870. COOK, SIR T. A., Rowing at Henley. Lond., &c., 1919, 8°. 182 pp.   38442 e. 33

Schools

2871. A bill to confirm and establish articles of agreement . . . between Archibald Hamilton of the one part and George Parker . . . and other trustees, of a charity therein mention'd of the other part, for exchanging certain lands in . . . Berks belonging to the said charity, for other lands. [For the maintenance of dame Elizabeth Periam's school at Henley.] n. pl., [1725], fol. 3 pp.

L. Eng. C 13 c. 1 (1714–27. 59)

— Act. (11 G. I, c. 8, Private.)

2872. FELL, H. F., Henley free schools on the national system [rules and regulations, signed H. F. Fell]. Henley, 1817, s. sh.

G.A. Oxon c. 317 (22)

2873. National school [to be established at Henley. Prospectus]. Henley, (1817), s. sh. G.A. Oxon c. 317 (22)

2874. Henley-on-Thames national and industrial schools. Report of the committee. 1864. Henley, (1864), 8°. 6 pp.

G.A. Oxon c. 317 (22)

2875. Henley training school for girls. Report. 1863, 1865, 66. n. pl., (1863–66), 4°. G.A. Oxon c. 317 (22)

2876. The book of sports of the Royal Grammar school. 2nd–6th issue. Henley, [1864–68], 8°. G.A. Oxon 8° 900 (38–42)

2877. A brief account of the United Charity schools. Henley, 1834, 8°. 20 pp. G.A. Oxon 8° 900 (36)

2878. Bye laws, orders, statutes, ordinances, rules and regulations . . . by the trustees for the United Charity schools. Henley, 1843, 8°. 23 pp. G.A. Oxon 8° 900 (37)

HENLEY DEANERY

2879. MANNING, P., Monumental brasses in the deanery of Henley-on-Thames. (Journ., Oxf. univ. brass-rubbing soc., 1898, vol. 1, p. 237–54, 286–306.) Soc. 2184 d. 50
— Repr. G.A. Eccl. top. 8° 38 (7, 8)

2880. PRIOR, C. E., Dedications of churches, with some notes as to village feasts and old customs. Deaneries of Aston and Henley. (Rept., Oxf. archaeol. soc., 1906, p. 14–22.) R. Top. 330

2881. PEARCE, S. S., The clergy of the deaneries of Henley and Aston and of the peculiar of Dorchester, during the settlement of 1559 and afterwards. (Rept., Oxf. archaeol. soc., 1918, p. 127–89.)

R. Top. 330

HENSINGTON

2882. An act for confirming articles of agreement and for effecting an exchange of lands [Hensington and Woodstock] between . . . George, Duke of Marlborough and . . . Merton college. . . . (9 G. III, c. 9, Private.) [Lond.], 1769, fol. 6 pp.

L. Eng. C 13 c. 1 (1769. 49)

2883. MARSHALL, E. The early history of Woodstock Manor, and its environs in Bladon, Hensington [&c.] Oxf. &c., 1873, 8°. 474 pp.
G.A. Oxon 8° 177
— Suppl. Oxf., &c., 1874, 8°. 122 pp. G.A. Oxon 8° 193

HENTON

2884. HASSALL, W. O., Henton and Wainhill. (Thame Gazette, Oct. 30, 1951.) N.G.A. Oxon a. 120

HETHE

2885. An act for dividing and enclosing the . . . fields . . . of Heath, otherwise Hethe . . . and for exonerating certain lands belonging to William Fermor esquire, from tithes and right of Common. (12 G. III, c. 103, Private.) n. pl., 1772, fol. 28 pp.
L. Eng. C 13 c. 1 (1772. i. 54)

2886. BLOMFIELD, J. C., History of . . . Hethe [&c.]. (Hist. of . . . deanery of Bicester. Pt. 5. Hethe. 39 pp.) Lond., [1890], 4°.
G.A. Oxon 4° 71

2887. Auction catal. Manor farm. 29 Oct. 1898. G.A. Oxon c. 317 (7)

HEYFORD-AT-BRIDGE

See LOWER HEYFORD

HEYTHROP

2888. An act for annexing the late duke of Shrewsbury's estate to the earldom of Shrewsbury and confirming Gilbert, earl of Shrews-bury's settlement. [Concerns Heythrop &c.] (6 G. I, c. 29, Private.) n. pl., [1720], fol.
— Repr. 1858. 16 pp. L. Eng. C 13 c. 1 (1714–27)
— 43 G. III, c. 40, Private.
— 1 G. IV, c. 40, Private.

2889. Heythorpe . . . the seat of the earl of Shrewsbury. [A description.] n. pl., [c. 1800?], s. sh. G.A. Oxon c. 317 (9)

2890. Places of meeting in the Heythrop hunt. [With map.] n. pl., [c. 1840], sq. 24°. 11 pp. Arch. AA g. 2 (3)

2891. An act for vesting part of the settled estates of . . . John, earl of Shrewsbury [in Heythrop &c.] . . . in trustees to be sold. (6 & 7 V., c. 28, Private.) Lond., 1843, fol. 60 pp.
L. Eng. C 13 c. 1 (1843. i. 28)

2892. List of masters and Hunt servants, and pedigrees of the Heythrop fox hounds, 1835–1886. Chipping Norton, 1886, 8°. 71 pp.
G.A. Oxon 8° 965

2893. North Oxon Benefit nursing association, Heythrop branch. Report for 1897. (Chipping Norton, 1897), fol. 4 pp.
G.A. Oxon c. 317 (9)

2894. Heythrop [house]. (Country Life, 1905, vol. 18, p. 270-76.)
Per. 384 b. 6

2895. BARROW, A. S., The Heythrop. (More shires & provinces, by 'Sabretache', 1928, p. 27-38.) 38445 c. 7

2896. ARKELL, W. J., The building-stones of . . . Heythrop house. . . . (Oxoniensia, 1948, vol. 13, p. 49-54.) R. Top. 340

HOLTON

2897. An act for enabling William Hall . . . to assign or surrender a term of one thousand years in estates [in Holton &c.] . . . unto . . . Elisha Biscoe. (53 G. III, c. 203, L. & P.) Lond., 1813, fol. 4 pp.
L. Eng. A 69 c. 6
See 3873 [Monumental brasses in the church. 1898].

2898. Auction catal. Holton park estate. 19 Nov. 1913.
G.A. Oxon b. 91 (11)

2899. Auction catal. Holton park. 15 July 1925.
G.A. Oxon b. 92* (19)

HOLWELL

2900. BROOKS, E. ST. J., Links with Peter Heylyn and sir Thomas More [Trinder family of Holwell.] (N. & Q., 1927, Feb. 19, p. 129-31.)
Ψ 2. 97

HOOK NORTON

2901. An act for sale of part of the estate of Richard Brideoake . . . and for confirming an agreement made between . . . Richard Brideoake and others, claiming common in Hooknorton Warren and Hook-norton Layes. . . . (9 Anne, c. 43, Private.) n. pl., [1710], fol. 4 pp.
B.M.

2902. An act for dividing and inclosing the . . . fields . . . within . . . Hook-Norton and Southrop. . . . (13 G. III, c. 114, Private.) n. pl., 1773, fol. 22 pp. L. Eng. C 13 c. 1 (1773. 46)

2903. Asylum at Hook Norton. (Rept., Metropolitan commissioners in lunacy, 1844, p. 42, 266.) 15191 d. 22

2904. Hook Norton. (Rept., Oxf. archaeol. soc., 1867, p. 6, 7.)
R. Top. 330

2905. TOMES, R. F., On the fossil corals obtained from the oolite of the railway cuttings near Hook Norton. (Proc., Geol. assoc., 1879, vol. 6, p. 152–65.)   Radcl.

2906. LEEDS, E. T., [Discovery of Romano-Celtic brooch at Hook Norton.] (Proc., Soc. of antiq., 1910, ser. 2, vol. 23, p. 406, 07.)
R. Top. 1

2907. KEYSER, C. E., Notes on the architecture of the churches of Great Rollright, Hook Norton and Wigginton. (Journ., Brit. archaeol. assoc., 1919, new ser., vol. 25, p. 1–23+55 plates.)   R. Top. 4

2908. DICKINS, M., A history of Hook Norton. Banbury, 1928, 4°. 200 pp.   G.A. Oxon 4° 489

2909. ARKELL, W. J., and WHITEHEAD, T. H., Report of a field meeting at Hook Norton and Sibford, Oxfordshire. (Proc., Geol. assoc., 1946, vol. 57, p. 16–18.)   Radcl.

2910. HEMP, W. J., A reused memorial at Hook Norton. (Trans., Monumental brass soc., 1949, vol. 8, p. 205, 06.)   Soc. 2184 d. 85

2911. Auction catal. Manor, Rectory or Mill farm, Hook Norton farm, tythe rents. 11 Nov. 1800.   G.A. fol. A 266 (33)

2912. Auction catal. Southrop farm. 28 May 1913.
G.A. Oxon c. 317 (9)

2913. Auction catal. Hook Norton mill and Southrop small holding. 25 Sept. 1918.   G.A. Oxon b. 92* (8)

HORLEY

2914. An act for dividing and inclosing the . . . fields . . . lying within . . . Horley and Hornton . . . (5 G. III, c. 25, Private.) n. pl., 1765, fol. 27 pp.   G.A. Oxon c. 184

2915. Pedigree of Goodwin of Horley, Oxfordshire. n. pl., [18—], 8°. 8 pp.   G.A. Oxon c. 317 (9)

2916. SEYMOUR, SIR J. H., A plain statement of facts, in a matter in which the parishioners of Horley are interested, by the vicar. [Concerning repairs to the parish church.] Banbury, [1839], 8°. 34 pp.
G.A. Oxon 8° 636 (5)
See 883 [Customs and charities. 1842].

2917. HEAVEN, C., [Letter appealing for funds for repair of schools, church & vicarage in the living of Horley & Hornton.] n. pl., [1879], 4°. 4 pp.   MS. Top. Oxon d. 42 (72)

2918. KEYSER, C. E., A visit to the churches of . . . Hanwell, Horley and Hornton. (Journ., Brit. archaeol. assoc., 1921, new ser., vol. 27, p. 129–58+76 plates.)   R. Top. 4

2919. STOCKTON, A., A history of the parish of Horley. [Typewritten.]
n. pl., 1939, 4°. 46 pp.   G.A. Oxon 4° 593

2920. Auction catal. Freehold cottages. 16 May 1888.
G.A. Oxon b. 85 *b* (40)

2921. Auction catal. Horley manor estate. 28 July 1892.
G.A. Oxon b. 85 *a* (35)

2922. Auction catal. Freehold properties. 2 July 1896.
G.A. Oxon b. 91 (12)

2923. Auction catal. Estate. 19 May 1898.   G.A. Oxon b. 91 (12 *a*)

HORNTON

2924. An act for dividing and inclosing the ... fields ... lying within ...
Horley and Hornton. ... (5 G. III, c. 25, Private.) n. pl., 1765, fol.
27 pp.   G.A. Oxon c. 184

See 2917 [Appeal on behalf of school and church. 1879].

2925. KEYSER, C. E., A visit to the churches of ... Hanwell, Horley and
Hornton. (Journ., Brit. archaeol. assoc., 1921, new ser., vol. 27,
p. 129–58+76 plates.)   R. Top. 4

2926. Auction catal. Estate. 31 Mar. 1864.   G.A. Oxon b. 85 *b* (36)

2927. Auction catal. Hornton manor. 28 July 1892.
G.A. Oxon b. 85 *a* (35)

2928. Auction catal. Hornton house estate. 2 June 1910.
G.A. Oxon b. 91 (13)
— 2nd ed. 26 Apr. 1911.   G.A. Oxon b. 91 (14)

2929. Auction catal. Hornton hill house. 28 Aug. 1912.
G.A. Oxon b. 91 (15)

HORSEPATH

2930. KNOLLIS, F. M., Horspath rent and shoe club [rules, signed
F. M. K.]. Oxf., (1851), s. sh.   G.A. Oxon b. 113 (61)

2931. An act to authorize the inclosure of certain lands ... [Horsepath].
(18 & 19 V., c. 14, Pub.) Lond., 1855, fol. 2 pp.
L. Eng. A 69 c. 1

2932. S. Kenelm's school, Horspath [prospectus]. n. pl., [*c.* 1880], 8°.
2 pp.   G.A. Oxon c. 317 (9)

See 3735 [Windmill, Horspath. 1925].

2933. Auction catal. Land. 19 Jan. 1820.   G.A. fol. B 71

2934. Auction catal. Agricultural estate of T. B. Morrell. 20 June 1903.
G.A. Oxon b. 91 (16)

2935. Auction catal. Horspath manor house. 16 July 1903.
G.A. Oxon b. 91 (17)

2936. Auction catal. Pasture land. 28 June 1913.
G.A Oxon b. 92 (22)

HORTON CUM STUDLEY

2937. An act for appointing jointures for the wives and . . . portions for
the younger children of . . . Willoughby, earl of Abingdon, and . . .
Peregrine Bertie his brother. [Horton &c.] (9 G. III, sess. 2, c. 10,
Private.) n. pl., 1769, fol. 43 pp. G.A. Oxon c. 192

See 1241 [Croke family. 1823].

2938. An act for inclosing lands . . . of Beckley [Horton and Studley].
(7 & 8 G. IV, c. 15, Private.) (Lond.), 1827, fol. 31 pp.
L. Eng. C 13 c. 1 (1827. i. 9)

2939. Studley 'Hand in glove' benefit society. Rules. Oxf., (1872), 8°.
10 pp. G.A. Oxon 8° 688 (1)

2940. Studley priory. (Country Life, 1908, vol. 24, p. 54–62.)
Per. 384 b. 6

2941. The visitation of the priory of Studley, 26 May 1445. (Cant. and
York soc., 1927, vol. 33, p. 361, 62.) R. 8. 26
— [Another issue.] (Lincoln record soc., 1929, vol. 21, p. 361, 62.)
R. Top. 260

2942. Visitations. Studley priory. (i) 26 April 1520. (ii) 20 Sept. 1530.
(Lincoln record soc., 1947, vol. 37, p. 107, 08.) R. Top. 260

See 1636 [Horton infirmary for Banbury. Rules. 1877].
See 1713A [Sir G. Croke's charity. 1880].

2943. Auction catal. Horton estates, with manor. 16 July 1844.
G.A. fol. A 266 (25)

2944. Auction catal. Studley priory estate. [3 eds.] 19 June 1897.
G.A. Oxon b. 85 *b* (51–53)

2945. Auction catal. Entire parish. 25 June 1919.
G.A. Oxon b. 92* (4)

HOWBERY PARK

2946. Auction catal. Howbery park. 20 June 1899; 17 June 1901.
G.A. Oxon b. 90 (26, 28)

2947. Auction catal. Village and manor. 28 May 1902.
G.A. Oxon b. 6 (35)

IDBURY

2948. An act for dividing and inclosing the ... fields ... of Idbury [&c.] (19 G. III, c. 78, Private.) n. pl., 1779, fol. 16 pp.
L. Eng. C 13 c. 1 (1779. ii. 12)

2949. MARSHALL, E., Idbury in ancient times. (Berks, Bucks, & Oxon archaeol. journ., 1895, vol. 1, p. 53–54.) R. Top. 100

2950. BUTLER, C. V., Village survey-making, an Oxfordshire experiment. [Relates to Idbury &c.] (Board of educ., educ. pamph. 61.) Lond., 1928, 8°. 36 pp.+4 maps. 2621 e. 187 (61)

2951. JONES, J. K., A village survey [Idbury]. [Reprod. from typewriting.] n. pl., (1933), 4°. O.C.L.

IFFLEY

General

2952. Iffley. (Gent's. mag., 1791, pt. 1, p. 499; 1818, pt. 2, p. 9, 232.)
Ψ 2. 44

2953. Church of S. Mary-the-Virgin, Iffley. [An account of the church.] (Oxf.), [18—], 4°. 4 pp. G.A. Oxon c. 317 (9)

2954. An historical and descriptive account of ... Iffley. Oxf., [18—], 8°. 12 pp. G.A. Oxon 8° 147 (18)

2955. An act for inclosing lands within the township or liberty of Yeftley, otherwise Iffley. (55 G. III, c. 102, Private.) [Lond.], (1815), fol. 25 pp. L. Eng. B 53 c. Land 3

2956. INGRAM, J., Iffley church and parish. (Memorials of Oxf., vol. 3.) Oxf., 1837, 8°. 16 pp. G.A. Oxon 8° 20

2957. PARKER, J. H., St. Mary's church, Iffley. (Archaeol. journ., 1847, vol. 4, p. 218–25.) R. Top. 5

2957A. Iffley rowing club. Rules. n. pl., [18—], s. sh.
G.A. Oxon c. 317 (9)

2958. MARSHALL, E., An account of the township of Iffley ... from the earliest notice. Oxf., &c., 1870, 8°. 164 pp. G.A. Oxon 8° 150
— 2nd issue, with additions. 1874. 176 pp. G.A. Oxon 8° 185

2959. An act to confirm certain provisional orders of the Local government board [concerning sewage works and distribution] relating to the districts of ... Oxford [Iffley &c.] ... (37 & 38 V., c. 182, L. & P.) Lond., 1874, fol. 23 pp. L. Eng. A 69 c. 6

See 1020 [Act concerning the supply of water. 1875].

2959A. Iffley parish. Statement of monies received and disbursed in 1880. Oxf., (1881), 4°. 4 pp. G.A. Oxon c. 317 (9)

2960. DRINKWATER, H., St. Mary's church, Iffley. (Journ., Brit. archaeol. assoc., 1891, vol. 47, p. 58–60.) R. Top. 4

2961. Iffley reading room [notice by the committee appointed to establish a club &c.]. n. pl., [1895?], s. sh. G.A. Oxon c. 23 (53)

2962. TAUNT, H. W., Iffley mill and its story. 2nd ed. Oxf., [1908], 8°. 15 pp. G.A. Oxon 8° 755 (1)
— 3rd ed., with additions. [1909.] 20 pp. G.A. Oxon 8° 755 (2)

2963. TAUNT, H. W., Iffley manor, church, and village. Oxf., [1909], 8°. 32 pp. G.A. Oxon 8° 755 (3)

2964. [St. Mary's church and the manor, Iffley.] (Trans., Bristol and Glouc. archaeol. soc., 1911, vol. 34, p. 18–21.) R. Top. 210

2965. S. Mary the Virgin, Iffley. [Extr. from the architect's report, and an appeal for funds to repair the church.] n. pl., (1911), 4°. 4 pp. G.A. Oxon c. 317 (9)

2966. ÖSTBERG, R., I discover England [Iffley church]. (Architect. journ., 1928, 11 Jan., p. 38–41.) N. 1863 c. 12

2967. An act to extend the boundaries of the city of Oxford and for other purposes [affecting Iffley &c.]. (18 & 19 G. V, c. 84, L. & P.) Lond., 1928, 8°. 68 pp. L. Eng. A 69 c. 6

2968. PARKES, G. D., and M., May day at Iffley. Oxf., 1934, 8°. 11 pp. 2806 e. 91 (11)

2698A. Auction catal. 'Freelands'. 2 Apr. 1919. G.A. Oxon c. 317 (9)

Charity School

2969. THOMAS, V., Thirty-seven reasons . . . for an early hearing of the case of mrs. Sarah Nowell's charity school, Iffley. Oxf., 1854, 8°. 20 pp. G.A. Oxon 8° 199 (20)

2970. THOMAS, V., The case of mrs. Sarah Nowell's endowed charity school for girls, in . . . Iffley . . . stated in a letter of complaint. Oxf., 1854, 8°. 34 pp. G.A. Oxon 8° 199 (19)

2971. THOMAS, V., A letter . . . to archdeacon Clerke, W. W. Woollcombe, H. Walsh, feoffees of the land and schoolhouse of mrs Sarah Nowell's school, Iffley. Oxf., 1854, 8°. 16 pp.
G.A. Oxon 8° 274

2972. THOMAS, V., A letter of complaint . . . in the case of mrs. Sarah Nowell's endowed charity school, Iffley. Oxf., 1855, 8°. 32 pp.
G.A. Oxon 8° 199 (22)

2973. Rules for Nowell scholars [at Mrs. Nowell's charity school, Iffley]. n. pl., 1880, s. sh. G.A. Oxon c. 317 (9)

Lock

2974. Copy of a letter . . . by the Conservators of the river Thames . . . in reference to the withdrawal of certain clauses of the Thames navigation bill [concerning the removal of flood waters at and above Oxford]. n. pl., 1870, s. sh. G.A. Oxon c. 317 (1)

2975. Form of petition presented to the Thames conservators, and to the Thames valley drainage commissioners (deprecating the removal of Iffley lock). n. pl., (1885), s. sh. G.A. Oxon c. 317 (1)

2976. FAUSSETT, R. G., The proposed abolition of Iffley lock [letter, signed R. G. Faussett]. n. pl., (1885), s. sh.
G.A. Oxon c. 317 (1)

2977. Thames valley drainage. Removal of Iffley lock. Reports and letters. Oxf., 1885, 8°. 43 pp. G.A. Oxon 8° 375

2978. CHILD, G. W., The removal of Iffley lock considered in relation to the health of Oxford. Oxf., 1885, 8°. 11 pp. 15012 e. 34

2979. Thames valley drainage. Report of the special committee appointed by the Thames valley drainage Commissioners . . . 12th June, 1886, to consider . . . the memorandum opposing the removal of Iffley lock. (Cirencester, 1886), 8°. 9 pp.
G.A. Eng. rivers 8° 5 a

IPSDEN

2980. FIELD, J. E., The Stapleton brass at Ipsden. (Berks, Bucks, & Oxon archaeol. journ., 1909, vol. 14, p. 107–10.) R. Top. 100

2981. KEYSER, C. E., Notes on the churches of Ipsden [&c.]. (Journ., Brit. archaeol. assoc., 1918, new ser., vol. 24, p. 1–32+67 plates.)
R. Top. 4

2982. D'ALMAINE, H. G. W., The Devil's ninepins, Ipsden. [A 19th century imitation of a Druid's temple.] (Proc., Soc. of antiq., 1919/20, 2nd ser., vol. 32, p. 111, 12.) R. Top. 1

2983. Auction catal. Arable and wood lands. 18 Sept. 1896.
G.A. Oxon b. 91 (4)

2984. Auction catal. Homer estate. 3 Sept. 1898.
G.A. Oxon b. 91 (18)
— 18 June 1900. G.A. Oxon b. 91 (19)

2985. Auction catal. Pocock's and Hailey farms. 21 Sept. 1900.
G.A. Oxon b. 92 (5)

2986. Auction catal. Little Stoke estate.
— 22 July 1901. G.A. Oxon b. 92 (2)
— 7 Sept. 1917. G.A. Oxon b. 92 (3)

2987. Auction catal. Basset and Ipsden woods. 23 Sept. 1910.
G.A. Oxon b. 91 (20)

ISLIP

See 412 [Sir S. Luke's victory at Islip. 1644].

2988. Islip. (Gent's. mag., 1788, pt. 2, p. 1051, 52, 1149; 1795, pt. 1, p. 459; 1861, pt. 1, p. 285.) Ψ 2. 44

2989. An act for inclosing lands in the parish of Islip. (44 G. III, c. 67, Private.) n. pl., 1804, fol. 19 pp. G.A. Oxon 4° 506

2990. PHILLIPPS, J. O. HALLIWELL-, Ancient paintings in the interior of Islip church. (Archaeologia, 1842, vol. 29, p. 420.) R. Top. 7

See 486, 87 [Railway. 1846, 1850].

2991. PHILLIPPS, J. O. HALLIWELL-, Notices of the history and antiquities of Islip. [Also appeared as no. 2992.] Lond., 1849, 8°. 15 pp. G.A. Oxon 8° 946

2992. PHILLIPPS, J. O. HALLIWELL-, Historical notices of Islip. (Journ., Brit. archaeol. assoc., 1850, vol. 5, p. 39–51.) R. Top. 4

2993. Islip. (Rept., Oxf. archaeol. soc., 1900, p. 17.) R. Top. 330

2994. MILLER, E., The history of the village of Islip. Oxf., 1930, 4°. 20 pp. G.A. Oxon 4° 505 (7)

2995. Three Westminster writs of king Edward the confessor [ed. by F. E. Harmer. Writ no. 2 concerns Islip and Marston]. (Engl. hist. review, 1936, vol. 51, p. 99, 102.) Ψ 2. 38

2996. Islip. (Archaeol. notes. Oxoniensia, 1937, p. 203.) R. Top. 340

See 31 [Stratigraphy at Islip. 1944].

2996A. SEABY, W. A., Late Dark Age finds from the Cherwell [near Magdalen bridge] and Ray [at Islip], 1876–86. (Oxoniensia, 1950, vol. 15, p. 29–43.) R. Top. 340

2997. Auction catal. Estate. 10 July 1849. G.A. Oxon b. 91 (46)

2998. Auction catal. Freehold properties. 17 Mar. 1921.
G.A. Oxon c. 317 (9)

2999. Auction catal. The Hall. 28 June 1933. G.A. Oxon c. 224*

ISLIP DEANERY

3000. PRIOR, C. E., Dedications of churches, with some notes as to village feasts and old customs. Deaneries of Islip & Bicester. (Rept., Oxf. archaeol. soc., 1903, p. 20–42.) R. Top. 330

KELMSCOTT

3001. An act for dividing, allotting and inclosing the . . . fields . . . of Kelmscot. . . . (38 G. III, c. 27, Private.) n. pl., 1798, fol. 26 pp.
L. Eng. C 13 c. 1 (1798. i. 20)

3002. MORRIS, W., Gossip about an old house on the upper Thames [Kelmscott manor]. New York, 1901, 16°. 26 pp.
G.A. Oxon 16° 159

3003. PAINTIN, H., Three village churches, Broughton-Pogis, Kelmscott, and Little Faringdon. Oxf., 1913, 4°. 21 pp.
G.A. Oxon 4° 262 (5)

3004. Kelmscott farm dairy. The achievement of an ideal [description of farm &c.]. [Lond., 1917?], obl. 8°. 14 pp.   G.A. Oxon 8° 977

3005. Kelmscott manor and William Morris. (Architect. rev., 1919, Apr., p. 67–69.)
Per. 17356 c. 8

3006. MORE, C., Kelmscott manor. (Country Life, 1921, vol. 50, p. 224–29, 256–61.)
Per. 384 b. 6

3007. Kelmscott church mural paintings. (Archaeol. notes. Oxoniensia, 1936, p. 202.)
R. Top. 340

See 4208A [Kelmscott manor in 'English country houses' by C. Hussey. 1951].

3008. WILLIAMS, A., Squire Turner's weird, a legend of Kelmscott Manor house. Cirencester, n.d., 8°. 8 pp.

3009. Auction catal. Broadwell and Kelmscott manor. 11 Nov. 1802.
G.A. fol. A 273*

3010. Auction catal. Manor farm and Plough inn. 23 July 1898.
G.A. Oxon b. 91 (21)

KENCOTT

3011. An act for dividing and inclosing . . . fields . . . in . . . Kencott. . . . (7 G. III, c. 6, Private.) n. pl., 1767, fol. 20 pp.
L. Eng. C 13 c. 1 (1767, p. 834)

3012. PAINTIN, H., Three Oxfordshire churches, Kencot, Broadwell and Langford. Oxf., 1911, 4°. 24 pp.   G.A. Oxon 4° 276 (16)

See 325 [Note on discovery of stone axe, by E. T. Leeds. 1938].

3013. Auction catal. Malthouse farm. 28 July 1910.
G.A. Oxon c. 317 (10)

3014. Auction catal. Kencot manor. 25 July 1923.
G.A. Oxon c. 224 (12)

KIDDINGTON

See 498 [Turnpike act. 1730, &c.].

3015. WARTON, T., Specimen of a history of Oxfordshire [Kiddington]. n. pl., 1782, 4°. 43 pp.   G.A. Oxon 4° 455 (2)
— 2nd ed. 1783. 71 pp.   G.A. Oxon 4° 455 (3)
— 3rd ed. [*entitled*] The history and antiquities of Kiddington. 1815. 82 pp.   G.A. Oxon c. 248

3016. Pedigree of the family of Babington of Kiddington. (Topogr. and geneal., 1846, vol. 1, p. 265–76.) Ψ 2. 10 *b*

3017. BUSBY, G., Memorial lines on Kiddington turnpike house. [In verse.] (Heyford, 1879), s. sh.   G.A. Oxon 8° 963 (1)

3018. BUSBY, G., Oxfordshire village [Kiddington] rhymes. Lond., 1899, 12°. 12 pp.   G.A. Oxon 16° 72

3019. The Catholic registers of the domestic chapel of the Browne-Mostyn family at Kiddington, 1788–1840, contributed by H. H. Ball, hist. notes by mrs B. Stapleton. (Publ., Cath. rec. soc., vol. 17, p. 455–78.) Lond., 1915, 4°.   G.A. Gen. top. 4° 220 (17)

3020. NORWOOD, R. P., A squirearchy for more than 600 years, a history of Kiddington. Long Compton, 1934, 4°. 43 pp.
       G.A. Oxon 4° 504 (4)

3021. SUTHERLAND, C. H. V., A late Roman hoard from Kiddington. (Num. chron., 1936, ser. 5, vol. 16, p. 82–87.)   Num. 03 d. 10

3022. SUTHERLAND, C. H. V., A late Roman coin-hoard from Kiddington. (Oxoniensia, 1936, p. 70–80.)   R. Top. 340

3023. Auction catal. Freehold estate. 21 Jan. 1802.
       G.A. fol. A 266 (34)

KIDLINGTON

3024. An act for confirming a partition made between Robert Dashwood . . . and Cholmley Turner . . . of certain . . . lands . . . [in Kidlington &c.]. (3 G. I, c. 22, Private.) n. pl., 1717, fol. 7 pp.
       B.M.

See 502, 505, 521, 527 [Turnpike acts. 1751, &c.].

3025. An act for inclosing lands . . . of Kidlington. . . . (50 G. III, c. 158, Private.) n. pl., 1810, fol. 23 pp.
       L. Eng. C 13 c. 1 (1810. i)

3026. Kidlington friendly society. Rules. Oxf., 1839, 8°. 34 pp.
       G.A. Oxon 8° 942

See 486, 87 [Railway. 1846].

3027. WING, W., Annals of Kidlington and its annexes, Campsfield, Gosford, Thrupp, and Watereaton. Repr. from the Oxf. chronicle. (Oxf.), 1881, 8°. 31 pp.   G.A. Oxon 8° 220 (5)

3028. Rules and schedule of the Kidlington poultry . . . and dog show. (28th–30th annual shows.) Kidlington, 1887–89, 8°.
G.A. Oxon 8° 856

3029. STAPLETON, MRS. B., Three Oxfordshire parishes. A history of Kidlington, Yarnton, and Begbroke. (Oxf. hist. soc., vol. 24.) Oxf., 1893, 8°. 400 pp.   R. 13. 700

See 1970 [Monumental brasses in the church. 1898].

3030. PAINTIN, H., Haydn's 'Creation' at the Church of St. Mary, Kidlington, Thursday, July 11th, 1907, with a few notes on the architecture of the church. Oxf., (1907), 4°. 3 pp.
G.A. Oxon 4° 186 (27)

3031. FYNMORE, R. J., Kidlington. [A letter about some of his ancestors.] (Berks, Bucks, & Oxon archaeol. journ., 1914, vol. 20, p. 94–96.)   R. Top. 100

3032. KURSBATT, I., The Kidlington bridges. (Journ., Inst. of civil engineers, 1939/40, vol. 13, p. 237–52; vol. 14, p. 524–26.)
Soc. 18611 e. 156

3033. NICHOLSON, P., Family album. 1st ed. [Reminiscences of Kidlington? in the late 19th and early 20th century, p. 1–34.] Lond., 1943, 8°.   211 e. 1033

3034. CHAMBERLAIN, F. W., Notes on local government in Kidlington. [Reprod. from typescript.] n. pl., 1946, 4°. 11 pp.   O.C.L.

3035. FREEBORN, H., The parish church of St. Mary, Kidlington; the history and architecture. (Brackley), [1947], 8°. 36 pp.
G.A. Oxon 8° 1204 (5)

3036. Kidlington. (Archaeol. notes. Oxoniensia, 1949, vol. 14, p. 76.)
R. Top. 340

3037. Auction catal. Tenement, formerly a public house, called The Old Crown. 17 Apr. 1811.   G.A. fol. B 71

3038. Auction catal. Estate. 6 Sept. 1848.   G.A. Oxon c. 317 (5)

3039. Auction catal. Estate. 31 May 1899.   G.A. Oxon b. 91 (37)

3040. Sale catal. St. Mary's lodge. [1904.]   G.A. Oxon c. 317 (10)

3041. Auction catal. Estate. 15 June 1910.   G.A. Oxon c. 317 (9)

3042. Auction catal. Freehold properties. 24 May 1911.
G.A. Oxon c. 317 (10)

3043. Auction catal. 'The Hill'. 17 Sept. 1913.
G.A. Oxon c. 256 (20)

3044. Sale catal. Grove house. [c. 1918].   G.A. Oxon c. 317 (10)

3045. Auction catal. Mill farm house, mill and house. 22 Sept. 1920.
G.A. Oxon c. 317 (10)

3046. Auction catal. Portions of Blenheim estate, comprising Gosford Hill farm, Manor farm, Village farm. 14 July 1920.
G.A. Oxon b. 92* (3)

KIDMORE END

3047. BUTLER, C. V., Village survey-making, an Oxfordshire experiment. [Relates to Kidmore End &c.] (Board of educ., educ. pamph. 61.) Lond., 1928, 8°. 36 pp.+4 maps.   2621 e. 187 (61)

3048. MASTERS, J. E. SMITH-, The history of Kidmore End [&c.]. (Leighton Buzzard, 1933), 8°. 87 pp.   G.A. Oxon 8° 1131

3049. Auction catal. Farm. 13 May 1824.   G.A. fol. B 71

KINGHAM

See 489 [Railway. 1860].

3050. An earnest appeal [to the Oddfellows and others at Kingham to raise a fund to settle in a business the widow of John Slatter, secretary of the Oddfellows club at Moreton-in-the-Marsh]. Kingham, 1881, s. sh.   MS. Eng. hist. d. 39 (515)

3051. FOWLER, W. W., Study of a typical mediæval village [Kingham]. (Quarterly journ. of econ., 1895, vol. 9, p. 151–74.)
Per 23211 d. 32
— Repr.   G.A. Oxon 4° 377

3052. FOWLER, W. W., Acrocephalus palustris [marsh warbler at Kingham] a breeding record of fourteen years. (Zoologist, 1906, no. 785, p. 401–09.)   Radcl.
— [Repr.]   G.A. Oxon 8° 976

3053. FOWLER, W. W., Kingham old and new. Oxf., &c., 1913, 8°. 216 pp.   G.A. Oxon 8° 873

3054. JARVIS, A. F., Fifty years of Kingham Hill, 1886–1936. Kingham Hill, 1936, 8°. 102 pp.   G.A. Oxon 8° 1165

3055. Kingham war record, 1939–1945. n. pl., [1948], 8°. 8 pp.
G.A. Oxon 8° 1204 (7)

See 449 [Estates of New college, 1659–75, p. 46–70].

KINGSEY

See 635 [Boundaries. 1895].

3056. An act to confirm a provisional order of the Minister of Health relating to the counties of Buckingham and Oxford [transferring Kingsey to Bucks and part of Towersey to Oxfordshire]. (23 G. V, c. 3, L. & P.) Lond., 1933, 8°. 29 pp.   L. Eng. A 69 c. 6

KINGSTON BLOUNT

3057. An act for vesting the real estate of Thomas Reade and Elizabeth Reade . . . situate in . . . Kingston Blount [&c.] . . . in Thomas, earl of Macclesfield. . . . (28 G. III, c. 6, Private.) n. pl., 1788, fol. 10 pp.
L. Eng. C 13 c. 1 (1788. 49)

3058. BROOKS, E. ST. J., Sir Thomas Blount, executed in 1400, and the Blounts of Kingston Blount. (Misc. geneal. et herald., 1929/31, 5th ser., vol. 7, p. 73–83, 114–24, 158–76, 215–22, 254–74, 315–25.)
Ψ 2. 10 f

3059. HASSALL, W. O., Dissent at . . . Kingston Blount [&c.]. (Thame Gazette, Jan. 30, 1951.)   N.G.A. Oxon a. 120

KIRTLINGTON

3060. An act for inclosing lands . . . of Kirtlington. . . . (51 G. III, c. 160, Private.) n. pl., 1811, fol. 22 pp.   L. Eng. C 13 c. 1 (1811. i)

3061. SAUNDERS, W. W., List of a few rare or interesting plants noticed in the neighbourhood of Kirtlington. (Magazine of nat. hist., 1839, new ser., vol. 3, p. 239–42.)   Per. 1996 e. 155

3062. British Association. Report of the committee . . . appointed to examine the ground [at Kirtlington] from which the remains of the Cetiosaurus in the Oxford museum were obtained, with a view to determining whether other parts of the same animal remain in the rock. [Extr. from Report, 1895.] [Lond., 1895], 8°. 2 pp.
G.A. Oxon 4° 375 (8)

3063. TAUNT, H. W., Kirtlington, Oxon., illustrated. (Oxf.), [1905], 8°. 40 pp.   G.A. Oxon 8° 718

See 362 [Manor. Survey of 1387. 1910].

3064. D., A., Kirtlington Park. (Country Life, 1912, vol. 31, p. 542–49.)
Per. 384 b. 6

3065. PARRY, T. R. GAMBIER-, A Tudor manor [Kirtlington]. (Bodleian quarterly rec., 1927, vol. 5, p. 179–88.)   R. 13. 178 f
— Repr.   G.A. Oxon 4° 403* (15)

3066. Kirtlington park, Kirtlington church. (Rept., Oxf. archaeol. soc., 1933, p. 16, 17, 20.)   R. Top. 330

3067. Kirtlington. Aves ditch. (Archaeol. notes. Oxoniensia, 1937, p. 202; 1946/7, p. 162.)   R. Top. 340

3068. Auction catal. Dashwood arms. 15 Sept. 1894.
G.A. Oxon b. 92 (43)

3069. Auction catal. Kirtlington estate. 15 June 1922.
G.A. Oxon c. 224 (11)

LANGFORD

3070. An act for inclosing lands . . . of Langford. (48 G. III, c. 54, Private.) n. pl., 1808, fol. 27 pp.   L. Eng. C 13 c. 1 (1808. i. 50)
— 50 G. III, c. 90, Private.

3071. TURNER, T., Unusual doorways in old buildings. [Langford church.] (Archaeol. journ., 1890, vol. 47, p. 58, 59.)   R. Top. 5

3072. WODEHOUSE, C. G., Church of St. Matthew, Langford. (Faringdon, 1900), 8°. 6 pp.   G.A. Oxon 8° 966

3073. PAINTIN, H., Three Oxfordshire churches, Kencot, Broadwell and Langford. Oxf., 1911, 4°. 24 pp.   G.A. Oxon 4° 276 (16)

3074. Langford church. (Rept., Oxf. archaeol. soc., 1935, p. 62.)
R. Top. 330

3075. WILLIAMS, A., Excavations at Langford downs . . . in 1943. (Oxoniensia, 1946–7, p. 44–64.)   R. Top. 340

LANGFORD (Peculiar jurisdiction of)

3076. PEARCE, S. S., The clergy of the deanery of Cuddesdon and of the peculiars of Langford, Thame and Great Milton during the settlement of 1559 and afterwards. (Rept., Oxf. archaeol. soc., 1920, p. 242–89.)   R. Top. 330

LANGLEY

3077. MACNAMARA, F. N., Historic houses. King John's palace at Little Langley, Oxfordshire. (Berks, Bucks, & Oxon archaeol. journ., 1899, vol. 5, p. 9–21, 44–47.)   R. Top. 100

LATCHFORD

3078. A bill for vesting the equity of redemption of the mannor . . . of Great Haseley with . . . lands in Haseley and Latchford . . . the estate of William Lenthall . . . to be sold for the discharging of incumbrances thereupon. n. pl., [1707], fol. 4 pp.   G.A. Oxon c. 247 (6)
— Act. (6 Anne, c. 23, Private.)

LAUNTON

3079. An act for inclosing lands . . . of Launton. . . . (50 G. III, c. 89, Private.) n. pl., 1810, fol. 25 pp.   L. Eng. C 13 c. 1 (1810. 2)

3080. Auction catal. 1750 trees on estate of F. J. Staples-Browne. 27 Feb. 1873.   G.A. Oxon 8° 959

3081. Auction catal. Hare Leys and Holly Breatch farms. 16 Aug. 1907.
G.A. Oxon b. 91 (24)

3082. Auction catal. Hare Leys farm. 12 June 1908.
G.A. Oxon b. 91 (25)

3083. Auction catal. Langleys farm. 2 May 1919.
G.A. Oxon c. 224 (3)

3084. Auction catal. Agricultural holdings. 9 June 1920.
G.A. Oxon c. 317 (10)

3085. Auction catal. Grassland and cottage property, including Spoil Bank field and the copyhold field. 4 Feb. 1921.
G.A. Oxon c. 317 (10)

LEAFIELD

3086. An act to authorize the inclosure of certain lands . . . [Leafield]. (21 V., c. 8, Pub.) Lond., 1858, fol. 2 pp.   L. Eng. A 69 c. 1

3087. An act to authorize the inclosure of certain lands . . . [Leafield]. (21 & 22 V., c. 61, Pub.) Lond., 1858, fol. 2 pp.
L. Eng. A 69 c. 1

3088. Coate and Leafield colportage assoc. Annual report. 1876–7. n. pl., 1877, 4°. 4 pp.   G.A. Oxon 4° 208 (34)

3089. (Records of the war activities of the inhabitants of . . . Leafield during 1939–1945, by a member of the Leafield Women's institute.) n. pl., [1948], 8°. 10 pp.   G.A. Oxon 8° 1184 (5)

3090. Auction catal. Cottage and land. 25 Aug. 1919.
G.A. Oxon c. 224 (6)

LEDWELL

3091. An act concerning certain estates heretofore of Francis Keck . . . in . . . Oxford and Wilts . . . [Leadwell &c.] . . . (18 G. III, c. 109, Private.) n. pl., 1778, fol. 46 pp.   L. Eng. C 13 c. 1 (1778. ii. 8)

3092. LONEY, J. E., A walk through a North Oxfordshire village, a sketch of the history of Sandford and hamlet of Ledwell. Oxf., 1925, 8°. 16 pp.   G.A. Oxon 8° 1046 (12)

3093. Auction catal. Ledwell house. 11 July 1893.
G.A. Oxon b. 6 (24)
— 3 Nov. 1948. G.A. Oxon b. 92* (ii)

3094. Auction catal. Outlying portions of Sandford park estate. 23 Sept. 1920. G.A. Oxon c. 224 (9)

LEWKNOR

3095. An act for vesting the real estate of Thomas Reade and Elizabeth Reade . . . situate in . . . Lewknor [&c.] . . . in Thomas, earl of Macclesfield. . . . (28 G. III, c. 6, Private.) n. pl., 1788, fol. 10 pp.
L. Eng. C 13 c. 1 (1788. 49)

3096. An act for inclosing lands . . . of Lewknor and Postcomb . . . (50 G. III, c. 157, Private.) n. pl., 1810, fol. 25 pp.
L. Eng. C 13 c. 1 (1810. 2)

3097. An act for inclosing lands in . . . Chalgrove [and Lewknor Mead]. (6 & 7 V., c. 7, Private.) n. pl., 1843, fol. 42 pp.
L. Eng. C 13 c. 1 (1843. 7)

3098. Lewknor. (Rept., Oxf. archaeol. soc., 1886, p. 1–7.)
R. Top. 330

3099. Auction catal. Farm, cottages and blacksmith's shop. 24 Jan. 1820.
G.A. fol. B 71

3100. Auction catal. Watercraft farm, Pound farm, Kensham farm, and Dell manor. 10 Aug. 1859. G.A. Oxon b. 92* (22)

3101. Auction catal. Aston Rowant estate. Cadmore estate. 30 Oct. 1889. G.A. Oxon b. 85 *a* (2)
— Aston Rowant & Cadmore estates. 22 July 1890.
G.A. Oxon b. 85 *a* (3)
— Aston Rowant estate. 1 July 1891. G.A. Oxon b. 85 *a* (4)

3102. Auction catal. Blenham farm. 30 Oct. 1889.
G.A. Oxon b. 92* (26)
— 22 July 1890. G.A. Oxon b. 92* (28)
— 1 July 1891. G.A. Oxon b. 92* (ii. 1)

3103. Auction catal. Moor and Beacon farms. 31 Oct. 1889.
G.A. Oxon b. 92* (27)

3104. Auction catal. Thame park estate. 24, 25 Sept. 1917.
G.A. Oxon b. 92 (23)

LIDSTONE

3105. Auction catal. 2 cottages. 25 Aug. 1919. G.A. Oxon c. 224 (6)

LITTLE BARFORD

See BARFORD ST. JOHN

LITTLE BOURTON

3106. An act for vesting the two undivided fourth parts, of Priscilla Allett [and others] . . . children of Alice Warner . . . of . . . the manors . . . of Great Bourton and Little Bourton . . . in trustees to sell. . . . (10 G. III, c. 84, Private.) n. pl., 1770, fol. 18 pp.
L. Eng. C 13 c. 1 (1770. 4)

3107. An act for dividing and inclosing the . . . field and commonable lands lying within . . . Great Bourton and Little Bourton. (17 G. III, c. 74, Private.) n. pl., [1777], fol. 31 pp.   G.A. Oxon c. 113 (5)

LITTLE CLANFIELD

See CLANFIELD

LITTLE FARINGDON

3108. An act for dividing, allotting, and inclosing the . . . fields . . . of Little Farringdon. (28 G. III, c. 34, Private.) n. pl., 1788, fol. 20 pp.
L. Eng. C 13 c. 1 (1788. i)

3109. MIDDLETON, J. H., Notes on the Little Farringdon chalice. (Archaeol. journ., 1882, vol. 39, p. 411.)   R. Top. 5

3110. Little Farringdon. (Rept., Oxf. archaeol. soc., 1885, p. 15.)
R. Top. 330

3111. PAINTIN. H., Three village churches, Broughton-Pogis, Kelmscott and Little Faringdon. Oxf., 1913, 4°. 21 pp.
G.A. Oxon 4° 262 (15)

LITTLE LANGLEY

See LANGLEY

LITTLE MILTON

See 515 [Turnpike act. 1770].

3112. Little Milton. (Gent's. mag., 1820, pt. 1, p. 9–11, 106–08; 1828, pt. 2, p. 203, 04.) Ψ 2. 44

3113. Rules of the 'Lamb' inn slate club, Little Milton. (Oxf.), [19—], 8°. 8 pp.   G.A. Oxon c. 317 (10)

See 31 [Stratigraphy at the Miltons. 1944].

3114. Auction catal. Mansion and prebendal manor. 3 Nov. 1810.
G.A. fol. B 71

3115. Auction catal. Ham farm, Blagroves farm house [&c.] 26 Mar.
1811.   G.A. fol. B 71

3116. Auction catal. Belcher's farm. 6 June 1903.
G.A. Oxon b. 91 (32)
— 30 May 1908.   G.A. Oxon b. 91 (33)

LITTLEMORE
General

3117. An act for allotting lands in the township or liberty of Littlemore.
(57 G. III, c. 11, Private.) [Lond.], (1817), fol. 26 pp.
L. Eng. B 53 c. Land 4

3118. Auction catal. Freehold property. 25 Feb. 1824.
G.A. fol. A 266 (35)

3119. Auction catal. Manor house. 29 May 1908.
G.A. Oxon b. 91 (28)

3120. Auction catal. Lawn Upton. 7 May 1919.
G.A. Oxon c. 317 (10)
— 18 May 1927.   G.A. Oxon c. 224*

Asylum

3121. Report of the committee of visitors [*and*] Superintendent's report
[*afterw.*] Oxford county and city mental hospital. Annual report.
1847–1947/8. [Oxf., 1848–1948], 8°.   O.C.R.L.
[Bodley has 1847–79: G.A. Oxon 8° 553.]

3122. Seventh annual report of the Commissioners in lunacy. (Oxford
county asylum, p. 85, 86.)   Pp. Eng. 1852/3, vol. 49
— 13th rept., p. 26.   Pp. Eng. 1859, sess. 2, vol. 14
— 18th rept., p. 29.   Pp. Eng. 1864, vol. 23
— 19th rept., p. 6.   Pp. Eng. 1865, vol. 21
— 20th rept., p. 4.   Pp. Eng. 1866, vol. 32
— 22nd rept., p. 5.   Pp. Eng. 1867/8, vol. 31
— 23rd rept., p. 208.   Pp. Eng. 1868/9, vol. 27
— 24th rept., p. 182.   Pp. Eng. 1870, vol. 34
— 25th rept., p. 35, 195.   Pp. Eng. 1871, vol. 26
— 26th rept., p. 173.   Pp. Eng. 1872, vol. 27
— 27th rept., p. 192.   Pp. Eng. 1873, vol. 30
— 28th rept., p. 36, 199–202.   Pp. Eng. 1874, vol. 27
— 29th rept., p. 31, 176.   Pp. Eng. 1875, vol. 33
— 30th rept., p. 33, 34, 215.   Pp. Eng. 1876, vol. 33

— 31st rept., p. 261, 62.   Pp. Eng. 1877, vol. 41
— 32nd rept., p. 231.   Pp. Eng. 1878, vol. 39
— 33rd rept., p. 287–90.   Pp. Eng. 1878/9, vol. 32
— 34th rept., p. 277.   Pp. Eng. 1880, vol. 29
— 35th rept., p. 284–86.   Pp. Eng. 1881, vol. 48
— 36th rept., p. 314.   Pp. Eng. 1882, vol. 32
— 37th rept., p. 258.   Pp. Eng. 1883, vol. 30
— 38th rept., p. 257–60.   Pp. Eng. 1884, vol. 40
— 39th rept., p. 265–67.   Pp. Eng. 1884/5, vol. 36
— 40th rept., p. 218–20.   Pp. Eng. 1886, vol. 33
— 41st rept., p. 242, 43.   Pp. Eng. 1887, vol. 39
— 42nd rept., p. 233–35.   Pp. Eng. 1888, vol. 52
— 43rd rept., p. 255–57.   Pp. Eng. 1889, vol. 37
— 44th rept., p. 237–38.   Pp. Eng. 1890, vol. 35
— 45th rept., p. 213–15.   Pp. Eng. 1890/1, vol. 36
— 46th rept., p. 231, 32.   Pp. Eng. 1892, vol. 40
— 47th rept., p. 230, 31.   Pp. Eng. 1893/4, vol. 46
— 48th rept., p. 74, 255, 56.   Pp. Eng. 1894, vol. 43
— 49th rept., p. 96, 286, 87.   Pp. Eng. 1895, vol. 54
— 50th rept., p. 312, 13.   Pp. Eng. 1896, vol. 39
— 51st rept., p. 300, 01.   Pp. Eng. 1897, vol. 38
— 52nd rept., p. 24, 25, 329, 30.   Pp. Eng. 1898, vol. 43
— 53rd rept., p. 28, 334, 35.   Pp. Eng. 1899, vol. 40
— 54th rept., p. 33, 336, 37.   Pp. Eng. 1900, vol. 37
— 55th rept., p. 35, 317, 18.   Pp. Eng. 1901, vol. 28
— 56th rept., p. 39, 324, 25.   Pp. Eng. 1902, vol. 40
— 57th rept., p. 341, 42.   Pp. Eng. 1903, vol. 27
— 58th rept., p. 351–53.   Pp. Eng. 1904, vol. 29
— 59th rept., p. 357, 58.   Pp. Eng. 1905, vol. 35
— 60th rept., p. 38, 361–63.   Pp. Eng. 1906, vol. 38
— 61st rept., p. 352–54.   Pp. Eng. 1907, vol. 30
— 62nd rept., p. 370–72.   Pp. Eng. 1908, vol. 33
— 63rd rept., p. 45, 393–95.   Pp. Eng. 1909, vol. 31
— 64th rept., p. 385.   Pp. Eng. 1910, vol. 41
— 65th rept., p. 6.   Pp. Eng. 1911, vol. 34
— 65th rept., pt. 2, p. 379, 80.   15191 d. 22
— 66th rept., p. 6, 7, 9.   Pp. Eng. 1912/13, vol. 39
— 66th rept., pt. 2, p. 401, 02.   15191 d. 22
— 67th rept., p. 7.   Pp. Eng. 1913, vol. 34
— 67th rept., pt. 2, p. 426–28, 510.   15191 d. 22
— 68th rept., p. 6, 30.   Pp. Eng. 1914, vol. 41
— 68th rept., pt. 2, p. 404–06, 490.   15191 d. 22
[Subsequent reports are to be found in 'Lunacy and mental deficiency. Board of control 1st—annual report. Pt. 1', publ. in the series of Reports, commissioners. Pp. Eng. 1916, vol. 13 &c.; Pt. 2, 1915–. Per. 15191 d. 37.]

3123.

Church

3124. UNDERWOOD, H. J., Elevations, sections, and details, of the church of St. Mary the virgin, at Littlemore. Oxf., 1845, fol. 14 plates. G.A. fol. A 325

3125. Littlemore parish magazine. Jan. 1893–Dec. 1906. n. pl., 1893–1906, 4°. Per. G.A. Oxon 4° 669

3126. SS. Mary and Nicholas', Littlemore. A memorial [to rev. Vernon Green in the form of a stained glass window. An appeal for funds]. n. pl., [1898], 8°. 4 pp. G.A. Oxon c. 317 (10)

3127. [Announcement of the completion, and a description, of the 4 new stained glass windows in Littlemore church. Signed J. R. B., i.e. J. R. Bloxham.] (Oxf.), [c. 1898], 4°. 4 pp.
G.A. Oxon c. 317 (10)

3128. Cowley Salesian fathers. Newman and Littlemore. Littlemore, 1945, 8°. 81 pp. 11132 e. 124

3129. LAMBORN, E. A. GREENING, Newman's church at Littlemore. (N. & Q., 1946, vol. 190, p. 46–49.) Ψ 2. 97

Minchery

3129A. [The Minchery or Nunnery of Littlemore, with a prospect from the N.W.] (Hist. and antiq. of Glastonbury, by T. Hearne. 1722, p. xvi–xxii; 285.) Mus. Bibl. II 73

3129B. Notes on the site of Roman pottery works at the Mynchery. (Scientific papers, by G. Rolleston, 1884, vol. 2, p. 937, 38.)
1652 d. 8

Priory

3130. The visitation of the priory of Littlemore, 1st June 1445. (Lincoln record soc., 1918, vol. 14, p. 217, 18.) R. Top. 260
— [Another issue.] (Cant. and York soc., 1919, vol. 24, p. 217, 18.)
R. 8. 26

3131. Visitations. Littlemore priory. (i) 17 June 1517, (ii) 2 Sept. 1518. (Lincoln record soc., 1947, vol. 37, p. 8, 11.) R. Top. 260

Public Utilities

3132. An act to confirm certain provisional orders of the Local government board [concerning sewage works and distribution] relating to the districts of . . . Oxford [Littlemore &c.] . . . (37 & 38 V., c. 182, L. & P.) Lond., 1874, fol. 23 pp. L. Eng. A 69 c. 6

See 1020 [Act concerning supply of water. 1875].

Schools

3133. Linden house school, Littlemore. . . . Prospectus. n. pl., [c. 1880], 4°. 4 pp.   G.A. Oxon c. 317 (10)

3134. Linden house school. The report of the Christmas examination. Dec. 1866–75. Oxf., 1867–76, 8°.   G.A. Oxon 8° 811

LITTLE ROLLRIGHT

General

3135. An act for vesting part of the settled estates of sir John Dixon Dyke, baronet, lying in the counties of Oxford, Sussex, and Kent, in trustees . . . to be sold. [Little Rollright &c.] (7 G. III, c. 69, Private.) n. pl., 1767, fol. 21 pp.
                    L. Eng. C 13 c. 1 (1767, p. 579)

3136. Rollwright. (Gent's. mag., 1806, pt. 2, p. 600.) Ψ 2. 44

3137. Excursion to . . . the Rollwrights and Chastleton. (Trans. of the Birm. archaeol. assoc. for 1888, p. 67–70.)   G.A. Warw. c. 2

3138. CHATWIN, P. B., Roman finds near Rollright stones. (Trans., Birm. archaeol. soc., 1940, vol. 60, p. 152.)   G.A. Warw. 4° 100

Rollright Stones

3139. BEESLEY, T., The Rollright stones. (Trans., North Oxf. archaeol. soc., 1853–55, p. 61–74.)   R. Top. 330

3140. Extracts from various authors relating to the Rollright stones. Chipping Norton, 1884, 8°. 75 pp.   O.C.L.

3141. EVANS, A. J., Rollright stones. (Trans., Bristol & Glouc. archaeol. soc., 1891–2, vol. 16, p. 38–40.) Ψ 1. 64

3142. EVANS, A. J., The Rollright stones and their folk-lore. (Folk-lore, 1895, vol. 6, p. 6–51.)   Per. 93 d. 36

3143. DRYDEN, SIR H., The Dolmens at Rollright and Enstone. (Rept., Oxf. archaeol. soc., 1897/8, p. 40–51.)   R. Top. 330

3144. TAUNT, H. W., The Rollright stones. Oxf., [1907], 8°. 71 pp.
                    G.A. Oxon 8° 746

3145. RAVENHILL, T. H., The Rollright stones and the men who erected them. (Birm., 1926), 4°. 51 pp.   G.A. Oxon 4° 399 a (13)
— 2nd ed. 1932. 62 pp.   G.A. Oxon 4° 504 (3)

3146. RENDALL, V., A glimpse of neolithic England [the Rollright stones]. (Sat. review, 1926, vol. 142, p. 307, o8.)   N. 2288 c. 8

3147. RAVENHILL, T. H., The Rollright stones, some facts and some problems. (Rept., Oxf. archaeol. soc., 1926, p. 121–43.)
R. Top. 330

3148. RAVENHILL, T. H., Notes on the Rollright stones. (Trans., Birm. archaeol. assoc., 1928, vol. 51, p. 43, 44.)   G.A. Warw. 4° 100

LITTLE TEW

3149. An act for annexing the late duke of Shrewsbury's estate to the earldom of Shrewsbury and confirming Gilbert, earl of Shrewsbury's settlement. [Concerns Little Tew &c.] (6 G. I, c. 29, Private.) n. pl., [1720], fol.
— Repr. 1858. 16 pp.   L. Eng. C 13 c. 1 (1714–27)
— 43 G. III, c. 40, Private.
— 1 G. IV., c. 40, Private.

3150. An act concerning certain estates heretofore of Francis Keck . . . in . . . Oxford and Wilts . . . [Little Tew &c.]. . . . (18 G. III, c. 109, Private.) n. pl., 1778, fol. 46 pp.
L. Eng. C 13 c. 1 (1778. ii. 8)

3151. An act for dividing and inclosing the open and common field . . . of Little Tew. (33 G. III, c. 72, Private.) n. pl., 1793, fol. 26 pp.
L. Eng. C 13 c. 1 (1793. i. 15)

3152. LOUDON, J. C., Account of the paper roofs used at Tew Lodge, Oxon [by J. C. Loudon]. Lond., 1811, 8°. 14 pp.   1863 e. 130
— New ed. [1824?]. 12 pp.   G.A. Oxon 8° 164 (2)

3153. LOUDON, J. C., Designs for laying out farms and farm-buildings, in the Scotch style; adapted to England; including an account of the buildings and improvements recently executed on Tew Lodge farm, Oxfordshire. [Prospectus. List of plates only.] Lond., [1824?], 8°. 4 pp.   G.A. Oxon 8° 164 (3)

3154. An act for vesting part of the settled estates of . . . John, earl of Shrewsbury [in Little Tew &c.] . . . in trustees to be sold. (6 & 7 V., c. 28, Private.) Lond., 1843, fol. 60 pp.
L. Eng. C 13 c. 1 (1843. i. 28)

3155. HEWLETT, E., Personal recollections of the Little Tew ghost. . . . Lond., 1854, 12°.   B.M.

3156. MARETT, R. R., The Little Tew ghost. (Folk-lore, 1933, vol. 44, p. 98, 99.)   Per. 93 d. 36

3157. Auction catal. Little Tew farm, Pomfret castle farm, Spring farm. 5 July 1894.   G.A. Oxon b. 6 (25)

LITTLEWORTH

3158. Auction catal. Farm and cottages. 2 Aug. 1854.
G.A. Oxon b. 85 b (44)

3159. Auction catal. Freehold enclosures and cottages. 30 May 1908.
G.A. Oxon b. 91 (33)

LONG HANDBOROUGH

3160. WILLSON, W. W., Mission church fund, 'God's acre', Long Hanborough. [Signed W. W. Willson.] n. pl., (1893), 8°. 8 pp.
G.A. Oxon c. 22 (38)

3161. A ring-ditch at Long Hanborough. (Oxoniensia, 1946–7, p. 175.)
R. Top. 340

LOWER HEYFORD

See 526 [Road over Heyford bridge. 1793, &c.].

3162. An act for dividing, allotting, and inclosing . . . lands . . . of Lower Heyford, otherwise Heyford-at-Bridge and Calcott. . . . (41 G. III, c. 71, Private.) n. pl., 1801, fol. 35 pp.
L. Eng. C 13 c. 1 (1801. iii. 15)

3163. Deddington, Heyford & Aston permanent building society. Rules. Lower Heyford, 1889, 8°. 32 pp.   G.A. Oxon 8° 567

3164. BLOMFIELD, J. C., History of Lower and Upper Heyford. (Hist. of . . . deanery of Bicester. Pt. 6. Lower Heyford. 90 pp.) Lond., 1892, 4°.   G.A. Oxon 4° 71

3165. FURNEAUX, H., [Letter, signed H. Furneaux, confirming his resignation from position of Rector of Lower Heyford.] Heyford, (1892), 8°. 4 pp.   G.A. Oxon c. 22 (41)

3166. BUTLER, C. V., Village survey-making, an Oxfordshire experiment. [Relates to Lower Heyford &c.] (Board of educ., educ. pamph. 61.) Lond., 1928, 8°. 36 pp.+4 maps.   2621 e. 187 (61)

See 449 [Estates of New college, 1659–75, p. 28–45].

LOWER TADMARTON

See TADMARTON

LYNEHAM

3167. An act for dividing and inclosing the . . . fields . . . in the parishes of Sarsden and Churchill, and tything of Lyneham Merriscourt and Finescourt. (27 G. III, c. 27, Private.) n. pl., [1787], fol. 23 pp.
L. Eng. C 13 c. 1 (1787. 17)

3168. CONDER, E., [Account of the exploration of Lyneham Barrow, Oxon.] (Proc., Soc. of antiq., 1895, ser. 2, vol. 15, p. 404–10.)
R. Top. 1

MADMARSTON

3169. RYE, A. B., The camp of Madmarston and its ancient town. (Trans., North Oxf. archaeol. soc., 1853–55, p. 51–55.)   R. Top. 330

3170. BEESLEY, T., Catalogue of coins found at Madmarston. (Trans., North Oxf. archaeol. soc., 1853–55, p. 56–60.)   R. Top. 330

MAPLEDURHAM

3171. Mapledurham church, May 2, 1644. (The Topographer, 1789, vol. 1, p. 410–14.)   Douce VV 14

3172. EYSTON, C. J., Historical notes on Mapledurham. (Newbury Field club, 1886, vol. 3, p. 232–36.)   Per. G.A. Berks 8° 95

3173. DRYDEN, SIR H. E. L., Maple Durham. (Rept., Oxf. archaeol. soc., 1888/9, p. 15–18, 27, 28).   R. Top. 330

3174. Mapledurham house. (Country Life, 1906, vol. 20, p. 274–76.)
Per. 384 b. 6

3175.

3176. COOKE, A. H., The early history of Mapledurham. (Oxf. record soc., 7.) Oxf., 1925, 8°. 216 pp.   R. 13. 702

3177. COOKE, A. H., New light on Mapledurham church. (Berks, Bucks, & Oxon archaeol. journ., 1927, vol. 31, p. 162–64.)   R. Top. 100

3178. MASTERS, J. E. SMITH-, The history of Kidmore End, with notes of . . . Mapledurham [&c.]. (Leighton Buzzard, 1933), 8°. 87 pp.
G.A. Oxon 8° 1131

MARSH BALDON

3179. March Baldon. (Gent's. mag., 1792, pt. 2, p. 980.)   Ψ 2. 44

3180. An act for dividing, allotting and laying in severalty lands in . . . Marsh Baldon and Toot Baldon. (6 & 7 W. IV, c. 16, Private.) Lond., 1836, fol. 32 pp.   O.C.R.L.

3181. RATHMELL, M., Nuneham Courtenay and Marsh Baldon: town planning survey. (Town planning review, 1937, vol. 17, p. 197–204.)   Soc. 2479115 d. 4

MARSTON

See 418 [Sir T. Fairfax at Marston. 1645].

3182. Marston. (Gent's. mag., 1799, pt. 2, p. 1097, 98; 1800, pt. 1, p. 105–07; 1816, pt. 2, p. 577.) Ψ 2. 44

3183. DRINKWATER, H. G. W., Architect's report [on S. Nicholas' church, Marston]. (Oxf., 1882), 8°. 8 pp. G.A. Oxon c. 317 (11)

3184. S. Nicholas church. [An appeal for funds to repair the church.] n. pl., [1883], 8°. 4 pp. G.A. Oxon 8° 715 (3)

3185. CLARK, G. N., Open fields & inclosure at Marston. Oxf., 1924, 8°. 24 pp. G.A. Oxf. 4° 430 (7)
— [Repr.] (Oxf. record soc., vol. 6.) 1925. R. 13. 702

3186. WEAVER, F. W., and CLARK, G. N., Churchwardens' accounts of Marston, Spelsbury, Pyrton. (Oxf. record soc., 6.) Oxf., 1925, 8°. 104 pp. R. 13. 702

3187. CLARK, G. N., Enclosure by agreement at Marston. (Engl. hist. review, 1927, vol. 42, p. 87–94.) Ψ 2. 38

3188. An act to extend the boundaries of the city of Oxford and for other purposes [affecting Marston &c.]. (18 & 19 G. V, c. 84, L. & P.) Lond., 1928, 8°. 68 pp. L. Eng. A 69 c. 6

3189. BUTLER, C. V., Village survey-making, an Oxfordshire experiment. [Relates to Marston &c.] (Board of educ., educ. pamph., 61.) Lond., 1928, 8°. 36 pp.+4 maps. 2621 e. 187 (61)

3190. CLARK, G. N., Marston church. (Rept., Oxf. archaeol. soc., 1930, p. 263–87.) R. Top. 330

3191. Three Westminster writs of king Edward the confessor [ed. by F. E. Harmer. Writ no. 2 concerns Islip and Marston]. (Engl. hist. review, 1936, vol. 51, p. 99, 102.) Ψ 2. 38

3192. Auction catal. Estate. 29 June 1813. G.A. fol. B 71

3193. Auction catal. Estate and a proprietary right in Marston forest. 5 Feb. 1821. G.A. Oxon b. 4 (6)

3194. Auction catal. Brook Close, Stock Leys. 24 July 1909. G.A. Oxon b. 92* (28)

3195. Auction catal. Calley's farm, Hill ground, and Morley's ground. 10 July 1918. G.A. Oxon b. 91 (29)

3196. Auction catal. 1 & 2 St. George's terrace. 23 July 1920. G.A. Oxon b. 92* (23)

MEDLEY

See 2626 [History, by H. W. Taunt. *c.* 1900].

MERTON

3197. An act for dividing and inclosing the . . . fields in . . . Merton. . . .
(3 G. III, c. 34, Private.) n. pl., 1763, fol. 12 pp.
L. Eng. C 13 c. 1 (1763, p. 159)

3198. Biographical sketches of the descendants of John Dunkin of
Merton, with some historical notices of that village. Bromley, 1816,
8°. 10 pp.   G.A. Oxon 8° 257 (3)

3199. MASSEY, E. R., Some reminiscences of John Dunkin. (Rept., Oxf.
archaeol. soc., 1901, p. 20–24.)   R. Top. 330

3200. MASSEY, E. R., An account of the parish registers of Merton and
of the recovery of a missing portion. (Rept., Oxf. archaeol. soc.,
1902, p. 23–26.)   R. Top. 330

3201. MAJOR, H. D. A., St. Swithun's church, Merton-on-Otmoor. Oxf.,
1951, 8°. 8 pp.   G.A. Oxon 4° 504 (12)

MIDDLE ASTON

3202. WING, W., Annals of Steeple Aston and Middle Aston. Repr.
from the Oxford Chronicle. [Oxf.], 1875, 8°. 84 pp.
G.A. Oxon 8° 161 (25)

3203. BROOKES, C. C., A history of Steeple Aston and Middle Aston.
Shipston-on-Stour, 1929, 8°. 359 pp.   G.A. Oxon 8° 1067

3204. Auction catal. Estate of sir J. T. Wheate. 30 May 1804.
G.A. fol. A 273*

3205. Auction catal. Middle Aston estate. 18 July 1896.
G.A. Oxon b. 90 (6)

MIDDLE BARTON

3206. An act for dividing the . . . fields . . . of Westcott Barton and . . .
Middle Barton. (35 G. III, c. 19, Private.) n. pl., 1795, fol. 33 pp.
L. Eng. C 13 c. 1 (1795. 22)

MIDDLETON STONEY

3207. Dye descriptie eñ contrefeytinge vande twee kinderen die in
Engelant, beginnen den dorpe vā Middleton inder plaetsen, aen
malcanderen geboren sijn den derden dach Augusti anno MD.LII
acht Engesche mijlen vande vniuersiteyt van Oxfoort. Tantwerpē,
[1552?], 8°. 8 pp.   Antiq. f. B. 1552. 1

3208. An act for sale of the estate of Henry late lord Carleton in the county of Oxon. [Middleton Stoney]. (8 G. II, c. 5, Private.) n. pl., [1735], fol. 3 pp.   L. Eng. C 23 c. Real prop. 1 (2)

3209. Middleton park. (Views of the seats of noblemen, by J. P. Neale, 2nd ser., 1829, vol. 5. 2 pp.)   G.A. Gen. top. 4° 43

3210. BLOMFIELD, J. C., History of Middleton and Somerton. (Hist. of . . . deanery of Bicester. Pt. 4.) Bristol, (1888), 4°. 160 pp.
G.A. Oxon 4° 71

3211. Catalogue of the Middleton Stoney state library. Heyford, (1893), 12°. 16 pp.   2590 f. Middleton 1. 1

3212. HUSSEY, C., Middleton Park. 1, 2. (Country Life, 1946, vol. 100, p. 28–31, 74–77.)   Per. 384 b. 6

MILCOMBE

3213. An act for dividing and inclosing the open and common field . . . of Milcomb. (33 G. III, c. 74, Private.) n. pl., 1793, fol. 28 pp.
L. Eng. C 13 c. 1 (1793. i. 16)

3214. Auction catal. Wigginton Glebe estate. 13 Nov. 1919.
G.A. Oxon c. 317 (14)

MILTON

3215. An act to authorize the inclosure of certain lands . . . [Milton Common fields]. (9 & 10 V., c. 16, Pub.) Lond., 1846, fol. 2 pp.
L. Eng. A 69 c. 1
See 1022 [Act concerning supply of gas. 1913].

3216. TYSSEN, A. D., The Presbyterians of Bloxham and Milton. (Trans., Unitarian hist. soc., 1920, vol. 2, p. 9–32.)
Per. 1116 d. 11

3217. Auction catal. Agricultural properties. 20 July 1922.
G.A. Oxon b. 92* (18)

MILTON-UNDER-WYCHWOOD

3218. RICHARDSON, L., The great oolite section at Grove's quarry, Milton-under-Wychwood. (Geol. mag., 1910, N.S., Decade V, vol. 7, p. 537–42.)   Radcl.

3219. GROVES, M., ed., Records of Milton and Shipton-under-Wychwood during the war 1939–1945. (Charlbury), [1948], 8°. 52 pp.
G.A. Oxon 8° 1204 (9)

3220. Auction catal. Arable and pasture land. 25 Aug. 1919.
G.A. Oxon c. 224 (6)

MINSTER DOWNS

3221. Oxfordshire anecdotes, with historical and topographical notes. [No. 1, 2. Minster Downs, &c.] n. pl., [c. 1826], 8°. 16 pp.
G.A. Oxon 8° 934*

MINSTER LOVELL

See 1225 [J. Leverett's will. 1783].

3222. Minster Lovel. (Gent's. mag., 1825, pt. 1, p. 25–30, 120–22.)
Ψ 2. 44

3223. PRICHARD, J., Views, elevations and sections of Minster Lovell church. Oxf., 1850, fol. 6 pp.+10 plates.   G.A. fol. B 36

3224. GILES, J. A., History of Witney, with notices of . . . Minster Lovel [&c.]. Lond., 1852, 8°. 107 pp.   G.A. Oxon 8° 13

3225. Minster Lovell. (Excursion. Archæol. and nat. hist. soc. of N. Oxf., 1868.)   Manning 8° 3

3226. Minster Lovel. (Rept., Oxf. archaeol. soc., 1891, p. 12–14; 1904, p. 7–9, 20–22.)   R. Top. 330

3227. [Minster Lovel church.] (Trans., Bristol and Glouc. archaeol. soc., 1911, vol. 34, p. 22–26.)   R. Top. 210

3228. Minster Lovel Castle estate, Oxfordshire. [Sale, with short history.] n. pl., [c. 1920], fol. 16 pp.   G.A. Oxon c. 224 (8)

3229. MONK, W. J., Minster Lovell, its ruins and its church. (Reading), [19—], 8°. 8 pp.   O.P.L.
— 2nd ed., with additions. (Cirencester), [1930], 8°. 13 pp.
G.A. Oxon 8° 1056 (8)

3230. Minster Lovel. (Trans., Bristol and Glouc. archaeol. soc., 1932, vol. 53, p. 48–54.)   R. Top. 210

3231. TAYLOR, A. J., The alien priory of Minster Lovell. (Oxoniensia, 1937, p. 103–17.)   R. Top. 340

3232. LAMBORN, E. A. GREENING, The Lovel tomb at Minster. (Rept., Oxf. archaeol. soc., 1937, p. 13–20.)   R. Top. 330
— [Repr.]   G.A. Oxon 8° 1175 (9)

3232A. LAMBORN, E. A. GREENING, The Lovel tomb at Minster. (N. & Q., 1947, vol. 192, p. 49, 50.) Ψ 2. 97

3233. HASSALL, W. O., Minster Lovell in 1602. (Oxoniensia, 1945, p. 101–04.)   R. Top. 340

3234. KIRK, J. R., The Alfred and Minster Lovel jewels [by J. R. Kirk]. (Univ. of Oxf., Ashmolean mus.) Oxf., 1948, 8°. 12 pp.   1756 e. 59

3235. Auction catal. Manor of Minster Lovel, with the quit-rents, royalty, fishery &c., and farms. 1811. G.A. fol. B 71

3236. Auction catal. Manor of Minster Lovel, with royalties, fisheries and quit-rents, and 8 farms. 18 July 1812. G.A. fol. B 71

3237. Auction catal. Minster Lovel estate. 23 Sept. 1920.
G.A. Oxon c. 224 (8)

MIXBURY

3238. An act to confirm an agreement for enclosing the . . . fields . . . of the manor of Mixbury. (3 G. II, c. 5, Private.) n. pl., [1730], fol. 11 pp. G.A. Oxon c. 191

3239. BLOMFIELD, J. C., History of Fringford, Hethe, Mixbury, Newton Purcell and Shelswell. (Hist. of . . . deanery of Bicester. Pt. 5. Mixbury. 58 pp.) Lond., [1890], 4°. G.A. Oxon 4° 71

MOLLINGTON

3240. An act for dividing and inclosing the . . . fields . . . in Mollington in the counties of Oxford and Warwick. . . . (37 G. III, c. 67, Private.) n. pl., 1797, fol. 30 pp. L. Eng. C 13 c. 1 (1792. 2. 17)

See 635 [Boundaries. 1895].

MONGEWELL

3241. Auction catal. Stonor estate. 26 Sept. 1894.
G.A. Oxon b. 92 (8)

3242. Auction catal. Homer estate. 3 Sept. 1898.
G.A. Oxon b. 91 (18)
— 18 June 1900. G.A. Oxon b. 91 (19)

MORETON

3243. An act for vesting in trustees, the several manors and lands [Tetsworth and Moreton] . . . the estate of Henry Perott in trust for him and his heirs. (2 G. II, c. 15, Private.) n. pl., [1729], fol. 7 pp.
G.A. Oxon c. 196

3244.

3245. Auction catal. Thame estate. 16 July 1844.
G.A. Oxon b. 92 (21)

MYCH MILTON

See GREAT MILTON

NEAT ENSTONE

See 526 [Turnpike act. 1793].

NEITHROP

3246. An act for dividing and inclosing one open and common field . . . and several parcels of land . . . within the township and liberties of Neithrop and Wickham. (32 G. II, c. 19, Private.) [Lond.], 1759, fol.   O.C.R.L.

3247. An act for vesting part of the estates of the late sir James Dashwood in trustees, in trust to sell the same. [Neithrop.] (37 G. III, c. 101, Private.) n. pl., 1797, fol. 30 pp.   L. Eng. C 13 c. 1 (1797. 4)

3248. PYE, H. J., The speech of H. J. Pye, esq., delivered to the electors of Banbury, Neithrop, and the hamlets, at the Flying Horse inn, on . . . Tuesday, 25th Sept., 1832. Banbury, (1832), 8°. 16 pp.
G.A. Oxon 8° 631 (4)

3249. Neithrop Working men's club. Fourteenth annual report and balance sheet. 1897. Banbury, 1897, 4°.   G.A. Oxon c. 22 (13)

3250. Auction catal. Map of an estate in Boddicote and Neithrop. 1838.
G.A. Oxon b. 85 a (11)

3251. Auction catal. Freehold estate. 20 Feb. 1872.
G.A. Oxon b. 85 b (37)

3252. Auction catal. Estate. 20 Aug. 1877.   G.A. Oxon b. 85 b (38)

3253. Auction catal. Freehold estate, including a public house, The Barley Mow. 23 July 1878.   G.A. Oxon b. 85 b (39)

3254. Auction catal. Stonor estate. 26 Sept. 1894.   G.A. Oxon b. 92 (8)

NETHERCOTE

3255. An act for the selling the reversion and inheritance of the farm of Nethercott . . . for payment of the debts and legacies of George Harrison. . . . (11 W. III, c. 18, Private.) 1699.

3256. An act for vesting part of the estates of the late sir James Dashwood in trustees, in trust to sell the same. [Nethercote.] (37 G. III, c. 101, Private.) n. pl., 1797, fol. 30 pp.   L. Eng. C 13 c. 1 (1797. 4)

NETHER WORTON

3257. WING, W., Two churches and parishes beyond the neighbourhood of Banbury. Over Worton and Nether Worton . . . [By W. Wing.] Repr. from the Banbury Guardian. n. pl., [c. 1880], 8°. 4 pp.
G.A. Oxon 8° 1184 (18)

3258. Auction catal. Nether Worton estate. 29 May 1854.
G.A. Oxon a. 116 (f. 211)

NETTLEBED

3259. The authentic trial, and memoirs of Isaac Darkin, alias Dumas, capitally convicted for a highway-robbery, near Nettlebed before mr. baron Adams at the Lent Assizes. Oxf., (1761), fol. 28 pp.
G.A. fol. A 240 (4)

3260. MORITZ, K. P., Travels, chiefly on foot, through several parts of England in 1782, tr. by a lady. (Nettlebed, p. 146–58.) Lond., 1795, 8°. Gough Gen. top. 293
— [*Orig. entitled* Reisen eines Deutschen in England, 1782.
G.A. Gen. top. 16° 27.]
— [Repr. in W. Mavor's British tourists companion, vol. 4. 1798, 1809.]
— [Repr. in J. Pinkerton's Collection of travels, 1808, vol. 2. 4°
BS 897.]
— [Another ed.] 1886. (Cassell's nat. hist.)

See 362 [Survey of 1387. 1910].

3261. PEAKE, A. E., Cave site at Nettlebed. (Proc., Prehist. soc. of E. Anglia, 1915, vol. 2, pt. 1, p. 71–80.) Soc. 247115 e. 30

3262. Nettlebed. (Berks, Bucks, & Oxon archaeol. journ., 1929, vol. 33, notes, p. 115.) R. Top. 100

3263. The official guide to Nettlebed. Croydon, [1949], 8°. 20 pp.
O.C.R.L.

3264. Auction catal. Huntercombe manorial estate. 26 July 1894.
G.A. Oxon b. 91 (38)

3265. Auction catal. Stonor estate. 26 Sept. 1894. G.A. Oxon b. 92 (8)

NEWBRIDGE

See 293 [History, by W. J. Monk. 1926].

3266. TOYNBEE, M. R., Radcot bridge and Newbridge. (Oxoniensia, 1949, vol. 14, p. 46–52.) R. Top. 340

NEWINGTON

3267. Newington. (Gent's. mag., 1796, pt. 2, p. 809, 10; 1797, pt. 1, p. 38.) Ψ 2. 44

3268. An act for inclosing lands in the liberty of Berrick Prior, and in the manor and parish of Newington. (50 G. III, c. 114, L. & P.) Lond., 1810, fol. 21 pp. L. Eng. A 69 c. 6

3269. PENDLEBURY, J. R., The church and parish of St. Giles, Newington, a sermon. Oxf., (1901), 8°. 10 pp.
G.A. Oxon 8° 973

3270. Newington Longeville charters, ed. by H. E. Salter. (Oxf. record soc., vol. 3.) Oxf., 1921, 8°. 117 pp. R. 13. 702

3271. BEAZLEY, F. C., Pedigree of Byseley, Bisley or Beazley, of Newington and Warborough. (Misc. geneal. et heraldica, 1926/28, 5th ser., vol. 6, p. 390–408.) Ψ 2. 10 f

3272. LAMBORN, E. A. GREENING, The painted window at Newington. (Rept., Oxf. archaeol. soc., 1938, p. 59–62.) R. Top. 330

3273. Auction catal. Greenfields farm. 31 Oct. 1889.
G.A. Oxon b. 92* (27)

3274. Auction catal. Holcombe estate. 25 Aug. 1911.
G.A. Oxon b. 91 (34)

NEWINGTON (Peculiar jurisdiction of)

3275. PEARCE, S. S., The clergy of the rural deanery of Oxford and of the peculiar of Newington with Britewell, at the time of the settlement of 1559 and afterwards. (Rept., Oxf. archaeol. soc., 1919, p. 198–234.) R. Top. 330

NEWNHAM MURREN

See 1324 [Patterns of inlaid tiles from churches, by W. A. Church. 1845].

3276. Auction catal. Huntercombe manorial estate. 26 July 1894.
G.A. Oxon b. 91 (38)

3277. Auction catal. Col d'Arbres estate. 28 June 1900.
G.A. Oxon b. 90 (27)

3278. Auction catal. Howbery park and Col d'Arbres. 17 June 1901.
G.A. Oxon b. 90 (28)

3279. Auction catal. Newnham Murren estate, comprising Newnham house and park, Newnham farm, and the village and manor of Newnham. 28 May 1902. G.A. Oxon b. 6 (35)

NEWTON PURCELL

3280. BLOMFIELD, J. C., History of . . . Newton Purcell [&c.]. (Hist. of . . . deanery of Bicester. Pt. 5. Newton Purcell. 24 pp.) Lond., [1890], 4°. G.A. Oxon 4° 71

NEW YATT

3281. Auction catal. New Yatt farm. 13 May 1824. G.A. fol. B 71
— 31 July 1902. G.A. Oxon c. 317 (9)

NOKE

3282. Noke. (Gent's. mag., 1789, pt. 2, p. 1011.) Ψ 2. 44

3283. An act for allotting lands . . . of Noke. . . . (58 G. III, c. 11, Private.) (Lond.), 1818, fol. 17 pp.
L. Eng. C 13 c. 1 (1818. i. 22)

3284. Auction catal. Noke estate and advowson to Noke rectory. 10 July 1849. G.A. Oxon b. 91 (46)

3285. Auction catal. Freehold estate. 15 Sept. 1909.
G.A. Oxon b. 91 (36)

NORTH ASTON

3286. An act for discharging certain manors [&c.] . . . part of the estate of Oldfield Bowles . . . from uses, estates, and trusts declared concerning the same, in and by the settlement made previous to the marriage of the said Oldfield Bowles, with Mary, his now wife, and for settling the manor of North Aston, and other lands . . . in lieu thereof. (27 G. III, c. 19, Private.) n. pl., 1787, fol. 28 pp.
L. Eng. C 13 c. 1 (1787. 22)

3287. WING, W., Annals of North Aston. Repr. from the Oxford Chronicle. (Oxf.), 1867, 8°. 50 pp. G.A. Oxon 8° 93 (8)

3288. FOSTER-MELLIAR, M., To the parishioners of North Aston [letter signed M. Foster-Melliar on disestablishment of the Church]. n. pl., [c. 1900], s. sh. G.A. Oxon c. 317 (4)

See 1278 [Heraldry, by E. E. Cope. 1929].

3289. LAMBORN, E. A. GREENING, The donor of the pulpit at North Aston. (Rept., Oxf. archaeol. soc., 1938, p. 65, 66.) R. Top. 330

3290. Auction catal. Estate of sir J. T. Wheate. 30 May 1804.
G.A. fol. A 273*

3291. Auction catal. Estate. 15 July 1857. G.A. Oxon b. 85 b (57)

3292. Auction catal. North Aston hall. 16 Oct. 1907.
G.A. Oxon b. 90 (5)

3293. Auction catal. Cold Harbour farm. 15 Sept. 1920.
G.A. Oxon c. 224 (7)

NORTH LEIGH

General

3294. An act for dividing and inclosing . . . Northleigh common fields and . . . Northleigh heath. (31 G. II, c. 29, Private.) [Lond.], 1758, fol. O.C.R.L.

3295. Church notes, &c. from North Leigh. (The Topographer, 1791, vol. 3, p. 128–30.) Douce VV 16

3296. Parish of North Leigh. Account of weekly offertory, 1872. n. pl., 1872, s. sh. G.A. Oxon c. 22 (14)

3297. St. Mary's church, Northleigh. [Appeal to pay off a deficit of £29 in the Tower restoration fund.] n. pl., [1914], 4°. 4 pp. G.A. Oxon c. 317 (10)

3298. PAINTIN, H., Oxford architectural and historical society. Visit to Northleigh. (Repr. from Oxf. journ. illustr.) n. pl., (1922), s. sh. G.A. Oxon a. 22

3299. MASON, V., Scraps of English folklore, XIX. Northleigh. (Folk-lore, 1929, vol. 40, p. 374–85.) Per. 93 d. 36

3300. LEEDS, E. T., Two Saxon cemeteries in North Oxfordshire [Chadlington and North Leigh]. (Oxoniensia, 1940, p. 21–30.) R. Top. 340

3301. TOYNBEE, M. R., Charles i and the Perrots of Northleigh. (Oxoniensia, 1946–7, p. 132–46.) R. Top. 340

3302. Auction catal. New Yatt farm. 13 May 1824. G.A. fol. B 71
— 31 July 1902. G.A. Oxon c. 317 (9)

3303. Auction catal. Field and Church farms. 9 June 1910. G.A. Oxon b. 91 (26)

3304. Auction catal. Hollycourt farm. 10 June 1911. G.A. Oxon b. 91 (27)

3305. Auction catal. Portion of the Blenheim estate. Perrotshill farm. 14 July 1920. G.A. Oxon b. 92* (3)

Villa

3306. A guide to Blenheim, Nuneham and the newly discovered Roman villa near Northleigh. (The Oxf. univ. and city guide, p. 151–96.) Oxf., 1818, 8°. G.A. Oxon 16° 137
[Other eds. in 1818, 19, 20, 21, 22, 23, 24, 25, 26, 27, 28, 29, 30, 1834, 1837, 1839, 1849, 1859, c. 1860.]

3307. HAKEWILL, H., An account of the Roman villa discovered at Northleigh . . . in the years 1813, 1814, 1815, 1816. (Extract from Skelton's Antiq. of Oxf.) n. pl., (1826), fol. 7 pp+5 plates. G.A. fol. A 123

3308. An account of the Roman villa near Northleigh. (A description of Blenheim. 12th ed., p. 117–19.) Oxf., [1836], 8°. G.A. Oxon 8° 71 (4)
— 13th ed. [c. 1840]. G.A. Oxon 8° 924

3309. HAKEWILL, H., Roman remains, discovered in the parishes of North Leigh and Stonesfield. Extr. from Skelton's Oxfordshire. Lond., 1836, 8°. 20 pp. G.A. Oxon 8° 164 (12)

3310. An account of the Roman villa near Northleigh. (New guide to Blenheim palace, p. 33–35.) Oxf., [1838], 8°.
G.A. Oxon 8° 232 (11)

3311. A description of . . . the Roman villa. (Stranger's guide and hist. & biogr. hand-book to Oxford. 6th ed. p. 248–50.) Oxf., [c. 1850], 8°. G.A. Oxon 8° 541

3312. Northleigh. (Rept., Oxf. archaeol. soc., 1908, p. 9–14.)
R. Top. 330

3313. HAVERFIELD, F., The Roman villa at Northleigh. [With plan.] n. pl., (1908), 8°. 4 pp. G.A. Oxon 8° 761 (4)

3314. TAUNT, H. W., The Roman villa, Northleigh. (Repr. from Blenheim, Woodstock, &c., p. 65–69.) [Oxf., c. 1909], 8°.
G.A. Oxon 4° 399A (1)

3315. HAVERFIELD, F. J., Roman country-house by the Evenlode river, Northleigh [by F. Haverfield. With plan.] [Oxf.]. (1916), 8°. 4 pp.
G.A. Oxon 8° 900 (18)

3316. TAYLOR, M. V., The Roman villa at North Leigh. Oxf., &c., 1923, 8°. 4 pp. G.A. Oxon 8° 1001 (9)

NORTHMOOR

3317. Northmoor, a general statement of the accounts for . . . 1872.
n. pl., (1872), s. sh. G.A. Oxon c. 22 (16)
— 1873. G.A. Oxon c. 22 (15)

See 12 [Act concerning draining of lands adjoining river Thames. 1871].
See 1297 [Parish registers. Marriages. 1909].

3318. Parish of Northmoor. [Appeal to the Rural district council of Witney for the provision of a bridge across the Thames at Bablock Hythe.] n. pl., (1910), fol. 4 pp. G.A. Oxon c. 317 (12)

3319. Parish of Northmoor. To the chairman of the . . . council . . . of . . . [in MS. Ducklington]. [Notification of no. 3318, asking for support of all neighbouring authorities.] n. pl., (1910), s. sh.
G.A. Oxon c. 317 (12)

See 293 [History, by W. J. Monk. 1926].

3320. STOWELL, J. H., Glimpses of Northmoor through 800 years. n. pl., [1930], 8°. 33 pp. G.A. Oxon 8° 1055 (17)

3321. Auction catal. Estate. 31 May 1893. G.A. Oxon b. 6 (23)

3322. Auction catal. Estate. 31 May 1899. G.A. Oxon b. 91 (37)

3323. Auction catal. Pasture land. 17 May 1919.
G.A. Oxon c. 224 (2)

3324. Auction catal. 2 cottages. 10 June 1920.　G.A. Oxon b. 92* (11)

3325. Auction catal. Northmoor portion of the Harcourt settled estates.
3 Sept. 1924.　　　　　　　　　　　　　　G.A. Oxon c. 226

NORTH NEWINGTON

3326. Universis Christi fidelibus . . . nos Joannes et Radolfus custodes
. . . cuiusdam capellae . . . ad honorem . . . S. Joannis Baptiste de
Northnewinton in parochia de Broughton [giving indulgences to
all who assist in the building & support of the chapel]. n. pl., 1521,
s. sh.　　　　　　　　　　　　　　　　　MS. Rawl. A 269 (f. 50)

3327. An act for indemnifying Thomas Twisleton and Francis Twisleton . . . the purchasers of certain lands . . . [North Newington &c.]
belonging to James Ness . . . (9 G. III, c. 88, Private.) n. pl., 1769,
fol. 7 pp.　　　　　　　　　　　　　L. Eng. C 13 c. 1 (1769. 76)

3328. An act for inclosing lands in Northnewton otherwise North-
newington in the parish of Broughton. (43 G. III, c. 119, Private.)
n. pl., 1803, fol. 22 pp.　　　　　　　　　　G.A. Oxon c. 113 (4)

3329. METCALFE, G., Some account of Broughton and North Newington. Lond., 1893, 8°. 18 pp.　　　　　　　　　G.A. Oxon 8° 968

3330. Auction catal. Paper mill. 15 March 1833.
G.A. Oxon b. 85 a (27)

3331. Auction catal. Freehold cottages. 16 May 1888.
G.A. Oxon b. 85 b (40)

NORTHSTOKE

3332. CHAMPION, W. S., On North Stoke church. (Proc., Oxf. architect.
and hist. soc., N.S., vol. 3, 1873, p. 112–15.)　　　　R. 13. 709

3333. The parson of North Stoke. (Oxf. diocesan mag., 1906/8, vol. 3,
p. 151–53.)　　　　　　　　　　　　　　　Per. 11126 d. 78

3334. KEYSER, C. E., Notes on the churches of South Stoke, North
Stoke [&c.]. (Journ., Brit. archaeol. assoc., 1918, new ser., vol. 24,
p. 1–32+67 plates.)　　　　　　　　　　　　　R. Top. 4

3335. WARNER, H. J., The church of Northstoke. Wallingford, [1933],
8°. 15 pp.　　　　　　　　　　　　　G.A. Oxon 8° 1079 (19)

3336. EVANS, H. F. O., Brasses to canons of Windsor [one at North
Stoke, the other in Magdalen College chapel]. (Trans., Monumental brass soc., 1939, vol. 7, pt. 6, p. 259, 60.)　　Soc. 2184 d. 85

3336A. North Stoke. (Archaeol. notes. Oxoniensia, 1950, vol. 15, p. 107.)
R. Top. 340

3337. Auction catal. North Stoke farm. 18 Sept. 1896.
G.A. Oxon b. 91 (4)

3338. Auction catal. Pocock's and Hailey farms; and the Grange.
21 Sept. 1900. G.A. Oxon b. 92 (5)

NORTH WESTON

3339. An act for vesting the . . . manors and estates [in North Weston &c.] of Charles Vere Spencer, an infant, in . . . Oxford and Denbigh in trustees, in order to effect the sale thereof. . . . (5 & 6 W. IV, c. 23, Private.) n. pl., 1835, fol. 44 pp.
L. Eng. C 13 c. 1 (1835. 23)

3340. M., P., Brass of a priest formerly at North Weston, Oxon. (Oxf. journ. of monumental brasses, 1900, vol. 2, p. 85.)
Soc. 2184 d. 50

3341. Auction catal. Thame estate. 16 July 1844.
G.A. Oxon b. 92 (21)

3342. Auction catal. North Weston farm, Manor farm, Field farm.
28 June 1913. G.A. Oxon b. 92 (22)

NUFFIELD

See 509 [Turnpike act. 1765, &c.].

3343. PEARMAN, M. T., Notices, manorial & ecclesiastical, of the parish of Nuffield. (Trans., Oxf. archaeol. soc., 42.) Banbury, 1901, 8°. 20 pp. R. Top. 330

3344. FIELD, J. E., The font at Nuffield. (Berks, Bucks, & Oxon archaeol. journ., 1916, vol. 22, p. 32.) R. Top. 100

3345. BRIERS, P. M., The history of Nuffield. [Oxf.], (1939), 8°. 178 pp.
Arch. AA d. 39

3346. Auction catal. Park corner and Ewelme park farms. 31 Oct. 1889.
G.A. Oxon b. 92* (27)
— 1 July 1891. G.A. Oxon b. 92* (ii. 1)
— 26 July 1894. G.A. Oxon b. 92 (10)

3347. Auction catal. Park corner farm. 22 July 1890.
G.A. Oxon b. 92* (28)

3348. Auction catal. Huntercombe manorial estate. 26 July 1894.
G.A. Oxon b. 91 (38)

3349. Auction catal. Stonor estate. 26 Sept. 1894.

G.A. Oxon b. 92 (8)

3350. Auction catal. Col d'Arbres estate. 28 June 1900.

G.A. Oxon b. 90 (27)

NUNEHAM COURTENAY

See 831 [Estate act. 1710].

3351. Nuneham-Courtenay, the seat of the earl of Harcourt, 1783. n. pl., [1783?], 8°. 18 pp.   Gough Oxf. 45 (8)

3352. MORITZ, K. P., Travels, chiefly on foot, through several parts of England in 1782, tr. from the Germ. by a lady. (Nuneham, p. 160.) Lond., 1795, 8°.   Gough Gen. top. 293
[Orig. entitled Reisen eines Deutschen in England, 1782. G.A. Gen. top. 16° 27.]
— [Repr. in W. Mavor's British tourists companion, vol. 4. 1798, 1809.]
— [Repr. in J. Pinkerton's Collection of travels, 1808, vol. 2. 4° BS. 897.]
— [Another ed.] 1886. (Cassell's nat. hist.)

3353. Description of Nuneham-Courtnay, in the county of Oxford. n. pl., 1797, 12°. 66 pp.   Gough Oxf. 45 (9)
— [Another ed.] 1806. 72 pp.   G.A. Oxon 8° 87

3354. The Oxford university and city guide . . . To which is added A guide to Blenheim, Nuneham, and the newly discovered Roman villa near Northleigh. Oxf., 1818, 8°. p. 151–96.   G.A. Oxon 16° 137
[Other eds. in 1818, 19, 20, 21, 22, 23, 24, 25, 26, 27, 28, 29, 30, 1834, 1837, 1839, 1849, 1859, c. 1860.]

3355. Nuneham Courtenay. (Views of the seats of noblemen and gentlemen, by J. P. Neale, 1820, vol. 3. 6 pp.)   G.A. Gen. top. 4° 42

3356. The perambulation of Oxford, Blenheim and Nuneham. New ed. Oxf., 1825, 8°. p. 191–220.   G.A. Oxon 8° 599
— [Another ed. 1826.]   G.A. Oxon 8° 599*

3357. HARCOURT, E. W., ed., The Harcourt papers. Vol. 1–14. Oxf., [1876–1905], 4°.   2182 H. e. 4–15*

3358. Catalogue of the library of E. W. Harcourt at Nuneham park. Lond., 1883, 4°. 366 pp.   2590 d. Nuneham 1

3359. WARREN, T. H., Nuneham Courtenay. (Country Life, 1913, vol. 34, p. 746–55.)   Per. 384 b. 6

3360. RATHMELL, M., Nuneham Courtenay and Marsh Baldon: town planning survey. (Town planning review, 1937, vol. 17, p. 197–204.)

Soc. 2479115 d. 4

3361. HUSSEY, C., and TAYLOR, G. C., Nuneham Courtenay (house). (Country Life, 1941, vol. 90, p. 866–70, 910–13.)   Per. 384 b. 6

3362. MINN, H., ed., The diary of an Oxfordshire rector [James Newton, rector of Nuneham Courtenay]. (Oxoniensia, 1945, p. 79–92.)   R. Top. 340

OATLANDS

3363. An act to authorize the inclosure of certain lands . . . [Oatlands]. (12 & 13 V., c. 7, Pub.) Lond., 1849, fol. 2 pp.   L. Eng. A 69 c. 1

ODDINGTON

3364. An act for dividing and inclosing certain . . . fields . . . of Oddington. . . . (31 G. III, c. 59, Private.) n. pl., 1791, fol. 25 pp.
                                                                 L. Eng. C 13 c. 1 (1791. 10)
See 486 [Railway. 1846].

3365. Reopening of the parish church. Repr. from the Oxf. Chron. 8th Nov. 1884. [Oxf.], 1884, 8°. 4 pp.   G.A. Oxon c. 317 (12)

3366. REITLINGER, G., The wall paintings at Oddington. (Burlington mag., 1926, vol. 49, p. 105–11.)   Per. 170 c. 25

3367. TORR, V. J. B., The Oddington shroud brass and its lost fellows. (Trans., Monumental brass soc., 1938, vol. 7, pt. 5, p. 225–35.)
                                                                         Soc. 2184 d. 85

3368. Auction catal. 1750 trees on estate of F. J. Staples-Browne. 27 Feb. 1873.   G.A. Oxon 8° 959

3369. Auction catal. Estate. 17 July 1909.   G.A. Oxon b. 91 (39)

OSNEY

3370. SWAINE, J., Memoirs of Osney abbey. Lond., 1769, 8°. 43 pp.
                                                                 Gough Oxf. 45 (6)
— 2nd ed., corrected, with suppl. 1773. 47 pp.
                                                                 G.A. Oxon 8° 218 (7)

3371. Osney. (Gent's. mag., 1771, p. 153.) Ψ 2. 44

3372. Annales monasterii de Oseneia, A.D. 1016–1347, Chronicon vulgo dictum Thomæ Wykes, A.D. 1066–1289. (Annales monastici, vol. 4.) Lond., 1869, 8°. 354+lxxxv pp.   Rolls Ser. 36 d

3373. Ex annalibus Oseneiensibus et Thomae de Wykes chronico. (Mon. Germ. hist., script., tom. 27, p. 484–503.) Hannoviae, 1885, fol.   R. 10. fol. 40

3374. CLARK, A., ed., The English register of Oseney abbey, written about 1460. (E.E.T.S., orig. ser., 133, 144.) Lond., 1907, 1913, 8°.
E. 2. 96 (133, 144)

3375. The visitation of the monastery of Oseney, 4 June 1445. (Cant. and York soc., 1927, vol. 33, p. 262–64.) R. 8. 26
— [Another issue.] (Lincoln record soc., 1929, vol. 21, p. 262–64.)
R. Top. 260

3376. SALTER, H. E., ed., Cartulary of Oseney abbey. 6 vols. (O.H.S., vols. 89–91, 97, 98, 101.) Oxf., 1929–36, 8°. R. 13. 700

3377. Visitations. Oseney abbey. (i) 10 June 1517. (ii) 8 May 1520. (Lincoln record soc., 1947, vol. 37, p. 39.) R. Top. 260

3378. An act to authorize the inclosure of certain lands . . . [Osney]. (12 & 13 V., c. 7, Pub.) Lond., 1849, fol. 2 pp. L. Eng. A 69 c. 1

3379. Osney bridge [report in connection with responsibility for repair and upkeep]. [Oxf.], 1886, fol. 4 pp. G.A. Oxon c. 317 (25)

3380. A half-yearly paper of the Sisterhood of s. Thomas ye martyr. 1891, 92, 1894. Oxf., 1891–94, 12°. Per. G.A. Oxon 16° 58

OTMOOR

3381. CROKE, A., A short view of the possibility and advantages of draining, dividing and enclosing Otmoor, with some proposals submitted to . . . the earl of Abingdon and the other proprietors. Lond., 1787, 8°. 27 pp. Gough Oxf. 45 (10)

3382. The case of Otmoore submitted to the attention of the members of the House of Commons, by the late Earl of Abingdon in the year 1788. Repr. Oxf., [1831], 8°. 24 pp. G.A. Oxon 8° 296 c

3383. An answer to lord Abingdon's case of Otmoor. n. pl., [1788], fol. 3 pp. G.A. Oxon b. 96 (4)

3384. A bill for draining and improving . . . Otmoor. [Lond.], 1788, fol. 31 pp. L. Eng. B 53 c. Enclos. 1

3385. CROKE, A., To the proprietors of the common of Otmoor [concerning the plan for draining and dividing Otmoor]. n. pl., (1800), fol. 3 pp. G.A. Oxon b. 96 (5)

3386. TAUNTON, W. E., The answer of mr. Taunton, of Oxford, to a letter written by dr. Alexander Croke of Studley, to the proprietors of the common of Otmoor. Oxf., (1800), 8°. 22 pp.
Gough Oxf. 45 (11)

3387. CROKE, A., A second letter to the proprietors of Otmoor, in reply to mr. Taunton's Answer to a former address. Lond., 1800, 8°. 40 pp. Gough Oxf. 45 (12)

3388. An act for draining and allotting Otmoor. (55 G. III, c. 100. L. & P.) [Lond.], 1815, fol. 39 pp.   L. Eng. B 53 c. Enclos. 2

3389. Rewards. Malicious injuries. Otmoor and the neighbourhood. [Notice, by the trustees appointed under the Otmoor drainage act, offering rewards for the discovery & conviction of persons damaging the property.] Oxf., [c. 1830], s. sh.   G.A. fol. A 139* (58)

3390. To the inhabitants of the seven Otmoor towns [signed A friend to the poor. Concerning the Otmoor riots.] Oxf., [1830], s. sh.
G.A. Oxon b. 96 (10)

3391. CROKE, SIR A., The case of Otmoor, with the Moor orders. Oxf., 1831, 8°. 40 pp.   G.A. Oxon 8° 71 (11)

3392. Oxford spring assizes, March 3rd, 1832. Proceedings on the trial of the information The king v. Smith . . . To which are prefixed, A plain statement of facts by the defendant. [Concerning the publ. of advertisements by Richard Smith, wine-merchant, inviting contributions to a fund aiding certain inhabitants of Otmoor, which were alleged to have provoked the Otmoor riots.] Oxf., 1832, 8°. 109 pp.   G.A. Oxon 8° 234 (4)

3393. PRIOR, C. E., Account of Otmoor. (Trans., Oxf. archaeol. soc., 40.) Banbury, 1900, 8°. 13 pp.   R. Top. 330

3394. DRUCE, G. C., Notes on the botany of Otmoor. (Trans., Oxf. archaeol. soc., 40.) Banbury, 1900, 8°. 3 pp.   R. Top. 330

3394A. HAMMOND, J. L., and B., The village labourer, 1769–1832. [Enclosure of Otmoor, p. 88–96.] Lond., &c., 1911, 8°.
247125 d. 14
— New ed. 1920, p. 64–72.   247125 e. 48
— 4th ed. 1927, p. 64–72.   247125 e. 49

See 120 [Close-ups of herons, &c., on Otmoor. 1932].

3395. Auction catal. 220 acres freehold grassland. 15 Oct. 1818.
G.A. Oxon b. 91 (40)

OVER NORTON

3396. An act for vesting part of the settled estates of . . . John, earl of Shrewsbury [in Over Norton &c.] . . . in trustees to be sold. (6 & 7 V., c. 28, Private.) Lond., 1843, fol. 60 pp.
L. Eng. C 13 c. 1 (1843. i. 28)

3397. LUCAS, J., Report . . . on the prospect of finding coal under the estate of Over Norton. Lond., 1891, 4°. 16 pp.
G.A. Oxon 4° 375 (6)

OVER WORTON

3398. WING, W., Two churches and parishes beyond the neighbourhood of Banbury. Over Worton and Nether Worton, otherwise Upper Worton and Lower Worton. [By W. Wing.] Repr. from the Banbury guardian. n. pl., [c. 1880], 8°. 4 pp.
G.A. Oxon 8° 1184 (18)

3399. Auction catal. Estate, including advowson of benefice of Over Worton. 4 Sept. 1913. G.A. Oxon b. 92 (40)

OVERY

3400. Auction catal. Dorchester and Overy estates. 16 July 1844.
G.A. Oxon b. 90 (33)

PEPPARD COMMON

3401. PEAKE, A. E., An account of a flint factory, with some new types of flints, excavated at Peppard common, Oxon. (Archaeol. journ. 1913, vol. 70, p. 33–68.) R. Top. 5

PIDDINGTON

3402. An act for dividing and inclosing the common fields . . . of Piddington. (30 G. II, c. 17, Private.) [Lond.], 1757, fol. O.C.R.L.

3403. RANDOLPH, J., bp. of Oxford. Case of the bishop of Oxford against the parish of Piddington in a cause of simony. Extr. from 'East's Reports for Easter and Trinity terms, 1806'. With an appendix containing the endowments of Ambrosden and Piddington. Oxf., &c., 1807, 8°. 27 pp. Gough Oxf. 7 (13)

3404. Auction catal. Chilling place farm. 12 June 1912.
G.A. Oxon b. 91 (41)

3405. Auction catal. Lower farm. 12 Nov. 1913.
G.A. Oxon b. 91 (42)

PIXEY MEAD

3406. Auction catal. Lammas meadow land. 10 July 1849.
G.A. Oxon b. 92 (36)

3407. Auction catal. Meadow land. 13 Nov. 1897.
G.A. Oxon c. 224 (1)

PLOUGHLEY HUNDRED

3408. DUNKIN, J., The history and antiquities of the hundreds of Bullingdon and Ploughley. 2 vols. Lond., 1823, 4°. 319 & 261 pp.
G.A. Oxon 4° 5

See 879 [Charities. 1826].

3409. WYNDHAM, H., A backward glance. [A reconstruction of the countryside of the Ploughley Hundred in 1793.] Lond., 1950, 8°. 79 pp.
G.A. Oxon 8° 1217

POSTCOMBE

See 404 [Prince Rupert's victory at Postcombe. 1643].

3410. An act for inclosing lands . . . of Lewknor and Postcomb. . . . (50 G. III, c. 157, Private.) n. pl., 1810, fol. 25 pp.
L. Eng. C 13 c. 1 (1810. 2)

See 534, 536 [Turnpike bill. 1833 &c.].

3411. Auction catal. Blenham farm. 30 Oct. 1889.
G.A. Oxon b. 92* (26)
— 22 July 1890.
G.A. Oxon b. 92* (28)

POUND COMMON

3412. An act to authorize the inclosure of certain lands . . . [Pound Common]. (20 & 21 V., c. 20, Pub.) Lond., 1857, fol. 2 pp.
L. Eng. A 69 c. 1

PRESCOTE

3413. Auction catal. Prescott manor farm. 6 Apr. 1797.
G.A. fol. A 273*

PRESTON CROWMARSH

3414. FIELD, J. E., [Note concerning a series of blocks of free stone included in a malthouse at Preston Crowmarsh, and now identified as part of Benson church.] (Berks, Bucks, & Oxon archaeol. journ., 1911, vol. 16, notes, p. 119.)
R. Top. 100

PUDLICOTE

3415. An act to authorize the inclosure of certain lands . . . [Whichwood (Pudlicot)]. (24 & 25 V., c. 38, Pub.) Lond., 1861, fol. 2 pp.
L. Eng. A 69 c. 1

3416. KIBBLE, J., Historical and other notes on the ancient manor of Charlbury and its nine hamlets . . . Pudlicote [&c.]. Oxf., 1927, 8°. 100 pp.
G.A. Oxon 8° 1053

3417. Auction catal. Manor of Pudlicot. 29 Jan. 1858.
G.A. Oxon b. 85 *b* (42)

3418. Auction catal. Pudlicote estate. 9 June 1874.
G.A. Oxon a. 116 (f. 242)

PYRTON

3419. An act effectuating an exchange between the dean and canons of Windsor, and Thomas Stonor [concerning Pyrton &c.] (34 G. III, c. 24, Private.) [Lond.], 1794, fol. 8 pp.
L. Eng. C 13 c. 1 (1794. ii)

3420. An act to authorize the inclosure of certain lands. . . . [Pyrton]. (12 & 13 V., c. 7, Pub.) Lond., 1849, fol. 2 pp.
L. Eng. A 69 c. 1

3421. COXE, H., Pyrton lectures, 1890. Oxf., 1890, 8°. 100 pp.
G.A. Oxon 8° 442

3422. PEARMAN, M. T., The descent of the manors of Pirton and Haseley. (Trans., Oxf. archaeol. soc., 27.) Lond., 1892, 8°. 24 pp.
R. Top. 330

See 1297 [Parish registers. Marriages. 1909].
See 359 [Honors and knights' fees. 1924].

3423. WEAVER, F. W., and CLARK, G. N., Churchwardens' accounts of Marston, Spelsbury, Pyrton. (Oxf. record soc., 6.) Oxf., 1925, 8°. 104 pp.
R. 13. 702

3424. HASSALL, W. O., Pyrton papers and Saxon woodlands on the Chilterns. (Oxoniensia, 1949, vol. 14, p. 89.)   R. Top. 340

3425. Auction catal. Standhill estate. 20 July 1910.
G.A. Oxon c. 317 (12)

RADCOT

3426. MYRES, J. N. L., The campaign of Radcot bridge in December 1387. (Engl. hist. review, 1927, vol. 42, p. 20–33.) Ψ 2. 38

3427. TOYNBEE, M. R., Radcot bridge and Newbridge. (Oxoniensia, 1949, vol. 14, p. 46–52.)   R. Top. 340

3428. Auction catal. Radcot house-estate. 20 July 1901.
G.A. Oxon b. 91 (22)

RADFORD

3429. Auction catal. Freehold estate. 21 Jan. 1802.
G.A. fol. A 266 (34)

RAMSDEN

3430. An act to authorize the inclosure of certain lands . . . [Ramsden]. (22 V., c. 3, Pub.) Lond., 1859, fol. 2 pp.　　　L. Eng. A 69 c. 1

3431. Ramsden. (Archaeol. notes. Oxoniensia, 1938, p. 167.)
R. Top. 340

3432. Auction catal. Arable and pasture land. 7 Dec. 1821.
G.A. Oxon b. 4 (5)

ROLLRIGHT STONES

See LITTLE ROLLRIGHT

ROTHERFIELD GREYS

3433. History of Rotherfield Greys. (The Topographer, 1791, vol. 4, p. 75–79.)　　　Douce VV 17

3434. Pedigree shewing the several persons of the family of Knollys, who have possessed the manor and Advowson of Rotherfield Greys. [Lond.], 1809, s. sh.　　　B.M.
— [Another ed.] 1810.　　　B.M.

3435. Rotherfield Greys. (Gent's. mag., 1824, pt. 1, p. 591, 92.)
Ψ 2. 44

3436. An act to authorize the inclosure of certain lands . . . [Rotherfield Greys]. (20 & 21 V., c. 20, Pub.) Lond., 1857, fol. 2 pp.
L. Eng. A 69 c. 1

3437. JONES, T. W., The Knolles or Knollys family of Rotherfield Greys. (Herald and geneal., 1874, vol. 8, p. 289–302.)　　Ψ 2. 10 d

3438. PEARMAN, M. T., Sir Francis Knollys. (Genealogist, 1884, new ser., vol. 1, p. 139–44.)　　　Ψ 2. 10 i

3439. Rotherfield Greys. (Rept., Oxf. archaeol. soc., 1888/89, p. 29–36.)
R. Top. 330

3440. WOOD, W., Church registers. Rotherfield Greys [account]. (Oxf. diocesan mag., 1908/9, vol. 4, p. 44–46.)　　Per. 11126 d. 78

3441. LAMBORN, E. A. GREENING, The armorial glass in the Knollys chapel, Rotherfield Greys. (Rept., Oxf. archaeol. soc., 1938, p. 62–64.)　　　R. Top. 330

3442. HUSSEY, C., Greys court. (Country Life, 1944, vol. 95, p. 1080–83; 1124–27.)　　　Per. 384 b. 6

3443. Auction catal. Estate. 15 Oct. 1844.　　　G.A. Oxon b. 92* (1)

3444. Auction catal. Stonor estate. 26 Sept. 1894.

G.A. Oxon b. 92 (8)

3445. Auction catal. Gillott's estate. 21 Sept. 1906.

G.A. Oxon b. 90 (17)

ROTHERFIELD PEPPARD

3446. An act to authorize the inclosure of certain lands . . . [Rotherfield Peppard]. (20 & 21 V., c. 20, Pub.) Lond., 1857, fol. 2 pp.

L. Eng. A 69 c. 1

3447. Auction catal. Estate. 15 Oct. 1844.　　G.A. Oxon b. 92* (1)

3448. Auction catal. Stonor estate. 26 Sept. 1894.

G.A. Oxon b. 92 (8)

3449. Auction catal. Gillott's estate. 21 Sept. 1906.

G.A. Oxon b. 90 (17)

ROUSHAM

3450. An act for establishing and confirming exchanges of divers lands and hereditaments in . . . Rowsham . . . pursuant to articles of agreement between sir C. C. Dormer, B. Holloway . . . and . . . H. Lee. . . . (15 G. III, c. 47, Private.) n. pl., 1775, fol. 23 pp.

L. Eng. C 13 c. 1 (1775. 68)

3451. DORMER, F. E. COTTRELL-, Account of Rousham, by F. E. C. D. [Bodleian copy contains newspaper cuttings, photographs &c. relating to the Dormer family.] Oxf., 1865, 8°. 52 pp.

G.A. Oxon 8° 228

— [Ed. in typescript, presented to the Bodleian in 1903 by the author. 84 pp.]　　　　　　　　　　　　MS. Top. Oxon d. 60

3452. WING, W., A charge to the Leet juries at the courts of Charles Cottrell Dormer, esq., lord of the manors of Rousham and Steeple-Barton-cum-Membris, Nov. 4, 1870. n. pl., (1870), 8°. 8 pp.

MS. Top. Oxon c. 6 (39)

3453. WING, W., Annals of Rousham. Repr. from the Oxf. Chronicle. [Oxf.], 1877, 16°. 32 pp.　　　　　　　　　G.A. Oxon 16° 154

3454. Rousham. (Country Life, 1910, vol. 27, p. 306–15.)

Per. 384 b. 6

3455. LENYGON, F., The work of William Kent at Rousham. (The Art journ., 1912, no. 883, p. 33–41.)　　　　　　　Per. 170 c. 3

3456. PAINTIN, H., The Cottrell-Dormers of Rousham. n. pl., [1915], s. sh.　　　　　　　　　　　　　　　G.A. Oxon c. 317 (12)

3457. HUSSEY, C., Rousham. (Country Life, 1946, vol. 99, p. 900–03, 946–49, 1084–87, 1130–33.)   Per. 384 b. 6

3458. Auction catal. Collection of prints and books of prints owned by sir C. C. Dormer. 19 Jan. 1764.   G.A. Oxon 8° 242 (1)

3459. Auction catal. Library of sir C. C. Dormer. 20 Feb. 1764.
G.A. Oxon 8° 242 (2)

3460. Auction catal. Choice old wines from Rousham park. 20 Mar. 1889.   G.A. Oxon 8° 242 (3)

3461. Auction catal. Cattle and hay from Rousham park. 20 Mar. 1889.
G.A. Oxon 8° 242 (4)

3462. Auction catal. Contents of Rousham rectory. 3 Apr. 1919.
G.A. Oxon 8° 242 (5)

3463. Auction catal. Furniture from Rousham park. 21 Sept. 1925.
G.A. Oxon 8° 242 (6)

RYCOTE

3464. An act for appointing jointures for the wives and . . . portions for the younger children of Willoughby, earl of Abingdon, and . . . Peregrine Bertie his brother. [Rycote &c.] (9 G. III, sess. 2, c. 10, Private.) n. pl., 1769, fol. 43 pp.   G.A. Oxon c. 192

See 2670 [Account of Rycote chapel. 1848].

3465. EDWARDS, W. G., Rycote chapel. (Oxf. diocesan mag., 1924, vol. 19, p. 161–68.)   Per. 11126 d. 78

3466. HUSSEY, C., Rycote (house). (Country Life, 1928, vol. 63, p. 16–24.)   Per. 384 b. 6

3467. Auction catal. Rycote estate. 31 May 1911.
G.A. Oxon b. 91 (44)

SALFORD

3468. An act to enable trustees to exchange lands of sir James Chamberlain . . . lying in the common hill or field of Salford in the county of Oxford, for like quantities of lands there, in order to the making an inclosure. (7 & 8 W. III, c. 16, Private.) 1695.

See 506 [Turnpike act. 1755].

3469. An act for dividing and inclosing certain . . . fields . . . in . . . Chipping Norton and Salford. (9 G. III, c. 75, Private.) n. pl., [1769], fol. 26 pp.   G.A. Oxon c. 185

3470. Auction catal. Village and Hill farms, the Cross hands inn &c. 12 Aug. 1896.   G.A. Oxon b. 91 (45)

SANDFORD-ON-THAMES

3471. Miscellanious epitaphs of the 16th and 17th century. Sanford. Aug. 8, 1660. (The Topographer, 1790, vol. 2, p. 370.)
Douce VV 15

3472. An act to confirm certain provisional orders of the Local government board [concerning sewage works and distribution] relating to the districts of . . . Oxford [Sandford &c.]. . . . (37 & 38 V., c. 182, L. & P.) Lond., 1874, fol. 23 pp. L. Eng. A 69 c. 6

3473. MAY, T., On the pottery from the waste heap of the Roman potters' kilns discovered at Sandford, in 1879. (Archaeologia, 1922, vol. 72, p. 225–42.) Ψ 3. 15

See 121, 126 [Bird population, Temple farm, Sandford on Thames. 1932, 1939].

3473A. LEYS, A. M., ed., The Sandford cartulary. 2 vols. (Oxf. record soc., 19, 22.) Oxf., 1938, 41, 8°. R. 13. 702

3474. Auction catal. Sandford estate. 10 July 1849.
G.A. Oxon b. 91 (46)

3475. Auction catal. Sandford farm. 9 June 1897.
G.A. Oxon b. 91 (47)

SANDFORD-ST.-MARTIN

3476. An act for dividing and inclosing . . . fields . . . in . . . Sandford . . . (7 G. III, c. 8, Private.) n. pl., [1767], fol. 20 pp.
L. Eng. C 13 c. 1 (1767, p. 1274)

3477. An act concerning certain estates heretofore of Francis Keck . . . in . . . Oxford and Wilts . . . [Sandford]. . . . (18 G. III, c. 109, Private.) n. pl., 1778, fol. 46 pp. L. Eng. C 13 c. 1 (1778. ii. 8)

3478. MARSHALL, E., An account of the parish of Sandford, in the deanery of Woodstock. Oxf., &c., 1866, 8°. 67 pp.
G.A. Oxon 8° 107

3479. Regulations for the management of the churchyard (Sandford St. Martin). Sandford St. Martin, 1884, s. sh.
G.A. Oxon c. 23 (8)

3480. Charity commission . . . 20 July 1885. [Statement concerning] Sandford-St.-Martin. Charities: allotments. [With letter from the vicar, E. Marshall.] n. pl., 1885, s. sh. G.A. Oxon c. 23 (10)

3480A. Charity commission. [Statement] In the matter of Thomas Giles's charity, and of the Poors allotment . . . 23 March 1875. [Repr. in 1885 with letter from E. Marshall.] n. pl., 1885, s. sh.
G.A. Oxon c. 23 (11)

3481 [Report of the Diocesan inspector, on his visit to the school.] n. pl., [1886], s. sh. G.A. Oxon c. 23 (12)

3482. MARSHALL, E., A few words [signed E. Marshall] for Christmas time, addressed to the parishioners of Sandford St. Martin. Heyford, 1886, 8°. 8 pp. G.A. Oxon c. 23 (16)

3483. Statement of (parish) accounts. 1889–1896/7. (Heyford), 1889–97, s. sh. G.A. Oxon c. 23

3484. National school. Copy of H.M. Inspector's report. 1890, 91. n. pl., 1890, 91, s. sh. G.A. Oxon c. 23 (27, 31)

3485. MARSHALL, E., A sketch of the history of Sandford St. Martin. n. pl., [c. 1890], 8°. 4 pp. G.A. Oxon c. 23 (3)

3486. MARSHALL, E., An address to the parishioners of Sandford St. Martin on the present state of religious education [in the village]. (Heyford), 1891, 8°. 2 pp. G.A. Oxon c. 23 (34)

3487. MARSHALL, E., An appeal to the proprietors, and to the inhabitants generally of Sandford St. Martin, in respect of the improvements required in the parish school by the Education department. (Heyford), 1893, 8°. 7 pp. G.A. Oxon c. 23 (41)

3488. MARSHALL, E., ed., Extracts from the vestry books . . . relating to the offices of parish clerk and cleaner of the church, with remarks by E. Marshall. n. pl., 1897, 8°. 4 pp. G.A. Oxon c. 23 (60)

3489. Office of parish clerk: Sandford St. Martin, 1897. n. pl., (1897), 8°. 4 pp. G.A. Oxon c. 317 (12)

3490. LONEY, J. E., A walk through a North Oxfordshire village, a sketch of the history of Sandford. Oxf., 1925, 8°. 6 pp. G.A. Oxon 8° 1046 (12)

3491.

3492. HUSSEY, C., Sandford park. (Country Life, 1940, vol. 87, p. 480–84.) Per. 384 b. 6

3493. Auction catal. Outlying portions of the Sandford park estate. 23 Sept. 1920. G.A. Oxon c. 224 (9)

SARSDEN

3494. An act for dividing and inclosing the . . . fields . . . in the parishes of Sarsden and Churchill. (27 G. III, c. 27, Private.) n. pl., [1787], fol. 23 pp. L. Eng. C 13 c. 1 (1787. 17)

SHELSWELL

3495. BLOMFIELD, J. C., History of . . . Shelswell. (Hist. of . . . deanery of Bicester. Pt. 5. Shelswell. 18 pp.) Lond., [1890], 4°. G.A. Oxon 4° 71

SHENNINGTON

3496. An act for dividing and inclosing the open and common field . . . of Shennington. (20 G. III, c. 49, Private.) n. pl., [1780], fol. 38 pp.   L. Eng. C 13 c. 1 (1780. 39)

3496A. MILLER, G., Rambles round the Edge hills. [Shennington, p. 180–87.] Lond., 1900, 8°.   G.A. Warw. 8° 129

SHIFFORD

3497. WILLIAMS, B., Account of officers in a manor in Oxfordshire [Shifford manor]. (Archaeologia, 1849, vol. 33, p. 269–78.)
R. Top. 7

3498. WILLIAMS, B., Additional remarks on hide of land, and on some ancient manorial customs in Oxfordshire [Shifford manor]. (Archaeologia, 1853, vol. 35, p. 470–74.)   R. Top. 7

SHILLINGFORD

3499. An act for repairing . . . the road from Shillingford [&c.] and for building a bridge over the Thames at or near Shillingford Ferry. (4 G. III, c. 42, Pub.) Lond., 1764, fol. 35 pp.   O.C.R.L.
— 24 G. III, c. 22, Pub.
— 45 G. III, c. 25, L. & P.   L. Eng. A 69 c. 6
— 7 & 8 G. IV, c. 19, L. & P.
— 15 & 16 V., c. 79, L. & P.
— 37 & 38 V., c. 95, Pub.

See 515, 534 [Turnpike acts. 1770, &c.].

3500. BROWNE, A. J. JUKES-, On a boring at Shillingford near Wallingford. (Midland naturalist, 1891, vol. 14, p. 201–08.)
Per. 1996 e. 158

3501. Auction catal. Strathbraen house. 29 May 1902.
G.A. Oxon b. 6 (33)

SHILTON

3502. An act to authorize the inclosure of certain lands . . . [Shilton]. (16 & 17 V., c. 3, Pub.) Lond., 1853, fol. 2 pp.   L. Eng. A 69 c. 1

3503. LEEMING, J. J., Shilton bridge. (Oxoniensia, 1940, p. 170.)
R. Top. 340

SHIPLAKE

3504. An act for vesting the mannor of Okeley and other lands . . . in trust for Charles lord Cadogan . . . and for settling other lands . . . in the counties of Berks and Oxon [Shiplake &c.] to the same uses. (3 G. II, c. 8, Private.) n. pl., 1730, fol. 10 pp.
G.A. Oxon c. 198

3505. An act to authorize the inclosure of certain lands . . . [Shiplake]. (27 & 28 V., c. 66, Pub.) Lond., 1864, fol. 2 pp.
L. Eng. A 69 c. 1

3506. CLIMENSON, E. J., The history of Shiplake. Lond., &c., 1894, 4°. 494 pp.
G.A. Oxon 4° 176

3507. Shiplake court. (Country Life, 1898, vol. 4, p. 16–19.)
Per. 384 b. 6

3508. Vicars of Shiplake. (Berks, Bucks, & Oxon archaeol. journ., 1900, vol. 6, notes, p. 60.)
R. Top. 100

3509. CLIMENSON, E. J., History of Shiplake church. n. pl., [1904], 4°. 16 pp.
G.A. Oxon 4° 224

3510. CLIMENSON, E. J., History of Shiplake church. (Berks, Bucks, & Oxon archaeol. journ., 1904, vol. 10, p. 5, 6.)
R. Top. 100

3511. PHILLIPPS, L. M., Shiplake court. (Country Life, 1906, vol. 20, p. 594–602.)
Per. 384 b. 6

3512. CHATWIN, C. P., and WITHERS, T. H., The zones of chalk in the Thames valley between Goring and Shiplake. (Proc., Geol. assoc., 1908, vol. 20, p. 390–421.)
Radcl.

3513. CLIMENSON, E. J., The poet Swinburne and Shiplake. (Berks, Bucks, & Oxon archaeol. journ., 1909, vol. 15, notes, p. 56.)
R. Top. 100

3514. CLIMENSON, E. J., The Shiplake virtuoso [H. C. Jennings]. (Berks, Bucks, & Oxon archaeol. journ., 1914, vol. 20, p. 26–28, 49–53.)
R. Top. 100

3515. CLIMENSON, E. J., Roman remains at Shiplake. (Berks, Bucks, & Oxon archaeol. journ., 1918, vol. 24, p. 34, 35.)
R. Top. 100

3516. DYER, A. S., Wilder family of Shiplake and the American Wilders. (N. & Q., 1934, 1 Sept., p. 148.)
Ψ 2. 97

3517. NORSWORTHY, L. L., The Plowden interest in Oxfordshire. (Trans., Shropshire archaeol. soc., 1948, vol. 52, p. 179–90.)
R. Top. 350

3518. Auction catal. Estate. 15 Oct. 1844. G.A. Oxon b. 92* (1)

3519. Auction catal. Portion of Crowsley estate. 29 July 1896.
G.A. Oxon b. 91 (48)

SHIPTON-ON-CHERWELL

3520. An act for dividing and inclosing the common fields . . . of Shipton upon Charwell. . . . (8 G. III, c. 66, Private.) n. pl., 1768, fol. 9 pp. L. Eng. C 13 c. 1 (1768. 43)

3521. Shipton-on-Cherwell. (Archaeol. notes. Oxoniensia, 1941, p. 88.)
R. Top. 340

3522. Auction catal. The whole parish, including the perpetual advowson of the rectory. 1 Sept. 1803. G.A. fol. A 266 (41)

3523. Auction catal. Shipton-on-Cherwell estate. 7 Aug. 1862.
G.A. Oxon b. 85 *b* (43)

SHIPTON-UNDER-WYCHWOOD

3524. Shipton court. (Views of the seats of noblemen, by J. P. Neale, 2nd ser., 1824, vol. 1. 1 p.) G.A. Gen. top. 4° 43

3525. An act to authorize the inclosure of certain lands . . . [Shipton-under-Wychwood]. (13 & 14 V., c. 66, Pub.) Lond., 1850, fol. 2 pp.
L. Eng. A 69 c. 1

3526. An act to authorize the inclosure of certain lands . . . [Shipton-under-Wychwood]. (22 V., c. 3, Pub.) Lond., 1859, fol. 2 pp.
L. Eng. A 69 c. 1

3527. PARKER, J. H., On Shipton-under-Wychwood. (Proc., Oxf. architect. and hist. soc., N.S., vol. 2, 1869, p. 132–35.) R. 13. 708

3528. Notes of an excursion to Shipton-under-Wychwood [&c.]. (North Oxf. archaeol. soc., 1870.) Banbury, [1870], 8°. 37 pp.
R. Top. 330

3529. BARTER, H., Shipton-under-Wychwood, restoration of the steeple [signed H. Barter and others]. n. pl., (1892), 4°. 4 pp.
G.A. Oxon c. 22 (18)

3530. Shipton-under-Wychwood tower restoration fund. Second list of subscribers. n. pl., [c. 1895], 8°. 4 pp. G.A. Oxon c. 22 (17)

3531. Shipton-under-Wychwood, church. (Trans., Bristol and Glouc. archaeol. soc., 1895–96, vol. 20, p. 364–67.) R. Top. 210

3532. Shipton court. (Country Life, 1900, vol. 7, p. 144–50.)
Per. 384 b. 6

See 362 [Manor. Survey of 1387. 1910].
See 1022 [Act concerning supply of gas. 1913].

3533. The history of Shipton-under-Wychwood. Lond., (1934), 8°. 61 pp.   O.C.L.

3534. GROVES, M., *ed.*, Records of Milton and Shipton-under-Wychwood during the war, 1939–1945. (Charlbury), [1948], 8°. 52 pp.
G.A. Oxon 8° 1204 (9)

3535. Auction catal. Contents of Shipton court. 23 July 1901.
G.A. Oxon c. 317 (12)

3536. Auction catal. Parsonage farm. 5 May 1911.
G.A. Oxon c. 317 (12)

3537. Auction catal. Agricultural portion of Shipton Court estate. 1913?   G.A. Oxon b. 92* (14)

SHIRBURN

3538. An act for vesting the estate of James Lucy Dighton . . . in . . . Sherborne . . . in trustees, to be sold. (7 G. III, c. 25, Private.) n. pl., 1767, fol. 12 pp.   L. Eng. C 13 c. 1 (1767, p. 567)

3539. An act for vesting the real estate of Thomas Reade and Elizabeth Reade . . . situate in Shirburn [&c.] . . . in Thomas, earl of Macclesfield. . . . (28 G. III, c. 6, Private.) n. pl., 1788, fol. 10 pp.
L. Eng. C 13 c. 1 (1788. 49)

3540. An act for inclosing lands in the parish of Shirburn. (45 G. III, c. 45, Private.) n. pl., 1805, fol. 14 pp.   G.A. Oxon c. 107 (68)

3541. Sherbourn castle. (Views of the seats of noblemen and gentlemen, by J. P. Neale, 1820, vol. 3. 2 pp.)   G.A. Gen. top. 4° 42

3542. Festivities at Shirburn castle. [Repr. from the Oxford journal, 11th Feb., 1865.] [Account of coming of age festivities of visct. Parker.] n. pl., [1865], 8°. 8 pp.   G.A. Oxon 8° 93 (12)

3543. MACCLESFIELD, M. F., countess of, Scattered notices of Shirburn castle. Lond., 1887, 16°. 46 pp.   G.A. Oxon 16° 156

3544. MONEY, W., A walk to Shirburn castle [from Whitchurch]. (Journ., Brit. archaeol. assoc., 1895, new ser., vol. 1, p. 285–95.)
R. Top. 4

3545. Shirburn castle. (Rept., Oxf. archaeol. soc., 1895/6, p. 18, 19.)
R. Top. 330

3546. Shirburn castle. (Country Life, 1900, vol. 7, p. 80–84.)
Per. 384 b. 6

3547. HASSALL, W. O., Shirburn castle. (Thame Gazette, Feb. 27, Mar. 13, 1951.)   N.G.A. Oxon a. 120

SHORTHAMPTON

3548. KIBBLE, J., Historical and other notes on the ancient manor of Charlbury and its nine hamlets . . . Shorthampton [&c.]. Oxf., 1927, 8°. 100 pp.   G.A. Oxon 8° 1053

3549. PAYNE, J. D., Notes on the history of the parish of Charlbury with Chadlington and Shorthampton. Oxf., 1935, 8°. 52 pp.
     G.A. Oxon 4° 702

3550. LONG, E. T., The wall paintings in Shorthampton Church. (Rept., Oxf. archaeol. soc., 1937, p. 8–11.)   R. Top. 330
— [Repr.] Long Compton, 1938, 8°. 4 pp.
     G.A. Oxon 8° 1230 (6)

3551. Auction catal. Manor of Shorthampton. 29 Jan. 1858.
     G.A. Oxon b. 85 b (42)

SHOTOVER

3552. An act to enable his majesty to grant the inheritance of part of the forest of Shotover and Stowood . . . to trustees, in trust for Augustus Schutz . . . and his heirs, upon a . . . consideration to be paid for the same. (17 G. II, c. 3, Private.) n. pl., 1743/4, fol. 7 pp.
     G.A. Oxon c. 183

3553. An act for allotting lands in . . . Shotover . . . (59 G. III, c. 85, Private.) n. pl., 1819, fol. 25 pp.
     L. Eng. C 13 c. 1 (1819. iv. 24)
— 18 & 19 V., c. 14, Pub.

3554. A description of . . . Shotover house. (Stranger's guide and hist. & biogr. hand-book to Oxford. 6th ed. pp. 251, 52.) Oxf., [c. 1850], 8°.
     G.A. Oxon 8° 541

3555. An act to authorize the inclosure of certain lands . . . [Shotover]. (18 & 19 V., c. 14, Pub.) Lond., 1855, fol. 2 pp.
     L. Eng. A 69 c. 1

3556. PHILLIPS, J., On the estuary sands in the upper part of Shotover hill. (Quart. journ., Geol. soc., 1858, vol. 14, p. 236–41.)   Radcl.

3557. POULTON, E. B., A walk from Oxford to Wheatley over Shotover hill [mainly geological observations]. (Oxf. mag., 1883, vol. 1, p. 169–71.)   G.A. Oxon 4° 141
— Repr.   G.A. Oxon 8° 683

3558. In Chancery. The president and scholars of Saint Mary Magdalen college in the University of Oxford v. Bateman and others. Bill of complaint [concerning the use of Shotover as common land]. (Lond.), 1872, fol. 20 pp.   MS. Top. Oxon b. 117 (166)

3559. BLAKE, J. F., Excursion to Headington, Shotover, and Wheatley. (Proc., Geol. assoc., 1902, vol. 17, p. 383–85.)   Radcl.

3560. MANNING, P., 'Old sir Harry Bath' [a legend of how Shotover was named]. (Oxford mag., 1903, vol. 21, p. 276, 77.)
G.A. Oxon 4° 141
— Repr.   G.A. Oxon 8° 705 (6)

3561. HUSSEY, C., Shotover park. (Country Life, 1926, vol. 59, p. 240–46.)   Per. 384 b. 6

3562. Forest Hill with Shotover. The village book. Oxf., 1933, 4°. 73 pp.
G.A. Oxon 4° 547

3563. COPPOCK, G. A., and HILL, B. M., Headington quarry and Shotover, a history. Oxf., 1933, 8°. 84 pp.   G.A. Oxon 8° 1115

3564. Shotover. (Archaeol. notes. Oxoniensia, 1940, p. 162.)
R. Top. 340

3565. HASSALL, W. O., Shotover and the old road. (Thame Gazette, Jan. 9, 1951.)   N.G.A. Oxon a. 120

3566. Auction catal. Ochre and clay pits. 18 Dec. 1847.
G.A. Oxon b. 91 (49)

3567. Auction catal. Shotover house, Grove and Thornhill, Lodge, West Hill and Hill House farms. 2 Aug. 1854.
G.A. Oxon b. 85 b (44)

3568. Auction catal. Pasture and arable land. 13 June 1855.
G.A. Oxon b. 4 (18)

3569. Auction catal. Land. 2 Sept. 1868.   G.A. Oxon b. 4 (35)

3570. Auction catal. Shotover estate. 1 Aug. 1871.
MS. Top. Oxon b. 117 (176)

3571. Auction catal. Agricultural estate of T. B. Morrell. 20 June 1903.
G.A. Oxon b. 91 (16)

SHUTFORD

3572. An act for dividing and inclosing the . . . field . . . and lands, lying within . . . Shutford. (5 G. III, c. 84, Private.) n. pl., 1765, fol. 23 pp.
G.A. Oxon c. 190

3573. Auction catal. Estate. 30 May 1872.   G.A. Oxon b. 85 b (47)

3574. Auction catal. Arable and pasture land, West Shutford. 1 May 1873.   G.A. Oxon b. 85 b (48)

3575. Auction catal. Two farm houses and land. 25 Sept. 1891.
G.A. Oxon b. 85 b (49)

3576. Auction catal. Estate, West Shutford. 4 May 1899.
G.A. Oxon b. 91 (51)

SIBFORD FERRIS

3577. An act for dividing and inclosing the . . . fields . . . within . . . Sibford Ferris. (29 G. III, c. 56, Private.) n. pl., 1789, fol. 26 pp.
G.A. Oxon c. 113 (3)

3578. ARKELL, W. J., and WHITEHEAD, T. H., Report of a field meeting at Hook Norton and Sibford [Ferris. Temple Mills quarry.] (Proc., Geol. assoc., 1946, vol. 57, p. 16–18.) Radcl.

3579. Auction catal. Folly farm, Field barn farm. 12 June 1873.
G.A. Oxon b. 85 b (50)

SIBFORD GOWER

3580. An act for dividing and inclosing the open and common field . . . within . . . Broad Sibford, otherwise Sibford Gower [&c.]. (13 G. III, c. 60, Private.) n. pl., 1773, fol. 25 pp.
L. Eng. C 13 c. 1 (1773. 80)

3580A. WOOD, H. E., The rhapsody Sibfordian, a fictitious description [in verse] of Sibford [Gower]. n. pl., 1900, 12°. 20 pp.
280 e. 3836 (1)

3581. Auction catal. Bunker's ground or Shaw's closes. 12 June 1873.
G.A. Oxon b. 85 b (50)

SIGNET

See UPTON AND SIGNET

SOMERTON

3582. An act for dividing and inclosing a certain open common field, common pastures, common meadows, and waste grounds, in the manor and parish of Somerton. (5 G. III, c. 83, Private.) n. pl., 1765, fol. 9 pp. G.A. Oxon 4° 349

3583. Church notes, &c. of Somerton. (The Topographer, 1791, vol. 3, p. 89–94.) Douce VV 16

3584. Somerton. (Gent's. mag., 1827, pt. 1, p. 113–17, 580, 81.)
Ψ 2. 44

3585. SHIRLEY, E. P., Extracts from the Fermor accounts [relating to Somerton] 1580. (Mem. chiefly illustr. of the hist. and antiq. of Oxf. Proc., Archaeol. inst., 1854, vol. 6, p. 83–90.)
G.A. Gen. top. 8° 528 (6)

3586. GOODMAN, T., Somerton, Oxfordshire [Repr. from the Cath. mag.]. n. pl., [c. 1870], 8°. 4 pp. G.A. Oxon 8° 147 (15)

3587. [Fermor pedigrees, with extracts from the parish registers of Somerton, and abstracts of wills of the Fermor family.] n. pl., [1880], fol. 24 pp. Hist. c. 92

3588. Fermor of Tusmore. [Pedigree.] n. pl., [c. 1880], s. sh.
Hist. c. 92

3589. BLOMFIELD, J. C., History of . . . Somerton. (Hist. of . . . deanery of Bicester. Pt. 4.) Bristol, (1888), 4°. 160 pp. G.A. Oxon 4° 71

3590. Rules for the government of a friendly and benefit society . . . Somerton. Heyford, 1892, 8°. 13 pp. 24786 e. 11 (23)

3591. BARNES, G. E., Church of S. James, A. & M., Somerton. (Rept., Oxf. archaeol. soc., 1898, p. 25, 26.) R. Top. 330
— [Another article in 1902, p. 12, 13.] R. Top. 330

3592. BARNES, G. E., Juxon's rectory at Somerton. (Rept., Oxf. archaeol. soc., 1900. p. 19–21.) R. Top. 330

3593. BARNES, G. E., Juxon coat of arms at Somerton rectory. (Rept., Oxf. archaeol. soc., 1902, p. 14, 15.) R. Top. 330

3594. GARNER, T., Juxon's arms (Glass). (Rept., Oxf. archaeol. soc., 1902, p. 20–22.) R. Top. 330

3595. Somerton church. (Berks, Bucks, & Oxon archaeol. journ., 1903, vol. 9, p. 68, 69.) R. Top. 100

3596. BALLARD, A., Seven Somerton court rolls. (Trans., Oxf. archaeol. soc., 50.) Banbury, 1906, 8°. 27 pp. R. Top. 330

SONNING

3597. An act for vesting the manor of Okeley and other lands in . . . Bucks in trust for Charles lord Cadogan and his heirs, and for settling other lands . . . in [Sonning] . . . to the same uses. (3 G. II, c. 8, Private.) n. pl., (1730), fol. 10 pp. G.A. Oxon c. 198

3597A. An act for vesting certain tenements and hereditaments in the counties of Oxford, Berks and Wilts, part of the settled estates of the earl of Macclesfield, in trustees, to be sold or exchanged. [Sonning &c.] (13 G. III, c. 49, Private.) n. pl., 1773, fol. 26 pp.
L. Eng. C 13 c. 1 (1773)

3598. An act to subject and charge the rectory . . . of Suning otherwise Sonynge in the counties of Berks and Oxford . . . to Doctor Thomas Greene. . . . (14 G. III, c. 44, Private.) n. pl., 1774, fol. 13 pp.
L. Eng. C 13 c. 1 (1774. 80)

3599. An act for inclosing lands in the parish of Sonning in the counties of Berks and Oxford. (56 G. III, c. 36, Private.) Lond., 1816, fol. 28 pp.   O.C.R.L.

See 3048 [History, by J. E. Smith-Masters. 1933].

3600. Auction catal. Estate. 15 Oct. 1844.   G.A. Oxon b. 92* (1)

SOULDERN

3601. A bill for the sale of part of the estate of John Weedon of Souldern . . . sufficient to pay his father's debts. [Lond., 1706], fol. 3 pp.
G.A. Oxon c. 195
— Act. (5 Anne, c. 38, Private.)

3602. DRYDEN, SIR H. E. L., The antiquities of Steeple Aston, by W. Wing. Together with a short description of Souldern, and of the sepulchral remains found there, by sir H. E. L. Dryden. Dedding-ton, &c., (1845), 8°. 87 pp.   G.A. Oxon 8° 92 (1)

3603. An act to authorize the inclosure of certain lands . . . [Souldern]. (16 & 17 V., c. 120, Pub.) Lond., 1853, fol. 2 pp.
L. Eng. A 69 c. 1
See 1228 [Account of John Horseman. 1872].

3604. GOUGH, J. H., and A. P., Notes on Souldern. Repr. from the Bicester Herald. Bicester, 1882, 16°. 62 pp.   G.A. Oxon 16° 155

3605. GOUGH, J. H., and A. P., Historical and descriptive notices of the parish of Souldern. (Trans., Oxf. archaeol. soc., 22.) Banbury, 1887, 8°. 36 pp.   R. Top. 330

3606. BLOMFIELD, J. C., History of Souldern. (Hist. of . . . deanery of Bicester. Pt. 7.) Lond., 1893, 4°. 100 pp.   G.A. Oxon 4° 71

3607. Appeal for means to build a fitting chancel for the ancient church of St. Mary, Souldern. n. pl., [1894], 4°. 4 pp.
G.A. Oxon c. 317 (13)

3608. Auction catal. Estate. 15 July 1857.   G.A. Oxon b. 85 b (57)

3609. Auction catal. Manor farm house and land. 24 Sept. 1896.
G.A. Oxon b. 91 (52)

3610. Auction catal. Chisnell farm. 13 Sept. 1900.
G.A. Oxon b. 91 (53)

3611. Auction catal. Tower farm. 6 June 1912.   G.A. Oxon b. 90 (54)

SOUTH LEIGH

See 3664 [Estate act. Johnson's farm. 1721].

3612. An act for dividing and inclosing the ... fields ... of Southleigh ... (32 G. III, c. 66, Private.) n. pl., 1792, fol. 22 pp.
L. Eng. C 13 c. 1 (1792. 2)

3613. Description of the mediæval paintings on the walls of Southleigh church, Oxon, discovered and restored 1872. Oxf., &c., [1872?], 8°. 11 pp. G.A. Oxon 8° 165 (12)

3614.

3615. WALLER, J. G., On recent discoveries of wall-paintings at ... South Leigh. (Archaeological journ., 1873, vol. 30, p. 52–58.)
R. Top. 5

3616. EAST, A., Southleigh 14th and 15th century mural paintings [by A. East]. n. pl., [c. 1900], s. sh. G.A. Oxon c. 107 (16)

3617. MOULTRIE, G., Six years' work at Southleigh [concerning the church, school, &c.]. Burford, 1875, 8°. 25 pp.
G.A. Oxon 8° 683 (5)
— Repr. with addendum. 1883. 16 pp. G.A. Oxon 8° 850 (1)

3618. St. James's coll. How we manage our affairs at South-Leigh, written by the little boys themselves. Lond., 1880, 8°. 30 pp.
G.A. Oxon 8° 215 b (6)

3619. St. James's coll. Commemoration, 1884. Introduction, speeches and sermon. Oxf. (1884), 8°. 27 pp. G.A. Oxon 8° 1148 (7)

3620. Southleigh. (Rept., Oxf. archaeol. soc., 1908, p. 8.) R. Top. 330

3621. GROSCH, A., Sowlye [Southleigh]. (Exeter), [1946], 8°. 25 pp.
G.A. Oxon 8° 1204 (3)

3622. Auction catal. Timber. 10 Dec. 1827. G.A. Oxon c. 317 (10)

3623. Auction catal. Tar farm. 10 June 1911. G.A. Oxon b. 91 (27)

SOUTH NEWINGTON

3624. An act for dividing and inclosing the ... fields ... of Southnewington otherwise Southnewton. ... (34 G. III, c. 90, Private.) n. pl., 1794, fol. 30 pp. L. Eng. C 13 c. 1 (1794. 45)

3625. An act for vesting part of the settled estates of ... John, earl of Shrewsbury [in South Newington, &c.] ... in trustees to be sold. (6 & 7 V., c. 28, Private.) Lond., 1843, fol. 60 pp.
L. Eng. C 13 c. 1 (1843. i. 28)

3626. ROYCE, D., History of . . . South Newington [by D. Royce]·. (Trans., North Oxf. archaeol. soc., 1875.) Oxf., 1877, 8°. 28 pp.
R. Top. 330

3627. BETTERIDGE, J. W., Restoration of South Newington Church. n. pl., [c. 1892], s. sh.   MS. Top. Oxon d. 42 (88)

3628. Restoration of S. Peter's church, South Newington. [Announcement of the completion of repairs, and appeal for funds to pay off a deficit.] n. pl., (1893), 4°. 2 pp.   G.A. Oxon c. 317 (12)

3629. WHITEHEAD, C. J., Notes on South Newington church and frescoes. (Rept., Oxf. archaeol. soc., 1907, p. 12–15.)   R. Top. 330

3630. South Newington vicarage. (Rept., Oxf. archaeol. soc., 1913, p. 129–30.)   R. Top. 330

3631. MORIARTY, G. A., South Newington and the Giffards. (Geneal. mag., 1933, Sept., p. 282–85.)   Per. 2183 e. 10

3632. TRISTAM, E. W., The wall paintings at South Newington. (Burlington mag., vol. 62, no. 360, 1933, p. 114–29.)
Per. 170 c. 25 (62)

3633. LAMBORN, E. A. GREENING, Arms in South Newington church. (Journ., Brit. archaeol. assoc., 1938, 3rd ser., vol. 3, p. 207–09.)
R. Top. 4

3634. Auction catal. Paradise farm. 20 July 1922.
G.A. Oxon b. 92* (18)

SOUTH STOKE

See 1324 [Patterns of inlaid tiles from churches, by W. A. Church. 1845].

3635. An act to authorize the inclosure of certain lands . . . [Southstoke-cum-Woodcote]. (13 & 14 V., c. 66, Pub.) Lond., 1850, fol. 2 pp.
L. Eng. A 69 c. 1

3636. Berks, South Oxon, and North Hants society for the preservation of public rights of way and open spaces. The proposed diversion of a Thames footpath [from Goring to South Stoke]. Repr. from the Reading standard, Jan. 7th, 1898. n. pl., (1898), 8°. 4 pp.
G.A. Oxon c. 317 (1)

3637. KEYSER, C. E., Notes on the churches of South Stoke, North Stoke [&c.] (Journ., Brit. archaeol. assoc., 1918, new ser., vol. 24, p. 1–32+67 plates.)   R. Top. 4

SOUTH WESTON

3638. An act to authorize the inclosure of certain lands . . . [South Weston]. (17 & 18 V., c. 48, Pub.) Lond., 1854, fol. 2 pp.
L. Eng. A 69 c. 1

See 359 [Honors and knights' fees. 1924].

SOUTHROPE

3639. An act for sale of part of the estate of Richard Brideoake [in Southrope, &c.]. (9 Anne, c. 43, Private.) n. pl., [1710], fol. 4 pp.
B.M.

3639A. An act for dividing and inclosing the . . . fields . . . within . . . Hook-Norton and Southrop. . . . (13 G. III, c. 114, Private.) n. pl., 1773, fol. 22 pp.　　　　　L. Eng. C 13 c. 1 (1773. 46)

SPELSBURY

3640. An act for dividing, allotting, and inclosing . . . lands . . . of Spelsbury. . . . (42 G. III, c. 81, Private.) n. pl., 1802, fol. 19 pp.
L. Eng. C 13 c. 1 (1802. ii. 8)

3641. Restoration of the church of All Saints, Spelsbury. [Appeal for funds.] n. pl., [1886], 8°. 4 pp.　　　　　G.A. Oxon c. 317 (13)

3642. OLDFIELD, J., A churchwarden's account book [at Spelsbury]. (Berks, Bucks, & Oxon archaeol. journ., 1910, vol. 16, p. 8–16.)
R. Top. 100

3643. WEAVER, F. W., and CLARK, G. N., Churchwardens' accounts of Marston, Spelsbury, Pyrton. (Oxf. record soc., 6.) Oxf., 1925, 8°. 104 pp.　　　　　R. 13. 702

3644. KIBBLE, J., Historical and other notes on the ancient manor of Charlbury and its nine hamlets . . . Spelsbury [&c.]. Oxf., 1927, 8°. 100 pp.　　　　　G.A. Oxon 8° 1053

3645. Spelsbury Women's institute. A history of Spelsbury, ed. by E. Corbett. Shipston-on-Stour, 1931, 8°. 272 pp.
G.A. Oxon 8° 1081

STADHAMPTON

3646. DE WATTEVILLE, H. G., A catalogue of the brasses in the churches of Stadhampton, Chalgrove and Waterperry, Oxon. (Journ., Oxf. univ. brass-rubbing soc., 1897, vol. 1, p. 110–20.)　　Soc. 2184 d. 50

STANDHILL

3647. An act for vesting the . . . manors and estates [at Standhill, &c.] of Charles Vere Spencer, an infant, in . . . Oxford and Denbigh in trustees, in order to effect the sale thereof. . . . (5 & 6 W. IV, c. 23, Private.) n. pl., 1835, fol. 44 pp.　　L. Eng. C 13 c. 1 (1835. 23)

STANDLAKE

3648. An act for the vesting . . . several manors and lands [in Standlake, &c.] . . . late the inheritance of W. Jennens . . . in trustees to be sold. (8 Anne, c. 10, Private.) n. pl., [c. 1709], 8°. 52 pp.
Radcl. e. 127
See 1225 [J. Leverett's will. 1783].

3649. An act to authorize the inclosure of certain lands . . . [Standlake]. (11 & 12 V., c. 109, Pub.) Lond., 1848, fol. 3 pp.
L. Eng. A 69 c. 1

3650. The Standlake parish magazine. No. 1, Jan. 1877–No. 61, Nov. 1882. n. pl., (1877–82), 8°. G.A. Oxon 8° 666

3651. Standlake and Stanton Harcourt Horticultural and cottage garden society's show. Rules & schedule of prizes. 1882. Witney, 1882, 4°. 4 pp. G.A. Oxon c. 22 (19)
— 1893. G.A. Oxon c. 208 (27)

3652. Standlake bell ringers' club. [Rules.] n. pl., [c. 1890], 4°. 4 pp.
G.A. Oxon c. 317 (13)

3653. CORNISH, C. J., A Royalist post: Gaunt house. (Country Life, 1903, vol. 13, p. 870–72.) Per. 384 b. 6

See 1297 [Parish registers. Marriages. 1909].
See 293 [History, by W. J. Monk. 1926].

3654. AKERMAN, J. Y., and STONE, S., An account of the investigation of some remarkable circular trenches and the discovery of an ancient British cemetery at Stanlake, Oxon. (Archaeologia, 1857, vol. 37, p. 363–70.) R. Top. 7

3655. STONE, S., Account of certain (supposed) British and Saxon remains, recently discovered at Standlake. (Proc., Soc. of antiq., 1857, ser. 1, vol. 4, p. 92–100.) R. Top. 1

3656. STONE, S., [Account of explorations at Standlake, &c.] (Proc., Soc. of antiq., 1858, ser. 1, vol. 4, p. 213–19.) R. Top. 1

See 310 [Traces of Early Britons. 1862].

3657. Notes of an excursion to . . . Stanlake [&c.] 1871. (North Oxf. archaeol. soc.) Banbury, [1871], 8°. 73 pp. R. Top. 330

3658. Standlake. (Archaeol. notes. Oxoniensia, 1938, p. 163; 1941, p. 88; 1942, p. 103; 1943/4, p. 199; 1949, vol. 14, p. 77; 1950, vol. 15, p. 107.) R. Top. 340

3659. BRADFORD, J. S. P., An early Iron age settlement at Standlake. (Antiquaries journ., 1942, vol. 22, p. 202–14.) R. Top. 2

3660. RILEY, D. N., A late Bronze age and Iron age site on Standlake downs. (Oxoniensia, 1946–7, p. 27–43.) R. Top. 340

3661. Auction catal. Manor and Yew tree farms. 29 Apr. 1896.
G.A. Oxon b. 92 (1)

3662. Auction catal. Estate. 31 May 1899. G.A. Oxon b. 91 (37)

3663. Auction catal. Gaunt house mill &c. 10 June 1920.
G.A. Oxon b. 92* (11)

STANTON HARCOURT

3664. An act to vest two fourth parts of a fee farm rent . . . in trustees to the like uses as lands called Johnson's farm in . . . Stanton Harcourt and Southly . . . were devised by dame Elizabeth Harcourt . . . and in lieu thereof for vesting Johnson's farm in visct. Harcourt. (8 G. I, c. 4, Private.) 1721.

3665. An act for . . . inclosing the . . . fields . . . of Stanton Harcourt. (13 G. III, c. 102, Private.) L. Eng. C 13 c. 1 (1773. 37).

3666. Stanton Harcourt. (Gent's. mag., 1783, pt. 2, p. 812; 1819, pt. 1, p. 393, 94.) Ψ 2. 44

3667. HARCOURT, G. S., 2nd earl, An account of the church and remains of the manor house of Stanton Harcourt [by George Simon, earl Harcourt]. (Oxf.), 1808, 8°. 28 pp. G.A. Oxon 8° 450

3668. DERICK, J. M., Views and details of Stanton Harcourt church. Oxf., 1841, fol. 2 pp.+11 plates. G.A. fol. A 117

3669. DYKE, W., Decorations in distemper in Stanton Harcourt church. (Archaeol. journ., 1846, vol. 2, p. 365–68.) R. Top. 5

3670. GILES, J. A., History of Witney, with notices of . . . Stanton Harcourt [&c.]. Lond., 1852, 8°. 107 pp. G.A. Oxon 8° 13

3671. STONE, S., [Account of explorations at Stanton Harcourt]. (Proc., Soc. of antiq., 1858, ser. 1, vol. 4, p. 213–19.) R. Top. 1

3672. Stanton Harcourt. (Excursion. Archaeol. and nat. hist. soc. of N. Oxf., 1868.) Manning 8° 3

3673. Stanton Harcourt, a general statement of accounts . . . 1872 (74). n. pl., (1872, 1874), s. sh. G.A. Oxon c. 22 (20, 21)

3674. Rules of the Victoria club held at the Harcourt Arms inn in Stanton Harcourt. Bampton, 1874, 8°. 12 pp.
G.A. Oxon c. 317 (13)

3675. HARCOURT, E. W., ed., The Harcourt papers. 14 vols. Oxf.,
[1876–1905], 8°.   2182 H. e. 4–16*

3676. Standlake and Stanton Harcourt horticultural and cottage garden
society's show. Rules & schedule of prizes, 1882. Witney, 1882,
4°. 4 pp.   G.A. Oxon c. 22 (19)
— 1893.   G.A. Oxon c. 208 (27)

3677. MONK, W. J., Stanton Harcourt. Repr. from the Witney gazette.
Witney, 1893, 16°. 32 pp.   G.A. Oxon 16° 157

3678. MONEY, W., Stanton Harcourt and its manor. (Berks, Bucks, &
Oxon archaeol. journ., 1908, vol. 13, p. 97–100.)   R. Top. 100

See 1297 [Parish registers. Marriages. 1909].

3679. OLDFIELD, J., Manor Courts [extract from 'Minute Book of
Courts' concerning manor of Stanton Harcourt]. (Berks, Bucks, &
Oxon archaeol. journ., 1913, vol. 19, p. 75–80.)   R. Top. 100

See 293 [History, by W. J. Monk. 1926].

3680. LAMBORN, E. A. GREENING, The shrine of St. Edburg [Stanton
Harcourt]. (Rept., Oxf. archaeol. soc., 1934, p. 43–52.)
                                                      R. Top. 330
— Repr.   G.A. Oxon 4° 504 (17)
— (Country Life, 1942, vol. 91, p. 1048, 49.)   Per. 384 b. 6

3681. Stanton Harcourt. An air-photograph of Black Ditch field.
(Antiquity, 1935, vol. 9, p. 478–79.)   R. Top. 6

3682. Stanton Harcourt. (Archaeol. notes. Oxoniensia, 1936, p. 201;
1937, p. 202; 1940, p. 161; 1941, p. 88; 1943–44, p. 200; 1945,
p. 94; 1950, vol. 15, p. 107.)   R. Top. 340

3683. HUSSEY, C., Parsonage house, Stanton Harcourt. (Country Life,
1941, vol. 90, p. 112–15, 160–63.)   Per. 384 b. 6

3684. HUSSEY, C., Stanton Harcourt, the romance of an Oxfordshire
manor. (Country Life, 1941, vol. 90, p. 628–31, 674–77.)
                                                      Per. 384 b. 6

3685. GRIMES, W. F., Excavations at Stanton Harcourt, 1940. [No. 1.]
(Oxoniensia, 1943, 44, p. 19–63.)   R. Top. 340

3686. HARDEN, D. B., and TREWEEKS, R. C., Excavations at Stanton
Harcourt, 1940. II. (Oxoniensia, 1945, p. 16–41.)   R. Top. 340

3687. Auction catal. Estate. 31 May 1899.   G.A. Oxon b. 91 (37)

3688. Auction catal. Stanton Harcourt portion of the Harcourt settled
estates. 3 Sept. 1924.   G.A. Oxon c. 226

STANTON ST. JOHN

3689. An act for dividing and inclosing the . . . fields . . . of Stanton Saint John. . . . (17 G. III, c. 73, Private.) n. pl., 1777, fol. 19 pp.
L. Eng. C 13 c. 1 (1777. ii. 27)

3690. [*Begin.*] Fire at Stanton St. John's. [Account of a fire which consumed 21 houses &c., and request to subscribe to relief fund for homeless.] n. pl., (1793), s. sh. Gough Oxf. 90 (20)

3691. An act for enabling William Hall . . . to assign or surrender a term of one thousand years in estates [in Stanton Saint John &c.] . . . unto . . . Elisha Biscoe. (53 G. III, c. 203, L. & P.) Lond., 1813, fol. 4 pp. L. Eng. A 69 c. 6

3692. Stanton St. John. (Gent's. mag., 1838, pt. 2, p. 651.)
Ψ 2. 44

3693. [Circular calling for subscriptions towards the restoration of the church, with list of contributions already received.] n. pl., [*c.* 1870], 4°. 3 pp. G.A. fol. A 139* (61)

3694. Stanton St. John [notes from the parish registers]. (Oxf. diocesan mag., 1904/5, vol. 2, p. 312.) Per. 11126 d. 78

3695. MANNING, P., Palimpsest brasses from Quarrendon, Bucks., and Stanton St. John, Oxon. (Oxf. journ. of monumental brasses, 1912, vol. 2, p. 153–56.) Soc. 2184 d. 50

See 449 [Estates of New college, 1659–75, p. 71–86. 1949].

3696. Auction catal. Jones' ground. 24 May 1911.
G.A. Oxon b. 90 (10)

STEEPLE ASTON

3697. An act for dividing and inclosing the common fields . . . of Steeple Aston. . . . (6 G. III, c. 11, Private.) n. pl., 1766, fol. 21 pp.
L. Eng. C 13 c. 1 (1766, p. 657)

3698. An act for vesting an estate in the parish of Steeple Aston . . . devised by the will of John Marten Watson . . . in trustees for . . . sale [&c.]. (7 W. IV & 1 V., c. 27, Private.) Lond., 1837, fol. 13 pp.
O.C.R.L.

3699. The Steeple Aston list for 1838. Woodstock, 1837, 12°. 15 pp.
G.A. Oxon 16° 33 (9)

3700. Steeple Aston. (Gent's. mag., 1842, pt. 1, p. 304, 05.) Ψ 2. 44

3701. WING, W., The antiquities and history of Steeple Aston [&c.]. Deddington, &c., (1845), 8°. p. 1–68. G.A. Oxon 8° 92 (1)

3702. WING, W., Charitable bequests and donations to . . . Steeple Aston . . . and to the parish church of St. Peter-the-apostle there. Oxf., 1873, 8°. 7 pp. G.A. Oxon 8° 147 (16)

3703. WING, W., Curiosities of law deeds of an Oxfordshire freehold . . . Title to a freehold at Steeple Aston. [By] W. W. n. pl., 1874, 8°. 2 pp. MS. Top. Oxon c. 6 (76)

3704. WING, W., Interesting antiquarian discovery [site of old Manor house] at Steeple Aston [by] W. n. pl., 1874, 8°. 2 pp. MS. Top. Oxon c. 6 (113)

3705. WING, W., [Lines] On the skeleton of a young female . . . found April 27, 1875, at Steeple Aston [signed A. L. A.]. n. pl., 1875, s. sh. MS. Top. Oxon c. 6 (72)

3706. WING, W., Annals of Steeple Aston and Middle Aston. Repr. from the Oxford Chronicle. [Oxf.], 1875, 8°. 84 pp. G.A. Oxon 8° 161 (25)

3707. Steeple Aston parish magazine. April 1899–Dec. 1914. (Oxf.), 1899–1914, 4°. G.A. Oxon 4° 326

3708. BALLARD, A., The management of open fields [extracts from the 'Parrish book' of Steeple Aston]. (Rept., Oxf. archaeol. soc., 1913, p. 131–44.) R. Top. 330

3709. BROOKES, C. C., A history of Steeple Aston and Middle Aston. Shipston-on-Stour, 1929, 8°. 359 pp. G.A. Oxon 8° 1067

3710. BROOKES, C. C., Fontes Rivorum, or The springs of the Brookes. [Brookes of Steeple Aston, p. 24–34.] Long Compton, 1931, 8°. 2182 B. e. 29

3711. Auction catal. Estate of sir J. T. Wheate. 30 May 1804. G.A. fol. A 273*

3712. Auction catal. Steeple Aston estate. 18 July 1896. G.A. Oxon b. 90 (6)

3713. Auction catal. Houses and cottages. 30 July 1902. G.A. Oxon b. 6 (65)

STEEPLE BARTON

3714. WING, W., Annals of Steeple Barton and Westcot Barton. Repr. from the Oxford Chron. (Oxf.), 1866, 8°. 61 pp. G.A. Oxon 8° 93 (2)

3715. WING, W., A charge to the Leet juries at the courts of Charles Cottrell Dormer, esq., lord of the manors of Rousham and Steeple Barton-cum-Membris, Nov. 4, 1870. n. pl., (1870), 8°. 8 pp. MS. Top. Oxon c. 6 (39)

3716. [Poster notifying proposed conference on temperance, 1884.] (Heyford, 1884), s. sh. G.A. Oxon c. 22 (23)

3717. The Bartons (Westcott and Steeple) Church of England mission & temperance hall (history). (Charlbury, 1937), 8°. 4 pp.
G.A. Oxon c. 317 (5)

3718. Auction catal. Manor of Steeple Barton. 28 Aug. 1782.
G.A. fol. A 266 (43)

3719. Auction catal. Estate of sir J. T. Wheate. 30 May 1804.
G.A. fol. A 273*

3720. Auction catal. Whistlow farm. 24 June 1882.
G.A. Oxon b. 6 (66)

3721. Auction catal. Horsehay farm. 2 Aug. 1902.
G.A. Oxon b. 92 (29)

STOKE LYNE

3722. An act for dividing and inclosing the . . . fields . . . of Stoke Lyne and Fewcott. (32 G. III, c. 27, Private.) n. pl., 1793, fol. 29 pp.
L. Eng. C 13 c. 1 (1793. i. 14)

3723. BLOMFIELD, J. C., History of . . . Stoke Lyne. (Hist. of . . . deanery of Bicester. Pt. 8. Stoke Lyne. 46 pp.) Lond., 1894, 4°.
G.A. Oxon 4° 71

3724. Auction catal. Estate. 15 July 1857. G.A. Oxon b. 85 b (57)

3725. Auction catal. Bainton farm. 15 July 1911.
G.A. Oxon b. 92 (6)

STOKE MOYLES

See 1258 [Note on family of Meols, by A. H. Cooke. 1929].

STOKE ROW

3726. An act to authorize the inclosure of certain lands . . . [Stoke Row]. (23 V., c. 17, Pub.) Lond., 1860, fol. 2 pp. L. Eng. A 69 c. 1

STOKE TALMAGE

3727. An act for vesting certain tenements and hereditaments in the counties of Oxford, Berks, and Wilts, part of the settled estates of the earl of Macclesfield, in trustees, to be sold or exchanged. [Stoke Talmage, &c.] (13 G. III, c. 49, Private.) n. pl., 1773, fol. 26 pp.
L. Eng. C 13 c. 1 (1773)

3728. An act for inclosing lands . . . of Stoke Talmage. . . . (51 G. III, c. 120, Private.) n. pl., 1811, fol. 17 pp.
L. Eng. C 13 c. 1 (1811, vol. 2)

3729. An act to authorize the inclosure of certain lands . . . [Stoke Talmage]. (17 & 18 V., c. 48, Pub.) Lond., 1854, fol. 2 pp.
L. Eng. A 69 c. 1

3730. Auction catal. Stoke Grange farm. 9 June 1863.   G.A. fol. B 71

STOKENCHURCH

See 495, 96, 524 [Turnpike acts. 1718, &c.].

3731. An act for vesting the real estate of Thomas Reade and Elizabeth Reade . . . situate in . . . Stokenchurch . . . in Thomas, earl of Macclesfield. . . . (28 G. III, c. 6, Private.) n. pl., 1788, fol. 10 pp.
L. Eng. C 13 c. 1 (1788. 49)

3732. An act to authorize the inclosure of certain lands . . . [Stokenchurch]. (20 & 21 V., c. 20, Pub.) Lond., 1857, fol. 2 pp.
L. Eng. A 69 c. 1

See 635 [Boundaries. 1895].

3733. DUNLOP, J. R., The family of Fettiplace. Pedigree, Fettiplaces of Stokenchurch. (Misc. geneal. et heraldica, 1916/17, 5th ser., vol. 2, p. 131–33.) Ψ 2. 10 f

3734. Visitation of Oxfordshire, 1668–9. Tipping of Chequers. (Misc. geneal. et heraldica, 1916/17, 5th ser., vol. 2, p. 161.) Ψ 2. 10 f

3735. PADDON, J. B., Windmills in the Midlands [Stokenchurch, Horspath, Great Haseley, Arncot]. Repr. from the Oxf. chronicle. [Oxf.], 1925, 8°. 16 pp.   18664 e. 12

3736. Auction catal. The Chequers' farm and Gibbons' farm. 10 Aug. 1859.   G.A. Oxon b. 92* (22)

3737. Auction catal. Aston Rowant estate and Cadmore estate. 30 Oct. 1889.   G.A. Oxon b. 85 a (2)
— Aston Rowant and Cadmore estate. 22 July, 1890.
G.A. Oxon b. 85 a (3)
— Aston Rowant estate. 1 July 1891.   G.A. Oxon b. 85 a (4)

3738. Auction catal. Coopers court and Eastwood farms. 31 Oct. 1889.
G.A. Oxon b. 92* (27)

STONESFIELD

General

3739. An act for dividing, allotting and inclosing the . . . fields . . . of Stonesfield. . . . (41 G. III, c. 30, Private.) n. pl., 1801, fol. 33 pp.
O.C.R.L.

3740. HULL, E., On the Blenheim iron-ore and the thickness of the formations below the great oolite at Stonesfield. (Geologist, 1860, vol. 3, p. 303–05.) Radcl.
— Rept., Brit. assoc., 1860, p. 81. Radcl.

3741. GOODRICH, E. S., On the fossil mammalia of the Stonesfield slate. (Quart. journ., microscop. sci., 1894, vol. 35, p. 407–31.) Radcl.

3742. British Association. Report (–3rd report) of the committee on Stonesfield slate. [Extr. from Report, 1894, 95, 96.] [Lond., 1894–96], 8°. 7 pp. G.A. Oxon 4° 375 (7)

3743. RICHARDSON, L., Excursion to Stonesfield and Fawler. (Proc., Cots. N.F.C., 1910, vol. 17, p. 28–31.) Per. 18855 d. 58

3744. Excursion to Oxford, Stonesfield and Fawler. (Proc., Geol. assoc., 1910, vol. 21, p. 25–29.) Radcl.

3745. DINES, H. G., Stonesfield slate-tips. (Antiquity, 1936, vol. 10, p. 93, 94.) R. Top. 6

3746. Auction catal. Portion of the Blenheim estate: North farm. 14 July 1920. G.A. Oxon b. 92* (3)

Roman Remains

3747. HEARNE, T., A discourse concerning the Stonesfield tessellated pavement. (Itinerary of John Leland, ed. by T. Hearne, vol. 8, p. vii–xxxv.) Oxf., 1712, 8°. Mus. Bibl. II 22
— 1745. Mus. Bibl. II 38
— 1769. Mus. Bibl. II 43

3748. This . . . tessellated pavement discover'd at Stunsfield . . . 1712 [coloured plate]. n. pl., [1712], s. sh. Gough maps 43 (f. 114)

3749. An exact delineation of the pavement in mosaick-work lately discovered at Stunsfield. n. pl., [1712], s. sh.
Gough maps 43 (f. 112)

3750. POINTER, J., An account of a Roman pavement, lately found at Stunsfield in Oxfordshire, prov'd to be 1400 years old. Oxf., 1713, 8°. 39 pp. Gough Oxf. 122 (1)

3751. HAKEWILL, H., Roman remains, discovered in the parishes of North Leigh and Stonesfield. Extract from Skelton's Oxfordshire. Lond., 1836, 8°. 20 pp. G.A. Oxon 8° 164 (12)

3752. TAYLOR, M. V., The Roman tessellated pavement at Stonesfield. (Oxoniensia, 1941, p. 1–8.) R. Top. 340

3752A. Stonesfield. (Archaeol. notes. Oxoniensia, 1950, vol. 15, p. 108.)
R. Top. 340

STONOR

3753. Stonor. (Views of the seats of noblemen and gentlemen, by J. P. Neale, 1820, vol. 3. 2 pp.)   G.A. Gen. top. 4° 42

3754. Minutes of the evidence given before the Committee of privileges to whom the petition of Thomas Stonor, of Stonor . . . claiming to be senior co-heir to the barony of Camoys, was referred. (1–9.) Lond., 1838, fol. 486 pp.   Hist. d. 214

3755. Camoys peerage. In the House of lords. Case of Thomas Stonor . . . claiming to be senior co-heir to the barony of Camoys [with pedigree]. Lond., [c. 1838], fol. 25 pp.   21851 b. 19 (1)
— Additional case. Lond., [c. 1838], fol. 13 pp.   21851 b. 19 (2)

3756. STONOR, T. S., The private printing press at Stonor, 1581. (Philo-biblon soc., Bibl. and hist. misc., vol. 1, no. 20.) Lond., 1854, 8°. 6 pp.   Soc. 3974 e. 207

3757. ALLNUTT, W. H., English provincial presses. The private press at Stonor park. (Bibliographica, vol. 2, 1896, p. 163–65.)
                    Per. 25805 d. 15

3758. PEARMAN, M. T., Murderous affray near Stonor, 1555. (Rept., Oxf. archaeol. soc., 1900, p. 22–24.)   R. Top. 330

3759. Stonor park, Henley. (Berks, Bucks, & Oxon archaeol. journ., 1907, vol. 13, notes p. 28).   R. Top. 100

3760. KINGSFORD, C. L., ed., The Stonor letters and papers, 1290–1483. 2 vols. (Camden soc., 3rd ser., vol. 29, 30.) Lond., 1919, 8°.
                    Ψ 2. 112

3761. OSWALD, A., Stonor park. (Country Life, 1950, vol. 108, p. 1094–99, 1188–92, 1282–86.)   Per. 384 b. 6

3762. STONOR, R. J., Stonor, a Catholic sanctuary in the Chilterns from the fifth century. Newport, Mon., 1951, 8°. 400 pp.
                    G.A. Oxon 8° 1232

3763. Auction catal. Stonor estate. 26 Sept. 1894.   G.A. Oxon b. 92 (8)

STOWOOD

3764. An act to enable his majesty to grant the inheritance of part of the forest of Shotover and Stowood . . . to trustees, in trust for Augustus Schutz . . . and his heirs, upon a . . . consideration to be paid for the same. (17 G. II, c. 3, Private.) n. pl., 1743/4, fol. 7 pp.
                    G.A. Oxon c. 183

3765. HASSALL, W. O., Royal Oak farm, Stowood. (Thame Gazette, Jan. 2, 1951.)   N.G.A. Oxon a. 120

STRATTON AUDLEY

3766. An act for dividing and inclosing the . . . fields . . . of Stratton Audley. (20 G. III, c. 50, Private.) n. pl., 1780, fol. 17 pp.
L. Eng. C 13 c. 1 (1780. 40)

3767. Auction catal. Stratton Audley park and village. 22 July 1891.
G.A. Oxon b. 92* (2)

3768. Auction catal. Stratton Audley hall estate. 30 Sept. 1910.
G.A. Oxon b. 92 (9)

STUDLEY

See HORTON CUM STUDLEY

SUTTON

3769. Auction catal. Farm house and homestead. 14 June 1842.
G.A. fol. B 71

3770. Auction catal. Estate. 31 May 1893.   G.A. Oxon b. 6 (23)

3771. Auction catal. Village. 3 Sept. 1924.   G.A. Oxon c. 226

SWALCLIFFE

3772. An act for dividing and inclosing . . . fields in . . . Swalcliffe. . . . (11 G. III, c. 70, Private.) n. pl., 1771, fol. 21 pp.
L. Eng. C 13 c. 1 (1771. 88)
See 530 [Turnpike act. 1802, &c.].

3772A. LONG, C. E., Descent of the family of Wickham of Swalcliffe, and their kindred to the founder of New college. [By C. E. L.] (Collectanea topogr. & geneal., 1835, vol. 2, p. 225–45, 368–87; 1836, vol. 3, p. 178–239, 345–76.) Ψ 2. 10

3773. An act to carry into effect a partition between John Michael Severne . . . and Anna Maria his wife, and others, of estates in the counties of Worcester [&c.] . . . Oxford [Swalcliffe-with-Epwell] and Leicester. (8 & 9 V., c. 28, Private.) Lond., 1845, fol. 94 pp.
L. Eng. C 13 c. 1 (1845)

3774. MARTIN, C. W., Was William of Wykeham of the family of Swalcliffe? (The Topographer and genealogist, 1858, vol. 3, p. 49–74.)
Ψ 2. 10 b
— [Repr.]   G.A. Oxon 4° 371
— Addenda. Who was William of Wykeham? (Herald and geneal. 1870, vol. 5, p. 225–35.) Ψ 2. 10 d

3775. Swalcliffe. (Rept., Oxf. archaeol. soc., 1867, p. 8; 1887, p. 1.)
R. Top. 330

3776. DRYDEN, SIR H. E. L., Notes on Swalcliffe parish church. (Rept., Oxf. archaeol. soc., 1887. 8 pp.)   R. Top. 330

3777. WILKINSON, J. T., Rectors or parsons [at Swalcliffe. List by J. T. Wilkinson]. Banbury [c. 1887], s. sh.   G.A. Oxon a. 22 (5)

3778. KEYSER, C. E., An architectural account of Swalcliffe church. (Archaeol. journ., 1904, vol. 61, p. 85–101.)   R. Top. 5

See 449 [Estates of New college, 1659–75, p. 87–93. 1949].

3779. Auction catal. Part of Far Old field and Grange close. 12 June 1873.   G.A. Oxon b. 85 b (50)

3780. Auction catal. Swalcliffe Lower Lea. 25 Feb. 1885.
G.A. Oxon b. 85 b (54)
— — 19 July 1893.   G.A. Oxon b. 85 b (55)

3781. Auction catal. Agricultural properties. 20 July 1922.
G.A. Oxon b. 92* (18)

SWERFORD

3782. An act for sale of part of the estate of Richard Brideoake [in Swerford, &c.]. (9 Anne, c. 43, Private.) n. pl., [1710], fol. 4 pp.
B.M.

3783. An act for annexing the late duke of Shrewsbury's estate to the earldom of Shrewsbury and confirming Gilbert, earl of Shrews-bury's settlement. [Concerns Swerford, &c.] (6 G. I, c. 29, Private.) n. pl., [1720], fol.
— Repr. 1858. 16 pp.   L. Eng. C 13 c. 1 (1714–27. 10)
— 43 G. III, c. 40, Private.
— 1 G. IV, c. 40, Private.

See 514, 529 [Turnpike acts. 1770, &c.].

3784. An act for dividing . . . and inclosing the . . . fields . . . and other . . . grounds within the liberties and precincts of Swerford. (42 G. III, c. 61, Private.) n. pl., 1802, fol. 20 pp.
G.A. Oxon c. 113 (1)
See 883 [Customs and charities. 1842].

3785. An act for vesting part of the settled estates of . . . John, earl of Shrewsbury [in Swerford, &c.] . . . in trustees to be sold. (6 & 7 V., c. 28, Private.) Lond., 1843, fol. 60 pp.
L. Eng. C 13 c. 1 (1843. i. 28)

3786. JOPE, E. M., Castle Hill, Swerford. (Rept., Oxf. archaeol. soc., 1938, p. 85–93.)   R. Top. 330

3787. Auction catal. Buttercomb farm, Pomfret castle farm, Spring farm. 5 July 1894.   G.A. Oxon b. 6 (25)

3788. Auction catal. House and cottages. 25 Sept. 1918.
G.A. Oxon b. 92* (8)

SWINBROOK

3789. Swinbrook. (Gent's. mag., 1792, pt. 1, p. 201.) Ψ 2. 44

3790. An act for inclosing and exonerating from tythes lands in . . . Swinbrooke. (53 G. III, c. 9, L. & P.) Lond., 1813, fol. 26 pp.
L. Eng. B 53 c. Enclosure 5

3791. Notes of an excursion to . . . Swinbrook . . . (North Oxf. archaeol. soc., 1870.) Banbury, [1870], 8°. 37 pp.   R. Top. 330

3792. Swinbrook church. (Trans., Bristol and Glouc. archaeol. soc., 1895–96, vol. 20, p. 367–68; 1911, vol. 34, p. 26–28.)
R. Top. 210

3793. Swinbrook. (Rept., Oxf. archaeol. soc., 1904, p. 10–16.)
R. Top. 330

3794. DUNLOP, J. R., Brasses commemorative of the Fettiplace family (Swinbrook, p. 112–16). (Trans., Monumental brass soc., 1911, vol. 6, pt. 2.)   Soc. 2184 d. 85

3795. DUNLOP, J. R., The family of Fettiplace. Pedigree, Fettiplaces of . . . Swinbrook. (Misc. geneal. et heraldica, 1916/17, 5th ser., vol. 2, p. 202–10.) Ψ 2. 10f

3796. HUSSEY, C., Swinbrook. (Country Life, 1945, vol. 98, p. 156–59.)
Per. 384 b. 6

3797. Auction catal. Cottages and land. 27 Nov. 1810.
G.A. fol. A 273*

SWYNCOMBE

3798. NAPIER, H. A., Historical notices of the parishes of Swyncombe and Ewelme. Oxf., 1858, fol. 454 pp.   G.A. Oxon c. 168

3799. St. Botolph's church. Restoration (account). n. pl., (1896), 8°. 4 pp.   G.A. fol. A 139* (71)
— Statement of accounts. n. pl., (1897), 4°. 4 pp.
G.A. fol. A 139* (72)

3800. PEARMAN, M. T., Notes on Swincomb. (Oxf. archaeol. soc., 48.) Banbury, 1906, 8°. 13 pp.   R. Top. 330

3801. Swyncombe churchwardens' accounts. 1910, 11. n. pl., (1910, 11), s. sh.   G.A. fol. A 139* (74)

3802. DUNLOP, J. R., The family of Fettiplace. Pedigree, Fettiplaces of Swincombe. (Misc. geneal. et heraldica, 1916/17, 5th ser., vol. 2, p. 242, 43.) Ψ 2. 10 f

3803. CHIBNALL, M., ed., Select documents of the English lands of the abbey of Bec. (Custumal, Swyncombe, p. 87–89). (Camden soc., 3rd ser., vol. 73.) Lond., 1951, 8°. Ψ 2. 112 (iii. 73)

3804. Auction catal. Park corner and Ewelme park farms. 31 Oct. 1889.
     G.A. Oxon b. 92* (27)
— 1 July 1891.   G.A. Oxon b. 92* (ii. 1)
— 26 July 1894.   G.A. Oxon b. 92 (10)

3805. Auction catal. Park corner farm. 22 July 1890.
     G.A. Oxon b. 92* (28)

3806. Auction catal. Red Pitts estate. 27 July 1899.
     G.A. Oxon b. 92 (11)
— 15 Aug. 1901.   G.A. Oxon b. 92 (12)

3807. Auction catal. Swyncombe estate. 27 May 1921.
     G.A. Oxon c. 224*

SYDENHAM

3808. An act for inclosing lands in . . . Sydenham. (4 G. IV, c. 8, Private.) Lond., 1823, fol. 21 pp.   L. Eng. C 13 c. 1

3809. BURROWS, M., History of the family of Burrows of Sydenham and Long Crendon. Oxf., 1877, 8°. 10 pp.   2182 B. d. 50

3810. Pedigree of the family of Burrows, of Sydenham and Long Crendon, 1877. n. pl., (1877), s. sh.
     MS. Top. Oxon c. 4 (f. 23)
— [Another ed.]   MS. Top. Oxon c. 4 (f. 25)

3811. HASSALL, W. O., Sydenham. (Thame Gazette, Jan. 23, 1951.)
     N.G.A. Oxon a. 120

3812. Auction catal. Thame park estate. 24, 25 Sept. 1917.
     G.A. Oxon b. 92 (23)

3813. Auction catal. Glebe farm. 28 Sept. 1920.
     G.A. Oxon b. 92* (18)

TACKLEY

3814. An act for vesting part of the estates of the late sir James Dashwood in trustees, in trust to sell the same. [Tackley.] (37 G. III, c. 101, Private.) n. pl., 1797, fol. 30 pp.
     L. Eng. C 13 c. 1 (1797. 4)

3815. WING, W., A church and parish beyond the neighbourhood of Banbury. Tackley. [By W. Wing.] Repr. from the Banbury guardian. n. pl., [c. 1880], 8°. 4 pp. G.A. Oxon 8° 1184 (17)

3816. Parish of S. Nicholas, Tackley. The Banner of faith. June, Sept., Oct. 1884, Jan., Mar., Apr. 1885. Oxf., (1884, 85), 8°.
Per. G.A. Oxon 8° 869

3817. BALLARD, A., Tackley in the 16th and 17th centuries [by A. Ballard]. (Rept., Oxf. archaeol. soc., 1911, p. 24–76.) R. Top. 330

See 359 [Honors and knights' fees. 1924].

3818. MILNE, J. G., and SUTHERLAND, C. H. V., A local collection of coins from Tackley. (Oxoniensia, 1937, p. 93–100.) R. Top. 340

3819. LAMBORN, E. A. GREENING, Arms on the . . . nave roof, Tackley. (Rept., Oxf. archaeol. soc., 1938, p. 57, 58.) R. Top. 330

3820. Auction catal. Old man's leys farm, Old farm, Malthouse farm, Whieveley farm, High wood, Sturdy's castle inn [&c.]. 9 Aug. 1809.
G.A. fol. B 71

3821. Auction catal. Tackley Park. 18 Dec. 1840. G.A. fol. B 71
— — 23 Nov. 1905. G.A. Oxon b. 92 (13)

3822. Auction catal. Estate. 11 May 1910. G.A. Oxon b. 90 (13)

3823. Auction catal. Outlying portions of the Blenheim estate. White-hill farm, Weaveley farm. 14 July 1920. G.A. Oxon b. 92* (3)

TADMARTON

3824. An act for sale of part of the estate of Richard Brideoake [in Tadmarton, &c.]. (9 Anne, c. 43, Private.) n. pl., [1710], fol. 4 pp.
B.M.

3825. An act for dividing and inclosing the open and common field . . . within . . . Upper Tadmarton and Lower Tadmarton. (15 G. III, c. 77, Private.) n. pl., 1775, fol. 32 pp.
L. Eng. C 13 c. 1 (1775. 81)

3826. BEESLEY, T., A chemical analysis of the water of Holywell, Tad-marton Heath, with an inquiry as to its fitness for the water-supply of . . . Banbury. Banbury, 1853, 8°. 9 pp. G.A. Oxon 8° 948

3827. Tadmarton. (Rept., Oxf. archaeol. soc., 1867, p. 10.)
R. Top. 330

3828. RIDDLE, A. E., Restoration of Tadmarton church [appeal for funds, signed A. E. Riddle]. n. pl., [c. 1890], 4°. 4 pp.
G.A. Oxon c. 22 (24)

3829. Tadmarton church bells and tower. [Report of the examination of the bells, and appeal for funds to renovate them.] n. pl., [1898], 4°. 4 pp. G.A. Oxon c. 317 (14)

3830. Auction catal. Tadmarton manor. 3 Oct. 1892.
G.A. Oxon b. 85 *b* (56)

3831. Auction catal. Austen's farm, Home farm and 7 cottages. 15 June 1899. G.A. Oxon b. 92 (15)

3832. Auction catal. Camp farm and another unnamed farm, a water corn mill, and cottages. 30 Sept. 1909. G.A. Oxon b. 92 (16)

TAPPEWELL

3833. KIBBLE, J., Historical and other notes on the ancient manor of Charlbury and its nine hamlets . . . Tappewell [&c.]. Oxf., 1927, 8°. 100 pp. G.A. Oxon 8° 1053

TASTON

3834. Spelsbury Women's institute. A history of Spelsbury, including . . . Taston [&c.] ed. by E. Corbett. Shipston-on-Stour, 1931, 8°. 272 pp. G.A. Oxon 8° 1081

3835. LATTEY, R. T., 'Thor's stone' at Taston. (Oxoniensia, 1949, vol. 14, p. 87.) R. Top. 340

TAYNTON

3836. An act for inclosing lands . . . of Taynton. . . . (1 & 2 G. IV, c. 6, Private.) n. pl., 1821, fol. 20 pp. L. Eng. C 13 c. 1 (1821. i. 3)

3837. An act to authorize the inclosure of certain lands . . . [Taynton]. (22 V., c. 3, Pub.) Lond., 1859, fol. 2 pp. L. Eng. A 69 c. 1

3838. STEVENSON, M. L., Taynton. [Letter on font & Church.] (Berks, Bucks, & Oxon archaeol. journ., 1914, vol. 20, p. 122, 23.)
R. Top. 100

3839. BROWNE, A. L., The manor of Taynton. (Rept., Oxf. archaeol. soc., 1935, p. 75–88.) R. Top. 330

See 614 [Building stones from Taynton for Abingdon abbey. 1948–9].

TEMPLE COWLEY

See COWLEY

TETSWORTH

3840. An act for vesting in trustees, the several manors and lands [Tetsworth, &c.] . . . the estate of Henry Perrott in trust for him and his heirs. (3 G. II, c. 15, Private.) n. pl., 1730, fol. 7 pp.
G.A. Oxon c. 196

3841. Tetsworth. (Gent's. mag., 1790, pt. 1, p. 17; 1793, pt. 2, p. 719.)
Ψ 2. 44

3842. An act for vesting the . . . manors and estates [at Tetsworth, &c.] of Charles Vere Spencer, an infant, in . . . Oxford and Denbigh in trustees, in order to effect the sale thereof. . . . (5 & 6 W. IV, c. 23, Private.) n. pl., 1835, fol. 44 pp.   L. Eng. C 13 c. 1 (1835. 23)

3843. WILLIAMS, B., Notice of a sculpture upon the tympanum of Tetsworth church, Oxon. (Archaeologia, 1853, vol. 35, p. 487.)
R. Top. 7
— [Repr.]   G.A. Oxon 4° 186 (8)

3844. Auction catal. Harlesford estate. 4 July 1894.
G.A. Oxon b. 92 (18)
— 20 July 1904.   G.A. Oxon b. 92 (19)

3845. Auction catal. Meadow land. 17 June 1897.
G.A. Oxon b. 92 (26)

3846. Auction catal. Goldpits' farm. 3 June 1902.
G.A. Oxon b. 92 (20)

3847. Auction catal. Latchford Hole farm, &c. 28 June 1913.
G.A. Oxon b. 92 (22)

THAME

General

3848. A bill for setling and securing part of the estates of Robert Barry, clerk, and Anne, his wife, for the benefit of the said Anne, and her children; and sale of other part of the estate . . . for payment of his debts. [Concerns Old Thame manor.] n. pl., [1706], 7 pp.
G.A. Oxon c. 197
— Act. (4 & 5 Anne., c. 60, Private.)

3849. An act for appointing jointures for the wives and . . . portions for the younger children of . . . Willoughby, earl of Abingdon, and Peregrine Bertie his brother. [Thame, &c.] (9 G. III, sess. 2, c. 10, Private.) n. pl., 1769, fol. 43 pp.   G.A. Oxon c. 192

3850. An act for inclosing lands in . . . Thame. (4 G. IV, c. 8, Private.) Lond., 1823, fol. 4 pp.   L. Eng. C 13 c. 1

3851. [Memoir of F. Lee.] (Confidence in God, by F. Lee, ed. by F. G. Lee, 1871, p. 3, 4, 18, 19.)   11125 e. 1

3852. LUPTON, H., The history of Thame and its hamlets. Thame, (1860), 8°. 147 pp.   G.A. Oxon 8° 472

3853. Thame. (Gent's. mag., 1865, pt. 1, p. 181–89.) Ψ 2. 44

3854. Rules and catalogue of books of the Thame institute. 1882. Thame, (1882), 8°. 20 pp.   2590 e. Thame 1. 1

3855. Pedigree of Lee of Thame. n. pl., [1882?], fol. 6 pp.
MS. Top. Oxon c. 4 (232)

3856. Thame horticultural society. Schedule of prizes &c., for 1888. (Thame, 1888), 8°. 15 pp.   G.A. Oxon 8° 441

3857. LEE, F. G., Thame, three hundred & eighty years ago. [Letter to the Thame Gazette.] n. pl., (1889), s. sh.
MS. Top. Oxon d. 41 (12)

3858. Thame. The official guide. (Lond.), [1928], 16°. 39 pp.
G.A. Oxon 16° 178

3859. Thame show, official catalogue of entries. 74th– annual show. Thame, (1934–), 8°.   Per. 19195 e. 421

3860. BROWN, J. H., and GUEST, W., A history of Thame. Thame, 1935, 8°. 286 pp.   G.A. Oxon 8° 1166

3861. LEEDS, E. T., A 15th century hoard from Thame. (Oxoniensia, 1940, p. 169.)   R. Top. 340

3862. EVANS, J., LEEDS, E. T., and THOMPSON, A., A hoard of gold rings and silver groats found near Thame. (Antiquaries journ., 1941, vol. 21, p. 197–203.)   R. Top. 2

3863. Auction catal. Houses, land and one third part of £100 secured on the Postcomb turnpike road, late estate of R. Stone. 1 May 1838.
G.A. fol. B 71

3864. Auction catal. Freehold estates. 28 June 1913.
G.A. Oxon b. 92 (22)

Abbey

3865. The visitation of the monastery of Thame, 1526 [ed. by G. G. Perry]. (Engl. hist. review, 1888, vol. 3, p. 704–22.) Ψ 2. 38

3866. The Thame cartulary, ed. by H. E. Salter. Vol. 1, 2. (Oxf. record soc., vol. 25, 26.) Oxf., 1947, 48, 8°.   R. 13. 702

See also Thame Park, 3877 &c.

Church

3867. Extracts from the accounts of the proctors and stewards of the prebendal church of the Blessed Virgin of Thame, commencing in 1529, and ending in 1641, and of the churchwardens of Thame, beginning in 1542 [ed. by H. Lupton]. Thame, 1852, 8°. 36 pp.
G.A. Oxon 8° 215 b (2)

3868. PAYNE, E. J., The building of the Trinity aisle, or north transept of Thame church, A.D. 1442 et seq. (Proc., Oxf. architect. and hist. soc., N.S., vol. I, 1863, p. 268–83.) R. 13. 707

3869. LEE, R., A new peal of bells for the prebendal church of the Blessed Virgin of Thame. Lond., 1876, 4°. 8 pp.
MS. Top. Oxon d. 41 (295)

3870. St. Mary's church, Thame [appeal signed R. Lee, in aid of the church bells]. n. pl., [c. 1876], 4°. 2 pp.
MS. Top. Oxon c. 3 (f. 431)

3871. LEE, F. G., The history, description, and antiquities of the prebendal church of the Blessed Virgin Mary of Thame. Lond., 1883, fol. 716 pp. G.A. Oxon b. 72

3872. Restoration of Thame church. [Appeal for funds.] n. pl., (1889), 4°. 4 pp. G.A. Oxon c. 317 (14)

3873. BARKER, W. R., Monumental brasses in the churches of Thame, Holton, and Great Tew. (Journ., Oxf. univ. brass-rubbing soc., 1898, vol. I, p. 137–69.) Soc. 2184 d. 50

3874. The churchwardens' accounts of the parish of St. Mary, Thame, transcr. by W. P. Ellis. (Berks, Bucks, & Oxon archaeol. journ., 1902, vol. 7, p. 113–19; vol. 8, p. 24–30, 50–59, 71–77; vol. 9, p. 51–57, 75–78, 117–20; vol. 10, p. 19–24, 55–58, 87–90, 105–07; vol. 11, p. 55–56, 116–18; vol. 12, p. 13–15; vol. 13, p. 49–52; vol. 14, p. 25–28, 86–88; vol. 16, p. 87–89; vol. 19, p. 20–24, 84–86; vol. 20, 1914, p. 115–19.) R. Top. 100

3875. Thame church. (Rept., Oxf. archaeol. soc., 1937, p. 6–7.)
R. Top. 330

3876. BROWN, J. H., A short guide to Thame church. (Thame), [c. 1940], 8°. 19 pp. G.A. Oxon 8° 1184 (14)

Directories

See 1390 [Directory. 1846].

Newspapers

See 1376 Thame Gazette.

Park

3877. LEE, F. G., The abbey and mansion house of Thame park. (The Building news, March 30, 1888, p. 455–57.)

MS. Top. Oxon c. 3 (f. 258 b)

3878. Thame park. (Country Life, 1909, vol. 26, p. 90–97.)

Per. 384 b. 6

3879. WILLS, G. B., Thame park, alterations. (Architect. rev., 1922, Jan., p. 16–19.)

Per. 17356 c. 8

3880. GODFREY, W. H., The abbot's parlour, Thame park. (Archaeol. journ., 1929, vol. 86, p. 59–68.)

R. Top. 5

3881. Auction catal. Thame estate. 16 July 1844.

G.A. Oxon b. 92 (21)

3882. Auction catal. Outlying portions of Thame park estate. 24, 25 Sept. 1917.

G.A. Oxon b. 92 (23)

Roads

See 494 [London inns frequented by Thame carriers. 1637].
See 515, 534 [Turnpike acts. 1770, &c.].

School

3883. Schola Thamēsis ex fundatione Johannis Williams militis domini Williams de Thame. [Statutes.] n. pl., 1575, 4°. 55 leaves.

Rawl. statutes 58

3883A. Preces matutinæ. Lond., [1578], fol. 5 leaves.

B.M.

3884. Endowed schools commission. Draft scheme for the management of 'the Thame school of the foundation of sir John Williams, Lorde Williams of Thame', and of the almshouses of Lord Williams united therewith at Thame. [Lond., 1872], fol. 15 pp.

MS. Top. Oxon c. 3 (f. 361)

3885. Some account of lord Williams, of Thame, founder of the Grammar school and the almes-houses, at Thame . . . with . . . copies of documents relating to the above charity. Thame, 1873, 8°. 128 pp.

G.A. Oxon 8° 958

3886. Scheme for the management of the 'Thame school' . . . and of the almshouses . . . united therewith. Thame, 1876, 8°. 23 pp.

MS. Top. Oxon c. 3 (f. 373)

3887. Lord Williams's grammar school, 1575. [Prospectus.] [Thame, 1894], 8°. 13 pp.

G.A. Oxon 8° 620 (20)

3888. Lord Williams's grammar school. The Tamensian. No. 1- .
(Thame, 1900-), 8°. [Bodleian no. 1-8: G.A. Oxon 8° 710]

3889. Thame school of the foundation of Lord Williams of Thame,
1575. [Prospectus.] n. pl., [c. 1903], 8°. 20 pp.
G.A. Oxon 8° 761 (2)

3890. Draft of a scheme made by the Board of education . . . for the
alteration of the scheme regulating lord Williams's school foundation. (2nd proof.) (Lond., 1908), fol. 14 pp.   G.A. Oxon c. 135

3891. BROWN, J. H., A short history of Thame school of the foundation
of sir John Williams. . . . Lond., 1927, 8°. 136 pp.
G.A. Oxon 8° 1052

3892. Auction catal. Thame grammar school and almshouses [&c.].
22 Aug. 1876.   MS. Top. Oxon c. 3 (f. 369)

THAME (Peculiar jurisdiction of)

3893. PEARCE, S. S., The clergy of the deanery of Cuddesdon and of the
peculiars of Langford, Thame and Great Milton during the settlement of 1559 and afterwards. (Rept., Oxf. archaeol. soc., 1920,
p. 242-89.)   R. Top. 330

3894. PEYTON, S. A., The Churchwardens' presentments in the Oxfordshire peculiars of Dorchester, Thame and Banbury. (Oxf. record
soc., 10.) [Oxf.], 1928, 8°. 340 pp.   R. 13. 702

THOMLEY

3895. An act for vesting certain mannors and lands in . . . Oxon and
Bucks, in dame Anne Tipping and her heirs . . . [Thomley &c.].
(12 G. I, c. 25, Private.) n. pl., [1725], fol. 11 pp.
L. Eng. C 13 c. 1 (1714-27. 104)

3896. An act for vesting . . . certain . . . lands . . . in . . . London, and
in the counties of Oxford and Bucks . . . the estate of Susanna
Letten . . . in trustees to be sold. [Thomley.] (7 G. III, c. 75,
Private.) n. pl., 1767, fol. 17 pp.   L. Eng. C 13 c. 1 (1767, f. 933)

3897. Auction catal. Worminghall and Thomley estate. 25 July 1911.
G.A. Oxon b. 92 (24)

THORN

3898. Auction catal. Manor of Thorn. 29 Jan. 1858.
G.A. Oxon b. 85 b (41)

THRUPP

3899. WING, W., Annals of Kidlington, and its annexes . . . Thrupp [&c.]. Repr. from the Oxf. chronicle. (Oxf.), 1881, 8°. 31 pp.
G.A. Oxon 8° 220 (5)

3900. Auction catal. Estate of sir J. T. Wheate. 30 May 1804.
G.A. fol. A 273*

TIDDINGTON

3901. Auction catal. Sandy Lane farm, Brimpton farm &c. 28 June 1913. G.A. Oxon b. 92 (22)

TOOT BALDON

3902. An act for dividing, allotting and laying in severalty lands in . . . Toot Baldon. (6 & 7 W. IV, c. 16, Private.) Lond., 1836, fol. 32 pp.
O.C.R.L.

3903. ROSS, J. C., [Parochial statistics, &c.] 1871. (Fruit for God, a pastoral charge, p. 12–19.) 1007 e. 2 (1)
— 1872. (The beautiful flock, p. 18–31.) 1005 e. 49 (19)
— 1873. (The whole duty of man, p. 34–70.)
G.A. Oxon 8° 161 (26)
— 1875. (The Gergesenes, p. 22–69.) 1007 e. 2 (1*)
— 1876. (The commemorative sacrifice, p. 15–42.) 1007 e. 2 (2)
— 1877. (Christian unity, p. 27–46.) 1007 e. 2 (3)
— 1878. (Fellowship unbroken, p. 49–69.) 1007 e. 2 (4)
— 1879. (Obedience and perseverance, p. 20–63.) 1007 e. 2 (5)

3904. Guild of St. Laurence, Toot Baldon [rules, &c.]. Oxf., [1886], 16°. 16 pp. 14021 f. 14 (1)

TUSMORE

3905. Fermor of Tusmore. [Pedigree.] n. pl., [c. 1880], s. sh.
Hist. c. 92
[See also under Somerton for further Fermor pedigrees, &c.].

3906. BLOMFIELD, J. C., History of . . . Tusmore. (Hist. of . . . deanery of Bicester. Pt. 3.) Bristol, (1887), 4°. 95 pp. G.A. Oxon 4° 71

3907. DRYDEN, SIR H., Granary and dovecot at Tusmore [by sir H. Dryden]. n. pl., [c. 1887], 4°. 3 pp. G.A. Oxon 4° 376

3908. OSWALD, A., Tusmore park. (Country Life, 1938, vol. 84, p. 108–13, 132–36.) Per. 384 b. 6

3909. LEGG, L. G. WICKHAM, *ed.*, Tusmore papers. (Oxf. record soc., 20.) Oxf., 1939 [really 1938], 8°. 110 pp.   R. 13. 702

3910. Auction catal. Tusmore estate. 15 July 1857.
G.A. Oxon b. 85 *b* (57)

TYTHROP HOUSE

3911. Tythrop house. (Country Life, 1904, vol. 15, p. 306–10.)
Per. 384 b. 6

UPPER HEYFORD

3912. An act for inclosing lands in . . . Upper Heyford . . . (4 & 5 V., c. 11, Private.) n. pl., 1841, fol. 43 pp.
L. Eng. C 13 c. 1 (1841. 11)

3913. WING, W., Annals of Heyford Warren, otherwise Upper Heyford. Repr. from the Oxford chronicle. (Oxf.), 1865, 8°. 20 pp.
G.A. Oxon 8° 93 (1)

3914. BLOMFIELD, J. C., History of Lower and Upper Heyford. (Hist. of . . . deanery of Bicester. Pt. 6. Upper Heyford. 64 pp.) Lond., 1892, 4°.   G.A. Oxon 4° 71

UPPER TADMARTON

See TADMARTON

UPTON AND SIGNET

See 503 [Turnpike act. 1753, &c.].

3915. A bill for dividing and inclosing the . . . fields of Upton. n. pl., [1773], fol. 11 pp.   Gough Oxf. 103 (21)
— Act. (13 G. III, c. 19, Private.)   L. Eng. C 13 c. 1 (1773. 95)

3916. ARBER, E. A. N., Concealed Oxfordshire coalfield [at Signet]. (Trans., Inst. of mining engin., 1916, June, p. 373–84.)
Soc. 1867 d. 114

3917. ARBER, E. A. N., Little-known concealed coal-field in Oxfordshire [borings at Signet]. (Proc., Cambr. phil. soc., 1916, vol. 18, pt. 4, p. 180–83.)   Radcl.

WAINHILL

3918. HASSALL, W. O., Henton and Wainhill. (Thame Gazette, Oct. 30, 1951.)   N.G.A. Oxon a. 120

WALCOT

3919. KIBBLE, J., Historical and other notes on the ancient manor of Charlbury, and its nine hamlets . . . Walcot [&c.]. Oxf., 1927, 8°. 100 pp. G.A. Oxon 8° 1053

3920. Auction catal. Manor of Walcot. 29 Jan. 1858.
G.A. Oxon b. 85 b (42)

WALLISCOTE

See WHITCHURCH

WARBOROUGH

3921. An act to authorize the inclosure of certain lands . . . [War-borough]. (11 & 12 V., c. 27, Pub.) Lond., 1848, fol. 4 pp.
L. Eng. A 69 c. 1

3922. COZENS, W., Ancient weapons found near Warborough. (Berks, Bucks, & Oxon archaeol. journ., 1900, vol. 6, notes, p. 95.)
R. Top. 100

3923. FIELD, J. E., Parish documents at Warborough. (Berks, Bucks, & Oxon archaeol. journ., 1908, vol. 14, notes, p. 94, 95.)
R. Top. 100

See 3271 [Pedigree of Byseley, Bisley or Beazley family of Warborough].

3924. Warborough. [Short account.] n. pl., [19—], 8°. 8 pp. O.P.L.

3925. Auction catal. Meadow at Hill Mead, arable land at Cupboard hill, and land on the village green. 17 Apr. 1896.
G.A. Oxon b. 92 (25)

WARDINGTON

3926. An act for dividing and inclosing the . . . fields . . . within Wardington [&c.]. (1 G. III, c. 30, Private.) n. pl., 1761, fol. 24 pp.
G.A. Oxon c. 113 (2)

3927. CHAMBERLIN, W. H., Valuation of Wardington, Wilscote and Coton. Banbury, 1833, 4°. 52 pp.

3928. WOOD, W., Note on an exchequer receipt found in Wardington church. (Rept., Oxf. archaeol. soc., 1890, p. 15–18.) R. Top. 330

3929. Wardington. (Rept., Oxf. archaeol. soc., 1892, p. 10.)
R. Top. 330

3930. Auction catal. Prescott manor farm. 6 Apr. 1797.
G.A. fol. A 273*

3931. Auction catal. Wardington house. 28 July 1892.
G.A. Oxon b. 85 *b* (58)

3932. Auction catal. High Wardington farm, Wardington farm, cottages, land [&c.] part of the Edgcote estate. 13 Nov. 1924.
G.A. Oxon c. 224 (17)

WATER EATON

3933. WING, W., Annals of Kidlington and its annexes . . . Watereaton [&c.]. Repr. from the Oxf. chronicle. (Oxf.), 1881, 8°. 31 pp.
G.A. Oxon 8° 220 (5)

3934. TIPPING, H. A., Water Eaton manor. (Country Life, 1907, vol. 22, p. 666–74.)
Per. 384 b. 6

3935. An act to extend the boundaries of the city of Oxford and for other purposes [affecting Water Eaton, &c.]. (18 & 19 G. V, c. 84, L. & P.) Lond., 1928, 8°. 68 pp.
L. Eng. A 69 c. 6

3936. Auction catal. Frize farm. 9 June 1863.
G.A. fol. B 71

WATERPERRY

3937. Church notes, &c. from Waterperry. (The Topographer, 1790, vol. 2, p. 362–65.)
Douce VV 15

3938. WALLER, J. G., Palimpsest sepulchral brass from the church of Waterperry, near Oxford. (Archaeologia, 1846, vol. 31, p. 510, 11.)
R. Top. 7

3939. Extracts of the name of Curson or Curzon from the parish register of Waterperry. (Misc. geneal. et herald., 1894, 3rd ser., vol. 1, p. 214–17.)
Ψ 2. 10 *f*

See 3646 [Catalogue of brasses in the church. 1897].

3940. HANSON, J. S., *ed.*, Catholic registers of the domestic chapel at Waterperry manor house . . . and St. Clement's church . . . 1701?– 1834. (Cath. record soc., 1909, vol. 9, p. 388–422.)
G.A. Gen. top. 4° 220 (7)

3941. SMITH, J. C., A note on the Curzon brass at Waterperry. (Trans., Monumental brass soc., 1914, vol. 6, pt. 9, p. 420–25.)
Soc. 2184 d. 85
— Repr.
G.A. Oxon 4° 262 (13)

3942. TODD, J., The palimpsest brass in Waterperry church. (Trans., Monumental brass soc., 1949, vol. 8, pt. 6, p. 246–50.)
Soc. 2184 d. 85

3943. Auction catal. Waterperry estate. 4 Mar. 1925.
G.A. Oxon b. 92* (20)

WATLINGTON

3944. An act effectuating an exchange between the dean and canons of Windsor, and Thomas Stonor [concerning Watlington &c.]. (34 G. III, c. 24, Private.) [Lond.], 1794, fol. 8 pp.
L. Eng. C 13 c. 1 (1794. ii)

3945. An act for inclosing lands . . . of Watlington. . . . (49 G. III, c. 128, Private.) n. pl., [1808], fol. 30 pp.
L. Eng. C 13 c. 1 (1808. ii. 26)

3946. Watlington. (Rept., Oxf. archaeol. soc., 1895, p. 18.)
R. Top. 330

3947. PEARMAN, M. T., A Watlington court roll of the 15th century. (Rept., Oxf. archaeol. soc., 1902, pp. 16–19.)   R. Top. 330

3948. SALTER, H., Watlington town hall. (Rept., Oxf. archaeol. soc., 1908, p. 16–21.)   R. Top. 330

See 362 [Survey of 1387. 1910].

3949. HAWKINS, H. L., Excursion to Henley and Watlington. (Proc., Geol. assoc., 1912, vol. 23, p. 250–53.)   Radcl.

3950. SALTER, H. E., A popular lecture on the history of Watlington [by H. E. Salter]. (Rept., Oxf. archaeol. soc., 1921/22, p. 290–318.)
R. Top. 330

3951. Watlington. The official guide. Lond., [1929], 16°. 24 pp.
— 2nd ed. [1935], 16 pp.; 3rd ed. [1936], 16 pp.
G.A. Oxon 16° 179

3952. HASSALL, W. O., Watlington tradesmen. (Thame Gazette, Feb. 13, 1951.)   N.G.A. Oxon a. 120

3953. Auction catal. Watlington Park estate and manor. 2 Sept. 1879.
G.A. Oxon b. 87

3954. Auction catal. Greenfield farm. 31 Oct. 1889.
G.A. Oxon b. 92* (27)

3955. Auction catal. Watcombe manor estate. 17 June 1897.
G.A. Oxon b. 92 (26)
— 2 Aug. 1911.   G.A. Oxon b. 92 (27)

3956. Auction catal. Howe farm. 15 July 1901.
G.A. Oxon b. 92 (28)

3957. Auction catal. Glebe farm. 28 Sept. 1920.
G.A. Oxon b. 92* (18)

WEALD

3958. OSWALD, A., Weald manor. (Country Life, 1946, vol. 100, p. 256–59.) Per. 384 b. 6

3959. Auction catal. Weald estate. 15 Aug. 1912.
G.A. Oxon b. 92 (41)

3960. Auction catal. Land. 15 Aug. 1912.   G.A. Oxon b. 92 (42)

3961. Auction catal. Cottage, paddock and 3 enclosures of arable and pasture land. 15 Aug. 1912.   G.A. Oxon b. 92 (43)

3962. Auction catal. Weald farm. 12 Sept. 1917.   G.A. Oxon c. 317 (4)

WEAVELEY

3963. An act for vesting part of the estates of the late sir James Dashwood in trustees, in trust to sell the same. [Weaveley.] (37 G. III, c. 101, Private.) n. pl., 1797, fol. 30 pp.
L. Eng. C 13 c. 1 (1797. iv)

3964. Auction catal. Land. [1st], 2nd ed. 6 June 1891.
G.A. Oxon b. 85 b (60, 61)

WENDLEBURY

3965. An act for dividing, allotting and inclosing the . . . lands . . . of Wendlebury. . . . (40 G. III, c. 10, Private.) n. pl., [1800], fol. 32 pp.
L. Eng. C 13 c. 1 (1800. ii. 23)
See 486 [Railway. 1846].

3966. Auction catal. Estate. 6 Oct. 1843.   G.A. fol. B 71

WESTCOTT BARTON

3967. An act for dividing the . . . fields . . . of Westcott Barton. (35 G. III, c. 19, Private.) n. pl., 1795, fol. 33 pp.
L. Eng. C 13 c. 1 (1795. 22)

3968. WING, W., Annals of Steeple Barton and Westcot Barton. Repr. from the Oxford chronicle. (Oxf.), 1866, 8°. 61 pp.
G.A. Oxon 8° 93 (2)

3969. MARSHALL, J., Memorials of Westcott Barton. Lond., 1870, 8°. 74 pp.   G.A. Oxon 8° 209

3970. The Bartons (Westcott and Steeple) Church of England mission & temperance hall (history). (Charlbury, 1937), 8°. 4 pp.
G.A. Oxon c. 317 (5)

3971. Auction catal. Horsehay farm. 2 Aug. 1902.
G.A. Oxon b. 92 (29)

WEST END

3972. Auction catal. Village. 3 Sept. 1924.　　　　　G.A. Oxon c. 226

WESTON-ON-THE-GREEN

See 505, 507, 521, 526 [Turnpike acts. 1755 &c.].

3973. Souvenir of Weston manor hotel, Weston-on-the-Green. (Bristol), [c. 1925], 8°. 12 pp.　　　　　O.P.L.

3974. CARR, HAMILTON, Weston manor. (Country Life, 1928, vol. 64, p. 268–74.)　　　　　Per. 384 b. 6

3975. O'CONOR, N. J., Godes peace and the queenes, vicissitudes of a house [Norreys family of Weston on the Green] 1539–1615. Lond., 1934, 4°. 154 pp.　　　　　G.A. Oxon 4° 553

3976. Weston on the Green. Methodist church centenary, 1838–1938. n. pl., [1938], 8°. 39 pp.　　　　　O.P.L.

3977. Auction catal. Weston-on-the-Green estate. 26 Sept. 1918.
　　　　　G.A. Oxon b. 92* (16)

WESTWELL

See 503 [Turnpike acts. 1753, &c.].

3978. An act for dividing and inclosing the . . . fields . . . within the manor and parish of Westwell. (10 G. III, c. 37, Private.) n. pl., [1770], fol. 21 pp.　　　　　G.A. Oxon c. 182

See 1278 [Heraldry, by E. E. Cope. 1929].

3979. ATKINSON, R. J. C., A henge monument at Westwell. (Oxoniensia, 1949, vol. 14, p. 84–86.)　　　　　R. Top. 340

3980. Auction catal. Westwell estate. 4 Mar. 1905.
　　　　　G.A. Oxon b. 92 (30)

WHEATFIELD

3981. An act for vesting certain mannors and lands [Wheatfield, &c.] in . . . Oxon and Bucks in dame Anne Tipping and her heirs. . . . (12 G. I, c. 25, Private.) n. pl., 1725, fol. 10 pp.
　　　　　L. Eng. C 13 c. 1 (1714/27. 104)

3982. An act for vesting . . . certain . . . lands . . . in . . . London, and in the counties of Oxford and Bucks . . . the estate of Susanna Letten . . . in trustees to be sold. [Wheatfield, &c.] (7 G. III, c. 75, Private.) n. pl., 1767, fol. 17 pp.
　　　　　L. Eng. C 13 c. 1 (1767, f. 933)

3983. Memorandum of Wheatfield. [Middlehill, 18—], s. sh.
Caps. 6. 24

3984. An act for vesting the . . . manors and estates [in Wheatfield, &c.] of Charles Vere Spencer, an infant, in . . . Oxford and Denbigh in trustees, in order to effect the sale thereof. . . . (5 & 6 W. IV, c. 23, Private.) n. pl., 1835, fol. 44 pp.   L. Eng. C 13 c. 1 (1835. 23)

3985. An act to authorize the inclosure of certain lands . . . [Wheatfield]. (17 & 18 V., c. 48, Pub.) Lond., 1854, fol. 2 pp.
L. Eng. A 69 c. 1

3986. Auction catal. Stoke Grange farm. 9 June 1863.
G.A. fol. B 71

WHEATLEY

3987. William Powell alias Hinson, esq., plaintiffe; The warden and fellows of All-soules colledge . . . defendants, in the Chancellors court of the University of Oxford. [Concerning lands let in Wheatley.] n. pl., 1656, 4°. 8 pp.   Wood 515 (16)

3988. An act for inclosing lands in . . . Wheatley. (49 G. III, c. 150, Private.) n. pl., 1809, fol. 25 pp.   G.A. Oxon c. 95

3989. B., W., Notice of a Roman villa recently discovered at Wheatley. (Archaeol. journ. 1846, vol. 2, p. 350–56; vol. 3, p. 92.) R. Top. 5

3990. Roman villa discovered near Oxford [Castle Hill]. (Illustr. London news, 1846, vol. 8, no. 206, p. 248.)   N. 2288 b. 6

3991. Order for the laying of a corner stone of the new church of St. Mary, at Wheatley, January 22nd, 1856. n. pl., (1856), 8°. 6 pp.
G.A. Oxon 8° 232 (6)

3992. POULTON, E. B., A walk from Oxford to Wheatley over Shotover hill [mainly geological observations]. (Oxf. mag., 1883, vol. 1, p. 169–71.)   G.A. Oxon 4° 141
— Repr.   G.A. Oxon 8° 683

3993. TAUNT, H. W., Anglo-Saxon graves found at Wheatley, May 1883. [10 photographs.]   G.A. Oxon 4° 184

3994. KENWARD, J., A first note on the Anglo-Saxon cemetery at Wheatley. (Proc., Birm. nat. hist. and phil. soc., 1884, vol. 4, p. 179–93.)   Per. 1996 e. 545
— Repr.   G.A. Oxon 8° 461

3995. LEEDS, E. T., [Account of an Anglo-Saxon cemetery at Wheatley.] (Proc., Soc. of Antiq., 1916, ser. 2, vol. 29, p. 48–63.)   R. Top. 1
— Repr.   G.A. Oxon 8° 611 (29)

3996. BLAKE, J. F., Excursion to Headington, Shotover, and Wheatley. (Proc., Geol. assoc., 1902, vol. 17, p. 383–85.)   Radcl.

3997. Eliza Carey Biscoe Home of rest, Wheatley. Report, Jan.–Dec., 1901. Birm., (1902), 8°. 7 pp.   24767 f. 16 (5)

3998. Excursion to Wheatley and Arngrove. (Proc., Geol. assoc., 1910, vol. 21, p. 234, 35.)   Radcl.

See 31 [Stratigraphy at Wheatley. 1942].
See 614 [Building stones from Wheatley for Abingdon abbey. 1948–9].

3999. HASSALL, W. O., The stones of Wheatley. (Thame gazette, Dec. 19, 1950.)   N.G.A. Oxon a. 120

4000. Auction catal. Freehold estates. 26 Oct. 1812, 14 Dec. 1812.   G.A. fol. B 71

4001. Auction catal. Freehold estate. 28 Apr. 1818.   G.A. fol. B 71

4002. Auction catal. Manor farm, with the Manor. 21 Feb. 1846.   G.A. Oxon b. 92 (31)
— 13 June 1846.   G.A. Oxon b. 92 (32)

4003. Auction catal. Rectory farm. 2 Aug. 1902.   G.A. Oxon b. 92 (33)

4004. Auction catal. Freehold enclosures and cottages. 30 May 1908.   G.A. Oxon b. 91 (33)

4005. Auction catal. The Old Manor house &c. 4 Mar. 1925.   G.A. Oxon c. 224*

WHITCHURCH

4006. An act for building a bridge, at or near the ferry over the river Thames, from Whitchurch, in the county of Oxford, to the opposite shore, in the parish of Pangbourn . . . Berks. (32 Geo. III, c. 97, Pub.) Lond., 1792, fol. 35 pp.   L. Eng. A 69 c. 1

4007. An act for dividing, allotting, and inclosing the open and common fields . . . and waste lands in the parish of Whitchurch. (40 G. III, c. 78, Private.) n. pl., 1800, fol. 31 pp.   L. Eng. C 23 c. Enclosure 2

4008. An act for inclosing Whitchurch Common and other waste lands . . . of Whitchurch. . . . (50 G. III, c. 102, Private.) n. pl., 1810, fol. 24 pp.   L. Eng. C 13 c. 1 (1810. ii. 46)

4009. Rules for the Whitchurch dancing assemblies. n. pl., [c. 1810], s. sh.   MS. Pigott c. 2 (7 b)

4010. Oxford county council. Whitchurch parish boundary. Report of the clerk of the peace to the Easter quarter sessions. [Oxf.], 1875, fol. 12 pp.   G.A. fol. A 139 (7)

4011. SLATTER, J., and DRYDEN, H. E. L., Whitchurch. (Rept., Oxf. archaeol. soc., 1888/9, p. 13–15, 21–26.)   R. Top. 330

4012. SLATTER, J., Some notes of the history of the parish of Whitchurch. Lond., 1895, 8°. 150 pp. G.A. Oxon 8° 625

See 2852 [Act concerning Whitchurch and district joint hospital district. 1904].

4013. Hardwick house. (Country Life, 1906, vol. 20, p. 90–97.)
Per. 384 b. 6
See 362 [Survey of 1387. 1910].

4014. GODLEE, SIR R. J., A village on the Thames, Whitchurch, yesterday and to-day. Lond., 1926, 8°. 283 pp. G.A. Oxon 8° 1048

4015. Auction catal. Walliscote estate. 24 Sept. 1800.
G.A. fol. A 266 (44)

4016. Auction catal. 2 proprietors shares of £100 each on the tolls of the New Bridge over the Thames from Whitchurch to Pangbourn. 8 Oct. 1800. G.A. fol. A 266 (31)

WHITEHILL

4017. An act for establishing . . . exchanges of . . . lands . . . within the hamlet of Wighthill . . . between . . . Corpus Christi college . . . and Simon Wisdome. . . . (17 G. III, c. 55, Private.) n. pl., 1777, fol. 14 pp. L. Eng. C 13 c. 1 (1777. ii. 62)

4018. An act for vesting part of the estates of the late sir James Dashwood in trustees, in trust to sell the same. [Whitehill.] (37 G. III, c. 101, Private.) n. pl., 1797, fol. 30 pp.
L. Eng. C 13 c. 1 (1797. 4)

WICKHAM

4019. An act for dividing and inclosing one open and common field . . . and several parcels of land . . . within the township and liberties of Neithrop and Wickham. (32 G. II, c. 19, Private.) [Lond.], 1759, fol. O.C.R.L.

4020. An act for vesting part of the estates of the late sir James Dashwood in trustees in trust to sell the same. [Wickham.] (37 G. III, c. 101, Private.) n. pl., 1797, fol. 30 pp.
L. Eng. C 13 c. 1 (1797. iv)

4021. Auction catal. Wickham tythes. 22 Oct. 1806.
G.A. fol. A 266 (26)

WIDFORD

4022. Widford. (Rept., Oxf. archaeol. soc., 1904, p. 17–19.)
R. Top. 330

4023. [St. Oswald's church, Widford.] (Trans., Bristol and Glouc. archaeol. soc., 1911, vol. 34, p. 28.) R. Top. 210

4024. Auction catal. Perpetual advowson of the rectory. 27 Nov. 1810.
G.A. fol. A 273*

4025. Auction catal. Widford manor farm, Widford mill farm, and Widford mill. 21 July 1926.   G.A. Oxon c. 224 (19)

WIGGINTON

4026. An act for sale of part of the estate of Richard Brideoake [in Wigginton &c.]. (9 Anne, c. 43, Private.) n. pl., [1710], fol. 4 pp.
B.M.

4027. An act for dividing and inclosing the . . . fields . . . of Wigginton. . . . (35 G. III, c. 21, Private.) n. pl., 1795, fol. 29 pp.
L. Eng. C 13 c. 1 (1795. 23)

4028. MOZLEY, A. D., Notes on Wigginton church. (Rept., Oxf. archaeol. soc., 1907, p. 10, 11.)   R. Top. 330

4029. KEYSER, C. E., Notes on the architecture of the churches of Wigginton [&c.]. (Journ., Brit. archaeol. assoc., 1919, new ser., vol. 25, p. 1–23+55 plates.)   R. Top. 4

4030. Auction catal. Estate of sir J. T. Wheate. 30 May 1804.
G.A. fol. A 273*

4031. Auction catal. Brooms barn. 25 Sept. 1918.
G.A. Oxon b. 92* (8)

4032. Auction catal. Wigginton Glebe estate. 13 Nov. 1919.
G.A. Oxon c. 317 (14)

4033. Auction catal. Agricultural properties. 20 July 1922.
G.A. Oxon b. 92* (18)

WIGHTHILL

See WHITEHILL

WILCOTE

4034. BUCKLER, J. C., Elevations, sections, and details, of Saint Peter's church, Wilcote. Oxf., 1844, fol. 6 plates.   G.A. fol. A 126

4035. BEAMES, W. A., and MOLESWORTH-ROBERTS, H. V., Wilcote church. (Builder, 1922, Oct. 13, p. 533–35.)   N. 1863 c. 1

4036. Auction catal. Oak, elm and walnut trees. 19 Nov. 1813.
G.A. fol. B 71

WILSCOTT

4037. An act for dividing and inclosing the . . . fields . . . within . . . Williamscott, otherwise Willscot [&c.]. (1 G. III, c. 30, Private.) n. pl., 1761, fol. 24 pp. G.A. Oxon c. 113 (2)

4038. CHAMBERLIN, W. H., Valuation of Wardington, Wilscote and Coton. Banbury, 1833, 4°. 52 pp.

WITNEY
General

See 422 [Witney wakes. 1646].

4039. ROWE, J., Tragi-comœdia, being a brief relation of the strange, and wonderfull hand of God discovered at Witny, in the comedy acted there February the third, where some were slaine, many hurt. Together with . . . three sermons on that occasion. Oxf., 1653, 4°. [90 pp.] [Madan 2221.] Gough Oxf. 45 (5)

See 1225 [J. Leverett's will. 1783].

4040. Witney benevolent society. Report from Jan. 1, 1824 to Jan. 1, 1827. Witney, (1827), s. sh. MS. Top. Oxon d. 213 (20)

4041. GILES, J. A., History of Witney [&c.]. Lond., 1852, 8°. 107 pp. G.A. Oxon 8° 13

See 670 [Register of voters, Witney polling district. 1859/60].

4042. Witney (Excursion. Archaeol. and nat. hist. soc. of N. Oxf., 1868.) Manning 8° 3

4043. Witney (and West Oxfordshire) horticultural society. [Rules and schedule of prizes for the annual show.] 1870–87. G.A. Oxon 4° 207

4044. New Mills bridge, near Witney. Report of the clerk of the peace upon the question of liability to repair the bridge. [Oxf.], 1873, fol. 4 pp. G.A. fol. A 139* (65)

4045. Witney Athenæum. Twenty-second annual report. Witney, 1874, 8°. 4 pp. G.A. Oxon 4° 208 (28)

4046. Witney choral society. Rules. n. pl., [1875?], 8°. 2 pp. G.A. Oxon 4° 208 (3)

4047. Witney choral society. [Report. 1895/6, 96/7.] Witney (1896, 97), 4° & 8°. G.A. Oxon 4° 183

4048. Mrs. Brown at Witney. [Humorous articles.] [Oxf., c. 1880], 8°. 32 pp. G.A. Oxon 8° 922

4049. Witney coffee tavern co. General balance sheet. 1880–1900. Witney, 1880–1900, fol. & 4°. G.A. Oxon c. 94

4050. Medical club for Witney and surrounding parishes. Rules. n. pl., [c. 1885], s. sh. G.A. Oxon 4° 208 (10)

4051. Witney church registry [for placing and assisting unemployed servants]. Report, 1890. n. pl., (1890), 8°. 4 pp.
G.A. Oxon 4° 208 (20)

4052. CROWTHER, G. F., On a pax penny attributed to Witney. (Num. chron., 1891, 3rd ser., vol. 11, p. 161–63.) Num. 03 d. 10

4053. NORRIS, W. F., Memoranda relating to Witney. (Journ., Brit. archaeol. assoc., 1891, vol. 47, p. 120–24.) R. Top. 4

4054. Witney. (Rept., Oxf. archaeol. soc., 1891, p. 12.) R. Top. 330

4055. MONK, W. J., History of Witney. Witney, 1894, 8°. 308 pp.
G.A. Oxon 8° 649
See 658 [Parliamentary history, by W. R. Williams. 1899].

4056. TAUNT, H. W., Witney, Oxon, and round it. Oxf., [1906], obl. 8°. 32 pp. G.A. Oxon 8° 738

4057. BALLARD, A., The Black death at Witney. (Rept., Oxf. archaeol. soc., 1909, p. 17–29.) R. Top. 330

4058. BALLARD, A., The Black death on the estates of the see of Winchester, by A. E. Levett. With a chapter on the manors of Witney [&c.] by A. Ballard. (Oxf. studies in soc. and legal hist., vol. 5, p. 182–204.) Oxf., 1916, 8°. S. Hist. gen. 5
See 293 [History, by W. J. Monk. 1926].

4059. The official guide. [1st]–3rd ed. Chelt., 1934–40, 8°.
G.A. Oxon 8° 1139

4060. Witney. (Country Life, 1942, vol. 92, p. 404–06.) Per. 384 b. 6

4061. HUSSEY, C., Merryfield's House, Witney. (Country Life, 1948, vol. 103, p. 26–29.) Per. 384 b. 6

4062. A visit to Witney and Witney mills [by J. V. Early]. Lond., (1898), 4°. 46 pp. G.A. Oxon 4° 701

4063. Auction catal. Staple Hall Inn &c. 9 Oct. 1812.
G.A. fol. B 71

4064. Auction catal. J. H. Usill estate. 26 July 1894.
G.A. Oxon b. 6 (31)

4065. Auction catal. Freehold and copyhold estate. 16 May 1895.
G.A. Oxon b. 92 (35)

4066. Auction catal. House, 11 cottages, land. 18 Sept. 1913.
G.A. Oxon b. 91 (1)

4067. Sale catal. Property including a chapel. Nov. 1922.
G.A. Oxon c. 256 (55)

Blanket Industry

See 4062 [Visit to Witney mills. 1898].

4068. The Witney blanket co. Handbook and price list of blankets, rugs and coverlets. n. pl., [1910], 8°. 16 pp. G.A. Oxon c. 317 (26)

4069. PLUMMER, A., The Witney blanket industry, the records of the Witney blanket weavers. Lond., 1934, 8°. 284 pp. 1784 e. 229

See 617 [Blanket trade, by R. P. Bickinsale. 1937].

4070. CROSBIE, M., Witney has woven wool for 700 years. (Country Life, 1942, vol. 92, p. 404–06.) Per. 384 b. 6

Directories

See 1390 [Directory. 1846].

Natural History

4071. Natural history & literary society. Report 1870–87/88. (Witney, 1870–88), 8°. G.A. Oxon 8° 667

4072. Natural history & literary society. A descriptive catalogue of fossil remains and other miscellaneous objects deposited in the museum, with, Rules and regulations of the society. . . . Witney, 1878, 8°. 18 pp. G.A. Oxon 8° 667

4073. Natural history and literary society. Rules & regulations. n. pl., [c. 1900], s. sh. G.A. Oxon 8° 667

4074. Natural history society. Catalogue of library. n. pl., [c. 1900], 8°. 4 pp. G.A. Oxon 8° 667

4075. RICHARDSON, L., Week-end field meeting in the Witney district, report. (Proc., Geol. assoc., 1935, vol. 46, p. 403–11.) Radcl.

See 34 [Geol. of Witney district. 1946].

Newspapers

See 1338 Guardian.
1377 Witney Express.
1378 Witney Gazette.
1379 Witney Telegraph.

Public Utilities

4076. Witney rural sanitary authority. Annual report, 1890–98, 1902, 1904. Witney, 1891–1905, fol. G.A. Oxon c. 88

4077. An act to confirm certain provisional orders made by the Board of Trade under the Electric lighting acts 1862 and 1888 relating to ... Witney. (1 & 2 G. V, c. 161, L. & P.) Lond., 1911, fol. 42 pp.
L. Eng. A 69 c. 6

4078. An act to confirm certain provisional orders made by the Board of Trade under the Gas and Water works facilities act 1870 relating to ... Witney and district gas. (1 & 2 G. V, c. 167, L. & P.) Lond., 1911, fol. 66 pp.
L. Eng. A 69 c. 6

4079. An act to confirm a scheme made by the Minister of Health under the Public works facilities act 1930, relating to the Urban district council of Witney. (24 G. V, c. 1, L. & P.) Lond., 1933, 8°. 23 pp.
L. Eng. A 69 c. 6

Railways

4080. An act for connecting the town of Witney with the existing railways in ... Yarnton and Wolvercot.... (22 & 23 V., c. 46, L. & P.) Lond., 1859, fol. 13 pp.
L. Eng. A 69 c. 6
— 24 & 25 V., c. 22, L. & P.

4081. An act to enable the Witney Railway company to make a road to their station at Witney.... (24 & 25 V., c. 22, L. & P.) Lond., 1861, fol. 4 pp.
L. Eng. A 69 c. 6

See 491 [Witney railway co. 1890].
See 493 [Oxford, Witney, and Fairford railway. 1931].

Religion

4082. Church notes, &c. at Whitney. (The Topographer, 1791, vol. 4, p. 155-60.)
Douce VV 17

4083. Witney parish magazine. Vol. 1, no. 1-vol. 3, no. 36. Witney, 1871-73, 8°.
O.P.L.

4084. [Announcement, in the form of a letter to his parishioners by W. F. Norris discontinuing the practice of allocating seats in the church to specific families.] n. pl., (1889), 4°. 4 pp.
G.A. Oxon c. 317 (26)

4085. NORRIS, W. F., Church work at Witney, 1888-9. n. pl., (1889), 8°. 39 pp.
G.A. Oxon 16° 33 (11)

4086. FOX, S., and PICKARD, E., The hat crusade. Vol. 1. [An account of the refusal by certain Quakers to remove their hats in church. Charlbury (where Fox lived for a time) and Witney churches are particularly mentioned.] Flushing, Corn., 1896, 8°.
11141 e. 8

4087. JONES, H. CUNLIFFE-, History of Witney Congregational church, 1662-1935. Milton-under-Wychwood, [1935], 8°. 16 pp.
G.A. Oxon 8° 1204 (13)

Roads

See 494 [London inns frequented by Witney carriers. 1637].
See 502, 512, 517, 529 [Turnpike acts. 1751, &c.].

4088. Witney rural district council. Estimate for district highways, 1897–98. Witney, (1897), 8°. 10 pp. G.A. Oxon 8° 648

Schools

4089. An act for the setling of a free school in Witney . . . being erected and endowed by Henry Box. . . . (15 Ch. II, c. 27, Private.) n. pl., 1663, fol.

4090. GOOLE, J., An answer to a scandalous pamphlet entitul'd The present state of the free-school at Witney. Oxf., 1721, 8°. 20 pp.
Gough Oxf. 45 (3)

4091. COLLIER, R., Remarks upon mr. Goole's Answer to the present state of the free-school at Witney in Oxfordshire. Lond., 1721, 8°. 32 pp. Gough Oxf. 45 (4)

4092. Witney grammar school. [Prospectus. 1882, 1893.]
G.A. Oxon 4° 208 (29, 30)

4093. Witney grammar school. Report of the examiner appointed by the Oxford delegacy of local examinations. 1899. n. pl., (1899), 4°. 4 pp.
G.A. Oxon 4° 208 (32)

4094. Board of education. Witney grammar and technical school. [Plan for altering scheme of the Charity commissioners.] (Lond., 1908), fol. 8 pp. G.A. Oxon c. 135

4095. [Account of the resolutions at a meeting which agreed 'that a society be now formed, entitled The society for promoting the instruction of the poor in . . . Witney, according to the general plan of the National society'.] (Oxf., 1813), fol. 4 pp.
G.A. Oxon c. 317 (26)

4096. Mr. Wells's school, Witney. Witney, 1832, s. sh.
MS. Top. Oxon c. 200 (17)

4097. Lynton House school. The Lyntonian. [Lithographed.] Vol. 1, no. 1–Vol. 2, no. 2. Witney, (1901–02), 8°. G.A. Oxon 8° 685

WITNEY DEANERY

4098. Witney deanery magazine.
— Jan. 1880–Dec. 1891. G.A. Oxon 8° 474
— No. 1–102. 1904–12. G.A. Oxon 4° 222
Burford, 1880–1912, 8° & 4°.

4099. MACRAY, W. D., Church plate in the deanery of Witney. (Rept., Oxf. archaeol. soc., 1890, p. 19–34.)   R. Top. 330

4100. PRIOR, C. E., Dedications of churches, with some notes as to village feasts and old customs. Deaneries of Woodstock, Deddington & Witney. (Rept., Oxf. archaeol. soc., 1904, p. 23–53.)
R. Top. 330

4101. PEARCE, S. S., The clergy of the deaneries of Witney and Bicester during the settlement of 1559 and afterwards. (Rept., Oxf. archaeol. soc., 1914, p. 180–237.)   R. Top. 330

WITNEY POOR LAW UNION

4102. The financial statements of the Witney union. 1891–98. Witney, 1891–98, 8°.   G.A. Oxon 8° 648

WOLVERCOTE

4103. An act for inclosing lands . . . of Wolvercot . . . and for commuting the tithes of the said parish. (1 & 2 W. IV, c. 18, Private.) Lond., 1831, fol. 33 pp.   L. Eng. C 13 c. 1

See 413 [Account of night march of Charles i. June 3, 1644, by V. Thomas. 1852].

4104. An act to enable the president and scholars of Saint John Baptist college in the university of Oxford to grant building leases of their lands in . . . Woolvercot. . . . (18 & 19 V., c. 10, Private.) Lond., 1855, fol. 15 pp.   L. Eng. C 13 c. 1

4105. An act for connecting the town of Witney with the existing railways in . . . Yarnton and Wolvercot. . . . (22 & 23 V., c. 46, L. & P.) Lond., 1859, fol. 13 pp.   L. Eng. A 69 c. 6
— 24 & 25 V., c. 22, L. & P.

4106. Oxford county council. Report of the Clerk of the peace as to Toll bridge, Wolvercot. [Oxf.], 1873, fol. 7 pp.   G.A. fol. A 137 (3)

4107. Oxford county council. Toll bridge, Wolvercot. Statement of the case, ex parte the County of Oxford submitted to mr. Cunningham Glen and mr. Alexander Glen, and their opinion. [Oxf.], 1874, fol. 4 pp.   G.A. fol. A 137 (4)

See 1020 [Act concerning water supply, 1875].

4108. PARKER, G., Bradfield, Berks, and Wolvercote, Oxon. Notes from the parish registers, 16th and 17th centuries [by G. Parker]. Oxf., 1888, 8°. 20 pp.   MS. Top. Oxon c. 166 (f. 405)

4109. S. Peter's, Wolvercote. Parish magazine. March 1891–Oct. 1895. Oxf., (1891–95), 8°.   G.A. Oxon 8° 593

4110. The proposed consecration of a portion of the Wolvercote cemetery. [Appeal for funds.] n. pl., 1897, 4°. 4 pp.
— [A second appeal 1897.] G.A. Oxon c. 317 (15)

4111. BELL, A. M., Implementiferous sections at Wolvercote. (Quart. journ., Geol. soc., 1904, vol. 60, p. 120–32.) Radcl.

4112. BLAIR, K. G., Some coleopterous remains from the peat-bed at Wolvercote. (Trans., Entom. soc. of Lond., 1923, pp. 558–63.)
Radcl.

4113. An act to extend the boundaries of the city of Oxford and for other purposes [affecting Wolvercote, &c.]. (18 & 19 G. V, c. 84, L. & P.) Lond., 1928, 8°. 68 pp. L. Eng. A. 69 c. 6

4114. FREEBORN, M. E., The church of St. Peter, Wolvercote. (Lond., &c.), [c. 1930], 8°. 40 pp. G.A. Oxon 8° 1230 (5)

4115. SUTHERLAND, C. H. V., A Wolvercote coin-hoard of the time of the civil wars. (Oxoniensia, 1937, p. 101–02.) R. Top. 340

4116. Auction catal. Wolvercote mills. 10 July 1849.
G.A. Oxon b. 92 (36)

4117. Auction catal. Land. [1st] 2nd ed. 6 June 1891.
G.A. Oxon b. 85 b (60, 61)

4118. Auction catal. Six houses in Elmthorpe road. 23 July 1920.
G.A. Oxon b. 92* (23)

WOODCOTE

4119. A descriptive account of the pictures in Woodcott house, the property of Adam Duff. Reading, 1839, 8°. 7 pp. 1706 e. 230

4120. An act to authorize the inclosure of certain lands . . . [Southstoke-cum-Woodcote]. (13 & 14 V., c. 66, Pub.) Lond., 1850, fol. 2 pp.
L. Eng. A 69 c. 1

4121. Woodcote in the War years. (Wallingford), [1948], 8° 16 pp.
G.A. Oxon 8° 1184 (7)

4122. Auction catal. Manor of Rawlings. 28 Aug. 1800.
G.A. fol. A 266 (45)

4123. Auction catal. Freehold house.
— 28 Sept. 1801. G.A. fol. A 266 (29)
— 9 Nov. 1801. G.A. fol. A 266 (30)

4124. Auction catal. Woodcote house. 28 June 1912.
G.A. Oxon b. 92 (38)

WOODEATON

4125. TAYLOR, M. V., Woodeaton. (Journ. of Roman studies, 1917,
vol. 7, p. 98–119.)　　　　　　　　　　　　　Ψ 3. 02
— Repr.　　　　　　　　　　　　　G.A. Oxon 4° 403 (1)

4126. Woodeaton. (Rept., Oxf. archaeol. soc., 1917, p. 91–119.)
R. Top. 330

4127. MILNE, J. G., Woodeaton coins. (Journ. of Roman studies, 1931,
vol. 21, p. 101–09.)　　　　　　　　　　　　Ψ 3. 02

4128. Wood Eaton. (Rept., Oxf. archaeol. soc., 1933, p. 19.)
R. Top. 330

4129. JOPE, E. M., and HUSE, G., Examination of 'Egyptian blue' by
X-ray powder photography. [Woodeaton.] (Nature, 1940, vol. 146,
no. 3688, p. 26.)　　　　　　　　　　　　　Radcl.

4130. JOPE, E. M., and HUSE, G., Blue pigment of Roman date from
Woodeaton. (Oxoniensia, 1940, p. 167.)　　　　R. Top. 340

4131. KIRK, J. R., Bronzes from Woodeaton. (Oxoniensia, 1949, vol. 14,
p. 1–45.)　　　　　　　　　　　　　　　R. Top. 340

4132. Woodeaton. (Archaeol. notes. Oxoniensia, 1949, vol. 14, p. 77.)
R. Top. 340

4133. Auction catal. Marston forest farm. 22 Feb. 1879.
G.A. fol. A 266 (36)

4134. Auction catal. Woodeaton estate. 2 Nov. 1912.
G.A. Oxon b. 92 (39)

WOODPERRY

4135. W. J., Antiquities found at Woodperry. (Archaeol. journ., 1846,
vol. 3, p. 116–28.)　　　　　　　　　　　　R. Top. 5

4136. Roman antiquities discovered at Woodpury in Oxfordshire.
(Archaeologia, 1847, vol. 32, p. 392.)　　　　　R. Top. 7

WOODSTOCK

General

4137. An acte for the reliefe and reedifiying of the borough of newe
Woodstocke. (18 Eliz., c. 21, Pub.) [Lond.], 1575, s. sh.
L. Eng. A 69 c. 1

4138. An inquisition taken [at Woodstock] in the county of [Oxford] the [xxth] day of [August] in the xiiiith] yeare of . . . Charles . . . of the price of graine, victuals, horse-meat, lodgings and other things. [The details completed in MS.] n. pl., [1639?], s. sh.

Gough Oxf. 80 (38)

See 421 [Taking of Woodstock. 1646].

4139. GREGORY, F., Votivum Carolo, or, A welcome to . . . Charles ii, from the master and scholars of Woodstock-school in the county of Oxford. [By F. Gregory.] [Oxf.], 1660, 4°. 28 pp.   Wood 319 (10)

4140.

4141. A collection of letters from several counties, cities and boroughs, containing instructions to their representatives in parliament to oppose any extensions of the Excise laws. (Woodstock, p. 25, 26.) Lond., 1733, 8°.   55 b. 138
— [Another ed. entitled] Excise: being a collection, &c. 1733.

Pamph. 399 (14)

4142. Woodstock. (Gent's. mag., 1749, p. 433; 1750, p. 83; 1792, pt. 1, p. 532.)   . Ψ 2. 44

4143. Woodstock: an elegy. Lond., 1761, fol. 24 pp.

Gough Oxf. 103 (14)

4144. An act for confirming articles of agreement and for effecting an exchange of lands [Hensington and Woodstock] between . . . George, Duke of Marlborough and . . . Merton college. . . . (9 G. III, c. 9, Private.) [Lond.], 1769, fol. 6 pp.   L. Eng. C 13 c. 1 (1769. 49)

4145.

See 883 [Customs and charities. 1842].
See 20 [Geology, by E. Hull. 1859].
See 22 [Geology, by A. H. Green. 1864].

4146. MOORE, J. J., Rambles and rides around Oxford, by rail, river and road. Sect. 2. Blenheim, Woodstock, and Bladon. (Shrimptons' hist. county handbooks.) Oxf., 1882, 8°. 103 pp.

G.A. Oxon 8° 964

4147. Agricultural and horticultural association. Twenty-ninth (–thirty-first) annual show. Catalogue [&c.] Woodstock, (1886–88), 8°.

G.A. Oxon 8° 857

4148. Agricultural & horticultural association. Catalogue of poultry, pigeons, dogs, cage-birds, rabbits, cavies and cats. Woodstock, (1889), 8°. 31 pp.   G.A. Oxon 8° 857

4149. The Bladon with Woodstock parish magazine. May, 1889. Woodstock, 1889, 8°.   G.A. Oxon c. 317 (19)

4150. DUNCAN, G., Woodstock debating society. [Announcement of meeting, signed G. Duncan.] n. pl., (1894), s. sh.
G.A. Oxon c. 22 (26)

4151. HIGGS, A. G., Proposed memorial to . . . Arthur Majendie. [Letter inviting subscriptions.] [Woodstock], (1895), s. sh.
G.A. Oxon c. 22 (34)

4152. In memoriam Arthur Majendie, rector of Bladon & Woodstock. Woodstock, (1895), 8°. 24 pp.   11126 e. 171 (9)

4153. BALLARD, A., Chronicles of the Royal borough of Woodstock. Oxf., 1896, 8°. 149 pp.   G.A. Oxon 8° 621
— Cheap ed. 1897.

4154. Woodstock. The official guide. Chelt. &c., [1935], 16°. 21 pp.
G.A. Oxon 16° 201
— 2nd ed. [1936]; 3rd ed. [1938]; 4th ed. [1941].
G.A. Oxon 16° 201

4155. Woodstock. (Archaeol. notes. Oxoniensia, 1936, p. 201.)
R. Top. 340

4156. HARDEN, D. B., Cast-iron water-pipes from Woodstock. (Oxoniensia, 1940, p. 171.)   R. Top. 340

4157. SHELMERDINE, J. M., Introduction to Woodstock. Woodstock, 1951, 8°. 47 pp.   G.A. Oxon. 8° 1237

See 4203 [Recollections, by I. W. Hutchinson. 1945].

4158. Historical manuscripts commission, National register of archives. List of the manuscripts and documents in the possession of the mayor and corporation of the borough of Woodstock. [Reprod. from typewriting, with a pr. title-leaf.] n. pl., [1952], fol.
R. 6 fol. 1

See also 4232, 4236–4239.

4159. Auction catal. Bear inn. 21 Aug. 1789.   G.A. fol. A 266 (46)

4160. Auction catal. Mansion near Blenheim park, and premises in the centre of Woodstock. 26 Oct. 1836.   G.A. fol. B 71

4161. Auction catal. Fletcher's house. 11 July 1924.
G.A. Oxon c. 224 (14)

Church

4162. The restoration of Woodstock church [Appeal, and list of subscribers]. n. pl., [1876], 4°. 4 pp.   G.A. Oxon c. 317 (19)

4163. The Church of St. Mary, Woodstock. [Appeal for funds for restoration with extracts from the architect's report, and 2 illustrations.] n. pl., (1896), 4°. 4 pp.   G.A. Oxon c. 317 (19)

See 1970 [Monumental brasses in the church. 1898].

4164. PEARCE, S. S., The parish church of Woodstock and an episode of the Civil war. (Rept., Oxf. archaeol. soc., 1927, p. 153–58.)

R. Top. 330

Corporation

4165. First report of the Commissioners appointed to inquire into the municipal corporations in England and Wales. (Woodstock, Appendix, p. 139–44.) Pp. Eng. 1835, vol. 23

4166. COCKBURN, A. E., Corporations of England and Wales. (New Woodstock, vol. 1, p. 208, 09.) Lond., 1835, 8°.

G.A. Gen. top. 8° 727 (1)

Directories

See 1390 [Directory. 1846].

Glove Industry

4167. JONES, H. A., Where Tommy Atkins' gloves are made [Woodstock]. (Black and White, Dec. 3 1898.) G.A. Oxon 4° 381

4168. SCHULZ, T. E., The Woodstock glove industry. (Oxoniensia, 1938, p. 139–52.) R. Top. 340

Manor

4169. The Woodstock scuffle, or, Most dreadfull aparitions that were lately seene in the Mannor-house of Woodstock [a ballad]. n. pl., 1649, 4°. 4 leaves. B.M.

4169A. The just devil of Woodstock, or, A true narrative of the several apparitions, the frights, and punishments inflicted upon the Rumpish commissioners sent thither to survey the mannors and houses belonging to his majestie [by T. Widows?]. Lond., 1660, 4°. 3 leaves+13 pp. B.M.
[Bodleian copy imperf. Gough Lond. 143 (3)]
— [Another ed.] 1649 [really 1660]. Harvard univ.

4169B. The genuine history of the good devil of Woodstock [and other stories]. New ed. Lond., (1802), 12°. p. 1–15. 930 f. 191

See 4187 [Act settling the honour and manor of Woodstock on John, duke of Marlborough. 1706].

4170. HOFFMAN, F., A poem on the mannour of Woodstock. n. pl., [c. 1710], fol. 7 leaves. Gough Lond. 143 (4)

4171. An account of the custom of the mannor of Woodstock. (Itinerary of John Leland, ed. by T. Hearne, vol. 8, p. xxxvi–xxxix.) Oxf., 1712, 8°. Mus. Bibl. II 22
— 1745. Mus. Bibl. II 38
— 1769. Mus. Bibl. II 43

4172. Queen Elizabeth's prison at Woodstock. [The mirror, no. 204.] n. pl., [1828], 8°. 2 pp.   G.A. Oxon 4° 355 (1)

4173. The ancient palace of Woodstock. (The mirror, no. 195.) n. pl., 1826, 8°. 8 pp.   G.A. Oxon 4° 355 (2)

4174. Remains of Henry the second's palace [Woodstock]. (The mirror, no. 465.) n. pl., 1830, 8°. 2 pp.   G.A. Oxon 4° 355 (3)

4175. Fair Rosamond; or, The bower of Woodstock. Lond., [1830?], 8°. 23 pp.   G.A. Oxon 8° 918

4176. Queen Elizabeth; her progresses and public processions. Her removal to Woodstock (castle). (Saturday mag., 1838, no. 372.)
G.A. Oxon c. 317 (19)

4177. MANNING, C. R., *ed.* State papers relating to the custody of the princess Elizabeth at Woodstock, in 1554, letters between queen Mary and her Privy Council, and sir Henry Bedingfield. (Norf. and Norwich archaeol. soc., 1855, vol. 4, p. 133–231.)   R. Top. 280

4178. MARSHALL, E., The early history of Woodstock Manor, and its environs. Oxf., &c., 1873, 8°. 474 pp.   G.A. Oxon 8° 177
— Suppl. 1874. 122 pp.   G.A. Oxon 8° 193
— [Another ed.] 1875.   Manning 8° 354

4179. BALLARD, A., Woodstock Manor in the thirteenth century. (Sonderabdr. aus d. Vierteljahrschr. für Social- u. Wirtschaftsgesch., VI, p. 424–59.) Stuttgart, 1908, 8°.
G.A. Oxon 8° 761 (1)

4180. CHAMBERS, E. K., Sir Henry Lee. [References to Ditchley and Woodstock manor.] Oxf., 1936, 8°. 328 pp.   22853 d. 37

Newspapers

See 1338 [The Guardian. 1838].
1380 [Woodstock herald and Charlbury messenger. 1875].

Parliamentary Representation

4181. Parliamentary representation. Report of Commissioners, and answers of returning officers. Report on the borough of Woodstock (p. 105–07).   Pp. Eng. 1831/2, vol. 37

4182. Parliamentary representation. Reports from commissioners on proposed division of counties, and boundaries of boroughs. (New Woodstock, p. 195–97.)   Pp. Eng. 1831/2, vol. 39

4183. [*Begins*] The following letter [signed J. Bowles, asking the Duke of Marlborough to recommend him for a magistracy in the Woodstock area] is submitted for the purpose of shewing the animus which prompted the rev. author to introduce C. L. Humfrey, to vilify the duke at the late Woodstock election, the petition having been rejected. n. pl., (1842), 4°. 4 pp.   G.A. Oxon 4° 119 (6)

4184. In the Queen's bench. The queen, on the application of the duke of Marlborough against L. C. Humfrey, esq., for a criminal information [arising out of speeches at the 1844 Woodstock election]. Birm., 1844, 8°. 71 pp. G.A. Oxon 8° 636 (7)

See 748 [County election squib. 1753].

4185. WING, W., Parliamentary history of the borough of Woodstock during the present century. (Oxf.), 1873, 12°. 6 pp.
G.A. Oxon 8° 220 (2)

See 658 [Parliamentary history, by W. R. Williams. 1899].

Railways

4186. An act for incorporating the Woodstock railway company. (50 V., c. 30, L. & P.) Lond., 1886, fol. 17 pp. L. Eng. A 69 c. 6

See 491, 92 [Railway acts. 1890, 1897].

Roads

See 494 [London inns frequented by Woodstock carriers. 1637].
See 496, 498, 513, 529 [Turnpike acts. 1718, &c.].

BLENHEIM PALACE

General

4187. An act for the settling of the honours and dignities of John duke of Marlborough upon his posterity, and annexing the honour and manor of Woodstock and house of Blenheim to go along with the said honours. (5 Anne, c. 3, Pub.) Lond., 1706, fol. 5 pp.
L. Eng. A 69 c. 1

4188. John, duke of Marlborough, appellant, Edward Strong, sen. and Edward Strong, junior, respondents. The duke of Marlborough's case [concerning payment for the building of Blenheim palace]. n. pl., 1721, fol. 4 pp. G.A. Oxon a. 110 (1)

4189. The most noble John, duke of Marlborough, appellant. Edward Strong, senior, and Edward Strong, junior, respondents. The respondents' case [concerning payment for the building of Blenheim palace]. n. pl., 1721, fol. 4 pp. G.A. Oxon a. 110 (2)

4190. Blenheim house. (Views of the seats of noblemen and gentlemen, by J. P. Neale, 1820, vol. 3. 23 pp.) G.A. Gen. top. 4° 42

4191. NEALE, J. P., Six views of Blenheim . . . with an historical description. Lond., 1823, 4°. 24 pp. G.A. Oxon 4° 3

4192. A bill intituled An act for repairing Blenheim palace. (20 July 1840. 4 V.) n. pl., 1840, fol. 13 pp. Pp. Eng. 1840, vol. 1
— An act . . . for the repairs of Blenheim palace. (5 V., sess. 1, c. 2, Private.) L. Eng. C 13 c. 1

4193. TIMBS, J., An excursion to Blenheim [by J. Timbs]. (Literary world, 1840, p. 326–30.) G.A. Oxon 4° 355 (3)

4194. RADCLYFFE, C. W., The palace of Blenheim, drawn and lithographed. Oxf., 1842, fol. 16 plates. G.A. fol. C 25*

4195. The fire at Blenheim palace. (Illustrated times, Feb. 16, 1861.) G.A. Oxon c. 317 (19)

4196. CHURCHILL, SARAH, duchess of Marlborough. Some unpublished letters of Sarah, duchess of Marlborough, relating to the building of Blenheim palace [ed.] by W. J. Churchill. (Trans. of the Birm. archaeol. soc. for 1887, p. 1–15.) G.A. Warw. c. 2 (4)

4197. WARREN, M. S., The duke of Marlborough and Blenheim palace. (Women at home [1897?], vol. 5, p. 263–73.) G.A. Oxon 4° 399 b (6)

4198. Blenheim palace. (Country Life, 1899, vol. 5, p. 688–92, 720–24.) Per. 384 b. 6

4199. HAVERFIELD, F., [On the excavation of a Roman road in Blenheim park.] (Proc., Soc. of antiq., 1899, ser. 2, vol. 17, p. 333–35.) R. Top. 1

4200. Blenheim palace. (Country Life, 1909, vol. 25, p. 786–98, 834–43.) Per. 384 b. 6

4201. Blenheim palace [Vanbrugh's architectural details and scheme of decoration carried out by Laguerre and Thornhill]. (Cabinet maker, 1915, 27 Feb., p. 187–89.) Per. 1753 c. 4

4202. Malvern [school] at Blenheim. (Country Life, 1940, vol. 87, p. 118–22.) Per. 384 b. 6

4203. HUTCHINSON, I. W., Recollections of Woodstock and Blenheim. (Geogr. mag., vol. 17, 1945, p. 468–76.) Per. 2017 d. 229 (17)

4204. GREEN, D., The mad earl [John, 2nd earl of Rochester] at High lodge [Woodstock park]. (Country Life, 1947, vol. 101, p. 510–11.) Per. 384 b. 6

4205. ARKELL, W. J., The building-stones of Blenheim palace [&c.] (Oxoniensia, 1948, vol. 13, p. 49–54.) R. Top. 340

4206. GREEN, D., and HUSSEY, C., Blenheim palace re-visited. (Country Life, 1949, vol. 105, p. 1182–86, 1246–50.) Per. 384 b. 6

4207. GREEN, D., Visitors to Blenheim. (Country Life, 1950, vol. 107, p. 648–51.) Per. 384 b. 6

4208. GREEN, D., Blenheim palace. Lond., 1951, fol. 348 pp. G.A. Oxon c. 320

4208A. HUSSEY, C., English country houses open to the public. (Blenheim palace, p. 119; Broughton castle, p. 34; Chastleton house, p. 79; Kelmscott manor, p. 81.) New York, 1951, 4°.

G.A. Gen. top. 4° 469

Contents
Books

4209. THORPE, T., Bibliotheca selectissima. Catalogue of books and engravings selected from the . . . library of the late duke of Marlborough [and others]. Lond., [1840], 8°. 119 pp.   2593 f. 9 (5)

4210. Catalogue of . . . library of books, fine paintings, prints, coloured drawings, musical instruments . . . fossils, &c. removed from Blenheim . . . sold by auction . . . May 28, 1840. n. pl., (1840), 8°. 30 pp.   Mus. Bibl. III 8° 465

4211. A catalogue of several small parcels of books of chiefly English and French literature; also a few miscellanies the property of the great duke of Marlborough, which will be sold by auction, Apr. 30. Lond., 1853, 8°. 10 pp.   Mus. Bibl. III 8° 524 (12)

4212. Catalogue of . . . books . . . surplus copies from a very celebrated library [Blenheim] . . . sold by auction . . . June 15, 1870. n. pl., (1870), 8°. 183 pp.   2591 d. 3

4213. THOMAS, V., Catalogue of the books in the library at Blenheim palace collected by Charles 3rd earl of Sunderland [by V. Thomas, revised by W. H. Bliss]. Oxf., 1872, 4°. 668 pp.   259 d. 39

4214. Bibliotheca Sunderlandiana, sale catalogue of the . . . Sunderland or Blenheim library. 1(–5) portion. [With] List of prices and purchasers' names. Lond., 1881–83, 8°. 1037+155 pp.

Mus. Bibl. III 8° 738, 39

Gems

4215. Gemmarum antiquarum delectus, ex praestantioribus desumptus quae in Dactyliothecis Ducis Marlburiensis conservantur. [By J. Bryant and W. Cole, with Fr. tr. by M. P. H. Maty and M. Dutens.] 2 vols. n. pl., 1780–90, fol.   Arch. Num. III 3, 4
— Repr. 1845.

4216. THOMAS, V., Thoughts on the cameos and intaglios of antiquity, suggested by a sight and survey of the Blenheim collection, by a lover of the fine arts [V. Thomas]. Oxf., 1847, 8°. 68 pp.

G.A. Oxon 8° 164 (8)

4217. MASKELYNE, M. H. N. STORY-, The Marlborough gems, a collection of works in cameo and intaglio, catalogued with descriptions. [Lond.], 1870, 4°. 118 pp.   1756 d. 34

4218. Catalogue of the Marlborough gems, a collection formed by George, 3rd duke of Marlborough . . . which will be sold by auction, June 26. Lond., 1899, 8°. 122 pp.   17156 d. 17

Pictures, &c.

4219. HAZLITT, W., Pictures at Oxford and Blenheim. (London mag., 1823, pp. 509–13.)   G.A. Oxon 4° 576 (11)
See 4210.

4220. SCHARF, G., Catalogue of the pictures and works of art in . . . Blenheim palace. (Lond.), 1860, 8°. 26 pp.   G.A. Oxon 8° 73 (5)

4221. SCHARF, G., Catalogue raisonné; or, A list of the pictures in Blenheim palace. Lond., 1861, 8°. 92 pp.   G.A. Oxon 8° 73 (6)

4222. Catalogue of the collection of pictures (and porcelain) from Blenheim palace, which . . . will be sold by auction, 1886. Portion 1–3. n. pl., (1886), 8°. 133 pp.   1707 d. 6 (18)

4223. Catalogue of the choice collection of Limoges enamels from Blenheim palace . . . which will be sold by auction . . . July 14, 1883. n. pl., (1883), 8°. 14 pp. & 68 photogr.   175 h. 125

Guides

4224. The new Oxford guide . . . To which is added A tour to Blenheim [&c.]. By a gentleman of Oxford. Oxf., 1759, 12°. p. 77–120.
                    G.A. Oxon 16° 27
[Other eds. in 1759, 1763, 64, 65, 1768, 1771? 1776, 77, 1781, 1785, 86, 87, 88, 1792, 1794, 1797, 1803, 1805, 1810, 1813, 1817.]

4225. A pocket companion [*afterw.*] A new pocket companion for Oxford . . . To which are added, Correct descriptions of the buildings . . . at Blenheim [&c.] New ed. Oxf., &c., 1759, 12°. p. 109–37.
                    G.A. Oxon 8° 176
[Other eds. in 1762, 63, 64, 1766, 1768, 69, 1772, 1776, 1782, 83, 1785, 1787, 88, 89, 90, 1793, 94, 95, 96, 97, 1799, 1800, 01, 02, 03, 04, 05, 06, 07, 08, 09, 10, 1812, 1814, 1816.]
See 4245 [Guide, by W. Mavor. 1787].

4226. MAVOR, W. F., New description of Blenheim. New ed. Lond., 1789, 8°. 172 pp.   Gough Oxf. 11
[Other eds. in 1797, c. 1800, 1803, 1806, 1810, 11, 1814, 1817, c. 1820, 1835, c. 1840.]

4227. The Oxford university and city guide . . . To which is added A guide to Blenheim [&c.]. Oxf., 1818, 8°. p. 151–96.
                    G.A. Oxon 16° 137
[Other eds. in 1818, 19, 20, 21, 22, 23, 24, 25, 26, 27, 28, 29, 30, 1834, 1837, 1839, 1849, 1859, c. 1860.]

4228. Blenheim. (Perambulation of Oxford &c. New ed., p. 191–220.)
Oxf., 1825, 8°.   G.A. Oxon 8° 599
— [Another ed.] 1826.   G.A. Oxon 8° 599*

4229. A description of Blenheim. 12th ed. Oxf., [1836], 8°. 139 pp.
                                                   G.A. Oxon 8° 71 (4)
— 13th ed. [c. 1840].   G.A. Oxon 8° 924

4230. A new guide to Blenheim palace. Oxf., [1838], 8°. 35 pp.
                                                   G.A. Oxon 8° 232 (11)

4231. A description of Blenheim. (The Strangers' guide through the
University and city of Oxford. 2nd ed. p. 101–14.) Oxf., 1839, 8°.
                                                   G.A. Oxon 8° 1222
— 5th ed. 1847, p. 135–48.   G.A. Oxon 8° 227
— 6th ed. [c. 1850]. p. 235–47.   G.A. Oxon 8° 541

4232. A new guide to Blenheim palace . . . To which is added An
account of the borough of Woodstock. 3rd ed. Woodstock, [c. 1850],
8°. 82 pp.   G.A. Oxon 8° 340
— 17th ed. [c. 1880]. 112 pp.   G.A. Oxon 8° 348

4233. Around Oxford: descriptive jaunts to Blenheim palace and park
[and 40 other places] ed. by the author of the 'Historical handbook
to Oxford'. (Shrimptons' popular handbooks, p. 86–124.) Oxf.,
1872, 8°.   G.A. Oxon 8° 161 (7)

4234. The penny guide to Blenheim. (Shrimptons' ser. of guides.) Oxf.,
[1874], 8°. 16 pp.   G.A. Oxon 8° 204 (2)

4235. MOORE, J. J., Rambles and rides around Oxford, by rail, river, and
road. Sect. 2. Blenheim, Woodstock, and Bladon. (Shrimptons'
hist. county handbooks.) Oxf., 1882, 8°. 103 pp.
                                                   G.A. Oxon 8° 964

4236. EMMOTT, J. T., Guide to Blenheim and Woodstock. Oxf., &c.,
[1897], 16°. 68 pp.   G.A. Oxon 16° 158

4237. TAUNT, H. W., Blenheim palace and Woodstock. Illustr. Oxf.,
[1906], obl. 8°. 24 pp.   G.A. Oxon 8° 736
— 3rd ed. [1914]. 28 pp.   G.A. Oxon 8° 883

4238. TAUNT, H. W., Blenheim, Woodstock, &c. Oxf., [c. 1909], 8°.
69 pp.   G.A. Oxon 8° 768
— 3rd ed. [1914]. 117 pp.   G.A. Oxon 8° 888

4239. TAUNT, H. W., Blenheim and Woodstock. Oxf., [c. 1909], 8°.
44 pp.   G.A. Oxon 8° 765
— 4th ed. [1914].   G.A. Oxon 8° 884 (1)
— [Another ed. entitled] Aldens' illustr. guide to Blenheim and
Woodstock. Oxf., [1924], 8°. 44 pp.   G.A. Oxon 8° 1001 (13)

4240. GREEN, D., Blenheim palace. [Illustr. guide, by D. Green.] Blenheim, 1950, obl. 8°. 34 pp.   G.A. Oxon 8° 1229

4241. Blenheim, a short guide to the interior. (Oxf.), [1950], 8°. 8 pp.   G.A. Oxon 8° 1184 (13)

Poems

4242. PHILIPS, J., Blenheim, a poem [by J. Philips]. Lond., 1705, fol. 22 pp.   Gough Oxf. 103 (11) [Other eds. in 1709, 1713.]

4243. HARISON, W., Woodstock park, a poem. Lond., 1706, fol. 10 pp.   Gough Oxf. 103 (13) — 2nd ed., revised. Lond., 1706, fol. 10 pp.   G.A. Oxon c. 194

4244. LYTTELTON, G., baron, Blenheim. [In verse, by G. Lyttelton.] Lond., 1728, fol. 6 pp.   Gough Oxf. 103 (12)

4245. MAVOR, W. F., Blenheim, a poem. To which is added, A Blenheim guide. Lond., 1787, 4°. 30+10 pp.   Gough Oxf. 103 (2)

4246.

WOODSTOCK DEANERY

See 1299 [Guide to architectural antiquities. Deanery of Woodstock, by J. H. Parker, &c. 1842].

4247. MARSHALL, E., Woodstock churchmen's union. [A letter, signed E. Marshall, announcing the dissolution of the union.] (Heyford, 1887), s. sh.   G.A. Oxon c. 22 (25)

4248. Woodstock deanery lay and clerical conference. Minutes of the fifth & sixth meetings. Woodstock, (1889), 8°. 8 pp.   G.A. Oxon c. 22 (27)

4249. Woodstock lay and clerical ruri-decanal conference. The eighth (9th) meeting. Woodstock, 1891, 92, 8°.   G.A. Oxon c. 22 (29, 31)

4250. Woodstock clerical assoc. Rules . . . and list of members. Woodstock, [c. 1890], 8°. 4 pp.   G.A. Oxon c. 22 (27*)

4251. MARSHALL, E., An inventory of church plate in the deanery of Woodstock, with historical and descriptive notices. (Trans., Oxf. archaeol. soc., no. 30.) Banbury, 1894, 8°. 33 pp.   R. Top. 330

4252. PRIOR, C. E., Dedications of churches, with some notes as to village feasts and old customs. Deaneries of Woodstock, Deddington & Witney. (Rept., Oxf. archaeol. soc., 1904, p. 23–53.)   R. Top. 330

4253. PEARCE, S. S., The clergy of the Woodstock deanery and the settlement of 1559. (Rept., Oxf. archaeol. soc., 1912, p. 89–110.)   R. Top. 330

4254. Woodstock ruridecanal magazine. Vol. 1, no. 1–vol. 9, no. 8. Woodstock, 1922–30, 4°. G.A. Oxon 4° 434

WOODSTOCK POOR LAW UNION

4255. Woodstock union directory. No. 3. Deddington, (1841), 8°. 10 pp. G.A. Oxon 16° 50

WOOTTON

4256. An act for dividing and inclosing certain . . . fields . . . in the parish of Wootton. (9 G. III, c. 96, Private.) n. pl., 1769, fol. 25 pp.
G.A. Oxon c. 170
See 879 [Charities. 1826].

4257. MARSHALL, E., Notices of parish of Wootton, 1066–1874. (Suppl., Hist. of Woodstock manor, 1874, ch. 4, p. 50–96.)
G.A. Oxon 8° 193
See 1297 [Parish registers. Marriages. 1909].

4258. HOLLAND, E., Wootton, a record of the war, 1939–1945 (by Ruth Holland). (Oxf., 1946), 8°. 6 pp. G.A. Oxon 8° 1204 (6)

4259. PONSONBY, C. E., Wootton. Oxf., &c., 1947, 4°. 140 pp.
G.A. Oxon 4° 637

4260. Wootton village history exhibition. (Oxf.), 1949, 8°. 7 pp.
G.A. Oxon 8° 1230 (17)

4260A. Wootton. (Archaeol. notes. Oxoniensia, 1950, vol. 15, p. 108.)
R. Top. 340

4261. Auction catal. Ludwell farm. 15 Sept. 1894.
G.A. Oxon b. 92 (43)

WORTON

4262. An act for confirming a partition made between Robert Dashwood . . . and Cholmley Turner . . . of certain . . . lands . . . in . . . [Worton &c.]. (3 G. I, c. 22, Private.) n. pl., 1717, fol. 7 pp. B.M.

WROXTON

4263. Wroxton. (Gent's. mag., 1797, pt. 1, p. 105–10.) Ψ 2. 44

4264. An act for inclosing lands . . . of Wroxton and Balscot. . . . (43 G. III, c. 146, Private.) n. pl., [1803], fol. 24 pp.
L. Eng. C 13 c. 1 (1803. ii. 42)

4265. Wroxton abbey. (Country Life, 1899, vol. 5, p. 240–43.)
Per 384 b. 6

4266. Wroxton abbey. (Rept., Oxf. archaeol. soc., 1901, p. 12–14.)
R. Top. 330

4267. The visitation of the priory of Wroxton, 16th June, 1445. (Cant. and York soc., 1927, vol. 33, p. 395, 96.) R. 8. 26
— [Another issue.] (Lincoln record soc., 1929, vol. 21, p. 395, 96.)
R. Top. 260

4267A. Wroxton. (Archaeol. notes. Oxoniensia, 1950, vol. 15, p. 108.)
R. Top. 340

4268. Auction catal. Contents of Wroxton abbey. 22 May 1933.
G.A. Oxon c. 224* (3)

WYCHWOOD FOREST

4269. PRIDE, T., Plan of Whichwood forest . . . made by T. Pride . . . in 1787, corrected by F. I. Insall, 1849. (Select comm. on woods and works.) [With] Enlargements. No. 1. n. pl., (1849), s. sh.
G.A. Oxon b. 115 (4, 5)

4270. A bill for disafforesting the forest of Whichwood. 9 June 1852. n. pl., 1852, fol. 8 pp. Pp. Eng. 1852, vol. 4
— 17 March 1853. n. pl., 1853, fol. 9 pp. Pp. Eng. 1852/3, vol. 7
— 6 May 1853, as amended by the Select Committee. n. pl., 1853, fol. 12 pp. Pp. Eng. 1852/3, vol. 7

4271. An act for disafforesting the forest of Whichwood. (16 & 17 V., c. 36, Pub.) Lond., 1853, fol. 12 pp. L. Eng. A 69 c. 1

4272. Forest of Whichwood. Declaration of the boundaries of the forest and purlieus, as ascertained and determined by the commissioners appointed under . . . 'An act for disafforesting the forest of Whichwood.' [With] Map. n. pl., 1854, fol. 11 pp.
G.A. Oxon b. 115 (1)

4273. WOOD, W. B., Reference to a map of the forest and purlieus of Whichwood, 1854. (Chippenham, 1854), fol. 4 pp.
G.A. Oxon b. 115 (2)

4274. AKERMAN, J. Y., A view of the ancient limits of the forest of Wychwood. (Archaeologia, 1857, vol. 37, p. 424–40.) R. Top. 7

4275. AKERMAN, J. Y., A view of the ancient limits of the forest of Wychwood. (From Archaeologia.) Lond., 1858, fol. 17 pp.
G.A. Oxon c. 107 (27)

4276. An act to authorize the inclosure of certain lands . . . [Chilson & Whichwood, Ascott and Whichwood, Leafield and Whichwood]. (21 V., c. 8, Pub.) Lond., 1858, fol. 2 pp. L. Eng. A 69 c. 1

4277. An act to authorize the inclosure of certain lands . . . [Whichwood]. (21 & 22 V., c. 61, Pub.) Lond., 1858, fol. 2 pp.
L. Eng. A 69 c. 1

4278. An act to authorize the inclosure of certain lands . . . [Whichwood]. (22 V., c. 3, Pub.) Lond., 1859, fol. 2 pp.
L. Eng. A 69 c. 1

4279. An act to authorize the inclosure of certain lands . . . [Whichwood (Pudlicot)]. (24 & 25 V., c. 38, Pub.) Lond., 1861, fol. 2 pp.
L. Eng. A 69 c. 1

4280. WATNEY, V. J., Cornbury and the forest of Wychwood. Lond., 1910, fol. 296 pp.
G.A. Oxon b. 75

4281. KIBBLE, J., Historical and other notes on Wychwood Forest, and many of its border places. Oxf., 1928, 8°. 121 pp.
G.A. Oxon 8° 1066

See 294 [History, by H. Paintin. 1929. Typewritten].

WYFOLD

4282. Auction catal. Manor of Wywold. 28 Aug. 1800.
G.A. fol. A 266 (45)

YARNTON

4283. An act for confirming a partition made between Robert Dashwood . . . and Cholmley Turner . . . of certain . . . lands . . . in . . . [Yarnton &c.]. (3 G. I, c. 22, Private.) n. pl., 1717, fol. 7 pp. B.M.

4284. [Begin] In the exchequer. The reverend Vaughan Thomas, clerk, versus Hall, and others. [Account of the vicar of Yarnton's suing certain parishioners for tithes.] n. pl., [1807], s. sh.
Gough Oxf. 80 (37)

4285. Alderman Fletcher's charities to the poor inhabitants of Yarnton, with directions for the distribution of them. Oxf., 1843, 8°. 13 pp.
G.A. Oxon 8° 900 (35)

4286. THOMAS, V., Copy of a statement to the Tithe Commissioners setting forth the . . . grounds upon which the vicar of Yarnton claims . . . adjudication in respect of the rent charge to be awarded in lieu of the small tithes of that parish. (Oxf., 1844), fol. 4 pp.
MS. Top. Oxon b. 19 (114)

4287. GOUGH, H., Heraldic notices of Yarnton church [by H. Gough]. (Oxf.), [1844], 8°. 16 pp.
G.A. Oxon 8° 944

See 413 [Account of night march of Charles i. June 3, 1644, by V. Thomas. 1852].

4288. THOMAS, V., Advice, pastoral and medical to those who stand in need of it, by the vicar [V. Thomas] now that cholera has reappeared, although at a distance from this village [Yarnton]. [Yarnton], 1853, 4°. 6 leaves.   1562 d. 23

4289. An act for connecting the town of Witney with the existing railways in ... Yarnton and Wolvercot. .... (22 & 23 V., c. 46, L. & P.) Lond., 1859, fol. 13 pp.   L. Eng. A 69 c. 6 — 24 & 25 V., c. 22, L. & P.

4290. THOMAS, V., Some account of Yarnton church and parish [by V. Thomas]. Yarnton, [c. 1860], 8°. 35 pp.   G.A. Oxon 8° 147 (19)

See 310 [Trace of Early Britons. 1862].

4291. ROLLESTON, G., Notes on archaeological discoveries at Yarnton, Oxfordshire. (Scientific papers and addresses by G. Rolleston, p. 942–44.) Oxf., 1884, 8°.   1652 d. 8

4292. Begbroke, Cassington and Yarnton horticultural society. Rules, list of subscribers, and schedule of prizes ... for 3rd annual show. Oxf., 1887, 8°. 12 pp.   G.A. Oxon c. 317 (5)

4293. STAPLETON, MRS. B., Three Oxfordshire parishes. A history of Kidlington, Yarnton and Begbroke. (Oxf. hist. soc., vol. 24.) Oxf., 1893, 8°. 400 pp.   R. 13. 700 (24)

See 1970 [Monumental brasses in the church. 1898].

4294. Yarnton manor. (Country Life, 1905, vol. 18, p. 90–95.)
Per. 384 b. 6

4295. Yarnton St. Bartholomew's. Quarterly paper. No. 1–59. (Kidlington, 1909–22), 8°.   G.A. Oxon 8° 779

See 1297 [Parish registers. Marriages. 1909].

4296. GRETTON, R. H., Lot-meadow customs at Yarnton. (Econ. journ., vol. 20, no. 77, p. 38–102.) Lond., 1910, 4°. 64 pp.
G.A. Oxon 4° 390 (2)

4297. EVANS, A., Drawing the lot-meadows at Yarnton. (The Field, 1910, vol. 118, p. 630.)   G.A. Oxon 4° 390 (1)

4298. GRETTON, R. H., Historical notes on the lot-meadow customs at Yarnton. (Econ. journ., 1912, vol. 22, no. 85, p. 53–62.)
G.A. Oxon 4° 390 (3)

4299. EVANS, A., Yarnton, and its story [by A. Evans] an appeal for help for the repair of the church of St. Bartholomew. (Repr. from the Oxf. journ.) [Oxf.], (1911), 8°. 8 pp.   G.A. Oxon 8° 900 (16)

4300. WESTON, F. H., [Notes on an old Oxford & Yarnton family. An attempted pedigree of Weston. Typewritten.] n. pl., [1914], 4°. 20 pp.   MS. Top. Oxon d. 134

4301. Yarnton. (Archaeol. notes. Oxoniensia, 1936, p. 201; 1945, p. 97–99; 1946–47, p. 175–81.) R. Top. 340

See 1322 [8 quarries in the church. 1944].

4302. Auction catal. Estate. 6 Sept. 1848. G.A. Oxon c. 317 (5)

4303. Auction catal. Lammas meadow land, Pixey mead. 10 July 1849.
G.A. Oxon b. 92 (36)

4304. Auction catal. Yarnton estate. [1st] 2nd ed. 6 June 1891.
G.A. Oxon b. 85 b (60, 61)
— 15 Sept. 1894. G.A. Oxon b. 92 (43)

4305. Auction catal. Land, pasturage rights in the Yarnton lot meadows.
5 June 1897. G.A. Oxon b. 90 (11)

4306. Auction catal. Freehold properties. 24 May 1911.
G.A. Oxon c. 317 (10)

4307. Auction catal. 'Sandy Croft' estate. 2 May 1951.
G.A. Oxon b. 92*

YELFORD

4308. STONE, S., [Account of explorations at Yelford.] (Proc., Soc. of antiq., 1858, ser. 1, vol. 4, p. 213–19.) R. Top. 1

4309. Notes of an excursion to Yelford, [&c.] 1871. (North Oxf. archaeol. soc., 1871.) Banbury, [1871], 8°. 73 pp. R. Top. 330

4310. Rectors of Yelford, 1200 to 1899. n. pl., [1900?], s. sh.
G.A. Oxon b. 96 (40)

See 293 [History, by W. J. Monk. 1926].

INDEX OF PERSONAL NAMES

Duplication of entries is shown by giving the subsequent references in parentheses.

Abbey, Charles John, 2060.
Abercrombie, sir Leslie Patrick, 1057.
Abingdon, Willoughby, 4th earl of, *see* Bertie, Willoughby, 4th earl of Abingdon.
Acland, sir Henry Wentworth, 2243.
Addington, Henry, 2391.
Adshead, Stanley Davenport, 1057.
Ægilbert, 2369.
Aikin, John, 167.
Airay, Henrie, 2033.
Akerman, John Yonge, 1863, 1864, 1865, 1901, 1902 (2556), 3654, 4274, 4275.
Albright, M. Catharine, 2030.
Alexander, Henry, 224.
Alexander, Wilfrid Backhouse, 121, 122, 127, 128.
Allen, Arthur Bruce, 854, 970 (2679).
Allen, G. W. G., 2388.
Allen, H., 2112.
Allen, John, 2418.
Allett, Priscilla, 2662 (3106).
Allnutt, Henry, 2640.
Allnutt, William Henry, 3757.
Almaine, H. G. W. d', 2982.
Antrobus, A. A., 868.
Aplin, B. D., 1619.
Aplin, Frederick Charles, 1619.
Aplin, Oliver Vernon, 111, 113, 1609.
Arber, Edward Alexander Newell, 3916, 3917.
Arkell, William Joscelyn, 31, 32, 33 (2909, 3578), 34, 36, 37 (613), 38, 39, 40, 41, 44A, 226, 329, 330, 332, 615, 616 (2189), 2612, 2896, 4205), 1448 (2591), 1818, 2463, 2742.
Arnold, Matthew, 295.
Arsic family, 2163.
Ashbee, E. W., 190.
Ashby, Arthur Wilfred, 598.
Ashby, Thomas, 2826.
Atkins, James, 620.
Atkinson, Richard John C., 1974, 2223, 2390, 3979.
Attlee, H. G., 116.
Audland, Anne, 435.
Ayres, Ph. B., 49.

B., G. E., *see* Barnes, G. E.
B., R., *see* Crouch, Nathaniel.
B., W., 3989.
Babington family, 3016.
Bacon, John, 1171.
Bailey, William, 1381, 1382.
Baker, George Barrington-, 2574.
Baker, H., 60, 63.
Baker, John Harold, 296, 2647.
Ball, H. H., 3019.
Ballard, Adolphus, 585, 586, 841, 1815, 1816, 2103, 2110, 2590, 3596, 3708, 3817, 4057, 4058, 4153, 4179.
Barentine family, 2017, 2018.
Baring, Francis Henry, 342.
Barker, sir Wilberforce Ross, 2482, 3873.
Barlow and Alden Ltd., 1307.
Barnes, George Edward, 2589, 3591, 3592, 3593.
Barnett, Herbert, 2611.
Barns, T., 2380.
Barnwell, Edward Lowry, 1260.
Barratt, Dorothy Mary, 2116.
Barrow, Albert Stewart, 1052 (1768, 2895).
Barry, Anne, 3848.
Barry, Robert, 3848.
Bartelot family, 1239.
Bartelot, Richard Grosvenor, 1239.
Barter, H., 3529.
Baskerville, Geoffrey, 1080.
Bateman, Thomas, 1169, 1170.
Bateman, William, 3558.
Bath, sir Harry, 3560.
Bather, Francis Arthur, 2548.
Batson, William, 830.
Baverstock, E. P., 1199.
Bawden, William, 348.
Baxter, Richard, 1159.
Baxter, William, 46.
Bayley family, 1240.
Bayley, William D'Oyley, 2086 (2131).
Beames, W. A., 4035.
Beauchamp, Maurice Henry, 2218, 2219.
Beauforest, abbot, 2403.

Beaumont, George, 158.
Beazley family, 3271.
Beazley, Frank Charles, 3271.
Beckinsale, Robert Percy, 617.
Beesley, Alfred, 1537.
Beesley, Sarah, 1576.
Beesley, Thomas, 1539, 1577, 1595, 1610, 1633, 1637 (3826), 3139, 3170.
Beeverell, James, 142.
Bell, A. M., 4111.
Bell, George, 1534.
Bennett's business directory, 1400.
Berkshire, earl of, see Howard, Thomas, earl of Berkshire.
Bertie, Peregrine, 1429 (1711, 2256, 2359, 2937, 3464, 3849).
Bertie, Willoughby, 4th earl of Abingdon, 1429 (1711, 2256, 2359, 2937, 3464, 3849), 3381, 3382, 3383.
Besse, Joseph, 1215A, 1215B, 1215C.
Betteridge, J. W., 3627.
Bignell, R., 1530.
Billing, Martin, 1395.
Billson, A., 2673.
Birch, Walter de Gray, 356.
Bird, W. Hobart, 1309.
Biscoe, Elisha, 2266 (2567, 2759, 2897, 3691).
Biscoe, Eliza Carey, 3997.
Blackall, John, 2668.
Blackstone, sir William, 729.
Blackwell, mr., of Bicester, 1765.
Blackwood, Beatrice, 848, 869.
Blair, K. G., 4112.
Blake, John Frederick, 2769 (3559, 3996).
Blaydes, Frederick Augustus, 1446.
Blome, Richard, 136.
Blomfield, James Charles, 1782 (1447, 1761A, 1906, 1979, 2205, 2585, 2588, 2752, 2886, 3164, 3210, 3239, 3280, 3495, 3589, 3606, 3723, 3906, 3914), 2563.
Blount family, 3058.
Blount, sir Thomas, 3058.
Bloxham, John Rouse, 3127.
Bonnett, Frank, 1045.
Boots, mr., pseud., see Bray, Thomas.
Boswell, Henry, 51.
Bouchier, Edmund Spenser, 1078, 1319, 1320.
Boulter, Edmund, 2668.

Bourdillon, Anne Francis C., 871.
Bourke, Dermot Robert W., 7th earl of Mayo, 479, 1057.
Bowen, Charles James, 1547, 1675.
Bowles, Joseph, 4183.
Bowles, Oldfield, 3286.
Box, Henry. For works connected with the Free school at Witney, see 4089 &c.
Boydell, John, 466.
Boydell, Josiah, 466.
Boyne, William, 618.
Brabant, Frederick Gaspard, 236.
Bradbrooke, William, 2307.
Bradford, J. S. P., 2389, 3659.
Braithwaite, William Charles, 1216, 1552.
Bray, Thomas, 693, 720.
Brenan, John Patrick M., 75, 76.
Bretherton, Russell Frederick, 88, 89, 90.
Brewer, James Norris, 179, 266.
Bricknell, William Simcox, 2517, 2518, 2519, 2580.
Brideoake, Richard, 2901 (3639, 3782, 3824, 4026).
Briers, Phyllis Mary, 3345.
Briggs, Martin Shaw, 216.
Brinkworth, Edwin Robert C., 1155, 1156.
Briot, Pierre, 2.
Britton, C. E., 68.
Brogden, James, 2324B.
Brooke, lord, see Greville, Robert, 2nd baron Brooke.
Brooke, Adela, 2181, 2182.
Brookes family, 3710.
Brookes, Charles Cunliffe, 3203 (3709), 3710.
Brooks, lord, see Greville, Robert, 2nd baron Brooke.
Brooks, E. J., and son, 843.
Brooks, Eric St. John, 2018, 2900, 3058.
Brooks, H. R. F., 1568.
Brooks, R., 2138.
Brown, mrs., pseud., 4048.
Brown, E. S., 81, 86.
Brown, G. J., 1811.
Brown, John Howard, 3860, 3876, 3891.
Brown, W. L., 1434.
Browne, A. L., 3839.

Browne, Alfred Joseph Jukes, 2859, 3500.
Browne, sir Richard, bart., 414.
Browne-Mostyn family, 3019.
Bruton, Edward George, 2055, 2056, 2157.
Bryant, J., 4215.
Buccleuch, Henry, duke of, see Scott, Henry, 3rd duke of Buccleuch.
Buchan, David, 9th earl of, 833.
Buchanan, doctor, 1634.
Buckell, R., and son, 839.
Buckland, Mary Wortley, 2457.
Buckler, Benjamin, 741.
Buckler, John Chessell, 4034.
Bugg, Francis, 1657, 1658.
Bull, Henry, 1099, 1100.
Bunton, W., 1659.
Burford, Barony of, 1925.
Burges, William, 2010.
Burgess, William, 2664.
Burlington, Charles, 164.
Burn, John Southerden, 2821.
Burnett, William, 182.
Burr, H., 577.
Burrows family, 3809, 3810.
Burrows, Montagu, 3809.
Busby, George, 858 (3018), 3017.
Butler, Christina Violet, 2950 (3047, 3166, 3189).
Buxton, Leonard Halford Dudley, 848, 869.
Byron, John, baron, 378.

C., 186.
Cadbury, James, 1540, 1574.
Cadogan, Charles, baron, 1983 (3504, 3597), 1984.
Calamy, Edmund, 1159, 1160, 1161, 1162.
Cam, Helen Maud, 298, 2317.
Camden, William, 260.
Campion, Thomas, 1981.
Cannan, Joanna, 221.
Carey, Lucius, 2nd viscount Falkland, 2709.
Carleton, Henry, lord, 3208.
Carpenter, Geoffrey Douglas Hale, 101.
Carr, Hamilton, 3974.
Carter, William Fowler, 1262, 2708.
Cassey, Edward, and co., 275 (1397).
Catesby, Robert, 2048.
Cattell, George Trew, 2259A.

Catton, W., 1665.
Cave, W., 1308.
Chamberlain, F. W., 3034.
Chamberlain, sir James, 3468.
Chamberlin, W. H., 2203 (3927, 4038), 2250.
Chambers, sir Edmund Kerchever, 2356, 2546, 4180.
Champion, W. Scott, 3332.
Chapman, mr., 2209.
Chapman, William Montague M., 126.
Chapple, J. F. G., 61, 77.
Charles I, king of Gt. Britain, see Civil War, 365 &c., 3301.
Chatwin, Charles Panzetta, 2656 (3512).
Chatwin, Philip Boughton, 3138.
Chaucer family, 2489.
Chaucer, Thomas, 2489.
Cheatle, Thomas H., 1928.
Cheney, Christiana S., 1578A.
Cheney, Christopher Robert, 1546A.
Cheney, John, 611, 1608A.
Chesterton, vicar of, 1829; see Price, Awbrey Charles.
Chibnall, Marjorie, 2206, 3803.
Child, Gilbert William, 1003, 2978.
Child-Villiers, George, 5th earl of Jersey, and Sarah Sophia, countess of Jersey, 2067.
Childrey, Joshua, 1, 2.
Chitty, Dennis Hubert, 133C.
Christy, Robert Miller, 105, 107, 112, 130.
Church, Alfred John, 473.
Church, Arthur Harry, 58.
Church, W. A., 1324.
Churchill, George, 4th duke of Marlborough, 1797 (2177), 2882 (4144).
Churchill, George, 6th duke of Marlborough, 4183, 4184.
Churchill, John, 1st duke of Marlborough, 4187, 4188, 4189.
Churchill, John Winston, 7th duke of Marlborough, 2136.
Churchill, Sarah, duchess of Marlborough, 4196.
Churchill, W. J., 4196.
Clack, Thomas Stanley, 2260.
Clapham, Arthur Roy, 59, 63, 65, 66, 78.
Clark, Andrew, 1113, 2627, 3374.
Clark, G. Rochfort, 2068.

C C

Clark, George Norman, 2111, 2461, 3185, 3186 (3423, 3643), 3187, 3190.
Clarke, Caleb, 1574.
Clayton, Horace Evelyn, 1110.
Climenson, Emily J., 2843, 3506, 3509, 3510, 3513, 3514, 3515.
Cobb, Arthur Kennedy, 2468, 2469.
Cobb, Thomas, 565.
Cockburn, A. E., 1563 (2094, 2848, 4166).
Coker, John, 759, 761.
Cole, George Douglas H., 2111.
Cole, W., 4215.
Coley, James, 2214, 2215, 2216.
Collett, Edward, 2178.
Collier, R., 4091.
Collinge, Walker Edward, 100.
Compton, lord Alwyne, bp. of Ely, 438.
Conder, Edward, 3168.
Conolly, John, 2803.
Cook, sir Theodore Andrea, 2869, 2870.
Cooke, A. H., 1258, 2061, 2652, 3176, 3177.
Cooke, George Alexander, 172.
Cooke, Selwyn Montagu, 2736.
Cooper, John, 2820.
Cooper, William Durrant, 976.
Cope, Emma, Elizabeth, 1192, 1278.
Cope, mrs. Hautenville, 1279.
Coppock, Gladys Annie, 2777 (3563).
Corbett, Elsie, 868, 3645 (2320, 2346, 2604, 3834).
Cornish, Charles John, 3653.
Cornwall family, 1925.
Cottrell-Dormer family, 3451, 3456.
Cox, Leslie Reginald, 39.
Cox, Thomas, 263.
Coxe, Hilgrove, 1872, 3421.
Cozens, William, 2381, 3922.
Crawford, Osbert Guy S., 316, 343, 2382, 2711, 2712.
Crawfurd, Gibbs Payne, 1764, 1769.
Crisp, Samuel, 1937.
Croke family, 1241.
Croke, sir Alexander, 1241, 3381, 3385, 3386, 3387, 3391.
Croke, sir George, 1713A.
Crosbie, Mary, 4070.
Crosse, Richard Banastre, 818, 826.
Crouch, Nathaniel, 138.
Crowder, Thomas Mosley, 814.
Crowther, George Francis, 4052.

Cruff, George, 2090.
Cruttwell, Clement, 173.
Culliford, William, 2090.
Cunningham, Timothy, 655.
Curzon family, 3939.
Cust, Arthur Perceval Purey-, 1092.
Cygnus, pseud., 2197.

D., A., 3064.
D., J., 1855, see Dalton, J.
D., J., 1890, 2302.
D., J. M., see Davenport, John Marriott.
Dalton, J., 97.
Dandy, James Edgar, 67.
Danvers family, 2169.
Darkin, Isaac, 3259.
Dashwood family, 1242.
Dashwood, sir James. For connexion with the 1754 election see 659 &c., 1531 (1824, 1961, 2255, 2456, 3247, 3256, 3814, 3963, 4018, 4020).
Dashwood, Robert, 1723 (1806, 1966, 2617, 3024, 4262, 4283).
Davenport, John Marriott, 276, 777, 778, 982, 2519.
Davenport, Thomas Marriott, 778.
Davey family, 1243.
Davey, Edward Charles, 1243 (2367).
Davies, Arthur Morley, 300.
Davies, E. A., 2270.
Davies, George Jennings, 2023.
Davis, Francis Neville, 292.
Davis, R., 2138.
Davis, R. H. C., 612.
Davis, Richard, 561.
Davis, T., 2138.
Davis, Thomas, 2466.
Dawkins, William Boyd, 310 (341).
Deacon, C. W., and co., 193 (1229, 1403).
Dearmer, Percy, 1067.
Defoe, Daniel, 263.
Delafield, Thomas, 2670.
De la Pole family, 1244, 2487, 2491.
De la Pole, William, 1st duke of Suffolk, 2502.
De Maré, Eric Samuel, 481A.
Derick, J. M., 3668.
De Sales la Terrière, B., 1956.
De Watteville, Herman Gaston, 2675 (3646).
Dicker, G. H. L., 92.

Dickins, Margaret, 2045, 2052, 2908.
Dighton, James Lucy, 3538.
Dillon, Harold, 2345.
Dines, Henry George, 34, 3745.
Disney, Henry, 158.
Ditchfield, Peter Hampson, 203, 284, 291, 1569.
Dodd, Joseph Arthur, 2485, 2489.
Dodsworth, Roger, 1072.
Donovan, Desmond Thomas, 44A.
Dormer family, 1245, 1246.
Dormer, Cottrell-, family, 3451, 3456.
Dormer, Charles Cottrell-, 3452.
Dormer, sir Clement Cottrell-, 759, 3450.
Dormer, Frances Elizabeth Cottrell-, 3451.
Dorset, Lionel, duke of, see Sackville, Lionel, 1st duke of Dorset.
Douglas, J. A., 42, 1613, 2463.
Draper, Eleanor, 1651, 1652, 1653, 1962.
Drewe, George Henry, 1506, 1508.
Drinkwater, H. G. W., 2960, 3183.
Druce family, 2636.
Druce, George, 2636.
Druce, George Claridge, 54, 55, 57, 2488, 3394.
Druse, Joseph, 2517, 2520, 2521.
Dryden, sir Henry Edward L., 1978, 2467 (3143), 2686, 3173, 3602, 3776, 3907, 4011.
Duckett, sir George Floyd, 630.
Duff, Adam, 4119.
Dugdale, James, 177.
Dugdale, Thomas, 182.
Dugdale, sir William, 1072, 1074.
Dumas, Isaac, see Darkin, Isaac.
Duncan, George, 4150.
Dunkin family, 3198, 3199.
Dunkin, John, 1782–1846, 264, 1432, (1760), 1908, (3408).
Dunkin, John, of Merton, 3198, 3199.
Dunlop, John Renton, 3733, 3794, 3795, 3802.
Dunn, F. T., 239.
Dutens, M., 4215.
Dutton and Allen co., 1396.
Dyer, A., Stephens, 3516.
Dyer, William Turner Thiselton, 52.
Dyke, sir John Dixon, 3135.
Dyke, William, 3669.

E., W. S., 1249.
Earle, John, 223.
Early, James Vanner, 4062.
Earwaker, John Parsons, 278.
East, Arthur, 2616.
Ecton, John, 1163, 1164, 1165, 1166.
Edburg, saint, 3680.
Edwards, H., 883.
Edwards, William Gilbert, 2677, 2678, 3465.
Elers family, 1798.
Elizabeth, queen of England, 4172, 4176, 4177.
Ellis, Arthur Erskine, 102, 103.
Ellis, Frederick, 1510.
Ellis, Thomas, 416.
Ellis, William Patterson, 3874.
Elton, Charles Sutherland, 131.
Emden, Cecil Stuart, 2187.
Emmet, Arthur Maitland, 91
Emmott, J. T., 4236.
Emslie, John Phillipps, 866.
Estcourt, Edgar Edmund, 1219.
Evans, Agnes, 4297, 4299.
Evans, Arthur Burroughes, 551.
Evans, sir Arthur John, 1714, 3141, 3142.
Evans, Evangeline, 2776.
Evans, H. F. Owen, 3336.
Evans, Herbert Arthur, 201.
Evans, J., 3862.
Evans, John Thomas, 1206.
Eyston, C. J., 3172.

Fairfax, Thomas, 3rd baron, 418, 420.
Falcon, Norman Leslie, 43.
Falconer, Adrian Wentworth Keith-, 827.
Falkland, lord, see Carey, Lucius, 2nd viscount Falkland.
Falkner, John Meade, 281, 282.
Farley, Abraham, 347.
Farrer, William, 359.
Faulkner, Charles, 1292.
Faunthorpe, John Pincher, 188.
Faussett, R. Godfrey, 2976.
Fea, Allan, 198, 204.
Fearson, W. W., 1418.
Fell, Hunter Francis, 2872.
Ferguson, William, 837, 1207.
Fermor family, 3587, 3588.
Fermor, William, 2885.

Ferryman, Augustus Ferryman Mockler-, 812, 815, 818.
Fettiplace family, 1247, 3733, 3795, 3802.
Fidoe, John, 428.
Field, John Edward, 864, 1735, 1737, 1742, 1743 (3414), 1744, 2403, 2644, 2980, 3344, 3923.
Firth, sir Charles Harding, 440.
Fisher, John, 1924.
Fitter, Richard Sidney R., 129.
Fitzpatrick, J. M., 74.
Fletcher, W., 227.
Fletcher, William, 4285.
Forbes, Charles, 1649.
Ford, Stephen, 2088.
Foster, Charles Wilmer, 362A.
Fowler, William Warde, 110, 115 (3052), 3051, 3053.
Fox, Augustus Henry Lane, 334, 2378.
Fox, Samuel, 1217 (2024, 4086).
Freeborn, Howard, 3035.
Freeborn, Miriam Elizabeth, 210, 4114.
Freeman, Edward Augustus, 2396.
Freeman, R. B., 95.
Freinshemius, Johannes, pseud., 754.
Fremantle, William Robert, 1099, 1100.
French, Joseph Milton, 443 (2571).
Frost, Maurice, 2333C–F.
Fuller, Thomas, 1224.
Furneaux, Henry, 3165.
Furse, Charles Wellington, 2269.
Fussell, George Edwin, 573.
Fynmore family, 3031.
Fynmore, R. J., 3031.

G., D., 715, 719.
Gage, John, 309.
Gammon, Laura M. P., 2011.
Gardner, Robert, 273 (1393).
Gardner, T. W., 579.
Garner, Thomas, 1306, 3594.
Garry, Nicholas Thomas, 1136.
Gaskell, Ernest, 1231.
Gatfield, George, 1230, 1274.
Gavazzi, Alessandro, 1674.
Gawthorp, Walter Edmund, 1290, 2080.
Gee, Charles Frank A., 2181.
Geoffrey of Monmouth, 1227.
Gepp, Henry John, 1420.

Gibbons, Alfred W., 1182, 1294.
Giffard family, 3631.
Giffard, Walter, bp. of Bath and Wells, 1857.
Gifford, Margaret Jeune, 1232.
Giles, John Allen, 1503, 1511, 4041 (2155, 2247, 2310, 2429, 2716, 3224, 3670).
Giles, Thomas, 3480A.
Glen, Alexander, 4107.
Glen, William Cunningham, 4107.
Godfrey, abbot of Eynsham, 2542.
Godfrey, Walter H., 1959, 3880.
Godlee, sir Rickman John, 4014.
Godley, Alfred Denis, 205.
Golightly, Charles Portales, 1090, 2276, 2277, 2278, 2280, 2289, 2294.
Gomme, sir George Laurence, 195 (279).
Goodman, Thomas, 3586.
Goodrich, Edwin Stephen, 3741.
Goodwin family, 2915.
Goole, John, 4090, 4091.
Gordon, Alexander, 800.
Gordon, Richard, 2459.
Gough, A. P., 3604, 3605.
Gough, Henry, 4287.
Gough, John Hill, 3604, 3605.
Gough, Richard, 165, 260.
Gove, Philip B., 1347.
Graham, Cuthbert Aubrey L., 828.
Graham, Rose, 1190, 1205.
Grant, J., 290.
Graves, Henry, 234, 551.
Graves, Robert, 2572.
Gravesend, Richard de, bp. of Lincoln, see Richard of Gravesend, bp. of Lincoln.
Gray, Howard Levi, 569, 570.
Greaves, Edmund, 2569.
Green, Alexander Henry, 22.
Green, David Brontë, 852, 4204, 4206, 4207, 4208, 4240.
Green, Vernon, 3126, 3127.
Green, William, 171.
Greene, Thomas, 3598.
Greenfield, Benjamin Wyatt, 1415, 2730.
Greenway, F. B., 1817 (2582, 2740).
Greenwood, George, 728.
Gregory, Francis, 4139.
Grensted, Lawrence William, 83, 84, 85, 93, 94.

Gretton, Mary Sturge, 283, 447, 984, 1236, 1944.
Gretton, Richard Henry, 1943, 4296, 4298.
Greville, Robert, 2nd baron Brooke, 373.
Grey, William, 1299.
Grimes, William Francis, 3685.
Grosch, Alfred, 3621.
Grose, Francis, 162.
Grosseteste, Robert, bp. of Lincoln, 1186.
Grove, L. R. A., 82.
Groves, Muriel, 3219 (3534).
Grundy, George Beardoe, 345.
Guest, Wiliam, 3860.
Gulliver, George, 1616.
Gunther, Robert William T., 289, 572.
Guppy, Henry Brougham, 1237.

Haberly, Loyd, 1325.
Hadow, Grace, 963.
Haines, Herbert, 1283.
Hakewill, Henry, 3307, 3309, 3751.
Hall, Anna Maria, 185.
Hall, Anthony, 264.
Hall, Hubert, 357.
Hall, John, 4284.
Hall, Samuel Carter, 185.
Hall, William, 2266 (2567, 2759, 2897, 3691).
Hall and son, 1339.
Halloway family, 1248.
Hamilton, Archibald, 2871.
Hamlet and Dulake, 840.
Hammond, Barbara, 3394A.
Hammond, John Laurence Le B., 3394A.
Hampden, John, 2015.
Hancock, Basil Lawrence, 70.
Hannam, Henry J., 2395.
Hanson, Joseph Stanislaus, 3940.
Harcourt family, 3357.
Harcourt, Edward William, 3357 (3675), 3358.
Harcourt, Elizabeth, 3664.
Harcourt, George Simon, 2nd earl, 3667.
Harcourt, Leveson Francis Vernon-, 14.
Harcourt, Simon, 1st viscount, 2139, 3664.
Harcourt, Simon, 2nd viscount, 2427.

Harden, Donald Benjamin, 30, 1439, 2384, 2713, 3686, 4156.
Harison, William, see Harrison, William.
Harmer, Florence Elizabeth, 2995 (3191).
Harper, Charles George, 202.
Harper, Edward James, 1897.
Harris, George, 1662–73.
Harrison, George, 3255.
Harrison, William, 4243.
Hart, George, 2427.
Hart, Susannah, 2427.
Hartford, marquess of, see Seymour, William, 2nd duke of Somerset.
Harvey, W. W., 2480.
Hassall, William Owen, 1208, 1223, 1480 (2083, 2257, 3059), 1481, 2258, 2271, 2462, 2494A, 2884 (3918), 3233, 3424, 3547, 3565, 3765, 3811, 3952, 3999.
Haverfield, Francis John, 335, 1766, 3313, 3315, 4199.
Hawkes, Charles Francis Christopher, 1436, 2829.
Hawkins, Edward Lovell, 1026.
Hawkins, H. L., 2860 (3949).
Hawkins, William, 747.
Hazlitt, W., 4220.
Headlam, Cecil, 208.
Hearne, Thomas, 262, 2358, 2502, 2616, 3129A, 3747, 4171.
Heath, James, 2151.
Heaven, Charles, 2917.
Hemming, Alice, 2003.
Hemp, Wilfrid James, 2910.
Henderson, Mary Sturge, see Gretton, Mary Sturge.
Herbert, George, 1578.
Herbertson, Andrew John, 197.
Heuman, G., 868.
Hewitt, W. H., 860.
Hewlett, Edgar, 3155.
Heylyn, Peter, 2900.
Heywood, Abel, 2842.
Higgins, Charles, 851.
Higgs, Arthur G., 4151.
Hill, Beatrice Mary, 2777 (3563).
Hill, Rosalind Mary T., 1192A.
Hinton, mr., 272.
Hinton, William, see Powell, William.
Hoare, 1946.
Hobbs, J. T., 602.

Hobson, Thomas Frederick, 1421.
Hodge, Robert Trotter Hermon-, baron Wyfold, 292A.
Hodgen, Margaret Trabue, 352.
Hodgman, M. G., 72.
Hodson, Toby, 1868.
Hoffman, Francis, 4170.
Hogg, A. H. A., 2387.
Holland, Edith, 4258.
Holloway, B., 3450.
Homespun, Ezakiel, pseud., 763.
Hone, Nathaniel J., 1204.
Hookins, Philip, 2175, 2587.
Hope, sir William Henry St. John, 1931, 2102.
Hopton, sir Ralph, 382.
Horde family, 1249, 1505.
Horseman, John, 1228.
House, J., 187.
Howard, Frank Ernest, 1318, 2330.
Howard, John, 991.
Howard, Thomas, earl of Berkshire, 377.
Hubbard, J. G., 1104.
Hucks, William, 2475.
Huddesford, George, 680, 695, 742.
Hudleston, Wilfred Hudleston, 2122.
Hudson, R., 1499.
Huggins, Margaret L., 2481.
Hugh of Wells, bp. of Lincoln, 1182, 1183, 1184.
Hull, Christopher, 2605.
Hull, Edward, 20, 21, 3740.
Humfrey, C. L., 4183, 4184.
Humphreys, Alfred Thomas, 2491.
Humphreys, John, 2050.
Hungerford family, 1250, 1798.
Hunt and co., 1390.
Hunt, T. H., 1922.
Hurman, Robert, 2240.
Hurst, Herbert, 1314.
Huse, G., 4129, 4130.
Hussey, Christopher Edward C., 1462, 1715, 1950, 1965, 2190, 2193, 2493, 2710, 3212, 3361, 3442, 3457, 3466, 3492, 3561, 3683, 3684, 3796, 4061, 4206, 4208A.
Hussey, Robert, 538.
Hutchinson, Isobel W., 4203.
Hutchinson, Walter, 209.
Huthname, mr., 800 (2098).
Huthnance, S. L., 578.
Hutton, doctor, 272.

Hutton, William Holden, 200, 1937.
Hyde, William, 299.

Iliffe, J. H., 1438.
Ingram, James, 2956.
Inman, Henry Turner, 235.
Insall, F. I., 4269.
Irving, John, 286.
Irwyn, David, visct., 832.
Isham, Arthur, 1093.

J., M., 2354.
Jackson, William, 1346, 1347.
Jarvis, A. F., 3054.
Jeanes, J., 428.
Jeffrey, Reginald Welbury, 2698.
Jennens, William, 1469 (1497, 1860, 1873, 1900, 2153, 2166, 2426, 2748, 3648).
Jennings, Henry Cecil, 1006, 3514.
Jersey, earl and countess of, 1829; see Child-Villiers, George, 5th earl; and Sarah Sophia, countess of Jersey.
Jeune, Margaret Dyne, 1232.
Jewitt, Llewellyn, 2761.
Johnson, J., 382.
Johnson, William Ponsonby, 1542, 1603.
Johnston, John Octavius, 1137.
Johnston, Philip Mainwaring, 2049.
Jones, David, 144.
Jones, H. A., 4167.
Jones, Hubert Cunliffe-, 4087.
Jones, Jessie K., 2951.
Jones, Mary Whitmore, 2046, 2048.
Jones, Thomas Wharton, 3437.
Jope, E. M., 614, 3786, 4129, 4130.
Jordan, John, 6, 2464.
Jourdain, Margaret Emily, 1945, 2051.
Juxon, William, abp. of Canterbury, 3592, 3593, 3594.

Keck family, 2705.
Keck, Francis, 2702 (3091, 3150, 3477).
Keck, lady Susan, 683.
Keeney, G. S., 2383.
Kelham, Robert, 347A.
Kelly's directories ltd., 1401, 1402, 1405.
Kennett, White, 1431, 1444.
Kent, William, 3455.
Kenward, James, 3994.

Keyser, Charles Edward, 1313, 1512, 1553, 1800 (1880), 2062 (2981, 3334, 3637), 2697, (2907, 4029), 2746 (2918, 2925), 3778.

Kibble, John, 2027 (2004, 2071, 2551, 2566, 3416, 3548, 3644, 3833, 3919), 2028, 4281.

King, William, 696, 697, 713, 747.

Kingsford, Charles Lethbridge, 3760.

Kirk, Joan Radcliffe, 3234, 4131.

Kirk, Kenneth Escott, 1202.

Kirkpatrick Herbert Francis, 2406.

Kirtland, Charles, 2099.

Knight, W. F. J., 1830, 1833.

Knollis, Francis Minden, 2930.

Knollys family, 3437, 3438.

Knollys family, claiming to be earls of Banbury, 1251–55.

Knollys, William, 1st earl of Banbury, 1981.

Knowles, lord, see Knollys, William, 1st earl of Banbury.

Knox, Edmund Arbuthnott, bp. of Manchester, 2293.

Kursbatt, Isaac, 3032.

L., C. E., see Long, Charles Edward.

Lambert, J. M., 73.

Lamborn, Edmund Arnold Greening, 353 (2132), 1280, 1281, 1311, 1321, 1322, 1793, 2017, 2492, 2709A, 2709B, 3129, 3232, 3232A, 3272, 3289, 3441, 3633, 3680, 3819.

Lambourne, Sineta, 1235.

La Pole, William de, see De la Pole, William, 1st duke of Suffolk.

Lascelles and co., 1394.

Lattey, Robert Tabor, 2471, 3835.

Laurie, Eleanor Mary O., 133B.

Leadam, Isaac Saunders, 364 (582), 2176.

Lee family, 1256, 1415, 3855.

Lee, B., 2178.

Lee, Frederick George, 1256, 3851, 3857, 3871, 3877.

Lee, H., 3450.

Lee, sir Henry, 2356, 4180.

Lee, Richard, 1268, 1276, 3869, 3870.

Leeds, Edward Thurlow, 315, 317, 318, 319, 320, 321, 322, 323, 325, 327, 337, 344, 1460, 1973, 2006 (3300), 2042, 2525, 2906, 3861, 3862, 3995.

Leeming, J. J., 2252, 3503.

Legg, Leopold George Wickham, 3909.

Leigh, Edward, 135.

Leland, John, 261, 2358, 3747, 4171.

Le Neve, John, 1062.

Lenthall family, 1955.

Lenthall, William, 2665 (3078).

Lenygon, Francis, 3455.

Leslie, Patrick Holt, 132.

Letten, Susanna, 3896, 3982.

Leverett, James, 1225.

Levien, Edward, 1925.

Leys, Agnes Monecrieff, 3473A.

Lickorish, W. H., 1608.

Liddell, H. A., 287.

Lipscomb, George, 170.

Littledale, Godfrey Armytage, 2106.

Litton, E. A., 1094.

Lloyd, John, 1164.

Lloyd, M., 422.

Lobel, Mary Doreen, 2008 (2321).

Loney, Julia E., 3092, 3490.

Long, Charles Edward, 3772A.

Long, Edward T., 1310, 1315, 1999, 3552.

Loudon, John Claudius, 563, 3152, 3153.

Loveling, Benjamin, 1658.

Lovell, W., 1567.

Lucas, Joseph, 3397.

Luke, sir Samuel, 412, 445.

Lupton, Harry, 3852, 3867.

Lupton, Mary G., 1799.

Lybbe family, 1257.

Lyell, Arthur Henry, 336.

Lyttelton, George, 1st baron, 4244.

M., A., 712.

M., P., 3340.

Macarthur, Wilson, 215.

Macclesfield, 3rd earl of, see Parker, Thomas, 3rd earl of Macclesfield.

Macclesfield, Mary Frances, countess of, see Parker, Mary Frances, countess of Macclesfield.

MacFadyen, Amyan, 87.

Macfarlane, William Charles, 2364, 2391.

MacIlwaine, Herbert C., 862.

Mackenzie, Frederick, 271.

Macklin, Herbert Walter, 1285, 1288.

MacLagan, Michael, 1246.

Macnamara, Francis Nottidge, 3077.
Macray, William Dunn, 1827, 2435, 2436, 2751, 4099.
Mais, Stuart Petrie B., 220A.
Majendie, Arthur, 1814 (4152), 4151.
Major, Henry Dewsbury Alves, 3201.
Malleson, J. P., 2709.
Manchester, A. J., 2081.
Manners, Janetha, duchess of Rutland, 2182.
Manning, Charles Robertson, 4177.
Manning, Percy, 199, 312, 315, 337, 857, 859, 1044, 1763, 1970, 2105, 2879, 3560, 3695.
Mansfield, Estrith, 1233.
Map, Walter, 1227.
Marett, Robert Ranulph, 3156.
Margrett, Edward, 1994, 2661.
Marlborough, dukes of, see under Churchill.
Marshall, Edward, 280, 1105, 1706, 2133A, 2325, 2949, 2958, 3478, 3480, 3480A, 3482, 3485, 3486, 3487, 3488, 4178 (1809, 2883), 4247, 4251, 4257.
Marshall, George William, 1237A, 1238, 1296.
Marshall, J., 1434.
Marshall, Jenner, 3969.
Marshall, Mary, 574 (1060).
Marshall, Rosa Mary, 211.
Marshall, William, 564.
Martin, Benjamin, 5.
Martin, Charles Wykeham, 3774.
Maskelyne, Mervin Herbert Nevil Story-, 4217.
Mason, Charlotte M., 191.
Mason, Violet, 3299.
Massey, E. R., 3199, 3200.
Massingham, Harold John, 297.
Masters, John Ernest Smith-, 3048 (1998, 2510, 3178).
Masters, Maxwell Tylden, 50.
Matthews, Andrew, 109.
Matthews, Arnold Gwynne, 1168.
Matthews, Henry, 109.
Maty, M. P. H., 4215.
Mavor, William Fordyce, 1808, 4226, 4245.
May, Thomas, 2167, 3473.
Mayo, 7th earl of, see Bourke, Dermot Robert W., 7th earl of Mayo.
Meades, Eileen, 2117.
Mee, Arthur, 241.

Melliar, Meliar Foster-, 3288.
Melville, R., 64.
Meols family, 1258.
Mercer and Crocker, 1399.
Metcalfe, Gilbert, 1893 (3329).
Middleton, Arthur Douglas, 130.
Middleton, J. H., 3109.
Miege, Guy, 139, 141.
Miles, P. M., 79, 80.
Mill, Hugh Robert, 18.
Millen, E. L., 1717.
Miller, Edith, 2994.
Miller, George, 3496A.
Miller, Sarah, 368.
Milne, Francis Alexander, 195 (279).
Milne, Joseph Grafton, 619, 621, 3818, 4127.
Milton, John, 443 (2571), 2569, 2572, 2573.
Minn, Henry, 3362.
Mockler-Ferryman, Augustus Ferryman, see Ferryman, Augustus Ferryman Mockler-.
Moll, Herman, 144.
Monck, George, 1st duke of Albemarle, see under Civil War, 365 &c.
Money, Walter, 2012, 3544, 3678.
Monk, William John, 206, 207, 293, 1930, 1934, 1936, 1940, 1947, 1948, 3229, 3677, 4055.
Moore, George, 2245.
Moore, James, 265, 1076.
Moore, James J., 1810 (4146, 4235).
Moorsom, William Scarth, 809.
Morden, Robert, 140.
More, Corona, 3006.
More, sir Thomas, 2900.
Moriarty, G. Andrews, 1261, 1265, 2163, 3631.
Morison, Cecil Graham T., 571.
Moritz, Karl Philipp, 2362 (2817, 3260, 3352).
Morley, Henry T., 1792.
Morris, William, 3002, 3005.
Mostyn, Browne-, family, 3016.
Moule, Thomas, 181.
Moultric, Gerard, 3617.
Mowat, C. L., 494.
Mowat, John Lancaster G., 192, 350.
Mozley, A. D., 4028.
Murray, John, 229, 233.
Myres, sir John Linton, 1435.
Myres, John Nowell L., 338, 2385, 3426.

Napier family, 1257.
Napier, Edward Hungerford D. Elers, 1798.
Napier, H., 56.
Napier, Henry Alfred, 2478 (3798).
Nares, Gordon, 2308.
Neale, John Preston, 1987, (2168, 3209, 3355, 3524, 3542, 3753, 4190), 4191.
Needle, William, 401.
Ness, James, 1527 (1888).
Neville, James Edmund H., 829.
Newbolt, sir Henry John, 817.
Newman, John Henry, card., 3128, 3129.
Newton, James, 3362.
Nichols, John, 1075.
Nicholson, B. D., 119.
Nicholson, Edward Max, 119.
Nicholson, Una Phyllis, 3033.
Nicolas, sir Nicholas Harris, 1269.
Niemann, Edmund J., 227.
Nightingale, Joseph, 175.
Norman, Alfred Merle, 96.
Norreys family, 1259.
Norris, William Foxley, 4053, 4084, 4085.
Norsworthy, Laura Lucie, 3517.
Norwood, Robert Pickman, 3020.
Nowell, Sarah, 2969-73.
Nuttall, P. Austin, 1224.

Oakley, Kenneth Page, 332.
O'Connor, H. E., 239.
O'Conor, Norreys Jephson, 1259 (3975).
Östberg, Ragnar, 2966.
Oldfield, William John, 1297, 1298, 3642, 3679.
Oldham, C. R., 912.
Ollard, Sidney Leslie, 305.
O'Neil, Bryan Hugh St. J., 331, 339, 444.
Orr, John, 571.
Osborn, George, 2136.
Oswald, Arthur, 1958, 2199, 2355, 3761, 3908, 3958.
Overton, Thomas, 2450.

P., 2369.
P., J., 951.
P., R., see Plot, Robert.
P., T., see Bray, Thomas.

Packer, George, 1923A.
Paddon, John Birch, 3735.
Paintin, Harry, 294, 1886 (3012, 3073), 1903 (3003, 3111), 1955, 2161, 2185 (2741, 3298), 2487, 2688, 3030, 3456.
Palmer, Arnold, 217.
Palmer, Francis Ingram, 13.
Palmer, Samuel, 1161.
Pantin, William Abel, 304.
Parker, Angelina, 855, 865, 867.
Parker, George, fl. 1725, 2871.
Parker, George, fl. 1888, 4108.
Parker, John Henry, 1299, 1302, 1303, 1926 (3527), 2365, 2377, 2622, 2762, 2957.
Parker, Mary Frances, countess of Macclesfield, 3543.
Parker, Thomas, 3rd earl of Macclesfield. For connexion with the 1754 election see 659 &c., 1985 (2509, 3597A, 3727).
Parkes, George David, 2968.
Parkes, Mary, 2968.
Parry, Thomas Robert Gambier-, 2653, 3065.
Patterson, R., 2830.
Paul, pseud., 2493.
Paul, Roland W., 2401.
Payne, E. J., 3868.
Payne, Edward, 1086 (2338).
Payne, J., 2158.
Payne, John Orlebar, 1219, 1220.
Payne, Julius D., 2029 (2005, 3549).
Peake, A. E., 3261, 3401.
Pearce, Stephen Spencer, 99, 1187, 1189, 1488 (2416, 2881), 1784 (4101), 2130 (2341), 2184, 2298 (2695, 3076, 3893), 3275, 4164, 4253.
Pearman, Morgan Thomas, 1254, 1734, 1857, 1993, 2057, 2058, 2073, 2305, 2671 (3422), 3343, 3438, 3758, 3800, 3947.
Pearson, Edwin, 1546.
Pearson, Martin K., 2108.
Peel, Albert, 1188.
Peel, John Hugh B., 219A.
Pendlebury, John Roger, 3269.
Peniston family, 2192.
Peniston, sir Thomas, 2192.
Periam, Elizabeth, 2871.
Perott, Henry, 3243 (3840).

Perrot family, 1260, 3301.
Perry, George Gresley, 1107, 3865.
Peters, George Hertel, 2831.
Peyton, Sidney Augustus, 1152 (1700, 2417, 3894).
Philip, Ian Gilbert, 445, 481, 1115.
Philips, J., 4242.
Philips, John, 2139.
Phillimore, William Phillimore Watts, 1297.
Phillipps, James Orchard Halliwell-, 2990, 2991, 2992.
Phillipps, Lisle March, 3511.
Phillipps, sir Thomas, 272, 1227, 1270, 1271, 2093, 2114, 2705, 3983.
Phillips family, 2114.
Phillips, mistress, 401.
Phillips, professor, 1862.
Phillips, Ernest, 2114.
Phillips, John, 3556.
Phillips, William Arthur, 2114.
Phizackerley, Peter Hugh, 44.
Pickard, Edward, 1217 (2024, 4086).
Pickford, P., 821.
Pidgeon, D., 1618.
Piggott, C. M., 2390.
Pigot and co., 184, 1384, 1385, 1388, 1389.
Pinsent, Ellen Frances, 1008.
Piper, John, 240.
Plomer, Henry Robert, 1511.
Plot, Robert, 3, 4.
Plowden family, 3517.
Plummer, Alfred, 4069.
Pointer, John, 333, 3750.
Pole, William de la, see De la Pole, William, 1st duke of Suffolk.
Ponsonby, Charles Edward, 4259.
Portland, earl of, see Weston, Jerome, earl of Portland.
Potts, John, 1566.
Potts, William, fl. 1842, 1581, 1582.
Potts, William 1868–1947, 1550, 1554, 1555, 1570, 1653.
Poulton, Edward Bagnall, 3557 (3992).
Poure family, 1261.
Powell, Mary, 2572.
Powell, William, 3987.
Poyntz, W. C. S., 2399.
Prestwich, Joseph, 17.
Price, Awbrey Charles, vicar of Chesterton, 2067.
Price, E. R., 1461 (2164).

Price, John Edward, 2041.
Prichard, John, 3223.
Pride, Thomas, 4269.
Pringle, James, 1448 (2591).
Prior, Charles Edward, 861 (1201, 1487, 1783, 2129, 2297, 2340, 2880, 3000, 4100, 4252), 2035, 2036, 2037, 2038, 3393.
Prosser, Richard B., 608.
Pudsey family, 2460.
Pulling, Alexander, 251.
Pye, H. J., 1623 (3248).

Quatremain family, 1262.

R., R., 146.
R., S., 379, 407.
Radclyffe, Charles W., 4194.
Radford, C. A. Ralegh, 2347, 2348, 2349, 2350.
Randolph, John, bp. of Oxford, 2488 (3403).
Rathmell, Miles, 3181 (3360).
Ravenhill, Thomas Holmes, 3145, 3147, 3148.
Rawlinson, Richard, 292, 1541.
Rawlinson, Thomas, 2615.
Read, Clare Sewell, 566.
Read, Thomas, 153.
Reade, Compton, 1263.
Reade, Edward Anderson, 2640.
Reade, Elizabeth, 1876 (3057, 3095, 3539, 3731).
Reade, Thomas, 1876 (3057, 3095, 3539, 3731).
Rede family, 1263.
Redford, E., 1575.
Reitlinger, Gerald, 3366.
Rendall, Montague John, 2699.
Rendall, Vernon, 3146.
Rhodes, P. P., 1791.
Richard of Gravesend, bp. of Lincoln, 1191.
Richardson, Linsdall, 34, 1448 (2591), 1614, 1615, 1829, 1938, 2124, 2549 (3743), 3218, 4075.
Rickard, Roy Llewellyn, 449.
Riddle, A. E., 3828.
Ridgway, James, 1989.
Rigaud, Gibbes, 439.
Riley, D. N., 328, 3660.
Riley, M., 1973.
Rimmer, Alfred, 231.

Ritter, Otto, 225.
Roberts, Cecil Edric M., 213, 214.
Roberts, D. F., 1974A.
Roberts, H. V. Molesworth-, 2407, 4035.
Robinson, Anne, 831.
Robinson, Charles John, 2562.
Robson, Ralph John, 679.
Robson, William, 1387.
Rodwell, George Edward C., 1513.
Rolleston, George, 3129B, 4291.
Rosamond, fair, 2618, 2621, 2625, 2626, 4175.
Rose, F., 69.
Rose, Geoffrey Keith, 822.
Rose, Lilian E., 2141.
Ross, James Coulman, 3903.
Round, John Horace, 1244.
Rowbottom, William, 632A.
Rowe, John, 4039.
Rowell, George Augustus, 1002.
Rowse, Alfred Leslie, 2573.
Royce, David, 2078, 2251, 2706 (3626).
Rupert, prince, 404.
Rusher, John Golby, 1579.
Rusher, Philip, 437, 1528 (2254).
Rushworth, J., 1530.
Russell, P., 159.
Rye, Arthur Brisley, 3169.

S., C. R., 1939.
Sabretache, pseud., see Barrow, Albert Stewart.
Sacheverell, Henry, 1526.
Sackville, Lionel, 1st duke of Dorset, 2757.
Salmon, Nathaniel, 147.
Salmon, Thomas, 150.
Salter, Herbert Edward, 358, 360, 362, 1151, 1153, 1185, 1218, 2115, 2162, 2402, 2543, 3270, 3376, 3866, 3948, 3950.
Salzman, Louis Francis, 285.
Sandars, N. K., 2390.
Sanders, Robert, 161.
Sandford, Kenneth Stuart, 19, 25, 27.
Saunders, James, 10.
Saunders, William Wilson, 3061.
Saye and Sele, 17th baron, see Twistleton - Wykeham - Fiennes, John, 17th baron Saye and Sele.
Scharf, George, 4220, 4221.

Schulz, T. E., 4168.
Schutz, Augustus, 3552 (3764).
Scott, Henry, 3rd duke of Buccleuch, 1411, 1412.
Seaby, W. A., 2996A.
Secker, Thomas, bp. of Oxford, 1081.
Segelhorst, Wilhelm, 2628.
Severne, Anna Maria, 3773.
Severne, John Michael, 3773.
Seymour, sir John Hobart, 2916.
Seymour William, 2nd duke of Somerset, 382.
Sharp, Cecil James, 862, 863.
Sharpe, Frederick, 1200, 1785.
Shaw, Stebbing, 168.
Shaw, W., 428.
Sheldon family, 1264.
Shelmerdine, Joan M., 4157.
Sherlock, R. L., 35.
Sherwood, George Frederick Tudor, 1295.
Shirley, Evelyn Philip, 3585.
Shorten, Monica Ruth, 133A, 133C, 133D.
Shrewsbury, earls of, see Talbot.
Shuffrey, James Allen, 237.
Shute, Hardwicke, 2284.
Sibthorp, John, 45.
Silver, Thomas, 2022.
Simmons, Lettice, 2646.
Simms, G., 2624.
Simms, George, 1004.
Simonds, William Blackall, 1986.
Simpson, Samuel, 151.
Sims, Richard, 1272, 1293.
Skelton, Joseph, 271, 3751.
Slater, Isaac, 1389, 1392.
Slatter, John, 4011, 4012.
Smith, Gyles, pseud., 747.
Smith, Henry, 2757.
Smith, Henry Stooks, 656.
Smith, J., 2138.
Smith, John Challenor Covington, 3941.
Smith, Lionel Graham H. Horton-, 1240.
Smith, Lucy Toulmin, 262.
Smith, Reginald Allender, 2827.
Smith, Richard, wine merchant, 3392.
Smith, Robert Henry Soden-, 1312.
Smith, Sineta, 1235.
Smith, T., 2138.
Smith, William, 190.

Southern, Henry Neville, 120, 133B.
Spence, Elizabeth Isabella, 174.
Spencer, Charles Vere, 3339 (3647, 3842, 3984).
Spencer, Nathaniel, *pseud.*, see Sanders, Robert.
Spicer, E. C., 24.
Spiker, Samuel Heinrich, 178.
Stallwood, J. St. L., 2013.
Stanford, William, 475.
Stanley, H. B., 1602.
Stanley, John, 2198.
Stapleton, mrs. Bryan, see Stapleton, Mary Helen Alicia.
Stapleton, Bryan John, 1203.
Stapleton, Mary Helen Alicia, 1221, 1726 (3029, 4293), 3019.
Sterne, Laurence, 2709A.
Stevens, C. E., 2383, 2387.
Stevens, C. G., 338.
Stevens, J., 311, 2824.
Stevens, John, 1074.
Stevenson, M. L., 3838.
Stevenson, Mill, 1287, 1289, 2059.
Stockton, Arthur, 2919.
Stone, James, 1674.
Stone, John, 1869.
Stone, Percy Goddard, 2650.
Stone, Stephen, 2430, 3654, 3655, 3656 (3671, 4308).
Stonor family, 3754, 3755, 3760.
Stonor, Robert Julian, 3762.
Stonor, Thomas, *fl. 1794*, 3419 (3944).
Stonor, Thomas, *fl. 1838*, 3754, 3755.
Stonor, Thomas Edward, 3756.
Stowell, John Hilton, 3320.
Strahan, sir Aubrey, 2658.
Stratton, Arthur, 1306.
Stratton, George Frederick, 2703.
Stretch, Richard, 1617.
Stretley family, 1265.
Strickland, Hugh Edwin, 2856.
Strong, Edward, sen., 4188, 4189.
Strong, Edward, jun., 4188, 4189.
Stubbs, Charles E., 114.
Stukeley, William, 145.
Sturges, Charles, 2681.
Summers, William Henry, 1211.
Sutherland, Carol Humphrey V., 324, 2526, 3021, 3022, 3818, 4115.
Sutton, Oliver, bp. of Lincoln, 1192A.
Swaine, John, 3370.
Swerford, Alexander de, 1227.

Swinburne, Algernon Charles, 3513.
Swinny, Henry Hutchinson, 2286.
Swinstead, John Howard, 2014, 2015, 2016.

Talbot, Charles, 15th earl of Shrewsbury, 1499.
Talbot, Gilbert, 13th earl of Shrewsbury, 2700 (2888, 3149, 3783).
Talbot, John, 16th earl of Shrewsbury, 2097 (2133, 2704, 2891, 3154, 3396, 3625, 3785).
Tandy, William, 1662–73.
Tanner, Thomas, 1073.
Tarrant, Leslie Hamilton, 43.
Tate, William Edward, 583, 584.
Tatham, Edward, 2178.
Taunt, Henry William, 469, 470, 471, 472, 2626 (1790), 2025, 2371, 2642, 2962, 2963, 3063, 3144, 3314, 3993, 4056, 4237, 4238, 4239.
Taunton, Robert Cropp, 761.
Taunton, sir William Elias, 3386, 3387.
Taylor, A. J., 3231.
Taylor, G., 67.
Taylor, George Crosbie, 3361.
Taylor, John, 261, 494.
Taylor, Margerie Venables, 3316, 3752, 4125.
Tenax, *pseud.*, see Taunton, Robert Cropp.
Thacker, Frederick Samuel, 476, 477, 478.
Thomas, Vaughan, 413, 2799, 2805, 2806, 2969, 2970, 2971, 2972, 4213, 4216, 4284, 4286, 4288, 4290.
Thompson, A., 3862.
Thompson, Alexander Hamilton, 1150, 1154.
Thompson, Flora, 845, 851, 853.
Thompson, William, 430, 431.
Thomson, Theodore, 1762.
Thorley, John, 2115.
Thorpe, Thomas, 4209.
Thoyts, Emma Elizabeth, see Cope, Emma Elizabeth.
Ticehurst, Norman Frederic, 124.
Tiddeman, Richard Hill, 18.
Timbs, John, 277, 4193.
Timm, E. W., 66.
Tipping family, 3734.
Tipping, Anne, 3895 (3981).
Tipping, Henry Avray, 1898, 3934.

Tit for Tat, *pseud.*, 760.
Todd, John, 3942.
Toldervy, William, 155.
Tollit, Henry James, 560.
Tomes, R. F., 2905.
Tomlinson, Mabel Elizabeth, 26.
Ton, *pseud.*, 819.
Torr, V. J. B., 2332, 3367.
Townsend, Charles, 1411.
Townsend, James, 1242.
Toynbee, Margaret Ruth, 2252, 3266, 3301, 3427.
Treacher, M. S., 330, 332.
Tregelles, Edwin Octavius, 1680A.
Trevor, J. C., 848.
Treweeks, R. C., 3686.
Trimen, Henry, 53.
Trinder family, 2900.
Tristram, Ernest William, 1316, 1317, 3632.
Trousdale, W. G., 2623.
Tucker, Bernard William, 123.
Tucker, J., 1097.
Turner, squire, 3008.
Turner, Cholmley, 1723 (1806, 1966, 2617, 3024, 4262, 4283).
Turner, sir Edward. For connexion with the 1754 election *see* 659 &c.
Turner, G. Lyon, 1209.
Turner, sir Gregory Osborne P., 180.
Turner, Mary Vane, 2331.
Turner, Samuel, 400.
Turner, T., 3071.
Turner, Thomas Hudson, 1301.
Turner, William Henry, 242, 1147, 1273.
Turnor, Christopher Reginald, 218.
Turrell, Walter John, 551.
Turrill, William Bertram, 71.
Twistleton, Francis, 1527 (1888, 3327).
Twistleton, Thomas, 1527 (1888, 3327), 1889.
Twistleton-Wykeham-Fiennes, John, 17th baron Saye and Sele, 1895.
Twopeny, Richard, 1088, 1089, 2281, 2282, 2283.
Tyler, Arthur A., 238.
Tymms, Samuel, 183.
Tyssen, Amherst Daniel, 1661, 1828 (3216).

Underwood, Henry Jones, 3124.

Valters, J. C., 1404.
Vanderstegen, William, 465.
Varley, Frederick John, 442.
Vaughan, Meredith, 2450.
Venables, 423.
Venables, A. M., 1050.
Venables, Edmund, 1107.
Venables, L. S. V., 132, 133.
Vinogradoff, sir Paul, 2707.
Virginia, *pseud.*, 2493.
Vivers, Margaret, 1656.

W., E., 1549.
W., J., 4135.
W., L., 2486.
W., P., 146.
W., T., 2033.
Wace family, 1266.
Wace, Edward Gurth, 1266.
Walford, Edwin Alfred, 1545, 1611, 1612.
Walford, Thomas, 176.
Walker, James John, 8.
Walker, John, 1167, 1168.
Walker, Richard, 47.
Waller, J. G., 3615, 3938.
Waller, sir William, 416.
Walpole, George Augustus, 166.
Walter, sir John, 2139.
Walton, H. M., 244.
Warburton, John, 1075.
Ward, G. H., 1848.
Warneford, Samuel Wilson, 2805, 2806.
Warner, Alice 2662 (3106).
Warner, H. J., 3335.
Warner, R. T., 1765.
Warren, Mary Spencer, 4197.
Warren, T. Herbert, 3359.
Warton, Thomas, 3015.
Washington family, 1267.
Wastie, John, 2669.
Watney, Vernon James, 2188 (4280).
Watson, Edmund Henry Lacon, 1894.
Watson, Hewett Cottrell, 48.
Watson, John Marten, 3698.
Watt, A. S., 605.
Weale, sir Thomas, 2450.
Weare, Thomas William, 2670.
Weaver, F. W., 3186 (3423, 3643).
Webb, Edward and Elizabeth Frances, 834.
Webber, Francis, 695.

Webster's directories, 1398 (1583).
Weedon, John, 3601.
Weinstock, Maureen M. B., 448.
Welles, Paul, 2265.
Wells, mr., of Witney, 4096.
Wells, Hugo de, see Hugh of Wells, bp. of Lincoln.
Wemyss, David, 4th earl of, 831.
Wenman, Philip, visct. For connexion with the 1754 election see 659 &c.
Weston family, 4300.
Weston, F. H., 4300.
Weston, Jerome, earl of Portland, 375.
Westwood, John Obadiah, 1713.
Whately, William, 1524.
Wheatley, H. B., 190.
Wheeldon, John, 2681.
Wheeler, 1946.
Wheeler, C., 824.
Whetham, Catherine Durning, 441.
Whetham, Nathaniel, 417, 424, 441.
Whetham, William Cecil Dampier, 441.
Whistler, Ellinor, 2646.
Whitaker, William, 21, 23.
White, Francis, 434.
White, Harold James Osborne, 2306, 2857, 2858, 2859.
Whiteaves, Joseph Frederick, 98.
Whitehead, C. J., 3629.
Whitehead, Talbot Haes, 33 (2909, 3578).
Whiteman, G. W., 2357A.
Whitmore, John Beach, 1238.
Whittaker, Robert, 1167.
Whyte, Dorothy, 220.
Wickham family, 3772A, 3774.
Widows, Thomas, 4169A.
Wigram, Spencer Robert, 1077.
Wikes, Thomas, 3372, 3373.
Wilcote family, 2708.
Wilder family, 3516.
Wilkinson, J. T., 3777.
Willan, Frank, 814.
Willan, Thomas Stuart, 480.
William of Wykeham, bp. of Winchester, 3774.
Williams, family, of Cote, 2195.
Williams, Adin, 3008.
Williams, Audrey, 3075.
Williams, Benjamin, 2195, 3497, 3498, 3843.
Williams, Ethel Carleton, 212, 2646, 2654.

Williams, John, baron Williams of Thame. For works connected with Thame grammar school see 3883, &c.
Williams, William Retlaw Jefferson, 658.
Williamson, George Charles, 618.
Willis, Browne, 654, 1063.
Willmot, G. F., 2318.
Wills, G. Berkeley, 3879.
Willson, William Wynne, 3160.
Wilmot family, 1415.
Wilson, John, 1850.
Wilson, Joseph Henry, 1087.
Wilson, William, 1609, 2150.
Windle, sir Bertram Coghill A., 313.
Wing, William, 657, 677, 678, 1787, 1820, 1968, 2174, 2326, 2706, 2725 (2731), 3027 (1964, 2659, 3899, 3933), 3202 (3706), 3257 (3398), 3287, 3452 (3715), 3453, 3602 (3701), 3702, 3703, 3704, 3705, 3714 (3968), 3815, 3913, 4185.
Wini, 2369.
Winstedt, Eric Otto, 1235.
Winstone, Reece, 2194.
Wisdome, Simon, 4017.
Wise, Thomas, 2475.
Withers, Thomas Henry, 2656 (3512).
Wodehouse, C. G., 3072.
Wodhams, John R., 1544.
Wood, Anthony à, 272, 292.
Wood, Helen E., 3580A.
Wood, W., 3928.
Wood, William, 3440.
Wood, William Bryan, 4273.
Woodforde, Christopher, 1322.
Woods, K. S., 609.
Woodward, Horace Bolingbroke, 2123.
Woodward, Michael, warden of New College, 449.
Wooldridge, Sidney William, 28.
Wyfold, lord, see Hodge, Robert Trotter Hermon-, baron Wyfold.
Wykeham family, 3772A, 3774.
Wykes, Thomas, see Wikes, Thomas.
Wymer, Norman, 219.
Wyndham, hon. Everard Humphrey, 450 (3409).
Wynslowe family, 1801.

Young, Arthur, 562.

INDEX OF SUBJECTS

Adminstration, 632A–797.
Agriculture, 561–603.
Almanacs, 1406–08.
Architecture and allied arts, 1299–1325.

Benefices, 1158–92.
Biography, 1224–98.
Birds, 109–29.
Botany, 45–78.
Boundaries, 633–37.
Brasses, 1282–90.
Bridges, 557–60.

Canals, 454–59.
Census, 779–95.
Charities, 872–87.
Churches, 1193–1206.
Clubs, 1025, &c.
Communications, 454–560.
County council, 638–39.
County finance, 640–52.

Dialect, 855.
Dissent, 1207–17.
Diocese, 1081–1206.
Directories, 1381–1405.

Ecclesiastical visitations and courts, 1146–57.
Economic history, 452–623.
Education, 914–70.
Elections, 674–776.
Enclosures, 580–84.

Family histories, 1237–67.
Farming, 561–603.
Finance, 640–52.
Fishes, 105, 106.
Floods and drainage, 9–16.
Folk-lore, 856–70.
Forestry, 604, 605.
Freemasons, 1025–28.
Friendly societies, 1029–33.

Gardens, 597–9.
Genealogy, 1224–36.

Geology, 20–44.
Guide books, 227–41.

Heraldry, 1268–81.
History, 242–451.
Husbandry, 561–603.

Incumbents, 1158–92.
Industries, 606–21.
Insecta, 79–95.

Law courts, 971–84.
Libraries, 1025, &c.

Mammals, 130–33.
Markets, 622, 623.
Military history, 798–829.
Mollusca, 96–104.
Monuments and records, 1282–98.

Natural history, 1–133.
Newspapers, 1326–80.

Open fields, 585, 586.

Parish registers, 1296–98.
Parishes, 1193–1206.
Parliamentary representation, 653–776.
Place names, 223–26.
Political history, 624–797.
Political societies, 1034, 1035.
Police, 985–88.
Poll books, 659–73.
Poor law, 888–913.
Post office savings bank, 1036, 1037.
Prisons, 989–1000.
Public health, 1001–19.
Public officers, 777–78.
Public utilities, 1020–24.

Railways, 482–93.
Religion, 1062–1223.
Reptiles and amphibians, 107, 108.
Rivers, 460–81.
Roads, 494–556.

Savings associations, 1036–77.
Smallholdings, 597–79.
Social history, 830–1061.
Social services, 871–1024.
Sport and pastime, 1043–56.
Statistics, 779–97.

Temperance societies, 1038–41.
Topography, 134–226.

Town and country planning, 1057–61.
Trades, 606–21.

Visitations (Ecclesiastical), 1146–57.
Visitations (Heraldic), 1268–81.

Water supply, 17–19.
Women's institutes, 1042.

Zoology, 79–133.

ADDENDA

Natural History. 12a. PHILLIPS, J., Notes on the drainage of the valleys of the Thames and Cherwell, near Oxford. (Comm. on the drainage of the valley of the Thames.) (Oxf., 1874), 8°. 7 pp. Radcl.

Place Names. 226a. GELLING, M., The place-names of Oxfordshire, based on material collected by D. M. Stenton. 2 pt. (Engl. place-name soc., vol. 23, 24.) Cambr., 1953, 54, 8°.   R. 9. 21 *p*

History. 259a. Historical manuscripts commission. National register of archives. [Oxfordshire. Reprod. from typewriting.]   R. 6 fol. 1

— 278a. FIENNES, C., Through England on a side saddle in the time of William and Mary. [Oxfordshire *passim.*] Lond., &c., 1888, 4°.
                    G.A. Gen. top. 4° 125
[Other eds. entitled 'The journeys of Celia Fiennes' in 1947, 1949:
                   G.A. Gen. top. 8° 1410, 1419]

— 301a. ENRIGHT, B. J., Rawlinson's proposed history of Oxfordshire. (Oxoniensia, 1951, vol. 16, p. 57–77.)   R. Top. 340

— 332a. RICHARDSON, K. M., and YOUNG, A., An Iron age A site on the Chilterns. (Antiq. journ., 1951, vol. 31, p. 132–48.)   R. Top. 2

— 340a. O'NEIL, B. H. ST. J., and O'NEIL, H. E., The Roman conquest of the Cotswolds. (Archaeol. journ., 1952, vol. 109, p. 23–38.)
                    R. Top. 5

Economic History. 453a. FLOWER, C. T. *ed.* Public works in mediaeval law. Vol. 2. (Oxfordshire lanes, mill streams, bridges, roads, p. 117–30.) (Selden soc., vol. 40.) Lond., 1923, 4°.   R. 9. 19 (40)

— 466a. FRASER, M., The Thames valley in pictures. Oxf., [1853], 8°. 14 pp.+34 plates.   G.A. Eng. rivers 8° 157

— 491a. Great Western railway. [Time-table of local trains. *Afterw.*] Dew's pocket time-table. Oct., 1891–April, 1918. [*Imperf.*] Hey-ford, 1891–1918, s. sh.   G.A. Eng. rlys. 16° 158

— 556. TEIGH, J., Along the Icknield way. (Country Life, 1952, vol. 112, p. 1948–50.)   Per. 384 b. 6

— 600a. Oxford cattle plague assoc. ltd. Memorandum of association. (Oxf., 1865), fol. 15 pp.   G.A. Oxon c. 317 (3)

— 603a. BLAND, G. R., Manuring of grass land in Oxfordshire. (Univ. coll., Reading, dept. of agric. and horticulture, bulletin 15.) (Reading, 1913), 8°. 64 pp.   Radcl.

— 605a. Forestry commission. Census report no. 5. Census of wood-lands 1947–49: woods of five acres and over. English county details. (Oxfordshire, p. 175, 76.) Lond., 1953, fol.   Radcl.

Economic History. 610a. Hunt, Edmunds & co., limited, 1896–1946. With an account of the earlier forms of the business [of brewing, malting, and wine and spirit making at Banbury, Burford, and Witney]. Banbury, (1946), 4°. 27 pp. 1783 d. 94

— 610b. JOPE, E. M., The development of pottery ridge tiles in the Oxford region. (Oxoniensia, 1951, vol. 16, p. 86–88.) R. Top. 340

Social History. 855a. BONAPARTE, PRINCE LOUIS LUCIEN, On the dialects of Monmouthshire . . . Oxfordshire [&c.] Read before the Philol. soc., 7th April 1876. [Lond., 1876], 8°. 12 pp. 30205 e. 3

— 855b. Dialectal words; from 'Kennett's Parochial antiquities, 1695'. (Engl. dialect soc., 1879, vol. 3, p. 1–22. Ser. B 18.) Soc. 30205 e. 2

— 870a. ETTLINGER, E., Novel approaches to the folklore of Oxfordshire. (Folk-liv, 1950/51, p. 87–94.) 247127 c. 4

— 871a. SMITH, W. P., and BATE, H. A., Family casework and the country dweller, an investigation carried out in Northumberland, county Durham, and Oxfordshire, 1950–51, ed. by A. V. S. Lochhead. Lond., [1954], 8°. 67 pp. 24724 e. 393

— 911a. Berks, Bucks, and Oxon poor-law officers' assoc. Rules. Oxf., [c. 1920], 8°. 7 pp. G.A. Oxon 8° 1255 (6)

— 964a. Oxford county council, educ. comm. Instructions to managers, correspondents, and teachers of public elementary schools. 2nd ed. [Oxf.], 1926, 4°. 54 pp. G.A. Oxon 4° 715

— 1032a. Oxford and Abingdon permanent benefit building society. Rules. Oxf., 1868, 8°. 23 pp. G.A. Oxon 8° 1308 (10)

— 1050a. GÊLERT pseud., Fores's guide to the foxhounds and staghounds of England. To which are added The otter-hounds and harriers. (Oxfordshire, p. 72–77, 139–41.) Lond., [1849], 8°.
49. 970
[Other eds. in 1849 and 1908: 38445 d. 36]

Religion. 1115a. MAJOR, K., A handlist of the records of the bishop of Lincoln, and of the archdeacons of Lincoln and Stow. Lond., &c., 1953, 8°. 122 pp. 111 e. 220

— 1115b. HOLTZMANN, W., ed., Papal decretals relating to the diocese of Lincoln in the twelfth century, with transl. of the texts by E. W. Kemp. (Publ., Lincoln record soc., vol. 47.) Hereford, 1954, 4°.
R. Top. 260

— 1146a. BRUERE, J., Letter to the clergy of the diocese of Oxford [attacking H. Beaver, the apparitor general, for taking larger fees from the clergy at visitations, than is permissible.] n. pl., (1763), 8°. 15 pp. Gough Oxf. 7 (9)

— 1156a. Bishop Wilberforce's Visitation returns for the archdeaconry of Oxford in the year 1854, transcr. and ed. by E. P. Baker. (Oxf. record soc., vol. 35.) (Banbury), 1954, 8°. 171 pp.
R. 13. 702 (35)

Religion. 1209a. Wesleyan Methodists, Oxford circuit. Plan and directory. No. 1–118. Oxf. (1886–1915), 8°. [The Bodleian set is imperf.] Per. G.A. Oxon 8° 1299

— 1215a. New road Baptist church [and circuit. Report of work, 1920]. (Birm.), 1921, 8°. 13 pp. G.A. Oxon 8° 884 (29)

— 1215b. The history of the life of Thomas Ellwood, written by his own hand. [Oxfordshire *passim*.] Lond., 1714, 8°. 478 pp.
8° C 731 Linc.
[Other eds. in 1714, 1791, 1827, 1855, 1885, 1900; 1906:
11139 e. 50]

Architecture. 1303a. WILKINSON, W., English country houses . . . views and plans. [Oxfordshire *passim*.] Oxf., 1870, 4°. 17363 c. 4
— 2nd ed. Lond., &c., 1875, 4°. 173 h. 85

Adderbury. 1413a. Adderbury fountain of friendship benefit society. (Rules and regulations.) Deddington, 1854, 8°. 52 pp.
G.A. Oxon 8° 1308 (3)

Alkerton. 1440a. An act for . . . inclosing . . . lands . . . of Alkerton. (16 G. III, c. 37, Private.) n. pl., 1776, fol. 25 pp.
L. Eng. C 13 c. 1 (1776. 1)

Ardley. 1446a. Memoir of . . . John Lowe, rector of Ardley. Repr. from the 'Bicester parish magazine'. Bicester, 1874, 8°. 4 pp.
G.A. Oxon c. 317 (4)

Arncot. 1450a. Arncott benefit society. Rules and regulations. (Bicester), [*c.* 1870], 8°. 8 pp. G.A. Oxon 8° 1255 (3)

Aston Rowant. 1481a. HASSALL, W. O., 'Hillwork'. (Oxoniensia, 1951, vol. 16, p. 89, 90.) R. Top. 340

Banbury. 1549a. BOSS, T. W., Reminiscences of old Banbury, a lecture. Banbury, 1903, 8°. 27 pp. G.A. Oxon 8° 1230 (18)

— 1581a. STONE, H., Moore's Almanac. [With Banbury notes.] 1845–48. Banbury, [1844–47], 8°. Alm. G.A. Oxon 8° 1289

— 1599a. Church passage infant school. 33rd report. (Banbury, 1866), 4°. G.A. Oxon c. 317 (16)

— 1676a. The fifteenth (24th, 29th, 40th, 42nd–45th, 48th, 50th) report of the (Banbury) Deddington and Chipping Norton district committee of the Society for promoting Christian knowledge (and for the propagation of the gospel.) Banbury, 1834–69, 8°.
G.A. Oxon 8° 641

— 1686a. Banbury district widows' society. Rules. Northampton, 1879, 8°. 7 pp. G.A. Oxon 8° 1255 (7)

Beckley. 1713a. BLACKMORE, R. D., Cripps, the carrier. 3 vols. [A novel, containing information concerning the countryside around Beckley.] Lond., 1876, 8°. 251 d. 605–07

Bicester. *General.* 1761a. FERGUSON, W., The daughters who excel, or, The mother, her daughters, and the boarding school. [Red House seminary, Bicester, *passim.*] Lond., &c., 1855, 8°. 24 pp.
100 g. 48 (25)

— 1761b. The Bicester magazine. Vol. 1–7. Bicester, 1858–64, 8°. [The Bodleian set is imperf.]　　　Per. G.A. Oxon 8° 1274; b. 183

— 1761c. Bye laws and regulations for the management of the Bicester new cemetery, by the burial board for the parish of Bicester. Bicester, 1861, 8°. 8 pp.　　　G.A. Oxon 8° 1308 (8)

— 1761d. Bye laws made by the Local board for the district of Bicester, Market End. Bicester, 1864, 8°. 24 pp.　　G.A. Oxon 8° 1308 (9)

— 1761e. Bicester national & infant schools. Treasurer's balance sheet. 1874. (Bicester, 1875), 4°.　　　G.A. Oxon c. 317 (18)

— 1761f. St. Edburg's chronicle. Bicester parish magazine. Jan. 1883–Jan. 1916. [Bicester], 1883–1916, 4°. [The Bodleian has 5 numbers only.]　　　G.A. Oxon c. 317 (18)

— 1761Aa. Bye-laws, made by the Local board for the district of Bicester acting as the urban sanitary authority, with respect to new streets & buildings. Bicester, [1894], 8°. 82 pp.
G.A. Oxon 8° 1301

— 1765a. Bicester urban district council. Waterworks. Rules and regulations. Bicester, 1905, 8°. 12 pp.　　G.A. Oxon 8° 1255 (13)

— 1765b. Photographic views of Bicester. Bicester, [c. 1905], obl. 4°. 14 plates.　　　G.A. Oxon 4° 713

— 1767a. Bicester urban district gas. A bill to confer upon the Urban district council of Bicester powers in relation to the acquisition of the Bicester gasworks, and the supply of gas and for other purposes. (2 G. V, session 1911.) (Lond., 1911), fol. 24 pp.
G.A. Oxon c. 323

— 1767b. Bicester urban district council. Bye-laws . . . with respect to a market. Bicester, 1913, 8°. 8 pp.　　　G.A. Oxon 8° 1255 (9)

— 1767c. Whizz-bang [a magazine of the Bicester Red Cross section hospital and Banbury Red Cross hospital]. Sept., 1916–May 1917. Bicester, 1916, 4°.　　　Per. 23173 d. 7

— 1772a. Bicester urban district council. Bicester guide & directory. Bicester, 1953, 8°. 72 pp.　　　G.A. Oxon 8° 1280

— *Directories.* 1775A. SMITH, E. AND CO., Moore's Almanack. [With notes relating to Bicester.] 1824–29, 1831, 1836, 1840. Bicester, [1823–39], 8°.　　　Alm. G.A. Oxon 8° 1285

— 1775b. SMITH, J. AND E., AND CO., Almanac, 1848(–74) with Bicester directory and almanac companion. Bicester, 1848–74, 8°.
Alm. G.A. Oxon 8° 1283

Bicester. 1776a. Hewiett's [*afterw.*] Boughton's Almanack (diary) and Bicester directory. 1861–95. Bicester, 1861–95, 4°.
Alm. G.A. Oxon 4° 709

— 1776b. Pankhurst's Almanack and directory. 1893, 1900–11. Bicester, 1893–1911, 8°. Alm. G.A. Oxon 8° 1284

— *Societies.* 1781a. Foresters (Ancient order of). Rules of court 'Loyal Oxonian' no. 5947 . . . held at the 'Red Lion' inn, Bicester. 1889, 1896. Bicester, 1889, 1896, 8°. G.A. Oxon 8° 1293

Bicester Deanery. 1782a. The Bicester deanery magazine. 1884– . Bicester, 1884– , 8° & 4°. [The Bodleian set is imperf.]
Per. G.A. Oxon 4° 708

Bicester Highway District. 1785A. General statement of receipts & expenditure on account of the highways of each parish, for the year ending 25 March 1878. [Bicester], (1878), s. sh.
G.A. Oxon c. 317 (18)

Bicester Poor Law Union. 1787a. Financial statement for the half-year ended 25 March (29 Sept.) 1878, 1881, 1883 (29 Sept. only). n. pl., 1878–83, s. sh. Per. G.A. Oxon b. 182

— 1787b. Abstract of the valuation lists of the parishes within the union, 25 March 1878 (1879). n. pl., 1878, 79, s. sh.
G.A. Oxon c. 317 (18)

— 1787c. Analysis of Report on the January school returns for 1878. n. pl., (1878), s. sh. G.A. Oxon c. 317 (18)

— 1787d. List of Guardians appointed as Union assessment committee, Finance committee, School attendance committee, and visitors to the workhouse, from 1879 to 1880. Bicester, (1879), s. sh.
G.A. Oxon c. 317 (18)

— 1787e. [List of Guardians of the poor]. Bicester, 1879, s. sh.
G.A. Oxon c. 317 (18)

— 1787f. Election of Guardians of the poor. Bicester, 1879, s. sh.
G.A. Oxon c. 317 (18)

— 1787g. Rural sanitary authority. Memoranda for the guidance of the inspector of nuisances. Woodstock, [*c.* 1880], 8°. 8 pp.
G.A. Oxon 8° 1255 (12)

— 1787h. Abstract of accounts of the guardians for the half-year ended March 1900(–Michaelmas 1916). Bicester, 1900–16, 8°.
Per. G.A. Oxon 4° 712

Bicester Rural District Council. 1787i. Bye-laws . . . with respect to new buildings. Bicester, 1904, 8°. 32 pp.
G.A. Oxon 8° 1230 (21)

— 1787j. Report of the medical officer of health, 1914. n. pl., [1915], 8°.
G.A. Oxon 8° 1230 (19)

Bicester Rural District Council. 1787k. Abstract of accounts for the half-year ended 30th Sept., 1916. n. pl., (1917), 8°.
G.A. Oxon 8° 1230 (20)

Bletchington. 1819a. Valentia club friendly society. Rules. [1856], 1872 [and] Bye rules, 1858. Oxf., [1856], 1858, 1872, 8°.
G.A. Oxon 8° 1296

— 1819b. Bletchington friendly society. Rules. [c. 1865, 1879]. Oxf., [c. 1865, 1879], 8°.
G.A. Oxon 8° 1307

Bucknell. 1905a. MAY, J. T., Words of farewell to the parishioners of Bucknell. Bicester, 1878, 8°. 12 pp.
G.A. Oxon 8° 1308 (14)

Burford. 1927a. DALLAS, A. R. C., Incidents in the life and ministry of . . . A. R. C. Dallas. [P. 226–35 concern the curacy of Burford, 1826, 27.] Lond., 1871, 8°.
210 j. 143

Cassington. 1974Aa. BRADFORD, J. S. P., Excavations at Cassington, 1947. (Oxoniensia, 1951, vol. 16, p. 1–4.)
R. Top. 340

Charlton on Otmoor. 2033a. Charlton benefit society. Rules and regulations. Oxf., 1880, 8°. 8 pp.
G.A. Oxon 8° 1255 (8)

— 2033b. The Charlton-on-Otmoor church monthly. 1891, 92. (Lond.), 1891, 92, 4°.
Per. G.A. Oxon 4° 706

Chesterton. 2068a. Chesterton sick club. Rules. Bicester, [c. 1870], s. sh.
G.A. Oxon b. 185

Chipping Norton. 2092a. ATKINS, J., A new almanack for 1821 (1824, 25). [With notes relating to Chipping Norton.] Chipping Norton, [1820–24], 8°.
Alm. G.A. Oxon 8° 1287

— 2092b. Laws and orders made by the jury at a court leet and court baron and view of frankpledge, holden by the bailiffs and burgesses of the borough of Chipping Norton, 15th Oct., 1821. Chipping Norton, 1821, 8°. 15 pp.
G.A. Oxon 8° 1230 (16)

— 2093a. SMITH, G. M., Moore's Almanack. [With notes relating to Chipping Norton.] 1832, 33. Chipping Norton, [1831, 32], 8°.
Alm. G.A. Oxon 8° 1290

Chiselhampton. 2132a. OSWALD, A., Chiselhampton house. 1, 2. (Country Life, 1954, vol. 115, p. 216–19, 284–87.) Per. 384 b. 6

Cowley. 2218a. Oxford movement centenary, 1833–1933. [Appeal for and account of Cowley parish church and hall.] [Oxf.], (1933), 8°. 8 pp.+3 plates.
G.A. Oxon 8° 1079 (20)

Cuddesdon Deanery. 2296a. Church of England temperance society. Boys' union. Cuddesdon deanery.
— Report. 1896, 97/8, 98/9, 1900/1–03/4.
— Roll of members. 1897–1901, 1903–05. (Birm., &c., 1896–1905), 8°.
G.A. Oxon 8° 1278

Culham. 2307a. Culham college directory. 1853/1948, 1853/1951. (Abingdon, 1947, 1951), 8°. Dir. Oxon e. 12

— 2308a. NAYLOR, L., Culham Church of England training college for schoolmasters, 1853-1953, centenary history. Abingdon-on-Thames, (1953), 8°. 141 pp. 26334 e. 120

Deddington. 2324Aa. Deddington and Steeple Aston self-supporting dispensary. Rules. Banbury, 1835, 8°. 7 pp. G.A. Oxon 16° 207 (3)

— 2324Ca. Deddington general friendly institution. Rules and regulations. Deddington, 1856, 8°. 16 pp. G.A. Oxon 8° 1308 (4)

— 2324Cb. The government deed relating to the Deddington national schools. Repr. from the North Oxfordshire monthly times, March 1856. Deddington, 1856, 8°. 11 pp. G.A. Oxon 8° 1255 (2)

— 2324Cc. Union beneficial society. Rules of the . . . society held at the Unicorn Inn, in Deddington. Deddington, 1873, 8°. 17 pp. G.A. Oxon 8° 1308 (12)

— 2324Cd. Whetton's Deddington almanack, commercial advertiser, & town and trade directory. 1877, 1881-83. Deddington, 1877-83, 8°. Alm. G.A. Oxon 8° 1286

— 2324Ce. Deddington, Heyford, & Aston benefit building society. List of members. 1877, 1879. Bicester, 1877, 1879, fol. G.A. Oxon c. 317 (8)

— 2325a. Deddington with Clifton and Hempton parish magazine. Vol. 1, no. 2-vol. 6, no. 12. Deddington, 1879-84, 8°. Per. G.A. Oxon 4° 710

— 2326a. Deddington prosecution association. [List of members.] Deddington, [c. 1880], s. sh. G.A. Oxon c. 317 (8)

— 2326b. Girls' friendly society, Deddington branch. Rules. (Heyford), [c. 1885], 8°. 4 pp. G.A. Oxon c. 317 (8)

— 2328a. Wesleyan reform union. Preachers' plan, Deddington circuit. 1895, 96. Deddington, 1895, 96, s. sh. G.A. Oxon c. 317 (3)

Fritwell. 2586a. Friendly society, held at the King's Head, Fritwell. Annual statement and balance sheet. 1867, 68, 1875-77, 1880, 1882-89, 1891-96. Bicester, 1867-96, s. sh. Per. G.A. Oxon b. 184

— 2586b. Rules of the friendly society established for the benefit of the parishioners of Fritwell and other adjacent parishes. Bicester, 1876, 8°. 12 pp. G.A. Oxon 8° 1308 (13)

— 2590a. St. Olave's, Fritwell, parish magazine. July 1907-May 1910. Lond., &c., 1907-10, 4°. [The Bodleian set is imperf.] Per. G.A. Oxon 4° 707

Godstow. 2633a. HARDEN, D. B., The Godstow 'foundation stone'. (Oxoniensia, 1951, vol. 16, p. 77, 78.) R. Top. 340

Great Haseley. 2670a. Oxford municipal charities. List of applicants for Cutler Boulter's charity . . . Great Haseley. September, 1890. n. pl., (1890), 8°.   G.A. Oxon 8° 592 (18)

Handborough. 2742a. BAILEY, R. C. S., Hanborough. (Oxf.), [1953], 8°. 58 pp.   G.A. Oxon 8° 1282

Hanwell. 2745a. An act for confirming . . . the inclosure of . . . fields . . . of Hanwell. (23 G. III, c. 43, Private.) n. pl., 1783, fol.
O.C.R.L.

Headington. *Warneford Asylum.* 2807a. THOMAS, V., A letter to the magistrates of the county of Oxford [commenting on No. 2807]. Oxf., 1857, 8°. 40 pp.   G.A. Oxon 8° 1308 (5)

Headington Poor Law Union. 2813a. Extracts from the quarterly abstract showing the number of paupers relieved, the amount of money expended, and the balances due to and from the several parishes, for the quarter ending Dec. 25th, 1841. n. pl., (1841), s. sh.
G.A. Oxon c. 317 (21)

Henley. 2831Aa. MOORE, C. N. RIVERS. Further excavations in the Roman house at Harpsden wood, Henley-on-Thames. (Oxoniensia, 1951, vol. 16, p. 23–27.)   R. Top. 340

Horsepath. 2932a. WOODS, M. L., A village tragedy. [Horsepath and district?] Lond., 1887, 8°. 229 pp.   256 e. 2925
— 2nd ed. 1889.   256 e. 16638

Islip. 2992a. Islip friendly institution. (Rules and regulations.) 1862, 1875. Oxf., 1862, 1875, 8°.   G.A. Oxon 8° 1305
— 2992b. Islip union fellowship. (Articles, regulations, &c.) Oxf., [c. 1870], 8°. 12 pp.   G.A. Oxon 8° 1255 (4)
— 2993a. FOWLE, T. W., Farewell address to the parishioners of Islip. Oxf., [1902?], 8°. 7 pp.   G.A. Oxon 8° 1255 (10)
— 2993b. Memoir of the rev. T. W. Fowle, late rector of Islip. Oxf., 1903, 8°. 26 pp.   24724 e. 76

Islip Deanery. 2999a. Islip rural-deanery magazine. Vol. 1, 2; 8–13. [Lond.], 1898–1910, 4°. [The Bodleian set is imperf.]
Per. G.A. Oxon 4° 705

Kingham. 3055a. Kingham Hill magazine. New ser. Vol. 1, no. 4– . Oxf., 1948– , 4°.   Per. G.A. Oxon 4° 703

Kirtlington. 3061a. Rules and orders agreed upon by a select company of persons, under the denomination of a friendly society, meeting at the Dashwood Arms inn, at Kirtlington. Oxf., [c. 1845], s. sh.
G.A. Oxon a. 126
— 3061b. Oxford arms friendly society. Rules. Oxf., 1859, 8°. 16 pp.
G.A. Oxon 8° 1308 (6)

Kirtlington. 3061c. Kirtlington provident friendly society. Rules. 1863, 1866, 1884. Oxf., 1863–84, 8°. 16 pp.   G.A. Oxon 8° 1298

— 3061d. The Kirtlington church monthly. Jan. 1892–Nov. 1895. (Lond.), 1892–95, 4°.   Per. G.A. Oxon 4° 704

Launton. 3079a. Oxford municipal charities. List of applicants for . . . Wootten's charity. Oct. 1885; Apr., Oct. 1887; Oct. 1889; May 1893. n. pl., (1885–93), 8°.   G.A. Oxon 8° 592

— 3079b. Launton provident society. Rules. 1894, 1898. Bicester, 1894, 1898, 8°.   G.A. Oxon 8° 1306

Littlemore. 3124a. Church of England temperance society. Littlemore branch.
— Register of members. 1892–1903.
— Rules, admission service, and maxims. 1887, 1893, 1898. Oxf., (1887–1903), 8°.   G.A. Oxon 8° 1279

Lower Heyford. 3162a. Heyford and Aston friendly society. Rules. 1851, 1879. Heyford, 1851, 1879, 8°.   G.A. Oxon 8° 1304

— 3162b. Heyford and Aston friendly society. Balance sheet for 1877–78. Heyford, (1878), s. sh.   G.A. Oxon c. 317 (9)

— 3165a. Oxfordshire assizes, Feb. 25th [really 5th], 1898. Action for slander between Eleanor Mary Godwin Cheesman of Lower Heyford, plaintiff, and William Kinch of Steeple Aston, defendant. Bicester, 1898, 8°. 4 pp.   L. Eng. C 25 d. Slander 1

Minster Lovell. 3232a. TAYLOR, A. J., Minster Lovell hall (official guide). (Ancient monuments & hist. buildings, H.M. Office of works.) Lond., 1939, 8°. 21 pp.   17356 d. 42 (91)
— Abridged version. 1947. 8 pp.   17356 d. 42 (129)

— 3234a. ZEUNER, F. E., A group vi Neolithic axe from Minster Lovell. (Proc., Prehist. soc., 1952, new ser., vol. 18, p. 240, 41.)
Per. 247115 d. 124

Murcot. 3245a. Murcott & Fencott benefit society. Rules and regulations. Bicester, 1872, 8°. 8 pp.   G.A. Oxon 8° 1308 (11)

Shipton-on-Cherwell. 3519a. Barbara Standard, spinster, a lunatick, sister and heir of R. Standard . . . and T. Pomfrett her committee and administrator (appellants). A. Meetkerke . . . P. Meetkerke and M. Wickham (respondents). The appellants case [concerning the manor of Shipton]. n. pl., (1736), fol. 4 pp.
L. Eng. C 25 b. Wills 1 (1)

— 3519b. Barbara Standard . . . and T. Pomfret . . . appellants. A. Meetkerke . . . P. Meetkerke, M. Wickham, respondents. The case of the respondents. n. pl., (1736), fol. 8 pp.
L. Eng. C 25 b. Wills 1 (2)

Shirburn. 3546a. S., C.R., Shirburn castle library. (Country Life, 1911, vol. 30, p. 176–78.) Per. 384 b. 6

Somerton. 3585a. Rules for the government of a friendly (and benefit) society to be held at the Railway Tavern inn, Somerton. [c. 1855], 1872, 1874. Deddington, [c. 1855]–74, 8°. G.A. Oxon 8° 1297

— 3586a. Somerton benefit society. Rules. 1873, 1884. Oxf., &c., 1873, 1884, 8°. G.A. Oxon 8° 1300

— 3588a. Somerton benefit society. The 24th annual statement. (Bicester), 1887, fol. G.A. Oxon c. 317 (13)

Souldern. 3601a. Souldern friendly society. Rules (and articles). 1843, 1864, 1876, 1881. Bicester, &c., 1843–81, 8°. G.A. Oxon 8° 1302

— 3607a. Souldern friendly society. Annual balance sheet. 1904. Banbury, 1904, 4°, 4 pp. G.A. Oxon c. 317 (13)

South Leigh. 3621a. GROSCH, A., Flowers from a Cotswold garden [poems and articles chiefly about Southleigh during World War ii]. Lond., 1953, 8°. 46 pp. 27001 e. 1933 (6)

Stanton Harcourt. 3686a. CASE, H., A cinerary urn from Stanton Harcourt. (Oxoniensia, 1951, vol. 16, p. 84, 85.) R. Top. 340

— 3686b. WILLIAMS, A., Excavations at Beard Mill, Stanton Harcourt, 1944. (Oxoniensia, 1951, vol. 16, p. 5–22.) R. Top. 340

Steeple Aston. 3701a. Steeple Aston friendly society. Rules. Banbury, 1861, 8°. 15 pp. G.A. Oxon 8° 1308 (7)

— 3701b. Steeple Aston co-operative industrial society ltd. Rules. 1872, 1881. Manch., &c., 1872, 1881, 8°. G.A. Oxon 16° 221

— 3706a. Steeple Aston friendly society. Annual balance sheet. 1876–77. Lower Heyford, (1877), s. sh. G.A. Oxon c. 317 (4)

— 3706b. Steeple Aston co-operative industrial society, ltd. 12th (14, 34, 64, 75–77) report. Heyford, 1878–1910, 4°. G.A. Oxon c. 317 (4)

— 3706c. Radcliffe's school, Steeple Aston. Balance sheet for year ended Feb. 28th, 1879. Heyford, 1879, s. sh. G.A. Oxon c. 317 (4)

— 3706d. Technical school. [Copy of document inserted in foundation stone.] n. pl., [1894], s. sh. G.A. Oxon c. 317 (4)

— 3706e. SPENCER, A., A sermon preached at Steeple Aston . . . in reference to the death of the rev. J. H. Brookes, rector. (Lond., 1896), 8°. 10 pp. 11126 e. 835 (6)

Swalcliffe. 3771a. Diego redivivus: or, The last will and testament of the pretended Humphrey Wickham [of Swalcliffe], alias William Morrel, alias Bowyer, &c. Lond., 1692, 4°. 10 pp.
G.A. Oxon 4° 6 (20)

Thame. 3855a. LEE, F. G., The French clergy exiles in England, 1792–97. (National review, 1888, vol. 12, p. 350–60.) Per. 22775 d. 14

Waterperry. 3936a. An act to enable John Barnewall Curson . . . to settle a jointure upon any woman or women he may hereafter marry. [Concerns Waterperry manor.] (17 G. III, c. 52, Private.) n. pl., 1777, fol. 15 pp. MS. Top. Berks b. 1 (95a)

Wendlebury. 3965a. Wendlebury benefit society. Rules and regulations. Bicester, [c. 1880], 8°. 8 pp. G.A. Oxon 8° 1255 (5)

Weston-on-the-Green. 3972a. Weston-on-the-Green friendly society. Rules. 1877, 1889. Bicester, &c., 1877, 1889, 8°.

G.A. Oxon 8° 1303

— 3972b. Weston-on-the-Green aerodrome workmen's social club. Rules. Bicester, [c. 1918], 16°. 14 pp. G.A. Oxon 16° 207 (4)

Westwell. 3979a. MITFORD, B. R., Westwell, a short history, B.C. 1700–A.D. 1951 [by B. R. Mitford with additions by B. Freeman-Mitford. Reprod. from typewriting]. n. pl., [1952], 4°. 50 pp.

G.A. Oxon 4° 698

Witney. 4039a. GOOLE, J., The contract [between the author, a master of Witney school, and Margaret Hudson] violated: or, The hasty marriage. Lond., [1733], 8°. 90+67 pp. Bliss A 92 (12)

Blenheim Palace. *General.* 4205a. ARKELL, W. J., Building stones of Blenheim palace. (Oxoniensia, 1951, vol. 16, p. 88, 89.)

R. Top. 340

— 4207a. GREEN, D., The Bernini fountain at Blenheim. (Country Life, 1951, vol. 110, p. 268, 69.) Per. 384 b. 6

— 4208Aa. BALSAN, C. VANDERBILT, The glitter and the gold [autobiography of the first wife of the 9th duke of Marlborough]. 1st ed. New York, 1952, 8°. 336 pp. 2142 e. 235
— [Another ed.] Lond., &c., 1953, 8°. 2142 e. 236

— *Contents.* 4217a. Catalogue of the Marlborough gems, which will be sold by auction, 28 June 1875. Lond., (1875), 8°. 112 pp.

17156 d. 17*

Yarnton. 4301a. NARES, G., Yarnton manor. (Country Life, 1951, vol. 110, p. 2096–99, 2162–65.) Per. 384 b. 6

PRINTED IN
GREAT BRITAIN
AT THE
UNIVERSITY PRESS
OXFORD
BY
CHARLES BATEY
PRINTER
TO THE
UNIVERSITY